CHANGING THE BULLY
WHO RULES THE WORLD

Also by author:

The Tomcat's Wife and Other Stories

The Passionate, Accurate Story:
Making Your Heart's Truth into Literature

Soil and Survival:
Land Stewardship and the Future of American Agriculture
(with Joe Paddock and Nancy Paddock)

Bad Government and Silly Literature

Backbone

Letters from the Country

CHANGING THE
BULLY
WHO RULES THE WORLD

READING AND THINKING ABOUT ETHICS

Carol Bly

MILKWEED
EDITIONS

Published 1996 by Milkweed Editions
Printed in the United States of America
Cover design by Sally Wagner
Interior design by Will Powers
The text of this book is set in Stone Serif and Stone Sans.
96 97 98 99 00   5 4 3 2 1
First Edition

Milkweed Editions is a not-for-profit publisher. We gratefully acknowledge
support from the Bush Foundation; Target Stores, Dayton's, and Mervyn's
by the Dayton Hudson Foundation; Ecolab Foundation; General Mills
Foundation; Honeywell Foundation; Jerome Foundation; The McKnight
Foundation; Andrew W. Mellon Foundation; Kathy Stevens Dougherty and
Michael E. Dougherty Fund of the Minneapolis Foundation; Minnesota
State Arts Board through an appropriation by the Minnesota State Legislature;
Challenge and Literature Programs of the National Endowment for the Arts;
I. A. O'Shaughnessy Foundation; Piper Jaffray Companies, Inc.; John and
Beverly Rollwagen Fund of the Minneapolis Foundation; The St. Paul Com-
panies, Inc.; Star Tribune/Cowles Media Foundation; Surdna Foundation;
James R. Thorpe Foundation; Lila Wallace-Reader's Digest Literary Publishers
Marketing Development Program, funded through a grant to the Council
of Literary Magazines and Presses; and generous individuals.

Library of Congress Cataloging-in-Publication Data
Changing the bully who rules the world : reading and thinking about
    ethics / [compiled by] Carol Bly. — 1st ed.
        p.   cm.
    Includes bibliographical references.
    ISBN 1-57131-205-6 (pbk. : alk. paper)
    1. Ethics.   2. Ethics in literature.   3. Ethical problems.
    I. Bly, Carol.
    BJ1012.C4543   1996
    170—dc20   96-403
                                                            CIP

This book is printed on acid-free paper.

To
Emilie Buchwald
good editor
good friend

Acknowledgments

The following people gave me substantive help in my research, but I thank them mostly for their unswerving hatred of bullying. My grateful thanks, therefore, to Dr. Mary Pipher, psychologist, University of Nebraska; Dr. Michael True, professor of English, Assumption College; Dr. George Shapiro, professor of speech communications, University of Minnesota; and Dr. Sarah Jeanne Snapp, M.S., L.I.C.S.W., L.M.F.T. of the Child Guidance Clinic, Wilder Foundation.

I am grateful to the following experts in their several fields who were patient with my necessarily generalist inquiries: Dr. Mary Ann Mattoon, Ph.D., Jungian analyst and licensed psychologist, Minneapolis; Dr. Sonja C. Matison, professor of social work, Eastern Washington University; Mary Peterson, L.I.C.S.W., M.S.W., cofounder and cochair, Collaborative of Teachers and School Social Workers, St. Paul; Mr. John L. Washburn Jr., United Nations; Dr. Sara Hunter, psychologist, St. Paul; Dr. Mary Bly, assistant professor of English, Washington University; Dr. Bridget Bly, Ph.D., psycholinguist; Mr. Noah M. J. Bly, executive director, Cooper Square Mutual Housing Association, New York; and the Reverend Robert W. Morse, Lincoln, Nebraska, who first introduced me to theories of ethical stage development.

My colleagues in the University of Minnesota course "Ethics in Ordinary Life," Dr. Terence Ball, professor of political science, and Dr. John Dolan, professor of philosophy, were of inestimable help. I am grateful to my students, Xandra Coe and Janet Koenen, for their remarkable, original suggestions about the combining of serious literature and psychotherapeutic ideas in the Master of Liberal Studies Program.

I want to thank Mr. David Bruce Marshall for his energetic and meticulous reading of the manuscript and substantive suggestions made.

Changing the Bully Who Rules the World

Contents

Preface

This book includes an anthology of first-rate literature, offered with a description of hopeful, elegant ideas from recent work in the helping professions of psychotherapy and social work.

Most of the discussion is about the stories and poems, and the social theories they touch upon. The essays in this collection are largely self-explanatory, and therefore are mentioned in connection with their own themes and wisdom.

My purpose in writing *Changing the Bully Who Rules the World* was to show general readers that some of the past half-century's most important insights and strategies about ethics come not from philosophy or political science but from social psychology. With no real home in the universities, helping professionals, in their offices, clinics, and conferences, have been developing several kinds of expertise for systemic change. Their amazing insights and experiences are waiting to be translated into action in our businesses, schools, civic organizations, and churches. If enough of us apply these new methods we have a real chance of transforming the age-old behaviors of bullying and coercion. What is most hopeful is that the modern breed of helping professionals offers methods for transforming privileged predators in nice clothes and nice places as well as ordinary bullies.

For centuries slave owners enslaved people. The process was normal and the slave owners were imperturbable. We don't practice slavery now in most countries, and nobody thinks slavery is acceptable. For centuries bullies in high places have felt entitled to push other people around. They have felt entitled to cheat little people of their life earnings. Now that there is some technology for changing their behavior, I suggest we pick it up and use it. Perhaps, soon, white-collar bullying, like slavery, will no longer be acceptable.

Introduction

Let us imagine that we are members of a very nice, classically educated, sensitive American family. Our Airedale, a terrific pet because she is big and romping and full of moxie, has mixed it up with a porcupine in the woods. Her face and paws are full of quills. She has dragged herself home, whining piteously, frantically snapping at such quills as she can get her teeth on. But dozens of other quills have dug themselves into her mouth and under her chin. Both parents have tried to yank out some quills, but God made porcupines as well as dogs so the quills are hook-shaped in order *(a)* to hurt when they go in and *(b)* once in to stay stuck so that the attacker will get infected and die.

The children of the family grieve. The Airedale goes into a fever. "Do something, Mom! Do something, Dad!" they cry. The parents shake their heads sadly. The mother is literary, so after she has consoled her children as well as she can, she slips into her study and works on a poem about destiny. The poem is on how dogs are as vulnerable to their destinies as human beings are to theirs. We share this terrifying mortality.

The father of the family gathers the children on the sofa. In a grave and loving way he tells them this is life. There is nothing one can do when life shows its claws. The darn thing is, he tells them, that it is in the nature of dogs to go after porcupines. And it is in the nature of porcupines to use such tools as they have—and powerful tools they are, too!—to save themselves. We love our Airedale, the father says, but the porcupine doesn't love our Airedale. This kind of trouble, the nice dad says gently, is an eternal verity. It is the essential fate. We don't want to get into denial here—we acknowledge we are sad—but we move on because there is nothing we can do.

The children listen. Into their minds seeps this idea: Dad and Mom tell us the truths we need about life. These truths stay true forever. In the eighteenth century, porcupine quills killed dogs. In the nineteenth century, porcupine quills killed dogs. In the twentieth and twenty-first centuries, quills will kill dogs.

There is such dignity in eternal truths. The children feel it.

They are horribly sad about the dog, but they also feel that Dad is giving strength to their own characters. The children already have noticed that the gloomier the eternal truth one hears the more dignified its ambience.

The children's minds are recording. The tape they make says, Dad and Mom, who are the spokespeople of our culture so far as we are concerned, have told us directly that they cannot save our dog. In their kind authority they have told us indirectly that quills cannot be got out of pet dogs. They have shared our sadness. We feel wonderfully close to Mom and Dad. "Poor girl," Dad says, on his knees now, touching the Airedale's burning nose.

Next day, fortunately before the dog died, an uninvited neighbor shows up as a guest. She takes a look and says, "Poor girl," in the same compassionate tone in which the father had said it. She is a veterinarian, so she removes a syringe from her bag, measures out 3 cc of ketamine and Valium, injects it into the dog's paw, and supports her head as it sinks to the floor. With surgical pliers the neighbor depresses each quill to break its vacuum and then removes it. Finally, she swabs the worst places with a disinfectant. After a while the Airedale wakes up, totters around, and in a half hour rejoices.

If we have been educated to "eternal truths," sad or happy interpretations of life that *stay put,* we may have wonderful liberal arts educations but, like the Airedale owners, we may be losing some winnable battles. Here is an example. In 1994 four experts on international affairs were being interviewed on public television about various aspects of Nazi Germany. One of them announced in a grave tone that "of course"—and he used those words—"there is no way we can know why the German people allowed and followed Adolf Hitler."

The others nodded sagely. These were men educated in the liberal arts and in political science, but they were utterly ignorant of the large, large body of psychological work in ethics that has been done. Not only are there several likely explanations for why the German people followed and loved Hitler, but some of the psychologists and stage-developmentalists who have investigated Nazi personality structures have drawn psychological parallels to other group phenomena. These findings are already of great use to us all. If we do not close our eyes to them we will find innumerable ways to head off or transform those Nazi characteristics that rightly frighten us.

My own education was in the liberal arts, so I have been late coming to the good of psychology and ethics. The thinkers about Nazi Germany who have surprised me with hope are Bruno Bettelheim, Hannah Arendt, Robert Jay Lifton and Eric Markusen, and Ervin Staub. Some thinkers about group psychology—how normal people do either evil or good in groups—have given me some rough insights that offer hope. They are Irving Janis, Irvin Yalom, and Murray Bowen. Some thinkers write about how human beings refine their perceptions, and it follows, their character, by growing from stage to stage. Those who have moved me and to whom I am most grateful are Erik Erikson, Tom Kitwood, Lawrence Kohlberg, and Jane Loevinger.

Some thinkers who do not write about Nazi Germany or about group psychology as such, or about stage development as such, have germane, immeasurable wisdom to offer: they are the psychotherapists and social workers who have deliberately studied *the conversations between people*. They now know that certain conversations are *not* "just common sense" or "just common courtesy." They have learned, and they model to their clients, a style of conversation between human beings for which Americans know only the name: it is *empathy*.

Why bring up a word that we are mostly sick to death of, even if we don't know what it means? When people get as sick of a word as most people are of the word empathy, they suppose that they do know what it means. Unfortunately, most people think that the word empathy means some slightly fancier kind of general sympathy.

I bring up empathy because a major position of this book is that when a person of indifferent or little ethical development can be mentored or parented or both by someone who will practice empathy with him or her—not just vague niceness, but real empathy—that person will move more quickly into the next more desirable ethical stage.

For the sake of clarity, here is an example of *anti*-empathy—that is, here is a young man speaking who had been motivated by parent and school teachers, but in early adolescence (in the streets) abandoned every potential *empathic* situation in order to validate himself with a brutal peer group. In brief, his adolescence reversed the ideal growth process.

> Through those guys, I discovered the strength and solace in camaraderie. It was a confidence booster, a steady support for my fragile self-esteem. Alone, I was afraid of the world and insecure. But I felt cockier and surer of myself when hanging with my boys. I think we all felt more courageous when we hung together. We did things in groups that we'd never try alone. . . .
>
> After I started hanging, the purpose of school changed completely for me. It seemed more like a social arena than someplace to learn. The academic rigors lost their luster and the reward of making the honor roll just wasn't the same.[1]

Later, the author takes his place near the end of the line in a gang rape, or "train," being run on a girl named Vanessa:

> While hovering near Vanessa, I remembered how Scobe had disgraced that guy. I wasn't about to let that happen to me. I wasn't about to let it be said that I was scared of pussy. I took a deep breath and tried to relax and free my mind. . . .
>
> After a few miserable minutes, I got up and signaled for the next man to take his turn.
>
> While straightening my pants, I walked over to a corner, where two or three dudes stood, grinning proudly. Somebody whispered, "That shit is *good*, ain't it?"
>
> I said, "Yeah, man. That shit is good." Actually, I felt sick and unclean.[2]

Before going further, I would like to explain an important distinction in social workers that may be unfamiliar to the general reader. There are both professionally trained and untrained social workers. People whose work is called social work are sometimes people with a bachelor of arts or higher degree in sociology, not social work. Sometimes they are psychologists with one or another degree in psychology. Sometimes they are people with literally no training of any kind. In some rural areas, in which counties have to operate their human services in straitened circumstances, people are hired as social workers who are not even college graduates. In this book, the term *social worker* is used to designate only a person with the master of social work degree — which for our purposes has this significance: that person will have taken one or more courses in "interpersonal skills" and "intentional interviewing" or "interactional skills" or "psychological practices in groups."

Professional psychotherapists and social workers know the commonalities among the following phenomena:

- Decent Germans who implemented deaths at Auschwitz
- Decent American high school kids who make themselves take part in gang rapes
- Decent college graduates who use their corporate standing or government power to cheat the helpless or kill innocent people or wreck our planet

Psychotherapists and social workers have some cures that work. These professionals are like the veterinarian who dropped in to visit the family with the hurt dog. They have the needed technology. Helping professionals already have skills for freeing not just children but adults stuck in low levels of ethical consciousness.

Highly educated people don't usually know much about veterinary medicine; they aren't against it but they regard it lightly, the way an algebra student regards a second grader's arithmetic solutions. Still, most families with a wounded Airedale will take it to a vet. But the same family, with the literary mother and the philosophically inclined and affectionate father, would sooner visit a witch doctor than acknowledge and use the wonderful insight of stage-developmentalists and the effective skills of therapists and social workers.

This habit of otherwise educated people accounts for international experts' announcing so sadly and authoritatively that there is no handle to be got on German followership.

This book is dedicated to beautiful literature and the beautiful theory of moral growth and to a few remarkable intervention skills. The three belong together. They may look like strange bedfellows, but then, astronomy and mathematics looked like strange bedfellows when everybody still thought the stars were no business of either one of them.

We are in a similar obdurate position now. Most of us suppose that problems of peacemaking belong in the field of international affairs. Not only do most of us readers and writers know scarcely anything about the past forty years of moral psychology, but stage-developmentalists and social workers and therapists don't know much of each other's work. To most social workers it sounds wild to say, "By the way, those skills you are using are good tools for speeding people up through the lower ethical-thinking stages." The stage-development theorists sometimes don't know that social workers and psychotherapists have invented ingenious conversations vital to the dynamics of how people move from stage to stage.

As for the field of ethics, I have never known a professor of philosophy to visit the office of a professor of psychology or a professor of social work and ask, "Are any of you people trying to figure out how one gets a hankering for goodness, as opposed to just the usual hankering for power? Oh, and have you people identified any factors that speed up or slow down the process?"

We know so little of each other's worthy thinking! We know so little of each other's work that we don't know which curious questions to ask one another. I interact with social workers a good deal, yet have never met one who knew Mary Oliver's "Lilies," which is an ode to activism. I have met a number of suicide-intervention team members, all of whom were surprised (and delighted) to be shown David Ignatow's poem "Above Everything." Even social workers with undergraduate degrees in English, of whom there are many, usually do not know the best writers of the 1980s and 1990s. I have not yet met a social scientist who has heard of Mark Helprin's "The Schreuderspitze," although it is one of the most subtle, modern, and compassionate stories in American literature.

And most of us in literature—readers, authors, teachers, and those in the bookselling and publishing industry—have a vague feeling that Erik Erikson thought that people graduate from stage to stage. We have heard of Abraham Maslow. We know it was B. F. Skinner, not Maslow or Erikson, who had the box. But that's about it for what we literary people know of moral stage-development theory. Most of us have never heard even the names Tom Kitwood, Lawrence Kohlberg, and Jane Loevinger, never mind more than a dozen others who have given us enormously interesting insights into how adults think about good and evil—how those adults behave themselves in a certain way for a while, and then change their moral tastes.

Certainly no one has suggested that we use moral psychology as a way of looking at both characters and authors of literature. We readers of classical literature have our habits. One of our habits of long standing is to figure that character is character: it is noble or endearing or mediocre or repulsive, just as in our personal lives we know people who are noble, endearing, mediocre, or repulsive. We are quite sure that people aren't going to change. We allow remarks like, "Yes, the more they change the more they stay the same" to sift through our conversations. Our education has been in eternal truths, not in this touted expertise of *change.* When social scientists tell us to be more flexible, we feel as if they are saying, "Be mushy. Be wobbly and uncertain. Relax your standards."

We like our standards. We don't want to do anything that remotely feels like relaxing them. We remember that Aristotle spoke of an appropriate hatred of evil, and we are proud to have such a hatred. When one isn't used to being around social scientists they seem to be saying, "Be uncertain! Join our pernicious junk culture." The most rigid of us see the American junk culture as blooming nearer their campsite than ours.

The impression is false. The best of social scientists are suggesting, as did Copernicus, that the universe is immeasurably larger than we took it for, and the paths of its fiery members are immeasurably more complicated than we thought they were. They don't ask us to be slack. They ask us to entertain more complex and scientific interpretations of everyday life than we are used to.

I have spoken enthusiastically about social science. Now I want to suggest with just as much enthusiasm that people read the literature in this book first for pleasure—certainly first for pleasure—but then with an eye for, "How might such and such an evil occasion have been avoided?" and "How might we behave differently in the situation than these characters behaved?"

We serious readers like to meditate upon villainy when we find it in life or in books. Such meditating makes us feel philosophical. Helping professionals are less peaceable. They think of human cruelty as something to study with the unswerving goal of getting rid of it. They interest themselves with, among other subjects, a spectacular specialty of villainy that would have made the poet Tom McGrath prick up his ears—that is, the villainous cunning by which a few human beings condition whole enclaves of other human beings dutifully to commit large-scale cruelty. They regard cruelty the way physicians regard a bacterium or a virus: first, they identify it as fast as they can—get its measure, so to speak, figure out its lifestyle and habitat of choice—and then second, they devise for it the most hostile environment that their technical prowess can invent. We would be furious if our doctor looked into our sore throat, drew back, and then cried out, "How utterly fascinating! How extraordinary, really, the way those germs writhe and thrive in the host's dark vault of throat!" We want the doctor to be a confrontational agent of change, not an aesthete. If our doctor won't get rid of those squatters we'll find another doctor who will.

If we literary people find ourselves anxious lest short stories be confused with case studies, we might be encouraged to know that once one has become a hopeful change agent, as opposed to merely a philosopher, one thenceforward hates passive emotionality about evil behavior. One despises literary rhetoric about catharsis and redemption and resolution and spirituality. For example, literary professionals have regarded the ending of Arturo Vivante's story "The Soft Core" as "lovely." Lovely—that the son can find beauty deep in the core of the bullying father. A family-systems therapy team would shake their heads and set to work on that family. What literature may call "redemption" is to them a grandiose exercise in pain avoidance. The son, who is the true "soft core" of the story, has pushed right out of his mind his father's marriage-long cruelty to the mother. To a therapy team, not confronting such a bully as that father is like watching a snake glide silently into the baby's room. Change agents have no taste for one person's redemptive feelings while the bully contin- / ues his bad work.

If even just one member of a family like this fictional family had consulted someone skilled in either of two practices—em- pathy and confrontation—the lives of the mother and the brother would have been enhanced. The personality of the father might have been nudged up a level from his self-centered bullying. / *bullies*

Psychologists and authors are only beginning the collegial sharing of their expertise. Bettelheim, Viktor Frankl, and Yalom read great literature, but typically social scientists do not know the best of literature. They have heard of popular writers in some- what the same way that readers of serious literature have heard of the old 1940s kind of psychology. We know that someone presses a bell and a rat jumps. We know the urban myths of industrial psychology. You apply some stimulus-response theory to a would- be union organizer and the guy gets scared and leaves the floor of your factory. In the same way, very few psychotherapists or social workers have heard of Denise Levertov or Scott Russell Sanders. This book is in part a call to psychotherapists and social workers: "Welcome to *wonderful* literature. You know about sensational vi- olence, à la mass commercial literature. Now have a look at some of our best!"

This book asks ordinary readers, some of whom may believe that they want to cut the funding to school social workers, "Please listen to a few social psychological ideas that would be useful to regular, normal people like you. These professionals know ways to help people free themselves from limited outlooks and violent behavior."

Changing the Bully Who Rules the World suggests tying new practices of moral psychology to the reading of literature. The book has this proposal to make: that we try out these ideas on the stories and poems and essays, and also try them for fit upon our own experience. We can settle a theory or two against our own lives, see if there is a fit, amend the theories for our own use, drop parts, or add our own insights to them. The fastest way to understand any theorem is to try it against familiar phenomena—in the case of normal psychology, then, against our own lives.

Creative-writing teachers have learned in the past two decades that no truth is real to a human being until that person writes it down in his or her own words and then bravely asks, "Is my take on this right? Is it partly right and partly not right so far? Have I got *some* of this right?"

This book therefore offers informal lists throughout, and like any creative-writing teacher, I suggest everyone else make lists, too.

We laypeople shouldn't worry about whether or not we are informed enough to have opinions about normal psychological dynamics or about how ethical thinking takes hold and develops in a person's lifetime. We ought to offer the experts our best guesses, our best hypotheses, our scattershot experimentation, our best assessments. Shakespeare decided intuitively that life is a stage and everyone an actor with some lines and stage business in each of seven acts. Erik Erikson, as gathered for imaginative leaps of thought as Shakespeare, said there were *eight* acts. Neither Shakespeare nor Erikson had a Ph.D. Lawrence Kohlberg decided to his own satisfaction that the development of moral reasoning fell into three levels, premoral, conventionally moral, and better-than-conventionally moral, with two stages in each. When challenged about a seventh "spiritual" stage, Kohlberg wrote equably enough that there might well be such a thing. He didn't see it, himself.

We should each make up our own stage theories. I think it is wasteful to pay attention to the notion that a little knowledge is a dangerous thing. A little knowledge is very much less dangerous a thing than no knowledge, especially in matters having to do with our own development. Laypeople shouldering around a little knowledge of a field may be irritating, but they are a lot less dangerous than experts who have lost their moral purpose. The sociologist Ernest Becker complained again and again of how the field of sociology had settled down to mere side issues, as if indifferent to the moral problems of human beings, despite the original charge of sociology—moral problems of human beings.

When I was forty-seven, I found out by accident that therapists have worked out a process by which people who have been proud (not embarrassed, but proud!) to take orders from a bully—people who enjoyed saluting and shouting "SIR!"—can actually change into people who take pride in *not* taking orders, in *not* making up to a muscly boss, in *not* having the easy, assertive answers about everything that bullies toss like sops to their recruits or parishioners or toadies. Psychotherapy has techniques for converting toadies. Dickens and other authors after him have vividly portrayed any number of toadies, but toadies don't change just because literature has shamed their type. That is because Dickens himself presented toadyism as an Eternal Verity, and toadies themselves believe it.

But why care whether toadies toady up to people or not? The answer is, we ought to care, because highly placed bullies use toadies, highly placed toadies, to keep the world going around the way it goes around. The way the world goes around is not good enough. A few bullies with enough toadies can rule the world for years, decades, at a stretch. That single skill—helping toadies leave off toadying in favor of becoming their own persons—is of great interest to people who resent the ease with which bullies manipulate followers.

New findings suggest that modern psychotherapists have been wise all along in telling people that we have several voices or selves inside ourselves—all the voices or selves worth heeding and respecting.[3] We respond to any given situation with emotions situated in several places in our brains, all firing presumably at the same time. This being true, we are one hundred percent better readers if we hear from even as few as two different voices inside ourselves than if we follow the old style of supposing we are only one person at a time, with one opinion.

In ethics, wise people have always taken note of *passing feelings* as scrupulously as they have taken note of new ideas. Anyone can remember *ideas;* what is hard to remember is each moment's moral gladness or moral indignation. Moral gladness and moral anger nearly always blindside us. They are as fleet as falling stars. Just when you realize that you are having a moral feeling, and that it has filled your whole sail, it evaporates like small gusts at dusk. The conventional wisdom has been until recently that if a feeling swiftly vanished it wasn't worth much. Now we know, however, that disparate areas of the brain light up with different feelings here and there like Saint Elmo's fire, only to wink back out of our consciousness. We cannot decide so easily what is a major feeling or what is a noble feeling. We need to pay more attention, more friendly attention, to our own confusing responses.

For people who like to do their own thinking, reading a book is like being in a safe house: as long as we are reading and taking our notes we are no one's minion. We can disagree with ourselves. We can have unsociable feelings. We sit in a living room, muttering to ourselves about three really bad characters in this anthology— Sam in "Cider 5¢ a Glass," Donald in "The Woman Lit by Fireflies," and Franzen in "The Schreuderspitze." I believe our anger is a sign of intelligence.

Specifically, this book suggests the following practices:

1. Reading serious literature expecting to experience several feelings about whatever we come across
2. Practicing the particular communication skill called *empathy* on the characters in the stories and poems, especially the part of empathy called *partializing*
3. Practicing a second particular communication skill, *confrontation*, on the characters and authors
4. Regarding people as moving along through, or stuck in, moral stages, rather than as being merely certain types of people
5. Making lists of our own values and our own theories
6. Doing "full-cost pricing" on every human action presented in the stories and poems and essays of this anthology

This last term, "full-cost pricing," is a ghastly but wonderfully accurate sample of ecologists' jargon. Full-cost pricing means figuring the actual number, the dollars, the millions of dollars, the cost in five years, in ten years, in fifty years, to everyone of a given action you are contemplating. If you were considering starting a new suburb to a city, for example, full-cost pricing would commit you to producing actual numbers for the cost in loss of river cleanliness, loss of forest, detriment to the air, cost of transport in ten years, cost of transport in fifty years, and so forth. You would calculate the prices to those of us now alive, and the costs to people and animals not yet born.

If we translate full-cost pricing from dollar cost to psychological loss, we instantly have an extraordinary, energetic way to look both at our own lives and at events presented in serious literature. Full-cost pricing has a brooding, heartening connection to the very old concept of atonement—namely, if there is an actual financial or psychological cost to a given act, then there is an actual financial or psychological atonement that could be begged or exacted of the human being who committed the act.

So far as literature is concerned, psychological findings give us a fresh way to contemplate the events reported in memoir or autobiographical fiction. (Such findings are discussed in chapter 1, with respect to Sam in "Cider 5¢ a Glass," and later, with respect to Alice Walker's "Brothers and Sisters.")

Much of what is customary in ethics seminars is omitted in *Changing the Bully Who Rules the World*, some with sorrow—especially moral reasoning. Moral reasoning is a fascinating form of inquiry, but the questions it asks have to do with distinctions between look-alike issues rather than with how the ethical potential wakens or doesn't waken in people.[4]

This book—its mixture of new social science and a few good stories and poems and essays—is meant to be of use to the ethics seminars springing up in the United States. It is based on literature because narrative is the best carrier of psychologically complex truths. Here and there, preeminent people of letters (for example, both Scott Russell Sanders and Wendell Berry, whose work is represented in this book) already lead ethics seminars based on essays, poems, and stories. Unlike those based on recognized ethics issues or on deliberately concocted or amalgamated case histories, discussions based on serious literature together with public issues or psychological realities have unlimited depth. No work of literature is the product of only one or two conscious ideas. A story is mysteriously dense of meaning.

We never do unearth all the telling points of literature. I think this is a reason for the traditional snappy temper of Zen masters. I think this is a reason that Jesus got witheringly cross with his disciples. He would tell them a parable that carried in its narrative fabric at least eight or nine moral or spiritual ideas, but the disciples would say, "Yes, but we certainly wish you would explain it." By "explain it" they meant tell us two or three of the ideas immanent in the story so that, armed with those two or three explained ideas, they would have permission to forget the story itself with its five other, less accessible ideas.

Literature, like any art or science, is wasted upon us at different moments. Throughout the ages critics and reviewers and teachers have stuck some desperately reductive interpretations onto one or another major work. Good literature, however, can survive bad reviewing and bad teaching, just as Mozart is not diminished though his scores have lain on the rack of children's recitals for two hundred years.

Works of good literature can also survive life in an anthology, with any argument an editor wraps around them. We needn't worry as we look at the twenty-three pieces in this book and ask our questions about goodness and bullying and the psychology of goodness and the psychology of bullying. If literature could be spoiled by how people cite it in order to forward one or another cause, it would have been spoiled long before now. Even if the only people who read David Ignatow's "Above Everything" were suicide/crisis clients and staff, and if someone reviewed Denise Levertov's "Like Loving Chekhov" as a discussion of women's sexuality, those two stunning poems would still wait for us, safe in their print.

A last point: Those of us who read and write literature know that writers are innately enthusiastic about life. Even Kafka was. Writers are like a very poor sidewalk chalk artist whom George Orwell described in *Down and Out in Paris and London:*

There was, clearly, no future for [the sidewalk artist] but beggary and a death in the workhouse.

With all this, he had neither fear, nor regret, nor shame, nor self-pity. . . .[5]

'The stars are a free show; it don't cost anything to use your eyes. . . . [Begging] don't need turn you into a bloody rabbit—that is, not if you set your mind to it.'[6]

No matter how he or she despises this injustice or that unmerciful behavior, a serious author goes headlong into life. Only such engagement in life could make anybody stick to the shockingly hard work of writing literature. Readers whose backgrounds are in the social sciences should take notice of the praise of life where it shows here: even though social psychologists and social workers and psychotherapists generally do more to improve human life than authors do, they do not tend to the same gaiety of mind.

So even though the new learning in this book *seems* to surge from the social sciences toward the stories, poems, and essays, it is actually the givers of literature—the authors—who make us these three huge offerings: their habit of not lying, their habit of going to the free show of the stars, and their determination not to become bloody rabbits.

Notes

1. Nathan McCall, *Makes Me Wanna Holler: A Young Black Man in America* (New York: Random House, 1994), 33.

2. Ibid., 46.

3. Daniel Goleman, "The Brain Manages Happiness and Sadness in Different Centers," *New York Times*, March 28, 1995, B9.

4. One characteristic question of moral reasoning is: Are you sure that if what you say is good, it will still be good if logically carried out in all circumstances? For example, a question in utilitarian ethics is: If good means what is good for the greatest number of the people, is it good to torture and kill an innocent person or two if their travail and death will help a preponderant majority?

Oxford University planned to honor President Harry S. Truman because he braved worldwide criticism when he ordered dropping the atomic bomb on Hiroshima and Nagasaki. Professor G. E. M. Anscombe, a moral philosopher, asked whether we should honor everyone for courage in braving adverse opinion whenever he or she does something grossly unjust to thousands of others. Oxford University withdrew the proposed honorary degree as a result of

Anscombe's paper. G. E. M. Anscombe, "Mr. Truman's Degree," in *Ethics, Religion, and Politics,* The Collected Philosophical Papers of G. E. M. Anscombe, vol. 3 (Minneapolis: University of Minnesota Press, 1981). That event, as much as any other, makes me sorry not to have a discussion of moral reasoning in this book. Moral reasoning sets itself to clarifying truths otherwise laughed off by cynics or slavered over with public sentimentality.

5. George Orwell, *Down and Out in Paris and London* (1933; reprint, New York: Harcourt Brace Jovanovich, 1961), 166.

6. Ibid., 164.

CHANGING THE BULLY
WHO RULES THE WORLD

Good News about Leaders and Followers

Ode for the American Dead in Asia

by Thomas McGrath

1.

God love you now, if no one else will ever,
Corpse in the paddy, or dead on a high hill
In the fine and ruinous summer of a war
You never wanted. All your false flags were
Of bravery and ignorance, like grade school maps:
Colors of countries you would never see—
Until that weekend in eternity
When, laughing, well armed, perfectly ready to kill
The world and your brother, the safe commanders sent
You into your future. Oh, dead on a hill,
Dead in a paddy, leeched and tumbled to
A tomb of footnotes. We mourn a changeling: you:
Handselled to poverty and drummed to war
By distinguished masters whom you never knew.

2.

The bee that spins his metal from the sun,
The shy mole drifting like a miner ghost
Through midnight earth—all happy creatures run
As strict as trains on rails the circuits of
Blind instinct. Happy in your summer follies,
You mined a culture that was mined for war:
The state to mold you, church to bless, and always
The elders to confirm you in your ignorance.
No scholar put your thinking cap on nor
Warned that in dead seas fishes died in schools
Before inventing legs to walk the land.
The rulers stuck a tennis racket in your hand,
An Ark against the flood. In time of change
Courage is not enough: the blind mole dies,
And you on your hill, who did not know the rules.

3.
Wet in the windy counties of the dawn
The lone crow skirls his draggled passage home:
And God (whose sparrows fall aslant his gaze,
Like grace or confetti) blinks and he is gone,
And you are gone. Your scarecrow valor grows
And rusts like early lilac while the rose
Blooms in Dakota and the stock exchange
Flowers. Roses, rents, all things conspire
To crown your death with wreaths of living fire.
And the public mourners come: the politic tear
Is cast in the Forum. But, in another year,
We will mourn you, whose fossil courage fills
The limestone histories: brave: ignorant: amazed:
Dead in the rice paddies, dead on the nameless hills.

Death Games

by Scott Russell Sanders

Humans are the last plentiful big prey. You have to be filthy rich, or
else live near one of earth's vanishing wild places, to get a shot at
grizzlies or tigers or rhinos. But there are people for the killing everywhere you look. You can take your pick of victims—both sexes, all
ages, any color of skin, any creed. Choose vicious ones, armed to
the teeth, if you have a taste for danger; or pussycat gentle ones, if
you prefer not to risk your own neck. In addition to the old-
fashioned guns and knives and lengths of pipe, there are dozens of
jazzy new weapons available, from lightning-quick poisons to lasers,
not to mention bombs, bombs the size of a wallet and bombs fat
enough to put a wobble in our orbit. No license is required,
although it helps to wear the uniform of an army or the get-up of a
guerrilla band. And there is no limit to the number of victims per
hunter.

It's hard to escape the feeling, under the barrage of the day's
news, that we've declared open season on our own kind. Coups
and invasions, border wars and civil wars; execution gangs scouring
the countryside, snipers crouched in tenements; explosives
delivered by jet and car and parcel post; firing squads and electric
chairs; plain old murder in our cities' mean streets: you know the
sort of news I mean. We hear so much of it that we forget how odd
it is, this epidemic of killing. Chewing on these reports of mayhem
with our breakfast cereal, swallowing a bit of the bitterness every
day, we gradually stop tasting it. Then a really sour slice of news
lands on our plate—depending on the year, the word might come
from Auschwitz or Johannesburg, from My Lai or Beirut, from
Moscow or New York—and suddenly we gag. Not that, we say,
stomachs turning. Lord, lord, not *that*. And for a spell we are
baffled by the bloodthirstiness of our species. We are astonished
and grieved.

When this aching amazement came over me recently, I couldn't
help noticing that all the killers—the heroes wrapped in flags and
goons wrapped in straitjackets—are male, and I couldn't help seeing

in their murderousness a grown-up version of the violent games we played back in boyhood.

Take the schoolyard, for instance. It was an acre of gravel and grass and weeds, bordered on one side by a farmer's electric cow fence, on the other two sides by the chain-link and barbed wire of a government munitions depot. This was in the country, in Ohio. Behind the farmer's boundary a lumbering bull patrolled, and behind the government's fence cruised guards in olive-drab Chevrolets. At every recess, dividing into tribes, we fought bitterly over that scuffed territory. Within each tribe there was a punching order, from the meanest big lugs down to the scrawniest wimps. The chief bully would bruise the runner-up, and the runner-up would shove the next in line, and so the punishment would cascade down. In nature films I have seen exactly the same thing happen among baboons: the alpha male starts a chain of growling and pushing that passes down through the ranks like a shock wave through a line of railroad cars, and when it reaches the end the puniest baboon, with no other beast to belt, gives a kick at the sand.

Unlike the female baboons, however, who take their lumps and give their lumps right along with the males, the girls rarely took part in our schoolyard bullying. Occasionally a tough sweetie would wallop the daylights out of a pestering boy. "If you don't shut up," she'd cry, "I'll put out your lights! I'll chop you up for stew! I'll move that ugly nose to the back of your head!" And she would bloody the lout. But most of the time the girls stood aside from our battles, mocking us and murmuring mysteriously, their faces like bread dough stretched into smiles, or they rode the swing with bare legs thrust skyward. I always envied them for that aloofness. I still do. To my ignorant eyes they seemed more sensible than we boys, so contained, more confident of who they were and where they stood in the scale of things.

Nor did the girls play with guns. Now and again they would wear fringed skirts or cowboy hats, but they never strapped holsters on their hips, never carried plastic grenades in their lunch buckets, never hid wooden machine guns behind the coal chute for battlefield use during recess. We boys played with all those weapons and more: model tanks, bombers, howitzers, bazookas; rubber knives

secreted in our hip pockets, pistols thrust under our belts. Our bedrooms were arsenals. The halls of our houses were awash with
imaginary gore. The westerns and war movies that crammed the
television after school showed us how it was done, this gleeful
killing.

When I was in kindergarten, during the Korean War, you could
buy plastic soldiers in the dime store, their bodies molded into fighting position, their chests crisscrossed with ammo belts, their waists
bejeweled with grenades. Of course the girls would have nothing to
do with them, those mysterious girls, but all the boys played war on
the dusty floors of bedrooms and in the dirt of backyards for hours
on end, slaughtering Chinese, Japanese, Russians, Germans. I don't
think we imagined actual people dying in our blustery assaults—we
were too young to know anything about death—but we understood
with utmost clarity that the world was divided, as in westerns and
GI-sagas, into good guys and bad guys. Our side deserved to live,
and the other side to perish. The notion of the perfectly evil enemy
hung in our minds like a blank target, waiting for a name to be written across it.

When our own son turned three and got the itch for guns, my wife
and I said no. "Why not?" he wanted to know. "Because it isn't
healthy," we'd say lamely; "it isn't good for you or for the world."
How could we recount for him what we had learned about real cow-
boys and Indians, about war, about genocide and assassination and
the extinction of animals? How could we explain to three-year-old
Jesse the sense of betrayal we felt upon discovering that we were
condemned to live our adult lives under the tyranny of the trigger?

Unconvinced, Jesse would halt in the aisles of department stores
and gaze longingly at water pistols, like a starving bum in a bakery.
In the library he would thumb his way through picture books, and
when he found soldiers or spacemen he would show them to us tri-
umphantly, as proof that every boy is entitled to bear arms. But we
stood firm. No guns. Most of his friends' parents—peacenik
holdovers from the Vietnam era like ourselves—also prohibited
weapons. No cowboy shoot-em-ups on TV, we declared; no war
movies, no cop shows. But here and there a grandparent delivered a

six-shooter for Christmas, or an older schoolmate passed along a snapping rifle, or a magazine ad for the Army inspired a yearning for tanks, and suddenly the boys were blasting one another with every pointed object they could find, from rulers to fingers. One day at lunch, still frustrated in his desire for an honest-to-goodness gun, Jesse nibbled his peanut butter sandwich into the shape of a revolver and sprayed us all with bullets.

The mayhem in Vietnam threw toy soldiers and their weapons into stinking disfavor, and for a while they disappeared from the stores. The manufacturers switched over to coochy-coo farm animals and road gangs. But as the gruesome images from Asia have faded, the business in war toys has begun to flourish once again. Now my son is in kindergarten, and all of his buddies keep an army or two in their closets.

"What kinds of stuff do they have?" I ask him.

"All kinds," he says warily, watching my eyes to see if I'll get on my high horse.

"Like what?"

Reassured because I have not growled at him, Jesse bursts into an excited inventory of the GI Joe set, the Star Wars fleets, the Masters of the Universe. "You ought to see them," he concludes passionately, "they're really neat."

This seems like good advice for a behind-the-times dad, so I leave an hour early on my daily run to pick up kids at school and pay a visit to one of the local toy emporiums. Infant amusements are heaped near the door, bright-colored beads and ticking rabbits and jovial pythons. Farther in, the store is divided by sex: girl things to the left, all in soothing pastels; boy things to the right, in lurid shades of flame and bruise and midnight. I make a quick leftward sweep to see what the mysterious females are up to, passing colonies of dolls, meadows of needlework kits, households of dishes and miniature vacuum cleaners. I am stopped in my tracks by a box labeled "Gettin' Pretty," a "Beauty Guide & Cosmetic Boutique" for teaching young girls how to cultivate their charms and give themselves the "high fashion" look. The cutie pictured on the front appears to be about seven; smoothing her wrinkles, she conquers nature's blemishes just in the nick of time. Stunned to find such a relic from what I thought was the dead-and-gone past—as if, in browsing through the tool racks at a hardware store I had discovered a stone ax for sale—I turn this box over and over. A clerk bustles up and tells me that this is only the starter kit. For more advanced cosmetics, I should look farther down the aisle. I drop "Gettin' Pretty" and flee to the other side of the store.

It takes no searching to find the war toys, which occupy more than half of the boys' department. The display for GI Joe ("A Real American Hero") fills both sides of a long aisle all by itself. Unlike the old days before Vietnam put a damper on things, when there was only a single figure called GI Joe, now there are fifteen or so, with a dozen assault vehicles and an armory of battle gear, from jetpacks to cross-country skis. The machinery of destruction and the lingo on the packaging have also been modernized. No more stodgy jeeps and gimpy halftracks. Now you get to choose from mobile missiles, artillery lasers, polar snowscooters, jet-powered helicopters and other whizzbang equipment, all "based on the U.S. Army's top secret weapons system." (Even now the Soviets are most likely smuggling these gizmos back to Moscow and copying the designs.) Collect every machine, the boxes urge us, and use them "to help GI Joe protect democracy from the evil enemy army of COBRA command."

The armies of COBRA, naturally, are also for sale. The molded figures are sinister, their faces masked with goggles or visors or bandannas, their eyes mere slits. ("Why are their faces all covered up?" I ask my son later. "It makes them more scary," he says, "like they're machines, you know, and don't have any hearts in them.") Each of the GI Joe characters has a code name, usually a macho monosyllable such as Grunt, Clutch, Zap, or Hawk; but the COBRA soldiers are all lumped under the single code name of "The Enemy." Whereas every good guy is supplied with a capsule biography, all the bad guys are covered with a blanket description: "Each is chosen for his physical strength and total dedication to evil." No weak adversary here, and no moral complications. Forces of light and forces of darkness. ("Does COBRA sound like the name of any country?" I ask during my son's next playgroup. After a moment's thought, one boy shouts, "China!" and another, "Russia!")

Keeping up with the times, the GI Joe folks include one female figure in their congregation of warriors. At least some things have changed since the Korean War, I reflect hopefully; in the benighted old days, women served only as nurses and captives and booty. Then I flip the box over and discover that her code name is—what? Smack? Fang? No, it's Cover Girl. With that alias, she probably caries a supply of "Gettin' Pretty" cosmetics in her fieldpack. Formerly a high-fashion model in New York and Chicago, now an efficient assassin, "Cover Girl finds that she must work against her beauty to prove herself. She's compelled to learn and master decidedly unfeminine disciplines. Her self-assurance and stunning good looks reduce most men to stuttering fools." Reading this account in the toy store aisle, I am reduced to a stuttering fool. I scan the passage again, to make sure I have not made this up. Sure enough, the words are there, describing the same old battlefield beauty, the nurse, the canteen dazzler, the sweetheart in uniform. If Grunt and Zap and the other tough guys have to put up with a female who is intent on proving herself in warfare, at least they can take comfort in her stunning good looks.

A boy of four or so, with a head of milkweed fluff, surprises me while I am clutching Cover Girl. "Look, Mommy," he exclaims, "they even got a lady in the army."

"Sure," the mother replies, "why shouldn't they?" She is carrying a baby on her hip, and wears the harassed look common to all parents who make the mistake of letting themselves be dragged by their children into toy stores. She gives me a suspicious glare. I hang Cover Girl back on the display rack.

"But I bet she doesn't carry a gun," says the boy.

"Of course she does," the mother insists. "Look at the picture."

The boy scrutinizes Cover Girl. "Yeah," he admits. "But she doesn't do any killing."

Exasperated, the mother snaps, "Don't be silly. Women are just as good at killing as men are," and as if to reinforce her point she yanks the complaining boy away by the arm.

In the next aisle I encounter the "Masters of the Universe." These are brawny lugs who are divided, like rival football teams, into groups of "Heroic Warriors" and "Evil Warriors" (labels that

the manufacturer claims as trademarks, lest someone else should
stumble upon these apt phrases). They are fantasy counterparts to
GI Joe, the good guys bearing names such as He-Man ("Most
Powerful Man in the Universe"), Man-at-Arms ("Master of
Weapons"), and Zodac ("Cosmic Enforcer"); and the bad guys
going by such titles as Skeletor ("Lord of Destruction") and Faker
("Evil Robot"). Swollen with muscles, none of the creatures looks
particularly human; if you met one on a sidewalk, you would have to
scramble into the street in order to squeeze by. One blunt fellow—
the "Heroic Human Battering Ram"—appears in fact to be a solid
lump of muscle, a sort of Platonic ideal of the weight lifter. But however meaty they may be, the heroes at least have humanoid faces,
while the villains wear the faces of bugaboos from the late-late show.

The makers of these cosmic warriors show that they also are up
with the times by including two women in their squadron, one for
the forces of light, one for the forces of darkness. Like Cover Girl
they are not only tough customers; they are also curvaceous charm-
ers, doubtless capable of reducing the muscle-bound he-men to
stuttering fools when the need arises. Rigged out in highheeled
boots, tiaras, and body suits that elevate their breasts and bare their
haunchy hips, looking in fact like professional cheerleaders (who are
dressed to look like hookers), these dangerous ladies are sorceresses
who fight with magic instead of swords.

Beyond the Masters of the Universe I spy other galactic armies,
battalion after battalion, with exotic weapons stacked in boxes to
the ceiling and names drawn from the most recent outerspace slam-
bang movies. But my eyes are beginning to glaze over. I retreat from
the aisles of bruise-and-flame-colored toys, past the "Screaming
Eagles" combat set, past electronic machine guns and laser pistols,
past falcon-faced missiles and alien bombers. After so many futuristic
weapons, it is almost touching to glimpse, as I hurry out, a flintlock
pistol with coonskin hat, a cowboy-and-Indian set called Fort
Courage, and a Lone-Ranger outfit complete with six-shooter, mask,
and silver bullets.

My son is intrigued, when I explain why I am a few minutes
late in picking him up from kindergarten, to learn that I took his

advice and went browsing among the war toys. Imagine that—old curmudgeonly Dad, who won't allow so much as a popgun into the house, out at the mall studying lasers and assassins. Jesse hopes for a miraculous conversion, for Dad to see the light and agree to arm the household.

"What do you think?" he asks cautiously.

"They're interesting," I answer vaguely.

"Did you like them?"

"I'm not sure."

"*I* think they're really *nifty,* " he cries, his wariness overwhelmed by his enthusiasm, "especially GI Joe. Just about the neatest thing there is."

"What's so nifty about them?" I ask him.

"There's all the soldiers, bunches of them, and all the stuff that goes with them, the backpacks and skis. And vehicles! Every kind you can imagine."

"You could have the same stuff with campers or forest rangers. Why not a set of mountain climbers?"

"But GI Joe's got planes, you know, and rockets, and rifles and . . ." He checks himself, mindful of the family taboo on guns. "And there's COBRA. You know—the enemy."

"Yeah, I saw them. Why are they enemies?"

"They just *are.* I don't know. They're bad. They're against GI Joe."

"So that makes it more fun, having an enemy?"

He shrugs. "It's the only way you can have a war."

We stop on our way home to buy milk at the supermarket. Waiting in the checkout line, I notice the headlines on one of the weekly scandal sheets: SECRET SAFARIS PREY ON POOR VILLAGERS. RICH HUNTERS KILL HUMANS FOR SPORT. FAT-CAT SPORTSMEN SHOOT CHILDREN LIKE RABBITS IN WILDS OF INDIA.

"What's that about?" says Jesse.

"Oh," I mutter, "just a story."

Unsatisfied, suspicious of a parental cover-up, he puts his brand new reading skills to use, stumbling over the bulky words. "Poor," he says. "Rich . . . fat . . . cat," and then he manages to sound out "shoot . . . children . . . like . . . rabbits." He repeats the phrase quizzically. "Shoot children like rabbits? What are they *talking* about?"

"It's just a made-up story," I assure him. Turn his attention elsewhere, I think. But there is nothing in sight except cigarettes, candy, horoscopes, and glamour magazines featuring scrawny models in unbuttoned dresses. As I pay for the milk, I grump at the cashier, "Why do you jam all this trash up here where we have to stand in line and look at it?" The clerk, a high-school boy wearing a clown's polka-dot bowtie and a have-a-happy-day button, blinks at me in consternation.

In the parking lot I tell Jesse, "People think up silly things like that to sell papers and magazines. Nobody's hunting children, believe me." But I'm not so sure what to believe myself, and I suspect that Jesse has already planted this bit of news in the patch of his child's memory devoted to dread, another seed of nightmare.

We find our car flanked by two pickups, each with a rifle in the gun rack of the cab window. Back when I worked as a carpenter in the Vietnam era, the builder I rode with carried a framing level on his rack. The other guys in our crew—bearded, pony-tailed, lanky young galoots who talked politics and karma while they hammered—displayed umbrellas or walking sticks in their trucks. But nowadays, here in southern Indiana, half of the gun racks I see are loaded.

"Why do they need those rifles?" Jesse asks, not for the first time. He can't understand why his mom and dad forbid him to own so much as a cap pistol when all these grown men are hauling arsenals around in their pickups.

I remember putting the same question to a fellow who was sharing a gas pump with me some time ago. While the two of us waited for our tanks to fill, I nodded at the rear window of his truck and asked, in a cordial way, why he carried three rifles. Just as cordially, he replied, "The twenty-two is for varmints, the twelve-gauge is for deer, and the thirty-ought-six is for people who mess with me." He had a fat, cherubic face, like an aging choirboy, and smiled as he spoke.

Not long after this gas-station chat, when a man pulled up at a stop sign near our house, three boys hiding in the bushes peppered his truck with kernels of field corn, a traditional Halloween stunt. Instead of laughing, the man grabbed a shotgun from the rack behind his head and fired blindly into the bushes, putting two of the boys in the hospital.

"They don't really *need* those guns," I tell Jesse, not for the first time. "It isn't as if they have to protect their lambs from mountain lions, or fight off highwaymen."

"I guess they just like having them up there to look at," says Jesse. "It kind of makes them feel good, you know. Like hanging pictures on the wall."

As we drive home, he turns around several times, studying our rear window. I imagine he is wondering if you can buy gun racks for compact station wagons.

Wherever it comes from—genes or movies, phallic fixation or the breeze—this hankering for guns seems to be as potent in young boys as the hankering for sex will be later on. The trouble, of course, is that too many boys refuse to surrender their six-shooters when their beards grow in. They trade in the toys for the real thing.

A lawyer I know owns a collection of machine guns, for which he has secured a special license. He's a neighborly sort of guy, who carries jumper-cables in his trunk and helps folks start their cars on winter mornings. He looks in regularly on an eightyish man who lives alone next door. He raises herbs in a backyard garden and shares them up and down the street.

"What do you want with machine guns?" I ask him.

"They're a good investment," he claims.

But every weekend he takes one of his gleaming investments to the firing range and burns up ammo worth more than any profit he's likely to make from selling his collection.

The firing range is crowded with shooters, and so is the countryside. Any day I'm feeling reckless I can take a hike in the hills south of town and hear gunfire, or I can watch marksmen blast floating junk in the abandoned limestone quarries. I find perforated cans squatting on stumps, and the shattered necks of bottles hanging by string from branches. On the ground, shell casings are scattered more thickly than hickory nuts. Here and there an abandoned car lies riddled and rusting in the ditch. Every road sign leaks daylight through bullet holes. It's as if private militias were constantly training in the woods.

There are sixty million or so handguns in our country, little pack-ages of annihilation within arm's reach, about one for every four of us. Two or three million new ones are sold each year. You can get a license to manufacture them for fifty bucks, and for ten bucks you can get a license to sell them. Unlike rifles, which hunters use as an excuse for hiking in the woods, handguns are worthless for hunting and next to worthless for target shooting. About all they are good for is putting large holes in people at close range, and for that they are very good. In recent years, handguns have been used in killing some twenty-five thousand people a year in the U.S., including mur-ders, suicides, and accidents. Knowing these numbers, when I am in crowds I don't worry about what other folks might pick from my pocket; I worry about what they might pluck from their own.

To judge from interviews on television, every third house or so has a basement stocked with two years' worth of food and a bedroom crammed with artillery. "We aim to survive," a grim-faced man announces to the camera. The barrels of guns, row upon row, gleam from the wall behind him. His son, a gap-toothed smiler about the age of Jesse, shows how to dismantle and reassemble a submachine gun. His wife holds up a jar of pickled beets for inspec-tion. "Survive what?" the interviewer asks. "Everything," the father declares, flinging his arms wide, "the whole mess. When it all comes apart, we're going to sit right here and stay alive."

At the newsstand I discover *Survival* magazine, aimed at those who are larding their basements with pickled beets and submachine guns. I browse through other magazines with titles such as *Knife Journal* ("How to Start Your Sword Collection"), *Shooting, Safari* ("Bagging a Pronghorn Despite the Ban"), *American Hunter, American Rifleman, American Handgunner, Guns & Ammo* ("The Most Powerful Rifle in the World"), and plain old *Guns*.

The most chilling selection at the newsstand is *Soldier of Fortune,* "The Journal for Professional Adventurers." When I buy a copy I ask the drowsy salesgirl to put it in a sack for me. This provokes a tilted smile from her. "Enjoy your reading," she says. From the cover, which shows U.S. Marines in battle gear landing on Grenada, through the articles about military hardware and bombing raids and Central American gun-running, to the classified ads for mercenaries and bounty hunters, the magazine is an exaltation of violence. It is a grown-up's version of GI Joe, complete with high-tech weapons, page after page of survival gear (bullet-proof vests and $300 knives), big-bosomed ladies for distracting the troops and for selling products, and a division of the world between Heroic Warriors (U.S. soldiers and our client armies) and Evil Warriors (Soviet soldiers and *their* clients). The ads offer Nazi hats and kamikaze headbands, instructions for making napalm or for evading lie-detector tests, ball-point pens that convert into stilettos, "Viet Cong Hunting Club" badges that show a guerrilla caught in the cross-hairs of a gunsight, or human skulls pierced by twelve-inch daggers. "Genuine Human skull (not plastic) zapped by USMC combat knife," the ad promises. "Unique Bizarre trophy for your den or gunroom . . . mind-boggling!" The lily-livered pacifists, whose minds really do boggle at all this bloody-mindedness, are in fact (as one essay observes) "on the *other side*—they are fighting the war, just as surely as a left-wing lobbyist in Washington or a . . . guerrilla in the bush." The other side, of course, belongs to COBRA, Satan, the evil warriors, the Commies, the perennial brutes in black hats.

Mystified and more than a little scared by this civilian arms race, I stop by a local gun shop to see what's for sale. The downstairs is heaped with clothes. The weapons are on the second floor. At the top of the stairs a noose dangles down—"RESERVED FOR SHOPLIFTERS"—and on the wall beside it is a plaque inscribed with the second article of the Bill of Rights, guaranteeing us all the freedom to bear arms.

Except for some tents and fishing tackle, the whole of this second floor is devoted to helping us fulfill our constitutional privilege: there are enough crossbows, rifles, knives, revolvers, and shotguns to equip most of the able-bodied folks in town. It is a candy store for gun lovers, case after case of gleaming weapons. In the faces of men who are gazing at the wares, there is a child's or a lover's undisguised hunger. One man in a three-piece suit actually presses his nose to the glass, the better to study a selection of pistols.

Another fellow, who has been handed a thirty-thirty for inspection, strokes the barrel and the satiny walnut stock with his eyes closed.

The stuffed heads of deer, bear, mountain goat, and moose peer down solemnly from the walls, their glass eyes glinting. Lesser beasts are represented by entire carcasses, including a turkey, a mallard, and a swordfish. Skins of fox and raccoon hang from nails. All these moldering trophies remind me of the prize teddy bears at shooting galleries. "Win one for your tootsie!" the barker would cry. "Five shots for a quarter!" Beside a shelf stacked with brochures from the National Rifle Association, a sheet of tin is on display, decorated with bullet holes that trace out the profile of an Indian in feathered headdress and signed by one Tom Frye, Remington Arms Co., 1971. I sit for awhile in a chair fashioned from a barrel and leaf through gun catalogs. The cover of the one for Winchester Sporting Arms shows John Wayne in cowboy get-up, his eyes fixed on the horizon, the air aswirl with smoke, and the sky blotted out by the Stars and Stripes.

At one end of this armory, set off by a split-rail fence and gate, there is a museum of hunting and military paraphernalia. The white-haired clerk who keeps watch nearby tells me, "Go right on in," and I thank him and do. Bayonets, mess-kits, medals, cartridge-belts, daggers, photographs of big game hunters kneeling beside deflated elephants and spread-eagled tigers: surrounded by these mementos of mayhem, I begin to feel the panicky smothering sensation that drove me from the toy store. Through a doorway that opens beyond this little museum into an inner sanctum, I glimpse the snowy pelt of a polar bear spread on the floor and the horns of a buffalo curling above the storekeeper's desk. Turning away, I imagine a succession of rooms opening beyond that one, gallery after gallery of corpses.

So where does the desire come from, this boy's compulsion to play at killing, this man's compulsion to kill for real? Pick your own answer. Original sin, the old mark of Cain, says a theologian. Too much testosterone, explains a biologist. Territorial imperative, insists an anthropologist. The will to power or the lust for death, say opposing psychologists. A historian assures us that it is all a legacy of life on the frontier. A feminist attributes it to male insecurity and the desire for sexual dominance. No, no, other pundits declare: it's television; it's food additives; it's the animal id.

"I just think playing with guns and soldiers is *fun*," says Jesse, and said the boy in me. Troubled about all this because *I* am troubled, he asks me, "What's so bad about playing war? It's all just pretend."

It *is* pretend when it starts, this toying with murder, and for most of us it remains make-believe. I swaggered around at cowboys-and-Indians, waddled about with six-shooters, shot up enemy armies, longed for and finally got my own BB gun and .22. Most of the men I knew in my childhood were hunters. Few things in life have given me more pleasure than tramping through the leafruck and dry grasses of October beside my father, on the lookout for anything covered in feathers or fur. And yet here I sit, fearing and hating every manner of weapon. If all the world's soldiers handed in their dog tags and uniforms tomorrow, I would dance with giddy pleasure.

Many of my old playmates, those boyhood soldiers, probably feel the same. If their trigger-fingers start itching, they content themselves with blasting aliens in a video arcade, or hunting rabbits and deer on weekends. But on the day of my graduation from high school, seven of my buddies drove to Cleveland to get themselves tattoos; on the next day, wanting to handle real guns, they all joined the Marines. I met another one of those playmates years later, in England, where he was resting up at a U.S. air base before returning to Vietnam for another bout of bombing. "It's beautiful," he said, describing night raids over Hanoi, "to see those fires blooming down there like flowers and to feel this whacking great machine turn in your hands." War is hell, say the generals; but it is also heaven, say many veterans. Remembering combat, ex-warriors will tell you they have never been so alive, never so happy, since the shooting stopped.

Soldiers or not, we veterans of childhood wars carry in our innermost ears the growl of machine guns, remember in our muscles the jab of a bayonet, preserve the star-image of bursting bombs. We know all about enemies. We understand how to divide the universe into the forces of light and the forces of darkness. On the edge of sleep, our hands curl and our fingers twitch. Massacres wait in us, like the lines of plays we rehearsed long ago. If we don't enact them ourselves, we feel little surprise when someone else does. Bang, bang, you're dead, we sing inwardly. And somebody really dies.

Lilies

by Mary Oliver

I have been thinking
   about living
   like the lilies
   that blow in the fields.

They rise and fall
   in the wedge of the wind,
   and have no shelter
   from the tongues of the cattle,

and have no closets or cupboards,
   and have no legs.
   Still I would like to be
   as wonderful

as that old idea.
   But if I were a lily
   I think I would wait all day
   for the green face

of the hummingbird
   to touch me.
   What I mean is,
   could I forget myself

even in those feathery fields?
   When van Gogh
   preached to the poor
   of course he wanted to save someone—

most of all himself.
   He wasn't a lily,
   and wandering through the bright fields
   only gave him more ideas

it would take his life to solve.
    I think I will always be lonely
    in this world, where the cattle
    graze like a black and white river—

where the ravishing lilies
    melt, without protest, on their tongues—
    where the hummingbird, whenever there is a fuss,
    just rises and floats away.

Good News about Leaders and Followers

by Carol Bly

I learned by lucky accident that what educators used to call "natural leadership qualities" are what modern counselors and psychologists and therapists consider to be *psychological health for everyone*. All my life before I had psychotherapy, I had fallen for the old siren song of entitlement: some people are natural leaders, some people are natural followers. That mistaken belief has accounted for institutionalized bullying of children and for stunted ethical and psychological growth. Here is how I experienced that myth.

My elementary schooling took place at the Tryon Country Day School, in North Carolina. Our classes of between two and five children broke off at eleven o'clock in the morning to spend the last half-hour singing English and French folksongs. Our singing teachers didn't know any Native American or Latin American songs. This was private schooling of the 1940s. We went light on German songs because we were at war for the second time with Germany.

The three, sometimes four, teachers who made up our faculty were intelligent, attentive to us, usually courteous. They were never the miserable bullies of George Orwell's prep school in *Such, Such Were the Joys*.

But our teachers were inveterate typecasters. With smiling faces they assigned us each our category of personality. So far as I know, each child stayed in the same category throughout his or her time at the Tryon Country Day School. Whatever the original assessment of a child, it stayed put, even if you backslid, even if you made enormous improvement.

From the start I was stamped Creative. A friend in the same class was put into the Practical, Factual category. We had no privacy. Every child seemed to have been told the faculty assessment of the other children. Our teacher explained over and over that the practical, factual child, Amy Timmons for one, thrived best with heavy structure. During the two years that we studied

French before we started Latin, our teacher made us understand, half directly, half by innuendo, that Amy was having trouble with French because it was such a subtle language; Amy would come into her own with Latin because Latin was a highly structured, mechanical [*sic*] language. Both Amy and I anticipated that she would "get her own back at me" once we started Latin.

But then there was trouble. In Latin, *Britannia est insula* makes sense to the most fact-minded and structure-suited person, but *quis est agricola* made Amy anxious: a farmer had no business being feminine. She said to our teacher, "You said that words ending in *a* were feminine, but here's this masculine noun being declined like a feminine noun." The three of us knew she was in trouble, although we would not have identified it as psychological trouble. Our language teacher made a great point of showing us how to enjoy, rather than fear, exceptions to the rule. I could always hear, under her inviting us into the joke about exceptions to the rule, that we had better enjoy those exceptions. Those who enjoyed them were treated like insiders; those who showed themselves anxious or indignant were flunking some tiny, invisible exam somewhere behind the teacher's eyes.

I have gone into this discussion about lack of flexibility because it illustrates a point about *natural followers* and *natural leaders,* as they were called in that school—in addition to an illusive and humbug-ridden category called *naturally creative people.* Flexibility of mind, being able to accept or even enjoy the fact that from time to time a feminine noun will have masculine meaning, was unmistakably identified by our teachers as a leadership quality.

What no one at the Tryon Country Day School dreamed of in 1943 was that *every* child is born with the potential for flexibility of mind—and what no one anywhere believed in 1943 is that if, for some reason, a child does have an inflexible mind, there are helps. No one made the connection between ego development and the ability to stomach ambiguity and shifts in data or doctrine. Ours was a stable, motionless world. You were what you were. You stayed that way.

Some kindnesses applied. We may have been categorized into

natural leaders and natural followers, but this latter declaration carried the postscript that "natural followers were not to be sneezed at." For the world, our teachers told us, needed followers as much as leaders.

Three of us children were shunted laterally into a side group of naturally creative people. The first was Frederick Buechner, later author and clergyman. We were told that Fred was both naturally creative and gifted. The second in our group was Noel Peattie, later poet and editor. Noel and I didn't quite make the cut of "gifted" the way Fred did, but we were still "naturally creative," which, like being a natural follower, was not to be sneezed at. A few children who kept up steady A averages were pronounced to be good workers but "not one whit creative, alas." The school mistresses were shameless gossips. We older children were told which of the younger children "did not have interesting minds." These announcements were made with genial, thoroughgoing authority.

How odd the language of nineteenth-century-style pedagogy seems now. Such language was also, in the case of my schoolteachers, the language of twentieth-century people longing for the nineteenth century—the language of Americans longing to be English, or of a modern urban people longing for pastoral stillness.

Much that we children heard sounded all right on the surface of it. Heroes were established—the natural leaders and in a tolerant way, the creative children. The hoi polloi were established—natural followers—and their understudies, those whose minds were not one whit original, alas. At twelve and thirteen I had scarcely a smudge of democratic morality about me. I simply played and studied, living the life of children in a rural school. Still, even I felt a faint worry: if some children were one way, others another way, and neither of these two "were to be sneezed at"—or sneered at—there must exist out there somewhere a third, shadowy contingent who *were* to be sneezed at or looked down upon.

Our we/they philosophy was presented to us as common sense. It was convincing enough. Anyone could see that Amy Timmons had never even tried to write a poem, whereas Fred Buechner did some lovely ones early and many later: that was common sense. Still, common sense or not, why should anyone be sneezed at? The first time I heard the phrase "sneezed at" I knew one and only one care: whoever those people undeserving of respect were, I wanted nothing to do with them. I didn't think about them. Whatever was wrong with them might be catching.

Most of them did not seem to be going to our school, in any case. I already felt the unfairness of such a division of the world, but I had my seat in the second row (behind Fred) on the fifty-yard line. If I had a drop of decency in my head at age twelve, it didn't show. My principal motivation was not to lose my spot. I dearly wanted never to be sneezed at.

I expect our generally kindly disposed, intelligent teachers labeled children as a sensible, timesaving distinction.

Once every few years, a qualified educator drove down to Tryon from Saluda, North Carolina, to give us our Stanford-Binet IQ tests. The test results were taken as eternal truth by my teacher, although, I found out later, the test administrator had repeatedly tried to explain that performance varied with a child's psychological condition at the time of testing. I think there were two reasons that she was unable to convince our faculty of how lightly one should take IQ test results. First, our teachers were mostly Northerners. I suspect the Saluda educator's protests may have been regarded as merely modest and charming Southern small talk. And second, the prevailing philosophy of our teachers was that if anything is any good it is long-lasting and unshakable. If the famous Stanford-Binet test was good enough to bother with, then its results were our IQs for life. Good things stay put. Spurious or feckless things shift about. Once it was decided that I was creative, I went on being regarded as creative though I never turned out a story or poem in a whole year. The children regarded as natural followers stayed tucked in their passive category.

A teacher who stereotypes a child is hardly like the mother bird who, upon seeing that one hatchling is weaker than the other, identifies it as a loser, stops feeding it, and later (in some species) helps its sibling peck and claw it open for easier eating. My schoolteachers were gentler, but they did let the natural followers drift free from the Socratic questioning that they practiced

with us natural leaders and creative types. There was a pronounced difference in treatment: I noticed even at the time the
difference between the quizzing I got and the quizzing the "less
promising" children got. I took it for kindness.

Here is how the discrimination worked. My classmates and I
were now thirteen years old, time (in those days) to learn to make
précis of essays, then and still a great way to teach people to pay
attention to other people's ideas. The point of the exercise is that
you can't reduce a thing to its essence unless you have made its
ideas your own, so to speak, so you've some idea of what the
essence of it would be. Précis writing divides men and women
from boys and girls, intellectually speaking.

The eighth graders were reading an essay by John Middleton
Murray about the difference between the "real" reason one does
something and one's "good" reasons for doing it. I got excited by
the work. It was the first time in my life I had been asked to have
psychological insight—definitely the first time in my life that a
psychological tool was put into my hand. I could hardly stay in
my seat. For one thing, I longed to go home and attack the aunt
whom I lived with. "Yeah," I planned to tell her, "that's what you
say is your reason, and it is a good reason, too, but what is your
real reason, I wonder I wonder I wonder?" *Stated motivation versus
real motivation* was the rod and staff I meant for my comfort and
protection against the adult in authority.

No sooner did we each read aloud our précis in class than it
was clear some people *could not analyze*. They did not understand
what Murray was getting at. I thought the teacher would say,
"You didn't get it, I'm afraid. You will have to rethink the whole
thing." I was so surprised by how my English teacher actually did
respond to their poor efforts. Instead of saying aloud, "Well, I am
afraid that what you did was simply cut out some sentences here
and there, which is *not* making a proper précis," what the teacher
in fact said was, "How did you like the essay?" The beleaguered
student grunted something. "What do you think is the best sentence in it?" the teacher went on. The student stayed red in the
face, but chose a sentence, obviously at random, and read it
aloud. "Good," the teacher said. "I like that sentence, too. Now—

if you had to help someone else find this essay, what information would you give him?" The student perked up and read off the title-author-publisher-date material on the copyright page. "First-rate!" the teacher said. "Right—we'll move on . . . ," et cetera. The rest of that year of serious eighth-grade English, the teacher did not ask weaker students a second, probing question if they had given an evasive or off-the-wall answer to a first question. Clearly she did not intend to harass anybody who seemed to be incapable of analysis. Just as clearly, she had given up moving that kid from concrete thinking to abstract idea.

She had slipped into two styles of teaching for her two styles of students—those who were being questioned rather carefully about what this author or that author had in mind, and the others who, being let off the hook about the substance of literature, were being guided to take their satisfaction from exactitude about footnotes. The less concept-minded children got less and less of the back-and-forth "partializing" questioning that makes all the difference.

We talk a lot about teaching kids to *think*—to think for themselves—as opposed only to learning data or doctrine by rote. But it is not easy to teach someone to think. Some teaching techniques terrify the student. Some increase the student's self-esteem minute by minute, such as that part of social work empathy called partializing.

Partializing helps people stop careening from one unclear emotion to the next. Partializing quiets a jerky, unclear mind. The teacher asks a student or client to divide what has seemed like a gleaming, immutable whole into bite-size pieces. A student has said, "I hate English." The teacher asks, "Which part of English were you thinking of?"

An analogy: Let us say that we are carrying a gunnysack full of agates and fieldstones and slivers of mica. "What's in there?" a mentor asks us with interest. "Beautiful stones," we say. "Like what?" the mentor asks. "Really really beautiful," we say, "all of them shining like mirrors from the world before God covered it with clay and laurel roots." "Amazing. Let's have a look," the mentor says, and adds, "You sit down, I'll sit down; you open the gunnysack and spread out everything." Grudgingly we sit. We dump out the bag and spread out the stones. Some *are* beautiful, their slivers shining as if they were indeed the remains of a world once made of crystal. Others look as if they had been laid down dully and gradually like sand in an ancient inland sea. Some have been gnarled bright by water. Some are ordinary gravel.

Partializing means breaking down a huge generalization by naming some specifics of it. Here is partializing, used in a discussion of *Charlotte's Web*. "Jimmy, you said that the love that Wilbur had for Charlotte was different from the love he had for her children and grandchildren. What made the two feelings different from one another—for example, what did he find so rare in Charlotte?" Such a question asks a child to partialize. A teacher staying with that discussion can lead children to see the difference between nostalgia-plus-love-of-fellow-creatures, which Wilbur felt for the balloonist spiders, and the love that his soul cherished for his mentor Charlotte.

Partializing is distinguished from Socratic questioning by its goal. Socrates's querying style was educative but some of his purpose was to catch out and crow over any discussants whose arguments showed logical flaws. Partializing in the hands of therapist, social worker, or good teacher, in contrast, has only the mission of showing someone the variousness of his or her *own* thinking and feeling. Partializing also helps children or adults to feel peaceful and mildly interested in the presence of a new, particular idea, even if they can't see a use for it straightaway.

Adults who typecast children or one another in the present day still teach or treat those whom they have identified as *natural followers*—or as having uninteresting minds—differently from how they treat *natural leaders*. The cruelty of it is that someone unable to get past "concrete thinking" (what page was this on? what color was Charlotte?) may have been culturally deprived or even culturally abused, by not being *taught* to make the jump from concrete to abstract thinking. Unfortunately, psychology is still a distasteful unknown to tens of millions of our teachers and statespeople. Children and adults, then, who happen to be in the power of such teachers or statespeople are unnecessarily at risk for staying stuck at whatever their present level of concrete thinking.

They stay stuck the same way the dog with the porcupine quills in its nose goes on being a dog with porcupine quills in its nose until someone is willing to focus on the dog and think: "That dog's agony is not the will of God. There are people with expertise in removing quills. Let's find one of them."

Whenever we let off an unsuccessful thinker with a technical, peripheral success, such as the ability to find the page of a citation, we once more reinforce his or her taste for technical, peripheral subjects (the page numbers, rather than the content, of books, for example). Since this particular dynamic has been exercised for generations of certain populations of children, it promulgates a kind of class dynamic. Kids early taken for "bright" develop an expectation inside themselves that they will do thinking in their lives. Kids early taken for less bright develop the expectation of organizing details, servicing the organization, being support staff. They are much more likely to put on khaki than to ask if such and such a war is right.

Even elementary school language arts teachers whose schools have social workers on staff often do not know the workers. They don't know what the social workers actually do, either. They do not ask the workers, "Have you any communication skills in your bag of tricks that would take a kid from fear of new ideas to enjoyment of ideas, new or old?" They do not ask, "Do kids come in types the way they seem to? Leaders . . . followers . . . ? Or is there a development angle to this?"

I want to return to the suggestion by our mentor that we dump out our gunnysack full of stones. Partializing shows us how to say, "Well, now that you have made me dump out the bag so we can both look, I see that *some*, but not all, of the rocks are as beautiful as mirrors. I do see that the mica is there, all right, but there are also fieldstones and other rocks I don't even know the names of," instead of saying, "Whatever is in my bag, it is beautiful," and later, by extension, "My country right or wrong." Partializing gives us two great political gifts: first, the savvy to acknowledge that we often treasure things that are not one hundred percent gorgeous even by our own standards, and second, the permission to go on treasuring that mixed bag (our country, our friends, a friend, an organization, a church). Once we have made ourselves look at the loved thing—let us say, our country—in its various pieces, we will never again love it so charismatically, so dreamily, so single-heartedly, as we did before. A parallel: In *Anna Karenina*, Tolstoy tells us that Levin eventually saw many mental limitations in Kitty. She was self-centered in her nesting instinct. She did not really care what he did about reordering the class system in his fields. Her beautiful eyes, which once had seemed to understand his very soul, actually missed the point of many issues. At the moment of noticing, Konstantin Levin became a whole person. Now he had to pull back all those projections of his own ideals from Kitty. If those ideals were going to come to anything, he himself would have to make it happen. He would go on loving Kitty, but never in the old way.

To be in love, blindly, with the whole of something or someone is less painful and certainly more ecstatic than to learn to partialize. And what is the return for loss of joyful enthrallment? You would think that enthrallment is about as enjoyable a feeling as there is. The return is that in the process of grasping that one can love a flawed thing or person, one finds oneself loving more and more things, even oneself. That is, partializing can lead to increased self-esteem. Partializing about oneself gives one the gift of self-tolerance, even forgiveness, even liking. What an unfamiliar concept this is—that the ability to analyze (coolly to take things apart for a look, as if any one thing or person were made of several elements) should increase one's self-esteem!

If I feel unhappy about a policy of my country and acknowledge that fact, I feel more self-esteem, and then, it sometimes follows, but not always, I feel more able to protest the national policy I don't like. I am no longer so psychologically needy that I have to be loyal to everything about my country. I am not loyal, let us say, to its foreign policy between 1966 and 1973 in either Asia or Latin America.

In his poem, "Ode for the American Dead in Asia," Thomas

McGrath inveighs against our educational class system. The "elders" of churches or schools have not taught the straight run of American kids to think for themselves—that is, to partialize. Since "no scholar put (their) thinking cap on," these young Americans of thirty years ago were left in the simpler, earlier levels of cognitive stage development. Their minds were full of jokes and "summer follies," no serious attitudes, only tennis. The stereotyping of children done in my school was pastel stuff compared to the broad brush of the 1990s American psychological class system. Children regarded as less promising than others are by the millions treated to hasty teaching or none. When people are not invited into complicated thinking, they will do the best they can: they will stay with simple thinking. Usually that means a combination of three of Lawrence Kohlberg's stages of ethical development. I have given short summaries of them below:

Looking at the world to see what it can do for me and my
   tribe (II)
Looking to determine what makes my crowd like me and
   molding myself so I will keep being liked (III)
Counting on nearby authorities with loud voices to define my
   duty for me, so I can do it (IV)

McGrath's poem pities the 58,000 American casualties because they were victims of *cultural abuse*. McGrath was not a typecaster. He argues that we are born not to

                    . . . run
As strict as trains on rails the circuits of
Blind instinct.

the way bees and moles are programmed to do. Nor are human beings programmed only for what is sometimes called "alpha-level thinking"—learning by copying or passively absorbing from whatever local stimulus is around. McGrath is indignant that church leaders and school teachers "confirm" a whole class of young Americans "in [their] ignorance."

Long before they sat in too-large classes taught by poorly trained teachers, they were victims of a haphazard unfairness.

Even when a baby is still a fetus, the American class system leans heavy against the walls of the womb. Some adults help the "psychological health" in their not-yet-born children, whereas other adults unwittingly hurt the psychological health of their children in utero.[1] We know the gross instances. If Mom drinks during any of the trimesters of our stay inside her womb, it affects our neural system. If Mom sings or plays certain music when she is pregnant with us riding passively inside her, our minds are helped. The effect of elegant music that isn't too thundering can't be measured yet, but it will be, since this effect has been repeatedly observed.[2]

We have identified parental activity that leads to psychological health in infants, such as the well-recognized influence of a child's being read to, for example. One more unfairness of nature is that in our early lives we are dependent on whomever our caretakers are, not only for physical well-being but for the first significant cognitive development and ego strength. Unfair.

Some cultural abuse is so cheery that we may fail to see it as cultural abuse. In fact, when we do identify it, our clue is not what the abuser has said but the blank inexpressiveness of the victims. How liberally and in what sensible tones cultural abuse still gets handed out! I heard the perfect case of cheery cultural abuse as recently as twenty years ago. The abuser was a clergyman in a rural community church that I belonged to. Some women were complaining to our pastor that their household life somehow didn't seem like enough. He told them that God has His purpose for each of us, and that some are called to work out His purpose in little lives and some in bigger. That was cultural abuse—on-site religious authority used to quash what that pastor, like any CEO, chose to perceive as a nagging personnel problem. At the time I was too ill-read in Christianity to realize that he had committed a crime that even Christian tradition recognized and defined as "a sin against the Holy Ghost." A translation for our century might be "an inappropriate, intrusive, overly directive comment made to a client." Psychotherapy has a canon, so to speak, against prophesying. Therapists constantly hear people ask, "How will I turn out?" or "He'll end up as a . . . , won't he?" Training invariably makes the therapist respond, "We can't know that" or "We don't know that." Prophesying, a subset of stereotyping, is spiritual abuse.

Our country pastor was cheerful, however. We trusted him. He made us run our discussions "lovingly." The minutes of our meetings recorded that "loving discussion followed." If you had been there and remembered the backbiting, the secretary who turned out the minutes was most valued player in hypocrisy. Still, the tone was loving and cheerful, and we trusted the tone. Country women were being indirectly told that living "little lives" for God was nothing to be sneezed at, just as the children in the Tryon Country Day School in the 1930s and 1940s had been told explicitly that being a natural follower was "nothing to be sneezed at."

That is the bad news. The recent good news, on the other hand, is inestimably beautiful: it is that there are no prototypes such as "natural leaders" and "natural followers." There are people in whom psychological and cognitive growth have received this much encouragement and people whose psychological and cognitive growth have received only that much encouragement, but the essential and democratic finding is that what were once loosely called "leadership qualities" are part of the formula for every member of the species.

Although the potential for thinking for oneself is a potential programmed into everybody, only some people seem to develop it. Cultural abuse is seen as normal behavior. It is so normal that when I have complained of it, otherwise nice people bring out the three classic responses of bullies: "Don't be so sensitive"; "You have to have a sense of humor, you know"; and, "Aren't you making an awfully big mountain out of an awfully small molehill?" They would be right, if what we grew up to be were only an amalgam of inborn traits. If the whole species were fated to be scared to inquire into politics, satisfied with moral chaos, unable to give up pain-avoiding denial, unable to imagine invisible hypotheses and make sense of them—if every one of our species were stuck like that—then indeed what we would need is the ability to josh one another.

In order to clarify our own ideas, along with ideas in the literary selections in this book, I suggest we make two lists: one a list of the human qualities that help a person *fulfill the expectations of our species* and the other a list of those human qualities that *sabotage anyone's fulfilling those expectations.*

We should make lists the way scientists enter labs—with expectation of further discovery. We expect to poke about through our thoughts and our notes, trying a hypothesis, trying a scenario or two, until we light on some new likely truth—and then we mean to use it to change one or another horrible aspect of our culture. I think we should let the titles and headings of our lists be large and clumsy so we don't edit out any of our thinking. There is one serious trouble with lists. They look too *right* and too authoritative. One forgets to check them for obviously missing items or those that have no business on the list.

I offer here my list of good psychological properties, but only in hopes that others will pencil in their own ideas:

1. The ability to look at new ideas with more curiosity than fear. ✗
2. The ability to ask for more information without feeling "loss of face."
3. The ability to keep an idea in mind long after its sensate sig-   ✗
nals disappeared—to remember, for example, that someone dying in a snowstorm ten minutes ago is still dying or dead in it, although we ourselves are back in the warm kitchen.
4. The ability to absorb and weigh painful information without   ✗
denial.
5. The ability to sin consciously. (I use the word sin because it means wrongdoing plainly understood by the doer to be wrongdoing and because it has psychological exactitude.) "An ability to sin consciously" is on the good-health list because it frees one from the delusion that one must do no wrong. Sophisticated moralists usually regard themselves as a "community of sinners," not because they mean to glamorize themselves but because sooner or later we all kill something innocent in order to eat it. Even vegetarians, who deprive themselves of easily found complete-protein meals for the sake of mercy to animals, pull up or cut off the lifestem of plants and eat them. Vegetarians allow medical

schools to experiment with animals. Lovers of nature take their children to look at the animals imprisoned without trial in the zoo. In other words, moralists know that, sooner or later, in dozens of ways, a human being hurts others in order to live better himself or herself.

6. The ability to imagine oneself as someone else, and to imagine oneself elsewhere. Nearly all acts of altruism and self-sacrifice at any level are tied to this particular ability of the human imagination.

7. The ability to invent hypotheses and try them and cheerfully reject any of them that don't fit all cases. A concept has to be universal or it isn't a truth, just as a scientific finding is not a proper finding if the experiment cannot be replicated.

8. The ability to maintain by willpower the idea that life has meaning. That means not letting that idea vanish in the presence of short-term psychological pain.

9. The expectation that you yourself will have a go at changing the system in which you live. This is the pinnacle of "leadership" in the nineteenth-century and prepsychology sense of the word. Social workers and family therapists today set this expectation as a goal for every single client they have. In some vague way most of us divide our acquaintances into those who will always prefer the status quo and those who are always trying to spruce up the campsite, but I don't think people realize that being a changer of the system is itself an aspect of psychological health. Being a changer of the system is the opposite of bumper-sticker-level group loyalty: "Don't like it? Try Moscow."

If we consider how present-day status quo people quarrel with present-day change agents, we see that reactionary people are typically loyal to what they see as the center-mass of the community, or the common denominator. Change agents are always looking either for novel ways of doing the old things or for the novelty of leaving off doing the old things. Likely the reactionaries, being the established majority or the established totalitarian leadership, have *always*, in prehistory as now, run change agents out of the village whenever they could. Some prehistory migrations of people may have had to do with the existing system being so strong that all dissenters had to leave or be punished for being original, or for being at odds with the common denominator. They would be acting out a sociological phenomenon repeated in the departure of dissenters from Europe to America in the seventeenth through the nineteenth century.

That is the end of my list and discussion of psychological properties that will allow human beings to take themselves seriously as beings in development. We can each make our own. Mine has glaring weaknesses. For one thing, every quality on it is of some use in the study of ethics, but none for the purposes of spirituality. What about openness to religious feeling as such? Should a welcoming attitude toward religious feeling be on such a list? Obviously no one list will do for everyone.

Here is a second list, called "The Properties of People Blocked by Psychological or Cultural Abuse"—properties formerly taken to be the markings of "natural followers":

1. Regarding nearly every issue as a practical or technical issue, and talking about it as practical, using technical language, even if the issue is loaded with implications of goodness or evil (such as the way some *Kommandants* of German concentration camps became absorbed in the problems of getting enough Zyklon-B gas).
2. Feeling much more easy in a crowd of like-minded people than in solitude, having very limited concentration when alone.
3. Clinging without examination to eternal verities, doctrines that don't swerve, styles that don't change, liking best any tradition that seems to go back to time immemorial— favored expressions being "world without end," "now and forever," and "stay put."
4. Using hierarchical terminology such as we/they, upper group/lower group, in-group/out-group, winner/loser thinking—in fact, either/or thinking of many kinds.
5. Having an aversion to system change. (Charities of choice are for disease research and organizations of tribal loyalty, such as one's own church.)

6. Enjoying having crushes on leaders, enjoying letting a dicta-
   tor do one's thinking, and then obeying that leader's orders.
   Formally educated (but psychologically blocked) people may
   jeer at charismatic leaders like Jim Jones who attract non-
   educated followers, but they themselves are vulnerable to
   charismatic leaders whom they perceive as more culturally
   or socially correct.

7. Typecasting and stereotyping others, the habit of seeing
   people as permanently of one caste or another, instead of
   seeing them as being at such and such a stage of personality
   growth.

8. Having a strong aversion to any modern psychology of
   which personal change is a goal. A psychologically blocked
   person can stomach the idea of psychiatry better than the
   idea of psychotherapy, psychiatry suggesting illness for
   which no one need feel implicated.

9. Lacking experience in, and therefore lacking a taste for, connecting particular experiences to universal concepts; or, vice
   versa, lacking experience in bringing up a personal story to
   illustrate or check a stated principle. For example, if A expresses a universal theory such as, "People sometimes drop
   into unfair behaviors when stressed," a blocked person, B,
   might exclaim, "Is that ever true!" A asks, "Were you thinking of some particular time you noticed that yourself?"
   B: "No—I don't know—but it sure is true." This particular
   property is inversely proportional to one's having experienced
   telling one's own story and having it *heard,* an experience
   classically *absent* in abusive homes and classically *emphasized*
   in all family therapy groups and individual sessions.

10. Having a tendency to describe every feeling at the midrange,
    tepid level. Condemnation is expressed as "not so hot," and
    praise shows up as "did a good job." When asked how they
    feel about happiness or sadness in life they frequently an-
    swer, "I just aim for contentment." The word *just* as a mini-
    mizer gets heavy use.

11. Being unable to name an emotion: a blocked person typi-
    cally answers the question, "Which emotion did you feel

when you saw such and such happening?" with a thinking
sentence rather than naming the emotion. Answer: "I didn't
think he had any business doing that." "No, he hadn't, but
what was the feeling you were feeling?" "I thought if he
went on like that he would paint himself into one real bad
corner." And so on.

12. Being self-oriented. If a blocked person drops a rock into a
    pond he or she does not squint at the far shore to see what
    effect the ripple had out there. Whoever is out there is *other.*

13. Reacting hostilely and rapidly to anyone of a more ethically
    complicated outlook. This response shows up dramatically
    in two cases of my experience: the obvious hostility that
    fundamentalist Christians feel toward Unitarians in a group
    and the resentful, even hateful, frame of mind of other, still-
    blocked family members at the point when one family mem-
    ber begins to become conscious of, and therefore both
    critical of, the family structure—and hopeful of change.

14. And finally, nearly always defining themselves as "not politi-
    cal" if liberal politics are under discussion, and as being "no
    crusader" when public ethics are under discussion.

If we expressed the main thrust of Thomas McGrath's "Ode for
the American Dead in Asia" in political terms, we could say that
he connects a young person's growing up without any education
in analyzing with that person's lack of political development.
Only the culturally privileged ask the abstract questions, such as,
"What is my duty, and to whom?" Some of the privileged could
arrive at answers like, "My duty is *not* to help kill 301,000 Southeast Asian people."

How much better it is to *think* than to know chapter and verse
(or page number) of anything! Of course our class system, like any
class system in history, is based mostly on inherited money and
inherited lifestyle, but a huge part of it is based on the difference
between an education devoted to learning to think about ideas
and feelings and an education devoted to concrete things—the
beam strengths of material, for example.

One cannot measure the exact extent to which habitual and

courteous questioning, asking for partialization of a child's or youth's generalizations, promotes the kind of freedom of mind that makes us able to resist obeying bad orders. What we do know is that a childhood and youth full of courteous questioning about one's life and ideas enhances the ego's development. And, conversely, we know that a childhood and youth full of being jeered at or even "just kidded" by parents slows or stalls the ego's development. Such influences are of course affected by the many dynamics that go on at the same time. One can't ascribe this or that outcome, such as a freethinking mind, to one or another discrete treatment received when one was young. In our 1.8 million years as *Homo sapiens* we are only now beginning to scratch the surface of how ego development and ethical maturity are systemically connected.

I want to take up a shadowy question that is germane to our concern with typing people as natural leaders or natural followers. This question is about the lies that society or family tells us. The lies that are passed to children are a principal subject of most literature, most psychotherapy, and nearly all family therapy. Here is Denise Levertov, one of the most serious poets of the United States, talking about several joyful feelings that come with what we have been calling "psychological health":

> . . . All humankind
> women and men,
> hungry,
> hungry beyond the hunger
> for food, for justice,
> pick themselves up and stumble on
> for this: to transcend barriers, longing
> for absolution each of each by each,
> luxurious unlearning
> of lies and fears,
> for joy, that *throws down the reins*
> on the neck of
>   *the divine animal*
> who carries us through the world.[3]

This stanza constitutes the final stanza of a long poem. Levertov is represented in this book with another poem, "Like Loving

Chekhov," in Chapter IX. This stanza is placed here because of the poet's beautiful and passionate way of saying things that intensely hopeful family-systems experts and psychotherapists feel, but express differently.

The following is a passage from Paula Gutlove, of the Center for Psychology and Social Change. Just as Denise Levertov has been an unswerving opponent of American wars abroad, the center has devoted its energy to psychological ways of peacemaking. Both poet and social scientist assure us that when human beings throw over the lies they had once accepted as national or family icons, annoying the older generation, shaking up their own, risking their colleagues' scorn—when human beings do that, there likely sets in a general, secret love of everybody.

> Family systems theory emphasizes relationships, interactive patterns, and context. Nations, like families, must be able to recognize when their belief systems are based on obsolete and constricted habits of thought that lead to undesirable actions and outcomes. Family systems therapy strives to disrupt and transform old patterns of belief and behavior, while fostering an openness to new information and the creation of fresh solutions. Family therapists have a repertoire of techniques to effect such changes.[4]

"A general, secret love of everybody" makes one open to joy, the offbeat happiness that human beings rise to when they aren't residually uneasy. Even if one doesn't get around to telling one's friends at coffee break, "I certainly feel as if I have thrown down the reins on the neck of some divine animal that is carrying me through the world," one's spirits pick up considerably when he or she stops being cramped by old lies ("obsolete and constricted habits of thought").

This chapter has dealt at length with the obsolete and constricted idea called typecasting people as natural leaders or followers. I am sad that my kindly teachers taught promising students one way and less confident students another way, thus preserving a psychological class system. But they were not genuine jerks. They were doing the best they could based on what they knew.

At age forty-seven, I decided to start making a list of lies that I once but no longer believed. My first list of lies did the bumpy first work of psychological health for me. The rest of what we do for our own freedom of heart is in comparison merely cognitive work—reminding ourselves to practice discernment and not to forgive and forget.

Why make such a point of focusing on old lies? It sounds handsomer to say, "Right! That lie was a mistake. I shall *forget* that my teachers typecast children! They were wonderful teachers. I shall remember only their good points."

Forgiving and forgetting is an immensely attractive nineteenth-century artifact. Modern psychology suggests that it is better health to tell oneself, "Right! That lie was a mistake. I shall always remember that my teachers typecast children, but I want to add this comment: in subscribing to such lies, they either *(a)* were doing the best they could at the time or *(b)* were genuine jerks, or a mix of both.

"But I will not forgive and forget, because the process of type-casting is still going on, so widely that it locks people into whole privileged and unprivileged populations. That process goes on inside ourselves, too, even though we don't want it to."

I have been working up to suggesting that we each jot down three lists to use for reference while reading "Ode for the American Dead in Asia," "Death Games," and "Lilies." The lists will be *essences*, like précis, taken from our own lives. When you take deeply felt thoughts from inside you, and lay them down outside you (in writing), far from locking you into self-orientation, they bring you closer to the deeply felt thoughts of serious authors like McGrath, Sanders, and Oliver. I have found listmaking a brisk, modern act of friendship between reader and writer.

Making lists, however, unlike deciding to write a journal, doesn't sound like much fun. I expect we associate lists with banality such as a Post-it on the refrigerator reminding us to get electrical tape and a Phillips screwdriver. Or listmaking reminds us of academic discipline from the era of our lives when academic discipline was an unpleasant experience. No one makes elementary school kids write lists, but teachers do encourage junior high school students to take systematic notes. Taking notes, to a fourteen-year-old, is antiglamour, knuckling under to the teacher, and knuckling under to the text assigned. No one with any pride would get mixed up in it. I think an ancient mouse in our psyches still, even when we are forty, twitches with scorn when someone suggests making a list.

I still would like to suggest three very personal, subjective lists to make in response to "Ode for the American Dead in Asia," "Death Games," and "Lilies." The idea is to awaken one's own feelings on the subjects that McGrath, Sanders, and Oliver feel so strongly about.

1. Thirty-six important good and bad qualities or abstract concepts in life—all earnest. No jokes. No "broken dental floss" entered as bad, for example; no "winning a sweepstake" entered as good. Thirty-six is deliberately a great number of values for anyone to name. It needs to be such a high number for two reasons: first, nearly everyone's first ten or fifteen items on such a list are simply off the media or the tops of our heads. We don't trust such a list, so we say whatever occurs—peace, war, not killing beef cattle—anything that strikes the mind. We feel we are being made to play the fool. If we stick with the job, a second stage sets in: we find that many events we thought of as mere practical realism are, in fact, moral values of our own. For example, torturing animals in a barn was once a painful sociological reality that I first noticed when I was married and went to live on a farm. I took it for just a sad fact. If only someone then had asked me to write it down, I would have noticed twenty years before I did notice it that torturing animals (or anything) is evil, not a fact of life. A long clumsy list surprisingly enables inexperienced moralists to move dozens of items from a previous mental drawer called "Oh, just the way it is, I guess" into the mental drawer called Good or Bad.
2. A list of lies about human goals that I have been told and have in the past lived by, and of truths I now feel confident of and try to steer by.
3. A list of only four good values and four evils, as *I* see them, to be followed by a list of four goods and four evils as *others*

—McGrath, Sanders, Oliver—see them. For example, to Scott Russell Sanders, making up one's own values, willfully standing apart from generally accepted morals, is a central business of good life. Although his essay is full of humor, every point in it rests on the idea that the general culture is too natural, too stuck at primitive tastes in killing, and one can't make a deep friendship with it.

A postscript to this list: Some find it easier to start with their *own* list of values and then glance at others' lists, to evaluate what those others (in the case of a book like this, the authors) are thinking. Another style of thinking is to start with *others'* values, and then later work inward, as with a shrinking circle, toward one's own.

A Few Suggestions for Thinking about McGrath's "Ode for the American Dead in Asia"

Like any first-rate poem, "Ode for the American Dead in Asia" moves into feelings and some literal argument at various levels. So that people with a primary interest in ethics not waste the poem, I suggest reading it first for pleasure and second for its shout against the American class system. The author points out several ways in which the United States government (through its schools), American teachers, and American clergy fritter away the cognitive development of young people. No cognitive development, no defense against daydreaming one's way to being cannon fodder. A. E. Housman's poems also come to mind, but McGrath has the particulars for Americans, and he is of a generation that understood psychological conditioning.

A Few Suggestions for Thinking about Sanders's "Death Games"

Scott Russell Sanders's "Death Games," about the conversations he has with his little boy, who longs for toy guns "like a starving bum in a bakery," is an awfully funny, engaging essay, considering that it is about males getting stuck at a boyhood-level love of guns.

Some questions to consider after reading "Death Games" include: How does the father respectfully practice empathy with Jesse? How is the conversation between Sanders and Jesse different from the conversation between the mother and her little boy while Sanders is holding Cover Girl? We note a rare empathic quality to the little boy's conversation: he actually asks his father to partialize a comment the father has just made. It takes considerable self-esteem to ask someone else to partialize, especially when the someone else is an adult in authority, and you are only a child. Why did the boy, from what we know in "Death Games," feel confident to ask his father to partialize? The father also asks the son to partialize. Such conversations can't be written off just as the conversations of any lucky, well-educated family, in which the father's business, whatever it is, gives him the leisure to fool around shopping and talking with his son. Their conversation is not normal for American privileged families, because this father and son listen to each other.

When the son *has* explained his feelings, the father doesn't come pounding in with "an interpretation"—he doesn't typecast the son. The father is humorous, but he is not a joker. Finally, an attribute far more important than it looks: Sanders is restful when talking to his son and to us. He lingers on this point or that point. He takes time. He comes back the next day. He keeps the focus. Jesse was charmed he'd gone to look at the toys. Any of us would have been charmed, too. These qualities are therapeutic. They are not just good manners, and they are not just common sense.

A Few Suggestions for Thinking about Oliver's "Lilies"

"Lilies" is such a good poem one could read it for its beauty of sound, for its kind sharing of thought, for its humor, for the poet's tying her worldview so beautifully to detail, for its high-mindedness. Who *else* has ever taken on Jesus on the subject of the lilies being so great, neither toiling nor spinning, got up better than Solomon in all his glory?

I suggest reading the poem first as an argument against ever accepting "natural followership" or stunted psychology or stunted ethical growth. The lilies and the cattle cannot, and the hummingbird will not, do the fierce, loving work of van Gogh—not just his beautiful painting, but his wanting to change the world. The idea is not to love nature less than we may now do, but to love the ethical potential of human beings *more* than we may now love it.

If schooling or willpower or psychology can help, no human being wants to be a hummingbird who just moves off when there's a fuss of some kind.

Notes

1. Jane M. Healy, "The Physically Deprived Brain," in *Endangered Minds: Why Our Children Don't Think* (New York: Simon and Schuster, 1990), 239.

2. "A four- or five-month-old fetus definitely responds to sound and melody—and responds in discriminating ways. Put Vivaldi on the phonograph and even the most agitated baby relaxes" (Thomas Verny and John Kelly, *The Secret Life of the Unborn Child* [New York: Dell, 1981], 21). Verny refers to the following studies: D. K. Spelt, "The Conditioning of the Human Fetus in Utero," *Journal of Experimental Psychology,* 38 (1948): 338-46; L. W. Sontag, "Parental Determinants of Post-Natal Behavior," in *Fetal Growth and Development,* ed. Harry W. Waisman and George R. Kerr (New York: McGraw-Hill, 1970); and Antonio Ferreira, "Emotional Factors in Pre-Natal Environment," *Journal of Nervous and Mental Disease,* 141 (1965): 108-17.

3. From the poem "Modulations," in *Life in the Forest* (New York: New Directions, 1978).

4. Paula F. Gutlove, "Transforming the Confrontation Mentality," *Center Review,* 5, no. 2 (1991). (Project on Promoting Effective Dialogue, Center for Psychology and Social Change, 1493 Cambridge St., Cambridge, MA 02139.)

Leaving the Casual Brutality of Nature

THE READING

Against Nature
Joyce Carol Oates

THE COMMENTARY

Carol Bly

Against Nature

by Joyce Carol Oates

> *We soon get through with Nature. She excites an expectation which
> she cannot satisfy.*
>
> Thoreau, *Journal*, 1854

> *Sir, if a man has experienced the inexpressible, he is under no
> obligation to attempt to express it.*
>
> Samuel Johnson

The writer's resistance to Nature.
*It has no sense of humor: In its beauty, as in its ugliness, or its
   neutrality, there is no laughter.*
It lacks a moral purpose.
It lacks a satiric dimension, registers no irony.
*Its pleasures lack resonance, being accidental; its horrors, even when
   premeditated, are equally perfunctory, "red in tooth and claw"
   et cetera.*
It lacks a symbolic subtext — excepting that provided by man.
It has no (verbal) language.
It has no interest in ours.
*It inspires a painfully limited set of responses in "nature-writers" —
   REVERENCE, AWE, PIETY, MYSTICAL ONENESS.*
It eludes us even as it prepares to swallow us up, books and all.

■   ■   ■

I was lying on my back in the dirt-gravel of the towpath beside the
Delaware-Raritan Canal, Titusville, New Jersey, staring up at the sky
and trying, with no success, to overcome a sudden attack of tachycardia that had come upon me out of nowhere — such attacks are
always "out of nowhere," that's their charm — and all around
me Nature thrummed with life, the air smelling of moisture and sunlight, the canal reflecting the sky, red-winged blackbirds testing their
spring calls — the usual. I'd become the jar in Tennessee,[1] a fictitious

center, or parenthesis, aware beyond my erratic heartbeat of the numberless heartbeats of the earth, its pulsing pumping life, sheer life, incalculable. Struck down in the midst of motion—I'd been jogging a minute before—I was "out of time" like a fallen, stunned boxer, privileged (in an abstract manner of speaking) to be an involuntary witness to the random, wayward, nameless motion on all sides of me.

Paroxysmal tachycardia is rarely fatal, but if the heartbeat accelerates to 250–270 beats a minute you're in trouble. The average attack is about 100–150 beats and mine seemed so far to be about average; the trick now was to prevent it from getting worse. Brainy people try brainy strategies, such as thinking calming thoughts, pseudo-mystic thoughts, *If I die now it's a good death,* that sort of thing, *if I die this is a good place and a good time,* the idea is to deceive the frenzied heartbeat that, really, you don't care: you hadn't any other plans for the afternoon. The important thing with tachycardia is to prevent panic! you must prevent panic! otherwise you'll have to be taken by ambulance to the closest emergency room, which is not so very nice a way to spend the afternoon, really. So I contemplated the blue sky overhead. The earth beneath my head. Nature surrounding me on all sides, I couldn't quite see it but I could hear it, smell it, sense it— there is something *there,* no mistake about it. Completely oblivious to the predicament of the individual but that's only "natural" after all, one hardly expects otherwise.

When you discover yourself lying on the ground, limp and unresisting, head in the dirt, and helpless, the earth seems to shift forward as a presence; hard, emphatic, not mere surface but a genuine force—there is no other word for it but *presence.* To keep in motion is to keep in time and to be stopped, stilled, is to be abruptly out of time, in another time-dimension perhaps, an alien one, where human language has no resonance. Nothing to be said about it expresses it, nothing touches it, it's an absolute against which nothing human can be measured. . . . Moving through space and time by way of your own volition you inhabit an interior consciousness, a hallucinatory consciousness, it might be said, so long as breath, heartbeat, the body's autonomy hold; when motion is stopped you are jarred out of it. The interior is invaded by the exterior. The outside wants to come in, and only the self's fragile membrane prevents it.

The fly buzzing at Emily's death.[2]

Still, the earth *is* your place. A tidy grave-site measured to your size. Or, from another angle of vision, one vast democratic grave.

Let's contemplate the sky. Forget the crazy hammering heartbeat, don't listen to it, don't start counting, remember that there is a clever way of breathing that conserves oxygen as if you're lying below the surface of a body of water breathing through a very thin straw but you *can* breathe through it if you're careful, if you don't panic, one breath and then another and then another, isn't that the story of all lives? careers? Just a matter of breathing. Of course it is. But contemplate the sky, it's there to be contemplated. A mild shock to see it so blank, blue, a thin airy ghostly blue, no clouds to disguise its emptiness. You are beginning to feel not only weightless but near-bodiless, lying on the earth like a scrap of paper about to be blown off. Two dimensions and you'd imagined you were three! And there's the sky rolling away forever, into infinity — if "infinity" can be "rolled into" — and the forlorn truth is, that's where you're going too. And the lovely blue isn't even blue, is it? isn't even there, is it? a mere optical illusion, isn't it? no matter what art has urged you to believe.

■   ■   ■

Early Nature memories. Which it's best not to suppress.

. . . Wading, as a small child, in Tonawanda Creek near our house, and afterward trying to tear off, in a frenzy of terror and revulsion, the sticky fat black bloodsuckers that had attached themselves to my feet, particularly between my toes.

. . . Coming upon a friend's dog in a drainage ditch, dead for several days, evidently the poor creature had been shot by a hunter and left to die, bleeding to death, and we're stupefied with grief and horror but can't resist sliding down to where he's lying on his belly, and we can't resist squatting over him, turning the body over . . .

. . . The raccoon, mad with rabies, frothing at the mouth and tearing at his own belly with his teeth, so that his intestines spilled out onto the ground . . . a sight I seem to remember though in fact I did not see. I've been told I did not see.

■   ■   ■

Consequently, my chronic uneasiness with Nature-mysticism; Nature-adoration; Nature-as-(moral)-instruction-for-mankind. My doubt that one can, with philosophical validity, address "Nature" as a single coherent noun, anything other than a Platonic, hence discredited, isness. My resistance to "Nature-writing" as a genre, except when it is brilliantly fictionalized in the service of a writer's individual vision—Thoreau's books and *Journal,* of course—but also, less known in this country, the miniaturist prose-poems of Colette *(Flowers and Fruit)* and Ponge *(Taking the Side of Things)*—in which case it becomes yet another, and ingenious, form of storytelling. The subject is *there* only by the grace of the author's language.

Nature has no instructions for mankind except that our poor beleaguered humanist-democratic way of life, our fantasies of the individual's high worth, our sense that the weak, no less than the strong, have a right to survive, are absurd.

In any case, where *is* Nature? one might (skeptically) inquire. Who has looked upon her/its face and survived?

■   ■   ■

But isn't this all exaggeration, in the spirit of rhetorical contentiousness? Surely Nature is, for you, as for most reasonably intelligent people, a "perennial" source of beauty, comfort, peace, escape from the delirium of civilized life; a respite from the ego's ever-frantic strategies of self-promotion, as a way of insuring (at least in fantasy) some small measure of immortality? Surely Nature, as it is understood in the usual slapdash way, as human, if not dilettante, *experience* (hiking in a national park, jogging on the beach at dawn, even tending, with the usual comical frustrations, a suburban garden), is wonderfully consoling; a place where, when you go there, it has to take you in?—a palimpsest of sorts you choose to read, layer by layer, always with care, always cautiously, in proportion to your psychological strength?

Nature: as in Thoreau's upbeat Transcendentalist mode ("The indescribable innocence and beneficence of Nature,—such health, such cheer, they afford forever! and such sympathy have they ever with our race, that all Nature would be affected . . . if any man should ever for a just cause grieve"), and not in Thoreau's grim mode ("Nature is hard to be overcome but she must be overcome").

Another way of saying, not *Nature-in-itself* but *Nature-as-experience.*

The former, Nature-in-itself, is, to allude slantwise to Melville, a blankness ten times blank; the latter is what we commonly, or perhaps always, mean when we speak of Nature as a noun, a single entity—something of *ours.* Most of the time it's just an activity, a sort of hobby, a weekend, a few days, perhaps a few hours, staring out of the window at the mind-dazzling autumn foliage of, say, Northern Michigan, being rendered speechless—temporarily—at the sight of Mt. Shasta, the Grand Canyon, Ansel Adams's West. Or Nature writ small, contained in the back yard. Nature filtered through our optical nerves, our "senses," our fiercely romantic expectations. Nature that pleases us because it mirrors our souls, or gives the comforting illusion of doing so. As in our first mother's awakening to the self's fatal beauty—

> I thither went
> With unexperienc't thought, and laid me down
> On the green bank, to look into the clear
> Smooth Lake, that to me seem'd another Sky.
> As I bent down to look, just opposite,
> A Shape within the watr'y gleam appear'd
> Bending to look on me, I started back,
> It started back, but pleas'd I soon return'd,
> Pleas'd it return'd as soon with answering looks
> Of sympathy and love; there I had fixt
> Mine eyes till now, and pin'd with vain desire.

—in these surpassingly beautiful lines from the Book IV of Milton's *Paradise Lost.*

Nature as the self's (flattering) mirror, but not ever, no, never, Nature-in-itself.

■   ■   ■

Nature is mouths, or maybe a single mouth. Why glamorize it, romanticize it, well yes but we must, we're writers, poets, mystics (of a sort) aren't we, precisely what else are we to do but glamorize and romanticize and generally exaggerate the significance of anything we focus the white heat of our "creativity" upon . . . ? And why not Nature, since it's there, common property, mute, can't talk back, allows us the possibility of transcending the human condition for a while, writing prettily of mountain ranges, white-tailed deer, the purple crocuses outside this very window, the thrumming dazzling "life-force" we imagine we all support. Why not.

Nature *is* more than a mouth—it's a dazzling variety of mouths. And it pleases the senses, in any case, as the physicists' chill universe of numbers certainly does not.

■   ■   ■

Oscar Wilde, on our subject: "Nature is no great mother who has borne us. She is our creation. It is in our brain that she quickens to life. Things are because we see them, and what we see, and how we see it, depends on the Arts that have influenced us. To look at a thing is very different from seeing a thing. . . . At present, people see fogs, not because there are fogs, but because poets and painters have taught them the mysterious loveliness of such effects. There may have been fogs for centuries in London. I dare say there were. But no one saw them. They did not exist until Art had invented them. . . . Yesterday evening Mrs. Arundel insisted on my going to the window and looking at the glorious sky, as she called it. And so I had to look at it. . . . And what was it? It was simply a very second-rate Turner, a Turner of a bad period, with all the painter's worst faults exaggerated and over-emphasized."

(If we were to put it to Oscar Wilde that he exaggerates, his reply might well be: "Exaggeration? I don't know the meaning of the word.")

■   ■   ■

Walden, that most artfully composed of prose fictions, concludes, in the rhapsodic chapter "Spring," with Henry David Thoreau's contemplation of death, decay, and regeneration as it is suggested to him, or to his protagonist, by the spectacle of vultures feeding off carrion. There is a dead horse close by his cabin and the stench of its decomposition, in certain winds, is daunting. Yet: ". . . the assurance it gave me of the strong appetite and inviolable health of Nature was my compensation. I love to see that Nature is so rife with life that myriads can be afforded to be sacrificed and suffered to prey upon one another; that tender organizations can be so serenely squashed out of existence like pulp,—tadpoles which herons gobble up, and tortoises and toads run over in the road; and that sometimes it has rained flesh and blood! . . . The impression made on a wise man is that of universal innocence."

Come off it, Henry David. You've grieved these many years for your elder brother John, who died a ghastly death of lockjaw, you've never wholly recovered from the experience of watching him die. And you know, or must know, that you're fated too to die young of consumption. . . . But this doctrinaire Transcendentalist passage ends *Walden* on just the right note. It's as impersonal, as coolly detached, as the Oversoul itself: a "wise man" filters his emotions through his brain.

Or through his prose.

■   ■   ■

Nietzsche: "We all pretend to ourselves that we are more simple-minded than we are: that is how we get a rest from our fellow men."

■   ■   ■

Once out of nature I shall never take
My bodily form from any natural thing,
But such a form as Grecian goldsmiths make
Of hammered gold and gold enamelling
To keep a drowsy Emperor awake;
Or set upon a golden bough to sing
To lords and ladies of Byzantium
Of what is past, or passing, or to come.
   William Butler Yeats, "Sailing to Byzantium"

Yet even the golden bird is a "bodily form taken from (a) natural thing." No, it's impossible to escape!

■   ■   ■

The writer's resistance to Nature.
Wallace Stevens: "In the presence of extraordinary actuality, consciousness takes the place of imagination."

■   ■   ■

Once, years ago, in 1972 to be precise, when I seemed to have been another person, related to the person I am now as one is related, tangentially, sometimes embarrassingly, to cousins not seen for decades, — once, when we were living in London, and I was very sick, I had a mystical vision. That is, I "had" a "mystical vision" — the heart sinks: such pretension — or something resembling one. A fever-dream, let's call it. It impressed me enormously and impresses me still, though I've long since lost the capacity to see it with my mind's eye, or even, I suppose, to believe in it. There is a statute of limitations on "mystical visions" as on romantic love.

   I was very sick, and I imagined my life as a thread, a thread of breath, or heartbeat, or pulse, or light, yes it was light, radiant light, I was burning with fever and I ascended to that plane of serenity that might be mistaken for (or *is*, in fact) Nirvana, where I had a waking dream of uncanny lucidity —

My body is a tall column of light and heat.

My body is not "I" but "it."

My body is not one but many.

My body, which "I" inhabit, is inhabited as well by other creatures, unknown to me, imperceptible — the smallest of them mere sparks of light.

My body, which I perceive as substance, is in fact an organization of infinitely complex, overlapping, imbricated structures, radiant light their manifestation, the "body" a tall column of light and blood-heat, a temporary agreement among atoms, like a high-rise building with numberless rooms, corridors, corners, elevator shafts, windows. . . . In this fantastical structure the "I" is deluded as to its sovereignty, let alone its autonomy in the (outside) world; the most astonishing secret is that the "I" doesn't exist! — but it behaves as if it does, as if it were one and not many.

In any case, without the "I" the tall column of light and heat would die, and the microscopic life-particles would die with it . . . will die with it. The "I," which doesn't exist, is everything.

But Dr. Johnson is right, the inexpressible need not be expressed. And what resistance, finally? There is none.

■   ■   ■

This morning, an invasion of tiny black ants. One by one they appear, out of nowhere — that's their charm too! — moving single file across the white Parsons table where I am sitting, trying without much success to write a poem. A poem of only three or four lines is what I want, something short, tight, mean. I want it to hurt like a white-hot wire up the nostrils, small and compact and turned in upon itself with the density of a hunk of rock from the planet Jupiter. . . .

But here come the black ants: harbingers, you might say, of spring. One by one by one they appear on the dazzling white table and one by one I kill them with a forefinger, my deft right forefinger, mashing each against the surface of the table and then dropping it into a wastebasket at my side. Idle labor, mesmerizing, effortless, and I'm curious as to how long I can do it, sit here in the brilliant

March sunshine killing ants with my right forefinger, how long I, and the ants, can keep it up.

After a while I realize that I can do it a long time. And that I've written my poem.

Notes

[1. A reference to Wallace Stevens's poem "Anecdote of the Jar."]

[2. A reference to a poem by Emily Dickinson, "I heard a Fly buzz— when I died—."]

Leaving the Casual Brutality of Nature

by Carol Bly

The introduction to this book proposed that each of us read the stories, poems, and arguments, taking care to hear our own various voices, the dissenting ones as well as the dominant or "proper" ones. When one deliberately welcomes one's own apparently contradictory feelings, the result is that still more feelings come to the fore. These new arrivals, much more philosophical than our earlier feelings, are generally more altruistic as well.

An example: A wildlife biologist, Terry DeBruyn, hunted bears occasionally between 1981 and 1989. Then a former United States Forest Service biologist introduced DeBruyn to a bear who had been habituated to people. Instantly DeBruyn was transformed from incidental hunter to a student of bear life. He has now spent a thousand hours following them about, tagging mothers and cubs, talking to them. He introduces bears as fellow creatures, not casual fodder, to present-day bear hunters.[1]

The question we want to ask is: if through mere lack of focus, we are at this moment *hunting* something or someone which or whom we could be *studying* instead—studying with intent to improve its lot, what's more—how do we work up consciousness about it? I make a mental image of a bear hunter before he has learned to know any one bear personally. Presumably if you say "Bear" to him, he automatically thinks, "Hunt." How might this natural, casual hunter have learned to *imagine* a bear so well that he could make the switch to Advocate of Bears? Advocacy on behalf of creatures not of one's own species is definitely *not casual* and it is *not natural*.

I have not heard a psychotherapist talk about turning oneself into a Committee of the Whole and then getting in some consultants to help. Nonetheless some part of psychotherapy asks for that process: realizing first that one has inside oneself both ideas one has recognized, and feelings, which are not-yet-but-developing-ideas, that one has not yet recognized, and that one's whole self consists of all of these voices. These voices want sometimes to consult with experienced people from the outside. When we read a book we are doing a kind of consulting.

Consulting in good faith is about as civilized a behavior as any that human beings pull off. All parties to a consultation agree to do no lying. They try hard to surface any secret agendas. When it is not the blind leading the blind and when it is not corrupt, consulting is wonderfully gratifying to both asker and adviser.

Because it works upon trust and shared insights, consulting is certainly most wonderfully subject to corruption. Anyone who has sat in nonprofit boardrooms has probably taken the soul scorching that egotistical consultants can hand out under the title of Troubleshooting. The useful point, I think, is that however many awful consultations may have taken place in the world, the process of consulting is, at its best, civilized. It gives stymied minds new play and hope. The key virtue of consulting is that it pulls people back to the *mission* of a project, when perhaps they have been trammeled up in the problems of staff, resources, and structure.

If we are not one hundred percent pleased with our species or its literature or both, then consulting about it is a good idea. One generally calls in consultants under one of two conditions: first, when there is threat of change, and second, when one *wants* change. We have found out that an enemy plans to invade us: we organize ourselves as consulting groups for information, goals, and strategies.

In the second case, when we want something to be different, and we are holding in our hands a work of literature—an essay by Joyce Carol Oates, whom we know for her stories, not her informal essays—we want to confer with one another and with her. Is this true? we want to ask. Do people casually, scarcely noticing, engage in little cruelties here and there as Oates seems to say in "Against Nature"?

We serious readers don't laugh off bad news when a good writer proclaims it. We do not want to be cool and supercilious. We are willing to listen to evidence, and even call in other consultants, to see if our bad fears are justified or exaggerated. We are willing to reconvene our own personalities as a kind of

Committee of the Whole so that every voice in us can speak freely. (One of the most cunning of Robert's Rules of Order is the process of a *Meeting* reconvening itself as a *Committee*—a "committee of the whole.")

For those readers who have not experienced modern psychotherapy I would like to point out that personal or group inquiry therapy begins in kind but firm agreement between client and therapist about the following:

1. This will be a safe place and time to express several inner, even secret, truths that may even conflict.
2. This will be a safe place in which to be earnest. No one will sneer. One need not put the winding-cloth of jokes around one's anxieties.
3. Some beliefs that we have supposed were Eternal Verities may well not be eternal verities. There may be hope where centuries of authorities have assured us there is no hope. There may be expert help where authority has assured us there is no technology.

The style of good therapy has many parallels to breaking up a rule-clad entity into a committee of the whole—and then suggesting that each of the committee members consult with one another and with any mentors they can buttonhole from the outside.

The assumptions one makes upon engaging in therapy are much like the assumptions one makes upon moral consultation: our selves say to each other, "We may have been ignoring or denying up to now, but we no longer intend to do so. We do not *want* to maintain a cool, vaguely polite demeanor. We don't want to give up humor, though. We will laugh at these authors' jokes if they make them, but only at such jokes as intensify, rather than divert from, the moral cloth."

In an exact and madcap poem called "America," Allen Ginsberg pretends to be a private citizen consulting with the United States about its general moral health. "America" is one of the funniest poems in our language, yet it points out the ominous low-level psychological and ethical development of 1950s cold

war leaders. The poem shows how profitably low-level ethics performs the marriage of television and business. The poem suggests
that *Time* magazine is a poor basis for anyone's theology. Finally
Ginsberg softshoes into a paranoid role-play done in Tonto's
English ("them Russians bad, and them Chinese") and winds up
with one of the best stanzas of satire in English:

> America this is the impression I get from looking in the
>   television set.
> America is this correct?
> I'd better get right down to the job.
> It's true I don't want to join the Army or turn
>   lathes in precision parts factories, I'm nearsighted and
>   psychopathic anyway.
> America I'm putting my queer shoulder to the wheel.[2]

Ginsberg's vivid lurch of poetics, his inventive devil-may-care
chunks of invention won him lots of disdain from the 1950s literary establishment. I suggest that we bear in mind that disdain of
forty years ago so that we can take in our stride the disdain we
might receive for reading literature for its idealistic content *now*. I
am thinking, too, of the ex-bear hunter who now, as the *New York
Times* writer admiringly pointed out, "Walks with Bears." I expect
unreconstructed bear killers feel disdain for him.

What exactly do we want from literature then? First of all, we
want literature for escape reading. I have always loved C. S.
Lewis's statement that whatever else we say we want out of literature we know we want it to take us away, away, away! into someone else's world.

We also want to see what these authors can show us consciously, or, if the author is half-unconscious, we want to guess at
what his or her story is symptomatic of. We want to think about
how to solve specific ethical problems they mention. We want to
think about how people, from their various psychological backgrounds or genetic makeup, ever got into those behaviors that
grieve us. We want to look at the love of life that some authors
demonstrate and share, even while they take exception to one or
another injustice or bad luck. Finally, if there are people in the

world who can help our species with some new insights, we want to refer ourselves to them.

First of all, in the age-old style of scholars we can take notes and make lists.

The women's movement inspired ordinary men and women to write journals but didn't mention making lists. In diaries and journals we leisurely fork through our impressions like gardeners turning over a plot in spring. Old scents rise up. We recall something touching—an expression on someone's face. Old strong feelings rise again.

We tend not to write down, "I deplore such and such a happening." We haven't any moral voice, but we've been told not to be preachy. Only those small circles of men on public television are fearless about being preachy; the rest of us have been warned off. We are led to believe that this is a coarse, greedy, and upwardly scrabbling culture: if we want to get anywhere in it, we had better refer to someone who steals as differently acculturated, not a habitual thief.

Yet first-rate authors keep trying to tell us, "By the way, you two hundred and seventy-odd million Americans and others in the world, you are unconsciously dying to identify your own moral ideas. You don't want to 'get your feelings *out*'; you want to put them together with some thinking about them, in the same way that one does an algebraic equation: first one lists whatever one is talking about, in our case, some moral feeling or other. Then one wants to list anything else that seems relevant. One needn't make an equation. One starts with a list of the entities in the case—let us say, in Joyce Carol Oates's "Against Nature," for example:

A list
This writer has known something of transformation first
hand.
She has set herself to write a poem.
She is against nature or some attributes of nature.
She says that when she saw herself mindlessly killing a lot of
ants she had her poem.

That is the barest outline of "Against Nature" but enough to start with. Joyce Carol Oates has some headlong, silvery ideas about *how* nature operates within us. Her essay is disarmingly messy-looking on the page. Despite its offhand disorder, its diary-like entries, Oates has carefully set down all sorts of insights about nature. She knows a cunning insight common to psychotherapy and religion and literature: when you find yourself listing feelings about a subject, some of the feelings may at first seem inconsistent with others on the same list. You stick with them, however, without deleting, for this reason: since you felt each of those feelings, each apparently has a claim to truth at some level. Do not erase them at this point. Hang onto everything. "Do not delete a fresh insight" is a moral equivalent of the brainstorming ground rule that "no contribution to the discussion is dumb."

Here is one reader's notes taken on the subject of Oates's disliking nature. No item on the list is "values-free" or "clean of emotion." The list hasn't one morally neutral item in it. Some of the list remains in the author's own words; some summarizes discussions of hers.

Nature—

It has no sense of humor.

It lacks a moral purpose.

It lacks a satiric dimension.

Its pleasures are merely accidental, its horrors merely perfunctory.

It lacks a symbolic subtext.

It has no verbal language.

It has no interest in ours.

It inspires a far-too-simple and far-too-rhetorical response in nature-writers: *reverence,* etc.

It eludes us, even as it prepares to swallow us up, books and all.

It is pleasant for sport.

It doesn't care whether I live or die.

Still, I feel it's my place and I'm at home in it.

Its repulsive and various violences are in my memories and
   memories shouldn't be suppressed.
Nature doesn't care two cents' worth for our value systems.
It gives us peace, the joy of its beauty, and consolation. It
   offers a lot more sensual pleasure than physics.
Thoreau had conflicting takes on nature: it is innocent and
   empathic; —it needs to be overcome.
      Thoreau claimed he liked the way nature kills things off
         by the millions so other things can eat: Oates thought
         him being precious about it. How would he have liked
         it if someone had told him it was good that his
         brother was being killed off so worms could gobble up
         the body, etc.? ("Come off it, Henry David.")
Landscape (nature) is mostly hobby.
We like nature when it seems to mirror *us* (Milton).
The human mind is what gives nature any *quality* (Oscar
   Wilde).
Nature is something culturally to evolve yourself out of, on
   purpose, whether or not you are stuck using the
   metaphors it gives us (Nietzsche and Yeats).
Nature, like any extraordinary stimulus, fills us up with
   consciousness but consciousness is a distraction from
   imagination (W. Stevens).
A fever once made me feel unified with everything, more like
   light or heat in everything than like a cool single human
   being. I felt so at one with everything I felt my body was
   inhabited not just by me but by other creatures.
There was an inexpressible feeling that I (separately) didn't
   exist but was only alive in everything, but since the idea
   is inexpressible it need not be gone into—or resisted.
I noticed I wanted to write a short tight mean work of art,
      but I took to killing, one by one, the ants in an unending
      column, bemusedly, as if outside myself . . . I found I
      can keep up that gratuitous murder a long time—a short
      tight mean finding like what I had thought I wanted for
      a poem.

Oates is not a babe in anyone's woods. When we read through her remarks, we see a good deal of comment that is neither spacious nor respectful. Thinking tough about nature is not depressing if one accepts two cheering assumptions of stage-developmentalists:

All human beings are potentially moral thinkers. We are as programmed for conscience as we are programmed for intellectual insights—both potentialities, of course, being pathetically dependent upon our psychological habitat.

Empathic treatment by mentoring *adults* is the major agent in helping a child (or, as we now know, a blocked or psychologically wounded adult) fulfill the human propensity for moral decision making. Vindictive mentoring, conversely, effectively stunts a human being from growing into conscientiousness.

These assumptions appear here because it is amazing to read Joyce Carol Oates in light of how willingness to consider unpleasant thoughts is at the core of ethical development. We know that some people go all the way through life practically shuddering if someone brings a new, not to mention critical, idea into the room. Their necks get red. Oates, on the other hand, has some moral genius in the area of Willingness Not to Deny Unpleasant Psychological Truth about *(a)* sacred cows and *(b)* herself.

I am grateful for her unpleasant insights. Her tone varies. Sometimes she makes her spare entries with a devil-may-care tone; sometimes she sticks flat-footedly to facts, such as the fact that she was perfectly capable of killing ants one by one as they sallied across her desktop. She reports to us about these low-affect murders by fingertip. The author has decided to tell us that the mercilessness of nature discussed earlier in the essay is unmistakably inside herself. There it is—with the classic low-level sadistic enjoyment—it is in there, all right—she goes on killing ants—but she is watching it, too. She is not lying about it.

We are so used to authors talking about whatever sensitive take they have on life: they, the authors, are always the sensitive ones. Their parents or their spouses or their employers or the other kids in the class are presented as the roughnecks without a half-ounce of mercy among them.

We could easily miss, out of pure habit, the moral genius of this particular writer who can say, "Here is an essay on natural cruelty, with moral undertones to it—but mind you, I am its villain, not the hero." Very few memoirists say, "I used to be quite morbid and what's more I see that as an adult, just when I think I have an aesthetic goal in mind—writing a poem—I settle for equably killing a string of ants instead."

Memoirists are willing enough to tell us about their childhood predations. They carried a slingshot on their Saturday walks and they dug up animals' graves—but their tone says, "Oh yes, I was a bloody-minded little kid, but of course I got over it." Oates's use of the childhood maggot watching, on the other hand, is not whimsical nostalgia for naughtiness: it forewarns us of her violence as an adult.

We can make some guesses about which qualities in human beings Oates respects. We know she believes in having self-control (from the lying-down scene) and we know she believes in humor to prevent grandiosity (a value that shows in several places). We know she has some level of ego development because she can regard herself with critical detachment. She believes that what makes art is psychological consciousness, not manipulation of words. We know that Oates despises soft-headedness. We know that she consciously enjoys her own sharp tongue.

From "Against Nature," we can hypothesize about several of her values. The central point of the essay may be one of them: that nature is lovely, outside of ourselves, and we are willy-nilly part and parcel of it; "the outside wants to come in," as she says. And some of it is already in there, inside ourselves. Some brutality comes naturally to us. In two ways, at least, there is too much of nature: when consciousness absorbs us so thoroughly that the imagination does nothing, and second, when we would just as soon kill something as not. At least, and this is the kernel of her essay, if we are someone who wanted to write a "tight, mean" poem, then we are someone who can kill a regiment of ants. Our natural, casual brutality will be subject enough for a poem.

What about leaving the brutality of nature? How is that done? The human brain is both hard-wired, like animals' brains, and soft-wired; that is, much of our thinking depends not on prebirth programming but on what our psychological habitat is like, what our mentoring has been like, if there has been any at all.[3] When McGrath pitied the soldiers, confirmed in their ignorance, who really had been brought up only to joking around, summer follies, and patriotism, he was pitying people who had not been helped to leave the brutality of nature.

If we look over the list of properties Oates attributed to nature—humorlessness, indifference to values, happenstance violence, random stimulation of various kinds, no verbal language, high proportion of mere sensate consciousness, no imagination, a tendency to kill for amusement if nothing better offers—we see those are properties of ignorance or lack of a contemplative education.

They are also the properties of people at risk to start, or willingly to serve in, wars.

The rest of this book is devoted to showing how empathy, the reading of imaginative literature, and a belief in the potential people have for moral development enhance one another.

Notes

1. David Binder, "Black Bears, Up Close and Personal," *New York Times*, April 4, 1995, C1.

2. Allen Ginsberg, "America," *Howl* (San Francisco: City Lights Books, 1956).

3. See a discussion of environmental influences on brain circuitry in the chapter titled "Neural Plasticity: Nature's Double-Edged Sword," in Jane M. Healy, *Endangered Minds: Why Our Children Don't Think* (New York: Simon and Schuster, 1990), 47.

The Brutality of Lucky Predators

THE READING

Cider 5¢ a Glass
Donald Hall

THE COMMENTARY
Carol Bly

Cider 5¢ a Glass

by Donald Hall

"When I heard Monica's
    voice on the telephone, I
knew what had happened. She
    spoke almost coldly, holding
the tears or hysteria back.
    Sam had pecked her goodbye
in bed that morning the way
    he usually did;
when she got up, she assumed
    he'd left for the office
on schedule until she
    looked out and saw the Buick
parked in the carport. Sam sat
    upright in the driver's
seat with his eyes open.

"Because I am sixty, I have
lost many friends (my mother
    who lived to be eighty-
seven looked at newspapers
    in her last years only
to read the obituaries)
    —but not friends like Sam:
We met at boarding school, roomed
    together in college,
and were best man at each
    other's weddings. It started
when we were new at Holderness,
    homesick and lonesome
as we watched the returning
    boys greeting each other
after their summers on the Cape.
    We took walks, we talked.

Our friendship endured college,
    political quarrels,
one drunken fistfight, dating
    each other's ex-girlfriends,
hitchhiking, graduation,
    and marriage; and survived
although Sam left the East
    to settle in Chicago
and drudge for a conglomerate's
    legal department,
pleading in court to deny
    workmen's compensation.
I write for the Boston *Globe,*
    considered liberal,
and whenever we met, Sam
    started right in on me
for the naiveté
    of my politics. Sometimes
we argued all night long . . .
    but I learned: If I refused
to fight, one night at the end
    of our visit, after
our wives had gone to bed
    and we drank one last bourbon
together, Sammy
    would confess that he hated what
he did—work, boss, and company.
    He wanted to quit;
and he *would,* too, as soon
    as he found another job.
One night he wept
    as he told a confusing story
about a man in Florida,
    paralyzed for life
when a forklift crushed
    his spinal cord, who was accused
of being drunk on the job,
    which he wasn't. When Sam's

department won its case,
    Sam got a bonus. Of course
he never quit his job
    and his salary to work
for Cesar Chavez or sail
    his boat around the world.
He spent ten years planning
    early retirement and died
six weeks before retiring.

    "Sam was a good father
and loyal husband most
    of the time; in private life
he was affectionate
    and loyal; many people
virtuous in public
    privately abuse their wives
and children. Then I think:
    'What about the night-watchman,
paralyzed and cheated?
    What about *his* family?'
Then I stop thinking.

    "Sam wrote letters rarely. We met
every couple of years, here
    or there, and he called up
impulsively. Last August
    Sam and Monica drove
to our place. He looked good
    although he wheezed a little.
He referred to someone
    by name, as if I should know
who she was, and shook his head
    sharply, two or three times,
insisting: 'It was only
    an infatuation.'

One night after dinner,
    neither of us drinking much
these days, he took his guitar
    from the trunk of the car
so that we could sing old
    songs and reminisce. On Labor
Day they headed back.

    "After Monica's call I dreamed
about Sam all night. Today
    I am ten thousand times
more alive in the rearward
    vision of memory
than I am editing stories
    by recent college
graduates or typing
    'graphs on a green terminal.
I lean back, closing my eyes,
    and my sore mind repeats
home movies of one day:

    "It's October, a Sunday
in nineteen-forty-four,
    Indian summer bright with
New Hampshire leaves: Sammy
    and I walk (happy in our
new friendship, sixteen and
    seventeen years old) under
tall sugarmaples
    extravagantly Chinese red,
and russet elms still thriving,
    enormous and noble
in the blue air.
    We talk about the war going on
overseas and whether we
    will fight in it; we talk

about what we will do
    after the war and college.
I admit: I want to write novels.
    Sam thinks maybe
he could be a musician
    (he plays guitar and sings
Josh White songs) 'but maybe
    it would be better to do
something that *helps* people . . .'
    Maybe he should think about
law school? (I understand:
    He feels that his rich father
leads a fatuous life
    with his Scotch and his girlfriends.)
Although we talk excitedly,
    although we mean what
we say and listen closely
    to each other, the real
burden of our talk
    is the affection that contains
and exalts us. As it turns dark,
    we head back toward school
on a shadowy gravel road;
    we are astonished
to see ahead (on a lane
    without cars in nineteen-
forty-four, as if an apparition
    conjured there
to conclude this day that fixed
    our friendship forever)
a small table with a pitcher
    on it, three glasses,
and a sign: CIDER 5¢
    A GLASS. A screendoor swings
open on the gray unpainted
    porch of a farmhouse,

and a woman (old, fat,
  and strong) walks down the dirt path
to pour us our cider.
  She takes our nickels and sells
us a second glass and then
  gives us a third. All day
today I keep tasting
  that Sunday's almost painful
detonation of cider sweet
  and harsh in my mouth."

The Brutality of Lucky Predators

by Carol Bly

What is a "lucky predator"? In Donald Hall's powerful poem "Cider 5¢ a Glass," four privileged people are the bad guys, one character, kept off-stage, is the victim, and a heroine appears so briefly as to be only a symbol of life outside the Ivy League. The poem is about two graduates of a prep school and an Ivy League college. The speaker of the poem is presumably a liberal. His friend Sam attended law school and later got a bonus from his gigantic Chicago firm for bilking a hurt workman out of the compensation due him.

The plot, in psychological and ethical terms, is that three very privileged people "enable" Sam to cheat the workman. They are the speaker, the speaker's wife, and Sam's wife. They enable Sam not to quit the bad corporation he works for. After Sam's death, the narrator says he feels nostalgia for their friendship more strongly than he has felt anything for a long time.

Information about Sam's bad work always comes through drunken conversations when the two couples get together. The other three privileged people enable Sam's drinking, as well as his crookedness. No one intervenes with Sam. No one even confronts Sam about his drinking, never mind his immorality, in the way that psychologically sophisticated people who love a drunk or a crook, or someone both drunk and a crook, confront or intervene. The speaker of the poem argued with Sam when they were drinking, but eventually gave up the drunken argument and settled for nonadversarial drinking with Sam, hearing him out, and waiting for Sam's confession of guilt. This confession would come late at night, long after the wives had gone to bed. Since Sam had years before jeered at the speaker for being naive and idealistic, the speaker understandably takes satisfaction from Sam's molten confession. The speaker takes no psychologically active or empathic action.

We can make intelligent guesses about the values of the poet and of the speaker of the poem. Perhaps these values are shared by the two wives and Sam. Abiding friendships, the beauty of New England, and the idealism of sixteen-year-old boys count as good. Heavy drinking, adultery, and using one's law education and prestigious association with a large firm to cheat hurt workmen are bad. There is some ironic equivocation at the end of the poem: should one's memories be of beauty or of treachery? Say that the teenaged boys talked about moral issues but really felt not the burden of those issues but only the burden of their love for each other. Isn't it all right just to remember the friendship? What's wrong with the freedom to be nostalgic? Don't we get to remember the good times, too? May we not, if we have pretensions to moral awareness, simply enjoy a poet's story of a nice poor woman who sells the boys cider at five cents and is so generous that she *gives* them the third glass they each want? Must we put together the anecdote of her generosity with money next to Sam's greed in being unwilling to leave his bad firm until he has another high-paying position? Aside from that, all issues seem clear enough. If that is so, why is the poem so shocking?

In some general ironic way we know that white-collar crime done by Americans of the most privileged backgrounds causes much more suffering, person by person, dollar by dollar, than all the street crime put together. Still, little of our serious poetry and fiction writing is about lucky predators. Although we writers, at least as much as people in other work, would embrace any psychology that might stop the rich from cheating the poor, our literary method is nothing more complicated than exposure. We write scenes showing the cruel events, and then expect someone else to exert themselves. Alas, people do not change because of what they read in literature. The work of Frank Norris, though loved and widely read, did not stop turn-of-the-century businessmen from preying on workmen. The vivid poetry of Allen Ginsberg did not break up the marriage of business and patriotism. Harold Grey's Daddy Warbucks delighted businessmen who read the comic strip "Little Orphan Annie" in the early 1930s. Far from regretting the irony of Daddy's manipulations of war and bucks, small businessmen were especially fond of that comic strip. A joke, of course, with his evening dress at all times of day,

Daddy Warbucks nonetheless was a natty financial and industrial hero, making it seem like a manly necessity to be the absent caregiver of the street-smart daughter who forgave him completely — and a no-nonsense hierarchical-style employer who kept his henchmen sweet and loyal; a man who had in his pocket low-life hoods who delighted readers with their occasional lifesaving of the boss's spirited kid. Literature, no matter how accurate its pictures of abuse or crime, is basically the stuff of which dreams, not systemic changes, are made.

Literature without reflection is wonderfully ineffective against white-collar predation. If it were effective, every estate lawyer who read Dickens's *Bleak House* would have taken the case of *Jarndyce v. Jarndyce* to heart and refused to bleed families dry in estate cases. Ironically, literature on its own normalizes and nearly vindicates the crimes it describes: people committing the same crimes sometimes feel validated, understood, even glamorized. If authors are writing about what they do, then what they do must be big — or at least real. Authors don't write whole books about cleaning up after a meals-on-wheels spread, after all.

The particular emotion we could call "wishing the rich would stop clipping the poor" is an extension of one of the ancient longings of our species. Whatever name we put on it, it is the emotion that made people think up the idea of having *laws*. Once people have experienced hatred of might-makes-right — the entitlement big people feel to manipulate smaller people — one feels a love of *law*. An example: Let us say there is a little boy who lives with his parents, not yet conscious of right and wrong — still a creature of nature, feeling love, feeling enjoyment, feeling frustration when a toy breaks, reading kids' books, having friends. One idle Sunday afternoon one of his parents takes him into the guest bedroom and rapes him. Now, for the first time, this child feels the emotion of wanting recourse. This child needs serious law that is enforced.

The poor are the little boy, and the rich are the parent. We have laws designed to stop Sam from cheating the workman. They work or they don't work. A roomful of people may feel that might does not make right, yet nearly everyone grins when someone says aloud, "I certainly wish we had some way to make the rich not *want* to cheat the poor!" The snickering comes from pessimism. People don't believe in any cure for this most ancient, most classic, most natural fate. Those who inherit power get to wield it against the weak. In a benignant democracy or in the occasional benignant era of any nation's life, one hand of the rich may be tied behind their backs, but seldom both. A well-organized predator can commit some injustice for a number of profitable years before the law weighs in, just as a parent-rapist may prey on his or her child for a long time before social services manage to intervene.

When a psychologically uneducated person has assessed a situation as hopeless, he or she, wanting to avoid the pain of further deliberations about the hopelessness, often practices this two-step defense: first, the person moves his or her thinking away from the hopeless problem itself. And why not? Why dwell on and get shrill about something that can't be fixed? Alternatively, the pain avoider attacks whoever just brought up the painful subject. The pain avoider points out how naive he or she was. Sam insults the speaker of the poem about his naïveté. If the pain avoider succeeds in creating embarrassment, then he or she has not only got rid of the conversation about the rich preying upon the poor but has experienced the fillip of bullying the idealist who just spoke.

A piece of normal psychology: People hang on to the conviction that such and such a situation cannot be cured. Sometimes people even go to someone who says there is a cure, especially in order to defeat that hopeful expert in the field. People have such an odd stake in declaring a situation hopeless.

I lived in western Minnesota for twenty-three years of my adult life. I was struck that some farmers took the trouble to attend all-day seminars in trash-surface farming in order to argue against it. Trash-surface farming, which has a number of names, is a means of saving soil from wind and water erosion, of lessening the compaction that comes from driving immense tractors over a field four or more times a year, and it saves farmers' time driving over the field for weed control. Its disadvantage is that it allows some buildup of pests.

In these all-day seminars, farmers used much of the question

period explaining to the seminar leaders that trash-surface farming wouldn't work. The leaders did what smart leaders do: they
cordially let everyone say their hopeless philosophies, knowing
that until people have spoken their objections to a new idea they
can't listen to you. The noise in a person's brain from the circuitry
that says, "That won't work!" may well be the loudest noise in
most people's heads most of the time. I underestimated that noise
until I found myself wasting one hundred and twenty dollars'
worth of psychotherapy sessions explaining to the therapist exactly how human nature cannot be changed.

I had shopped around until I found a therapist I could work
with. In the first five minutes I knew she would be first-rate, as
over the next two years she proved to be. I felt relieved and ready
to work, first through a grievous personal crisis, and second, to
transform my philosophy of life. In the first five minutes of the
first session I knew unmistakably that I was in the presence of
someone whose views about what makes human life beautiful, if
sometimes sad, were more spacious and benignant than my
views. My philosophy was like early Christian astronomy: I went
by measurements that wrote off humanity as much smaller, much
stiffer, more fatefully determined than our species really is.
Eratosthenes, Aristarchus, and other Greeks had hundreds of
years before Christianity postulated that earth size and our galaxy
size were much bigger than the figures that medieval Christians
clung to. The Greeks also knew that the stars' orbits were neither
"fixed" nor circular, as later Christian astronomists insisted they
were. Although Christian theologians were wrong in both measurements and celestial dynamics, they were willing, as we know,
to bloody the knees of outspoken astronomers who were right.
My approach to psychotherapy was a minuscule version of the
same defensiveness against a more limber, complex technology
than the conventional assumptions I had been brought up with.

In 1978 it cost me forty dollars a session to go to psychotherapy. I used the better part of each of the first three sessions explaining to the therapist that my particular crisis, of course, had
no cure and that, in any event, human nature cannot change. I
did that even though I had trouble scraping up the money for this

psychotherapeutic venture. My defense system apparently was not avaricious. It was willing to waste a lot of money to fight a new set of truths.

During those three weeks I told Chris, the therapist, the same remarks that people now make to me when I suggest we connect empathy and stage-development theory in order to help lucky predators improve their own missions in life. I told her that whatever her psychological program, it was not going to work.

I point this out so that readers of Donald Hall's "Cider 5¢ a Glass," the other works in this anthology, and the wraparound discussions may recognize and distinguish which of their own misgivings may be pain avoidance and which are indifference or cynicism, and which are wise and appropriate skepticism.

Good news: Without us laypeople knowing much about it, the twentieth century has produced a number of tools for stopping people in power from *wanting* to cheat as much as may be their present habit. One of these tools is basic empathy.

Here is an all-purpose working model of basic empathy. This particular model is called "basic" because it doesn't splice complex confrontations into certain places in the interview. Its goals are not so elaborated or scrupulously "on task" as the goals of intentional interviewing in use by professionally skilled therapists and social workers. Our empathy model will do, however, for hypothetical interviewing of the characters in "Cider 5¢ a Glass." This particular model helps one see fine-tuned truths in "The Schreuderspitze" and "Gryphon" as well. One can use an empathy model two ways: first, as a positive procedure to imagine a story's characters, and second, as a kind of civilized behavior that may be *absent* in a story's characters.

Empathy in Literature

The first step is to regard the conversation as intentional and not merely courteous. One makes a deliberate decision to hear the point of view of the other, which means absolutely to keep back one's own views or anecdotes.

The second step is to ask only open-ended questions so as to discover, in order, the relevant data, the interviewee's feelings about the data at that time, and the meaning the interviewee now attaches to that time.

The third step is to reflect back to the interviewee, in one's own words, what one believes he or she was saying, and to ask the interviewee if one got it right. Of all these steps, the third is the most loaded with positive psychological potential.

The fourth step is to ask the interviewee where we might go from here. This step says, given what we have, given what we know, how can we improve this corner of the world? Given the occasion or dilemma described, what shall we do?[1]

We can look at Donald Hall's poem about the cruelty of privileged people as if we meant to practice empathy on its characters—the speaker, Monica and Sam, and by implication, the speaker's wife. First, however, we get to read the poem through in the traditional way of reading stories and story-poems like this one: we read to engage with the story.

Whatever else it does, story takes us out of our own lives. The mind loves to be seeing one thing, such as a page with print on it, but to be imagining another—its characters in their New England setting, with the colored trees of fall. The second time we read it is soon enough for the work of empathy.

Anyone practicing the empathy steps is doing something that is practical, like common sense, and polite, like polite conversation, but empathy is more than either or both together. The interviewer is determined to hear out the other, because of a beautiful, but virtually unknown, twentieth-century finding—the idea that we cannot grow and change until we have been "heard out." The good news is that if we *are* heard out by an affectionate mentor, we can grow and change much more than ordinary people think adults can grow and change.

As with any new idea, there is a decades-long lag before people hear about it, accept it, begin trying to make use of it. Empathy is all the more unknown because the word itself has gotten around the way the word *quark* has gotten around. Few of us actually look up *quark* to see what it really means.

A twentieth-century wisdom: Until we have been heard out, not at the level of "How'd your day go, okay, I hope? . . . good, glad to hear it," but at a serious level, we are more likely to be stuck at a "self-referential level of communication." At least three kinds of professionals use empathy in everyday practice. The first is social workers, the second is psychotherapists (social workers as well as psychologists of various persuasions practice psychotherapy), and the third is a growing few, but not all, teachers of creative writing.

The purpose of *any* kind of empathy is to give someone a chance to have his or her story heard. The hearer will be not just the other human being or human beings in the room but—often for the first time ever—that speaker's elusive inward self. Already in just the purpose—being heard— we are talking about an experience that most people anywhere in the world have never had. Most people have never been heard out. Since they have never had the experience of being heard out themselves, they haven't developed a taste for hearing out anyone else. What comes naturally to human beings is self-referencing (discussed in some detail later): empathy is *not* natural. Empathy is a structure or tool only of civilization.

Here are three examples of self-reference, the second and third more ominous than the first. The first is a common kind that we all have heard. The second is a kind of self-reference that keeps people from getting to the moral center of literature. The third is a kind of self-reference that keeps reasonably idealistic groups from sticking to their initial desire for social change.

Example 1: Self-Reference with Respect to Data

(B is the person stuck in self-reference.)
A: I had surgery today.
B: Surgery, huh? My aunt had surgery. It took her forever before she was really on her feet again.

Sometimes people approach books in the way that B conducted the conversation—so absorbed in their own set of information that they can't hear out the details of someone else's. To lend one's mental-picturing energy to someone else's facts (A's fact having been that he or she had surgery that very day) is hard, imaginative work. Some children who have never been read to cannot do it at all. As soon as they hear "bear" or "polar ice" or "fairy godmother" their mind's intake machinery seems to identify what it is hearing as simply *other*, outside the creatures and objects of their own lives, and therefore not real. Such children just wait until you stop talking so that they can either tell you about *their* information, which is real, or they back away. Alas, especially about operations, adults, too, often cannot lend themselves to someone else's world. Memories of their own operation, or their aunt's operation, call to them like a dusky English horn full of longing; they can barely keep an expression of false interest on their faces because they so long to clamp a mute onto your talk about your operation. They nearly stamp, they are so anxious to make it clear to you how certain symptoms drove them to suspect that their own appendix was acting up, and not only that but it was such a queer thing that happened with their aunt's tubal ligation, a procedure that's supposed to go off like clockwork, but not in her case.

Example 2: Self-Reference with Respect to Feelings

(The reader is the person stuck in self-reference.)
Author: I want to tell you about my various feelings of disgust, yet wonder, for nature. One day, when I thought I had a purely aesthetic goal—that is, I thought I wanted to write a poem—I found out I myself enjoyed killing a lot of little ants. Look, I'm not saying it was ecstatic, but it was definitely *fun*.
Reader: Say what you like about nature, camping sucks. My family used to try to get me camping, and finally I just told them . . .

In this case, the last word the reader heard was the fifteenth, "nature." Hearing that one word flung the reader into an old remembered dislike of nature. The rest of whatever the author said never got through at all.

Example 3: Self-Reference with Respect to Thinking

A member of an ethics seminar: I think that people's values
    largely depend on the society they belong to.
A responding member: If you haven't any sense of community,
    you haven't got anything to work with.

This last exchange is called talking past one another, a group
conversation style so endemic to neighborhood improvement
groups, focus groups, town-hall discussions, and professional retreats that we sometimes feel disheartened about the democratic
structure called public assemblage. As long as the conversation is
made up of generic abstractions such as *values, people, society,*
background, community, and *sense,* people do not hear one another
beyond the first three or four words of the first sentence. For this
reason among others, moral ideas seem brighter in the hands of
Aesop and Jesus and other parabolists and storytellers than in
public-ethics discussions. What is the cure for this particular kind
of nonlistening?

Here is the preceding conversation again, but this time showing the intervention of a therapist at the third step in the empathy format—reflecting back. The therapist has heard that B is not
listening to A, and therefore asks B to paraphrase A's idea. B muffs
the paraphrase, so the therapist comes in again to show B his or
her own utter unconsciousness about having not listened.

A: I think that people's values largely depend on the society they
    belong to.
B: If you haven't any sense of community, you haven't got any-
    thing to work with.
Therapist: B, I don't think you heard what A said. I would like to
    cut in here, and ask you to repeat what A said in your own
    words.
B: You have to have some sense of community or what you have
    is zilch.
Therapist: No, that is what *you* said. And there is something to be
    said for that, too. What I want you to say, though, in your
    own words, is what A said.

But B can't think for the life of himself or herself what A said because B originally heard only a general smudge of abstract ideation from A, a smudge of normal, abstract terminology (values, society) that reminded B of a smudge of his or her *own* ideas.

Now the therapist says: A, would you repeat your idea so B can hear it again?

A: I think that people's values depend on the society they belong to.

Therapist: Thanks, A. B, would you please reflect back to A his or her idea?

B, crossly because this is the first time B has ever experienced *intervention:* Morals are culturally relative. That's what A is saying. (B feels he's over the worst of this so he adds with spirit) The very kind of crap-filled permissiveness that allows every moral lightweight to behave any way they like, the kind of slippery slope crap that caught on in the 1960s and—

Therapist: Stop, B. You will get your chance. You haven't checked with A to see if you understand his idea rightly. I want you to check with A right now.

B: Well, did I get you right, A? Is that what you were saying? That moral values vary from background to background?

A pauses.

Therapist: A?

A: Yes, B is right. I did say that. But—well—now that I've heard it coming back to me aloud like that, I am not so sure. For example, Eskimos are pretty different from the speaker in "Cider 5¢ a Glass" but both of them believe in hospitality. It's possible that what people think are virtues are really cross-cultural, just taking different forms.

Therapist: Would you like B to comment on this refinement or amendment of your original statement?

A: It is always wonderful when B shuts up—but yes, let B speak.

Everyone laughs.

B: If I have this right, you are considering the possibility that moral values are not, not in essence, culturally relative—but only in particular styles. Your example, hospitality, is interesting. Eskimos used to be famous for being so hospitable as to share their spouses with overnight visitors, a practice which neither Sam nor the speaker of "Cider" would condone. Yet, the reverence for the idea of hospitality might be an emotion shared by everyone.

A: That's right. I am rethinking this thing.

That is an idealized but not uncommon outcome of a therapist's intervention at the reflecting-back step. Not only does B learn that he has not been listening, but he learns how to bite the bullet and listen. Not only does A hear his idea dignified by another human being's reiterating it, but that double hearing—once in his own voice, once in B's voice—encourages his brain to look quietly and critically at the idea, and even to amend it.

Such amendments to someone's first presenting statement are one of the prime reasons that ethicists would benefit by practicing empathy. What if A's presenting statement had been "Change the rich? Look, once people feel entitled to use their power for their own retirement or for their family, they are sure not going to change their goals!" Then B would have shouted some tangential observation of his own. Then the therapist would have intervened and insisted that B paraphrase back to A. A, upon hearing his extraordinarily chill, hopeless conviction repeated back to him, might hear other voices inside himself—for example, a voice that says, "That sounds one hundred percent cynical . . . perhaps some part of everyone, some part even of the Sams of the world, really doesn't want to clip the poor."

B's reflecting back to A would thus have started A on the civilized path of partializing his own assumptions, one of which is that no one high up on the money chain has a critical mass of altruism inside him or her.

Empathy, at its best, leads to partialization. Partialization leads one to investigate one's own motivations with the idea that at a given moment on a given issue one may have three or four different emotions. Nearly invariably, the emotion one first recognized, and took to be the only one, is more practical and primitive than the secondary feelings brought to life through empathy and partializing. The first, "presenting" emotion is usually much nearer the kind of thing Joyce Carol Oates associated with "nature," as opposed to civilization.

I propose that we have a long look at "Cider 5¢ a Glass" in which we practice what empathy we can. We will have to make guesses. On the other hand, Donald Hall is an artist. He has *chosen* a few conversations and scenes to symbolize hundreds of conversations and scenes, so in a sense he has done much of our work for us.

We have to assume that each of us has been "heard out" enough, at one time or another, so that we can at least for a while leave behind our own story, our own thoughts, our own anxieties, our own passions, long enough to stay with the poem's characters. We will be unable, of course, to practice *reflecting back* since the characters of the poem aren't here to answer questions we want to ask them. The best we can do is to decide, first, that we will listen and, second, that we will listen as if Sam's life depended on it, or the speaker's life depended on it, or Monica's life depended on it. (Of course, the person whose life really did depend on it is the workman.)

The three steps of deciding to listen, then listening, and keeping notepads in front of us so we can make lists will work for reading "Cider." There is a fourth step that seems nearly magical to me. This fourth step will be especially helpful in showing why the Sams of the real world pay so little attention when protesters and ethicists speak sharply to them. This step is called *reversible thinking*, and it was developed and refined under the auspices of the Center for Psychology and Social Change associated with the Harvard Medical School and Cambridge Hospital.[2]

Staff members at the center regard reversible thinking as so important that during the cold war they sponsored retreats for highly placed Russians and Americans to learn the technique. We are doing reversible thinking when we deliberately pretend not only that we are inside another person but also that that other person is looking back at and judging us. The Russians and Americans were asked to imagine what clichés and stereotypes the others applied to *them* themselves.

Reversible thinking, like the empathy steps, does not come naturally. We don't develop such cordial, imaginative, and humorous acquaintance with someone other than ourselves in our bassinets, although the wonderful *potential* for doing so is inside our brains from the first. The ability to imagine you are your opposite number, on the other side of a possible or real war, has of course been horribly used. From Alexander to the Prussian military theorist Karl von Clausewitz to the U.S. Strategic Air Command, some war expert or other is forever setting groups of officers to focus on how the enemies are thinking of us, so that we can trick them.

Trickery seems to be the natural, brutal use of psychology as opposed to a principled use of psychology. Very likely there isn't a new technology in the world that hasn't within five minutes of its discovery been turned into a new way to trick someone's real or imagined enemies. It does not matter what foul uses military strategists, such as the psychological warfare people of the then Soviet Union, might make of *reversible thinking:* it is a great self-discipline and imaginative experiment for anyone to try.

Most adults have not once in their lives been asked first to pretend they are someone else and then to figure out that person's take on anything or anyone, least of all on themselves. I suggest we try out the following four empathic procedures on "Cider 5¢ a Glass":

1. We agree simply to "be with" the poem's characters
   and listen.
2. We pay close attention to their ideas and feelings.
3. We take notes so we can ask questions, on paper,
   since we can't ask them in person.
4. We pretend that we are *they*, looking back at us.

The four steps should give us a modern way to study four privileged people who have a good deal of sensibility—and their victim.

Right away a new difficulty presents itself—the American class system. A cat may look at a king, but can a family-systems therapist or a sociologist, never mind those of us who are interested lay students of such family systems and social philosophies, look at the plot of a good poem? And can we use that poem as if it were a "caseload" made up of four white, privileged people educated in the liberal arts? No one thinks anything of eliciting sociologists' insights into the works of Steinbeck, but Steinbeck's people were (1) poor and (2) back in the 1930s. Hall's people are rich, and each day's news in the *New York Times* would seem to assure us that their confreres are very much in power right now.

The poor had better figure that some insurance firms and some law firms intend to bilk them now and will continue to do so in future. Most rich people, however well educated in literature, tend not to take it seriously. And like any economic group, they give little time to reading theories of moral psychology. Typically, people of the speaker's and Sam's generation (people born around 1926–1930) did read the best current literature in college. Sam and the speaker were reading good literature at Holderness, well before they were eighteen. But within two years after college graduation most people of the 1950s generation stopped reading serious literature in favor of popular books. Donald Hall's "Cider" characters, people who had graduated from Harvard, were much more likely to have read books on the best-seller list of the moment than to know even the names of Jean Stafford, Mavis Gallant, Wallace Stevens, or Richard Wilbur. Majoring in English at no matter how good a college did not mean a lifelong acquaintance with serious literature.

Further, as to things psychotherapeutic: People like the speaker of this poem, his wife, Sam, and Monica, present themselves neither to psychotherapists for consciousness raising or learning nor to social workers for help with ethical problems arising in their workplace groups. We cannot yet call in teams of ethicists, as one can in Amsterdam, to get moral counsel about how we are making our livelihood.[3] What's more, and this specifically applies to Chicago-based attorneys like Sam, more than seven hundred interviews with Chicago lawyers have shown that lawyers' clients tend to be of the same political, religious, and social backgrounds as their own; that is, these lawyers connect with clients on the basis of client *type* rather than on the basis of *situation type.*[4] This adds up to a great deal of psychological homogeneity in our upper class.

Members of America's upper middle class make use of psychiatrists, not therapists, and never social workers. They consider their contact with psychiatrists as treatment, not as a learning experience. They suppose you go to a psychiatrist when you are in need. It is an admission of weakness. Such clients evaluate the psychiatrist as to whether or not he or she *addressed their needs* — such a curious, ominous expression. As users of psychiatry, the rich regard that work as only *intrapersonal*, not as education for changing our culture at all. Hardly any liberal arts educated person looks at psychology as a first-class approach for normal people to use in their communal life together and as citizens of a nation. Erik Erikson's idea that psychology is good for helping normal people cope with "the vicissitudes of life" is not an idea familiar to the hearts of most upper-middle-class people. They associate psychology with medicine. You take it when you are depleted or sick.

Isolating such privileged people further from the educational and ethical uses of psychotherapy is the fact that courts rarely adjudicate people like Sam to group therapy sessions, even though Sam participated in criminal activity. What judge has said, "This guy's morally limited by the values he was brought up with, all that entitlement he feels, just because his parents had money and he went to great schools. I order up six months of residential treatment for him. The guy's a menace."

Judges send lower-class people to "group," but rich people, wrapped as they are in the soft lashings of their networks, seldom stumble into the corral of social scientists. Their ethical issues are further confused by the fact that liberal arts graduates from good colleges know how to talk about civic responsibility and any other topic of moral interest. Their manners are so open and generous compared to the manners of poor people in trouble that any professional who does come to work with them must repeatedly make reality checks. A therapist working with the privileged must watch for intellectualized cover-ups, done so handsomely and habitually, in an affable, conversational tone, that the client himself or herself has the illusion of being a person of virtue. We hear a good deal about the moral complacency of fundamentalist believers—of how they seem to take themselves for the good, the only good people—but the complacency of the liberal arts-educated rich is granite bedrock in comparison.

Most psychologists or social workers don't deal with the lucky rich on a day-to-day basis, predator rich or nonpredator rich, nor do they expect to. I have read at least a dozen textbooks on social work interviewing, all of which advise the worker to use very simple, "down-to-earth" language, choosing the same clichés to repeat as the client uses and seems comfortable with. I have never seen a social work text that specifically prepared the worker to take authority and inspire respect in a client like Sam, who graduated from Holderness and Harvard. As it happens, the professional interviewing skills learned by master of social work candidates are so good and universally replicable that they will work with highly cultured people as well as with the more traditional social work clientele. What wants amending for use with the well educated is the language: it should be more various and grammatical, clichés should be left out when possible, and perhaps the point at which the social worker makes a firm, directive interventory move should be moved *forward*. That is, an educated person needs less ego building up front, and stiffer interventory conversational style further on. He or she has had the discipline of music lessons, rehearsing, making précis of essays, writing papers about other people's work, studying the history of faraway places—all of which enable a person to receive and consider tougher suggestions than otherwise. In fact, a highly educated person will regard a therapist as moldering around or gushing or stupid if that therapist doesn't move comparatively briskly to something incisive.

Any helping professional, then, embarking on psychoethical work with lucky predators like Sam and his three enablers must (*a*) consciously intensify his or her language and (*b*) take a directive, authoritative stance with dispatch. The ethics code of the National Association of Social Workers expressly stipulates that social workers are to take proactive steps to change "the system" that causes the griefs they are used to addressing on a patch-up basis (Article VI, Section 6). Unfortunately, however, American therapists and social workers have little expectation of acting as change agents to highly educated people — the people who negotiate and control our domestic and foreign policy.

Psychiatry has grown like moss upon the rich. I am certain that is because psychiatry, as a discipline, takes upon itself no such mission as changing the rich in order to lighten the griefs of the poor. Psychiatrists' values-free approach is wise as a serpent. For starters, it is wise as a serpent to call clients *patients*, too. The contract stays oriented to medicine, not to ego development.

I have always been moved by the story that Viktor Frankl told in *Man's Search for Meaning* about a highly placed American diplomat who came to see him.[5] This man had paid for years of psychoanalysis with a doctor in New York. After Frankl talked to him for a while, he determined that this man wasn't neurotic or in any way mentally disturbed: the man's work gave his life no meaning. Frankl told him that diagnosis. The man was delighted and went away to change to a more soul-serving job. There may be hundreds of people in New York City this year and next who see psychiatrists or psychoanalysts because they think they have defective personalities or defective minds, when in fact their lives are normal but so lacking in meaning, or virtue, that they suffer.[6]

Evil by Groups

The evil Sam did in the poem was to accommodate to his employer's mission. It is not literally evil by a group, but if the group (the legal department of the conglomerate) had not defined and paid for the evil action to be done by Sam and his department, Sam would not have done it on his own. We know from evidence in the poem (the teenaged Sam saying he ought to do something helpful) that he would not on his own have cheated the workman.

Although ethics discussion groups are springing up even in executive suites now, we have not developed a formal psychological and ethical understanding of groups who work together. We have sophisticated group therapies, but they are designed with the idea that the group will help each individual in it with his or her problems. The goal has to do with *each individual's outcome.* We haven't yet designed psychoethical groups to attend to the *group's problems*—we have, for example, no intentional groups to act specifically as change agents to legal departments of huge firms. So far as I know, we have not yet solidified a group psychology designed to act as change agent to whole boards as a unit. I don't think there is yet a group psychology designed for top leadership of any large corporations.[7]

We are only in the first stages of studying evil-by-profession. The level of unconsciousness is still very high. Most highly placed people in any profession still assure outsiders that groups are, after all, just made up of individuals. What they are saying is that there is no such thing as a group dynamic working for ill or for good. Privileged people will allow such realities as mass hysteria and crowd sickness, because they see them as lower-class artifacts. They are largely still in full-steam denial about group dynamics in their own class.

That denial is no doubt related to the studied ignorance of work already done and published by psychologists on evil by groups. People uneducated in social psychology often announce with the greatest complacency that there can be no way to know why people behave in such and such a way. Their tone is reminiscent of the grave, comfortable tone of the international affairs experts mentioned in the Introduction who denied that there was any way to understand why Germans followed Hitler as they did. When the devil wears the right school tie, and his voice is somber and authoritative, one believes nearly anything he says for about a half second. But in the next half second one feels disoriented, as if the owner of a 1995 single-engined Cessna had just explained to an audience of millions that there could never, of course, be such an invention as a Boeing 747. We want to believe eternal truths. They waft pleasantly into our hearing, like wisps of cloud, but then one remembers that ever since Pan Am first bought some 747s from Boeing on December 13, 1969, 747s have been the transoceanic airplane of choice.

Irving Janis's insights into management-level group dynamics and Irvin Yalom's *Group Psychology* give laypeople some clearly written twentieth-century savvy to help us think through the problem of evil that nice people do in their groups. Robert Jay Lifton and Eric Markusen report on psychological contrivances of as much interest in ordinary, everyday group decision making as decision making in Nazi Germany—how the teachers or elders or officers of an organization use fatherly camaraderie to inure new operatives to whatever evil actions the organization will ask them to perform.[8]

I suggest that we ordinary thinkers read the new group theories. Even though the insights of a handful of psychological scholars not only give us the bad news, which we suspected all along anyhow, that good people behave badly in some groups, they also offer hope. Our notepads begin to fill with information about *Homo sapiens*'s appalling vulnerability to adoration of leaders and passivity when in groups—but cures are suggested.

Why should the political experts discussing Germany know the work by Hannah Arendt, Bruno Bettelheim, Ervin Staub, Alice Miller, and Robert Jay Lifton and Eric Markusen? Why complain? Surely they, like any of us, have a right not to know someone else's field.

The drawback of such ignorance, however, is that sometimes what one is ignorant of is elegant, scholarly good news, whereas what has gotten about is fatalistic guesswork.

The good news, so far as lucky predators like Sam are concerned, is that accessible studies are already published that apply to Sam. If Monica or the speaker or the speaker's wife had known anything of such intervention skills, at least one if not all three of them might have invited Sam to get off the train of lucky predatorship.

I wrote earlier that a little knowledge is less dangerous than no knowledge. I would like to show now how that applies to Sam and the speaker and other members of their social background. Let us assume that none of them knows anything about psychological health and how psychological health interacts with one's ethics.

Let us make a new scenario now: let us pretend that we are a committee of a monstrous group whose goal is to draw upper-middle-class people into evil—specifically into evil in their workplaces. Our think tank is having a retreat. "How can we make Sam do bad work?" is up on the white board. "How can we make Monica go along with it?" is on the agenda. "How can we make the speaker, who is a liberal, somehow waste his chances to keep Sam from doing bad work?" is a third point. We agree to put together some proposals that would be effective not just with Sam but with well-heeled people in general.

Here are the ideas our horrible group handed to the secretary to get on disk:

• To make Sam do evil, have his pleasant-spoken peers and superiors describe the job to him as simply technical, values-free—simply a practical, sensible task.
• Introduce it by degrees. (This is the classic frog/ warm water method. You gradually heat the pot of water the frog is in without its noticing. It dies. If you had put in boiling water in the beginning, the frog would have jumped out.)
• Show Sam that his sense of self-identity, his pride in belonging, come from outside himself. No man is an island, one might remind him. Success, position, acquisition of goods—such are the facts of life. The more of Sam's personality that agrees to be externally fed like this, the less of Sam's personality will be capable of individual judgments. Sam himself will block his own conscience because he will surmise, accurately enough, that every dissenting feeling he has inside him is sabotage of the outer man, the Sam of litigious success, Sam of the stiff upper lip except when drunk.

Habit is next to ungodliness. The more Sam suppresses his private take on any issue, the more his conscience atrophies. After a while, Sam is a good fellow to choose when you need someone to do something foul because his unexercised conscience hasn't muscle enough to stop him from compliance.
• Give Sam, upon entering the evil-doing group, the sense that a virtuous life—that is, a life free of murder, cheating the poor, or whatever bad work a corporate group might ask of him—is

Sunday-school fluff. A real man or real woman gets past that. When talking to Sam, use the phrase "in the real world" as much as you can: it always means the same thing—in the world where wrongdoing is all right. To stand by one's scruples about not hurting innocent people looks chicken in the real world.

• Dress Sam like others in the group, so that he identifies with them in an external fashion—and secondarily, but more subtly, may develop decreasing awareness of character differences among the members. Our think tank took this idea from the ancient practices of soldier recruitment, of course, so this proposal needs adjustment for Holderness and Harvard graduates. That is, "dressing alike" would be translated into wearing beautifully cut suits and black or brown, never white, socks. The small group of our retreat section who brought in this proposal later dropped it because they recognized, when it was pointed out, that Sam's prep school and college had already done the work of look-alike anxiety for them.

• Choose for the group people who received too little love from their parents or significant authorities as children. Emotionally they will be brittle. They will have a useful uneasiness, even ambivalence, in love; in fact, longing for love may well translate, in their cases, into longing for status. Sam, with his hard-drinking and philandering father, would qualify for this selection.

Every one of these proposals loses its punch if the subject, Sam or someone like Sam, is familiar with a basic empathy process. Here is why: people who have not practiced asking others to partialize, reflecting back, asking them to speak again, and so forth, almost uniformly suppose that there are certain subjects you cannot bring up among friends and colleagues without wrecking the friendship or disrupting the workforce. They literally believe that the subjects closest to our interests can't be talked about openly because the only format they've seen for talking openly is the adversarial style of mutual accusation—a style that in immature males leads to fisticuffs (such as Donald Hall reports in "Cider") and in immature females to connivery. It is no wonder that most human beings think they can't get at what bothers them until they are drunk. No one has explained that the ground rules of empathic exchange—no personal gouging, no physical violence, no making the grand gesture of departing the room—actually preclude the discourtesy and distress of most conversations. No one has explained the relief one feels when someone else actually listens, and commits the kindness of paraphrasing our own ideas back to us.

In Nazi Germany there were nowhere near enough naturally criminal people among the eighty million Germans to implement the SS's mission. The SS needed a number of ways of getting decent people to brainstorm and supervise killings for them. Whatever the various psychological strategies that cruel intelligences apply, we must realize that they work. Any organization that wants some dirty work done need only ratchet down those psychological strategies to the level or style needed for their particular purposes. We pretended we were a monstrous organization trying to figure out the best way to get some Harvard graduates into our ranks. The exercise was not idle fantasy: its purpose was to show how one might lay out certain psychological pressures along a continuum, just as levels of cruelty in workplaces may be seen on a continuum, with the most virulent, like the work of the SS and other organizations specializing in torture and murder at the one end, and the comparatively mild-looking cheating of the poor, like Sam's crooked legal work in "Cider 5¢ a Glass" at the other. The same basic psychological dynamics, of which our think tank worked up six, can be brought to bear all along the continuum. One need only adjust the intensity to match the purpose one has in mind.

It doesn't take an Iago to plan such evil. The six psychological pressures that our evil think tank devised need scarcely be suggested for nature to take over. Primitive responses in our brains will help any think tank leader suppress better parts of our personalities. No taskmaster at Sam's firm told him to attack his old friend for being idealistic. Sam internalized that, and did it himself, first unconsciously *to* himself and then, to the speaker of the poem. Psychological pressures to go along with a bad group need no conspiracy to get them going—just a little ambience, a smile given for this behavior of the neophyte, a smile not given for some other behavior of the neophyte, and the neophyte, full—as Oates has told us—of natural forces, will do the rest.

We don't know all the reasons that Donald Hall wrote "Cider 5¢ a Glass," but at least one of them was to express his chagrin at Sam's evildoing and the speaker's enabling of Sam. We do know *our* mission to the poem as readers. After reading it through for plot, we want to be grateful for the beauty of the poem. It is real poetry when it tells you that the cider had a harsh detonation. A fiction writer or an essayist might think to remind us that New England's trees are noble, but only a poet would remember a harsh detonation in three glasses of cider.

I love it that the trees were noble. Nobody else in the poem was noble, but the trees made the cut. The word noble itself reminds us that nobility, the presence or the absence of it, is at issue.

Finally, the third part of our mission to this poem is to apply some psychotherapeutic know-how to its characters, to see what might have made them live differently.

We ought to pretend that we are each character in turn, not only those actually in "Cider 5¢ a Glass," but also characters who could have been in it—other grown-up Holderness and Harvard graduates with musical or literary tastes. We can pretend we are the cheated workman's wife. We can ask, If I were Monica or the speaker's wife, might I have intervened? Was I only on the gravy train—since this was the 1950s—when being on the gravy train of marriage to a rich man was meant to make up for being slighted in thousands of small ways? Or did I suffer? Or was I brought up in a cold house, and this marriage to Sam, as much as my gardening or anything else in my life, was a hobby with its drawbacks— I mean, was this the Real World?

"Cider 5¢ a Glass" touches on things we either know or can fantasize about—the prep school life, the fall colors of New England. Donald Hall is not a willful poet. He hasn't tucked into "Cider 5¢ a Glass" any weird information from his own past just because it is his past. Everything in "Cider" works off its controlled story line. Loaded with autobiographical material, the poem is not a slosh of autobiography with no unifying idea other than the fact that it all happened to one person.

Donald Hall's poem only *seems* to say that what takes us over at the end is nostalgia. That is not its true message, but a psychologically unconscious reader can mistake the point of nearly any work of art if he or she comes across nostalgic material somewhere in it: nostalgia is the weed of emotional life in our species. If no more elaborate feelings are cultivated, nostalgia will fill all the space. A seriously unconscious, "self-referential" reader could easily make it through Hall's "Cider" by concentrating on the nostalgia. "How terrific boys' friendships are," he would say, looking up from the page for a moment. "I remember having a friendship like the one this poet talks about. How well he nails it. How well he captures it about drunken weekends with old boys and their wives. And the crap you have to do for the firm, too. And Hall is a real writer. He uses beautiful words." What Hall is really about is showing us that both Sam and the speaker, whose adult friendship was too passive to be any force for good in their lives, were prone to nostalgia for simpler times—Sam with his guitar and the speaker leaning back in his office at the Boston *Globe*.

If we pretend that we are Donald Hall and then pretend that we are the speaker, we discover that the author and the speaker of this poem do not have the same mentality. One reason that Hall can present the speaker so well is that he understands the man's psychological limitations just as well as he understands Sam's defenses and moral collapse.

We readers want to ask Sam to pretend that he is the workman. We want the speaker *not* to "stop thinking" as he says he does, but to start thinking, right there.

Starting thinking is an ethical act. Stopping thinking is, as Hall, but not the narrator of the poem, knows, the second most classical method of pain avoidance in the human bag of tricks, the first being to deny that anything is wrong enough to make a fuss about. What really stops the Socrateses of this world from carrying the day for justice is not any of those combative people who argued back in the Dialogues but all the millions who for most hours of the day decide *not to think about justice at all.*

Anyone reading a book called *Changing the Bully Who Rules the World* must be a little like Joyce Carol Oates in "Against Nature." If we are cheerful, our cheer is like Oates's cheer—the cheer of people who are psychologically conscious enough to know there is bad news about, but we mean to find out the extent and the location of it, and if possible an antidote. We are willing to make lists the way studious readers do. We are also willing to try some "processes" like empathy, partialization, and confrontation.

Now I would like to propose that we borrow an approach from the modern practice of environmentalism.

Environmentalists nearly always take up the vantage of looking first at what naturally appeals to us (such as eating everything in sight and spreading our cities any place we feel like spreading them). Then they invariably want us to look at the results if we don't plan carefully.

I would like us to try out the environmentalists' practice called *full-cost pricing.* We will apply this procedure to the events in Hall's story-poem.

Full-Cost Pricing and "Cider 5¢ a Glass"

We need first to see what the physical environments are. What are the infrastructures? And what is the impact group? This kind of analysis will bring us close to the thinking of Wendell Berry when he looks at how farms influence the various members of the farm operation itself—the people, the soil, the animals, the plants— and next, how they influence creatures, land, and people *outside* the farm, elements that belong to the larger organization of which the farm itself is a part.

This environment-conscious kind of ethic is curiously parallel to stage-development theory. First a baby considers only itself. By the time it is an old man or woman we hope it sees itself as part of a universe, with a flowing connection to other motes in that universe. First a farm or a city thinks only of its needs. Later it must consider how it affects the well-being of things in ever wider sets of circles around it. The development of an environmental ethic in a person piggybacks on that person's development of empathy. First we are only self-referential; later, we hope, we can listen and respond to people in a circle around us, and thereafter in ever wider sets of circles. A poem, to a kid, is just something he or she "can really relate to." Adults want to read the poem as part of a gigantic grid of caring.

I suggest we read Donald Hall's poem in the way that people read Wendell Berry. Berry sees all things in concentric circles from the core of any one thing. Nowhere in Berry's work is this ecologically designed, almost graphable philosophy more explicit than in "Solving for Pattern" (see chapter 4). We expect Berry to show us a physical environment or two—he never fails us—and we expect him to urge us to love more widely than may be our habit. I suggest we take his expectations and see if we can live in their ambience long enough to read "Cider 5¢ a Glass" as if its physical settings, the community of its protagonists and offstage actors, and the "impact group" of its action deserved and needed our respectful attention. It might even be helpful to read "Solving for Pattern" before returning to "Cider 5¢ a Glass."

We will identify the physical environments of the poem, then the infrastructure of the community of the poem, and finally, the "impact group" of the poem's action.

The physical environments of the poem are (onstage) the autumn countryside of New England and an office at the Boston *Globe*. Offstage we know there is a boarding school for boys, a major Ivy League university, a Chicago Loop conglomerate, a Florida industrial site, and briefly, a driveway in front of a mansion or house in a Chicago suburb.

The Infrastructures

The infrastructures are a prep school in the United States, a college, a law school, the legal profession, the liberal newspaper profession, minimum-wage labor in industry, and upper-class 1950s marriage with its gender separation. The head of household's daytime ethics do not come into the family conversations: the wives

go to bed before the men get so far as to discuss any disappoint-
ments or evils in their workplaces.

The Impact Group

The impact group of this poem is principally the uneducated
poor, specifically a night watchman and his family. In a subtler
sense, the impact group includes the wives of Sam and the
speaker. Conventional wisdom, however, still says that it doesn't
hurt a wife if her husband does evil work provided she doesn't
know about it. When Barbara Bush, for example, spoke to a group
in Boston a few years ago, she told them with humor that she accounted for her years of happy marriage to the (then) president of
the United States by the fact that she didn't inquire into his business. That stance still has some cachet. If one's wife is considerate
enough not to interfere, how practical a free hand it gives us if we
are a lucky predator, and how attractive the wife comes off, too,
with her tolerance and loyal spousehood.

Moral psychology, on the other hand, suggests that when men
covertly do bad work for money, the dread and dislike of themselves that sift here and there in their consciousness eventually vi-
tiate their marriages. A book with interesting insights into this
marital problem is Melissa Everett's *Breaking Ranks*, which is about
men who finally left off doing shameful work for the CIA and
other war-related organizations.

A sophisticated judgment as to who makes up Sam's impact
group, then, would include Monica, no matter how well she benefits financially from his criminal activity.

Applying the Ethics of "Full-Cost Pricing" to Hall's Poem

To apply full-cost pricing to the world of "Cider," we make three
lists of material in the poem: a list of every character, a list of
every action taken (which includes absence of a responsive action
just after an action has been taken), and a list of all the victims—
those on scene and those outside the time and geography of the
poem. What we are doing is getting clear about the various griefs,
who causes them, and who suffers them.

Say that the workman was only forty when Sam's firm cheated

him of his compensation. We list his welfare payments as part of the pricing. If his wife's job had been helping keep the children in a pretty good college, the children may have to transfer to a vo-tech or a community college program. We could add in some zero-sum figures for Sam's firm: bonuses to hard-nosed attorneys like Sam pay off in the short run. Sam saved the company all the money it would have had to pay the workman. On the other hand, bonuses take budget away from potential pro bono cases. Full-cost pricing would include justice not meted out, at that firm's high level, to those needing the pro bono work. And so on.

That is financial full-cost pricing. Next, we look at full psychological costs to others of what Sam did. It is a long list, ending with anger, since at least for now sensible Americans entertain little hope that firms like Sam's will ennoble their *missions*. The psychological losses caused by Sam include an effect generated by unscrupulous business at any time: a kind of background anxiety. Evil in low places is frightening enough: no one wants knifings and shootings in dark avenues. But evil in high places, like Sam's, sends a constant disturbance of the air toward us—it grinds away like gray sound, always there, a steady-state resentment. It sands down the lightheartedness that depends on a modicum of civility in the marketplace.

As school social workers accumulate their findings about teenage suicide, it appears that after the largest cause (trouble with sexual identification), the second cause is this general, pervasive anxiety mentioned above. Since we are an animal whose maturation is long, with most of it done culturally—that is, after birth—we need to take seriously how it may or may not influence youth if they feel cynical about powerful *groups* in a society they have been told to revere. If most American youth had been told that materialism is low-minded and corporations are of course materialistic so you need not give their behavior the time of day, then Sam's legal work would have no more depressing effect on youth than a bad kid's pickpocketing has on a Boy Scout. But most American youth are brought up to respect lawyers, no matter what they do, just as most Americans feel respectful of large chemical companies, no matter what they do.

Although our general citizenry still pays little or no attention to evils done by corporations, several kinds of new ethics institutes and not-for-profit ecological organizations and miscellaneous change-agent organizations are cropping up among educated people. They run seminars. They offer retreats. They publish magazines and newsletters. Their members contribute money hard-won not from portfolios lying fat in the shade of the tax tree but from salaries. These people are at the hustings, embattled, every year having more cachet with radio and television programmers. Major news magazines give them more and more space.

Their efforts may seem laughable to America's glossy private sector, but if we weigh any project we want to try—its expense, for example, and the difficulty of starting it up—against the "full cost" of leaving things as they are, we find that leaving things as they are is what is laughable or naive.

The fourth step of the empathy format was asking the client, "Where do we go from here? What shall we try, to make things better?" In light of the full cost of Sam and the speaker to the rest of us, I would like to make a suggestion that the small ethics organizations and ecological organizations now engaged in public education and appropriate lobbying for legislation to restrain greed in the private sector might save money in the long run by addressing the psychoethical growth of young people.

Catching Sam and the Speaker at Age Eighteen

Example: Prep school kids, no matter how sweetly they say at age sixteen, "Maybe it would be better to do something that *helps* people," as Sam did, do not, in the main, grow up to do it. Most of them grow up to live by network rather than developing self-knowledge. They network their way through college and afterward. Donald Hall understood that perfectly well. He let us know (if we noticed!) that when the speaker and Sam were walking about in New England, they listened to each other, but they scarcely weighed each other's *ideas*: their focus was on their friendship, their stimulating feelings for each other. They really weren't awakened to public morality at all.

A few schools give a good deal of attention to public service—Groton and Andover, for example. But I don't think any American prep school supplies for its graduating seniors a pamphlet and a retreat day in which they are warned that such evils as they will be asked to do in their lives will not be private or individual evils. The devil, so to speak, will not come and pressure them into committing adultery, bank robbery, or murder; the devil will come as a legion of genuinely nice people in a corporation. These people will be avuncular and bracing. It will feel wonderful to be accepted as associates or junior partners in their organization. Liberals of lesser income and mealier lifestyles will look quite needlessly ratty, in comparison.

Mention of how liberals of lesser income look to lucky members of the status quo brings up *reversible thinking* again. If Sam had had some warning, when he was eighteen, that if he gave over his personal judgment to a profit-making organization later, any of his friends who were liberals would look mealy and gratuitously ratty to him, might that have given him pause at a future moment of need? That is, when he heard himself berating the speaker for being naive, would his memory retrieve for him the lesson of ten years earlier—that when one is about to do wrong, one feels disdain for holdouts against wrong?

The retreats and pamphlet material could give examples of evil done in American corporations: the sending of faulty propellers to P-47 Thunderbolt pilots stationed in England; the poisoning of Lake Onondaga in upstate New York; any one of various public positions of the Reynolds Company. Then group psychologists and psychologists who have done longitudinal studies could be asked to speak. If I were running an ethics wake-up retreat for young people I would try for Irvin Yalom on group dynamics and on existential meaning in life, and the inspiring George Vaillant, for example, author of *Adaptation to Life*, a thirty-year study of ninety-five psychologically healthy Harvard men. Some of their lives were meaningful to them; some of their lives exemplified nearly frantic passivity.

Authors of memoirs and biographies about doing bad work, and later regretting it and leaving it, could be asked to speak. I would carefully avoid speakers and writers, of which there a surprising number, who wear confessors' clothing but whose memoirs show the gray claws of apologists, not change agents.

Psychotherapists could identify for these kids some of the processes by which an organization immunizes its recruits to full awareness of what they are doing. Young people should be told that fear of dissent itself often makes executives nod when bad motions come up at meetings. A young person may grin at George Orwell's sidewalk artist being proud that he wasn't "a bloody rabbit," but that young person needs to see that bloody rabbithood is endemic in top-level boards and top-flight executive decision-making groups. Prep schools themselves are beehives of political intensity. Young people could be asked for parallels in the politics of their upper-middle and senior classes at school to what their presenters tell them of high-up workplaces.

One or two whistle-blowers' memoirs could be included.

Specific, comparatively novel kinds of corporate depravity could be discussed. For example, a loud complaint against American corporations in the 1990s is that top management licks up shareholder investment returns by giving "incentive" gifts to themselves, the directors, and even the noncorporate directors.

Law firms and legal departments of corporations are regarded as creatures, right or wrong, of their clients. When we hire an attorney, we want him or her to be our creature. Logical extensions of this should be discussed thoroughly in the presence of sixteen- to eighteen-year-olds. One of the most interesting ethical quandaries is about when a practice means that one lays aside one's values in order to serve one's employer. Republican doctors are supposed to cure Democratic patients. American soldiers are supposed "unquestioningly" to kill enemies when so ordered. Should Sam cheat the workman?

Most important: The pamphlet or retreat should be geared specifically to an audience of young Sams and Monicas. If its tone, or worse, grammar, is one whit less fastidious than the tone of other instructions coming Sam's and Monica's way, they won't even hear the content, never mind accept any of it.

However outlandish such a pamphlet or retreat might sound, it looks a lot better if we do some comparative pricing of Sam's behavior. For example, one pamphlet and two or three retreats could be run for less than one year's financial loss that Sam caused the workman and his family.

"Cider 5¢ a Glass" and the Brutality of Nature

What has nature to do with this poem? We may each have our own list of observations about nature, just as Joyce Carol Oates had hers, to which she added thoughts by other artists—Yeats, Thoreau, Stevens.

I want to refer to mine now. First off, big things eat little things, big things bully little things. Second, males herd together because they are afraid of one another's jeering.

In addition to helping one duck scorn, herding together is the structure of social life with the least risk of personal failure. The only trade-off of herding appears to be that in order to maintain a central, peaceable place in the middle of the herd, one must stay either unconscious or vague about one or another ethical issue that may rear its head. The pressure is on not to be seen as a difficult person.

It isn't herd instinct to attend a first-rate boarding school in New Hampshire, then a first-class private college, then a first-class private law school, then take employment at a first-class newspaper (the Boston *Globe*) or at Sam's first-class Chicago firm. That sequence is only ordinary career planning for people with those expectations.

What *is* herd instinct in "Cider" is the communication style of its main characters—the drunken mini-reunions, the wives sitting up until bored into a near coma; the men drinking more bourbon, until one of them confesses to shame over unethical behavior done for the sake of money. The other has a choice of arguing drunkenly or holding his peace drunkenly.

The speaker is following class conventions when he says nothing to Sam about cheating a workman. It is a privileged-male herd custom to let the other man blubber in his liquor and not once help him brainstorm how to undo the cruelty he devised for the nightwatchman.

The speaker of the poem exhibits another class marking or herd behavior in assuming that no one *can* keep from being bought when the price is high:

> ". . . When Sam's
> department won its case,
>   Sam got a bonus. Of course
> he never quit his job
>   and his salary to work
> for Cesar Chavez . . ."

That "of course he never quit" is cynical: it says that the Fates now had hold of Sam and he couldn't change. Since the speaker of the poem takes the situation to be hopeless, all he has to do is "be there" for Sam when Sam is drunk, himself also drunk.

The poem contains a fascinating selection of counterproductive conversations between highly educated people—where modern communication skills might have initiated different outcomes. This poem ought to be read aloud in social work classes. Social service people forget, if they ever knew, how really horribly the *lucky* people in our society can talk to one another! Old friends, even.

> "but I learned: If I refused
> to fight, one night at the end
>   of our visit, after
> our wives had gone to bed
>   and we drank one last bourbon
> together, Sammy
>   would confess that he hated what
> he did—work, boss, and company."

The speaker craved to hear Sam make the confession. It is time for a short list: if the speaker hasn't any plans to bring Sam around to decency, why does the speaker want to hear him confess? What satisfactions does the confession bring him? He appears to like the

power of hearing another man's moral troubles, rather the way ir-
responsible teachers sometimes encourage intimate revelations in
their students—teachers with neither the training nor the appropriate setting to follow them up with therapeutic procedures.
Another possible explanation is that when people don't know
how to be intimate together, they resort to personal revelations. If
the speaker in "Cider" gets a superior little flutter out of Sam's revelations, his satisfaction may be classic evidence of upper-middle-
class herd psychology. Sam's indifferent fragments, half-references
to an affair, for example, are part and parcel of his class. He is half
nice guy feeling sorry, half boasting. Playing something both
ways comes naturally. One kills two birds with one stone. Being
single-minded and clear is not nearly so psychologically self-
serving, and does not come naturally.

Bullying the poor and herding about with one's equals come
naturally and both are in this poem. What else of nature is here?
Some that is good—but not much; this is not a poem of affirma-
tion of how nice things are. We can pull an entry from the nature
list we made up for Joyce Carol Oates, based on her remarks:

> Nature gives us peace, the joy of its beauty, and consolation.
> It offers a lot more sensual pleasure than physics.

The beauty of New England autumn is here. Apropos of natural description, I don't want more than passing mention of literary technique, but this poetic device should be noticed: Hall
ironically gives to nature the moral qualities we would wish for in
the men: the trees are "noble" and the cider is "almost painful"
and "sweet" and "harsh." The men in this poem do not do the
sweet or harsh work of psychological and moral growth. They
drink. They're soft. They don't face pain sober. They slide on the
slippery slope of nostalgia.

Another view of nature: Here is a poem about a man whose father drank one kind of whiskey and cheated on his wife. The son
grows up to drink another kind of whiskey, to cheat on his wife,
and to cheat a workman. Both boys supposed that they wanted
good lives, though, as we know from their sixteen- and seventeen-

year-old conversation in 1944, Sam thinks "maybe it would be better to do something that *helps* people," and the speaker wants to write literature. The speaker tells us that at seventeen

> Although we talk excitedly,
>   although we mean what
> we say and listen closely
>   to each other, the real
> burden of our talk
>   is the affection that contains
> and exalts us . . .

What does it mean that the real burden of their talk is the affection between them, not the subject of their conversations? It points to a quality shared by Sam and the speaker that is more natural than civilized; that is, they felt joyful and rich in their love for what was nearby—each other. Michael Arlen, who wrote *Passage to Ararat,* once mentioned that it is hard being around provincial people because they are so taken up with their own affairs. A stage-development theorist would not be surprised that Sam and the speaker were absorbed in their own affairs when they were seventeen: time will pass and they will be capable of more generative interests later. Still, in a poem like "Cider" we look at everything because we are trying to guess at what went wrong. Personal friendships are simple emotional elements. When, how, should one jump to a wider ring of commitment? If we remember the list of six psychological pressures that an organization would put upon its executives in order to make sure they carried out the organization's, not their own, goals, the ability to be loyal to one's friends is not only no protection from wrongdoing, but it may put one further at risk. One might be too willing to ingratiate oneself with those close at hand.

Moral awareness, on the contrary, always involves seeing one's own situation in tandem with like situations among strangers. That is, if a happiness comes one's way, one wonders if others are on the subscription list, too. If an injustice interrupts one's life, then one wants legislation against the perpetrator for others of his or her victims as well. Moral ideas are innately communal, then universal, whereas feelings such as personal love are in our own psychological backyards. Sam and the speaker would need a philosophy far wider than their backyards in order to refuse to perpetrate the crime against the workman.

Donald Hall gives us information about Sam's class habitat. Perhaps he feels that habitat, psychological habitat or social class habitat, is somehow to blame.

Our childhood habitat tells us what is normal and what is extraordinary. For Sam and the speaker, friendship among peers was normal. Making a financial sacrifice for the sake of someone of another class would have seemed extraordinary. Displeasing other executive-level people in a profitable organization would certainly have seemed extraordinary.

This is a poem about white-collar people doing precisely what comes naturally. Sam and the narrator are of course glossier than Oates in her essay. Neither man, for example, would have a penchant for or admit to an interest in dead bodies. Neither man is morbidly attracted to nature's various forms of cruelty as Oates said she was. Their combined mores, however—Sam's feeling entitled as a big thing to prey upon a small thing, the speaker's not confronting Sam when they are sober, and both men's obliviousness to people outside their circle—these three perfectly natural proclivities enable hundreds of thousands of dollars' worth of cruelty. Oates's ant smashing is mere absentmindedness in comparison.

If there are more Sams in the economy today, a full-cost pricing ethicist might estimate their lucky predations in the millions and billions of dollars.

Notes

1. This model is one of two in use by the Collaborative of Teachers and School Social Workers, an organization committed to showing both elementary and high school teachers and their students how to practice empathy with the characters of the literature in their English courses.

2. The Center for Psychology and Social Change was originally called the Center for Psychological Research in the Nuclear Age.

3. Dutch philosopher Ad Hoogendijk started a philosophical consultation service in 1987. "Philosophers Helping Clients Think It Out," *Palm Beach Post*, January 1, 1990.

4. John P. Heinz and Edward O. Laumann, *Chicago Lawyers: The Social Structure of the Bar* (1983; reprint, Evanston, Ill.: Northwestern University Press, 1994).

5. Viktor E. Frankl, *Man's Search for Meaning: An Introduction to Logotherapy* (1939; reprint, Boston: Beacon Press, 1962), 161–62.

6. An odd usage of the second half of the twentieth century: The word "meaning" is used nearly interchangeably with "virtue." The cause may be self-consciousness about pretending one's life has any special moral quality to it. Or it may be exasperation with nineteenth-century sham about virtue. In any case, I think it is useful for teaching to ask people if they mean *goodness* when they speak of "meaning" in their lives.

7. Some ethics-centered organizations are looking at this problem. One is the Josephson Institute of Ethics, 4640 Admiralty Way, Suite 1001, Marina del Rey, CA 90292–6610, (310) 306–1868. Another is the Center for Psychology and Social Change (see note 2) at 1493 Cambridge St., Cambridge, MA 02139, (617) 497–1553.

8. Robert Jay Lifton and Eric Markusen, *The Genocidal Mentality: Nazi Holocaust and Nuclear Threat* (New York: Basic Books, 1990), 192–229.

C·H·A·P·T·E·R

14

Good News of the Twentieth Century:
We Can Combine Stage-Development
Philosophy with Empathy, Partialization, and Story

THE READINGS

A Mother's Tale
James Agee

Marooned on Gilligan's Island:
Are Women Morally Superior to Men?
Katha Pollitt

Solving for Pattern
Wendell Berry

THE COMMENTARY
Carol Bly

A Mother's Tale

by James Agee

The calf ran up the hill as fast as he could and stopped sharp.
"Mama!" he cried, all out of breath. "What *is* it! What are they
doing! Where are they *going!*"

Other spring calves came galloping too.

They all were looking up at her and awaiting her explanation,
but she looked out over their excited eyes. As she watched the mysterious and majestic thing they had never seen before, her own
eyes became even more than ordinarily still, and during the considerable moment before she answered, she scarcely heard their
urgent questioning.

Far out along the autumn plain, beneath the sloping light, an immense drove of cattle moved eastward. They went at a walk, not
very fast, but faster than they could imaginably enjoy. Those in front
were compelled by those behind; those at the rear, with few exceptions, did their best to keep up; those who were locked within the
herd could no more help moving than the particles inside a falling
rock. Men on horses rode ahead, and alongside, and behind, or
spurred their horses intensely back and forth, keeping the pace
steady, and the herd in shape; and from man to man a dog sped
back and forth incessantly as a shuttle, barking, incessantly, in a hys-
terical voice. Now and then one of the men shouted fiercely, and
this like the shrieking of the dog was tinily audible above a low and
awesome sound which seemed to come not from the multitude of
hooves but from the center of the world, and above the sporadic
bawlings and bellowings of the herd.

From the hillside this tumult was so distant that it only made
more delicate the prodigious silence in which the earth and sky were
held; and, from the hill, the sight was as modest as its sound. The
herd was virtually hidden in the dust it raised, and could be known,
in general, only by the horns which pricked this flat sunlit dust like
little briars. In one place a twist of the air revealed the trembling fabric of many backs; but it was only along the near edge of the mass
that individual animals were discernible, small in a driven frieze,

walking fast, stumbling and recovering, tossing their armed heads, or opening their skulls heavenward in one of those cries which reached the hillside long after the jaws were shut.

From where she watched, the mother could not be sure whether there were any she recognized. She knew that among them there must be a son of hers; she had not seen him since some previous spring, and she would not be seeing him again. Then the cries of the young ones impinged on her bemusement: "Where are they going?"

She looked into their ignorant eyes.

"Away," she said.

"Where?" they cried. "Where? Where?" her own son cried again.

She wondered what to say.

"On a long journey."

"But where *to?*" they shouted. "Yes, where *to?*" her son exclaimed; and she could see that he was losing his patience with her, as he always did when he felt she was evasive.

"I'm not sure," she said.

Their silence was so cold that she was unable to avoid their eyes for long.

"Well, not *really* sure. Because, you see," she said in her most reasonable tone, "I've never seen it with my own eyes, and that's the only way to *be* sure; *isn't* it."

They just kept looking at her. She could see no way out.

"But I've *heard* about it," she said with shallow cheerfulness, "from those who *have* seen it, and I don't suppose there's any good reason to doubt them."

She looked away over them again, and for all their interest in what she was about to tell them, her eyes so changed that they turned and looked, too.

The herd, which had been moving broadside to them, was being turned away, so slowly that like the turning of stars it could not quite be seen from one moment to the next; yet soon it was moving directly away from them, and even during the little while she spoke and they all watched after it, it steadily and very noticeably diminished, and the sounds of it as well.

"It happens always about this time of year," she said quietly while they watched. "Nearly all the men and horses leave, and go into the North and the West."

"Out on the range," her son said, and by his voice she knew what enchantment the idea already held for him.

"Yes," she said, "out on the range." And trying, impossibly, to imagine the range, they were touched by the breath of grandeur.

"And then before long," she continued, "everyone has been found, and brought into one place; and then . . . what you see, happens. All of them.

"Sometimes when the wind is right," she said more quietly, "you can hear them coming long before you can see them. It isn't even like a sound, at first. It's more as if something were moving far under the ground. It makes you uneasy. You wonder, why, what in the world can *that* be! Then you remember what it is and then you can really hear it. And then finally, there they all are."

She could see this did not interest them at all.

"But where are they *going?*" one asked, a little impatiently.

"I'm coming to that," she said; and she let them wait. Then she spoke slowly but casually.

"They are on their way to a railroad."

There, she thought; that's for that look you all gave me when I said I wasn't sure. She waited for them to ask; they waited for her to explain.

"A railroad," she told them, "is great hard bars of metal lying side by side, or so they tell me, and they go on and on over the ground as far as the eye can see. And great wagons run on the metal bars on wheels, like wagon wheels but smaller, and these wheels are made of solid metal too. The wagons are much bigger than any wagon you've ever seen, as big as, big as sheds, they say, and they are pulled along on the iron bars by a terrible huge dark machine, with a loud scream."

"Big as *sheds?*" one of the calves said skeptically.

"Big *enough,* anyway," the mother said. "I told you I've never seen it myself. But those wagons are so big that several of us can get inside at once. And that's exactly what happens."

Suddenly she became very quiet, for she felt that somehow, she could not imagine just how, she had said altogether too much.

"Well, *what* happens?" her son wanted to know. "What do you mean, *happens?*"

She always tried hard to be a reasonably modern mother. It was probably better, she felt, to go on, than to leave them all full of imaginings and mystification. Besides, there was really nothing at all awful about what happened . . . if only one could know *why*.

"Well," she said, "it's nothing much, really. They just—why, when they all finally *get* there, why there are all the great cars waiting in a long line, and the big dark machine is up ahead . . . smoke comes out of it, they say . . . and . . . well, then, they just put us into the wagons, just as many as will fit in each wagon, and when everybody is in, why . . ." She hesitated, for again, though she couldn't be sure why, she was uneasy.

"Why then," her son said, "the train takes them away."

Hearing that word, she felt a flinching of the heart. Where had he picked it up, she wondered, and she gave him a shy and curious glance. Oh dear, she thought. I should never have even *begun* to explain. "Yes," she said, "when everybody is safely in, they slide the doors shut."

They were all silent for a little while. Then one of them asked thoughtfully, "Are they taking them somewhere they don't want to go?"

"Oh, I don't think so," the mother said. "I imagine it's very nice."

"I want to go," she heard her son say with ardor. "I want to go right now," he cried. "Can I, Mama? *Can I? Please?*" And looking into his eyes, she was overwhelmed by sadness.

"Silly thing," she said, "there'll be time enough for that when you're grown up. But what I very much hope," she went on, "is that instead of being chosen to go out on the range and to make the long journey, you will grow up to be very strong and bright so they will decide that you may stay here at home with Mother. And you, too," she added, speaking to the other little males; but she could not honestly wish this for any but her own, least of all for the eldest, strongest and most proud, for she knew how few are chosen.

She could see that what she said was not received with enthusiasm.

"But I want to go," her son said.

"Why?" she asked. "I don't think any of you realize that it's a great *honor* to be chosen to stay. A great privilege. Why, it's just the most ordinary ones are taken out onto the range. But only the very pick are chosen to stay here at home. If you want to go out on the range," she said in hurried and happy inspiration, "all you have to do is be ordinary and careless and silly. If you want to have even a chance to be chosen to stay, you have to try to be stronger and bigger and braver and brighter than anyone else, and that takes *hard work. Every day.* Do you see?" And she looked happily and hopefully from one to another. "Besides," she added, aware that they were not won over, "I'm told it's a very rough life out there, and the men are unkind."

"Don't you see," she said again; and she pretended to speak to all of them, but it was only to her son.

But he only looked at her. "Why do you want me to stay home?" he asked flatly; in their silence she knew the others were asking the same question.

"Because it's safe here," she said before she knew better; and realized she had put it in the most unfortunate way possible. "Not safe, not just that," she fumbled. "I mean . . . because here we *know* what happens, and what's going to happen, and there's never any doubt about it, never any reason to wonder, to worry. Don't you see? It's just *Home,*" and she put a smile on the word, "where we all know each other and are happy and well."

They were so merely quiet, looking back at her, that she felt they were neither won over nor alienated. Then she knew of her son that he, anyhow, was most certainly not persuaded, for he asked the question she most dreaded: "Where do they go on the train?" And hearing him, she knew that she would stop at nothing to bring that curiosity and eagerness, and that tendency toward skepticism, within safe bounds.

"Nobody knows," she said, and she added, in just the tone she knew would most sharply engage them, "Not for sure, anyway."

"What do you mean, *not for sure,*" her son cried. And the oldest, biggest calf repeated the question, his voice cracking.

The mother deliberately kept silence as she gazed out over the plain, and while she was silent they all heard the last they would ever hear of all those who were going away: one last great cry, as faint almost as a breath; the infinitesimal jabbing vituperation of the dog; the solemn muttering of the earth.

"Well," she said, after even this sound was entirely lost, "there was one who came back." Their instant, trustful eyes were too much for her. She added, "Or so they say."

They gathered a little more closely around her, for now she spoke very quietly.

"It was my great-grandmother who told me," she said. "She was told it by *her* great-grandmother, who claimed she saw it with her own eyes, though of course I can't vouch for that. Because of course I wasn't even dreamed of then; and Great-grandmother was so very, very old, you see, that you couldn't always be sure she knew quite *what* she was saying."

Now that she began to remember it more clearly, she was sorry she had committed herself to telling it.

"Yes," she said, "the story is, there was one, *just* one, who ever came back, and he told what happened on the train, and where the train went and what happened after. He told it all in a rush, they say, the last things first and every which way, but as it was finally sorted out and gotten into order by those who heard it and those they told it to, this is more or less what happened:

"He said that after the men had gotten just as many of us as they could into the car he was in, so that their sides pressed tightly together and nobody could lie down, they slid the door shut with a startling rattle and a bang, and then there was a sudden jerk, so strong they might have fallen except that they were packed so closely together, and the car began to move. But after it had moved only a little way, it stopped as suddenly as it had started, so that they all nearly fell down again. You see, they were just moving up the next car that was joined on behind, to put more of us into it. He could see it all between the boards of the car, because the boards were built a little apart from each other, to let in air."

Car, her son said again to himself. Now he would never forget the word.

"He said that then, for the first time in his life, he became very badly frightened, he didn't know why. But he was sure, at that moment, that there was something dreadfully to be afraid of. The others felt this same great fear. They called out loudly to those who were being put into the car behind, and the others called back, but it was no use; those who were getting aboard were between narrow white fences and then were walking up a narrow slope and the men kept jabbing them as they do when they are in an unkind humor, and there was no way to go but on into the car. There was no way to get out of the car, either: he tried, with all his might, and he was the one nearest the door.

"After the next car behind was full, and the door was shut, the train jerked forward again, and stopped again, and they put more of us into still another car, and so on, and on, until all the starting and stopping no longer frightened anybody; it was just something uncomfortable that was never going to stop, and they began instead to realize how hungry and thirsty they were. But there was no food and no water, so they just had to put up with this; and about the time they became resigned to going without their suppers (for now it was almost dark), they heard a sudden and terrible scream which frightened them even more deeply than anything had frightened them before, and the train began to move again, and they braced their legs once more for the jolt when it would stop, but this time, instead of stopping, it began to go fast, and then even faster, so fast that the ground nearby slid past like a flooded creek and the whole country, he claimed, began to move too, turning slowly around a far mountain as if it were all one great wheel. And then there was a strange kind of disturbance inside the car, he said, or even inside his very bones. He felt as if everything in him was *falling,* as if he had been filled full of a heavy liquid that all wanted to flow one way, and all the others were leaning as he was leaning, away from this queer heaviness that was trying to pull them over, and then just as suddenly this leaning heaviness was gone and they nearly fell again before they could stop leaning against it. He could never understand what this was, but it too happened so many times that they all got used to it, just as they got used to seeing the country turn like a slow wheel, and just as they got used to the long cruel screams of the engine, and the steady iron noise beneath them which made the cold darkness so fearsome, and the hunger and the thirst and the continual standing up, and the moving on and on and on as if they would never stop."

"*Didn't* they ever stop?" one asked.

"Once in a great while," she replied. "Each time they did," she said, "he thought, Oh, now *at last! At last* we can get out and stretch our tired legs and lie down! *At last* we'll be given food and water! But they never let them out. And they never gave them food or water. They never even cleaned up under them. They had to stand in their manure and in the water they made."

"Why did the train stop?" her son asked; and with sombre gratification she saw that he was taking all this very much to heart.

"He could never understand why," she said. "Sometimes men would walk up and down alongside the cars, and the more nervous and the more trustful of us would call out; but they were only looking around, they never seemed to do anything. Sometimes he could see many houses and bigger buildings together where people lived. Sometimes it was far out in the country and after they had stood still for a long time they would hear a little noise which quickly became louder, and then became suddenly a noise so loud it stopped their breathing, and during this noise something black would go by, very close, and so fast it couldn't be seen. And then it was gone as suddenly as it had appeared, and the noise became small, and then in the silence their train would start up again.

"Once, he tells us, something very strange happened. They were standing still, and cars of a very different kind began to move slowly past. These cars were not red, but black, with many glass windows like those in a house; and he says they were as full of human beings as the car he was in was full of our kind. And one of these people looked into his eyes and smiled, as if he liked him, or as if he knew only too well how hard the journey was.

"So by his account it happens to them, too," she said, with a certain pleased vindictiveness. "Only they were sitting down at their ease, not standing. And the one who smiled was eating."

She was still, trying to think of something; she couldn't quite grasp the thought.

"But didn't they *ever* let them out?" her son asked.

The oldest calf jeered. "Of *course* they did. He came back, didn't he? How would he ever come back if he didn't get out?"

"They didn't let them out," she said, "for a long, long time."

"How long?"

"So long, and he was so tired, he could never quite be sure. But he said that it turned from night to day and from day to night and back again several times over, with the train moving nearly all of this time, and that when it finally stopped, early one morning, they were all so tired and so discouraged that they hardly even noticed any longer, let alone felt any hope that anything would change for them, ever again; and then all of a sudden men came up and put up a wide walk and unbarred the door and slid it open, and it was the most wonderful and happy moment of his life when he saw the door open, and walked into the open air with all his joints trembling, and drank the water and ate the delicious food they had ready for him; it was worth the whole terrible journey."

Now that these scenes came clear before her, there was a faraway shining in her eyes, and her voice, too, had something in it of the faraway.

"When they had eaten and drunk all they could hold they lifted up their heads and looked around, and everything they saw made them happy. Even the trains made them cheerful now, for now they were no longer afraid of them. And though these trains were forever breaking to pieces and joining again with other broken pieces, with shufflings and clashings and rude cries, they hardly paid them attention any more, they were so pleased to be in their new home, and so surprised and delighted to find they were among thousands upon thousands of strangers of their own kind, all lifting up their voices in peacefulness and thanksgiving, and they were so wonderstruck by all they could see, it was so beautiful and so grand.

"For he has told us that now they lived among fences as white as bone, so many, and so spiderishly complicated, and shining so pure, that there's no use trying even to hint at the beauty and the splendor of it to anyone who knows only the pitiful little outfittings of a ranch. Beyond these mazy fences, through the dark and bright smoke which continually turned along the sunlight, dark buildings stood shoulder to shoulder in a wall as huge and proud as mountains. All through the air, all the time, there was an iron humming like the humming of the iron bar after it has been struck to tell the men it is time to eat, and in all the air, all the time, there was that same strange kind of iron strength which makes the silence before lightning so different from all other silence.

"Once for a little while the wind shifted and blew over them straight from the great buildings, and it brought a strange and very powerful smell which confused and disturbed them. He could never quite describe this smell, but he has told us it was unlike anything he had ever known before. It smelled like old fire, he said, and old blood and fear and darkness and sorrow and most terrible and brutal force and something else, something in it that made him want to run away. This sudden uneasiness and this wish to run away swept through every one of them, he tells us, so that they were all moved at once as restlessly as so many leaves in a wind, and there was great worry in their voices. But soon the leaders among them concluded that it was simply the way men must smell when there are a great many of them living together. Those dark buildings must be crowded very full of men, they decided, probably as many thousands of them, indoors, as there were of us, outdoors; so it was no wonder their smell was so strong and, to our kind, so unpleasant. Besides, it was so clear now in every other way that men were not as we had always supposed, but were doing everything they knew how to make us comfortable and happy, that we ought to just put up with their smell, which after all they couldn't help, any more than we could help our own. Very likely men didn't like the way we smelled, any more than we liked theirs. They passed along these ideas to the others, and soon everyone felt more calm, and then the wind changed again, and the fierce smell no longer came to them, and the smell of their own kind was back again, very strong of course, in such a crowd, but ever so homey and comforting, and everyone felt easy again.

"They were fed and watered so generously, and treated so well, and the majesty and the loveliness of this place where they had all come to rest was so far beyond anything they had ever known or dreamed of, that many of the simple and ignorant, whose memories were short, began to wonder whether that whole difficult journey, or even their whole lives up to now, had ever really been. Hadn't it all been just shadows, they murmured, just a bad dream?

"Even the sharp ones, who knew very well it had all really happened, began to figure that everything up to now had been made so full of pain only so that all they had come to now might seem all the sweeter and the more glorious. Some of the oldest and deepest were even of a mind that all the puzzle and tribulation of the journey had been sent us as a kind of harsh trying or proving of our worthiness; and that it was entirely fitting and proper that we could earn our way through to such rewards as these, only through suffering, and through being patient under pain which was beyond our understanding; and that now at the last, to those who had borne all things well, all things were made known: for the mystery of suffering stood revealed in joy. And now as they looked back over all that was past, all their sorrows and bewilderments seemed so little and so fleeting that, from the simplest among them even to the most wise, they could feel only the kind of amused pity we feel toward the very young when, with the first thing that hurts them or they are forbidden, they are sure there is nothing kind or fair in all creation, and carry on accordingly, raving and grieving as if their hearts would break."

She glanced among them with an indulgent smile, hoping the little lesson would sink home. They seemed interested but some-what dazed. I'm talking way over their heads, she realized. But by now she herself was too deeply absorbed in her story to modify it much. *Let* it be, she thought, a little impatient; it's over *my* head, for that matter.

"They had hardly before this even wondered that they were alive," she went on, "and now all of a sudden they felt they under-stood *why* they were. This made them very happy, but they were still only beginning to enjoy this new wisdom when quite a new and different kind of restiveness ran among them. Before they quite knew it they were all moving once again, and now they realized that they were being moved, once more, by men, toward still some other place and purpose they could not know. But during these last hours they had been so well that now they felt no uneasiness, but all moved forward calm and sure toward better things still to come; he has told us that he no longer felt as if he were being driven, even as it became clear that they were going toward the shade of those great buildings; but guided.

"He was guided between fences which stood ever more and more narrowly near each other, among companions who were pressed ever more and more closely against one another; and now as he felt their warmth against him it was not uncomfortable, and his pleasure in it was not through any need to be close among others through anxiousness, but was a new kind of strong and gentle delight, at being so very close, so deeply of his own kind, that it seemed as if the very breath and heartbeat of each one were being exchanged through all that multitude, and each was another, and others were each, and each was a multitude, and the multitude was one. And quieted and made mild within this melting, they now entered the cold shadow cast by the buildings, and now with every step the smell of the buildings grew stronger, and in the darkening air the glittering of the fences was ever more queer.

"And now as they were pressed ever more intimately together he could see ahead of him a narrow gate, and he was strongly pressed upon from either side and from behind, and went in eagerly, and now he was between two fences so narrowly set that he brushed either fence with either flank, and walked alone, seeing just one other ahead of him, and knowing of just one other behind him, and for a moment the strange thought came to him, that the one ahead was his father, and that the one behind was the son he had never begotten.

"And now the light was so changed that he knew he must have come inside one of the gloomy and enormous buildings, and the smell was so much stronger that it seemed almost to burn his nostrils, and the smell and the sombre new light blended together and became some other thing again, beyond his describing to us except to say that the whole air beat with it like one immense heart and it was as if the beating of this heart were pure violence infinitely manifolded upon violence: so that the uneasy feeling stirred in him again that it would be wise to turn around and run out of this place just as fast and as far as ever he could go. This he heard, as if he were telling it to himself at the top of his voice, but it came from somewhere so deep and so dark inside him that he could only hear the shouting of it as less than a whisper, as just a hot and chilling breath, and he scarcely heeded it, there was so much else to attend to.

"For as he walked along in this sudden and complete loneliness, he tells us, this wonderful knowledge of being one with all his race meant less and less to him, and in its place came something still more wonderful: he knew what it was to be himself alone, a creature separate and different from any other, who had never been before, and would never be again. He could feel this in his whole weight as he walked, and in each foot as he put it down and gave his weight to it and moved above it, and in every muscle as he moved, and it was a pride which lifted him up and made him feel large, and a pleasure which pierced him through. And as he began with such wondering delight to be aware of his own exact singleness in this world, he also began to understand (or so he thought) just why these fences were set so very narrow, and just why he was walking all by himself. It stole over him, he tells us, like the feeling of a slow cool wind, that he was being guided toward some still more wonderful reward or revealing, up ahead, which he could not of course imagine, but he was sure it was being held in store for him alone.

"Just then the one ahead of him fell down with a great sigh, and was so quickly taken out of the way that he did not even have to shift the order of his hooves as he walked on. The sudden fall and the sound of that sigh dismayed him, though, and something within him told him that it would be wise to look up: and there he saw Him.

"A little bridge ran crosswise above the fences. He stood on this bridge with His feet as wide apart as He could set them. He wore spattered trousers but from the belt up He was naked and as wet as rain. Both arms were raised high above His head and in both hands He held an enormous Hammer. With a grunt which was hardly like the voice of a human being, and with all His strength, He brought this Hammer down into the forehead of our friend: who, in a blinding blazing, heard from his own mouth the beginning of a gasping sigh; then there was only darkness."

Oh, this is *enough!* it's *enough!* she cried out within herself, seeing their terrible young eyes. How *could* she have been so foolish as to tell so much!

"What happened then?" she heard, in the voice of the oldest calf, and she was horrified. This shining in their eyes: was it only excitement? no pity? no fear?

"What happened?" two others asked.

Very well, she said to herself. I've gone so far; now I'll go the rest of the way. She decided not to soften it, either. She'd teach them a lesson they wouldn't forget in a hurry.

"Very well," she was surprised to hear herself say aloud.

"How long he lay in this darkness he couldn't know, but when he began to come out of it, all he knew was the most unspeakably dreadful pain. He was upside down and very slowly swinging and turning, for he was hanging by the tendons of his heels from great frightful hooks, and he has told us that the feeling was as if his hide were being torn from him inch by inch, in one piece. And then as he became more clearly aware he found that this was exactly what was happening. Knives would sliver and slice along both flanks, between the hide and the living flesh; then there was a moment of most precious relief; then red hands seized his hide and there was a jerking of the hide and a tearing of tissue which it was almost as terrible to hear as to feel, turning his whole body and the poor head at the bottom of it; and then the knives again.

"It was so far beyond anything he had ever known unnatural and amazing that he hung there through several more such slicings and jerkings and tearings before he was fully able to take it all in: then, with a scream, and a supreme straining of all his strength, he tore himself from the hooks and collapsed sprawling to the floor and, scrambling right to his feet, charged the men with the knives. For just a moment they were so astonished and so terrified they could not move. Then they moved faster than he had ever known men could—and so did all the other men who chanced to be in his way. He ran down a glowing floor of blood and down endless corridors which were hung with the bleeding carcasses of our kind and with bleeding fragments of carcasses, among blood-clothed men who carried bleeding weapons, and out of that vast room into the open, and over and through one fence after another, shoving aside many an astounded stranger and shouting out warnings as he ran, and away up the railroad toward the West.

"How he ever managed to get away, and how he ever found his way home, we can only try to guess. It's told that he scarcely knew, himself, by the time he came to this part of his story. He was impatient with those who interrupted him to ask about that, he had so much more important things to tell them, and by then he was so exhausted and so far gone that he could say nothing very clear about the little he did know. But we can realize that he must have had really tremendous strength, otherwise he couldn't have outlived the Hammer; and that strength such as his—which we simply don't see these days, it's of the olden time—is capable of things our own strongest and bravest would sicken to dream of. But there was something even stronger than his strength. There was his righteous fury, which nothing could stand up against, which brought him out of that fearful place. And there was his high and burning and heroic purpose, to keep him safe along the way, and to guide him home, and to keep the breath of life in him until he could warn us. He did manage to tell us that he just followed the railroad, but how he chose one among the many which branched out from that place, he couldn't say. He told us, too, that from time to time he recognized shapes of mountains and other landmarks, from his journey by train, all reappearing backward and with a changed look and hard to see, too (for he was shrewd enough to travel mostly at night), but still recognizable. But that isn't enough to account for it. For he has told us, too, that he simply *knew* the way; that he didn't hesitate one moment in choosing the right line of railroad, or even think of it as choosing; and that the landmarks didn't really guide him, but just made him the more sure of what he was already sure of; and that whenever he *did* encounter human beings—and during the later stages of his journey, when he began to doubt he would live to tell us, he traveled day and night—they never so much as moved to make him trouble, but stopped dead in their tracks, and their jaws fell open.

"And surely we can't wonder that their jaws fell open. I'm sure yours would, if you had seen him as he arrived, and I'm very glad I wasn't there to see it, either, even though it is said to be the greatest and most momentous day of all the days that ever were or shall be. For we have the testimony of eyewitnesses, how he looked, and it is only too vivid, even to hear of. He came up out of the East as much staggering as galloping (for by now he was so worn out by pain and exertion and loss of blood that he could hardly stay upright), and his heels were so piteously torn by the hooks that his hooves doubled under more often than not, and in his broken forehead the mark of the Hammer was like the socket for a third eye.

"He came to the meadow where the great trees made shade over the water. 'Bring them all together!' he cried out, as soon as he could find breath. 'All!' Then he drank; and then he began to speak to those who were already there: for as soon as he saw himself in the water it was as clear to him as it was to those who watched him that there was no time left to send for the others. His hide was all gone from his head and his neck and his forelegs and his chest and most of one side and a part of the other side. It was flung backward from his naked muscles by the wind of his running and now it lay around him in the dust like a ragged garment. They say there is no imagining how terrible and in some way how grand the eyeball is when the skin has been taken entirely from around it: his eyes, which were bare in this way, also burned with pain, and with the final energies of his life, and with his desperate concern to warn us while he could; and he rolled his eyes wildly while he talked, or looked piercingly from one to another of the listeners, interrupting himself to cry out, '*Believe* me! Oh, *believe* me!' For it had evidently never occurred to him that he might not be believed, and must make this last great effort, in addition to all he had gone through for us, to *make* himself believed; so that he groaned with sorrow and with rage and railed at them without tact or mercy for their slowness to believe. He had scarcely what you could call a voice left, but with this relic of a voice he shouted and bellowed and bullied us and insulted us, in the agony of his concern. While he talked he bled from the mouth, and the mingled blood and saliva hung from his chin like the beard of a goat.

"Some say that with his naked face, and his savage eyes, and that beard and the hide lying off his bare shoulders like shabby clothing, he looked almost human. But others feel this is an irreverence even to think; and others, that it is a poor compliment to pay the one who told us, at such cost to himself, the true ultimate purpose of Man. Some did not believe he had ever come from our ranch in the first place, and of course he was so different from us in appearance and even in his voice, and so changed from what he might ever have looked or sounded like before, that nobody could recognize him for sure, though some were sure they did. Others suspected that he had been sent among us with his story for some mischievous and cruel purpose, and the fact that they could not imagine what this purpose might be, made them, naturally, all the more suspicious. Some believed he was actually a man, trying—and none too successfully, they said—to disguise himself as one of us; and again the fact that they could not imagine why a man would do this, made them all the more uneasy. There were quite a few who doubted that anyone who could get into such bad condition as he was in, was fit even to give reliable information, let alone advice, to those in good health. And some whispered, even while he spoke, that he had turned lunatic; and many came to believe this. It wasn't only that his story was so fantastic; there was good reason to wonder, many felt, whether anybody in his right mind would go to such trouble for others. But even those who did not believe him listened intently, out of curiosity to hear so wild a tale, and out of the respect it is only proper to show any creature who is in the last agony.

"What he told, was what I have just told you. But his purpose was away beyond just the telling. When they asked questions, no matter how curious or suspicious or idle or foolish, he leaned, toward the last, to answer them with all the patience he could and in all the detail he could remember. He even invited them to examine his wounded heels and the pulsing wound in his head as closely as they pleased. He even begged them to, for he knew that before everything else, he must be believed. For unless we could believe him, wherever could we find any reason, or enough courage, to do the hard and dreadful things he told us we must do!

"It was only these things, he cared about. Only for these, he came back."

Now clearly remembering what these things were, she felt her whole being quail. She looked at the young ones quickly and as quickly looked away.

"While he talked," she went on, "and our ancestors listened, men came quietly among us; one of them shot him. Whether he was shot in kindness or to silence him is an endlessly disputed question which will probably never be settled. Whether, even, he died of the shot, or through his own great pain and weariness (for his eyes, they say, were glazing for some time before the men came), we will never be sure. Some suppose even that he may have died of his sorrow and his concern for us. Others feel that he had quite enough to die of, without that. All these things are tangled and lost in the disputes of those who love to theorize and to argue. There is no arguing about his dying words, though; they were very clearly remembered:

"*'Tell them! Believe!'*"

After a while her son asked, "What did he tell them to do?"

She avoided his eyes. "There's a great deal of disagreement about that, too," she said after a moment. "You see, he was so very tired."

They were silent.

"So tired," she said, "some think that toward the end, he really *must* have been out of his mind."

"Why?" asked her son.

"Because he was so tired out and so badly hurt."

They looked at her mistrustfully.

"And because of what he told us to do."

"What did he tell us to do?" her son asked again.

Her throat felt dry. "Just . . . things you can hardly bear even to think of. That's all."

They waited. "Well, *what?*" her son asked in a cold, accusing voice.

"*'Each one is himself,'*" she said shyly. "*'Not of the herd. Himself alone.'* That's one."

"What else?"

"*'Obey nobody. Depend on none.'*"

"What else?"

She found that she was moved. "*'Break down the fences,'*" she said less shyly. "*'Tell everybody, everywhere.'*"

"Where?"

"Everywhere. You see, he thought there must be ever so many more of us than we had ever known."

They were silent. "What else?" her son asked.

"*'For if even a few do not hear me, or disbelieve me, we are all betrayed.'*"

"Betrayed?"

"He meant, doing as men want us to. Not for ourselves, or the good of each other."

They were puzzled.

"Because, you see, he felt there was no other way." Again her voice altered: "*'All who are put on the range are put onto trains. All who are put onto trains meet the Man With The Hammer. All who stay home are kept there to breed others to go onto the range, and so betray themselves and their kind and their children forever.*

"*'We are brought into this life only to be victims; and there is no otherway for us unless we save ourselves.'*"

"Do you understand?"

Still they were puzzled, she saw; and no wonder, poor things. But now the ancient lines rang in her memory, terrible and brave. They made her somehow proud. She began actually to want to say them.

"*'Never be taken,'*" she said. "*'Never be driven. Let those who can, kill Man. Let those who cannot, avoid him.'*"

She looked around at them.

"What else?" her son asked, and in his voice there was a rising valor.

She looked straight into his eyes. "*'Kill the yearlings,'*" she said very gently. "*'Kill the calves.'*"

She saw the valor leave his eyes.

"Kill us?"

She nodded, "*'So long as Man holds dominion over us,'*" she said. And in dread and amazement she heard herself add, "*'Bear no young.'*"

With this they all looked at her at once in such a way that she loved her child, and all these others, as never before; and there dilated within her such a sorrowful and marveling grandeur that for a moment she was nothing except her own inward whisper, "Why, *I* am one alone. And of the herd, too. Both at once. All one."

Her son's voice brought her back: "Did they do what he told them to?"

The oldest one scoffed, "Would we be here, if they had?"

"They say some did," the mother replied. "Some tried. Not all."

"What did the men do to them?" another asked.

"I don't know," she said. "It was such a very long time ago."

"Do you believe it?" asked the oldest calf.

"There are some who believe it," she said.

"Do *you?*"

"I'm told that far back in the wildest corners of the range there are some of us, mostly very, very old ones, who have never been taken. It's said that they meet, every so often, to talk and just to think together about the heroism and the terror of two sublime Beings, The One Who Came Back, and The Man With The Hammer. Even here at home, some of the old ones, and some of us who are just old-fashioned, believe it, or parts of it anyway. I know there are some who say that a hollow at the center of the forehead—a sort of shadow of the Hammer's blow—is a sign of very special ability. And I remember how Great-grandmother used to sing an old, pious song, let's see now, yes, 'Be not like dumb-driven cattle, be a hero in the strife.' But there aren't many. Not any more."

"Do *you* believe it?" the oldest calf insisted; and now she was touched to realize that every one of them, from the oldest to the youngest, needed very badly to be sure about that.

"Of course not, silly," she said; and all at once she was overcome by a most curious shyness, for it occurred to her that in the course of time, this young thing might be bred to her. "It's just an old, old legend." With a tender little laugh she added, lightly, "We use it to frighten children with."

By now the light was long on the plain and the herd was only a fume of gold near the horizon. Behind it, dung steamed, and dust sank gently to the shattered ground. She looked far away for a moment, wondering. Something—it was like a forgotten word on the tip of the tongue. She felt the sudden chill of the late afternoon and she wondered what she had been wondering about. "Come, children," she said briskly, "it's high time for supper." And she turned away; they followed.

The trouble was, her son was thinking, you could never trust her. If she said a thing was so, she was probably just trying to get her way with you. If she said a thing wasn't so, it probably was so. But you never could be sure. Not without seeing for yourself. I'm going to go, he told himself; I don't care *what* she wants. And if it isn't so, why then I'll live on the range and make the great journey and find out what *is* so. And if what she told was true, why then I'll know ahead of time and the one *I* will charge is The Man With The Hammer. I'll put Him and His Hammer out of the way forever, and that will make me an even better hero than The One Who Came Back.

So, when his mother glanced at him in concern, not quite daring to ask her question, he gave her his most docile smile, and snuggled his head against her, and she was comforted.

The littlest and youngest of them was doing double skips in his efforts to keep up with her. Now that he wouldn't be interrupting her, and none of the big ones would hear and make fun of him, he shyly whispered his question, so warmly moistly ticklish that she felt as if he were licking her ear.

"What is it, darling?" she asked, bending down.

"What's a train?"

Marooned on Gilligan's Island:
Are Women Morally Superior to Men?

by Katha Pollitt

Some years ago, I was invited by the wife of a well-known writer to
sign a women's peace petition. It made the points such documents
usually make: that women, as mothers, caregivers and nurturers,
have a special awareness of the precariousness of human life, see
through jingoism and cold war rhetoric and would prefer nations to
work out their difficulties peacefully so that the military budget
could be diverted to schools and hospitals and housing. It had the
literary tone such documents usually have, as well—at once superior
and plaintive, as if the authors didn't know whether they were brag-
ging or begging. We are wiser than you poor deluded menfolk, was
the subtext, so will you please-please-please listen to your moms?

To sign or not to sign? Of course, I was all for peace. But was I for
peace *as a woman?* I wasn't a mother then—I wasn't even an aunt.
Did my lack of nurturing credentials make my grasp of the horrors of
war and the folly of the arms race only theoretical, like a white person's understanding of racism? Were mothers the natural leaders of
the peace movement, to whose judgment nonmothers, male and female, must defer, because after all we couldn't *know,* couldn't *feel*
that tenderness toward fragile human life that a woman who had
borne and raised children had experienced? On the other hand, I
was indeed a woman. Was motherhood with its special wisdom
somehow deep inside me, to be called upon when needed, like my
uterus?

Complicating matters in a way relevant to this essay was my
response to the famous writer's wife herself. Here was a woman in
her 50s, her child-raising long behind her. Was motherhood the only
banner under which she could gain a foothold on civic life? Perhaps
so. Her only other public identity was that of a wife, and wifehood,
even to a famous man, isn't much to claim credit for these days.
("To think I spent all those years ironing his underpants!" she once
burst out to a mutual friend.) Motherhood was what she had in the
work-and-accomplishment department, so it was understandable

that she try to maximize its moral status. But I was not in her situation: I was a writer, a single woman, a jobholder. By sending me a petition from which I was excluded even as I was invited to add my name, perhaps she was telling me that, by leading a non-domestic life, I had abandoned the moral high ground, was "acting like a man," but could redeem myself by acknowledging the moral pre-eminence of the class of women I refused to join.

The ascription of particular virtues—compassion, patience, common sense, nonviolence—to mothers, and the tendency to conflate "mothers" with "women," has a long history in the peace movement but goes way beyond issues of war and peace. At present it permeates discussions of just about every field, from management training to theology. Indeed, although the media like to caricature feminism as denying the existence of sexual differences, for the women's movement and its opponents alike "difference" is where the action is. Thus, business writers wonder if women's nurturing, intuitive qualities will make them better executives. Educators suggest that female students suffer in classrooms that emphasize competition over cooperation. Women politicians tout their playground-honed negotiating skills, their egoless devotion to public service, their gender-based commitment to fairness and caring. A variety of political causes—environmentalism, animal rights, even vegetarianism—are promoted as logical extensions of women's putative peacefulness, closeness to nature, horror of aggression and concern for others' health. (Indeed, to some extent these causes are arenas in which women fight one another over definitions of femininity, which is why debates over disposable diapers and over the wearing of fur—both rather minor sources of harm, even if their opponents are right—loom so large and are so acrimonious.) In the arts, we hear a lot about what women's "real" subjects, methods and materials ought to be. Painting is male. Rhyme is male. Plot is male. Perhaps, say the Lacanian feminists, even logic and language are male. What is female? Nature. Blood. Milk. Communal gatherings. The moon. Quilts.

Haven't we been here before? Indeed we have. Woman as sharer and carer, woman as earth mother, woman as guardian of all the small rituals that knit together a family and a community, woman as beneath, above or beyond such manly concerns as law, reason, abstract ideas—these images are as old as time. Open defenders of male supremacy have always used them to declare women flatly inferior to men; covert ones use them to place women on a pedestal as too good for this naughty world. Thus, in the *Eumenides,* Aeschylus celebrated law as the defeat by males of primitive female principles of bloodguilt and vengeance, while the Ayatollah Khomeini thought women should be barred from judgeships because they were too tenderhearted. Different rationale, same outcome: Women, because of their indifference to an impersonal moral order, cannot be full participants in civic life.

There exists an equally ancient line of thought, however, that uses femininity to posit a subversive challenge to the social order: Think of Sophocles' Antigone, who resists tyranny out of love and piety, or Aristophanes' Lysistrata, the original women's strike for peace-nik, or Shakespeare's Portia, who champions mercy against the savage letter of the law. For reasons of power, money and persistent social structures, the vision of the morally superior woman can never overcome the dominant ethos in reality but exists alongside it as a kind of permanent wish or hope: If only powerful and powerless could change places, and the meek inherit the earth! Thus, it is perpetually being rediscovered, dressed in fashionable clothes and presented, despite its antiquity, as a radical new idea.

"Relational" Women, "Autonomous" Men

In the 1950s, which we think of as the glory days of traditional sex roles, the anthropologist Ashley Montagu argued in "The Natural Superiority of Women" that females had it all over males in every way that counted, including the possession of two X chromosomes that made them stabler, saner and healthier than men, with their X and Y. Montagu's essay, published in *The Saturday Review* and later expanded to a book, is witty and high-spirited and, interestingly, anticipates the current feminist challenge to male-defined categories. (He notes, for example, that while men are stronger than women in the furniture-moving sense, women are stronger than men when faced with extreme physical hardship and tests of endurance; so when we say that men are stronger than women, we are equating strength with what men have.) But the fundamental thrust of Montagu's essay was to confirm traditional gender roles while revising the way we value them: Having proved to his own satisfaction that women could scale the artistic and intellectual heights, he argued that most would (that is, should) refrain, because women's true genius was "humanness," and their real mission was to "humanize" men before men blew up the world. And that, he left no doubt, was a full-time job.

Contemporary proponents of "difference feminism" advance a variation on the same argument, without Montagu's puckish humor. Instead of his whimsical chromosomal explanation, we get the psychoanalytic one proposed by Nancy Chodorow in *The Reproduction of Mothering:* Daughters define themselves by relating to their mothers, the primary love object of all children, and are therefore empathic, relationship-oriented, nonhierarchical and interested in forging consensus; sons must separate from their mothers, and are therefore individualistic, competitive, resistant to connection with others and focused on abstract rules and rights. Chodorow's theory has become a kind of mantra of difference feminism, endlessly cited as if it explained phenomena we all agree are universal, though this is far from the case. The central question Chodorow poses—Why are women the primary caregivers of children?— could not even be asked before the advent of modern birth control, and can be answered without resorting to psychology. Historically, women have taken care of children because high fertility and lack of other options left most of them no choice. Those rich enough to avoid personally raising their children often did, as Rousseau observed to his horror.

Popularizers of Chodorow water down and sentimentalize her thesis. They embrace her proposition that traditional mothering produces "relational" women and "autonomous" men but forget her less congenial argument that it also results in sexual inequality, misogyny and hostility between mothers and daughters, who, like sons, desire independence but have a much harder time achieving it. Unlike her followers, Chodorow does not romanticize mothering: "Exclusive single parenting is bad for mother and child alike," she concludes; in a tragic paradox, female "caring," "intimacy" and "nurturance" do not soften but *produce* aggressive, competitive, hypermasculine men.

Thus, in her immensely influential book *In a Different Voice,* Carol Gilligan uses Chodorow to argue that the sexes make moral decisions according to separate criteria: women according to an "ethic of care," men according to an "ethic of rights." Deborah Tannen, in the best-selling *You Just Don't Understand,* claims that men and women grow up with "different cultural backgrounds"— the single-sex world of children's play in which girls cooperate and boys compete—"so talk between men and women is cross-cultural communication." While these two writers differ in important ways— Tannen, writing at a more popular level, is by far the clearer thinker and the one more interested in analyzing actual human interactions in daily life—they share important liabilities, too. Both largely confine their observations to the white middle class—especially Gilligan, much of whose elaborate theory of gendered ethics rests on interviews with a handful of Harvard-Radcliffe undergraduates— and seem unaware that this limits the applicability of their data. (In her new book, *Meeting at the Crossroads,* Gilligan makes a similar mistake. Her whole theory of "loss of relationship" as the central trauma of female adolescence rests on interviews with students at one posh single-sex private school.) Both massage their findings to fit their theories: Gilligan's male and female responses are actually quite similar to each other, as experimenters have subsequently shown by removing the names and asking subjects to try to sort the test answers by gender; Tannen is quick to attribute blatant rudeness or sexism in male speech to anxiety, helplessness, fear of loss of face—anything, indeed, but rudeness and sexism. Both look only at what people say, not what they do. For Tannen this isn't a decisive objection because verbal behavior is her subject, although it limits the applicability of her findings to other areas of behavior; for Gilligan, it is a major obstacle, unless you believe, as she apparently does, that the way people say they would resolve farfetched hypothetical dilemmas—Should a poor man steal drugs to save his dying wife?—tells us how they reason in real-life situations or, more important, what they do.

But the biggest problem with Chodorovian accounts of gender difference is that they credit the differences they find to essential, universal features of male and female psychosexual development rather than to the economic and social positions men and women hold, or to the actual power differences between individual men and women. In *The Mismeasure of Woman,* her trenchant and witty attack on contemporary theories of gender differences, Carol Tavris points out that much of what can be said about women applies as well to poor people, who also tend to focus more on family and relationships and less on work and self-advancement; to behave deferentially with those more socially powerful; and to appear to others more emotional and "intuitive" than rational and logical in their thinking. Then, too, there is the question of whether the difference theorists are measuring anything beyond their own willingness to think in stereotypes. If Chodorow is right, relational women and autonomous men should be the norm, but are they? Or is it just that women and men use different language, have different social styles, different explanations for similar behavior? Certainly, it is easy to find in one's own acquaintance, as well as in the world at large, men and women who don't fit the models. Difference feminists like to attribute ruthlessness, coldness and hyperrationality in successful women—Margaret Thatcher is the standard example—to the fact that men control the networks of power and permit only women like themselves to rise. But I've met plenty of loudmouthed, insensitive, aggressive women who are stay-at-home mothers and secretaries and nurses. And I know plenty of sweet, unambitious men whose main satisfactions lie in their social, domestic and romantic lives, although not all of them would admit this to an inquiring social scientist. We tend to tell strangers what we think will make us sound good. I myself, to my utter amazement, informed a telephone pollster that I exercised regularly, a baldfaced lie. How much more difficult to describe truthfully one's moral and ethical values—even if one knew what they were, which, as Socrates demonstrated at length, almost no one does.

So why are Gilligan and Tannen the toasts of feminist social science, endlessly cited and discussed in academia and out of it too, in gender-sensitivity sessions in the business world and even, following the Anita Hill testimony, in Congress? The success of the difference theorists proves yet again that social science is one part science and nine parts social. They say what people want to hear: Women really are different, in just the ways we always thought. Women embrace Gilligan and Tannen because they offer flattering accounts of traits for which they have historically been castigated. Men like them because, while they urge understanding and respect for "female" values and behaviors, they also let men off the hook: Men have power, wealth and control of social resources because women don't really want them. The pernicious tendencies of difference feminism are perfectly illustrated by the Sears sex discrimination case, in which Rosalind Rosenberg, a professor of women's history at Barnard College, testified for Sears that female employees held lower-paying salaried jobs while men worked selling big-ticket items on commission because women preferred low-risk, non-competitive positions that did not interfere with family responsibilities (see Jon Wiener, "Women's History on Trial," September 7, 1985). Sears won its case.

Mother Knows Best

While Chodorow's analysis of psychosexual development is the point of departure for most of the difference feminists, it is possible to construct a theory of gendered ethics on other grounds. The most interesting attempt I've seen is by the pacifist philosopher Sara Ruddick. Although not widely known outside academic circles, her *Maternal Thinking* makes an argument that can be found in such mainstream sources as the columns of Anna Quindlen in *The New York Times*. For Ruddick it is not psychosexual development that produces the Gilliganian virtues but intimate involvement in child-raising, the hands-on work of mothering. Men too can be mothers if they do the work that women do. (And women can be Fathers—a word Ruddick uses, complete with arrogant capital letter, for distant, uninvolved authority-figure parents.) Mothers are patient, peace-loving, attentive to emotional context and so on, because those are the qualities you need to get the job done, the way accountants are precise, lawyers are argumentative, writers self-centered. Thus mothers constitute a logical constituency for pacifist and antiwar politics, and, by extension, a "caring" domestic agenda.

But what is the job of mothering? Ruddick defines "maternal practice" as meeting three demands: preservation, growth and social acceptability. She acknowledges the enormously varying manifestations of these demands, but she doesn't incorporate into her theory the qualifications, limits and contradictions she notes— perhaps because to do so would reveal these demands as so flexible as to be practically empty terms.

Almost anything mothers do can be explained under one of these rubrics, however cruel, dangerous, unfair or authoritarian— the genital mutilation of African and Arab girls, the foot-binding of pre-revolutionary Chinese ones, the sacrifice of some children to in-crease the resources available for others, as in the killing or malnour-ishing of female infants in India and China today. I had a Caribbean student whose mother beat all her children whenever one got into trouble, to teach them "responsibility" for one another. In this country, too, many mothers who commit what is legally child abuse *think* they are merely disciplining their kids in the good old-fashioned way. As long as the practices are culturally acceptable (and sometimes even when they're not), the mothers who perform them think of themselves as good parents. But if all these behaviors count as mothering, how can mothering have a necessary connec-tion with any single belief about anything, let alone how to stop war, or any single set of personality traits, let alone nonviolent ones?

We should not be surprised that motherhood does not produce uniform beliefs and behaviors: It is, after all, not a job; it has no stan-dard of admission, and almost nobody gets fired. Motherhood is open to any woman who can have a baby or adopt one. *Not* to be a mother is a decision; becoming one requires merely that a woman accede, perhaps only for as long as it takes to get pregnant, to thou-sands of years of cumulative social pressure. After that, she's on her own; she can soothe her child's nightmares or let him cry in the dark. Nothing intrinsic to child-raising will tell her what is the better choice for her child (each has been the favored practice at different times). Although Ruddick starts off by looking closely at maternal practice, when that practice contradicts her own ideas about good mothering it is filed away as an exception, a distortion imposed by Fathers or poverty or some other outside force. But if you add up all the exceptions, you are left with a rather small group of people— women like Ruddick herself, enlightened, up-to-date, educated, upper-middle-class liberals.

And not even all of them. Consider the issue of physical punishment. Ruddick argues that experience teaches mothers that violence is useless; it only creates anger, deception and more violence. Negotiation is the mother's way of resolving disputes and encouraging good behavior. As Ann Crittenden put it in *The Nation* during the Gulf War: "One learns, in theory and in practice, to try to resolve conflict in ways that do not involve the sheer imposition of will or brute force. One learns that violence just doesn't work." Crittenden would have a hard time explaining all those moms in uniform who participated in Desert Storm—but then she'd have a hard time explaining all those mothers screaming at their kids in the supermarket, too.

As it happens, I agree that violence is a bad way to teach, and I made a decision never, no matter what, to spank my daughter. But mothers who do not hit their children, or permit their husbands to do so, are as rare as conscientious objectors in wartime. According to one survey, 78 percent approve of an occasional "good, hard spanking"—because they think violence *is* an effective way of teaching, because they think that hitting children isn't really violence, because they just lose it. Even *Parenting* found that more than a third of its readers hit their kids. And *Parenting*'s audience is not only far more educated, affluent and liberal than the general population; it consists entirely of people who care what experts think about child development—and contemporary experts revile corporal punishment. Interestingly, the moms who hit tended to be the ones who fretted the most about raising their children well. Mothers who think too much?

Like old-style socialists finding "proletarian virtue" in the working class, Ruddick claims to be describing what mothers do, but all too often she is really prescribing what she thinks they ought to do. "When their children flourish, almost all mothers have a sense of well-being." Hasn't she ever heard of postpartum depression? Of mothers who belittle their children's accomplishments and resent their growing independence? "What mother wouldn't want the power to keep her children healthy . . . to create hospitals, schools, jobs, day care, and work schedules that serve her maternal work?" Notice how neatly the modest and common-sensical wish for a healthy child balloons into the hotly contested and by no means universal wish of mothers for day care and flextime. Notice too how Ruddick moves from a mother's desire for social institutions that serve *her* children to an assumption that this desire translates into wanting comparable care for *all* children. But mothers feature prominently in local struggles against busing, mergers of rich and poor schools, and the placement of group homes for foster kids, boarder babies and the retarded in their neighborhoods. Why? The true reason may be property values and racism, but what these mothers often say is that they are simply protecting their kids. Ruddick seems to think Maternal Thinking leads naturally to Sweden; in the United States it is equally likely to lead to Fortress Suburbia.

As Gilligan does with all women, Ruddick scrutinizes mothers for what she expects to find, and sure enough, there it is. But why look to mothers for her peaceful constituency in the first place? Why not health professionals, who spend their lives saving lives? Or historians, who know how rarely war yields a benefit remotely commensurate with its cost in human misery? Or I don't know, gardeners, blame-lessly tending their innocent flowers? You can read almost any kind of work as affirming life and conferring wisdom. Ruddick chooses mothering because she's already decided that women possess the Gilliganian virtues and she wants a non-essentialist peg to hang them on, so that men can acquire them too. A disinterested observer scouring the world for labor that encourages humane val-ues would never pick child-raising: It's too quirky, too embedded in repellent cultural norms, too hot.

Man's World, Woman's Place

Despite its intellectual flabbiness, difference feminism is deeply appeal-ing to many women. Why? For one thing, it seems to explain some important phenomena: that women—and this is a cross-cultural truth—commit very little criminal violence compared with men; that women fill the ranks of the so-called caring professions; that women are much less likely than men to abandon their children. Difference feminists want to give women credit for these good behaviors by raising them from the level of instinct or passivity—the Camille Paglia vision of femininity—to the level of moral choice and principled decision. Who can blame women for embracing theories that tell them the sacrifices they make on behalf of domesticity and children are legitimate, moral, even noble? By stressing the mentality of nurturance—the *ethic* of caring, maternal *thinking*—Gilligan and Ruddick challenge the ancient division of humanity into rational males and irrational females. They offer women a way to argue that their views have equal status with those of men and to resist the customary marginalization of their voices in public debate. Doubtless many women have felt emboldened by Gilliganian accounts of moral difference: Speaking in a different voice is, after all, a big step up from silence.

The vision of women as sharers and carers is tempting in another way too. Despite much media blather about the popularity of the victim position, most people want to believe they act out of free will and choice. The uncomfortable truth that women have all too little of either is a difficult hurdle for feminists. Acknowledging the systematic oppression of women seems to deprive them of existential freedom, to turn them into puppets, slaves and Stepford wives. Deny it, and you can't make change. By arguing that the traditional qualities, tasks and ways of life of women are as important, valuable and serious as those of men (if not more so), Gilligan and others let women feel that nothing needs to change except the social valuation accorded to what they are already doing. It's a rationale for the status quo, which is why men like it, and a burst of grateful applause, which is why women like it. Men keep the power, but since power is bad, so much the worse for them.

Another rather curious appeal of difference feminism is that it offers a way for women to define themselves as independent of men. In a culture that sees women almost entirely in relation to men, this is no small achievement. Sex, for example—the enormous amount of female energy, money and time spent on beauty and fashion and romance, on attracting men and keeping them, on placating male power, strategizing ways around it or making it serve one's own ends—plays a minute role in these theories. You would never guess from Gilligan or Ruddick that men, individually and collectively, are signal beneficiaries of female nurturance, much less that this goes far to explain why society encourages nurturance in women. No, it is always children whom women are described as fostering and sacrificing for, or the community, or even other women—not husbands or lovers. It's as though wives cook dinner only for their kids, leaving the husband to raid the fridge on his own. And no doubt many women, quietly smoldering at their mate's refusal to share domestic labor, persuade themselves that they are serving only their children, or their own preferences, rather than confront the inequality of their marriage.

The peaceful mother and the "relational" woman are a kinder, gentler, leftish version of "family values," and both are modern versions of the separate-spheres ideology of the Victorians. In the nineteenth century, too, some women tried to turn the ideology of sexual difference on its head and expand the moral claims of motherhood to include the public realm. Middle-class women became social reformers, abolitionists, temperance advocates, settlement workers and even took paying jobs in the "helping professions"— nursing, social work, teaching—which were perceived as extensions of women's domestic role although practiced mostly by single women. These women did not deny that their sex fitted them for the home, but argued that domesticity did not end at the front door of the house, or confine itself to dusting (or telling the housemaid to dust). Even the vote could be cast as an extension of domesticity: Women, being more moral than men, would purify the government of vice and corruption, end war and make America safe for family life. (The persistence of this metaphor came home to me this summer when I attended a Women's Action Coalition demonstration during the Democratic National Convention. There—along with WAC's funny and ferocious all-in-black drum corps and contingents of hip downtown artists brandishing Barbara Kruger posters and shouting slogans like "We're Women! We're Angry! We're Not Going Shopping!"—was a trio of street performers with housecoats and kerchiefs over black catsuits and spiky hair, pushing brooms: Women will clean up government!)

Accepting the separate-spheres ideology had obvious advantages in an era when women were formally barred from higher education, political power and many jobs. But its defects are equally obvious. It defined all women by a single standard, and one developed by a sexist society. It offered women no way to enter professions that could not be defined as extensions of domestic roles—you could be a math teacher but not a mathematician, a secretary but not a sea captain—and no way to challenge any but the grossest abuses of male privilege. Difference feminists are making a similar bid for power on behalf of women today, and are caught in similar contradictions. Once again, women are defined by their family roles. Child-raising is seen as women's glory and joy and opportunity for self-transcendence, while Dad naps on the couch. Women who do not fit the stereotype are castigated as unfeminine—nurses nurture, doctors do not—and domestic labor is romanticized and sold to women as a badge of moral worth.

What's Love Got to Do with It?

For all the many current explanations of perceived moral difference between the sexes, one hears remarkably little about the material basis of the family. Yet the motherhood and womanhood being valorized cannot be considered apart from questions of power, privilege and money. There is a reason a non-earning woman can proudly call herself a "wife and mother" and a non-earning man is just unemployed: The traditional female role, with its attendant real or imagined character traits, implies a male income. Middle-class women go to great lengths to separate themselves from this uncomfortable fact. One often hears women defend their decision to stay at home by heaping scorn on paid employment—caricatured as making widgets or pushing papers or dressing for success—and the difference feminists also like to distinguish between altruistic, poorly paid female jobs and the nasty, profitable ones performed by men. In *Prisoners of Men's Dreams,* Suzanne Gordon comes close to blaming the modest status of jobs like nursing and flight attending on

women's entry into jobs like medicine and piloting, as if before the
women's movement those female-dominated occupations were respected and rewarded. (Nurses should be glad the field no longer
has a huge captive labor pool of women: The nursing shortage has
led to dramatic improvements in pay, benefits and responsibility.
Now nurses earn a man-sized income, and men are applying to
nursing school in record numbers—exactly what Gordon wants.)
   It's all very well for some women to condemn others for "acting
like men"—i.e., being ambitious, assertive, interested in money and
power. But if their husbands did not "act like men," where would
they be? Jean Bethke Elshtain, who strenuously resists the notion
of gendered ethics, nevertheless bemoans the loss to their communities when women leave volunteering and informal mutual support
networks for paid employment. But money must come from somewhere; if women leave to men the job of earning the family income
(an option fewer and fewer families can afford), they will be eco-
nomically dependent on their husbands, a situation that, besides
carrying obvious risks in an age of frequent divorce, weakens their
bargaining position in the family and insures that men will largely
control major decisions affecting family life.
   Difference theorists would like to separate out the aspects of traditional womanhood that they approve of and speak only of those.
But the parts they like (caring, nurturing, intimacy) are inseparable
from the parts they don't like (economic dependence and the subor-
dination of women within the family). The difference theorists try
to get around this by positing a world that contains two cultures—
a female world of love and ritual and a male world of getting and
spending and killing—which mysteriously share a single planet. That
vision is expressed neatly in a recent pop-psychology title, *Men Are
from Mars, Women Are from Venus*. It would be truer to say men are
from Illinois and women are from Indiana—different, sure, but not in
ways that have much ethical consequence.

The truth is, there is only one culture, and it shapes each sex in
distinct but mutually dependent ways in order to reproduce itself.
To the extent that the stereotypes are true, women have the
"relational" domestic qualities *because* men have the "autonomous"

qualities required to survive and prosper in modern capitalism. She needs a wage earner (even if she has a job, thanks to job discrimination), and he needs someone to mind his children, hold his hand and have his emotions for him. This—not, as Gordon imagines, some treason to her sex—explains why women who move into male sectors act very much like men: If they didn't, they'd find themselves back home in a jiffy. The same necessities and pressures affect them as affect the men who hold those jobs. Because we are in a transition period, in which many women were raised with modest expectations and much emphasis on the need to please others, social scientists who look for it can find traces of empathy, caring and so on in some women who have risen in the world of work and power, but when they tell us that women doctors will transform American medicine, or women executives will transform the corporate world, they are looking backward, not forward. If women really do enter the work force on equal terms with men—if they become 50 percent of all lawyers, politicians, car dealers and prison guards— they may be less sexist (although the example of Russian doctors, a majority of them female, is not inspiring to those who know about the brutal gynecological customs prevailing in the former U.S.S.R.). And they may bring with them a distinct set of manners, a separate social style. But they won't be, in some general way, more honest, kind, egalitarian, empathic or indifferent to profit. To argue otherwise is to believe that the reason factory owners bust unions, doctors refuse Medicaid patients and New York City school custodians don't mop the floors is because they are men.

The ultimate paradox of difference feminism is that it has come to the fore at a moment when the lives of the sexes are becoming less distinct than they ever have been in the West. Look at the decline of single-sex education (researchers may tout the benefits of all-female schools and colleges, but girls overwhelmingly choose coeducation); the growth of female athletics; the virtual abolition of virginity as a requirement for girls; the equalization of college-attendance rates of males and females; the explosion of employment for married women and mothers even of small children; the crossing of workplace gender lines by both females and males; the cultural pressure on men to be warm and nurturant fathers, to do at least some housework, to choose mates who are their equals in education and income potential.

It's fashionable these days to talk about the backlash against equality feminism—I talk this way myself when I'm feeling blue—but equality feminism has scored amazing successes. It has transformed women's expectations in every area of their lives. However, it has not yet transformed society to meet those expectations. The workplace still discriminates. On the home front few men practice egalitarianism, although many preach it; single mothers—and given the high divorce rate, every mother is potentially a single mother—lead incredibly difficult lives.

In this social context, difference feminism is essentially a way for women both to take advantage of equality feminism's success and to accommodate themselves to its limits. It appeals to particular kinds of women—those in the "helping professions" or the home, for example, rather than those who want to be bomber pilots or neurosurgeons or electricians. At the popular level, it encourages women who feel disadvantaged or demeaned by equality to direct their anger against women who have benefited from it by thinking of them as gender traitors and of themselves as suffering for their virtue—thus the hostility of nurses toward female doctors, and of stay-at-home mothers toward employed mothers.

For its academic proponents, the appeal lies elsewhere: Difference feminism is a way to carve out a safe space in the face of academia's resistance to female advancement. It works much like multiculturalism, making an end-run around a static and discriminatory employment structure by creating an intellectual niche that can be filled only by members of the discriminated-against group. And like other forms of multiculturalism, it looks everywhere for its explanatory force—biology, psychology, sociology, cultural identity —*except* economics. The difference feminists cannot say that the differences between men and women are the result of their relative economic positions because to say that would be to move the whole discussion out of the realm of psychology and feel-good cultural pride and into the realm of a tough political struggle over the distribution of resources and justice and money.

Although it is couched in the language of praise, difference feminism is demeaning to women. It asks that women be admitted into
public life and public discourse not because they have a right to be
there but because they will improve them. Even if this were true,
and not the wishful thinking I believe it to be, why should the task of
moral and social transformation be laid on women's doorstep and
not on everyone's—or, for that matter, on men's, by the you-broke-
it-you-fix-it principle. Peace, the environment, a more humane
workplace, economic justice, social support for children—these are
issues that affect us all and are everyone's responsibility. By promising to assume that responsibility, difference feminists lay the ground-
work for excluding women again, as soon as it becomes clear that
the promise cannot be kept.

No one asks that other oppressed groups win their freedom by
claiming to be extra-good. And no other oppressed group thinks it
must make such a claim in order to be accommodated fully and
across the board by society. For blacks and other racial minorities, it
is enough to want to earn a living, exercise one's talents, get a fair
hearing in the public forum. Only for women is simple justice an in-
sufficient argument. It is as though women don't really believe they
are entitled to full citizenship unless they can make a special claim to
virtue. Why isn't being human enough?

In the end, I didn't sign that peace petition, although I was sorry
to disappoint a woman I liked, and although I am very much for
peace. I decided to wait for a petition that welcomed my signature
as a person, an American, a citizen implicated, against my will, in
war and the war economy. I still think I did the right thing.

Solving for Pattern

by Wendell Berry

Our dilemma in agriculture now is that the industrial methods
that have so spectacularly solved some of the problems of food production have been accompanied by "side effects" so damaging as to
threaten the survival of farming. Perhaps the best clue to the nature
and the gravity of this dilemma is that it is not limited to agriculture.
My immediate concern here is with the irony of agricultural methods
that destroy, first, the health of the soil and, finally, the health of
human communities. But I could just as easily be talking about sanitation systems that pollute, school systems that graduate illiterate
students, medical cures that cause disease, or nuclear armaments
that explode in the midst of the people they are meant to protect.
This is a kind of surprise that is characteristic of our time: the cure
proves incurable; security results in the evacuation of a neighborhood or a town. It is only when it is understood that our agricultural
dilemma is characteristic not of our agriculture but of our time
that we can begin to understand why these surprises happen, and
to work out standards of judgment that may prevent them.

To the problems of farming, then, as to other problems of our
time, there appear to be three kinds of solutions:

There is, first, the solution that causes a ramifying series of new
problems, the only limiting criterion being, apparently, that the new
problems should arise beyond the purview of the expertise that produced the solution—as, in agriculture, industrial solutions to the
problem of production have invariably caused problems of mainte-
nance, conservation, economics, community health, etc., etc.

If, for example, beef cattle are fed in large feed lots, within the
boundaries of the feeding operation itself a certain factory-like order
and efficiency can be achieved. But even within those boundaries
that mechanical order immediately produces biological disorder, for
we know that health problems and dependence on drugs will be
greater among cattle so confined than among cattle on pasture.

And beyond those boundaries, the problems multiply. Pen
feeding of cattle in large numbers involves, first, a manure-removal

problem, which becomes at some point a health problem for the animals themselves, for the local watershed, and for the adjoining eco-systems and human communities. If the manure is disposed of without returning it to the soil that produced the feed, a serious problem of soil fertility is involved. But we know too that large concentrations of animals in feed lots in one place tend to be associated with, and to promote, large cash-grain monocultures in other places. These monocultures tend to be accompanied by a whole set of specifically agricultural problems: soil erosion, soil compaction, epidemic infestations of pests, weeds, and disease. But they are also accompanied by a set of agricultural-economic problems (dependence on purchased technology; dependence on purchased fuels, fertilizers, and poisons; dependence on credit)—and by a set of community problems, beginning with depopulation and the removal of sources, services, and markets to more and more distant towns. And these are, so to speak, only the first circle of the bad effects of a bad solution. With a little care, their branchings can be traced on into nature, into the life of the cities, and into the cultural and economic life of the nation.

The second kind of solution is that which immediately worsens the problem it is intended to solve, causing a hellish symbiosis in which problem and solution reciprocally enlarge one another in a sequence that, so far as its own logic is concerned, is limitless—as when the problem of soil compaction is "solved" by a bigger tractor, which further compacts the soil, which makes a need for a still bigger tractor, and so on and on. There is an identical symbiosis between coal-fired power plants and air conditioners. It is characteristic of such solutions that no one prospers by them but the suppliers of fuel and equipment.

These two kinds of solutions are obviously bad. They always serve one good at the expense of another or of several others, and I believe that if all their effects were ever to be accounted for they would be seen to involve, too frequently if not invariably, a net loss to nature, agriculture, and the human commonwealth.

Such solutions always involve a definition of the problem that is either false or so narrow as to be virtually false. To define an agricultural problem as if it were solely a problem of agriculture—or solely a problem of production or technology or economics—is simply to misunderstand the problem, either inadvertently or deliberately, either for profit or because of a prevalent fashion of thought. The whole problem must be solved, not just some handily identifiable and simplifiable aspect of it.

Both kinds of bad solutions leave their problems unsolved. Bigger tractors do not solve the problem of soil compaction any more than air conditioners solve the problem of air pollution. Nor does the large confinement-feeding operation solve the problem of food production; it is, rather, a way calculated to allow large-scale ambition and greed to profit from food production. The real problem of food production occurs within a complex, mutually influential relationship of soil, plants, animals, and people. A real solution to that problem will therefore be ecologically, agriculturally, and culturally healthful.

Perhaps it is not until health is set down as the aim that we come in sight of the third kind of solution: that which causes a ramifying series of solutions—as when meat animals are fed on the farm where the feed is raised, and where the feed is raised to be fed to the animals that are on the farm. Even so rudimentary a description implies a concern for pattern, for quality, which necessarily complicates the concern for production. The farmer has put plants and animals into a relationship of mutual dependence, and must perforce be concerned for balance or symmetry, a reciprocating connection in the pattern of the farm that is biological, not industrial, and that involves solutions to problems of fertility, soil husbandry, economics, sanitation—the whole complex of problems whose proper solutions add up to *health:* the health of the soil, of plants and animals, of farm and farmer, of farm family and farm community, all involved in the same internested, interlocking pattern—or pattern of patterns.

A bad solution is bad, then, because it acts destructively upon the larger patterns in which it is contained. It acts destructively upon those patterns, most likely, because it is formed in ignorance or disregard of them. A bad solution solves for a single purpose or goal, such as increased production. And it is typical of such solutions that they achieve stupendous increases in production at exorbitant biological and social costs.

A good solution is good because it is in harmony with those larger patterns—and this harmony will, I think, be found to have the nature of analogy. A bad solution acts within the larger pattern the way a disease or addiction acts within the body. A good solution acts within the larger pattern the way a healthy organ acts within the body. But it must at once be understood that a healthy organ does not—as the mechanistic or industrial mind would like to say—"give" health to the body, is not exploited for the body's health, but is *a part* of its health. The health of organ and organism is the same, just as the health of organism and ecosystem is the same. And these structures of organ, organism, and ecosystem—as John Todd has so ably understood—belong to a series of analogical integrities that begins with the organelle and ends with the biosphere.

It would be next to useless, of course, to talk about the possibility of good solutions if none existed in proof and in practice. A part of our work at *The New Farm* has been to locate and understand those farmers whose work is competently responsive to the requirements of health. Representative of these farmers, and among them remarkable for the thoroughness of his intelligence, is Earl F. Spencer, who has a 250-acre dairy farm near Palatine Bridge, New York.

Before 1972, Earl Spencer was following a "conventional" plan which would build his herd to 120 cows. According to this plan, he would eventually buy all the grain he fed, and he was already using as much as 30 tons per year of commercial fertilizer. But in 1972, when he had increased his herd to 70 cows, wet weather reduced his harvest by about half. The choice was clear: he had either to buy half his yearly feed supply, or sell half his herd.

He chose to sell half his herd—a very unconventional choice, which in itself required a lot of independent intelligence. But character and intelligence of an even more respectable order were involved in the next step, which was to understand that the initial decision implied a profound change in the pattern of the farm and of his life and assumptions as a farmer. With his herd now reduced by half, he saw that before the sale he had been overstocked, and had been abusing his land. On his 120 acres of tillable land, he had been growing 60 acres of corn and 60 of alfalfa. On most of his fields, he was growing corn three years in succession. The consequences of

this he now saw as symptoms, and saw that they were serious: heavy
dependence on purchased supplies, deteriorating soil structure,
declining quantities of organic matter, increasing erosion, yield
reductions despite continued large applications of fertilizer. In addition, because of his heavy feeding of concentrates, his cows were
having serious digestive and other health problems.

He began to ask fundamental questions about the nature of the
creatures and the land he was dealing with, and to ask if he could
not bring about some sort of balance between their needs and his
own. His conclusion was that "to be in balance with nature is to be
successful." His farm, he says, had been going in a "dead run"; now
he would slow it to a "walk."

From his crucial decision to reduce his herd, then, several other
practical measures have followed:

1. A five-year plan (extended to eight years) to phase out entirely
   his use of purchased fertilizers.
2. A plan, involving construction of a concrete manure pit, to increase and improve his use of manure.
3. Better husbandry of cropland, more frequent rotation, better
   timing.
4. The gradual reduction of grain in the feed ration, and the con-
   current increase of roughage—which has, to date, reduced the
   dependence on grain by half, from about 6000 pounds per cow
   to about 3000 pounds.
5. A breeding program which selects "for more efficient roughage
   conversion."

The most tangible results are that the costs of production have
been "dramatically" reduced, and that per cow production has
increased by 1500 to 2000 pounds. But the health of the whole
farm has improved. There is a moral satisfaction in this, of which Earl
Spencer is fully aware. But he is also aware that the satisfaction is not
purely moral, for the good results are also practical and economic:
"We have half the animals we had before and are feeding half as
much grain to those remaining, so we now need to plant corn
only two years in a row. Less corn means less plowing, less fuel for

growing and harvesting, and less wear on the most expensive equipment." Veterinary bills have been reduced also. And in 1981, if the schedule holds, he will buy no commercial fertilizer at all.

From the work of Earl Spencer and other exemplary farmers, and from the understanding of destructive farming practices, it is possible to devise a set of critical standards for agriculture. I am aware that the list of standards which follows must be to some extent provisional, but am nevertheless confident that it will work to distinguish between healthy and unhealthy farms, as well as between the oversimplified minds that solve problems for some X such as profit or quantity of production, and those minds, sufficiently complex, that solve for health or quality or coherence of pattern. To me, the validity of these standards seems inherent in their general applicability. They will serve the making of sewer systems or households as readily as they will serve the making of farms:

1. A good solution accepts given limits, using so far as possible what is at hand. The farther-fetched the solution, the less it should be trusted. Granted that a farm can be too small, it is nevertheless true that enlarging scale is a deceptive solution; it solves one problem by acquiring another or several others.
2. A good solution accepts also the limitation of discipline. Agricultural problems should receive solutions that are agricultural, not technological or economic.
3. A good solution improves the balances, symmetries, or harmonies within a pattern—it is a qualitative solution—rather than enlarging or complicating some part of a pattern at the expense or in neglect of the rest.
4. A good solution solves more than one problem, and it does not make new problems. I am talking about health as opposed to almost any cure, coherence of pattern as opposed to almost any solution produced piecemeal or in isolation. The return of organic wastes to the soil may, at first glance, appear to be a good solution *per se*. But that is not invariably or necessarily true. It is true only if the wastes are returned to the right place at the right

time in the pattern of the farm, if the waste does not contain toxic materials, if the quantity is not too great, and if not too much energy or money is expended in transporting it.

5. A good solution will satisfy a whole range of criteria; it will be good in all respects. A farm that has found correct agricultural solutions to its problems will be fertile, productive, healthful, conservative, beautiful, pleasant to live on. This standard obviously must be qualified to the extent that the pattern of the life of a farm will be adversely affected by distortions in any of the larger patterns that contain it. It is hard, for instance, for the economy of a farm to maintain its health in a national industrial economy in which farm earnings are apt to be low and expenses high. But it is apparently true, even in such an economy, that the farmers most apt to survive are those who do not go too far out of agriculture into either industry or banking—and who, moreover, live like farmers, not like businessmen. This seems especially true for the smaller farmers.

6. A good solution embodies a clear distinction between biological order and mechanical order, between farming and industry. Farmers who fail to make this distinction are ideal customers of the equipment companies, but they often fail to understand that the real strength of a farm is in the soil.

7. Good solutions have wide margins, so that the failure of one solution does not imply the impossibility of another. Industrial agriculture tends to put its eggs into fewer and fewer baskets, and to make "going for broke" its only way of going. But to grow grain should not make it impossible to pasture livestock, and to have a lot of power should not make it impossible to use only a little.

8. A good solution always answers the question, How much is enough? Industrial solutions have always rested on the assumption that enough is all you can get. But that destroys agriculture, as it destroys nature and culture. The good health of a farm implies a limit of scale, because it implies a limit of attention, and because such a limit is invariably implied by any pattern. You destroy a square, for example, by enlarging one angle or lengthening one side. And in any sort of work there is a point past which more quantity necessarily implies less quality. In

some kinds of industrial agriculture, such as cash grain farming, it is possible (to borrow an insight from Professor Timothy Taylor) to think of technology as a substitute for skill. But even in such farming that possibility is illusory; the illusion can be maintained only so long as the consequences can be ignored. The illusion is much shorter lived when animals are included in the farm pattern, because the husbandry of animals is so insistently a human skill. A healthy farm incorporates a pattern that a single human mind can comprehend, make, maintain, vary in response to circumstances, and pay steady attention to. That this limit is obviously variable from one farmer and farm to another does not mean that it does not exist.

9. A good solution should be cheap, and it should not enrich one person by the distress or impoverishment of another. In agriculture, so-called "inputs" are, from a different point of view, outputs—*expenses*. In all things, I think, but especially in an agriculture struggling to survive in an industrial economy, any solution that calls for an expenditure to a manufacturer should be held in suspicion—not rejected necessarily, but *as a rule* mistrusted.

10. Good solutions exist only in proof, and are not to be expected from absentee owners or absentee experts. Problems must be solved in work and in place, with particular knowledge, fidelity, and care, by people who will suffer the consequences of their mistakes. There is no theoretical or ideal *practice*. Practical advice or direction from people who have no practice may have some value, but its value is questionable and is limited. The divisions of capital, management, and labor, characteristic of an industrial system, are therefore utterly alien to the health of farming—as they probably also are to the health of manufacturing. The good health of a farm depends on the farmer's mind; the good health of his mind has its dependence, and its proof, in physical work. The good farmer's mind and his body—his management and his labor—work together as intimately as his heart and his lungs. And the capital of a well-farmed farm by definition includes the farmer, mind and body both. Farmer and farm are one thing, an organism.

11. Once the farmer's mind, his body, and his farm are understood

as a single organism, and once it is understood that the question of the endurance of this organism is a question about the sufficiency and integrity of a pattern, then the word *organic* can be usefully admitted into this series of standards. It is a word that I have been defining all along, though I have not used it. An organic farm, properly speaking, is not one that uses certain methods and substances and avoids others; it is a farm whose stucture is formed in imitation of the structure of a natural system; it has the integrity, the independence, and the benign dependence of an organism. Sir Albert Howard said that a good farm is an analogue of the forest which "manures itself." A farm that imports too much fertility, even as feed or manure, is in this sense as inorganic as a farm that exports too much or that imports chemical fertilizer.

12. The introduction of the term *organic* permits me to say more plainly and usefully some things that I have said or implied earlier. In an organism, what is good for one part is good for another. What is good for the mind is good for the body; what is good for the arm is good for the heart. We know that sometimes a part may be sacrificed for the whole; a life may be saved by the amputation of an arm. But we also know that such remedies are desperate, irreversible, and destructive; it is impossible to improve the body by amputation. And such remedies do not imply a safe logic. As *tendencies* they are fatal: you cannot save your arm by the sacrifice of your life.

Perhaps most of us who know local histories of agriculture know of fields that in hard times have been sacrificed to save a farm, and we know that though such a thing is possible it is dangerous. The danger is worse when topsoil is sacrificed for the sake of a crop. And if we understand the farm as an organism, we see that it is impossible to sacrifice the health of the soil to improve the health of plants, or to sacrifice the health of plants to improve the health of animals, or to sacrifice the health of animals to improve the health of people. In a biological pattern—as in the pattern of a community—the exploitive means and motives of industrial economics are immediately destructive and ultimately suicidal.

13. It is the nature of any organic pattern to be contained within a larger one. And so a good solution in one pattern preserves the integrity of the pattern that contains it. A good agricultural solution, for example, would not pollute or erode a watershed. What is good for the water is good for the ground, what is good for the ground is good for plants, what is good for plants is good for animals, what is good for animals is good for people, what is good for people is good for the air, what is good for the air is good for the water. And vice versa.

14. But we must not forget that those human solutions that we may call organic are not natural. We are talking about organic *artifacts,* organic only by imitation or analogy. Our ability to make such artifacts depends on virtues that are specifically human: accurate memory, observation, insight, imagination, inventiveness, reverence, devotion, fidelity, restraint. Restraint—for us, now—above all: the ability to accept and live within limits; to resist changes that are merely novel or fashionable; to resist greed and pride; to resist the temptation to "solve" problems by ignoring them, accepting them as "trade-offs," or bequeathing them to posterity. A good solution, then, must be in harmony with good character, cultural value, and moral law.

Good News of the Twentieth Century:
We Can Combine Stage-Development Philosophy with Empathy, Partialization, and Story

by Carol Bly

In the Good News/Bad News jokes we always get the good news first, then the bad. The good news is moderate, the bad news so disproportionately bad that it undoes the good news by a thousandfold. In stage-development theory, the good news gives hope beyond anything we expected. Psychological discoveries or inventions, like stage-development theory, aren't much like mechanical inventions, but they have this in common with mechanics: once they are pointed out, they seem so sensible and logical we half wonder why no one thought them up hundreds of years ago. In stage-development theory, the only bad news is that most human beings live out their lives, not only their childhoods, in circumstances that stunt human development.

The good news is that people are not immutably certain types of people. Rather, they are on a continuum that runs from plain natural behavior to highly civil behavior, from plain practical response (Help! Fight! Run!) to highly ethical reflection (if I do that, how will that affect people near and people afar?).

We are all somewhere along that continuum. At any one time we are pausing at one stage level or another. Often we are stuck. Perhaps we are not only *not* stuck but just about to make a leap into much more complex thinking and feeling. Perhaps we will get to stage six or seven. Perhaps we will spend our lives stuck at stage one, two, three, four, five. . . .

It is good news that we are growing and changing, not locked into types. It is exponentially greater news that certain communications skills can affect how quickly we do that growing and changing.

I would like to present a layperson's all-purpose moral-thinking and moral-growth stage-development format. Its best points are ideas learned from Jean Piaget, Lawrence Kohlberg, Jane Loevinger, and Tom Kitwood.

Professional stage-developmentalists make not one but several sets of schemes: some of their schemes have to do with increasing consciousness of others. Some stage schemes show levels of rational judgment about right and wrong. Some show levels of likely behaviors in given situations—for example, six levels of how well one behaves in such and such a situation, despite pressures from one's background society or present community. Some stage systems focus on personality development. Some focus on improving levels of cognition. There are stage graphs that show how a human being's motivation for doing certain moral actions grows from stage one, which we may consider as instinctive self-serving, to conscious, considered self-serving, to conscious, considered serving of others of our acquaintance to—finally—conscious consideration of others we do not know and very likely will never know, such as people in lands we will not visit or the grandchildren of our grandchildren.

Some stage systems concentrate on how a human being, stage by stage, does the serious, central work of character development (impulse control, ability to maintain a goal past its initial sensate stimulus, ability to imagine someone else's needs and respect them, even if you don't know that someone else and may never be a friend).

Any psychological theory comes to life when we try it on ourselves. No sooner did I begin reading Kohlberg than I found I could tie the stage idea to my own life, to myself, and to people I know. The concepts that follow here are greatly influenced not just by Kohlberg but by the ego-developmentalist Jane Loevinger. For the interest of readers who would like to glance at some professional stage layouts, the Appendix offers commonalities and differences among a few stage development schemes, as charted by Jane Loevinger.

A Layperson's All-Purpose Moral Stage-Development Scheme

A reader will notice straight off that the first two levels aren't moral at all. The person in Stage I or II is still only practical, thinking of what *works* as opposed to what is conscientious. The second two levels are conventional: the person is taking his or her cue from others in the social or national group. Only the final two stages have any aspect of what people nowadays call "taking responsibility for yourself":

I: One is at a premoral utterly selfish stage.

II: One is still selfish, but at least one sees there are others out there, and one decides they have a right to be selfish, too.

III: Whatever seems to win strokes from the crowd is the highest good.

IV: Whatever authority says is right, is right.

V: One has developed one's own code of rights and wrongs, which one applies universally—such as honesty, hospitality, murder: one supposes that everyone in every culture should be honest and hospitable and eschew killing people. (Stage V people may be cultural relativists so far as *styles* of honesty and hospitality are concerned, but the underlying principles apply to all.)

VI: One has to disobey one's own code of rights and wrongs in order to make the best judgment in a given predicament. For example, one would lie to the Gestapo in order to save innocent lives.

Before going into each of these stages, let me describe some of the philosophical underpinnings of any stage-development theory.

First, the stages are not tied to age. Some people are in Stage V by the time they are fourteen years old. Other people never get past a patriotic Stage IV: at eighty they are saying, "What's wrong with a little my-country-right-or-wrong? Sounds like plain simple loyalty, if you ask me!" Some people, especially those whose childhoods were not blessed with kind treatment and wise mentors, stay at Stage II all their lives; that is, the bounds of their love are so close around them, they include only those of nearest kin. They are like the man whom the cold wind blew and blew at, trying to get his coat off. He only gathered it the more frantically about himself. Such a person's attitude toward anyone outside the circle of self and spouse and very few others of the same tribe is like a nation's foreign policy: one chooses one's actions on the basis of whether they are practical and properly defensive. A nearly ideal case of Stage II thinking was the British acquisition of the "Elgin marbles." The British took the ancient Greek friezes home to their museum because they would be a gorgeous acquisition for the British Empire. No one else's wishes, no ownership by geographical placement, operated in the British mind at all. Responsibility was to one's own people, not those foreigners who happened to have the works of art on their land. Since the British had the power to take them, they took them. A Stage II person is totally practical. In foreign policy we call such a-ethical practicality "Realpolitik." One does anything that won't bring home grief.

Some people stay at Stage I all their lives. They do not even include relations or loved ones in their considerations: their affections end at their own skin. They see nothing but the self. They can scarcely even make out anything but their own drives and wants. In babies, Stage I is appropriate and life-enhancing. When an adolescent human being is at Stage I, we use expressions like "poorly brought up," "undersocialized," or "showing poor ego development." In adults, someone stuck at Stage I is said to be *not* socialized. I suppose sociopaths could be described as extreme cases of people stuck at Stage I. In adults such selfishness and self-orientedness are ominous, and the behaviors are poor, ranging from inactivity with no affect to casual criminality in which the person often shows no particular emotion more intense than, "Well, he had it, and I wanted it, so I killed him."

Some stage-development thinkers partly link stages to actual human age. We do not yet know enough about the brain to be sure whether one can ever pass certain cognitive stages if one has not done so by a certain age. Children compensate for earlier lack of brain use: other circuitry in the brain appears sometimes to do the work of damaged areas. But we don't yet know some key information, such as whether a child can still learn to do imaginative symbolic work if he or she has done none at all by age eighteen. Let us say you sit a child in front of a television for all the hours of its life other than when it is eating or sleeping. After many years—sixteen or seventeen, let us say—you remove the TV, introduce hours and hours of physical exercise and read stories aloud to this young person. The young person's brain has been operating on what is sometimes called "alpha level" thinking—passive absorption of information given in pictures—for those 93,440 hours (sixteen hours a day for sixteen years). Can that brain jump out of its chemoelectric habits? Can it wake up the millions of dendritic connections in the neocortex that do such work as making a mental image of eleven goats in the woods when a parent says, "Once upon a time there was a nanny goat who had ten kids . . ."?

We haven't sure answers to such questions yet. Jean Piaget, the father of stage-development philosophy, felt certain that by the age of fourteen a child needed to be able to think conceptually. I believe learning-research people feel much more hopeful now. Still, the "use it or lose it" philosophy has some currency in learning.

For our purposes here, stage-development theory assumes that no one skips a stage, whether or not there is any age connectedness to the stages. Crawling first, then walking. Thinking selfishly first, then less selfishly, then even less selfishly, and so on. A curious finding of twentieth-century psychotherapy has been that women who have been conditioned by their class backgrounds to think only of others and never develop their own interests or convictions have to be taken back to the self-awareness and self-interest level of Stage I to learn self-honor. When they have learned self-honor, with the help of the therapist, they can and will move gradually forward into tribal loyalty (Stage II) and into peer-group honoring (Stage III) and into patriotism and authority honoring (Stage IV). Only then, after experiencing that gradual refinement of a growing ego, can they get to the altruism and principled notions of Stage V *without losing the health of their own personalities.* In terms of stage development, one could say that their culture, their psychological habitat, their background, had assaulted their ego development. The job of the psychotherapist in such cases is partly to undo years of cultural abuse, and help women rebuild their own personalities.

Here follow a few introductory remarks about the general stage-development theory discussed thus far.

Stage I
A premoral stage: Everything is myself. I am all there is.

In the beginning, when I am a baby, Good equals myself because I am all there is. It isn't that I object to others or to *other* in the abstract: I don't see them at all. If I am a baby, I even think my mother and I are the same person. If I am a baby, I howl or reach for what I want and express happiness when I have it. A baby in Stage I is living in a world of simple nature.

Let us say that I am a Stage I child, as opposed to a Stage I baby. You, my mother, return from a day's work at the food shelves and tell me that kids are hungry out there. I say, "No, I'm full. I just made myself a sandwich from the stuff you left in the refrigerator."

If I am a Stage I adult, and you tell me you are about to have an operation, and you even explain to me that this operation is being undertaken late in the course of the illness in question and likely won't do what you wish it would do, I respond, "I had an operation once. In 1984. No, 1985. No, it was too 1984, November." I scarcely take in your data about your operation and your approaching death. I have sunk deep into a mental gloaming of what happened to *me* and how *I* felt. Your speaking to me served only as a key into my own material. You used the word "operation" and my mind glommed on to it. "Operation!" my mind explained to my circuitry inside. "*We* know about operations, don't we?" I have all but forgotten you: I probably see you simply as a face to tell my story to. If you try to cut back into my daydreaming about my operation with some theory of life that you may have, I either do not take it in or, if I do, I don't like it because it is not familiar. If you keep talking when I want to think about myself and my affairs and mosey through my memories of my operation, I may get very hostile feelings toward you. I will save up these feelings for when I am next with my friends. I will snicker about you to them. And now, with you still here talking, I think of my absent friends, good buddies all, whom I trust to stick by me, not you, with your crazy ideas.

This premoral Stage I is appropriate for babies. If a third-world baby were starving in the next bassinet, a lucky first-world baby would still cry for its mother's breast milk and would not take it in good part if she nursed the other baby instead.

Stage I selfishness in adults, however, is dangerous. Examples: Clare's parents in "The Woman Lit by Fireflies," the man in "Death Games" who had a 22 for varmints, a .12 gauge for deer, and a 30.06 for people who messed with him.

Stage II
Another premoral stage: I see there are others out there.

If I am at Stage II, I have realized I am not the only one in the world. I still define *good* as having my wants met, but presumably those people out there also have their wants. At least now I can see there *are* others. Since I want what I want and will get it any way I can, those others have the right to pull off anything they can pull off, too. All considerations are practical. Anything that works—I do it.

There are fine points to my live-and-let-live selfishness. I am capable of doing a little foreign-policy thinking: I feel that I have my sphere of influence and that others have theirs. If we have to overlap, we deal. I strike as sharp a deal as I can. Why shouldn't I? This is reality. This is also the foreign policy of nearly every government in nearly every era in nearly every case. In such realpolitik I still have no sense of responsibility to any others, beyond agreeing that in their spheres of influence they have the natural right to use people and things as resources, just as I do. I obey my parents or rules about crossing the street, because it is practical: obeying prevents my getting spanked or in the case of traffic rules, it prevents my death. My loyalties are to me, my family, my church or professional group, my nation, in widening (and sequentially weakening) circles. If you draw a picture with me at the center, my family represented as a circle around me, and my

church or professional group or workplace organization as a concentric circle around the family, then the nation farther out
around the groups, my feelings are down to one hundred percent
indifference beyond the nation group. This allows me frequently
to say that I put America first. I put it first before other nations or
peoples, because a psychological mist or smokescreen envelopes
anything beyond my country. Whoever might be out there is fair
game.

Stage III
*I am now thinking like a moral person; that is, some of the things
I believe in require some short-term sacrifice of pleasure on my part.
I can see that much. I now think of good or virtue as whatever
qualities bring me acceptance or strokes from my peers.*

I believe that the ideas of the group must be right, or the group
wouldn't have those ideas. I feel dubious about any ideas I may
have that don't agree with the societal ideas around me.

A behavioral description of a Stage III morality is elaborated in
"A Mother's Tale." The mother cow neither believes nor dis-
believes the major myth or religion of her group, because the
group was torn one way or the other about it, and in the end the
cows she knew did nothing about it anyway.

Cognitively, a Stage III person hasn't got so far as to organize
his or her own ideas and has no particular code to live by. Thus,
the group of peers fills that philosophical or ego vacuum quickly.

Behaviorally, a Stage III person will betray self and anyone *outside* the immediate group in order to maintain popularity within
the group. Irving Janis's study of the bad psychology of groups in
Groupthink is a marvelous analysis of the pressures of a group on its
members.[1] I commend Janis's book because it is so well organized
that a layperson can read it easily. One need not be a government
expert or a psychologist. It has lists of the ominous tendencies of
people thinking together in groups, lists of the outcomes of these
proclivities, and steps to prevent "groupthink." Janis gives six pol-
icy-group examples in some detail, showing how groupthink
brought about poor American policy. One horrible example of a

bad group is the feasibility consultants who allowed the Bay of Pigs disaster to play itself out. In careful analysis, Janis shows a few examples of what makes a group be a good group, not a bad group—for one, Averill Harriman's group that implemented the "Marshall" program.

In his essay "The Inner Ring," C. S. Lewis points out the inane cruelty a man will practice in order to stay in good grace with the in-group of his choice. A question we might ask of the speaker in "Cider 5¢ a Glass" is: Was belonging to the old Holderness School crowd experienced by the speaker as pressure to stay in the good graces of the right group? Did it influence the speaker not to confront Sam about his behavior when they were both sober? Lest such inquiry into two characters of a poem seem gratuitously ill-willed, we remind ourselves that the classic white-collar crime of swindling the poor causes most of the suffering in human history. Rich powerful males and rich powerful females, and the spouses of rich powerful males and rich powerful females, are pleasant about supporting symphonies and museums, but in their daytime groups—corporations and governments—they pull off the policies that hurt people and despoil the planet. When we remember that, then trying for new insights into peer pressures and how they may work among entitled-feeling people seems not only justified but urgent.

Stage IV
Fealty to my sovereign group: I enjoy obeying authority.
It gives me a sense of belonging and it enlarges me.

At this stage one kills Southeast Asians if one's national leaders want it done. One defines *good* by citing authority. The authority is not always the president or the Congress or the army. Sometimes the words "America" or "my country" are the salient language. That is why national propagandists on television talk so much about "what Americans want" and "the people of this country." That kind of talk dismisses other countries and peoples of other countries by nonmention—a psychological phenomenon that women will always remember from the days before inclusive language. One doesn't need to be underaware of other countries in order to adore one's own and mindlessly obey its leaders, but most leaders try to lock it in either by directly promoting hatred of other countries (cold wars) or by indirectly making them vaporous by nonmention. When one wants some unthinking servants, there's hardly a psychological tool more effective than to validate and reinforce Stage IV citizens at the expense of Stage V or Stage VI citizens. Senator Joseph McCarthy was a twentieth-century monument to this particular strategy of punishing persons in stages above IV.

In Stage IV, I not only obey laws, I believe in them precisely because they *are* laws: they are formal, external proof that there is a government around someplace. If there is a government about, and it's mine, I love to feel bound to it in a mindless shoulder-to-shoulder citizenry with others. My loyalties, as with Stage II and Stage III people, are not to ideas but to geographical entities: at the center is myself, still a strong emotional component, then my family, then my tribe or my community. Next is my sovereign group—the United States, for example. An important point here is that *I feel no loyalties to anything outside the wide circle of my sovereign group.* Anything out there is fair game, just as anything is fair game in foreign policy—which I take as a matter of practicality, not ethics.

Those who report themselves as "having no politics" or "being very unpolitical" are frequently Stage IV people. That is, they live their personal lives to the greatest satisfaction they can, and give no attention to government. In time of crisis, however, when their government makes any demands upon them, they dutifully comply without thinking. If the government tells them to love their country, they of course love it. They have no particular reason not to.

Here is a perfect Stage IV statement:

> I never had the slightest interest in politics. The circles in which I moved had no contacts with the world of Naziism or the Nazi creed, and I never joined the Hitler Youth Movement. True, in my last year at school, I did some voluntary work on the land during the summer holidays, which I thoroughly

enjoyed. In fact, the chairman of the local parish council thanked me officially, which duly impressed the school authorities. But I took good care to keep out of any organization, except of course the sailing-club.

Naturally I realised that as an officer I would have to obey all orders without question. But I knew too that it would be in a service where every man has his own duties and responsibilities, a service bound by its traditions and the code it has built up.[2]

At the end of his book, Heinz Schaeffer, a U-boat commander, remarks, "And to Argentina I have taken with me the greatest thing the Second World War left me—a faith unshaken in the German people."[3] That unshaken faith in the German people might make a social worker want to ask for some particulars. "Which qualities of the German people were you thinking of?" An ethicist, less effective than members of the helping professions, more given to driving home points, might ask Captain Schaeffer: "For example, have you faith that the German people in future will not vote in governments who kill off *(a)* the mental patients and *(b)* the Gypsies, Jews, Jehovah's Witnesses, and political prisoners of Slavic ethnicity?"

Stage V
I have finally developed my own ethical code.

At last I think for myself. I know a few crimes I disapprove of and I do not intend to commit them. Should I in fact commit them, I won't be deluded into thinking I am behaving justly or mercifully when I do. I will be sinning. I have finally arrived at a polyglot code of what I consider right and what I consider wrong. If my country forces me to commit an atrocity, I will do it if I am terrified, but I will not think it is right.

It takes me longer to deliberate on my feelings and thoughts than it did when I was in Stage IV. I need more time. When an issue comes up I have to think it through for myself. I take responsibility for my own actions, as well. I no longer say, "Someone made me do it," or, like Adolf Eichmann, "I was just following orders." A Stage V person's lip curls at the phrase, "Look, I just work here," because a Stage V person would quit a job at a workplace that was manufacturing an evil product.

Stage V people can be seriously exasperating. They are so pleased not to be Stage IV people anymore that they tend to think they are pure. They are quick to denounce other individuals and groups as having sold out when those people and groups succeed in some public benefit; they have so recently occupied Stage IV, and they despair so constantly of what authority organizations do, that they find it difficult to relax in any group. If life gets comfortable around these comparatively ethical colleagues, they often wonder if they are selling out in some unconscious way.

A huge improvement of Stage V thinking over Stage IV thinking is that Stage V ethics are universal. If a virtue is a certain right or a certain kindness for me and mine, then it is right and merciful for peoples of other nations. Some Stage V people even want mercy and fairness not only for everyone in our species but for other species. They do not want animals to be treated cruelly. They feel it almost viscerally when some clod carves his initials into a living tree.

In Yukon Territory, I met a Stage V naturalist. She was guiding a straggling group of us about some slopes. I pinched and uprooted a little of what I took for lichen. "Would this lichen grow differently," I asked her, "if it were living in twenty degrees less north latitude?" "No," she said equably, "it wouldn't. It isn't lichen. It is dwarf birch. Rather, it *was* a living dwarf birch, I should say. Until you yanked it up." Some people who spend a lot of time in solitude get skilled at floating their imaginations lightly as gossamer over to other species. I think that naturalist felt a genuine pity for the three-quarters-of-an-inch tree that I had killed.

Stage VI
In this stage I realize I will get my hands red.
I can no longer be pure and think very well of myself.

For example, we find that even if being truthful is a part of one's proud (Stage V) personal code, one must lie in certain situations or evil will result. We must treat every situation individually. We cannot simply bring out our hard-won personal code of behavior like a ruler and apply it. One must imagine all the *others*, especially the invisible, peripheral, or future victims, involved in a situation—and then design a plan that will savage as few creatures and devastate as few landmarks as possible.

Such ruminations, a kind of "full-cost pricing," mean making choices. Whenever one has to choose the lesser of two evils, one gets one's hands red. One can exercise bad judgment and make a serious mistake. In any case, one must do some rendering unto Caesar of what is his. That is to say, one does not go to every battle for justice, because if one did one could not go in strength to the great ones. Jesus frequently "slipped through the crowd." He wasn't cowardly: he was at least at Stage VI. Abraham Lincoln voted for some legislation that wouldn't brighten anyone's halo, and thus kept power for the moments when he would need it. On the surface, such Machiavellianism may sound more Stage II than Stage VI.

Here is a Stage VI story. A Gestapo officer has come to my door. Am I hiding any Jews in the attic? I was a Stage V person until this minute. I hated lying, as Chekhov advises us to do, like the plague. Now I must lie. "Who, me?" I say, snarling like a Stage IV Nazi. "You'd never catch me hiding such scum! I'm a good German!" After the officer leaves, I wait hours to be on the safe side—and then let the people upstairs climb out of their hiding places.

A Stage VI person is never a cultural relativist. To this person, character is universal. Cruelty is still cruelty wherever it takes place and regardless of who did it to whom. Killing of the innocent is unjust. Beaten children, like battered wives, sometimes don't seem to mind much but it is still wrong to beat them. Stage VI people are in some sense always in court about something. They don't need someone else to bring the case. That is because either plaintiff or defendant is internalized—imagined, permanently, inside Stage VI people's minds.

A side aspect of Stage VI shows up in sports. A Stage VI person has enough imagination to honor cultural structures previously built. Cultural structure, such as a priest's performing the Mass, or a baseball player stepping up to bat, requires *sacrifice*. There come hundreds of Sundays in a priest's life when he or she does not feel like "celebrating"—the clerical term for saying the Eucharist. I know this is true, because I badgered a number of Anglican friends (priests, lay readers, and deacons) into confession on this point. Each admitted that in their youth they were able to recover the glorious feelings because the words were reminders, but by the time they were middle-aged they often couldn't. The point is, they perform the Mass anyway, because it is a structure with rules that benefit people.

Like Anglican priests, baseball players have bad days. A batter, as the philosopher John Rawls points out in "Two Concepts of Rules," must accept as prior rule the rule of the game:

> If one wants to play a game, one doesn't treat the rules of the game as guides as to what is best in particular cases. In a game of baseball if a batter were to ask "Can I have four strikes?" it would be assumed that he was asking what the rule was; and if, when told what the rule was, he were to say that he meant that on this occasion he thought it would be best on the whole for him to have four strikes rather than three, this would be most kindly taken as a joke.[4]

Rawls's example is classical Stage IV as well as Stage VI thinking. The Stage IV person would abide by any rules explained by anyone perceived as authority. A Stage VI person gives priority to and acknowledges the authority of a rule of practice, over personal convenience. A Stage VI person chooses to break a rule of practice, such as not lying to the official police of one's own government, only when he or she is acting on a higher, more demanding level of ethicality rather than a lower one—such as protecting self and friends from police inquiries into a scam. Breaking the particular rule of practice mentioned—that is, lying to the police of one's own country—is painful to a principled person.

Stage VI is the most ethically conscious stage that I can think of. If I had any genuine feeling for a Stage VII, I would offer it.

This particular crux—how to describe a stage of moral think-ing and feeling that one hasn't reached oneself—suggests that one needs some humor about one's own stage development. Kohlberg noticed that when asked what they supposed was their general stage of moral-reasoning development, a great many people reported themselves one stage, but never two stages, higher than the one they had tested out in. Kohlberg gathered from this that their imaginations had already begun to visualize and want the next stage of thinking, perhaps the way a bright, motivated fifth grader may have grasped fractions and decimals, and already half grasps and longs to understand the idea of per-centage. No one, however, he believed, had a moral taste for moral reasoning *two stages* above his or her present stage. I expect an example of that would be, if one were at Stage III, guiding one's principles by what seemed to be accepted by the peer group, one might already be glimpsing a finer way to judge—namely, by harking to those who know more than one's peers—authorities, those who appear powerful and wise and older. That is to say, one might be ready to spring into Stage IV thinking, taking one's obligations from tradition, sovereign power, or established superi-ors in one's life. But a peer-group follower would never admire Stage V thinking—making up one's own standards for good and bad and being willing to stand alone for them. Standing *alone* for any principle seems like madness to a Stage III person, just as dressing in bizarre clothes would appall most fourteen-year-olds.

Lawrence Kohlberg noticed that although some of his col-leagues could make quite clear certain lower moral-reasoning stages to their students, their explanations of the upper stages were muddy or frantic. He concluded that these particular teach-ers had likely not yet reached those upper stages, and therefore were gamely and intellectually trying to *guess* at what feelings one would have if one were in those stages. Further, he remarked on an irritability, too, when their students pressed those professors for more clarity. Kohlberg supposed that perhaps one tends to be irritable about higher moralities than one's own. I regard that as an exquisite understatement. We can sense the presence of a more elegant moral being than ourselves. I have noticed that I feel extraordinarily irritable when philosophers or students talk comfortably about Stage VII, a spiritual stage. I met a sometime colleague of Lawrence Kohlberg's and was pleased when she could corroborate some information I had about Kohlberg's research and what Carol Gilligan said about Kohlberg's research. I felt immensely lucky to be having that conversation with a full-fledged psychologist. Then gradually, she began to talk about a spiraling kind of thinking that one does in the spiritual stage, Stage VII, for example. I felt a burst of unmistakable fury. I thought to myself, How could anyone talk such humbug?

That is how people can react to more elaborate, more intricate human accomplishment than their own.

People seem to have a tremendous stake in rejecting stage-development theory. How curious that seems. Since I feel keen on the subject, like someone proposing electricity in a land of candlelighters, I try it on anyone willing to listen and on some who are courteous rather than willing. Invariably people to whom stage-development language is new tell me promptly, with amazing dispatch and confidence, "But of course that won't work. You said yourself people get stuck in their stages. If they get stuck in their stages, what's the operating difference between stage theory and *type* theory?"

When we hear instant rejection of a quarter- or half-understood idea, the best way to understand it is to unearth the assumptions of this new idea.

The Assumptions of Stage-Development Theory

Stage-development theorists do not always agree, but for all the diversity of concepts, they share a number of philosophical assumptions, every one of which is respectful of human potential, sociologically hopeful, and anticlassist.

These assumptions have a simple, pleasing, and naive tone: that is because they invariably are cast in ancient language that we use for things we regard as holy—merciful, just, moral, challenge, love. Such words, along with their sociological equivalents—socialized, detached, values-rich, and the like—are familiar. But also familiar are our daily lives in the cities shuddering from violence, the repeated announcements of new corruptions among lucky people, repeated reports of sexual sadism among the young. I believe it is because the reality seems to belie its hopeful language that stage development gets cold greetings—knowing, confident smiles.

The sad fact is that most human beings do not make these assumptions. They don't believe in any cheerful ideas, first, because no one has bruited them about enough, and second, the last time they heard anyone sounding this sanguine about human morality it was their Sunday school teacher. Everyone knows that Sunday school teachers, like alcoholics, take it one day at a time.

Here are the assumptions of stage-development theory:

1. Our species has certain potential for thinking. Therefore the brain wants to think and gets angry when balked.
2. Sooner or later, some of the thinking our brain wants to do is setting values—deciding what is merciful, what is just, what is vicious or unfair.
3. We engage in the various kinds of cognitive learning, in certain progressions: one solves practical, technical problems first, moral problems later. No one solves moral problems (in a given area of endeavor) before solving the how-to problems in that area. No baby tries to decide if the switch from crawling to walking will have unkind outcomes: *all* able babies decide to make the switch from crawling to walking. They take it on as a how-to challenge.
4. People stay at given stages of thought (before moving on) for longer or shorter periods—some of this no doubt depending on neurophysiological heritage. But the significant arbiters are how much *(a)* love and respect that person has received at some point from someone (the place-in-the-sun theory) in combination with *(b)* the level of civil, questioning, story-hearing mentorship that person has received, at some point, *from an adult in authority.* Peer listening doesn't do it.
5. Once a complicated higher level of thinking has entered someone's head, that person will regress to a simpler idea *only* if brainwashed or interfered with neurophysiologically.

6. Everyone appears to start at the bottom stage of any system,[5] and no stages are ever skipped. No one, for example, goes from total self-orientedness, such as in feeling, "My mother and I are one, and we are all that there is," to supposing that any dictum from the Pentagon must be right. Everyone moves upward, slowly or quickly, with or without halts and blockages, and some get to whatever the top stage is. Others don't seem to.

7. Everyone tends to feel greatest comfort when moving along in the middle of a stage, when not yet about to change concepts. There's some trepidation as one leaves an old paradigm in favor of a new one, no matter how stimulating the new one may seem.

8. The psychological reason that people tend to report themselves in a stage *immediately above the one they are in* is that the human mind admires achievements greater than its own, never mind that the person himself or herself doesn't yet practice the discipline of that higher stage. Even if one bristles with envy, one's mind admires and feels happy when it hears ideas better than its own. For example, socially intolerant people sometimes claim to be pluralists and will speak in favor of diversity, though they still feel a horror of the idea of being in relationship with anyone unlike themselves.

10. The brain craves complication. The brain loves to associate some new event it has just heard of with something it already knew about. If not discouraged by either cultural abuse or psychological abuse, every human being will live by some sort of philosophy. Our brains are not just sightseers, noting down this *pith* or this *gist* (to use Clare's language, in "The Woman Lit by Fireflies," for scattershot ethical notetaking): at our full potential, we constantly make connections. At our full potential, we want to make a lot of connections, even if we go astray and proclaim ideas from which we may have to retreat tomorrow or next week. We make them anyway, because at our full potential, apologies for mistaken ideas don't bother us much.

Contemporary American culture doesn't reinforce the craving for complicated ideas. Someone, in fact, is always trying to sell us on a *simple* way to accomplish large projects. Most people are therefore quite sure that they would prefer a list of *Fifty Simple Things You Can Do to Save the Earth*[6] to a shorter list of difficult things we might try. The ominous reward of being satisfied to pick up some beer tabs off the beach is that it keeps the mind distracted from the exceedingly painful work the mind needs to be doing—namely, thinking about how nice people *in groups* ruin the world. We need to remember Bristol-Myers Squibb and the other companies who turned Onondaga Lake, in upstate New York, into a chemical dumping vat.[7] We need to remember that, not in order to revisit our own indignation, but in order to consider the psychological and ethical habitat of *groups*, like boards of directors or top management of anything.

Trying to think about boards of directors of chemical companies is not one of the fifty simple things one can do for the planet. Unfortunately, making things simple and finding commonalities, as opposed to studying differences, have so much cachet now that it is hard to propose that people think of complicated subjects in ethics. Physicists and mathematicians are willing to think of complicated likelihoods in their fields, but people who teach civic issues and the like are expected either to reduce complex ideas to one or two simple components of the ideas or to limit discussion to simple issues. Sometimes I have the fantasy that at any one moment in the United States, a thousand teachers are saying in adult seminars, "Now I am going to make this as simple as I can for you."

Yet the main idea of any development theory, whether of human beings or of geological processes, is that we ought to look at everything with the idea that it is made of complicated parts that enable us to do complicated tasks or to be complex entities.

Things start inchoate and looking much like other objects around them. We are used to the idea, so far as it applies to physiology. Any one entity begins with a legion of events whose trickle of direction is not clear. A farmer examining rills of a disked field knows that left alone, these twig-shaped creeks will feed into a stream that in turn will contribute to a river. Then the new entity—in this case, the river, but the same pattern applies to a human personality, or even, in chaos theory, to a given tangle of mathematical ideas—gains what will be its characteristic identity. At its periphery it will create new small likenesses of itself.

What had been inchoate is now child, adolescent, and adult, discrete from his or her background and family and associates, a being whom we gather facts about and make judgments on. Look, we say, there is so-and-so, an honest woman, tactless, lazy, one-third conservative, two-thirds liberal in temperament, humorless, and trustworthy. Look, we say, there is the Mississippi, still cutting new channels at its upper ends, roaring away in its main riverbed, diffusing itself in delta buildup at the end. Look, we say, here is the universe. If it started with a bang, the bang probably came of millions of trivial factors of gases and other entities, just as the Mississippi came of uplift of landforms followed by millions of creeks and the erosion of farmers' fields.

The mouth of a river, the part that has slowed, lost some water to capillary-like branchings and oxbow lakes, then reached the sea, we call "old." When most or all of a whole river has slowed and widened and rilled away here and there, we call it "an old river." First its delta, eventually the whole river, resembles an uncanny, cunning reverse of its original start-up webbing of tributaries.

Developmental theorists spend little time arguing primogeniture of chicken or egg. They spend *a lot* of time wondering and testing to see which and how many factors go into an entity, how an entity has the characteristic, identifiable life that makes us give it a name such as "river" or "creature" or "person." Since developmentalists are developmentalists, they respectfully note but don't spend much time studying how the entity eventually slows within the accumulations of its own culture. It will lose its selfness. It will return to the universe. If the entity in question is a dying human being it will be conscious that it is returning to the universe. If the entity in question is a vibrant human being in early or middle life it will be conscious that eventually it will return to the universe. If it is a vibrant enough human being so that it keeps that painful idea (eventually returning to the universe) somewhere on its mental shelves but not right on the desktop, then it will feel itself to be in some powerful relationship with the universe, even now, long before the end of its life.

The work of the psychological stage-developmentalist and of a therapist is to help human beings balance a psychic sense of being in relationship with the universe with an exuberant, dynamic choice as to their own direction.

Ethical stage-development theory tells us that we proceed from simple intellectual expectations, tiny, start-up ego development, and low moral-reasoning levels to *higher* thinking levels, *fuller* development of the ego, and more complex, *more altruistic* moral-reasoning levels. The main idea of this book is that we progress to those more complex and altruistic levels in spectacularly direct proportion to how much empathic mentoring we have received from those who are important in our lives.

Empathy is so powerful a tool that school social workers succeed in using it to help seriously disturbed children put themselves together into functioning human beings. The general public has no idea how much success social workers have in modeling and teaching kids to look at their wants and others' wants, their plans and others' plans—to get the hang of being individual people who can plan some of their lives. Social workers' empathy helps kids see that home may not be fixable—at least, the social worker isn't going to be able to make every home safe or happy—but inside the kid himself or herself are a few safe places. School social workers use empathy to help kids get conscious of those places.

Psychotherapists using empathy have been able to "turn around" some people who had been locked in rigid notions, poor self-development, and extravagant fear of any change and dislike of anything unlike themselves.

Sometimes it is easier to understand an unfamiliar process if we talk about its opposite, especially if the opposite is familiar to us. To get a sense of the magic of empathy, then, I would like to describe its opposite, which is equally powerful—the magic of

anti-empathy. Beginning geometrists sometimes come to new understandings by making a hypothesis they suspect is opposite to
the truth. They are looking at a certain figure. It looks bizarre.
They propose that it is a triangle, and then step by step try the figure against what they know of triangles. As they work through
successive revelations about the figure, its nontriangularity becomes clearer and clearer. They are all the more certain in their
own minds about what a triangle is because they have thoroughly
investigated a figure that fails in the particulars, and therefore the
impact, of a triangle. (For example, builders would not use this
parallelogram or whatever the figure is instead of a triangle for
making a building rigid.)

The anti-empathy example will be this story, one familiar to
most of us. A man is joining the Marines. Our start-up assumption is that it is for the most part a harmless experience to go
through boot camp. Our assumption is that of course the training
is specifically suited to make recruits into (1) skillful killers and (2)
survivors of other killers' efforts. "But it can't hurt a man, anyway," we suppose.

The drill instructor needs to turn someone who thinks for
himself or herself, has a high level of curiosity about what's new
and a low level of fear, with no instinct to murder, into someone
passive and fearful enough to obey authority without pause,
someone who will kill without any personal knowledge of the victim—namely, a soldier. How does one do it? We know it can be
done because for millennia noncommissioned officers in all the
world's armies have been turning civil people into soldiers, com-
mandos, special forces, interrogators, and torturers.

The way noncommissioned officers make soldiers and killers
out of autonomous, intelligent people is by diminishing the ego
development of the recruit, an aim exactly opposite to the mentor's or therapist's aim of enhancing the ego development of a
student or client.

The drill instructor looks at the recruit before him and deter-
mines to practice anti-empathy with each recruit. He doesn't call
it anti-empathy, but it is what he means to practice.

1. He means to insult the recruit to break his present sense of well-being. The recruit must understand that he individually is worth nothing.
2. The drill instructor will make him fearful of disgracing his unit.
3. He will reduce the recruit's conscious ideals down to mere pride in his unit.
4. The sergeant will screen back the recruit's consciousness of any complex relationships in his life: conscious affections need to be replaced by mere pack loyalty to the squad or platoon.
5. The sergeant will insult the recruit whenever he pauses to consider a command.
6. He will not allow the recruit to look into his own, the sergeant's, eyes when at attention. The recruit must glaze.

As we look at all six of these practices, they seem sadistic. They are. It is sadistic deliberately to destroy another person's confidence and individuality, yet military personnel feel justified in boot camp practices because war is an uncivilized situation in which, to stay alive and effective, one must have a number of attributes precisely opposite to those one needs in a lawful culture. Many of the six *anti-empathic* practices are ways in which wolf packs and other highly organized animal units control their members. There is a hidden deal in it: the state (or the Marines or the wolf pack) *must* be served by the individual. The individual will be drummed out of the group if he or she doesn't comply. On the other hand, when the individual does comply, the payback is a sense of *worth in belongingness*.

Before leaving the description of anti-empathy I suggest we see it as a long continuum that at one end is training for the SS or a modern equivalent and at the other end, is training for a pleasant career with a company or for membership in a given social class. In the middle range of this continuum of anti-empathy lies the family style of nearly all families in which wives are battered or children molested. In such families, the equivalent of the drill instructor, namely, the predator, makes it very clear to spouse and children that individually they are nothing. Their only value lies in belonging to the group (the family), so they had better be loyal to that group. This explains what a phenomenal psychological turnaround a battered woman has to exercise in order to leave the batterer and not return.

On my notepad I have an item called "Very Mild Sadism." Very mild sadism is not the shrieking "What are you, a fairy or what?" that we associate with a DI's dressings-down. Very mild sadism is, in the case of Clare in "The Woman Lit by Fireflies," making fun of anyone's spiritual life—making fun of it gently. Or very mild sadism is the attack by Sam on the speaker of "Cider 5¢ a Glass" for being "naive" in his idealism. Very mild sadism uses derision to control the individual in favor of the group's goals—which are usually *less humane* than the individual's goals. Sam's goal, for example, is to protect the unconscionability of prep school and Ivy League graduates, as a class. He needs for that goal to stay in place, so he won't feel besmirched as he practices his appalling law career.

Psychological Properties of Empathy

Here are six aspects of empathy. A glance through them shows that the empathist's goals are service to the client's best potential, not service to any group or to any goal or secret agenda of his or her own. (But not serving one's own secret agenda is an extraordinarily hard thing to learn. Great therapists have reported that they look back with horror on their early years of practice: as young therapists they had been unconscious of ways in which their own driving wills occasionally skewed their work for clients.)

1. The empathic person assures the interviewee or client or child that he or she is worthwhile.
2. The interviewee need not worry about being loyal to his or her close-in group—family, tribe, church, town, nation— for now. This is a safe place where he or she is honored. The interviewer or therapist makes it very clear that, perhaps

for the first time in their lives, the anxious clients and scared children have permission to say disloyal remarks about the authority figures and established groups (families) in their lives. The therapist clearly indicates that he or she is utterly willing to hear complaints against authority or family. The therapist is on your side. The last thing in the world to worry about is disgracing your family or committing sedition against the person you have always perceived as your sovereign.

3. People practicing empathy make every effort to release the other from binding, limiting attitudes which that person hangs on to, taking it for loyalty to family or tribe or nation. The psychotherapist or teacher or social worker tries hard to release the person from servitude to others' expectations.

4. The empathic person encourages the client to explore many complex relationships, and to let them be complex. The last thing in the world the empathic person does is to try to simplify relationships down to pack or herd loyalty.

5. The empathic person encourages the person to explore new ideas, to express himself or herself in new ways.

6. And finally, empathic people look into the faces of people they talk to unless there is a specific ethnic awkwardness involved.[8] Some group therapists make it a ground rule that the whole group maintain eye contact with anyone who is speaking.

Applying Stage-Development Theory and Communication Skills to the Lucky, the Rich, and the Powerful

Any population can be a population "at risk" to harm others. If a rule is truthful it applies to all cases. Two apples plus two apples must make four apples if two and two make four. The addition is spurious if two oranges plus two oranges make four oranges but two apples plus two apples make five apples. If both of those sums were correct we would have to reject the hypothesis that two of anything plus two more of the same thing make four of whatever it is.

If people move more rapidly to higher personal ethics under certain conditions and more slowly or hardly at all under other conditions, those conditions must apply to the rich, the lucky, and the powerful as well as to the more traditional clientele of social work and psychotherapy. But whoever heard of applying developmental theory to the rich? Whoever heard of practicing social work communication skills with the rich? Even the most scrupulously trained social workers, L.I.C.S.W.s and D.S.W.s, scarcely ever approach the rich with theories of normal psychology and normal ethics.

Still, the rich, like the poor and everyone in between, are "at risk" to do evil.

Before looking at how a therapeutic, developmental approach might work with the rich, let's do a reality check on how moralists have dealt with the rich up to now.

The usual ways in which civic-minded people try to influence the rich and powerful don't work. Demonstrating for peace outside the Pentagon is a perfect case in point. Defense Secretary Robert S. McNamara watched at least one of the peace marches from behind a window. When the demonstrators begged him, by name, to open the window and talk to them, he refused to do so. He is one of the rich and powerful predators who throughout their active adult years make money and win political clout from wars and preparations for wars—who thirty-odd years later turn out books that are attempts at self-exoneration dressed up as apologies. Such books do nothing for whatever fraction of the dead, let us say, a third, died after the predator, midwar, realized he was wrong but said nothing. In the case of the Vietnam War one third of our dead would number nineteen thousand young men and women who would have come home if strong public steps had been taken. The predator would, of course, have had to be making a mental picture of those American dead, in order to get psyched up to make a public statement. He could not be making a mental picture of the frequently acerbic Lyndon Johnson's displeasure with him.

The pattern of the immunity of power figures to protesters is vitally important. Admiral Hyman Rickover, for example, stood adamantly for increasing our nuclear submarine fleet. The amazing antisubmarine demonstrations didn't seem to touch him. Then, in his eighties, he wrote an apology. He had been wrong, he said.

Immunity to protesters is made up of a number of psychological factors. When men stood untouched by anti-Vietnam War protest they were firmly, attractively, richly supported by their groups of privileged males—the cabinet, the Pentagon, the Atomic Energy Commission, the National Security Council, and myriad other civilian agencies of defense. In their eighties, when no one is requesting acquiescence from them, perhaps these rich, powerful people feel lonely for the old public attention. Whenever powerful leaders write a genuine or phony confession, some public candles are relit around them. But the candles are of the votive sort: they light up memory of the unjustly killed as much as they give the old man some tagalong glamour.

An old apologist might well count on the American people's low level of dissent.[9] We like happiness, so we try not to rise to scorn when reading books by the powerful. Our ambience is generally amiable. Besides, more than thirty years of television since 1965 has likely further raveled our moral feelings. Another present-day cultural dynamic is people's habit of learning about the existence of books, or even reading a little of them, at least knowing titles, but not reading the books all the way through. An author might logically count on not reaping scorn from people who haven't read his or her book: scanners and light readers would keep all comments general and in tune with whatever the going opinion seemed to be. Robert McNamara's book was said to give us a window on the thinking of those who managed our war in Vietnam. "Giving a window onto some thinking" is a mild enough and ethics-free enough remark. Captain Schaeffer's book gave us a window onto the thinking of a U-boat captain. Albert Speer's memoir gave us a window onto the thinking of a number of people close to Hitler who adored him. Windows onto people's thinking makes engaging history. In the case of Secretary McNamara's memoir, the surprising anger of readers may come from the fact that unlike him, the then-protesters are not in their eighties. They are in their sixties, fifties, and forties. They are still making mental pictures of all those useless deaths. They remember losing jobs, too, because of being called long-hair protest types or Communists, so they are not touched by the secretary's trying to keep folks peacefully together at the top.

I would hope that as we learn to use insights into normal psychology on ourselves and on the rich and powerful, the consciousness of rich and powerful leaders will wake up to options other than spending their salad years being loyal to bosses and groups and doing work they know is bad—and then writing books about it in their old age.

If the rich are a demographic grouping at risk to harm others, what is the definition of an at-risk population, and what makes any population prone to bad behavior?

On a superficial level the question is easy to answer. Greed incites people to selfish behavior, and this behavior worsens when the greedy perpetrator is frightened. The greed of all the muggers in the world put together has much in common with whatever the greed is that lets hospital administrators complain of hospital costs and keep shaving down the services offered, while maintaining their national average of $300,000 to $400,000 salaries. Directors of corporations who are not otherwise employees of those corporations swap hundreds of thousands of dollars in annual bonuses from one another's organizations. If greed is alike in a pickpocket and a corporate director, other psychological elements will be alike as well.

I would like to define what social workers mean by the term *at-risk populations* and then show how young white rich people with expectations of taking power fit the definition.

An at-risk population is those people who are made vulnerable to antisocial or criminal behavior by a confluence of circumstances. We can think of a confluence of circumstances as analogous to a coming together of germs, cold weather, depressed feelings, and poor self-care. If germs are proliferating at an accelerated rate in my throat, let us say, and the house is cold, and I am feeling low in spirit for some reason, and am not wearing enough clothes, I am experiencing a confluence of circumstances that make me vulnerable to catching a cold.

The confluence of circumstances that makes a population at risk for antisocial or criminal behavior includes the following:

1. Poor parenting or too little parenting during childhood.
2. Being born into a social class whose values are repeatedly described as practical. ("Do what works, hey," a class background may tell young people between the lines. Or: "You want it? No cops around? Or the only cops around are cops you can manage? Take it!" On a more courteous statesman-like level: "Would that we didn't have to do some of the things we have to do. It isn't always easy." Sage tone or not, these remarks are all alike. They all say, "Do what it takes to achieve *your* group's ends.")
3. Poor education or no education.
4. Poor physical and mental endowment.
5. Having parents who have either never been psychologically conscious of any responsibility to others, or who have given up taking responsibility because the whole scene seems inevitably hopeless, or who *deny* that a human being has responsibilities other than the most primitive loyalty to the immediate tribe.

I suggest we check the preceding list of factors making a person at risk to do harm to others against what we know of the rich and powerful. We can check out the influences on some of the characters in the readings in this book. Then we can check the list again for how those characters conduct the power-wielding segments of their lives. Were Sam and the speaker of "Cider 5¢ a Glass" in any determinable way at risk of becoming predatory white males, for example? Were Sam's parents mainly self-serving? Did both Sam and the speaker demonstrate a sleepy, unconscious subservience to the prep school tribe?

Another set of social work findings usually applied to the poor that will help us understand the rich is the information about bullies being studied in Scandinavia. If what the Scandinavian school experiences indicate is true of bullies—how they act, how they feel "entitled" to act like bullies, how victims' behaviors often have the effect of doubling the bullies' pleasure in torturing them—if all those findings are scientific, they will give us useful bearing on rich American adult bullies as well as Norwegian and Swedish youth.

The feeling called "entitlement" to push other people around, however, works out well and is a classic characteristic of school-yard bullies. Most Americans think that a bully is a (usually male) person of low self-image, but the modern research on school bullies now states outright that, in general, bullies like being bullies. It works out fine for them. They get a little fillip from knocking some "whiner" around, anyhow.[10] Dan Olweus, working with Norwegian schoolchildren, lists the following characteristics of bullies:

aggression towards peers
aggression towards adults
positive attitude towards violence
impulsivity
strong need to dominate others
little empathy with victims
relatively positive view of themselves
(if boys) physically stronger than peers
unusually little anxiety and insecurity or were roughly
    average on such dimensions
did not suffer from poor self-esteem
popular to average, or slightly below average level—less
    than average after grade 9
bullying is only one component of their antisocial/rule-
    breaking behavior patterns; they begin such behaviors
    at a relatively early age[11]

The Difficulties of Applying Any Ideas
from the Helping Professions to the Rich

One reason that we Americans have not looked seriously enough at our own rich predators for clues to their bullying behaviors is that we have been made to believe that bullies are without exception people of low self-image. Even when evidence shows that many bullies have high self-images, we have clung to the view that the bully can be bullied himself or herself. That view of the suffering bully is less galling than the view that the bully is grinning at us as we fasten on our bandages.

We will want the stamina of a Viktor Frankl or an Irvin Yalom if we are going to study and work with the rich. They are immune in dozens of ways. On the surface, they have so much money they can leave the room. The poor never get to leave the room. When the level of violence in the United States makes some rich people uneasy, they buy into armed, walled enclaves that even have their own power plants. They abdicate from the United States. Obviously nobody that rich is going to hang about for a day of consciousness-raising unless some force is exerted so that the pain of staying will be less than the pain of leaving.

On a less superficial level, the rich know about building immunity to other people's suffering just as well as the poor. The *style* of immunity building, perhaps, may differ, but the essential task, of making oneself and one's children not feel others' pain, is made of the same psychological elements. Experienced rich people are oddly at ease, even when feeling neurotic. Even as they explain how damnable they feel, you can't help picking up on their basic, if patchy, contentment. Perhaps they feel entitled not to feel neurotic. They have a right to happiness. That feeling of entitlement to happiness seems germane to the schoolyard bully's feeling of entitlement to push around weaker boys.

Even trained masters of social work—who are a different professional from otherwise educated social services persons— scarcely ever approach the rich or their spouses with theories of *normal* psychology and ethics that might beautifully apply to their cases. They beg off a good deal, even though theirs may well be the very skills that might change how the rich collect and distribute their spoils. "We have no access to them," the social workers—and indeed, other mental health workers—point out.

They are right enough about that. In our present society, psychological helping professions get access only when someone who is in pain presents himself or herself with a request for help, or when a judge rules that an offender must undergo counseling, therapy, or residential treatment. But because helping professionals have at present no access to the rich doesn't mean some other enclave in American life shouldn't draw attention to this lack of access. Authors, for example, might agitate for helping professionals to publish applications of their theories to the rich. Authors, after all, agitated for the protests against the Vietnam War. They could look at publicizing group dynamics, for example, in such corporations as make decisions that negatively impact upon the rest of us.

I said we will want the verve of a Frankl or a Yalom. One reason it is hard to approach the rich is that their manners engage us as pals. I have never seen a liberal arts-educated person of some power who couldn't make a number of people in the room feel that they shared a good deal of human experience with him or her. One may walk into the room wishing to say something sharp. Within a half hour one wants to be a good sport, someone willing to see their side of things in the pleasant way that they have been willing to see everyone else's. What one is experiencing here is a psychological phenomenon sometimes called "satellization."

A beaten or raped child is participating in satellization when he or she identifies with a large scary power figure—a predatory parent, for instance. The child gives up its own psychological needs in service to the adult's, the way a fairy-tale page might serve a knight. It is a tony folly: the child feels cared for, involved in an in-group (self and the powerful parent), conspiratorially, often proudly, separate from other parents and children. The child wears that relationship like a secret club insignia. It works because the parent claims to love the child, claims to be including the child in on "our little secret," claims that the loyalty between them will make the child safe. Thus the child sees himself or herself as a little moon going around the earth-parent, a satellite in the cosmos of life.

We who have no power or less power are constantly tempted to satellite ourselves to the rich. When we do that we are still in their pocket. If we don't let ourselves be satellites of the rich, then we feel the most frightful anguish being around those who do evil work in government or corporations. Why do we feel such anguish? I believe we agonize because we feel certain that rich people who are immoral will always do what they want, and what they want will always be of lifetime benefit to them and their families and constitute the long-term devastation of others.

One way that people behave when they feel that justice cannot prevail is to develop a jocular good sportsmanship about evil and evildoers. They exercise a behavior style we could call "Louisa May Alcotting."

Alcotting the Rich

When the women's movement erupted, it developed new psychological language for males and females. This new language in itself gave release and power to the movement. The early feminists developed appropriate insults, which is to say, words and phrases that drove the conversation from mere how-things-are to how-things-bloody-shouldn't-be. The language itself propagated a change in attitude. Women called men "male chauvinist pigs." That single expression, which now seems funny and nostalgic, liberated hundreds of thousands of people from just putting up with "the way he is, don't you know, I mean, he's got the male ego, so what can you do?"

Louisa May Alcott, a century earlier, has Jo referring to Laurie and his Harvard friends as "lords of creation"—a jolly, fun-loving term that says, "Yes, males are entitled to run the place; that's how it is, right enough, and you won't find us lacking in good sportsmanship about it!"

As long as that jocular, sporting attitude survived, women couldn't move the conversation from realism ("that's how it is, right enough") to a moral attitude ("is this right? is this really right enough?"). Is it moral, we women should have been asking 35,000 years before we did, for men to hog the freedoms for themselves, to cheat and undercut women in the workplace and reduce their ego development and subjugate them in their homes? "Of course that's how it *is*," we should have been saying all those years, "but is it fair?" But we were not saying it, because like Louisa May Alcott's Jo, we exercise cheerful forbearance about males.

Most men and woman in America today exercise cheerful forbearance about the greedy rich (as opposed to the nongreedy rich). This cheerful forbearance is like Jo March's forbearance of the male lords of creation. Educated, employed, responsible people try to keep a jocular, sporting attitude toward the rich. We are envious, of course; the rich run the place with their million-dollar salaries and huge portfolios of extras. But we are also appropriately angry with them. They start the wars that we go to. Back home in their directors' rooms, they turn down shareholders' proposals that their companies' top people *not* be paid more than twenty-five times as much as the average pay of company employees. They despoil the Great Lakes until they get caught. They lie to uranium miners about the effects of exposure, again until they get caught.

Our attitude is too much Louisa May Alcott's attitude: you won't catch *us* being shrill and unattractive about the rich. That is because, like Alcott, we think it is hopeless. Besides, as alcoholics always assure their first-session counselors, we know such a lot of really nice people who happen to have this particular habit (being alcoholic or being rich directors of corporations with bad policies). A confirmed Alcottlike good sport will say, just as all bullies nearly always get away with saying, "You are making a gigantic mountain out of a very small molehill." And then—this being the *second* remark typically made in first sessions to psychotherapists—"You'll never change human nature anyway."

I propose we deliberately lay aside for a minute our feeling that it is hopeless. With notepads out, we might ask the classic question of all change agents: "Is there already any set of regimens or philosophies out there that we could get our hands on and put to use here?"

We need a *normal psychology* to try for fit. At present, the very rich and powerful tend to have heard only of psychiatry and psychoanalysis as medical models of treatment for the disturbed or mentally ill. Most rich and powerful people know scarcely anything about psychotherapy as a means of learning, or about ethical stage development as a hopeful philosophy or about empathy as a means of each of us helping one another to discover and then understand our complexity. At the moment, most very rich powerful people have little access to the kind of social scientist who helps with our ethical growth. What an irony—that it is the comparative losers in the workplace, in the street, in love, and in the justice system—we losers are the people whom chance or juvenile court judges or common sense have shoved into the faces of modern therapists and social workers.

We need, for example, a normal psychology for the wives of the middle-aged and elderly rich, whether the husband is noble or ignoble. Such a remark seems outrageously sexist to young people not highly placed in the private sector, but among those over fifty in American corporations and government the gender separation, with its allotted, different tasks, is still in force. The psychological situation of the rich wife is not the same as the psychological situation of the breadwinner in such a family.

Part of the point of Jim Harrison's brilliant "The Woman Lit by Fireflies" is that a nice enough person with lots of money can and will erect a wall between conventional self and real self. Such a wall may last for years, or even for a whole marriage. In any event, most people suppose out of hand that the rich spouses of greedy males have self-selected themselves as mates of alpha wolves.

There are studies out now about the wives of Los Alamos scientists, some of whom were career-bound for top policy making in the United States. The studies suggest that these wives deliberately tried to keep a cheerful mien. In their own telling, they largely kept their minds off what the men were doing. They decided to stay unconscious.

Deciding to stay unconscious at one level or another is very likely the most telling characteristic of rich, powerful men's wives. What if we could change that? Unconsciousness is a good defense for little children. When the perpetrators are huge and your chances of wiping out their evils are none, wise kids hide in psychological denial. But unconsciousness as a way for rich wives to maintain childlike comfort while the husbands lack the scruples to leave off doing well-paid gouging of others is bad for everyone, even though it is utterly normalized in the upper class.

Empathy for the Rich Predator

The major outcome of empathy is the client's discovery that he or she had three or four feelings about something he or she either took as a completely nonemotional practical issue or recognized only one feeling about.

A helping professional would set about showing the rich predator that he or she had a whole range of responses to any one event or situation. Human beings have several takes on everything.[12] Thinking through one's various feelings about dropping two bombs on Japan, one might find that

1. one felt it was practical to drop two bombs instead of one;
2. one felt aggrieved by the dropping of the first bomb;
3. one felt appalled and aggrieved by the dropping of the second bomb;
4. one felt glad, because one had lost a child at Iwo Jima;
5. one felt a low-level anxiety that didn't stay put. Now one felt about subject A, now about subject B. It didn't seem to have anything to do with the bomb dropping, though it came on in late August 1945.

That will be a huge milestone. The next step after recognizing a plethora of emotions when you thought you had only one is easier and it is fun: the client will charge himself or herself with listing those emotions in their order of importance. Taking control of what has been unconscious material is one of the most interesting of cognitive experiences people have. If the social workers or therapists have been responsible, their clients fairly quickly learn to ask themselves the empathic, partializing questions that help them lay out their thoughts and feelings.

I expect we should all accept the anguish of listening to the rich, the way therapists patiently and carefully listen to highly defended, unconscious clients. Let's say that we are determined, with pen and notepaper, hoping to make a list, to find some *new* way for us less powerful people to approach the more powerful people. We are looking for some way for those powerful people to come closer to whatever is inside them that dislikes cruelty.

What is our goal? We want lucky predators to know and speak all their own feelings *now*, not later, before more eighteen-year-old males kill other eighteen-year-old males in wars and the earth is wrecked by corporate dumping and extracting. Any person can feel sorry in his or her eighties. What is the psychology needed to help a rich person feel sorry enough at forty to stop doing bad work—lying about nicotine, devising new germ warfare at Fort Detrick, removing the restrictions on clean air and water, polluting, cutting the funding of our cultural truth-keepers—arts and humanities funds, libraries, public television?

The lucky predator's wife might be wakened to her power as an individual person. Might she not define her marriage as something more complex, yet free, than mere help-matism? Might she help the husband stand up to his daytime group of males (his corporation or the gathering in the Oval Office or at the secret think-tank retreat)?

Might she not help him redefine their social lives, too, so that their evenings are not just a recreational extension of the daytime group of males?

Sometimes we don't need a new idea. Sometimes we need to combine two ideas that haven't been brought together before. Working with such rich people will be especially difficult because of their natural immunity to any process that they know perfectly well is trying to erode their defenses. An expression used at hunt clubs comes to mind. If you are about to jump a horse, you may decide to let the horse see the jump and do its own timing. Alternatively, you may "rate" the horse—that is, decide when its forefeet should leave the ground and then direct the animal so that its forefeet leave the ground at that time. Whichever you do, you must encourage the horse to be "gathered" for the effort. The muscle system must be in the brain's loop. "Going to jump," the brain sends out, and the muscle system says "Yes!" One can feel it in a horse, the being gathered or not.

We shall need to be gathered if we mean to combine the two ideas of moral stage development and basic empathy with the idea of making social change among powerful groups.

The people who have thought up the various development schemes and the various empathy schemes have not yet said, "Let's try this in tandem with that other idea—empathy to go with the developmental stuff, or let's try stage-development philosophy to go with this empathy process. Let's try the paired wisdom, if it is wisdom, with very privileged people and see if they can perceive *potential* ethical goals in themselves that they don't bother even to scoff at now."

I am sorry that psychology and psycholinguistics researchers are so necessarily stuck with using undergraduate college students for subjects. How much more interesting it would be if they could E-mail to the Amherst Alumni Association or the Wellesley Club of Minnesota or the thirty-, forty-, and fifty-year-old alumnae and alumni of other institutions or other colleges-of-the-lucky. These subjects, unlike undergraduates, would be people presently *at risk* of causing public suffering through omission or commission. The rest of us are in some sense their "impact group."

There are a hundred blessings for readers in George Vaillant's *Adaptation to Life,*[13] but one that especially gratified me was that in this longitudinal study of ninety-four psychologically normal Ivy League college graduates, Vaillant paid attention to and told the stories of, with rich detail, middle-aged people. Among the Harvard men of Vaillant's Grant Study were people like Sam in Donald Hall's "Cider 5¢ a Glass." Outside of such rare studies, the Sams and Monicas of the United States rarely are questioned. No one helps them break down the chunks of their philosophies into small, accurately reported feelings about things.

A psychotherapist might well have talked to Sam about his conviction that there was nothing he could do to leave his firm or make atonement until he found another job. What therapists do, among their other procedures, is keep asking someone to produce and describe aloud more and more accurate mental images of what happened, and to tell the story of the present or of the past, and to lay out courses for the future, in ever more accurate focus. They constantly try to make people able to tell the various true stories of themselves. They listen to material over and over, in hopes of hearing the one slight change, the new item remembered, which shows that the mind is investigating *differently* from how it investigated last week.

Looking at Literature from the Point of View of Stage-Development Philosophy

Like any enthusiastic layperson, I am afraid of bowdlerizing or skewing the scholars' and professionals' elaborate ideas. We laypeople who get interested in certain work by professionals are always in difficulties: we want to participate, yet we feel respectful of the demanding scholarship that has gone into designing and replicating studies. We feel daunted by the broad base of scholarship that underlies the Ph.D. in psychology, education, or social work—a broad base we shall never have time to duplicate or approximate.

We desperately need the general reading and thinking public to make much more use of recent twentieth-century social sciences, not to keep reiterating the ideas of the 1940s. Many outgrown ideas still look like authority, even in psychology departments. There are still people teaching that our souls are run by sexual drive. There are professors still treating students' and clients' emotions as *affect*—something to be worked away from, when sometimes those emotions are idealism with a surround of sadnesses. Medical schools are still teaching Freud, not as an original thinker to whom we owe much, but as the definitive psychoanalyst, as if there had been no amended theory since his death.

To get a Ph.D. in psychology one must study rigid, outmoded, or impersonal material and pretend it seems central to one's focus. Finally, clear of academia, practicing in the field, clinicians are busy or glad enough not to renew the academic connection. That may partly explain why 1940s psychological philosophies, often preserving a mechanistic and deterministic take on the human mind, keep chugging along on the lay-by track of so many American universities.

Meanwhile, the life-giving practices of therapists are of a different and increasingly more existential mode. They both model and teach empathy. For thousands of Americans, the empathy of the social work therapist or the philosopher-therapist is their first experience of being attended, the first experience of being asked a *question*, not to mention a *second* or *third question*, about anything they have just said. The rich are no less deprived in this than the poor.

I think we underestimate the general American rudeness. It cuts across all classes. We underestimate the relationship between constant rudeness and stunted ego development. We vastly underestimate the relationship between stunted ego development and that person's failure to develop moral thinking.

Hundreds, especially in New York City, still taxi themselves and their children to a "shrink" when what they need may well be meaning in life, not medication. Existential or philosophical and ethical psychotherapy, as such, has never had much of a home in American universities. Irvin Yalom points out that Ludwig Binswanger, Medard Boss, Eugene Minkowski, Viktor von Gebsattel, Roland Kuhn, Caruso, Frederik Buytendijk, G. Bally, and Viktor Frankl were "almost entirely unknown to the American psychotherapeutic community until Rollo May's highly influential 1958 book *Existence*. However, today, more than twenty years after May's book, it is striking that these figures exert little influence upon American psychotherapeutic practice."[14]

Perhaps adherence to a medical model of therapy for nonmedical situations is like the stubbornness with which some professors and secondary school teachers teach literature as individual bunches of textural techniques. Perhaps every field has its technology barnacles that spoil our clean passage through any seas of truth.

The three works by James Agee, Katha Pollitt, and Wendell Berry are unlike in content, in form, and certainly in their authors' intentions. They are the literary selections for this chapter on moral stage-development theory because all three beautifully illuminate basic points in stage-development philosophy.

None of the three authors could be called a developmental philosopher. Only one, in fact, Katha Pollitt, actually argues the way stage-development theorists argue: that is, she fine-tunes and fully lists those qualities in people that are *not* inborn traits but responses to present habitat, responses to the kind of mentoring or lack of mentoring people have received, and—given their habitat and past mentoring or conditioning—responses to such expectations as they may now have. I value Pollitt's against Carol Gilligan's and others' *trait* philosophy—that is, the notion that people of one gender are good and kind and people of the other less so. I value Pollitt's distinction between psychological underbrush and serious analysis.

Agee's parable, "A Mother's Tale," gives a wonderfully thoroughgoing, dreadful view of how conventionality makes us cling to habit, follow peers and not leaders, and refuse to look at bad news, thus not empowering our offspring to avoid disaster. Agee, who had theological interests and friendships with theologians, was interested in the processes by which conventional people (in the story, cattle) dilute and fragment messages from any authentic leader who tries to teach and save them. The One Who Came Back, a cow that somehow survived the slaughterhouse to return with dire warnings, is obviously a parallel to Jesus, leaking both blood and water. Further, Agee had the aesthete's dislike of people manipulating others through seduction (note the relationship of mother cow to son cow). I don't know that Agee minded sexual devices in themselves: what he seems to despise in this parable is the use of sensual pleasure to distract a thinking person (the young steer) from a harsh reality that he needs to know.

A useful way to look at this engrossing story is to see it as a very full set of characteristics of people stuck in Stage III—that is, people longing for psychological comfort, people taking the word from *peers*, not from great leaders, people whose response to great leaders is to be thrilled by hymns about them but to forget their actual, revolutionary teachings. Agee's parable is at least half about how Western civilization, with its love of everyday inventions and industry and everyday lifestyle, has been able to keep itself immune to serious moral teaching, while knowing the hymn tunes. I am not joining the California mystique that says the East is more profoundly holy than the West; I argue only for Agee's having described *our particular style* of ignoring spiritual leadership. Asia and the Near East and North Africa may have other kinds of social contrivances for keeping life morally flat—or for keeping on doing what Bruno Bettelheim called "business as usual."

Why not simply live along flatly? How tiresome always to be taking one high ground or another! Agee's point is partly that if one avoids painful thoughts and ignores prophecies by people who have gathered the relevant data, one is the perfect mark for a totalitarian government. Totalitarian government in "A Mother's Tale" is the Men, who breed, fence, and murder the cattle for their own convenience.

"Marooned on Gilligan's Island: Are Women Morally Superior to Men?" is a catchy, journalists' kind of title for what is a thoroughgoing and finely tuned discussion of how acculturation, not inborn traits, influences people's levels of kindness and unkindness, their tendency or lack of tendency to protest injustices, their acumen for civic and public life or the lack of it, and whether they conduct their lives in provincial self-centeredness or with spacious vision. In summary, Pollitt points out some particular qualities we associate with leadership, others we associate with followership, and says they are not gender-specific qualities but adaptations to habitat.

Pollitt's essay properly assigns gender less importance in how we identify and categorize people's ethics than some 1970s and 1980s feminists—and ironically, a good many male chauvinists—have noisily given it. Her carefully argued essay frees us all from the idea that people are stuck with one kind of personality or another: we may indeed be stuck at a certain stage of development but that is a much less dire, hopeless diagnosis than that we simply are some *kind* of person, predetermined by our sex.

The kind of argumentation in this essay is the very stuff of stage-development theory. Like stage-development theorists, Pollitt champions a position that doesn't look as cozy as the feminist-separatist position, but in the long run is a thousand times more hope-giving. After all, if certain supportive experiences and certain kinds of mentoring would make it possible for women not to be dominated by males, then we have our work clearly cut out for us: we must go get those experiences and those kinds of teaching for women.

"Solving for Pattern" is not the kind of Wendell Berry writing that most people know. It is essential—that is, analytical and full of social conceptualizations—whereas most people know Berry for his charming but less enterprising storytelling. I regard "Solving for Pattern" as one of the most effective pieces of philosophical writing in our time. It is too succinct to be popular with casual readers. Perhaps it is less known for this reason, just as Mark Helprin's "The Schreuderspitze," in which he condensed his most deeply felt understandings of life, is less known than Helprin's easier work, such as *A Winter's Tale*.

Berry's "Solving for Pattern" is an essay in ecological ethics. It is based on the idea that goodness in organizations, such as farms, means being good to the environment or impact group around the organization as well as to the organization's own members. Berry's thinking is very like ecologists' thinking: let us see ourselves as we influence others in ever widening circles around us. Let us see that whoever or whatever lives in those wide circles are not merely resources for us to scarf up: their well-being is not just a matter of practicality, but a moral concern of ours.

This short essay is a gem of philosophical theory. We don't need the slightest interest in farming in order to benefit from Berry's systemic thinking. From the author's fourteen good solutions relevant to "farming" we can read good solutions for

any business organization
any public, adult-level project
the conducting of a family-systems healing process[15]
an adult life itself—actively planned by the person living it.

Berry, already revered for the loving particularity of his essays and stories, is a first-rate and concise philosopher. Of all his work, sage and humorous and affectionate, I think "Solving for Pattern" is the best teaching, life-giving essay. In the general scheme of

moral stage development, Berry's ecological point of view illustrates Stage VI thinking: to run a good organization, one must not
be self-absorbed (Stage I) or merely competitive with other organizations (Stage II) or obedient to conventional peer advisories
such as overbuying equipment or overspecialization (Stage III) or
merely follow dicta from "authorities"—authorities on farming
or on business, for example—(Stage IV) or rigidly glommed onto
one's own code of ethics, without constantly scanning about to
see how one's code affects unlike fellow creatures (Stage V).
People who can discipline themselves to act according to the
principles in "Solving for Pattern" are behaving, so to speak, at a
Stage VI level.

Lest such remarks horrify people who dislike linear and hierarchical psychology, I want to say for myself that I love reading
Stage VI thinking like Berry's. I may never get there myself, but I
know a good thing when I see it, just the way a child still crawling
watches with unreserved envy and anticipation a larger child who
can walk. I hope that no one would suppress that child's admiration for walking. No one should try to convince the child to crawl
forever because it is less hierarchical and more democratic.

I feel no trepidation in suggesting that we look at literature—both
at content and, if we are scholarly enough, at the authors themselves as their own works show them to us—from the point of
view of stage-development philosophy. The literary criticism of
the 1990s has filled American literature with so much nihilism, so
much high-tech attention to word texture only, and so much un-
willingness to distinguish between profound work and shallow
work, between unartistic work and beautiful first-rate writing,
that one more approach can do no harm.

Tradition in the field of literature always warns against mining
instances from fiction or poetry to illustrate social theory. The
scholar's concern, a good one, is that the reader won't openheart-
edly enter the world of the poem itself or the world of the story itself, but instead will read it with a mind looking only for proofs of
ideas already implicit in his or her mind. Scholars are right to fear
and dislike that practice.

On the other hand, we readers have to keep telling ourselves that mountains of beautiful literature in all the languages have been around since history started. In this book, we want purposely to read literature as descriptions of bullying and of bullies. We want to take literary works as messages to the bullies of the world and to those whom they bully.

In any case, you can't harm literature by talking about it. Let us say that someone wrote a stage-development application for James Agee's parable "A Mother's Tale." If one can accept Agee's cattle as characters, we have a number of examples to consider of behavior at various levels of ethical-thinking development. The mother is clearly at Stage II, although she has been vaguely catechized in Stage VI ideas through the hymn and folk traditions of the One Who Came Back. I expect her religious experience is parallel to any Stage II member's religious feeling. She pivots desperately between lies and myths, as people do who have developed so many defenses against worry. Her approach is "business as usual" unless shaken. Pain avoidance—not wanting to acknowledge mortally bad news—is her flag.

The least mechanistic, most surprising way to apply any stage-development theory to literature is to think about communication style at the same time. For example, if a reader copied out all the conversations in the literature included this book, starting with the talk between Sam and the speaker in "Cider 5¢ a Glass" and continuing through all the stories, and then asked, for each individual conversation, "What might have happened for these characters if the talk had gone differently?" And, "If something *needed* to happen for these characters—for example, Sam needed to be a lot more honorable and merciful and less rat-fink an attorney than he was—what *kind* of conversation might have done some good? If someone were to practice empathy with Sam, what would be a start?" That is a question from the field of social work, not from any tradition of belles lettres. We aren't used to it, and on first exposure we don't like the sound of it.

My grandmother-in-law and I visited for a half-hour nearly every day when she lived in the Madison (Minnesota) Lutheran Home. We talked religion, because she was interested in evangelical Lutheranism in America (now the ELCA). One day I told her, "Religion or no religion, a person has to accept scientific evolution. Evolution does not mean there was no God. It means God is a lot more complicated than people thought he was and that is the end of it." She had the kind of aged eyes that have lightened yet kept many separate stars in them. "*You* may be descended from monkeys," she explained to me, "but I am not. And *that* is the end of it." Traditional readers look at any proactive use of literature in somewhat that way.

Besides, we want to use literature as an escape. Escape, or having a second life, is one of the eternal pleasures of reading. This happened, then that happened—all of it blessedly outside of our own lives: then it is autumn in New England and *that* happened, then there was a telephone call saying such and such had happened, then there is a workplace scene in Boston, and so forth.

What is at issue is this: how long can one hide in escape reading, and how soon can one acquire a taste for sharp social truths in one's reading? An interesting example: The father in Arturo Vivante's "The Soft Core" was a great reader, and he had been a writer, too. Still, in his personal life, his self-absorption, his maneuvering of his family to serve him, his discounting of the inner life of one son and of his wife, he seemed like a Stage II bully—an energetic primitive, really, painted over with gracious habits. But those habits are just class background. He really treated everyone outside his own skin as people to be used, tenderly, but nonetheless used.

Reading science and reading literature, then, do *not* in themselves bring about new insight and changes of heart. They just make people feel faintly sensitized. Sensitization, if we have been unconscious, is a starting place, of course, but we need mentoring about what to do once sensitized. Otherwise we will just continue to be sensitive. The world is bejeweled with people who are sensitive, but their sensitivity doesn't come to much. We need to learn some of the social psychology skills. I know that it sounds repellent: like Clare, we would rather collect our miscellaneous "piths and gists."

Literature is half about how life goes along—the love affairs, the adventures of work, the journeys made, the illnesses finally succumbed to—and half about how the good guys leave off being just natural like the lilies in Oliver's poem, or it is condemnation by description of the bad guys, like Sam in "Cider" and the hummingbird in "Lilies." That general morality is admirable but readers don't necessarily grow just by being exposed to bad or good models.

I don't want to be pushed outside my own personality by some social "process" that someone is wishing on me. Still, the idea of stage development interests me. Perhaps I can avoid feeling shoved off my center by trying what I know of stage development against my own life history. After all, I am an expert in the field of myself. Here is an example of trying a notion of the development of ethical consciousness on oneself.

As mentioned in chapter 2, I recognized at twelve that unequal treatment went to promising and unpromising children in my school. I noticed it but made no quarrel about it, because I was in the favored group. I would have been frightened to displease my teachers by questioning their treatment of other children. What stage of moral development was I in? Without putting a label to it, we can amass useful insight on any issue in our past if we do this social work or therapist's trick: write down the *names of the emotions* we think we felt at that time, not the emotions we assign to it now:

pride of position as a promising child
fear of losing that favorable position
some genuine compassion for the children treated less well,
    but nowhere near enough to act on
a pleasant sense of personal security—in favor with
    authority
powerlessness in the system: What can a child of twelve do to
    influence teaching methods? Almost nothing.

Even such a short list of feelings reminds us of characters we know in dozens of works of literature, and other adults of our personal acquaintance. Amy, in *Little Women*, Prince Bolkonsky in *War and Peace*, Eustace in the Narnia series—they had pride of position, feelings of entitlement. The children in Katherine Mansfield's "The Garden Party" are the perfect example of people with an attractive but painless level of compassion for a dead working-class man. Most of the narrator figures in Somerset Maugham's novels enjoy a pleasant entitlement—a sense of being socially correct enough to meet whatever is going to happen. The poor children in Dickens are powerless in the system, and know it. We all know adults who don't get around to changing a single unjust corner of their world: perhaps their hearts are strapped around with one or more of the feelings listed earlier. Questions we can begin with, with ourselves, are, When did I feel powerless in whatever system I was brought up in? What was the system like? How did I get such power as I did have, and when was that?

After writing that down for ourselves, we reverse the process. Instead of recalling situations of our own, and letting them remind us of parallels in literature, we can try to think empathically of literary characters, make lists on their behalf, give them places in their continuum of development, and so on, and then let what we know of them remind us of our own lives. Scientists may rightly feel skeptical, because either procedure—starting with literature and moving to self, or starting with self and moving to literature—is nothing if not anecdotal. Anecdote, telling the story of what happened that day to those people, however, is the genius of literature, and when it appears in social science reports it wonderfully illumines otherwise grubby argument.

Notes

1. Irving Janis, *Groupthink: Psychological Studies of Policy Decisions and Fiascoes* (Boston: Houghton Mifflin, 1983).

2. Heinz Schaeffer, *U-Boat 977* (New York: W. W. Norton, 1952; reprint, New York: Bantam Books, 1981), 189–90.

3. Ibid., 190.

4. John Rawls, "Two Concepts of Rules," *Philosophical Review*, 64, no. 1 (January 1955): 26.

5. We still have so few tools for measuring intellectual influences on unborn children that I wrote "appears to start at the bottom." There is more and more evidence, however, that some children well before birth have received incredible blessings to their hearts and minds. It appears that we all start together, but perhaps, by the end of the twenty-first century, we will have measured ways in which some sperm and some eggs, even before they meet, have been acculturalized differently.

6. Earthworks Group (Berkeley, Calif.: Earthworks, 1989).

7. Constance Hays, "Bristol-Myers Pleads Guilty to Pollution," *New York Times*, April 25, 1992, 25.

8. Some Native American nations take eye contact as intrusive or even belligerent. Out of respect for the soul of the other, they avoid staring into the eyes.

9. Noam Chomsky in *Manufacturing Consent* and *Chronicals of Dissent* at length, and briefly in a published transcription of his remarks to the Northwest Broadcast News Association in Minneapolis on February 4, 1984, discusses a kind of propaganda that democracies are especially prone to—a propaganda of nonissues and side distractions from intense moral issues. An instance of propaganda: the government refers to one or another war policy as a "peace policy," which diffuses attention and furs over our perception of the violent happenings. See Edward S. Herman and Chomsky, *Manufacturing Consent: The Political Economy of the Mass Media* (New York: Pantheon, 1988); Chomsky, *Chronicles of Dissent: Interviews with David Barsamian*, intro. Alexander Cockburn, (Monroe, Maine: Common Courage Press, 1992); and Chomsky, "1984: Orwell's and Ours," intro. John M. Dolan, *Thoreau Quarterly*, 16, nos. 1–2 (winter–spring 1984): 13.

10. Dan Olweus, "Bullying among School Children: Intervention and Prevention," in *Aggressions and Violence throughout the Lifespan,* ed. R. D. Peters, R. J. McMahon, and V. L. Quincy (Newbury Park, CA: Sage Publications, 1992).

11. This translation and organization of Dr. Olweus's material is reprinted with the permission of Dr. Sarah Jeanne Snapp at the Child Guidance Center, Wilder Foundation, St. Paul, MN.

12. New brain research has shown that when something happens, the human brain responds to it with emotions from different centers; that is, we have several different responses at once (a phenomenon that psychologists have known but not neurophysiologically demonstrated). See Daniel Goleman, "The Brain Manages Happiness and Sadness in Different Centers," *New York Times*, March 28, 1995, B9.

13. George Vaillant, *Adaptation to Life* (Boston: Little, Brown, 1977). This book reports on the thirty-five year Grant Study, conducted at Harvard, whose aim was to see how ninety-four normal adults of privilege live out or don't live or expand their ideals for the good life.

14. Irvin D. Yalom, *Existential Psychotherapy* (New York: Basic Books, 1980), 17.

15. If one sets a list of Berry's suggestions alongside a list of the strategies of family-systems therapists one sees an amazing parallel between them. This similarity between a literary giant's thinking and psychotherapists' thinking may not rejoice everyone's heart, but it does mine. Berry is much more than the charming, soothing Southern writer a good many literature teachers take him for, and family therapy is a much more subtle and intellectual learning tool than most people suspect.

The Psychological and Moral Habitats
of American Children and Adults

THE READINGS

The Woman Lit by Fireflies
Jim Harrison

White Canyon
Susan Lowell

THE COMMENTARY
Carol Bly

The Woman Lit by Fireflies

by Jim Harrison

She had not yet accepted as real the quiver in her stomach and the slight green dot of pain in the middle of her head that signaled an incipient migraine. Her husband on the car seat beside her punched in a tape called *Tracking the Blues* which contained no black music, but rather the witless drone of a weekly financial lecture sent from New York City. This particular tape was seven days stale and had been played three times on their trip, but Donald repeated it to get "fair value" for his money. The tape, not incidentally, replaced Stravinsky's *Histoire du Soldat* from an Iowa City FM station, a piece she always enjoyed.

"Do you mind, darling?" he asked.

"Not at all, dear," she replied, partly because the pain clinic she had attended in Arizona that spring had emphasized giving up resistance to outside phenomena at the possible onset of a migraine under the notion you wanted to starve rather than feed the affliction. For instance, she shouldn't have been driving—sitting with her eyes closed listening to music would have been helpful, but she drove to avoid reading to him, which is what he required when he drove. An additional, insurmountable problem was that his car, an Audi 5000, was low-slung and the early August corn beside Interstate 80 in Iowa presented itself as a dense green wall. She preferred the higher vantage of her own nine-year-old Toyota Land Cruiser, a functional clumsy old machine that she and her beloved friend Zilpha used on their outings, or so they called them, which were somewhat famous in their neighborhood in Bloomfield Hills, a suburb of Detroit.

Clare would be fifty in another week, Donald was fifty-one and eager to get on with life, a matter about which she had mixed feelings. They had just been visiting their daughter Laurel, who at twenty-nine was a veterinarian married to a veterinarian, the both of them ministering to horses and cattle in a clinic outside of Sioux City, Iowa, up near the Nebraska border. The visit had been cut short two days by a quarrel between Laurel and Donald. On the way home they were to spend the weekend with Donald Jr., who at twenty-seven was a commodities market whiz in Chicago.

"I love you, Mom, but I can't understand why you don't leave that asshole," Laurel had said.

"Please, Laurel, he's your father."

"In name only," she had replied, and then they kissed goodbye as they always did, with Clare's heart giving a breathless wrench at separation.

A specific giddiness began to overtake her when she thought of the goodbye. *This is the way, after all, I've spent my life,* she thought. You could not fault Donald for being Donald, any more than you could fault Laurel for being the same as she was at three years, a cantankerous little girl with a sure though general sense of mission, a personality so specific as to be sometimes offensive.

"The overloaded leverages are coming home to roost," Donald brayed so loud she applied the brakes. She quickly reset the cruise control at a modest seventy considering that most cars passed her at that speed. The week before at the club she attempted a witticism about how all the lives saved by the Mothers Against Drunk Driving were being lost to the raising of the speed limit. The luncheon ladies were used to Clare and let the quip pass, but not a new member who found it "dreadfully morbid." Suddenly it occurred to her that Donald didn't feel really good about making money unless others were losing theirs, which made it all, to her mind, a silly game to spend your life on rather than the grave process with which he was totally obsessed.

An ever so slight tremor of head pain made her dismiss the thought about Donald and money as true but banal. She forced her thoughts back to a pleasant morning with Laurel, spent hiking on some bluffs above the Missouri River. Laurel had discovered a rattlesnake that had difficulty getting out of their way because of a huge lump in its belly—no doubt, Laurel said, from swallowing a gopher. They both laughed when Laurel added, "Poor thing, also poor gopher." The laughter was nervous relief. The first hour of their walk had been spent lifting Clare's confusion over a pamphlet an antivivisectionist neighbor had given her concerning a doctor down south who, on a defense contract, had shot several thousand cats in the

head for research. Laurel habitually defended the scientific community but this one puzzled her, as the brain of a cat was dissimilar
enough to that of a human as to make the research appear useless.
She did not tell Clare that it would have made more sense to shoot
several thousand dogs, or better yet chimpanzees, though the latter
were very expensive. The purpose of the research, of course, was to
better treat head wounds in soldiers. Then Clare had brought up another item that she had brooded about for two years without mentioning. Laurel had sent her an article from *Orion Nature Quarterly,*
by a Spanish fellow, Lopez, called "The Passing Wisdom of Birds," in
which the author described Cortez's vengeful burning of the aviaries
in Mexico City in the sixteenth century. Clare loved birds and cats
and could easily overlook the fact that Cortez had destroyed the city
and murdered hundreds of thousands of citizens — that was to be expected — but the burning of Montezuma's aviaries seemed to stand
for something far more grotesque and the image of the conflagra-
tion passed through her mind daily. So she had asked Laurel, a scant
fifteen minutes before they saw the gorged rattlesnake, why she had
sent the article, and Laurel had said, "People who love each other
try to explain themselves to each other. I wanted you to see again
why I work with animals. I can't stand people. Now it's your turn to
explain yourself to me." That, as they say, was that, until the poor
snake appeared as a convenience, almost a stage prop if it weren't
for the immensity of the sky above and the wide, brown Missouri
River below them.

Back on Interstate 80 she wondered why they bothered teaching
us the things they did — the grandeur, sweep and intricacies of civilization at its best — when there was little enough to do with the
knowledge. Clare's criticisms of the human condition were sharp but
basically mid-range and items like Cortez and the birds shifted her
off balance as did, to a lesser degree, the three thousand holes in the
heads of three thousand cats. Now she tried to reduce the growing
pain by an act of will, dimming the fluttery green energy to a
pinpoint if only for a moment as she had been taught to do in
Arizona. There was a sign for a rest stop in ten miles and it was 2:50
which meant she would beat the phone call by a minute. The tape
about blue chip stocks had mercifully finished but now Donald was

whistling "The Colonel Bogey March" and tapping out the rhythm on the cellular car phone, anticipatory to his daily broker call. His lips pursed and the whistling and tapping stopped as he made a notation in red pencil on the day's *Wall Street Journal*.

"I'm going to have to stop while you phone. I'm not feeling all that well," she said, stiffening at his possible reaction.

"Fine, honey. We've got time to kill." Donald glanced at his watch. "There's room for your nappy in Davenport."

She never understood quite how "nap" became "nappy" but had always judged an inquiry as not quite worthwhile. She looked at him with a longing close to homesickness that the troubled at heart feel for those who treat the world as their lovely private apple. Donald was a passably good man, or so everyone thought, a citizen so apparently solid that, as a club jokester had said, he could throw a successful fund raiser for a crack dealer. A business associate had organized a dinner for ten at a hotel in Davenport, which Donald looked forward to as an orphan would his first circus. He was being especially tender because Clare was the daughter of one of the founding partners of the accounting firm which had branches throughout the Midwest, and the Davenport office was doing espe- cially well. The Davenport people would be thrilled to meet Clare. It would be all bows by the men and curtsies by the ladies. He had even alerted them about Clare's taste in wine which he thought a wasteful vice she had inherited from her mother. Frequently, he noted, the wine on a dinner bill equaled the price of the food, and when he picked up a case of Meursault or Chambertin at the wine store he liked to joke out loud: "Here goes three shares of General Motors." The old clerk at the wine store invariably smiled his mask of a smile knowing it was Clare's money in the first place, a point which would appall Clare herself in that she was so fair-minded as to be frequently rendered immobile.

But not now. She eased the car into the rest stop, slowing to a creep for fear of hitting the children darting in and out of campers and cars in the crowded parking area. Across a green swath semis were parked with the muffled drone of their engines at rest only at destinations. One of the semis held squealing pigs in metal-slatted layers while another was full of silent cattle. Clare got out, taking the leather and canvas Buitoni bag Donald had bought her on their trip to Florence. At the time she could not believe his brusque affability translated so well. They had dined nearly every evening with Italians he had met in his tours of brokerage offices, several times in their homes, allowing Clare a look into the life of Florence never allowed the ordinary tourist. Donald waved at her with the other hand on the phone, antsy to make his daily call. She watched him dial, then walked toward the Iowa Welcome Center and the adjoining bathrooms, her head beginning to thrum in the noisy heat. It occurred to her that the tourists all looked blowzy and fatigued because they were headed back east at the end of their vacations.

When she thought about it later Clare was surprised again by how clear and cool her painful mind had felt. Every human and object, the landscape itself, had the distinct outlines found in a coloring book before the crayons are applied. The green wall of the cornfield behind the Welcome Center became luminous and of surpassing loveliness. She turned and walked back toward Donald in the car but he was in his brokerage trance, his clipped business voice saying, "But what the hell happened to Isomet?"

In the bathroom stall she checked her bag for certain items: Donald Jr.'s Boy Scout compass she used on hikes with Zilpha, a small can of cranberry juice, the addresses of three orphan children she wrote to and helped support in Santo Domingo, Mexico and Costa Rica; in a leather packet was her passport and a copy of the new translation of the *Tao Te Ching* given to her by a counselor at the pain clinic, and at the bottom, and most important, was the tan beret she had bought thirty years before on Rue St.-Jacques and had never worn. As a comparative literature senior at Michigan State she was to spend a year studying in Paris which lasted only three weeks when her father died and the family sent her boyfriend Donald to fetch her home. At the time Donald was her act of rebellion, a left-wing political science major who wore lumberjack shirts, the only son in a working-class family from Flint, who intended to be a writer or labor leader. On dates they read John Dos Passos's *U.S.A.* trilogy aloud to each other. Curiously her father had rather liked Donald, and perhaps this was foresight into the man Donald would become. So each morning for three weeks in her tiny *pension* Clare would look at her beret but was too timid to put it on.

Now in the toilet stall she finally put on the beret and laughed softly to herself. It was so easy. For luck she also slipped on a conch pearl ring Zilpha had given her in March as a remembrance. Among her last words had been "We never got around to the Amazon," a trip they had planned since they were girls when they were convinced they'd discover a pleasanter civilization somewhere in the jungle. Clare took out a Cafergot pill, then put it back, preferring pain-ridden consciousness. She tried to remember something René Char had written, "Blank blank blank the legitimate fruits of daring," but the growing pain blinded her memory. The note itself was simple enough: "I am in a small red car driving east. My husband has been abusing me. Do not believe anything he says. Call my daughter." She added Laurel's number, wrote "To The Police" on the envelope and stuck it to the side of the stall with a postage stamp. She noted that someone had scratched "Bob is cute" with a sharp object on the paint and she smiled with the confusion of female and male.

Behind the Welcome Center a small boy walking the family dog held Clare's bag as she climbed the fence which was more difficult than she anticipated. She wobbled and the wire cut into the soles of her tennis shoes. On the other side she lost a few moments explaining to the boy why he couldn't go along, but then the dog started barking and she hurried off down between two corn rows, toward the interior, wherever that might be.

Within a scant five minutes Clare would have liked to turn around, had turning around not already become so improbable. A hundred yards into the cornfield the beret made her feel silly so she took it off and stuffed it into her bag. The moment the hat came off the pain became so excruciating she fell to her hands and knees and retched up her lunch of iced tea and a club sandwich. The pain was such that she could not balance herself on her hands and knees, but pushed her legs backward until she lay on her stomach. She closed her eyes a moment but the world became bright red and whirling. There was the slightest memory of a pain lesson but it was too abstract to be of much use: the secret was to maintain your equilibrium in the face of incomprehension, as pain, finally, could not be understood.

At eye level she looked at the way the roots of the corn broke up the earth. She tried to let go of her brain which it now seemed would boil over with its brew of knots and hackings, clots, soft lumps against sharp hot stones. She rolled over onto her back. By the time the sun made its way down through the tassels, leaves and stalks, it was weak and liquid. There was a crow call so close it startled her, the bird flapping low over her row, then twisting, darting back for another look, squawking loudly in warning at the intruder, then a third pass up the row out of curiosity. She had never been so close to a crow, she thought, and tried closing her eyes a moment to rehearse crows from the past. The red storm had somewhat subsided and she saw the open mouth of a rooster at her grandmother's, and herself as a child stooping near the rooster as he swelled his throat, craned his neck outward and crowed as if he could not stop himself. As a child she had liked cellars because they frightened her, and now she longed for a cool, black cellar with a rooster for company, for her grandmother's dog whom the rooster pretended to chase though he kept a safe distance, as if he and the dog had agreed upon a reasonable pace for the dog to walk away. Grandfather told her that the rooster felt the whole world was after his hens, and that was all he thought about.

Now she heard a siren, but only gradually understood the sound, from back toward the rest stop. She scrambled to her feet and they moved off quickly down the row as if informed by their own panic. The siren became louder, then stopped abruptly. She continued to run, holding her hands and the bag up against the slapping of the leaves. There was an image of Donald explaining himself to the police, who she hoped would call Laurel despite Donald's usual cagey aplomb. But then Donald passed away with her breathlessness and her flayed brain began to play the rest of the Stravinsky Donald had truncated, then she tripped on a clod of earth and fell sprawling in a bare row where the corn turned direction. Now she was far enough from Route 80 so that she no longer could hear the trucks, only the crows, as the one had become five, and she twisted her neck for a look as they passed over, apparently discussing her. Perhaps the police could see the birds far out in the cornfield and guess that she was there, but she hoped they would believe the "small red car driving east." The sun was warm in the narrow clearing and she moved her upper body into the shade. She drew out the cranberry juice, drank it, then looked at the Boy Scout compass, deciding to head west along the wider row after a rest. She curled up, noting the earth smelled like a damp board after rain, then more heat. She looked at a dirty hand and thought idly with a smile, despite the pain, that for the first time in her life she did not know where her next shower was coming from.

Clare slept for a few minutes but was startled awake by her first dream in several months. She was a girl again, out in her rowboat on Burt Lake, and Dr. Roth was on the dock calling out and asking her why she had died. That was all there was to the dream and then she awoke. The pain had localized toward the right side of her head and within it Dr. Roth continued to call after she woke up. Clare was difficult to push off balance and ignored the phenomenon which was not unlike certain other symptoms of classic migraines. Besides, she liked Dr. Roth very much; he was not only her doctor and confidant, up to a point, but also had been Zilpha's doctor. Dreams are no respecter of time and Dr. Roth couldn't have been more than a child when Clare was a girl in a rowboat. She turned over and thought, at the very least, she had her first dream since Zilpha died, and then two weeks later when Clare's dog died her sleep had become even blacker. The dream wasn't ominous to Clare: death simply didn't hold her interest, but there was the nagging angle of Dr. Roth who Clare at the very moment realized she had been in love with for a brief period.

This recognition jolted her to her feet and she continued to head west, wondering if "maize" and "maze" were somehow connected. She normally walked a great deal because she was essentially claustrophobic and walking made the world appear larger. The fact that the field offered no variation was moot. Dr. Roth's lighthearted question meant something different to her than might appear. Once, when they had a drink after a library board meeting, he had said that most of his patients were already dead, and life herself was merely a technicality that allowed them to get up in the morning to collect a paycheck. They shared this sort of acerbic wit that made them both somewhat mistrusted in what are known as the better circles. The characteristic was harder on Dr. Roth than on Clare because this sharp wit, added to his slowness to write unnecessary prescriptions, limited his practice to those who desired honesty in medicine.

But on another evening after another library board meeting, when they had had to deal with a group of evangelical nitwits who wanted *The Catcher in the Rye* and *Slaughterhouse Five* banned from public consumption, Dr. Roth had looked up from his melancholy brandy and said, "You should be careful. You've lived your life with the kind of will that could later cause a lot of problems."

"I know it," she had said. But she didn't know it; the statement only brought forth the familiar feeling of an unpleasant truth.

That was half a year ago and the morning after, when she heard Donald pull out of the driveway she began to weep, an act so strange to her she couldn't pinpoint the event that had made her weep before. A few weeks later both Zilpha and Clare's dog had been diagnosed, Zilpha with lung and the dog with fibroid cancer.

Down toward the end of the row the greenness narrowed and blurred, and then there seemed to be a line of taller greenery. Her pace quickened in wan hope for a change of view, but she slowed down as the pain redeveloped with the swiftness of pace, though luckily enough the pain had moved to the left side of the head where it was more confinable. On the left side Clare could reduce the pain to a diffuse green light, then work consciously on reducing the dimensions of the light. The only side effect was that her sense of time became utterly jumbled, which was vertiginous but preferable to the pain. During one of these seizures, and at this particular state, the best she could do was to remember to feed the dog. Out in the field all that was required was to walk a straight line.

In fact, she thought she was moving within the heart of time. Normally she stood aside and lived on her comments to herself on what was happening to her, but when the pain moved to the left she moved inside herself, and this had the virtue of being novel within the framework of suffering. The pain was always a moment behind her as if she stood on the platform of a caboose watching the world go away. There was a sudden impulse to pray but she found the act embarrassing because, of course, she could *see* herself praying. As a child up near Petoskey on summer vacation her parents had allowed her to go to Daily Vacation Bible School with the maid's daughter. The maid was a mixed-blood Chippewa but her religion was Evangelical. Clare's parents had once discovered their daughter out in the garage praying over a three-legged cat that lived in the neighborhood. This was viewed as highly amusing and became part of a repertoire of "Clare stories" her parents shared with their friends during the rites of the martini hour. Now, to her surprise, this made Clare angry. What was the point of being angry at her parents for something that happened forty years ago, but then what was so funny about a child praying for a three-legged cat? In defiance she dropped to her knees but couldn't think of anything to say so got up again. Dr. Roth should see her now. He liked to think that, all efforts of the glitz media to the contrary, life is Dickensian, and that pathos is invariably the morning's leading news item. Clare with dusty knees and a verbless prayer would, no doubt, amuse him.

It had taken Dr. Roth several years to set Clare straight over the fact that Donald was an anti-Semite, albeit a quiet one. Clare had invited Dr. Roth and his wife to a large dinner party and late in a rather boozy evening Dr. Roth had made an acid but very funny comment about Richard Nixon which everyone had laughed at but Donald, to whom Nixon was an object of reverence. "Golly, but you guys can be smartasses," Donald had said, and the table had become so quiet that Zilpha had plunged courageously ahead with a lame joke. When everyone left Clare was instantly furious, partly at herself for letting the first incident pass. Years before, they had been visiting friends in Palm Beach with the real purpose of the trip being to pick up the dog from other friends. They had all eaten dinner at the Everglades Club and their host had proudly announced that the club was off limits to Jews. Clare had merely said that she found the fact odd just twenty-five years after World War II and let it drop, though the comment put everyone on edge. Before bedtime Donald had said something critical about her dinner behavior, admitting quite pompously that he agreed with the club policy. She had only looked at him and said, "I see." Next morning the joy of picking up the yellow Labrador, who was being given away for littering the pristine lawn with stray coconuts and palm fronds, made her overlook the issue.

Curiously, Dr. Roth was remote and analytical on the subject of

anti-Semitism. He had grown up in Ann Arbor in a sheltered academic family, and after medical school had married a Jewish girl from
Memphis whose family had been in the country from well before the
Civil War. His experience was limited to a number of minor incidents
similar to the one with Donald. He tried to tease his way out of
Clare's questions by saying that being Jewish couldn't be as bad as
being a manic depressive or a woman, and his wife was all three.
When Clare insisted, he finally admitted that his own Jewish experience could be likened to her acute migraine, not in the degree of
pain but in the utter uncertainty of when something unpleasant was
going to occur. The incident could be a small item in the paper, say
an inept political statement, or the recent suicide of one of his
favorite authors, Primo Levi. The condition of being Jewish bred a
perpetual wariness shared by all minorities, and the wariness tended
to become an irksome cliché in life unless one was careful. The true
burden of awareness had been carried by his parents' generation
where the threat was all too specific.

One late afternoon over drinks he said something that disturbed
Clare, to the effect that they shared an economic condition that was
out of sync, and definitely out of sympathy with ninety-nine point
ninety-nine percent of the rest of the world, and they had to walk an
extremely narrow line not to die from being rich freaks. He asked
how Clare and Donald got their home and she said it had been a
wedding gift from her mother. Dr. Roth said his own home had
come from his father-in-law on the same occasion, and when had
either of them given more than nominal consideration to the
purchase of anything—food, clothing, wine, books, cars, vacations?
He said he would have gone mad long ago without the single day a
week he spent as a volunteer at Detroit Receiving, a hospital that
serviced the black ghetto and the poorest whites. Then he noticed a
hurt look quickly pass across her face before she could conceal it.

"What about me?" she said.

"Oh, your reading in unpleasant areas and your migraines keep
the tips of your toes in the real world."

"That's not very much, is it?"

"It's usually enough. Our sort doesn't need a great deal of
consciousness to get by. Most often sending a check will do."

"I'm not leaving this shitheel fern bar on that sour note." She signaled the waiter for another glass of wine. Clare swore on the order of once a year. "This can't be another monkey occasion." She was referring to a benefit ball they had attended, the purpose of which was to raise money for new accommodations for the chimpanzees at the Detroit Zoo. Donald was in Atlanta for a few days and Dr. Roth's wife had entered a manic shopping phase that could best be resolved in New York City. Zilpha had only recently died and Dr. Roth thought it important for Clare to get out of the house. Unfortunately they were seated at a table with two self-important General Motors executives whose wives ignored everyone, and an exhausted neurosurgeon whose wife obviously wanted to be at a zippier table. Despite a normal aversion for talking shop in front of laymen, Dr. Roth and the neurosurgeon began some heavy-hearted joking on the effects of crack cocaine on the nervous system of newborn infants, the neurosurgeon's punch line forcing everyone to drink hard and fast.

"We're going to have to look at Detroit as a vast rookery for psychotics," the man said.

"What's a rookery?" a GM wife asked.

"A breeding ground. Our dominant product is psychosis. It's moved ahead of automobiles."

"That doesn't speak well for the future of the work force," an executive huffed.

"Not unless you're producing worker-tested automatic rifles," Dr. Roth quipped.

That evening had been effectively deadened and in the shitheel fern bar they tried to work themselves out of the hole that they had dug.

"I'm tired. Can't you look in your catalogue of piths and gists?" Dr. Roth was referring to a ledger Clare had started at the university and continued to the present where she recorded passages of literature she cherished. Dr. Roth had been amazed at Clare's ledger, the range was boggling, all recorded in a neat, almost lapidary script, from Aeschylus down to E. M. Cioran, with a preponderance coming from the early modernist period in world literature from 1880 to 1920. Her intended but never finished senior honors thesis was to be

on Apollinaire and there were many translated quotes, but her temperament seemed to have been most captured by Rilke. Dr. Roth's
own sense of balance had been disturbed when he came across
Yeats's notion to the effect that life was a long preparation for something that never occurred.

"My piths and gists don't work since Zilpha and Sammy died."
Sammy was the name of the female Labrador. In an instant Clare
relived Dr. Roth's stricken look when he had stopped by late one
afternoon for a drink and found her and Zilpha listening to the
Beethoven "Last Quartets" while Zilpha held the fat, stinking,
cancerous Sammy on her lap, smooching with the dog, hugging
its bulk to her breast, both of them within a month of death.

"I'm thinking hard," Dr. Roth said. "Let's not come to this place
again. It's full of binge shoppers trying to sedate themselves. Now,
I know you have an aversion to anything Oriental as being too passive, even though you're utterly passive yourself. A Wayne State
University student suffering from obvious malnutrition said it to me.
The general notion is that the only use for today is today. The only
reality you are ever going to get is the ordinary one you make for
yourself. In other words, there's no big breakthrough."

"That's awfully grim. Does that mean there's no Christmas on
earth? And what does he do with the information?"

"The 'he' is a 'she.' I gave her ten bucks and made her promise
she'd go eat a good meal. Then I loaded her up with vitamin
samples. I don't know what she does with this information. I only
know she doesn't take care of herself."

"Can I make a donation?" Clare had become nervous.

"Not at the moment. Perhaps later when a donation doesn't
mean you're delaying doing something about yourself."

"When you say 'doing something about yourself' it sounds like
psychobabble. You know the big section in Borders Bookstore that
covers self-improvement."

"Pathology can only be imaginative up to a certain point. If you
like, I'll work on the sentence."

Clare found herself nearly at the end of the row and presented with
a barrier she hadn't allowed herself to comprehend while thinking

about Dr. Roth. It was a dense thicket, apparently as impenetrable as any of the topiary hedges she had seen in England and France. The thicket grew into the cornfield so she couldn't turn right or left. She stepped back twenty feet for a better view and thought she could make out the top of a cottonwood; as her breathing calmed she was sure she heard flowing water, then she remembered that a mile or so before they reached the rest stop there had been a creek or river named after a cow—Guernsey, she thought. Her watch said that had been over two hours ago which didn't seem possible. A creek crossed at seventy miles an hour in a split second doesn't look threatening, but now she felt tears welling up. She had expected a barnyard and farmhouse at the end of the row, and now the compass said that was a possibility only in a southerly direction since north was the interstate. Millions of women merely leave their husbands; why had she fled? She swallowed with difficulty, wishing she had saved some of the cranberry juice, then looked up at the thunderheads, their edges lined with silver from the descending sun. She sat down and made traceries in the dirt with the compass bracket. She had an impulse to discuss the situation with Zilpha but she felt that would further loosen her tenuous grip. Laurel was a better choice.

"Laurel, you little bitch, this is partly your idea. What do I do now?" There was an urge to be angry, cheap, vulgar.

"You could have waited until Davenport and taken a cab to the airport when Dad was in the shower." This was so like Laurel who was matter-of-fact even in the cradle.

"I knew the pain was coming and I lost my good sense." The pain was increasing a bit with the tinge of self-pity so she stiffened up. At the clinic one of the first lessons was never to adopt a "why me?" attitude which might precipitate a collapse.

"You know very well your good sense is bullshit. Remember when I came home from college years ago and said that you act as if you're living three feet from yourself? You were angry but it's true."

"I suppose so, but let's get back to the situation right now. I'm sitting here in the dirt and I don't know what to do. Like most people I'm only prepared for the life I've already lived, none of which included this sort of thing." Clare remained cool with this admission.

On all the trips she had made to beautiful places with Zilpha they had never camped out, though twice they had bought a lot of expensive equipment that was donated to the Boy Scouts on return. Laurel and her husband had backpacked everywhere, even in the winter on cross-country skis.

"For Christ's sake, Mother, you're going to have to toughen up. You said you read that book on camping I sent. You're going to have to get some water in your system to avoid hypothermia. You know that from a lifetime of tennis which I always thought was a waste of time. You might have to go back to the rest stop for water."

"I refuse. It looks like it's going to rain. My bag is canvas so maybe I could catch some water."

"It's important that you crawl into that thicket to stay dry. No matter how warm it is now, if you get wet you'll be cold by nightfall. Don't drink any water from that creek unless you find a way to boil it. If you get desperate, don't forget why you're doing this. I'd say you're in for a long night unless you're willing to hoof it back to the interstate. I hope you'll come to spend a few months with us."

"That's kind of you but I have my heart set on Paris."

"That's silly of you. Paris isn't the same as it was thirty years ago. You'll be disappointed."

"I don't care. I've passed through a few times since and I don't care if I'm disappointed."

Clare signed off on the phantom conversation with a wave at the oncoming thunderheads that had begun to rumble. She rechecked the edge of the thicket, noting that there were narrow breaks and holes that raccoon and perhaps deer made. She crawled in a small opening in the greenery and looked upward, seeing enough of the sky to know it would still be wet in a hard rain. She remembered with a smile something she had overheard her gay decorator say on the phone, to the effect that his friend should fasten his seat belt because it was going to be a bumpy night. President Reagan had also liked to quote from the movies. Then she recalled as a child at Thanksgiving time on her grandparents' farm how she liked to make small caves in dried corn that had been stacked in shocks. She felt this memory comprised her first bright idea of the day other than leaving Donald, and she busied herself uprooting the green stalks which came up easily, and which she layered on top of the thicket. It was easy so she erred on the side of excess until, when she crawled into the thicket hole, there was a large area that blocked out the sky. If she hadn't been so thirsty she would have been happy in the choice. She emptied out the bag containing her small purse, compass, address book, the beret, the empty juice can (she didn't want to litter), and the passport. It had been Zilpha's notion that the act of taking your passport with you everywhere added drama to life. She arranged these objects like talismans, then scooted back out and spread the bag's mouth open.

The thunder deepened in its volume and she looked up to see lightning shattering the sky like luminous tree roots. The thunderclap that followed had a sharp edge as if the sky were being torn, and the wind came up suddenly so that the leaves down the row were pale and flapping. Clare backed into her makeshift cave with a feeling that things were well in hand, at least for the moment, but the torrent that followed, brief as it was, cast her behavior in a fresh light. When she gave birth to Laurel that early May so long ago she could hear a cloudburst beyond the walls and windows of the delivery room, and there was a tinge of déjà vu in the present rain. *I had two children and lived with a man nearly thirty years. I don't seem to have a real idea what occurred to me. Maybe nobody does, or just a few.*

The driving rain splattered mud upward and formed puddles in the opening, but she was dry and warm and drowsy, the remnants of pain merely diffuse and endurable. She froze then, startled at the slightest movement to her left, but then saw it was only a cottontail, the same kind of rabbit that made her put chicken wire around her herb garden back home. The rabbit studied Clare from half a dozen feet away, then continued feeding on wild clover shoots, but with its ears alertly erect and its nose trying to determine if Clare presented a danger. Within its ears on the pinkish lobes wood ticks dotted the flesh, gorging on blood. Clare counted seven. She and the rabbit stared at each other so long that Clare didn't notice that the rain had stopped and the water caught by her bag was both being absorbed and draining slowly out. The rabbit's ears stiffened for an instant at the sound of a cock pheasant crowing from the direction of the creek, followed by the sharp clear notes of red-winged blackbirds.

There was a new dimension of stillness in all of this and Clare felt somehow heartened that the rabbit didn't feel in danger, much less know what a human was. She stayed absolutely quiet, breathing soundlessly and not even blinking her eyes for fear the rabbit would leave her alone. Laurel should see her now, she thought, well within her body, moving gracefully in the heart of time, but then the rabbit hopped off for reasons of its own. The message was dim but Laurel seemed to be asking a question.

"Mother, what about the water?"

Clare scrambled out, her hands skidding in the fresh mud. "Oh fuck!" she yelled, for the first time in her life. The bag was soaked but nearly empty with scarcely a gulp left down in a corner. She pressed her face into it for fear of losing any of the precious water, which tasted a little of the sunscreen lotion that had leaked there years ago.

How dumb. There was the sense that she was stuck in a children's story of enormous dimensions, one of those old Europeans out of *The Book House: Ramona fled, watching the barbarians destroy the village, hiding herself behind a tree on the edge of the dark forest.* Clare supposed that even if she did make her way back to the rest stop and drop a quarter in the pay phone the world could never repair itself. With a smile she imagined Donald's umbrage when the police asked him if he had abused his wife. And did he know who might own the red car traveling east? It was she who had set fire to the village before running into the dark forest, and now the consequences enlarged themselves as the sun reappeared casting a golden late afternoon light off the tassels. She was a free woman but would gladly have traded anything for a quart of cold water. Donald was also free to go home and soothe his wounds with his Bing Crosby collection that he liked to tell visitors "was known far and wide," at least among other collectors. Clare was not a bully, though, and raised in her mind some of Donald's good points: he was, surprisingly, a relentless lover; he had taken Laurel and Donald Jr. everywhere, from Disneyland to Busch Gardens, the Smithsonian, and the Museum of Natural History in New York (while Clare was at the Whitney), to Detroit Pistons games, to the Lions, to the Red Wings, to their corporate box for the Detroit Tigers, while Clare

stayed home and read or went on outings with Zilpha. Donald
loved the life outside the mind and slept like a rock, though he had
recently surprised her with a first edition of *Tar* to round out her
Sherwood Anderson collection. And last Christmas he had managed
to find Faulkner's book of poems *A Green Bough,* which, she overheard him telling a friend, cost him "an arm and a leg."

Clare cleaned the drying mud off her hands with a sharp stone
and tried not to think of water. Perhaps the beginning of the end
had been five years ago just after Donald Jr. had graduated from the
University of Michigan. Clare and Zilpha, on whim, had been late
additions to a list of matrons who wished to go on a Detroit Institute
of Arts tour of the museums of Moscow and Leningrad. Zilpha's visa
had come in ten days but Clare's had never arrived despite repeated
phone calls from her travel agent to Washington, and they had
missed the trip. Zilpha's husband, whom Donald loathed, was a big-
time liberal dope lawyer, and through the intercession of a black
congressman he discovered that Donald had jinxed the visa with a
phone call to a friend in the State Department, the sort of favor that
is due a major Republican fund raiser like Donald. When Clare con-
fronted him he had affected a minor breakdown, saying he couldn't
have borne up under the strain of his beloved wife's visiting the "evil
empire." Untypically, Clare thought of shooting him while he slept,
but instead she and Zilpha went off to Costa Rica to visit one of the
children whose survival the brochure and a letter said she
sponsored. This trip had also made Donald frantic despite the assur-
ances of his State Department friend that Costa Rica was "as safe as
Switzerland."

Clare was beginning to feel the mild dizziness brought on by hypothermia, a lightness in the head from her extreme thirst; vomiting
plus the long hot walk had pushed her to the edge of tolerance,
and though the late afternoon sun was cooling she found it unen-
durable. Back in her green cave she felt she was due another reassuring message from Laurel when her eyes lit on the cranberry juice
can. The camping book said to boil suspicious water for fifteen minutes. Of course. She grabbed the can and scrambled on her hands
and knees through the dense thicket toward what she thought of as
the distant sound of water, much increased after the cloudburst.

Unfortunately the Guernsey was less than twenty feet distant and Clare nearly catapulted down the slick, muddy bank into the sluggish, dark brown water, an inadvertent baptism by immersion, but she came up waist deep and laughing. The world that had been so narrowed by her physical and mental anguish became quite suddenly larger as she filled the cranberry juice can, resisting the strong temptation to drink the water straight.

Half an hour later Clare had the water bubbling away, the can stuck in a small mound of dirt and the fire crackling around it, with the dry grass and reed stalks kindling the dampish sticks found beneath the cottonwood tree. To extend her patience to the advised fifteen minutes she looked at her only book, the *Tao Te Ching,* for a few minutes but she was far too excited about the boiling muddy water to concentrate. The counselor at the pain clinic had told her that if she adapted all the principles of the volume to her life she could very well be cured of her migraines. Dr. Roth had not been sanguine on this prospect, saying that if she were Pope John XXIII or Martin Buber or Saint Theresa she would also be free of the disease. Clare carried the book along, though she had a childish aversion to Orientals, because the translator was the same as that of her favorite volume of Rilke, *The Sonnets to Orpheus.* The aversion had been occasioned by her father's service as a major during World War II, though he never got beyond Washington, D.C. One day Clare stayed home from kindergarten in order to ride along with her mother when she took her dad to the train station. He had been home on leave for only a few days when he was called back to Washington, and both of her parents had wept at the station. After the train pulled away her mother had told her that "he's off to fight Tojo." Clare knew that Tojo chopped the heads off American soldiers and she was terribly frightened at the idea of a headless father.

At the clinic in Arizona she had become friendly with a wheat farmer from Fort Dodge, Kansas, who was suffering a spinal defect, the accompanying spasms of which could strike him to the ground at any time. When they had all been given the *Tao* one evening at dinner he had been irritable, but in the morning he assured Clare that the "secrets" of the book might save them. She was startled at

this statement because Frank, the farmer, was critical of their counselor whom he referred to as a "goofy bastard," partly because the
counselor wore an earring. Frank had also been outspoken against
an Italian from Albany with a bone disease who had told Clare at the
dinner table that she had "nice stems." Frank had fairly shouted at
the Italian to mind his language. A plump woman from Pasadena
had piped up that there was nothing dirty about good legs, and the
table had agreed, with Frank leaving in a huff before dessert. After
that, despite the heat, Clare had worn slacks rather than hiking
shorts.

She carefully eased the can out of the mound of dirt with her
handkerchief, managing to burn the tip of a finger which she
ignored. Now she had to wait for the water to cool sufficiently and
glanced to the west at the setting sun, guessing that she had
another hour of daylight. She hoped to do at least three more of the
six-ounce cans, plus an extra for the night, before dark, and the sure
thought of removing this manic thirst made her feel giddy. It was so
utterly ordinary, this thirst, that it returned her solidly to earth, the
only concern being for immediate comfort.

"Laurel, I'm doing rather well considering. I was just wondering
if there were rattlesnakes around here."

"That's unlikely. They prefer rocky hillsides where they can find
rodents. I heard there are a few moccasins in the southern part of
the state but they'd be a rarity and you're well up in the middle.
The main problem might be mosquitoes."

"I've already noticed that. At what point does the daughter
become the mother?"

"You're not ready for that. I bet you still get a few passes."

"Perhaps. I certainly don't want to talk about it to my daughter."

"Back in high school my friends and I used to wonder if you and
Zilpha had some boyfriends stashed on your outings. We thought
you two were so thrilling."

"Everyone suspected that we might have gentleman friends,
and it was fun to let them think so. It used to drive your father a bit
crazy, and I'd say, 'But dear, you go on business trips at least once
a month and I don't wonder about you.'"

"You never suspected him?"

"I didn't really care."

"Then why did you hold on so long?"

"I had my friends, my books, dogs, garden, my children. Why does a husband have to be the absolute center of a married woman's life?"

"I don't know but they always are. Actually, I know you're the center of his life, with making money a close second."

"Are you suddenly getting warm about your father?"

"No, it was only an observation."

"I'm the center like a prized possession. Remember when I wouldn't go to any more fund raisers after I was introduced as a 'prominent Republican wife,' with no name attached. It seemed to stand for something quite out of focus."

"That was funny, also sad. I'm sure you were sorely missed. Dad always liked to pretend we had more money than we did. I mean, we had plenty so why pretend? Kevin pointed out my trust would have grown as much in a savings account as it did under Dad's care."

"Was Kevin upset?"

"Not at all. It's just Dad always treats him as if as a veterinarian he has his head in the clouds, when if you pull a difficult calf or help a mare drop a foal it's pretty realistic."

"Businessmen would be utterly destroyed if they didn't think they were the most practical men on earth. Lawyers tend to be that way too. Zilpha's husband used to say that a lawyer was society's proctologist. Sadly, that was the only charming thing he ever said."

"You miss her terribly, don't you? And Sammy too?"

"More than I dreamed possible. Strangely, I couldn't have done this if they had still been with me. It was a pleasure to give so much to them because I loved them. Then they were gone and I had to do something. I just tasted my hot water. It's somewhere between truck stop coffee and the average veal glacé in a Detroit restaurant, the kind where they slip in a bouillon cube. I'd better get busy now."

"Keep me posted. Remember, you don't have to spend the night. There's still time to make it back to the highway if you hurry."

"No thanks, dear."

Clare finished her first can of water with pleasure, spitting out a bit of grit that had accumulated at the bottom and setting out for the next. It was similar to weeding her large herb garden because she didn't think about anything except what she was doing, though thoughts might float easily in and out. The difference was that she didn't try to hold on to the thoughts so that the bad ones disappeared on their own accord.

On the third trip, when her thirst was somewhat abated and the sun was beginning to set, she made her way down the riverbank searching for more wood. Just past the single cottonwood tree there was a large branch she tugged away from clinging vines as if she had found the mother lode. If she could keep a small fire going she wouldn't miss a flashlight so much. If you're going to leave your husband, take a flashlight. That was about as sensible as the rules could get for the time being. A movement in the vines startled her and an opossum scurried out, looked at Clare and flopped over in fake death. She had seen this twice before in her garden back home and it was difficult not to draw certain parallels, amusing ones, though if you played dead long enough the act of coming back to life was questionable. Of the seven women who had been in her tennis group (the A class) a decade ago, four had been divorced in the past few years and none of them were doing very well, but then it was so easy to be smug about her own passivity, the way she let the years float gently by, relying on Zilpha's natural ebullience, two long walks a day with Sammy, hours of reading and cooking, the latter more for herself than for Donald who ate everything she cooked him with equal gusto.

Back at the campsite she coaxed the dwindling fire back to life, broke up the branches and put the sticks in a neat pile, stooping there, impatient for the water to boil. There was a reassuring chatter of birds but she guessed there was at most only a half hour of daylight. She put down a layer of corn leaves, then pulled enough dry marsh grass to cover them, to protect her sleep from the ground's dampness. She took off her skirt and blouse, hung them on a stick and held the clothes over the fire to draw out the slight amount of moisture left from her river plunge. It was a balmy night, but with nothing to wrap herself in but her own arms she was sure she would be cold by morning.

It was so strange to stand there nearly naked, feeling the smoke and heat purl up her body, with just enough darkness to make her legs and tummy golden. She felt good enough for the moment not to have to think of herself as an admirable person. If Zilpha had been there she would have been smoking the cigarettes that killed her. It had been her nature to defy everything, just as many intelligent men drink themselves to death. Right up until the last day Zilpha had said she had no regrets about dying, and on the last day she had only joked, "I'm not absolutely sure this is a good idea. Too bad I can't call and let you know." With her husband her eyes had brimmed with tears and she had merely shook her head. It was by common consent the lousiest marriage in the neighborhood and everyone wondered why they bothered to hang on.

Clare stuck her clothes stake in the ground and decided once again to make sense out of the *Tao,* especially a single line Frank had thought was so wonderful. The line was disappointingly sparse: "Thus whoever is stiff and inflexible / is a disciple of death." Frank had said that he'd spent thirty years being angry at the United States Department of Agriculture over grain prices and all of that energy had been wasted, and the anger had vastly accelerated his back problems. Clare and Frank had been talking in the shade of an enormous boulder; hiding, in fact, from the counselor who was being especially captious and unnerving that day, or so they thought. The twelve of them were being led on a "meditation hike" and were supposed to be dispersed in a boulder-strewn valley to sit alone and concentrate on a double-faced question: "Do you want to live?" and, simply enough, "Who dies?" There was also an admonition to keep alert for rattlesnakes. To break up the obvious tedium and anguish of the questions, Frank and Clare, through hand signals, had met behind the boulder for a chat.

"What the hell does that hippie mean? Suicide's not Christian."

"It's not supposed to be something to get angry about," Clare said without a good deal of conviction. "He says that our bodies are quarreling with themselves and that makes them hard to heal. He's not the USDA. They don't wear earrings."

Frank smiled, then developed a stricken look so Clare massaged his back and shoulders. Clare had seen one of his seizures the first day of the clinic and had doubted that she could handle one behind the boulder. He had twisted on the floor of the dining area and at one point his entire weight was supported by his heels and the back of his head, his trunk thrusting upward. Now his back softened from iron to clay under her hands and they embraced for a moment but he began weeping after he kissed her. At the time she wished she had the gumption to seduce him despite the consequences, whatever they might be. After that incident Frank was embarrassed when talking to her, as if he had behaved badly, and she didn't know how to tell him otherwise. At the end of the clinic Frank's wife picked him up and she looked overplump and spiteful to Clare.

Back at the fire Clare felt the warm smoking clothes and decided she wasn't inflexible, at least compared to Donald, but maybe that was one thing wrong with marriage, or smallish social settings, where the comparisons were so limited. Her brother felt he never drank more than his three best friends, but the four of them had all nearly drunk themselves to death, and were at present all leading lights in the AA for the Detroit area. The sheer taffy in self-awareness exhausted her. Saying that you were no more inflexible than your husband was small-minded dogshit, and she laughed out loud. She wanted more life, not *Robert's Rules of Order.* Crossing a fence was certainly a start, a flexible one at that. It occurred to Clare that while Zilpha swore occasionally, and Laurel repeatedly, she had never learned how. "Fuck you, Donald, you jerkoff," she whispered to the gathering dark, but the oath was froth. "Jerkoff" was what the boys who worked at the neighborhood gas station called each other. They always glanced down at her legs while they were doing the windshield. If she was wearing a tennis skirt they did an especially good job at the windshield. Quite suddenly a blush rose to Clare's face as she thought of Zilpha's son Michael. It had been an unforgivable mistake, and constituted her only secret from Zilpha.

"It's okay, Mother. It was the right thing to do."

"No it wasn't. I was never so ashamed of myself. How did you know?"

"Michael told me way back when. I think it was four years ago, right after it happened. He called to say he was going to ask you to run away to New York with him. He wondered if I thought it was a good idea." Laurel and Michael had been close since childhood, an unlikely pair, with Michael as obsessed with art as Laurel was with the life sciences.

"How absurd. It was stupid of me to let it go that far. I must have been sleepwalking." Clare put on her warm, smoky clothes in defense. The clothes felt wonderful against her skin.

"I doubt that. The last thing I ever felt when I was making love was asleep."

"You're simple-minded if you think I'm going to talk to you about it."

"Suit yourself. What I'm trying to say is that your night is going to be long enough without feeling guilty about something so innocent. If you get hungry just roll a couple of ears of that field corn in that wet clay and lay them at the edge of the fire. By the time the clay dries and hardens the corn will be ready. Not great, but better than nothing. I love you. Good night."

"I love you. You didn't tell anyone, did you?"

"Of course not. And I doubt Michael will ever write his memoirs.

"Thanks. Good night."

Clare picked two ears of corn and rolled them in the remains of a mud puddle until they were covered with a thickish layer of clay. It was a messy business and she dried her hands before the fire until she could flake off the clay. Perhaps Laurel was right. She felt guilt because she had pretended she only made love to Michael to get out of an uncomfortable situation, but then Michael was as removed from a rapist as could be imagined. A modest "no" would have pushed him over. Also, it was soon after Donald's nasty interference in her Russian trip, but she recognized that was only a minuscule part of it. In fact, Donald hadn't been given a thought.

"Be honest with yourself," Laurel chimed in from the dark.

"Why? Okay, then. At the moment Michael reminded me of a young English instructor I studied with as a freshman. I knew we both wanted to make love but there were rules against it and besides we were too shy. When I came back as a sophomore I found out he had committed suicide that summer in New York City. Every time I got a crush on someone, they moved to New York. I chose badly."

"Did he leave a note?"

"Not that I know of. Once we had coffee at a cafeteria and he gave me some bad advice. He told me that literature was so rich with possibility that I could safely ignore life itself. I asked him why Pasternak had said that despite all appearances, it took a lot of volume to fill a life. He told me Pasternak's reputation had been discounted by the higher critics. Two of his colleagues passed our table and one of them winked at him as if I were his bimbo."

"Which is what you wanted to be."

"You might say that. When I met your father I made sure he didn't get away."

"I know all about that one. It fails to interest. Anyway, Michael said you only had that single event. As they say, don't sweat it. I made love to him once myself when we were fourteen. We smoked a marijuana cigarette, drank some wine and did it. We decided afterwards that we wouldn't let it ruin our friendship. Actually we fell asleep and Zilpha caught us. She broke out laughing and closed the door."

"So I heard. We didn't come to any conclusions when we discussed it."

"You two never had any secrets, did you?"

"I never told her I made love to her son. It still bothers me.

"Oh, for Christ's sake, Mother. The corn should be roasted by now."

"Good night, dear."

"Keep in touch if you get lonely."

"I will."

Clare tapped the baked clay with her knuckles to no effect, then used a stone to break it. The green shucks steamed on the night air and she waited for them to cool. What had happened one day was that she and Zilpha were supposed to help Michael pack up to move to New York after a morning tennis game. Zilpha looked terrible, having spent the night arguing with her husband, plus she had a summer cold, so Clare volunteered to go solo on the packing chores. She went straight to his studio apartment from the tennis game and found him untypically organized. Michael had given all of his furniture to friends, and he wandered around the apartment stuffing what he called simply his "art" into portfolios, wearing pajamas which was all he ever wore unless it was absolutely necessary to wear clothes. If the trip was to the grocery store or to his mother's house he'd slip a raincoat over the pajamas.

Clare began by disassembling some large unstretched frames. Michael, more than anyone she had ever met, had no abilities outside of his imagination, nor was he interested in any. Michael and his father had given up on each other in his early teens, and he kept his doting mother at an affectionate distance. He developed a few friendships among other burgeoning artists at Cranbrook, and he and Laurel kept close though she went to Country Day, but Michael had been considered pretentious and unlikable in the neighborhood. He had not been at the club since his fourteenth birthday when he took off his clothes and pissed in the fireplace. He was flunked out of Rhode Island School of Design for a total lack of interest, spent a year in Paris and Florence, then came home for a few years in Detroit where his paintings caused a minor rage in the art community. The paintings were a bit of a puzzle to Clare because Michael painted only what he called "the insides of things": animals, engines, clouds, trees, women. For a year or so on his return from Europe Clare and Michael had become close again, just as they were when he was young. She helped him hang his paintings at several galleries, bought not a few of them and had lunch with him at least once a week at a restaurant that indulged him his pajamas. Donald didn't begrudge the time she spent with Michael, never referring to him as anything but "the poor little bugger," though Michael was of average size. Of course he seemed a bit effeminate, but then Donald and his cronies were sure that all men but themselves betrayed gay tendencies, even professional hockey players. This was a mystery to Clare when she listened to their after-dinner jokes. Sadly to her, Michael sensed charity in her continued purchase of paintings and began to keep her at a distance. Only in the last few weeks before his move to New York had they become quite friendly again.

That day in the dull, humid heat of a Detroit July Michael surprised her with her favorite wine, a Château d'Yquem, saying that he wished he had swiped it from his father but he had bought it himself. They drank the wine on the floor, her back against the wall, but Michael sprawled in front of her. He told her about a recent adventure with a lovely black girl who had decided he was too crazy and went back to her musician. He was a bit sad about that and said so. The wine was nearly gone and they had lapsed into silence when he looked at her strangely.

"I'm finding you quite exciting," he said.

"I'm the same person I've always been."

"That's not what I mean."

"Michael, I don't believe that. You're teasing me." She blushed deeply, unable to look at his eyes. "You shouldn't tease about such things."

"I'm not teasing."

He put a hand around her ankle and she let a leg straighten out. His other hand covered the crotch of his pajamas where it was obvious that he wasn't teasing. She closed her eyes and said, "Oh, well," with her ears buzzing. He made love to her quickly there on the floor and she was embarrassed at her excitement. Afterwards, they stood in the kitchen apologizing to each other in miserable half sentences, then went back into the main room where she tried to think of a graceful way to pick up her panties on the bare floor. They stood there for a few minutes, then he embraced her strongly and they took off everything and made love for quite a long time, ending with exhaustion, then laughter. He yelped when she put hydrogen peroxide on his raw knees.

The ear of corn was much better than Clare had reason to expect, lacking sweetness but full-flavored. It was now dark but a three-quarter moon was rising, a cream-colored globe barely above the horizon. A full moon would have been too dramatic, she reflected. One of the grandest times ever with her father had been a long walk one night in the summer during a full moon up near their cottage on Burt Lake. They had taken the long way through a virgin oak forest down to a Chippewa graveyard near the lake, and her father, who was inventive for an accountant, made up new variations on the Robin Hood stories. When they reached the white picket fence of the cemetery she clutched his hand tightly as they looked out over the crosses at the sheen of the moon on the lake. At this juncture her father always tried to spook her by saying in a whisper,

"Perhaps there'll be a message from the spirit world," but this time when he finished they heard from far out on the lake the tremulous wail of a loon as if it had been arranged. He clutched her hand as hard as she did his, then they laughed at their fright and made unsuccessful loon imitations.

Clare considered saving the second ear for morning, then thought why bother, since she was surrounded by virtually millions of them. The idea that she probably wouldn't have married Donald if her father hadn't died was less interesting at the moment than Robin Hood. Michael had sent her a book of poems called *Roots and Branches* by Robert Duncan, whom she had never heard of; the poems were splendid though difficult, and now she could remember an entire passage she had copied in her ledger:

> Robin Hood in the greenwood outside
> Christendom faces peril as if it were a friend.
> Foremost we admire the outlaw
> who has the strength of his own
> lawfulness. How we loved him
> in childhood and hoped to abide by his code
> that took life as its law!

The day after her lovemaking with Michael she and Zilpha had a final lunch with him, then a trip to the airport. It was an unsuccessful event with the only lighter moments provided by the memory of the time the three of them had packed a picnic basket to search for Michael's car which he had "misplaced" a week before. They had driven all the way to Zug Island near Wyandotte to consult an actual Gypsy fortune teller who, startlingly enough, had pinpointed the lost car within a block of Wayne State University. It seemed terribly funny when they had arrived at the car and found the tires were gone.

At the restaurant Zilpha went off to the bathroom and Michael suggested, half seriously, that they get rid of her and make love in the airport parking lot. Clare became angry and said, "Never again," and Michael paled. He was quite hopeless and she didn't hear from him again for several years until his mother's funeral, where he looked harsh, thin, hardened, which she supposed was part of living in New York. They were both weeping over Zilpha when they embraced, and Michael pinched her bottom and whispered, "I'm willing when you are." She stepped back sensing the kind of humor that arises out of grief, but no, he wasn't kidding.

Clare stirred the fire and wondered if her diminished pile of sticks would last, but then even the slightest of fires would suffice to leaven the balmy night. She feared the dissociation of waking up in the middle of the night to total blackness, though the moon should be a modest compensation. She rearranged the wood where she could reach it from her green cave, and firmed some dirt around her can of water so she wouldn't inadvertently tip it over. She wished she felt a little stronger when she curled up for sleep and thought again of the notion of prayer, but she lacked the solace of a religion that does not depend on ignoring the human condition. When she prayed as a child God's face in her mind was similar to her father's — the graying hair, the furrowed brow, the essentially kind look that was still not interested in trivialities. Her childhood prayer from Sunday school was simple enough: "Now I lay me down to sleep, I pray the Lord my soul to keep. If I should die before I wake, I pray the Lord my soul to take." Curled there on her bed of leaves and grass, Clare thought this prayer lacked a great deal in terms of reassurance. She didn't want the Lord to take her soul in the night; she wanted to go to Europe without having to listen to Donald's incessant business prattle. In the nave of Notre-Dame he had whispered, "Remind me to make a call," as if he ever forgot. In the Uffizi he couldn't stop saying, "I wonder what this would bring at Parke-Bernet."

The world itself was a marketing possibility. Before he had played his *Tracking the Blues* tape today in the car he had interrupted a favorite Stravinsky passage by saying that local acreage was recovering from the 1985 downturn, though Donald Jr. had said pork bellies had the flutters but would really firm up by Labor Day. A signal announcement had been that the black walnut tree in their backyard was worth seven thousand bucks as furniture veneer, and that walnut tree thieves were circulating the Midwest waiting for the innocent to go on vacation. Curiously enough, Donald didn't mind when she asked him to write a large check for the American Indian

College Fund or the NAACP, two of her favorite charities, saying something to the effect that "those folks got the wrong end of the stick," as if all American history had been a business deal. Maybe it was. Donald had tried to hedge at her support of the Nature Conservancy and Greenpeace because he felt the bird watchers and "little old ladies in tennis shoes" were cramping certain resort complexes in northern Michigan that were otherwise good investment potentials. Clare reminded him that if she wasn't already a little old lady in tennis shoes, it could clearly be seen on the horizon.

But how could you blame Donald for so fulsomely taking on the colors of the workaday world? Perhaps the lines were drawn more clearly than she had ever thought, and that was why she lay curled in a thicket staring at the weak light of a cottonwood fire. One autumn afternoon when she was helping her father comb burrs out of the long hair of their English setters she had asked him why the Bible said it was easier for a camel to get through the eye of a needle than for a rich man to enter heaven. He treated the question gravely and said that if all your mind is full of is money you become crazy, and that insane people live in a private hell without even knowing it, and that insane rich people created a hell for a lot of other people without knowing or caring about it. As simplistic as this seemed Clare still essentially believed it. Her father said it and he looked like God, though he had done a lot of bad things to her without knowing it. He couldn't have done them on purpose.

Clare sat up as a lump had begun to form beneath her breastbone at the first indication of certain childhood memories. She put a fresh stick on the fire and watched its brief, feverish blaze. She always read herself to sleep and the absence of this routine was haunting. She would have read the footnotes in the *Tao* if there had been enough light. She studied a book of matches from a truck-stop restaurant in Illinois called R Place where they had stopped for lunch on the way out. The restaurant gave a special award and inscribed the name on a plaque of anyone who could eat a four-pound hamburger. The waitress had told Clare that the meat patty was only a little over three pounds but the bun and all the fixings brought the weight up to an even four. For some reason this disgusted Donald who thought the idea "lowlife." The waitress pointed out a burly trucker on the other side of the room who was on his way to victory. Clare excused herself to wash her hands and passed by the trucker on the way to the bathroom, though the trucker was well out of the way. She paused at the table.

"I hope you manage. It looks wonderful," she said.

"You look pretty damn good yourself. I'd give you a bite but I'd be disqualified."

She waved and passed on, wondering if the man had a wife and what she looked like.

Now she reached out and put her beret on tight for extra comfort. She took off her watch and stowed it in the bag thinking if she kept looking at it time itself would swallow her. It was extraordinary that at one moment she could be thinking of making love to Michael on the floor and at the next she was trying to devise a prayer appropriate to the situation. Back to the basics, she joked: religion, fucking and Dad at the cemetery.

When and if she emerged her friends and acquaintances back in the neighborhood were bound to prate "nervous breakdown" or "depression" during countless phone calls and lunches. One of the favorite local psychiatrists was an ardent pill pusher in his efforts to remove any socially embarrassing symptoms. The probable cause in her case would be obvious to all—the deaths of Zilpha and Sammy—but her marriage, which was considered to be improbably solid, would not be questioned. The same psychiatrist had offered nothing when she had gone to him, troubled about Donald Jr.'s apparent lack of morals in school. He seduced innocent, homely girls and kept a tally, cheated wherever possible on school work, plagiarized term papers and, as a school leader, made problems for teachers who didn't give him good grades. The psychiatrist had dismissed all of this as Donald Jr.'s effort to take short cuts into his father's world, and when sufficient negative reinforcement came from his "peer group" the behavior would cease. Unfortunately for this theory Donald Jr. continued to be widely admired as charming and capable. His SATs were too mediocre to get him into an Ivy League college, which his father hoped for, but strings were pulled and he was accepted at University of Michigan where he became the president of his fraternity. Donald Jr. had always been impeccably dressed, even for a trip to the 7-Eleven, while Laurel, who had gone to Northwestern, was a slob, drank beer and smoked marijuana, and graduated summa cum laude. She had also been the best student in her class at Michigan State's veterinary school, neither of which honors made more than a cursory dent in her father's consciousness.

There was a rustling in the thicket off to the left and Clare's pulse quickened, but then a barred owl called from the cottonwood and Clare supposed the other creatures were making adjustments to keep out of the owl's way. At one time Donald Jr.'s character had been puzzling because she was blinded by the fact that he had been a much more loving child than Laurel, helping Clare in the garden, arranging his Audubon cards, building bird houses, acting as a deft little "sous chef" when she cooked. It was as if during puberty he woke up, looked around and decided to become a child of his time.

Clare wriggled closer to the opening for a look at the moon and stars, then sat up and stuffed her bag with dry grass for a pillow. This camping had its moments but she was claustrophobic enough to dread tents, elevators and theater lines, and the stars and moon were a tonic after the dark lid of her thicket. There was still the slightest twinge of pain in her left lobe and she monitored the size of the speck of green light. She heard a strain of Monteverdi, then a bar of *The Firebird,* and the light diminished. With Laurel the light was steady but the images of Donald and Donald Jr. increased it. She searched for good memories to control her fear of another attack.

When they were first married and Donald had just entered the firm as an assistant office manager he still wore his lumberjack shirts in the evening and on weekends. He hadn't finished his senior thesis, an essay, ironically enough, on Thorstein Veblen's *Theory of the Leisure Class,* so through the long winter of the pregnancy Clare had actually written most of the thesis. She thought Donald talked brilliantly but didn't write well, while she was shy but wrote well, if a little too carefully. Some of Donald's politically active friends from Michigan State were back in the Detroit area and they all met at least once a week. Donald would regale them with stories about the "bourgeoisie" at work and in the neighborhood near their Birmingham apartment.

Clare's mother had busied herself in her grief by drinking even

more than usual and shopping for a perfect home for her daughter.
Clare's brother Ted, younger by five years, was in his junior year at
Kent, a prep school in Connecticut, his fourth in four years. When
her mother had finally found the home, she and Clare had spent a
great deal of time overseeing the redecorating. Clare was uncon-
cerned and felt the project was good therapy for her mother.
Meanwhile she and Donald and their scrubby friends ate at inexpen-
sive Polish, Italian, Chinese and Greek restaurants, and went to the
wonderful movies of those times: all of Bergman, Fellini and the
early Antonioni. They marched with other civil rights protesters,
hand in hand with blacks, and listened religiously each Sunday
morning to the wild-eyed sermons of the Reverend C. L. Franklin,
Aretha's father. They actually shook hands with the great man himself, Martin Luther King. He had said to Donald, "Keep up the good
work, brother," and Donald had beamed. Like so many others they
had been paralyzed with fear by the Cuban missile crisis. Clare had
been reading William Faulkner's *The Reivers* when she heard on WJR
that President Kennedy had been shot in Dallas. Donald rushed
home from work and they wept together, glued to the icy, catatonic
replays on television.

One evening, before they had moved into the house, all of their
friends had come over for dinner and to listen to blues and jazz
records on their new stereo. Donald discoursed on Charlie Parker,
Muddy Waters, B. B. King and the primitive discs recorded by Alan
Lomax, before carefully putting the needle on the record. Among
their favorites were Forest City Joe singing "Chevrolet" and Vera
Hall's "Can't You Hear That Wild Ox Moan." Clare thought that perhaps that evening had been the beginning of the end. Laurel had
been sick with a cold, and Clare at the time was a distinctly amateur
cook. Hearing of the party, her mother had volunteered to send over
a little something from the club. Two waiters showed up at 8 P.M.
sharp when the guests were groggy from Gallo burgundy and fam-
ished to despair. Clare went into the bathroom, embarrassed to the
point of tears when the food arrived. She primped herself, wiped
away her tears, blew her nose and emerged when she heard the
shouts of joy from the other room. There were only ten of them but
her mother had sent over a huge prime rib roast, a Smithfield ham,

side dishes including six dozen oysters, a mixed case of French wine and two cases of imported beer. Their friends were utterly thrilled with the food, without a single negative comment. They ate, drank, danced and laughed, and at the bleary end of the party Clare wrapped up ample packages of leftovers for each of the guests.

In the morning they had the first serious argument of their marriage, over, oddly enough, a novel by James Baldwin and a profile of Malcolm X in a Detroit newspaper. A week later they moved into the house and things were never the same again, nor were they meant to be. Despite his jokes about work Donald had become a well-concealed predator, a skilled manipulator, something he had learned as a political activist, and was earning a degree in accounting at night school at the University of Detroit. During the longish evenings alone Clare began reading again and hadn't stopped since. Over the long haul she couldn't have endured Donald without her books, but now the idea of the books without Donald seemed rather nice. Two years after Laurel, who had been nicknamed "Papoose," Donald Jr. was born, and when Donald arrived late at the hospital with three dozen roses he announced, in his first tailored suit, that he had been elected a member of the Detroit Athletic Club. Clare put down the book she was reading, a novel called *The Deer Park* by Norman Mailer, in which there were no deer to be found but lots of intriguing bad behavior. She remembered looking closely at Donald, a long pause where she waited patiently for him to mention the birth of his son.

Clare dozed for a half hour, waking fearfully with a deep chest pain, then smiled because she had rolled over and clenched a fist against her heart, mistaking it for an attack. The fire was down to embers and she decided to use the largest of the sticks in hope that it would last until she slept long and deeply, if ever. She strained above the hiss and sputter of the fire to hear something just on the edge of the audible. There it was again. And again. A dog barking far to the south, she imagined in some barnyard at the outer edge of the arc thrown by a porch light, the dog's body stiffening as it barked at the night as Sammy's body had every single night just before bedtime. It was an unimaginably comforting sound and tears of joy formed in her throat. How wonderful it would have been to have the dog with her, not for protection, as Sammy's bravura was mostly fake, but for companionship. Sammy had been afraid of cats and snakes, but her thunderous bark warned away possible intruders and door-to-door salesmen and the irksome approach of Jehovah's Witnesses. For unclear reasons she liked the Federal Express man but loathed the one for UPS. The black furnace repairman once threw her into a fearsome rage which caused Clare to offer an embarrassed apology after she had closed Sammy up in the garage. The black man, who was about her age, looked at her strangely, then offered his hand. It turned out they had been in a civil rights march together well over twenty years before, and the man's little son who had played with Laurel in Hart Plaza now taught high school science in Ypsilanti. When the repairman left it wasn't the happiest occasion because the intervening years acquired the sharpest of focuses. The man had mentioned seeing her name in the *Detroit News* where she had been referred to rather nastily as a "well-heeled liberal environmentalist."

At dinner when she brought up the repairman Donald had become vague and nearly morose for a minute. It had been difficult for him lately as one of his minor saving graces was an abiding concern for probity in government, and the successive scandals in Pentagon procurement, HUD, and the enormity of the savings-and-loan mess disturbed him deeply. She tended to go easy on him on the rare occasions when he became vulnerable, but two summers before, near Bay View in Petoskey, they had come upon a ragged Chippewa selling Korean-made moccasins. Clare had bought several pairs, quipping that the Chippewa apparently didn't own any oil wells, a reference to a Reagan gaff. They usually avoided political discussions, settling for canceling each other's vote at the polls.

Laurel, however, was merciless and could redden Donald's face by saying that she wanted to go to Costa Rica and speak Latin just like Dan Quayle. Laurel was never particularly interested in novels or poetry, and her single misquote was from Yeats, the sense being that while the best lacked all conviction, the worst were full of passionate intensity. That appeared to sum up Laurel's feelings toward the political world. Donald Jr. tended merely to be a more cynical version of his father. Clare herself had come to the point that all the highest hopes of her twenties had dissembled to the degree that she was relegated to writing checks to distant organizations and trying to save the occasional pond, creek or sorry woodlot in Michigan. The heady idealism of the Labor State had died with Walter Reuther, and the prospects for social services and the environment had become dismal in the face of lobbyists' opportunism.

Fortunately, the thought of politics made her sleepy, though sodden might be a better word, she thought. She heard the dog's bark a little more clearly and there was an eerie moment when she thought it might be her own ghost dog, but the image of it barking out its loneliness under the porch light was dominant. The stars and the moon didn't seem quite high enough, and she remembered Donald's chagrin when they added a master bedroom with a sixteen-foot ceiling. Clare couldn't stay in newish hotels where the windows didn't open. She often regretted her mother's gift of a house so soon after they were married. Money tended to derange people when it arrived so abruptly, and the house wasn't, ultimately, fair to Donald. The ceilings were high in Europe but less equitable societies made her nervous after a few weeks. When this was over she intended to live in an apartment or in a smallish house on the far edge of a town. It would be near a woods and farm country. She would find a job in a library or bookstore where she could make herself useful, a sense she had lost since Donald Jr. had gone off to college. The woman who ran the local office for the charity in Costa Rica had said she was an overworked volunteer and that sounded good to Clare. The woman had advised against visiting the child and she was right. The family had been fearful that something might be taken from them, that they were being judged, but they had warmed to Zilpha and the atmosphere had become relaxed in the one room stucco cottage near Punta Arenas.

Clare traced a finger across the dew gathering on her face. She had learned enough Spanish to translate the thank you notes from the child who was now in her early teens. The parents had been painfully shy but the second child, a boy of seven, was perfectly round and had thought everything about Zilpha was funny. Clare's mother definitely had been a problem drinker and Clare thought again of the nightmares caused by rich, overgenerous alcoholics.

The new, homely word "yuppie" had been devised for the grandchildren of the Depression and she wondered how gracefully they
would age. Another ugly word was "schmucks." Last Christmas
when Donald Jr. came home from Chicago with a rather pretty but
vacant girl, he told Clare her "main problem" was that she expected
too much from people when they were really only schmucks.

Sleep was too far away for the clumsiest of prayers. She got up,
put another stick on the fire and looked at her bed in the brief
yellow flare-up. It was the nest of a not very skilled animal, a temporary measure like a deer bed in high grass. She turned and the wider
row she had come down a lifetime ago was now aligned with the
moon, a darkling path between silvered leaves which a breeze was
lightly rustling. It was a path from a children's book of the twenties
in the golden age of illustration, lovely, foreboding, irresistible. She
decided to walk herself to sleep as she did so often with her dog at
home. Donald had bought her a small pistol which she never took
along because the presence of a pistol would have changed the nature of the walk. And Sammy, though still frightened by cats,
thought she was a grizzly bear after dark. Besides, she was in fine
trim, and asked Donald why they'd remained in so otiose a
neighborhood if it wasn't the safest in the Detroit area. She could
tell he didn't know what "otiose" meant but pretended he did as he
watched Pisor, his favorite late-news baritone. *Oh, fuck Donald,* she
reminded herself. *I am here because he isn't.*

She set off at a relaxed but steady pace, fixed on the moon as if
she were trying to walk to a place directly under it. After a few hundred yards she quickened her gait and felt that delightful sense that
her joints had become oiled, and the night air was sweet and drink-
able. Dr. Roth liked to say that the overexamined life was not worth
living, and that the quasi-upper-class life had become the shabbiest
of self-improvement videos. Goddamn but her mind was so
exhausted with trying to hold the world together, tired of being the
living glue for herself, as if she let go, great pieces of her life would
shatter and fall off in mockery of the apocalypse. Or it would simply
deflate, letting off its sour air like a punctured rubber ball. She was
delighted when she thought she saw the moon move a bit as it
must. Time moved the moon. You should be lucky enough to be

there when the tree falls in the desert. Dr. Roth, who was fascinated with the history of religions, gave her what he called a "nice Jewish present," *The Unvarnished Gospels,* a new translation by Gaus. The language was so stark and commonplace as to be almost unreadable.

The world is likely commonplace, she thought. There was the amusing memory of the second term of her sophomore year when East Lansing was frozen in dirty ice. She had met a boy in the periodicals room who was reading her favorite literary journal, *Botteghe Oscure,* edited in Rome by Marguerite Caetani. Clare's secret ambition was to be Marguerite Caetani's secretary and meet the French poet René Char, whose long poem "To a Tensed Serenity" was in the latest issue. The boy reading the journal was shabby, condescending, an avowed "beatnik" who smelled strongly of potato chips. She found him exciting though he looked down his pale, mottled nose at her pleated skirt and gray cashmere cardigan. The boy let her sit near him at Kewpee's, a cafeteria favored by the intellectual and artistic types, the latter having the advantage of smelling like paint rather than something else.

She and the boy would sit as close as possible to a table of seniors dominated by a strange-looking young man who, on alternate days, wore army surplus or the kind of suit and Chesterfield coat worn in her hometown. He was more vigorous and arrogant than her suicidal instructor and she and the boy listened raptly as the young man droned on about Rimbaud, Verlaine, Laforgue, Péguy, Alain-Fournier, Camus, Kierkegaard, Yesenin and the "obvious" structure of Joyce's *Finnegans Wake.* He had taken to glancing at her legs, now and then and once loudly told a story about fucking a fat, drunken waitress who wore an ankle bracelet which spelled "Herbert." One day the man looked over at her and asked her if she had read Dostoevsky, especially the new translation of his *Notebooks* wherein there was an entry about a girl who, one cold St. Petersburg afternoon, drank a bottle of wine and committed suicide out of boredom. She answered that she hadn't read Dostoevsky but Turgenev's *Sportsman's Sketches* was one of her favorites (it was actually her father's favorite). "That's good," he said, "but read *Fathers and Sons.* I'm actually Bazarov. Get off your pretty

ass and read all of Dostoevsky or you'll become a punching bag for
some Grosse Pointe fraternity boy." Then the man stood up and announced to his cronies that it was time to get drunk and play pool.
On the way out the man paused by her chair and pronounced
loudly that she was "edible" which confused her somewhat.

After she said goodbye to the boy she cut a class and went
immediately to the campus bookstore and bought all of the
Dostoevsky in the Modern Library editions, the Constance Garnett
translations. She read *The Idiot, The Gambler, Notes from Underground, The Possessed, Crime and Punishment* and *The Brothers
Karamazov.* Her eyes were hot red balls in her head but her life was
changed. The great Russian had devoured another piece of her each
time she wept over a hero or heroine, a grand conception, the marriage of heaven and hell that was his peculiar genius, and spat her
out in bones and gristle. But after she and the beatnik boy had
returned on three successive empty days they finally heard the
young man had suffered a nervous breakdown and had run off to
New York City, leaving a wife and child in married housing. Clare
stayed in her room for a week until a dorm counselor escorted her
to the campus psychiatric clinic where a sluggish doctor advised
her to construct some effective shields against her emotional life, a
project at which she proved most successful.

Her skin was moist and her breathing harder as the darkness of the
path ahead yielded to a lighter shade of gray. There was a hissing,
clicking sound which could have been a flying saucer had she not
recognized the sound of irrigation sprinklers from the golf course
near their home. The cornfield gave way to another huge field she
guessed must be soybeans, the sprinklers tossing water into the
moonlight as far as she could see to the east. Off to the north were
the soundless lights of trucks and cars on Route 80, with the illusion
at that distance that they were traveling slowly, creeping toward
Chicago or back west toward Omaha. There was a two-track lane
between the soybeans and corn and she walked south for a while,
hoping to see the light of a farmhouse. She wanted to hear the dog
bark and there was nothing, but she suspected everyone must be
asleep by now. She followed a thumping in the ground to a tall

thicket of grass and weeds growing up around the main outlet and valve for the irrigation system. She slid in a big puddle but maintained her balance, the water pleasantly icy on her hot feet. Where the main pipe curved up and out of the ground there was a wheel to turn the water off and on, and a large connecting pipe to the field, out of which came a steady gout of water from a bad fitting. Clare cupped her hands, pausing to let their warmth cut the water's icy edge to avoid the onset of a headache. The water was clean and marvelous after the tea-colored sludge from the creek and she stooped there drinking until she felt a little bilious. She slipped off her blouse, skirt, panties and bra, bathing herself slowly with her hands. She did not feel remotely sorry for herself which there had been a trace of earlier. Dr. Roth had a theory that self-pity was the most injurious emotion to mental and physical health. In the small desert town near the pain clinic a trinket store sold T-shirts that read, "The Pain People," which they all bought with irony and humor.

Clare let the breeze dry her off. People used to say "buck naked" and that's what she was, with more than a twinge of desire for Dr. Roth at the moment his image shifted out of the dark in connection with Dostoevsky. She felt quite free to think about making love to him because she knew it would never happen. It would break the etiquette of their affection for each other. For an uncharacteristic few seconds she thought that any farmer would do, or even the trucker who ate the four-pound hamburger, but certainly not Donald, who would not be caught dead out here unless he was bent on buying the farm. She was nearly dry and thinking about nothing in particular except how smooth and strong her body was for her age, when Dr. Roth arrived again. She had told him about the Dostoevsky incident at the bar of the Townsend Hotel and was miffed when he began laughing.

"Life is so unforgiving when you're nineteen," he said.

"And that makes my sad tale funny?"

"If it's not funny by now you might have to shoot yourself. That's what I mean by unforgiving. Actually, if you shoot anyone it should be the psychiatrist. All he did was try to lower the ceilings."

"I suppose he was tired of the anguish of hundreds of nineteen-year-olds."

"Then he should have gotten the fuck out of the business. You have to remain vulnerable to treat the vulnerable."

"I'm not so sure he could have said anything valuable."

"Of course he could. He might have said that neurotic intellectuals can be as dangerous as cheese-brained fraternity boys. He could have said if you really wanted the guy you could have closed the deal before you read all the books, but it probably wouldn't have been a good idea."

"But I didn't know I could have closed the deal."

"That's ladylike bullshit. You knew that on a particular level. I think it's intriguing that you wanted to fuck someone for their mind. I sure could have used that at nineteen." Dr. Roth nearly blushed at this, the first mention of sex between them, albeit abstract.

"I would have been twenty-six at the time, already an old lady for a nineteen-year-old." She was going to let him fry for a moment.

"That's not the way it works. I'd feel more comfortable talking about religion."

"I remember when I wrote about Apollinaire that he said Jesus held the world's high-altitude record. Is that religious enough?"

"It's definitely safer. We always like to think we're on the verge of danger when we're nearly immobile, don't we?"

"I suppose so. It's nice to hear that you think of yourself as no more adventurous than me."

"Now it's my turn to suppose so." He had become strained and distraught. "That's what is finally unforgiving. All of this mythological freedom we grow up on which we usually get to express standing around in a field wearing a baseball mitt. Or sailing a quarter-million-dollar sailboat down the Detroit River hoping the water won't corrode a hole in the bottom."

On the long walk back to her nest Clare remembered that Apollinaire left his wife by merely getting on a train and disappearing, but the idea of her own escape was too obvious to attribute to the poet. The beauty and dread of time was that nothing was forgiven. Not a single minute. The years she had spent in consideration of this act were not only lost, irretrievable, but the recognition of the loss was so naïve as to leave her breathless. And she lacked the convenient excuse of children to care for, or the most central excuse of all, poverty. The bondage for most women was not enough money to live on, especially if there were children. And for men there was the perpetual bondage of work and debt, to which was added so frequently a level of spending far beyond their means. In Clare and Donald's class it meant something quite different. Donald had explained several personal bankruptcies after Black Monday. A number of their club members had been making five hundred thousand a year but regularly spent seven hundred. This fact dumfounded Clare whose extravagances were limited to a good bottle of wine a day and rare books. On vacations she liked deluxe hotels but flew tourist class, which had always irritated Donald. She liked to send the difference to a charity so that it wasn't a matter of being an unpretentious skinflint.

Her brother Ted always seemed a more elegant version of Donald and tended to avoid seeing her except around the holidays when it was pro forma. He had been to Hazelden in Minnesota three times to dry out, and the last trip was to the Betty Ford which still didn't do the trick. What finally worked was a panel of doctors' absolute guarantee that he'd die within a year if he continued drinking. His three failed marriages and obsession with racing sailboats in the Great Lakes and the Caribbean had diminished his trusts by two-thirds, until he was forced to live quite modestly. Clare had loaned him a great deal of money over the years and this made Donald quarrelsome. Her brother liked to make her feel guilty by repeating that she had inherited all the good genes from their father, while he was stuck with the unstable propensities of their mother. Unfortunately, Dr. Roth had said, that was a possibility. The bottom line, Clare thought, was that her brother had been a bully since he was an infant, and had tended to bully himself into the middle of any misery he could find. To an unimaginable degree he had ruined his life and caused a great deal of pain to his wives and children. He was a living poster child for the evil potential of inherited wealth.

Clare was absurdly happy when she reached her nest, as if returning home from a tiring day. She tended to the remaining embers of the fire, bringing them to life with dry grass and sticks. There was a lightness in her body brought about by the fact that she did not give a flat fuck if she ever saw her brother or Donald again. It was as simple as that. She repeated the phrase "flat fuck" with the avowed intent to take up swearing as a pressure valve. The phrase was used by April, a rotund woman Clare and Zilpha met up near Pellston the October before on an outing. It was at a small county park on a lake, the autumn colors so stridently lovely as to approach banality, with Sammy swimming through the red and yellow leaves on the lake. When Sammy finished swimming she came up to Clare and waited patiently for Clare to pick the wet maple leaves off her back, then rolled vigorously in the dust and ashes of a campfire site. Zilpha had started a fire in the small Weber grill they traveled with, using the dry split oak that was kept neatly tied in a bundle. From home Clare had brought the salad, the dressing, and a pheasant Donald had shot at a hunting preserve near Holly. The pheasant had looked a bit lean so she had split it in half before daylight that morning, puréed butter, fresh thyme and sage and forced the mixture gently up under the skin while Donald was already barking on the phone in the breakfast nook.

April was driving down the gravel road when she blew a tire with a shotgun sound not fifty yards from them, and Sammy rushed into the woods, remembering the few times she had been used as a bird dog in her youth. April got out of the car with her five-year-old daughter, a chubby miniature of her mother.

"I can't believe this fucking shitass car," April hollered with a volume that brought Sammy running back from the woods.

Zilpha and Clare went to her aid. There was a bald spare tire but no jack among the hundreds of returnable beer cans in the trunk. Zilpha got the jack from the Toyota and swiftly changed the tire which amazed April. Zilpha's husband was a car buff, and before their marriage had ruptured into boredom they had restored a number of old cars together.

"Lady, you could get a job in a flat-fucking garage," April said. She continued to talk, bearing down on the day's problems, with every sentence peppered with phrases polite folks think of as filth. Zilpha and Clare couldn't help but begin to laugh and April said she was sorry but she always talked that way. Meanwhile the child was off throwing a stick into the lake for the dog, her voice pealing out, "Bring it back, you son-of-a-bitch." Clare asked April if she'd like a drink or something to eat. April said she had just had lunch but "I could use a fucking drink to turn the day around."

They sat at the picnic table drinking white wine with Clare getting up now and then to tend the broiling pheasant, watching the child wrestle with the wet dog. April was a local and worked as a barmaid up the road. Her ex-husband was a welder in Detroit but was in jail on assault. She had had his checks garnisheed but he wasn't getting paid in jail so times were hard. Zilpha took down the information, saying that her husband might be able to look into it. Then April said, "Where do you gals work?" and there was an embarrassed silence.

"We're sort of housewives," Clare said, and April said she had tried that once but it "bored the shit out of me." She liked working in the bar because you could shoot the shit with the customers, and if you got a little horny you could always find someone. Clare had set out a small wheel of Camembert and cut a wedge for the daughter who was eyeing it. The child smelled the cheese, announced loudly that it smelled like poop and ran off again with Sammy. When April left she thanked them profusely, took one more swig from the bottle of wine and said, "You fucking ladies got it all." When she was gone their laughter was mixed with a little melancholy. The pheasant was delicious and Sammy got a chunk of raw shin bone of beef that had been packed for her in a cellophane sack.

That had been their next to last outing before Zilpha's diagnosis had come, right after Thanksgiving. In early December they went off to a spa near Tecate in northern Sonora, just a few hours south of San Diego. The trip had its moments but the diagnosis was too fresh in mind to try to ignore. After the first day of group exercise they gave up the program in favor of hiking in the mountains, most of the time well off the marked trails.

They had been at the spa together a decade earlier, and since then it had vastly upgraded its facilities, and the clientele had become a bit more hard and glitzy. One evening in the dining hall Zilpha said, "We're all the same here," and it was true. Other than a dozen men there were nearly ninety women, between the ages of forty and sixty, but a concentration around fifty. More than age, the women seemed to be fighting a malaise of fatigue and dissociation, of free-floating anxiety so deeply ingrained as to be invisible to the bearer. The regimen of a vegetarian diet and relentless exercise in a lovely setting far from home, the source of the gray-area angst, worked quite well, and within two days spirits were lifted. It was a break, not a cure, a shifting into a pleasant neutral where the body's exhaustion supplanted the brain's dreary machinations. Unfortunately, given the death sentence of Zilpha, the function of the place was too clearly scribed, so they took refuge in the mountains, packing along water bottles, hard-boiled eggs and oranges, descending in the late afternoon to start a fire in the fireplace and drink a glass of wine before dinner. Clare had been thrilled to discover that their small villa had once been used on a regular basis by Aldous Huxley, one of her earliest reading enthusiasms. Zilpha was a steady reader herself but disliked Huxley's brittle intelligence which reminded her of her husband. At dinner every evening Zilpha would look out over the assembled ladies and whisper, "Don't you wish April was here to sweeten them up?"

One afternoon they were sitting on a boulder halfway up Mount Cuchama when a Pacific front swept in over a distant ridge and within a few minutes they were looking down at the roiling tops of clouds with far less security than is felt in an airplane. They were excited and girlish at the experience, noting the occasional hawk or raven that would pop up through the clouds, circle around, then dive back down into the moving fleece. "These clouds aren't comforting enough for the afterlife," Zilpha said, just before they heard a rattle of stone and a ragged, desperate Mexican man appeared before them. He gestured at his mouth in hunger and they handed down a remaining orange and hard-boiled egg from their perch on the boulder. The man pocketed the food, smiled, bowed and scampered up the steep mountain at an alarming rate, with physical verve that Clare pointed out none of the fitness instructors could have managed. Zilpha became depressed that the man was headed for America and might be disappointed, then she began coughing so they headed down the mountain.

Clare sat before her fire and decided that at last she was ready for sleep. She felt a trace of something new and feared she might be like a patient emerging from an asylum, using a cornstalk as a scepter, and saying, "As of today I'm giving up control of the entire world and all of its inhabitants." A half-dozen fireflies had gathered in the darkness around her green cave, and the tiny beams seemed to trace the convolutions of her thought. Life outside the asylum was not necessarily more pleasant. It could be, but it didn't have to be. She tried to recall what her beloved Camus said about "terrible freedom," that once you decided not to commit suicide, whether physically or figuratively, you assumed the responsibility of freedom. The thought blurred with a firefly's movement past her nose. She curled up fetally, rejected the position and stretched out strenuously on her back until there were bone crackles.

When she woke up a few days before this trip she noted that her feet were getting old, and laughed. She met Dr. Roth downtown for lunch because it was his volunteer day. He looked grim in the foyer of the Caucus Club and she feared a bad morning at the hospital, but it turned out an auto dealer had called to tell him his wife was intent on buying the same car she had bought the day before. The restaurant seemed suddenly inappropriate so they walked down the street and bought two coney islands apiece. Clare admitted she had never eaten one in her life but found the frankfurters covered with onions, mustard and chili quite delicious.

"You just saved a hundred bucks," he said, examining a splotch of mustard on his necktie. Clare had always insisted on the check.

"Too bad they don't sell these out our way."

They ducked into a bar, had a quick beer and removed the mustard from his tie. When they left and began walking again it was by common consent they decided not to be witty.

"What would you think if I left Donald?"

"I'd think you were sane"—his reply was quick—"but that's as much as I'll say. When did this come up?"

"About seven years ago. Why won't you say any more?"

"Because I've seen dozens of divorces in my practice and the act is so utterly intimate that outside advice only confuses the issue. Also, anything I'd say would be an abridgment of your freedom."

"I understand that. I've actually reduced it to an abstract principle." She hesitated, feeling foolish.

"Let's have it. Don't leave me hanging. This will be a first."

"I want to evoke life and he wants to dominate it. Is that too simple?"

"No, I don't think so. I'll have to spend an evening with that one. When are you going to do it?"

"I have no idea."

"Where are you going?"

"I don't know."

"Well I don't believe you don't know. In the ten years we've known each other you've mentioned a number of places you'd like to live. Let's see, there was Flagstaff, Minneapolis, Durango in Colorado, Pendleton in Oregon, and Duluth. And the obvious Paris."

"You have a remarkable memory for my nonsense."

"I've never been to any of them, but when you'd mention a place I'd look it up in the atlas and think it over." He was nervous with this admission and looked at his watch. It was then that she understood that at one time, at least, he had cared for her. They walked on in silence for a few minutes, her heart swelling in her throat. When they reached her car he hugged her and rushed off.

Clare was sinking into the ground, into a point well past sleep, or so she thought, with her body sweet, warm, deadened, giving itself up to the bed of leaves and grass, the green odor transmitting a sense she belonged to the earth as much as any other living thing. *I don't need to change. I'm just this.* Her brain had grown larger, its outer reaches vertiginous, grand, so that she could move within it as if taking an evening walk. She understood that she had been abandoned there by her mother and father, Donald, her children, Sammy and Zilpha, and that only being abandoned by Sammy and her children was natural. Zilpha was torn off the earth, taken away. Donald had disfigured himself beyond recognition and bore no resemblance to the man she in innocence had once been proud to love. Her mother smelled of allspice, martinis. Her ears smelled of gin. *Be careful because they'll always try to put their thing in you, dear. No matter what they say, that's what they're trying to do.* Her father had said, *Clare, look at your mother and don't drink anything stronger than wine,* and she hadn't except an occasional brandy. But when she slept in her birthday tent out by the grape trellis with the English setter, Tess, the dog had growled when her mother covered her in a mink coat, then she heard her mother vomit in the yard. Her legs were so thin and she died a year after him, unable to stand on thin legs still smelling of gin after death, beside him in the cemetery Clare could not bear to visit. Now she would, to say goodbye. As a child puzzled by age she'd say, Why is Dad older? Why does he say, *Take the best bite first?* We went for a drive that took all day from the cottage to a man's farm near Gaylord to get Tess bred. We dropped her off and he didn't want me to see it so we went to town for lunch. Mother was in the hospital so I got to eat French fried potatoes, then we went to see the Hartwick Pines, the biggest trees left, then we went to the wilderness where there were only huge old stumps. He said all but a few white pines five feet thick were cut down. *They're like the buffalo,* but I didn't understand. At Christmas he gave me a silver dog whistle with three small diamonds set in it because I could make the setters mind. Sit, stay, come, heel, slow. I never got to go hunt-ing. My brother hated it. Girls don't hunt, he said. My brother hit the dogs with a stick and got spanked. He would always hit me but Mother said I did the bruises myself to make my brother look naughty. The clock said three and I didn't hear Sammy's breath and I knew she was gone. It was May and the lilacs had just come out. I wore my nightgown and put on my hiking boots. I carried her down the hall and Donald looked out of his bedroom door and I said, *Go back to bed Donald this is my dog.* Out at the end of the garden I began digging and it was more than an hour before the hole was deep enough. I got down in the hole chest deep and could see that dumb bastard Donald staring at me out the kitchen window, then he went away. I lifted Sammy in after I kissed her goodbye and cov-ered her with the dirt, and sat down out of breath. At Zilpha's grave they covered the dirt with a rug of fake grass the color of grass in Easter baskets.

Something brushed against her leg and she bolted upright from the waist in alarm with hundreds of yellow dots whirling about her and above the rabbit that paused beside the dim coals of the fire. The moon made shadows of the rabbit's twitching ears. She scrambled out of the green cave and stood, gulping air in fright, the rabbit shooting back into the thicket. She prayed for her heart to stop thumping and looked up at the moon, and there were fireflies above her. As her heartbeat slowed she still did not want to look down at her body or touch herself because she thought she might be seven again. The fireflies were thicker in some places above the thicket, blinking off and on, whirling toward each other so if you blurred your eyes there were tracers, yellow lines of light everywhere. She thought, *Laurel should see this, Laurel would love this,* and then she was no longer seven.

Clare rebuilt the small fire to break the unearthly mood but the fireflies weren't disturbed. She walked up the row fifty feet, turned and looked back, hoping that she wouldn't see herself standing there. The countless thousands of fireflies stayed just outside and within and above the thicket. Quite suddenly she felt blessed without thinking whether or not she deserved it. She went back to her nest, lay down and wept for a few minutes, then watched a firefly hovering barely a foot above her head. She tried out *Now I lay me down to sleep* despite its failure to reassure. *All souls will be taken, including the souls of fireflies.*

She closed her eyes and felt herself floating in memory from her beginning, as if on a river but more quickly along the surface than what had happened to her. Now she saw when it was she had slept on the ground without covers up at the cottage when she was seven, with Tess curled up in her arms, smelling like a skunk Tess had bothered. In March that year, 1947, there was a serious bout of pneumonia and the doctors had given her too much of the new wonder drug, penicillin. At first she was better, though she hated the hospital and asked her parents daily if she could go home and they kept forgetting to bring along her small ceramic dog. All her joints began to redden and swell and her fever rose precipitously. The doctors diagnosed rheumatoid arthritis, a terrible disease, and then she lapsed into a coma for five days. All that she could remember from the coma was that her grandfather had brought into her hospital room his huge Belgian draft horse mare with the rooster perched on its back. When her grandfather left with the horse and rooster, her grandmother came in leading a black bear with a red

leash. Her grandmother said nothing but the bear had sat down beside her and talked in a soothing language, and before the bear said
goodbye she put Clare's ceramic dog on the nightstand so it was
there when she woke up with a big needle putting juice in her arm.
No one was there when she woke up though she thought she still
smelled the bear in the room. A specialist from the university said
she was allergic to penicillin and the drug had poisoned her system.
Her parents were happy she didn't have rheumatoid arthritis (they
kept saying it) but Clare felt things were never quite the same again.
In her child's mind she felt that they had abandoned her because
she had frightened them with her illness, an almost imperceptible
withholding of affection that became directed to her little brother,
or so she believed. When she got out of the hospital it was nearly
time to move up to the summer place, but when they got there she
was told she was too ill to go fishing with her father. He kept saying,
Maybe next month. One evening her parents went to a party down
the lake, the babysitter was awful just sitting out on the porch with a
boyfriend, and her little brother had purposefully broken the tail off
her ceramic dog by hitting it against the fireplace. She stayed up late
to show the broken dog to her parents, but they came home a little
drunk and spanked her for staying up late. She crawled out the window with Tess and slept under the bushes near the garage where
the three-legged cat had visited them. Tess liked cats and tried to
lick their fur. Early in the morning she was discovered when Tess
started barking at a motorboat, and she was spanked for sleeping
outside. She never did get to go fishing that summer though she
happily threw her brother's favorite teddy bear off the dock and
stood there a long time until it drowned. Then her mother had to go
to the hospital down near Ann Arbor, Mercy Wood, because she
drank too much, though her dad said she was just sick. The good
trip was to take Tess to Gaylord to find her a "husband." That's what
he said though there was no church, just a farm with English setters.
Then came the lunch, the big trees and the buffalo stumps.

When Clare awoke again the fireflies were gone. She rummaged in
the bag until she found her watch, lit a match and saw it was
four A.M., with dawn less than two hours away. She felt drowsy and

unafraid so didn't bother to rekindle the fire. It was pleasant to know she had no idea what she was going to do other than wear a beret in Paris on at least a single walk, she hoped on a rainy August afternoon. Barring small children most women in her neighborhood in broken marriages ran afoul of sheer idleness. Clare knew she was bright enough to make herself useful somewhere, especially when she wouldn't be running the house, which she tended at the moment to look upon as a preposterous imposition put on her by her mother. Her father tended to be naturally morose, taciturn, but the times her mother began drinking again after a supposed cure were hard on him. Once Clare came upon him crying in the den after her mother had fallen down the stairs. She hadn't really injured herself but the family doctor thought it an opportunity for a quick cure. His eyes had also become moist when Clare was dressed up for her first formal dance at fourteen. He had just arrived home from a business trip to New York and stood in the hall with his ponderous briefcase, and as she was leaving, he turned and nodded to her boyfriend standing on the porch, kissed her and said, *This can't be, this is too sudden,* and off she went. The last time was when, despite the pressures of business, he drove her up to East Lansing to enter college. Going to Michigan State was Clare's first act of total defiance against her mother to whom the college was unmentionable. Her mother had insisted on her own alma mater, Smith, and Clare had said, *You're not much of a recommendation, the only thing I've seen you read is Vogue,* and her mother had slapped her for the last time. Clare's favorite teacher had gone to MSU and had set up a program with old professor friends so that after basics Clare would have clear sailing in comparative literature. She envisioned a career that allowed her to read world literature, think about it, and anything beyond that was an irritation. Her father was fairly strict about her spending but gave her free rein with books. Sadly, Clare thought, the only time he truly defended her against her mother was in the choice of a college. But he had become quite upset when he dropped her off at her dorm, and they had talked with an intimacy previously unknown to them about her mother. He nearly begged her to come home as often as possible, if only for his sake. It was an unnerving moment for her, this first time her father was not quite her father but an intimate. Why had he waited until she was eighteen to try to become close, a time when it was no longer achievable, though it might have been later, had he lived? *Oh Father don't worry I'm doing fine,* and then she slept a pure, deep, dreamless sleep.

At first light there were more birds than she had ever heard at one time. It was as if she were *within* the birds, and wrens fluttered skillfully through the branches of the thicket. She heard whippoorwills, mourning doves, the resurgence of the red-winged blackbirds from the marsh beyond the creek. She ran a finger through the dew on her face which was slick as fine oil, and her movement disturbed something beside her. She turned and her heart stopped as a very long, thick, black snake eased himself off into the deeper reaches of the thicket. *Holy Jesus I have slept with a snake.* She laughed as her heart restarted. She gathered up her bag, took a sip of the boiled creek water, which had settled somewhat during the night and scrambled out into the dawn. If someone would just bring coffee she might stay a few hours more. She began to walk down the row, then turned around, having forgot the cranberry juice can. When she picked it up there was a clear view of her nest, and it reminded her in the first light of a swamp near their cabin where her father said a bear slept. She made a little goodbye bow to the green cave, examined her filthy clothes and set off down the row toward the east where a burnished orange sun was rising. She thought that in the future any place she lived would have to have a clear view of the east.

Two weeks later in a not altogether pleasant room in a small hotel a block off Rue St.-Jacques Clare's view was a scant dozen feet in whatever direction, but the ceiling was high. The room was as close as she could get to the *pension* she had stayed in for three weeks thirty years before, and twenty times as expensive. She had had her walk in an August shower in her beret, without an umbrella, until she was quite wet, and then a coffee and calvados at Café de Flore, where she had overheard an American couple her age asking a waiter where Camus had sat. There are other pilgrims, she thought, without a trace of self-mockery. She read Guillevic and Sarraute in her room, reread Alain-Fournier's *The Wanderer* and planned a train trip into the countryside. In the café where she took her lunch every day she knew she was referred to as "the schoolteacher." This pleased her though it wasn't meant to.

On long walks in the overwarm city she had occasion to think of the cool breezes that came in the evening off Lake Michigan. If she had the whole thing to do over she would have done it differently, but then no one has anything to do over. Down near the end of the corn row a pickup truck passed and she hid as an old man turned off the irrigation for the soybean field which was tinged orange and glistened in the morning sun. She followed the path of the pickup to the back of a barn where there was a field of pigs with small, low-slung sheds in rows, and a smell that would take some time to get used to. She went through a gate into a barnyard where the old man had the hood up on his pickup and was tinkering. A collie mongrel rushed at her, barking, but Clare said a quiet hello and the dog wagged its tail. The old man looked at her without alarm and put his hands in his denim jacket.

"What can I do for you?"

"I've been misplaced. I'd like a cup of coffee."

"If it's coffee you want, we got coffee. You must be the woman we heard about all evening on the radio. You're supposed to be in a red car."

"I spent the night in your field." Her voice began to quiver.

"You had to get loose. The radio said he was beating on you."

The old man led her toward the porch where a very large old woman was standing with her arms crossed. "She looks just like Grandma, doesn't she, Ed?" she said. At the screen door with a tuft of cotton on it to keep away flies the old man nodded in assent. Ed disappeared into the house and came back with an antique gold-leaf mirror with a photo portrait of a woman framed on the back of it. The woman wore a stiff necked black dress and had an amazing re-semblance to Clare who was momentarily disoriented.

"That picture was took in 1890," said the old woman.

"I suppose I should make some phone calls," Clare said.

Laurel arrived in two hours from Des Moines in a police car with a state trooper who talked farm prices and drank coffee with Ed while

Laurel and Clare sat on a porch swing. Laurel had come down from
Sioux Falls and spent the night in vigil with Donald in Des Moines.
"I never thought you would do it," Laurel kept saying.

"How's Donald?"

"He's unhappy but he'll survive. He told the police you had a
nervous breakdown, but I had them call Dr. Roth. You have to tell
the trooper that he didn't abuse you within Iowa state lines."

"The poor thing," Clare said, and began to cry.

Clare spent a scant hour talking with Donald in a room at a Best
Western motel in Des Moines. There was more than a trace of the
vulnerability in him that she once had cherished. He wanted to put
off any decision "in depth" until Clare "came to her senses," which
is precisely what she thought he'd say. She sat next to her suitcase
on the bed near the open window, as always. She couldn't help but
notice the day's *Wall Street Journal* and a note pad covered with
numbers on the nightstand. He was the same Donald, only paler,
and she waited fearfully for some tremor to come, but it didn't.
There were a few surprises.

"I can't say I didn't see this coming, but I hoped we'd carry on."

"I don't have anything left to carry on." It was so utterly painful
to say it.

"Is it Dr. Roth?" He looked away when he asked this, as if fearing
a blow.

"No. Don't be absurd. You were always more than enough."

"What about the house? What about everything, for God's
sake?"

"I hope you'll still look after everything. I don't care about the
house. I want my books, but the house was Mother's idea." She
found that she was three feet from her body again, but craving the
immediacy of the thicket. What did fireflies do in the daytime?
Perhaps Laurel would know.

"I had a good talk with Laurel last night. Per usual she told me
what was wrong with me. When she was little she even told me how
to shave. She said you were tired of the life you were living and
wanted to do something else. Is it as simple as that?"

Clare looked up and saw that he had begun to cry, but it was

Donald crying, not her father. She nodded yes, it was as simple as that. She got up and hugged him, and saw herself hugging him in the wall mirror, with a wave of claustrophobia sweeping through her body.

"We'll talk it over in October," she said, because that was what Laurel told her to say.

Laurel was dozing in the car and awoke with a start when her father put Clare's suitcase in the back seat. Laurel got out and began to cry which was so untypical that both Clare and Donald were nonplused, though it seemed Donald might have felt some subdued pleasure. They consoled Laurel, and it occurred to a couple driving up to the entrance that they were seeing a happy, if tearful, reunion.

In Paris at a newsstand Clare bought a *Rand McNally Road Atlas* of America. Due to the strength of the franc many prosperous French were visiting the States. In her room she spent a warm, humid afternoon looking at the locations that interested her, letting the maps bring back Zilpha, and Sammy sitting expectantly in the back seat waiting for a lunch break or a rest-stop stroll. Clare felt a little lost but then she always had, and supposed easily that it was the condition of life. Lying back on the bed, under the whir of the fan on the nightstand, she decided that she felt less lost than before her night in the thicket, and when the afternoon cooled she would write letters to Dr. Roth and Laurel. If it rained, she would wear her beret to dinner.

White Canyon

by Susan Lowell

I

Two dead deer were hanging in the juniper tree outside the window. They had appeared in the night.

Screaming, my little brother and I escaped from our cribs, built toe-to-toe by our father at the front of the trailer, and we crashed into our parents' bed in the back. We lived on the rim of White Canyon, in Utah, almost a day's drive from the nearest town. As recreation from hunting for uranium, some of the other geologists in the camp had gone hunting for deer and had hung the carcasses in the tree. Our parents explained that the deer would be made into jerky, which we ate often, powdered like us with fallout from the nuclear tests going on in Nevada, farther west.

One deer dangled upside down, roped by its miniature hoofs. The other was suspended apparently in mid-leap across a branch. Their legs were dry sticks, their fur iron.

Fifty yards from the trailer camp, the ground fell away suddenly, but I do not remember the canyon as white. The cliffs were streaked and layered: rust, pink, bone. The Little Colorado River glistened like a knife at the bottom. My brother and I were forbidden to go to the edge of the canyon alone.

In St. George, Utah, two hundred miles southwest of us, parents roused their children from bed to watch the atomic explosions bubble up in the sky. It was as good as the Fourth of July.

We never saw a mushroom cloud. Sometimes violent rainstorms swelled the Little Colorado, washed out the road to town, and turned the camp into sticky red mud that glued my brother's boots in place until he was rescued.

In a small deckle-edged photograph we play beside the trailer, and our big spaniel watches us. I hold my arms akimbo; a straight black ponytail sprouts from either side of my head. My brother, wearing a knitted cap, sits behind the wheel of a bulldozer built from an orange crate.

When my father nailed on the finishing touch, an empty Vienna sausage can for a smokestack, my mother cried: "It's perfect!"

And although the snapshot shows them as gray, I know that my denim jacket was marvelously studded with jewels of red plastic. In the picture I am three; my brother is eighteen months old.

Memories, like snapshots, are always in the present tense.

I stare upward through bars, and several strange adults stare down. Something is happening. I am a prisoner, a freak, a specimen. Where is my mother?

At St. Mary's hospital in my parents' home town of Tucson my brother has just been born.

The can of evaporated milk is too heavy for my hand. It slides into the bassinet on top of him and causes a surprising amount of noise.

The three of us fly north again to meet my father, who works for the Atomic Energy Commission. The airplane is silver, like our trailer, but narrower and somewhat longer. The stewardess wears a heavy navy blue uniform and a round wool cap. I glare suspiciously as she dares to hold our baby.

Those trailers were just that, not pseudo-houses. Besides beds, ours contained a tiny galley and a bathroom. A table unfolded beside a sofa, where the dog slept, and every spare inch of wall was fitted with small cupboards of irregular sizes, in blond wood with stiff latches. We owned few possessions and each had its place. At night my doll and my brother's truck disappeared into a cupboard beyond our reach.

For weeks I checked the juniper tree as soon as I woke in the morning. One up, one down, the deer hung in my nightmares.

My father's Geiger counter sometimes served as a doorstop. It was the size of a shoebox, with wrinkled black paper skin and glass-covered dials marked in arcs of red numbers against a sallow green background. It was too heavy for me to lift.

The narrow aluminum door opened high above the ground. Even to reach the step my brother and I must stretch our legs. A dozen other trailers surrounded ours, housing couples and families;

across the Colorado Plateau in the early Fifties the uranium boom was on, and it had generated jobs for young engineers, physicists, and geologists. Exploring for mineral deposits was a much better job than working underground, my father thought, and he began to dream of graduate school.

The catskinners—Caterpillar tractor operators—lived together in a barracks near the mess hall and wash house. Some of them were Navajo Indians; their reservation lay south of us. But we were not near anything.

My brother and I traveled in the back seat of the Jeep with the dog, who would start each long trip on the floor, gradually moving up to the seat and pushing my brother to the floor and me to the corner. Then our mother would restore us to the original order, and the process would begin again. When we hit bumps I clung to the rim of the seat with both hands. I could feel the shape of a pipe beneath the thin padding.

On a map of the Four Corners area I know these names: the Bear's Ears, the Valley of the Gods, Moab, Shiprock, Gallup, Lukachukai, Chinle.

Outside the window the mesas seemed to be carried past upon a tray. Clouds formed another landscape. Bound by barely visible wires, power pole giants marched in single file. There were two kinds: male and female? But which was which? They reminded me of the pair of Hopi kachinas that my parents kept in one of the highest cupboards at home.

My brother and I made up a song for riding through dips: "Uppee go—downee go!" Because of the way our father drove, we had to sing it fast. Our stomachs flipped pleasurably.

We were always driving straight for a pool of shining water across the pavement ahead of us. It always faded before the splash, which I never stopped expecting.

Real water was brown. I knew that. And I knew that before we forded it my father would stop and wade impatiently across it to make sure that the Jeep could pass.

Once, when we moved to White Canyon, we towed the trailer onto a ferry and crossed a wide river. My mother preferred to stay in the car with the baby, but my father and I rode outside.

In my memory, the wind lifts my bangs from my forehead. The ferry is made of rickety wooden latticework. The water looks like torrents of chocolate whipped into little waves and blobs of creamy foam, but it smells like mud. I enjoy looking at it; I have no fear of falling in.

Once a month we used to drive to the small town of Blanding to shop. Because of the size of the trailer refrigerator, we only ate fresh food one week in four, and my brother and I drank diluted canned milk. It still tastes of childhood to me. Much of our fruit was dried, and the big glass jar of jerky was kept low enough for me to reach for snacks.

The road from Blanding to White Canyon turned into dirt and then got rough. A tall sign stood at this point, and when my uncle came out from medical school in Boston to visit us, my mother took his picture there.

It is summer. He wears a white T-shirt, and the old color transparency film has put blue highlights in his black hair. Deadpan, he lolls against the signpost, while above his head the text jumps out of the brilliant sky:

> **DANGER AREA**
> Four-wheel-drive vehicles mandatory.
> Before entering, leave notice of your whereabouts.
> Carry food and water.
> Blinding sandstorms and flash flooding may occur.
> Do not attempt to cross dips when flooded.
> Proceed at your own risk.

The sign told us nothing new. I did not understand why the adults found this scene so remarkably funny, both then and each time the slide snapped into focus on the screen afterward. Now I see. In Boston the picture was a trophy. My uncle's foot was planted casually upon a beast. And to my parents, too, it stood for adventure, a push at the limits, the joy of laughing at dangers survived, or discovered to be imaginary after all. And youth: they were twenty-six; he was twenty-four. Neither failure nor grief had touched them closely yet.

The shadow of the Jeep used to stretch across the buttes, with our necks and heads pulled into long grotesque shapes. Then it would tumble onto flat ground—a fleeing box with two large and two small loose pegs inside. At the sight or sound of us, deer like giant jackrabbits went lofting through the scrubby trees. Coyotes melted away. Vultures sliced their invisible circles overhead.

"Buzzards in the sky know the time is nigh," my mother used to sing.

My uncle's summer visit coincided with a plague of stinging gnats so bloodthirsty that they kept us briefly indoors. The adults sat and talked. I played with my doll, an eight-inch blonde with a snarled wig.

My uncle pointed at the Geiger counter.

"But what about the hazards in this job?" he asked.

"Hazards?" said my father.

"Radiation exposure. You're dealing with uranium, aren't you?"

"Small amounts," said my father, shrugging.

The A.E.C. had given his team a fleet of Jeeps and plenty of money, and he enjoyed the field work, climbing up and down the canyons and deducing the patterns in the rocks. Once he found an Indian pot no bigger than a walnut tucked in a niche in a cliff. Inside was a pinch of dust, perhaps the remains of a sacrifice long ago.

At night my brother and I used to swarm into his khaki lap and tug out the hand lens he always wore on a chain around his neck. The steel cover glided off a disk of magnifying glass about the size of the ball of his thumb, where swirls of whitish ridges ran beside pink ditches where I could almost see the rush of blood. The sofa cover was as coarse as a basket. My mother's wedding ring was uninteresting. But two kinds of freckles spotted her arm, uniform round dark ones and pale ones with irregular edges like stains.

My hands strongly resembled my father's, even down to the network of lines in the palms. Longer, more slender, my brother's hands had crooked little fingers hereditary in my mother's family.

Sometimes we looked at the grains that, crushed together, made rocks. I learned that yellow meant uranium; red, iron; blue, copper. Then the rocks would return to the pile of canvas sample sacks in the corner where the pick also leaned. Recently another pick had shattered against a rock and lodged a splinter of steel in my father's chin, which bled when he shaved.

My little brother ran away one day. Turning from the clothesline, our mother saw only me. The search and panic spread through the camp to the edge of White Canyon. Finally someone found him playing pinball in the mess hall with a Navajo catskinner who had caught him on the path to the cliff.

The first fallout storm came at about that time. In a camp full of Geiger counters it was impossible to miss. Suddenly one morning they all began to chatter: radioactive particles showered us, three hundred miles downwind from the nuclear explosions over Nevada.

Hiroshima and Nagasaki had been bombed eight years before, and the implications of fallout were clear enough to people with scientific training, though not perhaps the implications of low dosages. In a way it was still an innocent age. There was a residue of awe — and of V-J Day. Also, familiarity breeds carelessness. Everyone in camp knew about the Nevada tests. Yet the Atomic Energy Commission was everyone's boss; the object of the job was to find uranium, the source of the problem. They had never agreed to be contaminated, but there seemed to be no escape. Perturbed, everyone stayed indoors until the radiation level dropped off, like the gnats, and life returned to normal.

There were many picnics, one in the middle of a skeleton of the carnivorous dinosaur Allosaurus. It lay on its side like a chicken with a three-foot skull, and suddenly after lunch all the young geologists started a rock fight with fossils.

I think that my mother, who had majored in anthropology, suggested our trips to a Hopi snake dance and to the Gallup Ceremonial. My clearest memory is of a Navajo squaw dance.

I ride on my father's shoulders above the heads of the crowd. The other men all wear black cowboy hats with wide flat brims. Some of the women are dressed in velvet blouses; their long tiered skirts sway as they move. I stare at the other children. A bonfire streams into the night sky, a drum beats, and the dancers take a few steps forward, a few steps back. My brother and I lie upon a sleeping bag at the fringes of the orange light. A few steps forward, a few steps back. I pry open my eyelids. Can it be that my parents are dancing too?

Another time, a sing or curing ceremony for a sick young girl was held at her home. This I remember only faintly, having been told the details years later. We arrived at dawn, and there was little to see besides the other visitors and their wagons and pickup trucks. The sand painting and singing had all been done inside the round log hogan. But as the sun came up we did watch a shaman throw the girl's clothes out of the smoke hole at the top of the hogan. They caught a breeze and drifted to the ground, and she was purified.

The second fallout storm was heavier than the first. It was impossible to stay indoors long enough. When my father ran the Geiger counter along the dog's back, the needle surged up the green dial, and the machine clicked faster. My parents looked at each other.

A letter arrived from my uncle.

"Can't you evacuate?" he wrote. "Why don't they warn you before blowing off these bombs?"

"They don't know we're here," my mother suggested.

"It's like getting an X-ray," said my father.

In Washington President Eisenhower observed that it was probably just as well to keep the public in the dark about atomic matters —confused about the difference between fission and fusion, as he put it.

More fallout came down. My father started to apply to graduate schools. He might, he explained, become a rock doctor. I puzzled over this and finally abandoned the mystery as insoluble. Rocks could not be sick or hurt, I was sure.

My doll is shut in the high cupboard, and I am alone in the trailer. I know that I should not climb upon the back of the sofa and from there find a toehold on the cupboard handle. Clinging to the wall with my right hand, I stretch out the other toward the door that hides my doll. My fingers graze her silky hair.

Slowly, slowly, guiltily I lose my balance. I fall. The bone above my left eyebrow strikes the floor first, and a lump swells up. My mother is not angry. My brother peeks past her knee. I have a headache, I am sick, I turn green. Someone mentions the word "Blanding."

"He's out in the field," my mother says.

She means that my father has gone to work.

Another man, a neighbor, is driving us in a strange Jeep. At first my eyes behave oddly; they seem to see through water. Each hill is endless, vertical. Jolt by jolt, my head ringing, we fight against gravity. But as the hours pass I begin to feel better. We arrive in Blanding at dusk and find the doctor. I lie on a silver table, his face balloons in mine, and then a horrifying instrument—a needle?—stabs straight at my eye but misses.

II

"Who's the president of the United States?"

I struggled through layers of murk, broke the surface, and answered: "Jimmy Carter."

Then I gave a start. The baby was in the bed with me! No, she wasn't after all. My arms were empty, but I felt a great pain behind my left eyebrow.

The man sitting across the room from me made no response. I recognized him now; he wore a gold Rolex watch big enough to manacle both my wrists at once. I had met him in the emergency room. He was a neurologist.

"What's the date today?" he asked.

I struggled again. The sky was blue outside. The baby had been born in this hospital at night, but that was weeks ago, before my head began to hurt. I seemed to have paused in the midst of a long journey. Was it one or many nights that I remembered like a blow in the diaphragm?

"I'm not sure. August, 1980."

"Where are we?"

"Dallas, Texas."

I had a house, a husband, and a job teaching poetry. I lived on a street called Hillcrest, which was quite flat. My students, who drank Dr. Pepper for breakfast, included one excellent poet.

"What drugs have you taken?"

"Ice!" I said angrily. "That's all. What's the matter with my head?"

"We're working on that."

He never looked at me directly except when he shone a penlight in my eyes. When he had gone I lay back and listened to the interminable discord inside my head.

I remembered how once in a museum of medical curiosities I'd seen the skull of a Victorian railroad worker who was brained by a crowbar and survived. Also bequeathed to science, the crowbar neatly fitted into the cleft it had made.

Needle marks speckled the inside of my left arm. A large television screen tilted over me. Someone had arranged the cushions of an easy chair in the shape of a bed upon the floor.

A nurse came to collect a flabby ice pack from a pool of water on the table beside me. She was not the tall black woman capped with a purple wig who had brought the ice the night before. No other painkiller was allowed. It might confuse the diagnosis.

"Where's my mother?" I said, beating down panic. "And my husband? And my baby?"

"Did they check you in last night?"

So it had only been one night. Memories jammed against one another without logic, the dial flipping from channel to channel. I must have acted strange yesterday afternoon.

The headache spirals me up a peak impossibly narrow and steep, but I refuse to go to the hospital. Clenching her fists, the baby screams and sweats.

I am holding a telephone. My doctor uncle speaks calmly into my ear. "After childbirth, women are in an unusual condition," he says. "Why not have a checkup?"

His hair is no longer blue-black, but his voice never changes.

My husband responds to trouble by increasing his self control. In the hospital corridor he takes my arm with the lightest possible touch. His fingertips are icy.

The obstetrician wears a foolish look on his youthful face. "I only know them from here to here," he explains to someone over his shoulder. His hair is still wet from the swimming pool.

Stripped to the waist, shivering, I lean into the chest X-ray machine. "This is stupid," I think. "It's my head that's killing me. And I don't need any extra radiation."

The nurse was gone. How much time had passed?

In the dark my mother spreads the cushions on the floor.

"I won't leave you," she whispers.

The baby is falling and I cannot catch her. No, she's safe in bed with me. No. She's vanished.

The purple wig bends over me, smelling sweet. "Try this, honey."

The ice. For a moment it dulls the sensation behind my eye, and words begin to tap in my head: "About suffering they were never wrong,/The Old Masters. . . ."

"They haven't found anything yet," said my husband, at his coolest. "They're going to do an EEG today—test your brain waves."

A game show host called from the television: "The question is this. If you could change any part of your body, would it be the top half or the bottom half?"

"Is your hair clean?" said the bored technician. She screwed my scalp full of electrodes, hunched over her table, and dimmed the lights.

"Sleep if you can."

Ballpoint pens scribbled automatically upon a conveyor belt of paper.

"Messages from the spirits," I said.

"Quiet, please."

Lights sparkled in geometric patterns, and I soared into the void.

"I have felt like this before," I thought. "When?"

Every move precise, my husband sets up his camera; the metal petals of the shutter expand and contract; the strobe light multiplies itself on my eyeballs.

In college, I stay up all night to see Janis Joplin at the Fillmore Ballroom. Black air above the dancers seethes with sound, light, smoke. I focus upon a single fixed point to keep my balance as I whirl.

While my father is a graduate student, my little brother starts to spin. He revolves quickly in corners until he is too dizzy to stand. Merely a nervous tic, the pediatrician tells my mother. The habit continues for years. Finally it is replaced by others.

Studying in London I fall ill, but the weather is so bitter, inside and out, that I never feel hot. Instead I have fits of shivering; I compose a long poem about the Underground. But when I wake in my dim rented room, the words melt away. I am not a great poet, after all.

"I have a fever," I said out loud.

"I'm testing," said the technician brusquely.

The fever, they decided, was insignificant. The auger continued to grind at my skull. My mother brought the baby to me, and she tangled her hands in my hair and cried. My scalp was covered with small scabs.

"The EEG is normal," my husband said.

Grease dribbled through two kitchen strainers on the TV screen.

I carried the baby to the window. The hospital was one of a row of blue medical monoliths rising above the north Texas prairie, which was tiled with tiny houses. An occasional steeple jabbed up among them: one had a clock face marked with black Roman numerals and the words, "Night Cometh." No mountains, no canyons. I was homesick for the far West. The sky was wide enough here, however, and perfectly clear.

Dallas was trapped in a heat wave. For fifty consecutive days the temperature had passed a hundred degrees, without rain. Deep cracks opened in the clay beneath the singed lawns, and people stumbled into them.

The maternity ward lay somewhere beneath us. I did not know the name or number of the floor where I stood.

Their eyes glittering, their hair glued into rich curls, two men in white dress shirts hurled an inert body onto a bed and crept off. Organ music rippled from the television.

Time collapsed like folded paper. My mother must have taken the baby away. My husband sat in the dark beside my bed, watching a musical comedy. A Chinese princess and a Renaissance nobleman performed a love duet in a ruined pagoda.

"Marco. . . ." she sang.

And he answered, "Polo. . . ." His lips did not synchronize with the music.

"After the CAT scan tomorrow," said my husband, without expression, "we're calling in another doctor."

"What kind?"

"A psychiatrist."

"No!" I shouted. So I was in the psycho ward. "I'm not crazy. There must be a cause."

The deer hang in the juniper tree. Inverted images: the quick and the dead.

The mesas are on the move. They cruise over my shadow. "Basin and range topography," says my father, gesturing. We travel from house to house, each full of rocks, maps, transits, and magnetometers. A pill bottle of uranium, yellow and lumpy as dry mustard, remains forgotten in the medicine cabinet for many years.

Among the specimens in my father's mineral collection are an Allosaurus vertebra and a chunk of its femur. They are radioactive. The dinosaur's organic material has been replaced by high-grade uranium ore.

Madame Curie derived her radium from fossil wood from Utah.

Trepan—in mining, a rock-boring tool used for sinking shafts. In surgery, a trephine.

Trephine—a surgical tool with circular serrated edges for cutting out disks of bone, usually from the skull.

My brother finds school difficult but shows a gift for mechanics. At ten, wearing a homemade parachute, he jumps off the roof and breaks his leg.

I have a gift for standardized tests. I write short-lived poems. I begin to travel on my own.

My brother drives an old school bus to Oregon and lives in it, repairing small engines and skydiving.

I graduate, I marry. My Navajo rugs look barbaric in the Dallas house, but after all I have never stayed anywhere for long.

I am pregnant.

The baby's body is born with a rubbery wriggle. The obstetrician duly says, "It's a girl," and turns her around. The faces of several relatives in extremis look back at us before dissolving into her own.

There was no real pain in all of that. Now *this* was a territory I did not know. Then I recognized the bare feet plodding below the hem of the hospital gown.

"You have dull feet," my husband used to tease.

Square, thick, they matched my hands. They looked like my father's. They stopped.

DANGER AREA
Birdless night country.
Outer space. No stars.
Travel at your own risk.
Major test underway.
Some will not get out alive.
Blood will be drunk.
No clues.

"Are you allergic to fish?" asked the young male technician.

"No, why?"

"We inject radioactive iodine dye. When it reaches your brain, we take pictures."

Words drummed: "O the mind, mind has mountains; cliffs of fall/ Frightful. . . ."

"Lie still."

The machine clamped me in its white enamel jaws. I lay alone in an underground chamber while a voice quacked through a perforated metal plate in the ceiling.

"CAT scan? CAT scan? Are you there?"

The machine clicked gently.

Pure blankness. I woke with the same chrome piston apparently pounding my left eye. Where was I? *"Untrumra monna hus,"* came the answer. The Anglo-Saxon poet Caedmon, dying, was carried to the "unhealthy men's house." He held my hand. "About suffering—" I began. I saw that he wore a Rolex watch.

"What number between one and ten did I just trace in your palm?" asked the neurologist.

"Seven," I said.

He waved a tiny vial beneath my left nostril. "What do you smell?"

"Nothing."

He moved it to the other nostril.

"Flowers," I said.

"I'm taking myself off this case," said the neurologist.

For the first time a nurse brought me a paper frill, like a nut cup at a children's party, filled with colored pills. She sat on the bed while I swallowed them.

"Did you know," she said, "that this was the hospital where they brought J. R. Ewing on *Dallas* when he was shot?"

Encircled by rings of pink and periwinkle paint, her eyes rose hopefully to the TV screen. A middle-aged man peered through a barred window. "I've got to get out of here somehow," he muttered. In a garden below him another man prowled with a machine gun in his hands.

My husband said, "You have a brain tumor. They found it with the CAT scan. They're calling it a benign meningioma, but we won't know for sure until after the operation."

"I'm not crazy?"

"We told the psychiatrist to go away. You'll like the surgeon."

I dug my fingers into his familiar shoulders. His upper body, usually so calm and set at a lower temperature than my own, was shaking.

"Don't cry," I said. "I'm happy."

I went into surgery as to a bridegroom, washed and exalted. Saying goodbye, faces loomed up in a mist: husband, father, mother, and baby. I reached for her fuzzy head and fell back. The big nurse with the purple wig was taping my wedding ring to my third finger.

The neurosurgeon slit my scalp from ear to ear. He sawed a two-inch hinged square from my skull, lifted up the frontal lobe of my brain, and removed the tumor. Then he reassembled my head with wax, thread, and staples.

I watched opaque waves as they divided and rose into crests, precipices, watersheds. There was no smell of mud. I was staring through a row of bars. A green bottle floated up to my mouth.

"Oxygen, ma'am?"

"Yes, please."

The ferry docked, and I put the dark river behind me. My head, half shaved, was wrapped in gauze, harsh to the touch.

"Lady Lazarus," I said.

Nurses unplugged me from various plastic tubes; I sat up, solid and ravenous.

"You're leaving ICU now, sugar. Good luck."

On the regular surgical floor, rings, chains, and a triangle jingled above my bed, as though gymnastic exercises would be required.

"On the day of your operation," said my brother on the telephone from Oregon, "I went skydiving and made a special jump for you."

"Thank you." My throat ached, but still I had not produced one tear. "Be careful, Icarus."

"Me? What about you?"

Making rounds the neurosurgeon bent his wide pink face over his work and admired it. He moved in an atmosphere of Panama hats and white linen suits.

"Benign meningioma, just as I thought," he said, gratified. "Before the CAT scan, we used to operate blind."

"Or lock madwomen up," I thought.

There should be no further problems, he told us. He had scraped the bone clean. He might have been a Southern country lawyer or a gourmet butcher. "Of course I did have to take the left olfactory nerve. But that's why they come in pairs."

I buried my nose in the baby's neck. Newborn, she'd had an acrid yeasty smell, but now it was insipid baby lotion and sour milk. I saw my cranium, an ivory artifact in a glass case.

"But why did it happen?" said my father.

"Who knows?" said the surgeon. "Pregnancy makes everything grow. But the tumor had to be started first."

"When she was three," said my mother thoughtfully, "she had a concussion in just that spot."

"Head trauma!" The surgeon brushed it away. His hands seemed too bulky for his job. "Everyone has head trauma."

"What causes tumors?" I said.

He paused in the doorway, impatience now reducing his dignity. "Oh, genetics. Viruses. Radiation. Who knows?" He relented slightly. "Studies do show more mutations in populations near the equator. Sun."

"It doesn't matter," said my husband with finality.

From this window the ground was much closer; the details of houses and cars and quivering leaves were rich and sharp. A mass of moist clouds had bubbled up in the sky. Behind my back the others went on talking.

"The bone will regenerate," my mother said. "I've seen fossil skulls that had been trepanned and then grew back, partly."

"I wanted to give up," my husband said. "Once I even went to the telephone to call someone, to resign. But who do you call when you want to give up? Everyone was depending on me. So I came back."

That night I could not sleep.

"Nurse—nurse—nurse," called the old woman across the hall, but nobody ever came.

I turned the television volume very low and huddled at the foot of my bed. Doomed lovers moved in triangular patterns. Parents betrayed their children, children their parents. Natural disasters rained down, followed by war. There was a short spell of hope, but at the end a woman lay sick in a thunderstorm. They found her in the morning, her hungry infant nuzzling at her cold breast.

I hugged my own knees. The hospital breathed painfully around me, and I tried to hush my rude joy.

A cylinder soared across the screen and burst, red, white, and blue. It was a giant beer can.

We would camp in remote places, I thought. We were still young. Together we would see orange cliffs, hot blue sky. The baby could ride in a backpack. We would get sunburned and muddy. We would sleep like the dead under the stars. The North Rim, I thought, Canyonlands, Bryce, Zion.

The Psychological and Moral Habitats of American Children and Adults

by Carol Bly

We still don't know enough about the brain to be certain of the extent to which some people's brains make them innate criminals and bullies, and how much criminal lives and the habit of bullying are acculturated. The strong evidence suggests that creatures live in what we can call *psychological habitats* and adjust to those habitats as inevitably as people in thin jackets turn their backs to the wind.

In stage-development theory, the rightful business of children is play, the development of their ego, and the formation of enough character to live affectionately and without enormous suffering.

Children go about their play wherever they are placed or left by adults. Their personalities develop and their character builds among the adults around them. Wherever their home is, if they have one, and the streets or fields around it—that is their psychological habitat. The children's spirits pick up unbidden messages from our culture, hour by hour. These are our expectations of you, the voiceless messages say. In verbal families the messages are actually spoken. In either circumstance, children accumulate the social expectations of parents and neighborhood. They may not like those expectations, but they know what they are.

If no one in the family and no one in the neighborhood has ever heard of psychological consciousness as a valuable accomplishment in life, the child won't hear of it, either.

The literary selections for this chapter, Jim Harrison's "The Woman Lit by Fireflies" and Susan Lowell's "White Canyon" have two characteristics in common: both families in the stories are without psychological consciousness and both stories have psychological consciousness as their principal subject—this despite the vast differences in culture and privilege between the two families presented.

Some children live in happy enough households, but the culture immediately outside the apartment or house is inimical or sordid. For some children, school is the bright center of their lives: each afternoon they dread returning home to cruelty or sadness or emptiness. Some children live in homes that look lucky on the outside, and go to schools that are not crowded or ill run or full of drug use or sexism—yet a subtle, ironic kind of humor floats down to them from their parents. In other homes, the mother and father and siblings are gray presences compared to the brilliant television, its sounds and pounding, its repetitive, hearty talking heads, and the average of 144 murders shown each day. A child's emotional life blooms or wilts in the house. If there is no home, then the child feels that wherever the parent or parents sleep is home. Wherever that is, that is the physiological home. However adult human beings are treating other human beings or animals or plants in that home—that is the child's psychological habitat.

Economic class is not in itself a factor, but all too often, poor parents are scrabbling at two or three jobs to keep the household going: they scarcely find the leisure to have relaxed conversations and fanciful storytelling and other cultural cheer. They are physically tired, psychologically distracted, often frantic. Lack of money isn't what blocks a person's psychological growth, but poverty brings a dozen low-level irritations during any day. The windowsill paint is checked and flaking: it can't be got clean. A stream of insects comes up through holes between walls and floor. Linoleum no longer lies flat, but is curled up at the seams. The washing machine is miles away and takes quarters. Every single household job takes a long time because the tools needed are wrong for the job or missing or broken. Machinery once broken often gets repaired with whatever is around instead of with appropriate parts. If the poverty is rural poverty, one wraps duct tape because there aren't any lag bolts of the right size. Wire repairs are done with the wrong gauge of wire because that's what's around, and electric appliances are run on undergauge extension cords. When the cotter pin breaks on a well, someone runs a twist tie through the two eyes instead. Everything breaks again.

Every job takes longer than it should and cannot be done

without greater exertion than rich people expend on the same chore. People spend hours of the day slightly or hugely out of temper.

In a discussion of cultural effects on moral development, Elizabeth Léonie Simpson gives this pathetic news of habitat:

> It is also likely that preindustrial and traditional societies do not provide their members with means for gratifying the basic psychic needs that would allow the development of motivation toward personal growth and the values of equality and justice, which are the core of autonomous moral judgment. Evidence for this formulation may be found in Kohlberg's report (1968) that children of low socioeconomic status are slower than higher-status children in passing through his stages of moral development, as well as less likely to achieve the highest levels. Evidence supporting this analysis also appears in research indicating that delinquents do not show expected age-developmental changes in moral reasoning (Selman, 1974). Although neither Kohlberg nor Selman infer the following relationship, from my revised version of the cognitive-developmental theory it can be reasoned simply that lower-socioeconomic-status children and delinquents have been less able to satisfy the psychic needs that must be met before higher moral development can occur.[1]

Jim Harrison's "The Woman Lit by Fireflies" is a study of the psychological habitat of a very rich person educated in the liberal arts. Harrison's story gives full pictures of several characters, not just of Clare, the protagonist. Here are rich parents with B.A.s in comparative literature who are capable of providing terrible psychological habitats for their children. Clare's parents were ironic and cold.

The parents in "White Canyon" were scientists, people in their twenties, with no background in the kind of thinking we associate with the humanities. They were still much like teenage hobbyists. Their attitude seems to say, "Oh, look at this, pick it up—it's interesting. An artifact." They are cheerful, affectionate people, who don't bother their heads about the radiation that should have concerned them. Nothing taught them the idea that being grown-ups means analyzing what is happening in the world that might affect their lives, hearing, if necessary, bad news and be-lieving it. They and their friends haven't got the idea of acting on information received. They laugh off serious worry. Their psycho-logical habitat supports them adequately for life, provided there are no major enemies in the field: their expectations have de-signed them for the little life—the job pays well, so you ask no questions. There are fun trips to go on, and sprees of touristing. Religion is enjoying other people's religious fetes.

Here is a list of nine characteristics of habitats in which our egos develop as well as they can. These psychological habitats are where we learn any moral reasoning that we may acquire.

Please note that although I believe the solid argument of Dr. Jane Loevinger that ego development and moral-thinking devel-opment are absolutely intertwined or interdependent, I am leav-ing the two phrases separate. I want to preserve the weight and slightly different psychological texture of both words—ego and moral. Although no one could arrive at top-flight ethical thinking without top-flight ego development, one could have arrived at top-flight ego development yet be an immoral person. They are therefore not quite part and parcel of each other.

1. A childhood and youth in which one receives respect and affection from at least one adult

The visiting aunt, incidental friend of parent, teacher, or sports coach whose inner life is still intact can provide respect as well as parents. A parent or parents usually have so much one-on-one time with their children that if they are disrespectful and unlov-ing to the children it is hard to overcome the hour-for-hour im-pact of their unkindnesses. Still, all it takes to keep kids' small egos bolstered well enough so that they can strengthen, however, is one affectionate and courteous teacher or mentoring adult.

When the adults around a child are civil and full of accurate insights, a child experiences conversations with them almost like a starry vaulting overhead. Sometimes children nearly shine when adults who care for them name things, gently but accurately. The adults' insights can be on the smallest subjects, just so long as they are mildly philosophical. For example, nearly everyone at some point in childhood has an ant colony. You came across a brigade of ants dragging crumbs or dead smaller insects from somewhere to somewhere. You set down sugar or bread crumbs in a kind of food depot. Soon all the ants come. Then it occurs to you that it is hard work for them to totter around, bearing their loads over bumps and gutters and around grass, so if you are any kind of a ten-year-old socialist you make them a smooth double-lane highway with your index finger. But they keep on carrying their loads all-terrain style. Then an adult comes. "Yup, that's right," the adult says after studying the colony, "they just don't use highways. They haven't got the idea in their ideas. You've got that idea, not they." It is the universality of that comment that fires a person up: how respectfully that adult looked over one's engineering, and how philosophical his or her analysis! No one was right or wrong, so there was nothing scary about the conversation. Wisdom got shared casually. It all sounds obvious, and if it were not for the shocking rarity of easy, amiable, philosophical conversations between children and their adults I wouldn't have described it.

Reflections on a more serious level: If a child asks a grandparent, "Was so-and-so a bad person, Grandpa? Is that what you're saying?" and the old man answers, "Bad! Lower than a copperhead in a wagon-wheel rut!" the child laughs with joy. That laugh is like a ferris-wheel laugh: there is more to it than just amusement.

I have been thinking about how children laugh or even jump at certain metaphors. I think it is partly because metaphors give off gaiety and partly because children love truths about character, life, death: they are always delighted when an adult will comment on things more inward than "Go get a cloth and wipe that up." Metaphor is a narrow way to tell a truth: that is, any given metaphor can say only one thing about something, but it says it sharply and five times more emotionally than a similar truth explained in abstractions. For example, "My feeling is that so-and-so's greatest fault was a thoroughly corrupt character" is experienced as a companionable, unemotional comment. "He was lower than a copperhead in a wagon-wheel rut" cuts fast below the conversational surface into a strong narrow feeling. Neither adults nor children want a continuous diet of metaphor for the same reason that one doesn't want a continuous diet of basil or roe.

2. A childhood and youth in which words are used a lot

Even the use of words in a sentence such as, "Here, pass me that induction coil, would you, Dale?" is a different experience for Dale from "Here, pass that over, no, not that one, the other thing, yeah, that one, thanks" because of the naming of the induction coil and even better, the naming of Dale himself aloud, affirmed by a human voice. Educated people who have spent their lives in cities where one networks among people of one's own lifestyle tend not to have the least idea how few exact nouns are used by uneducated people. The horrible, unfair truth is that a child's mind rejoices in learning particular nouns, yet people unused to reading or speaking distinctly don't use nouns much.

Lest this seem like a strange argument, here is a list of non-words regularly used instead of nouns by people who haven't the habit of words: *thingamajig, what's-it* (chiefly British), *that thing, whatdoyoucallit,* and the word *deal* used to mean party, business arrangement, county fair, reception after a wedding. Behavioral psychology, the form of psychology that most Americans think makes up all of psychology, has taught us or implied to us two impressive psychological dynamics: first, that not mentioning people, such as saying "mankind" and "he" instead of "our species" and "he or she" is a form of hostility to or putdown of the unmentioned person; second, using a general piece of slang—that is, slapping an inexact, slack tag onto something—as opposed to specifically naming that thing or person, takes away the formal tone that our souls need. Despite Emily Dickinson's insight on the subject, a remark like "our souls need a formality" gives the cynic his or her chance to grin. In the preceding example, however, Dale's being called by his own name is a more pleasant experience for him than being called "Hey" or "Hey, you" or "Kid." That much is obvious. In addition, some part of Dale's mind experiences the use of the word "induction coil" as more pleasant than "that thing, the one on the right."

I have spent a number of years in a small town, in which no one lives by network; that is, our important conversations took place among people of several educational levels. I worked every day with people who used language more carefully than I and people who used language less carefully than I. I was struck by the fact that hundreds of people address their children by common names instead of proper names, and also identify objects by toneless generic words. I know that such language has a psychological effect on children far more salient than the mere cultural deprivation of hearing only clumsy language use. "Thingamajig" and the gerund "putzing around" tell us that everything is a practical jumble of who cares what, what'd you expect anyway.

This issue of formality versus inexact slang comes up among psycholinguists but is ignored elsewhere. People who live in the country experience homogeneous community rather than life in a given educational stratum. They therefore recognize the feeling aspects of language, because they daily hear people using language either more formally or less formally than they themselves use it. We need a couple of Ph.D. theses on the psychological effects of informal language in a child's habitat. If such scholarship has already been done, we need to know about it. Groups like MOTHERREAD would be interested, perhaps helped, just as such groups are helped by their members' hearing, usually for the first time in their lives, that a child benefits cognitively if you tell him or her stories.

3. A childhood and youth in which abstract concepts are spoken of, by name, at the supper table

Words for invisible qualities exercise the imagination just as naming aloud invisible victims exercises the imagination. Since altruism is entirely to do with imagining creatures and people who are *other*, one needs early experience in imagining anything other— children's books, talk, geography lessons, history, second languages. Otherwise one might stay stuck in self-orientation—stuck in a self-interest later glossed over with whatever conventional behavior is needed to make one seem attractive to one's peers at school, in the family, and eventually in the workplace.

Inexperience in imagining *other* is not automatically built into "working-class" backgrounds like Donald's background in "The Woman Lit by Fireflies." Sometimes children from the least leisured families—families not given to cordial philosophical conversations over dinner—still hear a good deal of abstract language. They may even memorize abstract language. The kind of church-going that liberals scoff at has this virtue: for two hours a week, one hour of Sunday school and one hour of church, in the case of Protestant churches, words never heard in television dramas and sports reporting, and scarcely ever in most American homes, come crowding into children's ears. In fact, the duller the preacher, the more shrill and exhortative, the less given to interesting anecdote the minister or priest, and the more galling the hymn lyrics and the more rigid the liturgy, the more likely it is that a child hears words having to do with character formation. *Love, service, honor,* and so forth become some kind of norm to any child hearing them repeated by adults outside the home (clergy and Sunday school teachers), provided they are adults whom the community seems to treat with respect.

Conversely, if we never hear the words *service, honor, integrity, mercy to strangers,* and so on, the potential for those moral artifacts begins to atrophy in the brain. The brain won't do much unless it can get into the act, wrap itself around some abstract concepts, try them against stories pulled up from its storage. Of course, much preaching is a hodgepodge of great phrases carelessly slung from pulpit over the nave like spit from exuberant actors flying over the first row of stalls. Still, hearing obvious rhetoric about great purpose is not bad, as liberals sometimes assume.

Children who never hear words like mercy do not know there is such an autonomous virtue as mercy. If that sounds precious, we see it more clearly in another example: wives who are battered begin to know that they are battered when they hear the phrase *battered wives.* If they do not hear those words, the exact name of their own predicament, they cannot cognitively recognize that they are battered wives. People who never hear the word *atonement* will hardly think to make atonement. What if Sam's wife or his friends in "Cider 5¢ a Glass" had mentioned atonement to him, say, twenty times a year for three years? Sooner or later the idea would be a conceptual reality, even inside Sam's brain with its liquor-sluiced neurons.

We all suppose it is good for children to name things. We tend exponentially to underestimate how important naming or *failing to name* is to *adults'* ethical growth. I regret the current fashion of carping at abstract language for its being "awfully abstract" as if *abstract* were a pejorative adjective. It is like saying that ideas are too much like ideas.

Professor Michael Levin says that abstract morals can't be taught. He is talking about teaching abstract values to adults, however; he is not talking about children hearing those words at earlier cognitive stages. In an essay called "Ethics Courses: Useless" he writes:

> Moral behavior is the product of training, not reflection. As Aristotle stressed thousands of years ago, you get a good adult by habituating a good child to doing the right things. Praise for truth-telling and sanctions for fibbing will, in time, make him "naturally" honest.
>
> Abstract knowledge of right and wrong no more contributes to character than knowledge of physics contributes to bicycling.[2]

Professor Levin's either/or thinking (you either do or do not need physics to ride a bike) is logical enough, but psychologically and cognitively the situation is more complicated. First, one does make conscious use of simple physics in riding a bike. Second, one can't invent a bike without applying, consciously or unconsciously, several physical laws to do with mechanical exchanges — such as the belt-geared/rotary exchange that translates up/down or pistonlike pedaling into rear-wheel rotation — and centrifugal force, against which bike riders lean and with which they steer. Most important of all, *if one were to improve a bike* or figure out new, surprising uses for bicycles, one would need physics.

The same is true of improving the morals of a society: people need to be able to talk about principles, and puzzle out how to use the same old ideas of virtues and vices for new, site-specific applications. Montesquieu was right: ethics must have characteristics appropriate to a given place. But if one is not comfortable with abstractions, one can't or won't take an ancient concept, no matter how good it is, and adapt it to a new era or setting. There is no serious creative activity that doesn't first require analysis, then theory, then a rough trying out of the theory, then checking.

What Professor Levin's idea doesn't encompass is the possibility that when students of the professions have heard the language of principles and have been invited to participate in discussions of the ethical properties, as they apply to their chosen profession, these students develop more ethical sensitivity. A study done with first- and second-year dental students at the University of Minnesota showed that conversation, talking as such, about professional situations demanding ethical decisions woke up the students' moral nature.[3] An especially interesting finding of these researchers was the clear suggestion that *talk* nudged forward the dental students' ethical growth more than solving written ethical ideas or situational problem solving. The talk, furthermore, needed to involve moral ideas tied specifically to professional situations. It was no good, in other words, to have all moral talk on Sunday mornings at an institution dedicated to moral talk, and then to practice one's profession at an institution that taught only practical technology.

Not thinking conceptually stunts maturity in two different characters in "White Canyon": the scientist-father and the narrator's husband. Neither can face the truth about radioactivity and the evil perpetrated by the Atomic Energy Commission upon them and those they love because they are not in the habit of using moral abstractions.

When a brain makes abstractions it is doing several intricate tasks, one of which is dividing things into categories. Geiger counters, rain gauges, and seismographs are instruments of mensuration. Engineers, like the narrator's father in "White Canyon," are accustomed to such categorization. One may be lithe and enthusiastic about categorizing concrete objects—or spirited and enthusiastic about identifying cultural artifacts, as is the narrator's mother—and yet have failed in the tougher job of identifying appalling news and categorizing it—the work we associate with ethics.

Misrepresenting danger to a group, lying to employees, and perpetrating that danger in the first place belong in a category called "evil by those with power used against those with less power or no power." The narrator's parents' brains did not organize data received into that category or any category like it. Rudeness, offhandedness, and evasion with hospital patients, self-orientation in medical staff at the expense of patients—those behaviors belong in a category perhaps called "gratuitous low-level bullying by those with professional responsibilities." The narrator's husband and parents were too morally inexperienced to form that category in their brains.

4. A childhood and youth during which the parents protect the child's solitude and provide a desk in the child's room

One needn't have enough money to give a child a desk or the inestimably valuable room of one's own, however: I have heard both poor and lower-middle-class parents point out to their children a secret hiding place just for that child. That is not ideal, but it will do. Children leap to it the moment someone says, "Do you need a secret place? We'll work it out." At the least, the secret place can be a notebook or scrapbook and pencil respectfully protected by a parent from the child's siblings, and when possible, from the child's own destructive tendencies. For children experience self-doubt when writing alone, just as adults experience "writer's block" or "the inner critic." A child finds it hard to keep up self-esteem when apart from friends, gang, or parents—yet one must have some experience of being apart or one can't write down one's own ideas. The well-known sociological finding that the first child of a large family usually does better on the Scholastic Aptitude Test than the other siblings suggests much about families. One insight this offers is that the first child had

more time, hour for hour, free of sibling peers in which to validate
the brainwork we have to do alone.

School libraries with computers are filling this need in a way
not dreamed of thirty years ago. Learning-disabled children do
amazing conceptual work on computers. Adults who never kept
journals are writing down their own hypotheses about life because they can hide their ideas on the hard drives. If Virginia
Woolf could have seen the phenomenon of computers, she would
have joyfully proposed a laptop for every Mrs. Brown in a second-
class carriage.

**5. *A childhood and youth in which, just after a child has given
an opinion, an adult asks the child to enlarge upon it or to
clarify it***

Such ego enhancement and mental challenge are easy to perform,
yet rare.

**6. *A childhood in which the caretakers speed up the pace of
imagination whenever a chance offers***

Let us say we are walking down Randolph Avenue in St. Paul,
Minnesota. A child walks along, hand in hand with an adult.
Here is what the child knows just from the fact that the adult has
taken his or her *hand*, not *wrist*: this is not a zoo with safely imprisoned animals of which I am one. This adult likes me and will
keep me safe.

In the next second the adult says, in the same tone we use to
tell the carryout person that we want paper, not plastic: "I am trying to think: if I were a lioness, where would I hide on this corner."

"But Mama, you aren't a lion."

A parent needs not to be discouraged by the conventionality of
children. Conventionality is more neatly programmed into human beings than imagination, and it gets so much support early
on that it is a wonder we ever do develop much imagination. "But
Mama, you aren't a lion" is nothing more than the last cry of the

collective-culture beast. A half second later the child is all set to go into the lioness's strategy.

Adult: "I know one thing. I would not hide in that plastic-walled metro bus waiting station, where everybody could see me right out in the open, not to mention the people already waiting for the bus in there."

"You could climb up the streetlight pole in front of the bank," the child offers.

"Good idea," the parent answers. "It'd take nerve, though, because if someone did see a lioness hanging on for dear life up there, they'd fuss."

"With her claws scratching around where the four light things are stuck!" cries the child.

"Well, maybe they would be so shocked they would tell themselves they never did really see her up there at all. People do that," the parent says. "They might do that even though her tail, hanging down with the switch of hair at the end, is swatting back and forth so it has slapped that man's visor cap right off."

A brief list of what has happened in the scene above:

The child has been invited to share a deliberately nutty
    scenario.
The child has been invited to see a dilemma from a large, wild
    animal's point of view—a very *other* view, indeed.
The child has been invited to participate in an extended
    image.
The child has seen a person of great authority, Mama, at play,
    which means human and vulnerable, not in her
    persona as parent-mentor.
The activity was quiet. There was no noise above the sound of
    the two human voices and whatever traffic sounds made
    up the background. I emphasize this point because many
    households full of electronically heightened sound have a
    deleterious effect on cognitive faculties.

A magnificent aspect of the human brain is that it is willing to fire up its millions of little chemoelectrical nerve endings with the tiniest amount of outside stimulus. It doesn't need a mentor-adult every day; it scarcely needs one playful imaginative conversation a month. It remembers the conversations and darts ahead, tying them to something else here, tying them to something else there. A child who has participated in just two or three imaginative conversations with adults is not the same person as he or she was beforehand.

Jules-Henri Poincaré admired the predilection of great scientists for trying hypotheses, everywhere, whenever they have time. A child's parallel to such play of mind can be only fancy, like the hypothesis of a lioness hiding on the corner of Snelling and Randolph, or it can be metaphor, like Richard Wilbur's imagining the drying clothes to be angels, then not angels, then clothes for thieves being hanged (see "Love Calls Us to the Things of This World" in chapter 9).

Any imaginative exercise given by an adult to a child (or to another adult) counts as what W. N. Dember would call having a "pacer": that is, the adult danced the child into a far more exuberant scenario than most children wander into by themselves. Dember's analogy is to a track runner, who will increase his or her own speed if led off by a pacer. The aspect of "adult pacers" that I love is that Dember squarely says neither people nor animals run faster just out of physiological need: they run faster out of *interest*. They like novelty and mental complexity.[4]

7. *A childhood and youth in which a child has protection from putdowns and insults close in (which is to say, within the house, from the primary adults), and as much as possible from attack outside the home (in the neighborhood or on the school grounds)*

Being verbally bullied inculcates so much fear of further ridicule that the mind shudders lest it express anything unsafe—that is, anything that has not been said over and over by nearby adults in power. Later, when peers are as influential on one's well-being as adults have been during childhood, a frightened young person will express only the views of those young people who seem most powerful—that is, popular. If one's self-esteem is very low, one doesn't even bother emulating the most popular of one's school-mates. One clings instead to the lowest common denominator—the least admired, even the outcasts of the class. Since the others in this low common denominator of moral opinion or imaginative level are also validating only group ideas they have anxiously assimilated from the outside, they keep reinforcing a frightened, rigid conventionality in one another.

We know that the families of abused children are signally rigid, authoritarian, isolated from one another, given to either tyrannizing or cowering, depending on their roles in the family. They are chilled through. According to the *Harvard Mental Health Letter*,

> They are said to lack warmth, humor, and sensitivity to the rhythms and needs of their children. They talk to the children mainly to give orders, ask peremptory questions, and hurl derisive epithets. They treat the child's behavior as though it were intended to annoy them.[5]

That is the extreme case. Nearer the center of the continuum between abusive and beneficent stand the majority of families. Tens of millions of parents may be mildly rigid, mildly authoritarian, mildly isolated, mildly chill-hearted, with everyday patterns of low-key tyranny and tyranny-enabling, lacking humor and sensitivity and tending to speak briefly and peremptorily to their children, allowing themselves a constant sense that the children are deliberately trying their patience.

It would take a fortune to monitor enough households to estimate how many millions of parents quietly, regularly, never noticing, dull their children's spirits. (A sharp example would be how the parents of Clare in "The Woman Lit by Fireflies" made fun of her for praying over a three-legged cat. "Clare stories" were even a genre of cocktail-hour wit, stories to regale their friends with, in front of the little girl.)

8. *A childhood and youth in which adults do not reinforce groupthink or passive public relations and tact skills in girls while allowing solitary study and individual decision making in boys*

Spending all one's time with others encourages relationship smoothing, but not originality. Here is why: original ideas sound harsh, the way freshly gathered herbs smell rank, not nostalgic. If one takes as one's goal making a roomful of people feel comfortable, one tones down bright ideation—at least down to the common denominator. If someone has just said, "That news anchor said we were in danger of getting rain by night and we should watch for it," a tact-driven person would not remark, "Because Americans get so little major international news on television, the poor anchors have to make good theater out of the weather—pretending there is danger in a half-hour of rainfall, for example. Pathetic." Such a remark is about as welcome as it would be if two people were chewing the fat while idling their engines next to each other and suddenly both pickups were lifted up thirty feet in the air by a huge invisible gantry.

Teaching any category of people, little girls or non-liberal-arts-educated adults or any other grouping, to accustomize themselves to low-key group amiability, while allowing others imaginative development, is a form of cultural abuse. Katha Pollitt's essay "Marooned on Gilligan's Island" casts particular light on such separatism.

Ironically, some gender separatism originates with feminists. Here is an instance for which Carol Gilligan's and others' work[6], promoting the idea that women do best in little groups, may be indirectly to blame. Ursuline College, in Cleveland, Ohio, actually revamped its curriculum so that the women were expected to spend key learning time in groups. The *New York Times* quoted Ursuline Professor of Sociology Gary Polster as saying, "Our approach reflects the different ways boys and girls are socialized." The same news story quotes Judith Shapiro, provost of Bryn Mawr, as describing the girl-grouping approach as "dangerous." She went on to say, "I think it can be feminism doing the work of sexism."[7] If boys and girls are socialized in different ways, as Polster contends, we need to consider that difference as cultural abuse, not as appropriate diversity of style.

If pictures are really better than words, here are two. In the first, Virginia Woolf is trying to write *Three Guineas* with a helpful little group around her. "I really like that, Ginny," one says. "I think you are working through something that is real for you, Vir," says another.

In the second scenario Clara Schumann is composing music with a support group urging her to get the kinks out of a rondo. "If you make it more like other rondos, then it will be more accessible," one of them explains. But another intervenes: "Clara, we're behind you all the way."

In a word, the most serious work of the world has to be thought through, at some point, by someone who is *alone*. Group dynamics experts point out that when a group discusses ethical problems, it tends toward "moral drift." That is, any one or two strong dissenters from the general group idea begin to lighten their subversive commitment, until finally their dissent is scarcely more passionate than objecting to the punctuation. Women have practiced moral drift on their own ideas for centuries, calling it being considerate of male egos. Whatever the motivation, the result is rubbery conversation.

The trustees or the legislature or the faculty of a college deliberately plans the psychological habitat in which students will grow, even if they don't call it psychological habitat. It's a culturally abusive plan that allows female students so little solitude that they feel anxious unless they are yarding up together like deer in winter—at the very time of life (ages seventeen through twenty-five) when men or women need to learn to honor and trust the complex brain they each have. I have seen full-scale sadness pour into students' faces when told they must break into small groups. Why? In the large group, only people of serious interest and considerable confidence participate in the discussion; in small groups, people who have not done the reading or the thinking nevertheless allow themselves to barge into the discussion, even prefixing their slack remarks with "I'm not sure where this is going. . . ." If one's mission is to arrive at new truth, not social comfort, an undisciplined small group can make you feel like a painter chained to a tree four feet from your palette.

9. *A childhood and youth spent in an environment that is absolutely free of violence*

Violence on television, which is so normal and omnipresent that we may take it for just one more aspect of "how things are," is seriously hurtful to children. Children have their beautiful, intricate work to do, work best done during childhood and not by patchwork later: play, ego development, and character formation.

One can't do play, ego development, and character formation in a violent habitat.

The human mind is ingenious, even if largely unconscious. Like a chess player with a large piece being threatened, the mind runs through its crisis responses. In chess these responses are: kill the threatener; failing that, put an obstruction between your piece and the threatener; or failing that, run. The lower, ancient part of the mind lays out choices like that for its child—fight, block, or flee—when the psychological habitat is cruel or violent.

A child usually cannot use the first of the chess defenses, killing the threatener, though in the United States younger and younger children attempt to murder abusive parents. A child's mind usually chooses distraction or flight. The forms of flight from violence seem to fall into either denial or numbing—the numbing, if kept up too long or too deeply, turning into nihilistic feelings—cynicism—and following the cynicism, a moral boredom. I think we should use the phrase "moral boredom" because what bores a cynic is the moral workings of the mind, the part that takes an interest in deciding what's ideal or what's bad.

The mind wants the child to survive, and will make every effort. Its one idea seems to be, once it has registered that terrible psychological pain exists, "Let's avoid this pain. Let's practice pain avoidance in any way we can. Let's start with *denial*. We will therefore not call this pain 'pain' but just 'how-things-are.'"

Children tend, in any case, to think everything that happens is happening the same everywhere else: they think it is reality.

Denial, popularly thought of as undesirable because it is indeed undesirable in adults, can be a lifebelt for children. A child seemed sad, but not disturbed, after his parents' divorce. He played Dungeons and Dragons nearly constantly. A psychoherapist said, "Sounds good to me. That's where *I'd* go if I were he. And if I were his parent, I would just leave him right there for now."

But violence in the family is even harder on a child than divorce. When there is violence in the family or in the streets right around the home, children use another kind of pain avoidance that is a larger cloud of the unconscious than denial. This psychological defense is called numbing. Denial is an adjunct form of numbing; that is, one has numbed one's own awareness of misery about a given cause, such as Daddy's beating Mommy or raping me. Numbing itself, on the other hand, applies to any number of emotions in any number of situations. It is a general flattening of feeling. When the news is too bad to bear, people numb.

I remember an instance I read of in someone's memoir of trench warfare in World War I. Some officers doing rounds through a trench, asking the usual questions, reminding sergeants to check feet, and so forth, came to a group of men who had hung up some of their kit above their heads, against the sandbagging. "What's that!" one officer said suspiciously, indicating the projection around which the soldiers had slung straps. It looked like someone's leather boot and leg. "Oh, that's just Jerry, sir," one of the men said. "Well, get rid of it," the officer snapped. Such numbing of sensitivity to the uses of an enemy's dead body is practical in horrible circumstances. What is *not* practical is numbing for so long or so deeply that it sticks and becomes one's emotional habit. Numbing can be the germ of serious nihilism.

If children practice too much numbing while their cognitive development is in its early stages, they become poorly socialized people, people indifferent or even habituated to violence. A short, clear, specific discussion of this dilemma by two physicians and two social workers concludes that of all the awful results, the one we need to pay serious attention to is the fact that "early scenes of violence make a child vulnerable to a nihilistic, fatalistic orientation to the future."[8]

Nihilism and sadness are not rare in children, so we cannot write them off in the way that thinkers write off the fact that some children are born with one or another rare physiological defect. Unfortunately, sadness and cynicism are rising in the populations of the young.

The psychologist and therapist Mary Pipher has given scrupulous attention to the psychological habitats in which young people live.[9] Young girls are especially endangered by the violence in the school culture. By the time they are in the sixth grade, most children have been introduced to drugs. One-third of American children think they will die before they are twenty-one. They desperately need parents, but their parents are often separated, absent, distracted, or frantic. The extended family, so calming to children, is disappearing.

A dreadful aspect of childhood nihilism is that it spoils some of the cognitive work that a happier mind needs and wants to do. Children's work is partly play, which along with being read aloud to, is the greatest developer of the imagination. How ordinary it sounds: "I'll be the mother. You be an escaped beast from the zoo dressed up as a UPS woman."

That proposal doesn't seem psychologically noteworthy unless we make a scenario of two little kids who have *not* been able to develop imagination: one *cannot* imagine being the mother or the doll being sick or the card table being a lion's den. The other just waits, stupefied, if someone does propose such fantasy. That child waits through the senseless words until something comes along that he or she gets, such as, "Time to wash your hands for lunch, kids."

A number of forces can lead to such blankness, nihilistic feelings being the most ominous. They destroy the concentration. A person who feels that nothing really is any good and that no one counts for anything tends not to dwell on one mental image or maintain one sequence of daydreaming. Yet the brain, excitable and distractable as it is, nonetheless is programmed to think a thing over leisurely — to think this, then pause, then suppose *that*, and so forth. The brain expects and wants some hours a week, here and there, even if only in ten-minute slots, to muddle through some rankling or ecstatic task it has set itself until it has arrived at what social workers call "a handle on it." If the mind doesn't get to do that muddling because the child has been psychologically too disturbed, then the child is at risk for what C. G. Jung called psychological "poison." That is, the mental gift of being able to imagine oneself in this situation or that situation, the gift of enjoying such imaginings, turns bad and is moribund and then toxic to the child.

A low level of imagining means little mental work is going on. Introverts, especially, use fantasies for mental stimulation. If there is no fantasizing, some skill of the brain wilts for lack of that particular kind of stimulus. Ours, unfortunately, is a culture that kids its "introverts" and pays extroverts the highest salaries, even though human beings need to do inward thinking. "Daydreaming is not going to get you much of anywhere," an unimaginative parent says to a child, and the child, heartbroken, in turn passes along that moribund advice to his or her children, in the same way that a heartbroken victim of incest passes along heartbreaking incest to his or her children. Some, but not all, of the dynamics of physical abuse apply to cultural abuse.

Sometimes the boredom experienced by people whose thinking is "other-directed," to use David Riesman's term, or extroverted, goes unnoticed. I think that extroverts experience a kind of cultural suffering: they seem to go to boat fairs and look at motors in a random way. They read a book people are talking about. They have tickets for the game next week. Their life looks cheerful enough; when you glance at their snapshots, everyone is smiling on the beach towel, or, in Susan Lowell's "White Canyon," smiling underneath a sign that says DANGER AREA.

A dozen aspects of our early psychological habitat can halt the growth of inward consciousness; one is violence in the home — violence figuratively rattling the brain, shaking up the little planning, hoping structures in there. The habit of not reflecting sets in the way rubble settles around a seriously damaged building.

Finally, when no reflection occurs, one doesn't recognize evil for evil: everything is of a piece, "the way things are." An ominous, newer expression in the United States is "whatever." People even say it to each other by way of response to someone's comment. "Listen," we tell someone, "I've got this new idea to add to my philosophy of life." The other person says, "Whatever." That was a silly example in which one naïf speaks to one discourteous person. I offer it, however, as a sad parallel to what thousands and thousands of people whose minds haven't been encouraged say to themselves inside themselves.

"Listen, I've got this new idea to add to my philosophy," says one self in there — the ego trying to organize concepts the way the ego loves to do.

The half-conscious self replies, "Whatever."

Psychologists call it *internalized* material. The anti-empathy of the person's background now is being practiced by the self against the self. We are a brainy species, so this kind of violence to the mind is serious.

A curious question to ask, when we think about the life of Clare and the life of the "White Canyon" woman, is this: What did these women *internalize* from their psychological habitats? How do they repeat, inside themselves, one side thinking one thing, the other opposing, the casual brutalization of their habitats?

Jim Harrison's "The Woman Lit by Fireflies" is an amazing story of a woman with a complex set of blessings and curses in her life. She didn't have a clear outlook, but she did have an outlook. She contemplated her life and she judged herself. She had many pleasures to distract her, and her journal was not a connected essay but fragments, done here, done there, "piths and gists." She had a beginner's taste for reflecting on life.

In this novella, the author shows us more than thirty characters, fascinating, horrible or sweet people. And most astonishingly, in the United States of the 1990s, Jim Harrison gives us an accurate picture of a very rich person.

Most of us are too bad-tempered to look at the rich carefully, too cross to honor their struggles when they have them, too rude to find out what their agenda really is. Harrison's story is wonderfully good-tempered. Several of its characters watch, with sympathy, while others struggle to be livelier and more ethical than their social background and education conditioned them to be.

Even the woman alongside the road took an interest in Zilpha and Clare, and praised them with great sweetness. Clare's daughter encouraged her. Dr. Roth was sympathetic, and helped Clare be conscious of her knee-jerk class responses—writing a check in order not to feel guilty, for example. Since human beings of goodwill often *do* watch one another's struggles to get free and be good, it was nice to find it so in this story.

In two ways this is the best story I have seen in English. First, it takes on the whole pageantry of people's psychological habitats—where they are coming from—and how far into meaningful life each of them can get from there. Second, "The Woman Lit by Fireflies" is the only amiable, accurate treatment of cultured people with substantial private incomes. Clare is psychologically engaging, charming in a wandering, insubstantial way, and morally ridiculous. Even in the end, all she manages to do is what not particularly intellectual rich people ordinarily *do* do: go to Paris, affect bohemian headwear, and resume one or another cultural interest aborted in her youth.

American reading audiences are not used to thinking of people who support symphonies as morally ridiculous. For one thing, most of us see them from the outside or not at all. Jim Harrison gives us a prolonged look at a few. This woman, Clare, from the beginning of the story to its end, performs one morally wasteful act after another. We could put together a list of her life interests, her judgments on one issue and another, and finally her actions, then write across the bottom: "The above thoughts and actions were chosen and executed by a college-educated American with a portfolio yielding an income of between half a million and a million a year."

With the exception of Dr. Roth, the story's characters come from no particular ethnic background; they have no disabilities, no record of physical abuse, and no divergent sexual choices.

Well, then, why should we care two cents' worth what Clare does, when so many are openly suffering worse situations? So she is a rich woman married to someone who turns off her classical music in order to listen to a financial lecture? So what? a conventional reader might ask. Why should her story be included in anything called an ethics reader?

This story ought to be of the greatest interest to people who would like to stop the world's bullying. First and last, in its little and big scenes, the story is about big and little bullying.

Clare belongs to a powerful class of people. Her kind of people could make America a merciful place, but the Clares, with their beastly Donalds, don't bother to think about the economic system. Clare never thinks about *changing* her class prerogatives. When she thinks of Donald's rotten behavior she thinks about it as a bad part of her marriage, not as Donald doing bad things out in the world. That's why her moral notes (the "piths and gists") are so piecemeal. She is *still* swaddled safe from systemic thinking. That is why Dr. Roth warns her about her having the illusion that she is helping: he knows that she repeatedly comforts herself with that very illusion.

What is her psychological habitat?

As a child, she was made fun of by her parents. They told their friends "Clare stories." Such friendly, ironic teasing of one's own children in front of one's adult friends, often during cocktails, was still acceptable among the rich in the 1960s and 1970s. Friendly teasing that slightly puts down the child forwards a number of learning goals dear to Clare's parents' class. First, the friendliness teaches the child that manners must and will be maintained even in a conversation in which some people are smiling but you personally feel diminished. You must smile, too. One learns double messages. Second, the child must learn not to be "centered" but to distance himself or herself from strong feelings. A child must focus not on learning to be conscious of and grateful for one's own take on things, but on a set of social graces one must practice with others. Until recently, children like Clare were routinely taught to offer the trays of canapés to adults. Such graceful gestures help socialize a person, and children love getting good at them. To be asked to learn and practice some formalities is a bless-ing. People eat it up. I only object to how few hours were spent by parents in encouraging Clare's life of thought in comparison to the many hours spent showing her practical skills like how to stoop with the tray and hold it still without smirking while some-one has trouble picking up the toothpick full of lamb kidney from which the wrapped bacon is coming undone.

Another disadvantage of such training is that it is very hard to drop these class markings when one needs to save one's own spirit. This point is more important than most people guess. People of less formal socialization than Clare's have little trouble dropping their class markings when they go into psychotherapy. Their class markings have visible drawbacks—perhaps the men grunt instead of speaking, listening to, or speaking respectfully to women; per-haps the women, with a mouse around one eye and bruises under left and right forearm (from raising the arms to protect the face from a beater), have been acculturated to lie. They say, "No biggie. I'm just tired, is all." Such styles are easy to drop once one gets in-terested in becoming psychologically conscious. They are easy to drop because they get in the way of kindness and truthfulness. But what Clare was taught goes on looking rather beautiful, even to a psychiatric patient or social work client. Graceful early training be-comes one more hurdle that she has to look at, tear free from, as-sess with some distance, and resist nostalgia for.

Clare's adult life: her father saw through the fiancé's persona of left-wing liberal. Clare's father recognized an absolutely values-free capitalist when he saw one.

Clare discovered her husband's vicious attitudes—his anti-Semitism, his willingness to promote anything if there was money in it.

She found out he was an exquisite liar.

She was in some denial about misery. She had migraine headaches.

Her life had a number of most pleasant distractions in it, however.

Her adulthood was informed by sensitivity, but might a person of lifelong sensitivity be able to initiate a confrontation with the husband and carry it through? Probably not. More likely, she will simply exit. She won't reorganize the neighborhood. After twenty years of being pleasantly distracted, recognizing the good things, what does she do? She goes to Paris, on her private income.

American women could probably change this particular dynamic of rich women's thinking. We would have to get over the terror of stereotyping, first. No one thinks it is stereotyping when someone proposes that we do something for disabled people, but when we propose looking at rich wives it sounds as if a pterodactylic generalization is about to fly across the room. Physiological groupings are treated differently depending on their needs. We ought to do the same with psychological groupings. If a number of people raised in a certain psychological habitat seem to be needing help in a way that suggests their troubles are peculiar to their habitat, we should be open to looking at them.

A second philosophy might be deciding that it cannot be solved. Somewhere in the background of everyone's awareness is Martha Mitchell, the wife of Nixon's attorney general, John Mitchell, who spoke out fairly clearly and was put into an insane asylum. Muscle might be used against one's own life.

A third philosophy: Life is nothing but various sets of triages in any event. The trade-offs here are good. If one is Clare, for example, one has enough money to take the pleasant trips with Zilpha. Discreet affairs take money, too. One has enough money for them. If we are married to a rich powerful person who enables some of the world's bullying, well, a sensible voice says, what we were promised was a rose garden, and we got it—*not* a chance for changing a bullying organization or two. That was not promised.

In chapter 4 I mentioned a book by George Vaillant, *Adaptation to Life*. Vaillant's remarks about happiness, mental health, and successful adaptation might give some clue to how hard it will be for the rich to change the venue of the rich.

In his summarizing remarks about the Grant Study, a longitudinal study of ninety-five Harvard men over thirty years of their lives, Vaillant warmly reiterates his idea that a good adaptation to the lives given us is what makes us healthy and happy. He believes in mental health. He believes in happiness. He remarks,

"The healthy individual is a conservative—not in the sense of being penny-pinching or 'anal-retentive,' but in the sense of being capable of conservation and of assessing personal costs. Hans Selye is wrong; it is not stress that kills us. It is effective adaptation to stress that permits us to live."[10] Perhaps Vaillant's voice is the voice of the true, conservative establishment: healthiness and happiness are adaptation to the psychological habitat. One would risk those things if one became some kind of a change agent.

The first thing that any society does to an active change agent is to try to make him or her unhappy. One jeers at, one isolates, one takes to court (if that works) anyone who proposes we make sacrifices we have not been making.

Harrison's Clare would have had to stand up against such opposition, in addition to putting up with her appalling husband.

"White Canyon" is best read first for its beauty of telling, and second as the story of the kind of people a government easily manipulated. These are people who have believed any pain-avoiding aphorism cast toward them, for example "[Radiation] is like getting an X-ray."

At the time of the nuclear-bomb testings in western America, there was a strong protest movement around the country. Humanities-educated young people *knew* that strontium 90 got into breast milk and babies' bones. They knew about cobalt 60 and cesium 137. They already, by 1950, felt wretched about the bombing of Japanese civilians.

"White Canyon" is not about those alert and angry Americans. Lowell's people were of another psychological habitat. Their story makes a companion piece to the implied biographies of the men in Tom McGrath's poem, "Ode for the American Dead in Asia."

Both the story about the uranium hunters and the poem about Vietnam War casualties have to do with how, if one hasn't learned to question authority, and if one wants to have fun—that is, not register painful realizations about what is going on—one is vulnerable to being dangerously used by the United States.

In both cases, our atomic energy policy and our Vietnam War

policy, the people brought up *not* to contemplate and *not* to judge policies were the victims: Americans of disadvantaged psychoethical habitat worked in radioactive places and went to the Vietnam War.

But how can someone talk about the majority of people's childhood upbringings as "disadvantaged"? It sounds like a shrill exaggeration, but an irony of social psychology is that whatever it says sounds like an exaggeration until we read the story of some particulars. When the particulars come in, such as the jaunty, fun-loving, devil-may-care stances of the narrator's parents in "White Canyon," and the coarse manners of the official males in the hospital, then a phrase like "disadvantaged psychoethical habitat" gathers meaning.

The characters in Lowell's story and McGrath's poem, like any of us who have little penchant for reflecting on life, just live along, like zombies, but with a fun-loving surface to their lives. They are short on hard information that they need, such as whether this much or that much radiation is safe or kind, but they have macho stances. In terms of psychological consciousness, a stance is any hypothesis that one accepts on a permanent basis because one does not expect to receive further information on the given subject. Stances are an interesting artifact of denial of anxiety. For example, here is a story of stance, instead of information absorption, being practiced. A is a questioner. B is engaging in stance and denying force of fact.

A: I see you leave your front door unlocked. In St. Paul, even.
B: You bet I do.
A: You're not nervous about it? I mean, with all the people walk-
    ing into people's houses and attacking them?
B: Look, the day I have to lock my own darn front door is the
    day I check out.

Lowell's people live largely by stance.

Here is the author's canny description of the cheerful car rides up and down the great sweeping roads of American desert country, past the DANGER signs:

The shadow of the Jeep used to stretch across the buttes, with our necks and heads pulled into long grotesque shapes. Then it would tumble onto flat ground—a fleeing box with two large and two small loose pegs inside. At the sight or sound of us, deer like giant jackrabbits went lofting through the scrubby trees. Coyotes melted away. Vultures sliced their invisible circles overhead.

Lowell's passage works, of course, at the level of mere description of parents and children in a car. Desert rabbits do "loft" away from cars. Families do cast shadows when the sun's out and motion distorts them. But the way Lowell has put the images together is what shows us how ominous our species is—with its people like shadows, grotesque shapes, and oddly mechanical like wooden pegs. That is our species whose passage frightens the rest of nature.

It is the *patterns* of things, not things themselves, that are invisible, and Lowell's characters, like McGrath's, needed to have been seeing those patterns.

Notes

1. Elizabeth Léonie Simpson, "A Holistic Approach to Moral Development and Behavior," in *Moral Development and Behavior: Theory, Research, and Social Issues,* ed. Thomas Lickona (New York: Holt, Rinehart and Winston, 1976), 162.

2. Michael Levin, "Ethics Courses: Useless" *New York Times,* November 25, 1989, 23.

3. Muriel J. Bebeau, Ph.D., James R. Rest, Ph.D., Catherine M. Yamoor, M.A., "Measuring Dental Students' Ethical Sensitivity," a paper presented at the International Association of Dental Research, in New Orleans, March 1982, and at the American Educational Research Association meeting in Montreal, April 1983.

4. W. N. Dember, "The New Look in Motivation," *American Scientist,* 53 (1965) 409–27, quoted in Jane Loevinger, *Ego Development: Conceptions and Theories* (San Francisco: Jossey-Bass, 1976), 308–9.

5. *Harvard Mental Health Letter,* 9, no. 11 (May 1993): 2–3.

6. Mary Field Belenky, Blythe McVicker Clinchy, Nancy Rule Goldberger, and Jill Mattuck Tarule, *Women's Ways of Knowing* (New York: Basic Books, 1986).

7. Susan Chira, "An Ohio College Says Women Learn Differently, So It Teaches That Way," *New York Times,* May 13, 1992, A1.

8. Betsy McAlister Groves, Barry Zuckerman, Steven Marans, and Donald J. Cohen, "Silent Victims: Children Who Witness Violence," Division of Developmental and Behavioral Pediatrics, Boston City Hospital, Talbot 214, 818 Harrisons Avenue, Boston, MA 02118.

9. Mary Pipher, *Reviving Ophelia: Saving the Selves of Adolescent Girls* (New York: Ballantine Books, 1994). Dr. Pipher offered these observations in her April 4, 1995, lecture in St. Paul, Minnesota, to the Distinguished Women Foundation, at the College of St. Catherine.

10. George Vaillant, *Adaptation to Life* (Boston: Little, Brown, 1977), 374.

CHAPTER **16**

Genuine Jerks and Genuine Jerk Organizations

The Soft Core

by Arturo Vivante

It was suppertime. The bell had rung. Everyone was around the table except his father, nearly eighty. Sometimes he didn't hear the bell. So Giacomo went and knocked at his bedroom door.

No answer came. Going in, he found his father lying on the bed with his shoes on. His eyes were open, but they didn't seem to recognize Giacomo.

"Papa, dinner is ready."

"What? What is it?"

"Dinner," Giacomo said, without any hope now that he would come to it.

"Dinner," his father echoed feebly, making no effort to get up but rather trying to connect the word. Dinner where, when, his eyes seemed to be saying.

"You are not feeling well?"

"Yes, I'm well," he said, almost inaudibly. "I am well, but . . . you . . . you are . . . ?" His father could not quite place him.

"Giacomo. I am Giacomo," the son said.

His name seemed to make little or no impression on his father. Indeed, he seemed to have forgotten it already and to be groping for some point of reference, something familiar to sustain his mind, which was wavering without hold in space and time.

Quickly Giacomo stepped out of the room, through an anteroom, and opened the dining-room door. His wife, his sister, their children, and a guest were round the table eating, talking. He called his wife.

She rose and hurried over. "Is he all right?"

"No."

"Like last time?"

"No, no, not as bad."

They had in mind a time five or six months before, when Giacomo's sister had called from Rome for a phone number that their father had in his address book. Giacomo, then as now, had gone to call him in his room, and found him on his bed, unconscious, breathing thickly, and in a sort of spasm. A stroke, he thought. Thoroughly alarmed, he rushed back to the phone, hung up after a few hurried words of explanation, and called the doctor. In a few minutes, everyone in the house was round his father's bed. It seemed to Giacomo that the end had come. Its suddenness appalled him. He wasn't prepared for it. He had been so unfriendly to his father lately—almost rude. Why, only the day before, when his father had asked him to drive him into town, as he often did, Giacomo told him that he couldn't, that he was too busy, which wasn't really true. And other things came to mind—his curt replies to his father's questions, the long silences at table, and when there was some conversation, his father's being left out of it, ignored; his not laughing at his father's little jokes; not complimenting him on the fruit that came from trees he had planted, and for which he so much expected a word of praise when it was served at table. If Giacomo had only had some warning, to make up for his behavior— oh, he would have been his father's chauffeur, if he had known, talked with him about his books, his philosophy, his fruit trees, laughed at his jokes, listened keenly to the things he said and pretended it was the first time he heard him saying them. With a sense of anguish, he watched his father, unconscious, on the bed. He couldn't die just yet; he must talk again. The prospect that he mightn't—that he might live on paralyzed and speechless on that bed—was even worse.

They waited for the doctor. Yet, even before the doctor came, something might be done. He couldn't just wait and watch his father die in this awful, sunken state. To ease his breathing, Giacomo took out the dentures, which seemed to lock his father's mouth, and opened the window, because the radiator, going full steam, had made the room stiflingly hot. Then he hurried upstairs. In the drug cabinet, there were some phials of a relaxant—papaverine—that had once been prescribed for his father to help his circulation. Giacomo gave him two, by injection—a certain knowledge of medicine having remained from when he had studied it, and even practiced it, long ago—then waited for the effect. But even before the drug could possibly have had one, his father seemed to improve, to rise from his prostration. The breathing was easier. His limbs were slowly relaxing. It seemed that whatever had commanded them to stiffen was easing its hold, loosening up. His eyes began to look and not just gaze; the sounds coming from his mouth were not just moans but language, or the beginnings of it—monosyllables, bits with which words and phrases could be made. And the improvement was continuous. By the time the doctor arrived, he was moving his limbs and uttering words, though the words were disconnected. As the doctor examined him and prescribed treatment, his voice gained strength. He answered questions; he sat up; he even asked for food. An hour or two later, he was reading, making notes, pencil in hand and postcard on the page, in case he should want to underline a word or a sentence that had struck him. And he looked very sweet there on the bed in his pajamas, reading under the light, thin and ethereal, all involved in that spiritual form of exercise. His body—the material aspect of it, his physique—which had been so much in the foreground and had so preoccupied them a few hours before, now seemed quite forgotten, back where it should be, something one is hardly aware of, that works better when one's mind is off it.

So his father had been given back to life, and Giacomo had another chance to be warm and friendly to him. At intervals that night, he slipped into the room to see how he was doing, or, if the light was out, afraid to wake him, listened outside with his ear to the door. Oh, this was easy enough to do, and it was easy to be solicitous the next day—ask how he was, and help him with the half-dozen drugs the doctor had prescribed, and with the diet. But when his father—well again, his usual self, full of the same old preoccupations and requests—resumed getting about and Giacomo heard his aged yet determined step coming toward his room, something in him stiffened as if in defense, and he waited for the door to open.

His father came in without a knock, as was his custom. "After all, cars now are pleasingly designed," he said in a slightly plaintive, slightly polemical voice, from just inside the doorway.

For a moment, Giacomo wondered what he was talking about. Then he remembered his father's arguing a few days before against an ordinance barring cars from the main street of the town. Giacomo had disagreed, and now his father was bringing the subject up again, bothered as always by anyone's disputing his view-point. "You like them?" Giacomo said.

"Well, they are certainly more pleasant to watch than were carriages drawn by panting, weary horses. Besides, people put up with much more disturbing things than cars without complaining."

His father had his own peculiar ideas about traffic, about where Giacomo should park his car, about driving—about practically every-thing, in fact. He insisted on the frequent use of the horn, and if the person driving didn't blow it and he thought there was danger of a collision, he would shout to let the other party know that the car he was riding in was coming. It was almost as irritating as his bringing up an old argument and wanting to prove his point though a long time had passed. For him an argument was never closed. He went on pondering over it, debating it in his mind. One saw him doing it—wandering in the garden, pausing, starting to walk again, a true peripatetic—and if some new thought came to him he didn't hesitate to let you know it, wherever you might be.

About this matter of the ordinance, in the end Giacomo just nodded. Appeased, his father asked him for a favor. It was a way of showing he was on good terms with him. "Are you going into town tomorrow afternoon?"

Giacomo never planned his days ahead if he could help it. "Well, yes, I can go in, if you like."

"Would you? I need to buy some brown paper to line the crates of cherries with."

The cherries weren't ripe yet.

"Ah, yes, yes, I'll take you," Giacomo said.

"At about three o'clock?"

"The shops, you know, don't open until four."

"Say at half past three."

It took ten minutes to drive into town.

"Ah, yes, yes, all right."

Two or three times the next day, his father would remind him of the trip, and at a few minutes past three be at his door, ready to go. Giacomo would prevent himself from making any comments, but the very effort not to make them would keep him silent. "You are so silent," his father would observe in the car. "What is it?"

"Nothing. I am sorry."

"You have such a long face."

It was the hardest thing for Giacomo to look cheerful when he wasn't. He had no more control over his face than over his mood, and felt there was no poorer dissembler in the world than he. "I'm sorry if I can't be gayer," he would reply.

Sometimes his father would come into his room to ask him for advice on where to send an article he had written. But it seemed to Giacomo that he was asking for advice only in order to discard it. "I would send it to Wyatt, if I were you," Giacomo would suggest. But his father had already made up his mind whom to send it to, and it wasn't to Wyatt.

Speaking of his works, his father would say to him, "It is a *new* philosophy."

"Yes," Giacomo would reply, and be quite unable to elaborate. It was a pity, because his father yearned for articulate assent and recognition. People found his work difficult; some said they couldn't understand it. Nothing irked him more than to hear this. "Even Sylvia," he would say, referring to a guest, a pretty girl with a ready smile and pleasant manner, "who I don't think is very widely read in philosophy, found it clear." He never doubted that praise was offered in earnest. And no praise seemed more important to him than that which came from girls, from pretty women. Then a blissful smile would light his face and linger in his eyes.

With the single-mindedness of someone who has devoted his whole life to a cause, he gave or sent his articles around. He was so surely entrenched in his ideas that nothing could budge him from them. Each problem, each concept he came on had to be thrashed out and made known. Intent on it, if he met you—no matter where —he might stop and, pronouncing each word as if he were grinding it out, say without preamble, "Creativity is an underived, active, original, powerfully present, intrinsic, self-sustaining principle— something that cannot be resolved or broken up into preexistent, predetermined data, and that is fraught with a negative possibility."

Giacomo would nod. He had been brought up to the tune of phrases such as these, had grown up with them, and though he had only begun to understand them he had finished by believing in them. At any rate, he was convinced there was a good measure of truth in what his father said. And yet he couldn't make it his own. "Negative possibility," *"causa sui,"* "psychic reality," "primal active"—these terms perplexed him. He knew they were full of meaning, for his father, but he couldn't grasp what lay beneath. They weren't in his language, and he looked on them with the detachment of one who is given instruments he can never use.

The extraordinary importance his father gave his work! One had the feeling that nothing—not his wife, not his children—mattered to him quite so much as the vindication of certain principles. He probably saw his family, house, fruit trees, and philosophy as a whole— he had a unified view of everything—and felt that one could never damage the other; he probably even thought that his work was the key, the solution, to a host of problems, financial ones not excluded. Since he didn't teach and lived isolated in the country, to advance his views he tirelessly went to the post office to send off his manuscripts and books, as well as reprints of his articles, which he ordered by the hundreds. He sent them assiduously, and impatiently he waited for acknowledgments and answers that often failed to come.

It was all very admirable, but Giacomo couldn't really admire it. He was more inclined to admire his mother, who painted and often hid her paintings in a cupboard. He thought of some of the landscapes she had done, particularly one of a row of vines, a study of green done with such love of leaf and branch and sod and sky its value couldn't be mistaken, yet, because his father—perhaps with a slight frown or tilting of his head—told her it was not among her best, she had put it in a cupboard, and it had never been framed until after her death. Paintings, his father said, looked better unframed. "Let's wait till we have a bit more money before buying one," he would say, which meant never to everyone but him.

His father wrote and spoke about the value of spontaneity in art and literature and all things, but was he spontaneous? He seemed the opposite to Giacomo sometimes—very deliberate and willful. And how he wanted to escape his father's will. He still felt it upon him as he had when he was a child, a boy, a young man. His father's will shaping his life. His brother's life, too. At school, his brother had been good at all subjects, including mathematics, so his father must have a scientist in the family and had strongly advised him—and wasn't advice, especially the advice of someone whom you admired, harder to disobey than a command?—to study physics and mathematics at college, subjects for which he had no special gift. His brother hadn't, as a result, fared well at college. And as for Giacomo, when he was twenty-two and had been away from home, overseas, for seven years—it was wartime—his father had written, making it seem urgent that he come back immediately. "You are coming home to save your mother," one of his letters said. And Giacomo, who would have wished to delay his return another year—there was a girl, there were his studies, well begun—had gone back only to find that his father had exaggerated, sort of been carried away.

Then his father had a way of asking Giacomo to do things that instinctively made him wish to disobey. He seemed to like asking favors, to ask them for the sake of asking. Giacomo had never answered a flat no; he wasn't that familiar with his father. Recently, though, he had done something worse. His father had called to tell him once again about a cistern whose drainage had become a fixed idea with him. Giacomo had made the mistake of contradicting, and now his father, pencil and paper in hand, came after him so he would get a thorough understanding of his plan. But Giacomo, who had heard enough of it, went off, leaving his father in a rage. Never before had he refused to listen. Now, doing so, he experienced a strange sense of freedom, as though he had shaken off the bonds of childhood. For a moment, he felt almost snug and comfortable in his attitude toward his father. Perhaps it wasn't all unjustified, he thought, and old, childhood resentments came back to him. He remembered a fall from horseback when he was a boy: limping home, with a gaping wound about the knee that needed stitching, his father scolding him for it, and the words of his mother—soothing, like something cool upon a burn—and her taking him to the hospital, the doctor telling her it might be better if she left the room, her replying that she had once been a nurse, staying with him, holding him by the hand while the doctor put the stitches in. His father had scolded him, instead. No, he thought, perhaps I am not altogether in the wrong.

But seeing his father watch the sunset in the garden as he so often did, absorbed in light, a man whom beauty had always held in sway, or hearing him recite a poem—though now he rarely did—enunciating the words in all their clearness, slowly, in a voice that seemed ever on the verge of breaking yet never broke and that seemed to pick each nuance of rhythm and of meaning, Giacomo felt his old love, respect, and admiration come back full to overflowing as when he was a child and it seemed to him that his father never could be wrong—in the realm of the spirit, a man of mighty aims and wider grasp.

And chancing to meet him late at night going into the kitchen for food, looking so frail and thin in his pajamas and so old without his dentures, Giacomo felt ashamed of himself. Oh, his unfriendliness was revolting. That he should be distant and cold toward his father now when he was weak and wifeless, now when he was so old he had become almost childish in some ways—laughing and crying with ease. It was unforgivable, horrible, inhuman. If it hadn't been for his father, where would they be, Giacomo asked himself. If his father hadn't taken his family out of Italy in time, they might all have perished in a German concentration camp. And he had seen that his children learned English almost from babyhood. And he had never raised a hand against them. And he had been generous with those who needed money or lodging or employment.

Well, there was nothing for it but to change his attitude. He must make more of an effort. No week went by without Giacomo's telling himself this. He would talk to his father as to a friend, about any subject that came to his mind. "What this town needs, I think," he said to him at lunch one day, trying to be nice, "is a newspaper. I'd like to start one."

"It would be a very bad idea," his father said.

"Why?"

"But it's obvious why," his father snapped with irritation and perhaps even dislike.

"Well, I wish you would explain it."

"But anyone can see that if there were only one newspaper in the country it would have a better chance of being a good one."

This wasn't like his father at all. He seemed only to want to contradict.

"I thought that to encourage writers and the arts, as well as trade, a local paper . . ." Giacomo didn't finish his sentence. Why should he? His father's face seemed full of aversion, as though Giacomo were saying something blasphemous.

The meal went on in silence. Giacomo looked up at his father. The lines of his face were still set in anger, and he was looking down at his plate, the segment nearest to him, almost at his napkin. No, one could not change, Giacomo thought. His father could not change. He himself could not change. Perhaps if one could fall into a state of oblivion one could change, but otherwise?

And then came the evening when his father did not turn up for supper and Giacomo went to call him in his room. It wasn't nearly as bad as the earlier time, when he thought his father had had a stroke—after all, now he was conscious, his breathing was normal, he wasn't in a spasm, and he could speak. Yet Giacomo had the same feeling that the end had come. His father seemed so tenuously, so delicately attached to life, like down of a thistle in the wind. And when he spoke he was like a flame that wavered in the air this way and that, sometimes almost detached from the body that fed it.

It seemed as though he were living in another century and in another land. "We'll have to ask the Byzantine government," he said.

"What Byzantine government?" Giacomo asked.

"In Constantinople," his father replied, as if he found it odd for anyone to ask a question with such an obvious answer.

It was strange he should speak of the Byzantines. His father's ancestors were from Venice, and Giacomo sensed that his father was talking of the affairs of six or seven centuries ago.

To bring him back to this one, he began to speak to him, to explain just what had happened and to reassure him. He told his father that his memory would all come back to him in a little while, after he had drunk some coffee. And he went on to tell him who he was, and, when his wife appeared with a cup of coffee, who she was, and about the house, his fruit trees, his articles and books, the recent letters; he went over all his life with him, in a fashion.

Intent on reconnecting himself to the past and those around him, patiently, like someone threading beads, the present not quite with him, his father sat up on the bed and, speaking very gently, asked him questions. "Where is Mama?" he said, referring to his own wife.

For a second, Giacomo didn't answer. He had expected and feared the question. Then he said, "She died. You know, she died three years ago."

"Ah, yes," he said sadly, and for a moment father and son seemed not so much to look at one another as to survey the last days of her life.

"And you say we went to England?"

"Yes, do you remember, in 1938? You took us there."

"Yes. You children were so good on that crowded train."

"And when we got to England you saw a sign that read, 'Cross at your own risk,' and you said it was worth coming just to see that sign, and that in Italy it would have said, 'It is severely forbidden to cross.'"

His father smiled. "It was a sign of freedom."

"Yes."

"And then we came back here?"

"Yes, by boat, after the war. The bailiff met you in Naples, all the money he had for you stuffed under his garters, in his socks. He was afraid of thieves."

They laughed together. Laughter, it has the power to reconcile lost friends, to bridge the widest gaps.

"Your wife . . . tell me her name again."

"Jessie."

"Ah, yes, so dear," he said tenderly. He got up slowly and went to his desk for a pencil. He said he wanted to write the name down before he forgot it once more. He looked at the desk aimlessly, then pulled out the wrong drawer. "My little things," he said, "where are they?" He looked like a child whose toys a gust of wind has blown away.

Giacomo found a pencil for him, and his father wrote the name Jessie on a piece of paper. Next, he paused by the bookcase. All the books in it he had annotated, but now he looked at them as if for the first time.

"This one you wrote," Giacomo said.

His father looked at it closely. "This one I know. But the others . . ."

He stroked his head as if to scold it. "And these are your poems," he said, seeing a flimsy little book with his son's name. "I remember the first one you wrote, about the stars, when you were ten. Strange, your mother's father, too, wrote one about the stars—his best one."

"You see, you remember a lot."

"About the distant past. Such a long time . . . for you, too." He smiled, then, looking at him warmly, said, "Our Giacomo," and it was as it had been when Giacomo was a boy and his father used to look at him and say "Ajax," because he considered him generous and strong.

Strangely, now, Giacomo found that he *could* talk to his father, easily, affably, and with pleasure, and that his voice was gentle. When his father was well, he couldn't, but now he was reaching the secret, soft core—the secret, gentle, tender core that is in each of us. And he thought, *This* is what my father is really like; the way he is now, this is his real, his naked self. For a moment it has been uncovered; he is young again. This was the young man his mother had met and fallen in love with; this was the man on whose knees he had played, who had carried him on his shoulders up the hills, who had read to him the poems he liked so much. His other manner was brought on by age, by a hundred preoccupations, by the years, by the hardening that comes with the turning of the years.

Already, with coffee, with their talk, his father was recovering his memory. Soon he would be up and about, and soon Giacomo wouldn't be able to talk to him as he did now. But though he wouldn't, he would think of his father in the way he had been given back to him, the way he had been and somewhere—deep and secret and only to be uncovered sometimes—still was.

Dismantling the Castle

by Linda McCarriston

May all of your children be writers,
or makers of movies, or sculptors
who will caste you in bronze forever
and stand you in the village square,
your hand lifted into the generations
in a characteristic gesture of love or
destruction from afternoons you may forget,
your feet in their heavy shoes walking
your daughter up the hill at dusk,
or kicking her, the hands of the clock
at six, across the linoleum.
May their words put your words back into
your mouth, verbatim, precise as how
animals learn—crystalline memory:
cowed once, forever cowed—the mare
who will never be touched at the ear
where the first year the twitch
was twisted. May they write your stories
for you, as you told them to their flesh,
make vivid on the page or on the screen
or raise on pedestals of stone, framed
by a city's green, what has passed
as the castle, body to body, in private:
the unforgettable sound of a man's
fist stopping the breath of a child,
the muzzled crying a small body makes
pinned in a grown man's bed, the arc the foot
or the hand cuts in domestic air. And the mouth
carved writhing—for the life of the granite—
in the ugliest curse a man can imagine
as he spits it on his little girl,
public—biography—once and for all.

In the Garden of the North American Martyrs

by Tobias Wolff

When she was young, Mary saw a brilliant and original man lose
his job because he had expressed ideas that were offensive to the
trustees of the college where they both taught. She shared his views,
but did not sign the protest petition. She was, after all, on trial herself—as a teacher, as a woman, as an interpreter of history.

Mary watched herself. Before giving a lecture she wrote it out in
full, using the arguments and often the words of other, approved
writers, so that she would not by chance say something scandalous.
Her own thoughts she kept to herself, and the words for them grew
faint as time went on; without quite disappearing they shrank to remote, nervous points, like birds flying away.

When the department turned into a hive of cliques, Mary went
about her business and pretended not to know that people hated
each other. To avoid seeming bland she let herself become eccentric
in harmless ways. She took up bowling, which she learned to love,
and founded the Brandon College chapter of a society dedicated to
restoring the good name of Richard III. She memorized comedy rou-
tines from records and jokes from books; people groaned when she
rattled them off, but she did not let that stop her, and after a time
the groans became the point of the jokes. They were a kind of tribute to Mary's willingness to expose herself.

In fact no one at the college was safer than Mary, for she was
making herself into something institutional, like a custom, or a mas-
cot—part of the college's idea of itself.

Now and then she wondered whether she had been too careful.
The things she said and wrote seemed flat to her, pulpy, as though
someone else had squeezed the juice out of them. And once, while
talking with a senior professor, Mary saw herself reflected in a
window: she was leaning toward him and had her head turned so
that her ear was right in front of his moving mouth. The sight
disgusted her. Years later, when she had to get a hearing aid, Mary
suspected that her deafness was a result of always trying to catch
everything everyone said.

In the second half of Mary's fifteenth year at Brandon the provost called a meeting of all faculty and students to announce that the college was bankrupt and would not open its gates again. He was every bit as much surprised as they; the report from the trustees had reached his desk only that morning. It seemed that Brandon's financial manager had speculated in some kind of futures and lost everything. The provost wanted to deliver the news in person before it reached the papers. He wept openly and so did the students and teachers, with only a few exceptions—some cynical upperclassmen who claimed to despise the education they had received.

Mary could not rid her mind of the word "speculate." It meant to guess, in terms of money to gamble. How could a man gamble a college? Why would he want to do that, and how could it be that no one stopped him? To Mary, it seemed to belong to another time; she thought of a drunken plantation owner gaming away his slaves.

She applied for jobs and got an offer from a new experimental college in Oregon. It was her only offer so she took it.

The college was in one building. Bells rang all the time, lockers lined the hallways, and at every corner stood a buzzing water fountain. The student newspaper came out twice a month on mimeograph paper which felt wet. The library, which was next to the band room, had no librarian and no books.

The countryside was beautiful, though, and Mary might have enjoyed it if the rain had not caused her so much trouble. There was something wrong with her lungs that the doctors couldn't agree on, and couldn't cure; whatever it was, the dampness made it worse. On rainy days condensation formed in Mary's hearing aid and shorted it out. She began to dread talking with people, never knowing when she would have to take out her control box and slap it against her leg.

It rained nearly every day. When it was not raining it was getting ready to rain, or clearing. The ground glinted under the grass, and the light had a yellow undertone that flared up during storms.

There was water in Mary's basement. Her walls sweated, and she had found toadstools growing behind the refrigerator. She felt as though she were rusting out, like one of those old cars people thereabouts kept in their front yards, on pieces of wood. Mary knew that everyone was dying, but it did seem to her that she was dying faster than most.

She continued to look for another job, without success. Then, in the fall of her third year in Oregon, she got a letter from a woman named Louise who'd once taught at Brandon. Louise had scored a great success with a book on Benedict Arnold and was now on the faculty of a famous college in upstate New York. She said that one of her colleagues would be retiring at the end of the year and asked whether Mary would be interested in the position.

The letter surprised Mary. Louise thought of herself as a great historian and of almost everyone else as useless; Mary had not known that she felt differently about her. Moreover, enthusiasm for other people's causes did not come easily to Louise, who had a way of sucking in her breath when familiar names were mentioned, as though she knew things that friendship kept her from disclosing.

Mary expected nothing, but sent a résumé and copies of her two books. Shortly after that Louise called to say that the search committee, of which she was chairwoman, had decided to grant Mary an interview in early November. "Now don't get your hopes *too* high," Louise said.

"Oh, no," Mary said, but thought: Why shouldn't I hope? They would not go to the bother and expense of bringing her to the college if they weren't serious. And she was certain that the interview would go well. She would make them like her, or at least give them no cause to dislike her.

She read about the area with a strange sense of familiarity, as if the land and its history were already known to her. And when her plane left Portland and climbed easterly into the clouds, Mary felt like she was going home. The feeling stayed with her, growing stronger when they landed. She tried to describe it to Louise as they left the airport at Syracuse and drove toward the college, an hour or so away. "It's like *déjà vu*," she said.

"*Déjà vu* is a hoax," Louise said. "It's just a chemical imbalance of some kind."

"Maybe so," Mary said, "but I still have this sensation."

"Don't get serious on me," Louise said. "That's not your long suit. Just be your funny, wisecracking old self. Tell me now—honestly— how do I look?"

It was night, too dark to see Louise's face well, but in the airport she had seemed gaunt and pale and intense. She reminded Mary of a description in the book she'd been reading, of how Iroquois warriors gave themselves visions by fasting. She had that kind of look about her. But she wouldn't want to hear that. "You look wonderful," Mary said.

"There's a reason," Louise said. "I've taken a lover. My concentration has improved, my energy level is up, and I've lost ten pounds. I'm also getting some color in my cheeks, though that could be the weather. I recommend the experience highly. But you probably disapprove."

Mary didn't know what to say. She said that she was sure Louise knew best, but that didn't seem to be enough. "Marriage is a great institution," she added, "but who wants to live in an institution?"

Louise groaned. "I know you," she said, "and I know that right now you're thinking 'But what about Ted? What about the children?' The fact is, Mary, they aren't taking it well at all. Ted has become a nag." She handed Mary her purse. "Be a good girl and light me a cigarette, will you? I know I told you I quit, but this whole thing has been very hard on me, very hard, and I'm afraid I've started again."

They were in the hills now, heading north on a narrow road. Tall trees arched above them. As they topped a rise Mary saw the forest all around, deep black under the plum-colored sky. There were a few lights and these made the darkness seem even greater.

"Ted has succeeded in completely alienating the children from me," Louise was saying. "There is no reasoning with any of them. In fact, they refuse to discuss the matter at all, which is very ironical because over the years I have tried to instill in them a willingness to see things from the other person's point of view. If they could just *meet* Jonathan I know they would feel differently. But they won't hear of it. Jonathan," she said, "is my lover."

"I see," Mary said, and nodded.

Coming around a curve they caught two deer in the headlights. Their eyes lit up and their hindquarters tensed; Mary could see them trembling as the car went by. "Deer," she said.

"I don't know," Louise said, "I just don't know. I do my best and it never seems to be enough. But that's enough about me—let's talk about you. What did you think of my latest book?" She squawked and beat her palms on the steering wheel. "God, I love that joke," she said. "Seriously, though, what about you? It must have been a real shockeroo when good old Brandon folded."

"It was hard. Things haven't been good but they'll be a lot better if I get this job."

"At least you have work," Louise said. "You should look at it from the bright side."

"I try."

"You seem so gloomy. I hope you're not worrying about the interview, or the class. Worrying won't do you a bit of good. Be happy."

"Class? What class?"

"The class you're supposed to give tomorrow, after the interview. Didn't I tell you? *Mea culpa*, hon, *mea maxima culpa*. I've been uncharacteristically forgetful lately."

"But what will I do?"

"Relax," Louise said. "Just pick a subject and wing it."

"Wing it?"

"You know, open your mouth and see what comes out. Extemporize."

"But I always work from a prepared lecture."

Louise sighed. "All right. I'll tell you what. Last year I wrote an article on the Marshall Plan that I got bored with and never published. You can read that."

Parroting what Louise had written seemed wrong to Mary, at first; then it occurred to her that she had been doing the same kind of thing for many years, and that this was not the time to get scruples. "Thanks," she said. "I appreciate it."

"Here we are," Louise said, and pulled into a circular drive with several cabins grouped around it. In two of the cabins lights were on; smoke drifted straight up from the chimneys. "This is the visitors' center. The college is another two miles thataway." Louise pointed down the road. "I'd invite you to stay at my house, but I'm spending the night with Jonathan and Ted is not good company these days. You would hardly recognize him."

She took Mary's bags from the trunk and carried them up the steps of a darkened cabin. "Look," she said, "they've laid a fire for you. All you have to do is light it." She stood in the middle of the room with her arms crossed and watched as Mary held a match under the kindling. "There," she said. "You'll be snugaroo in no time. I'd love to stay and chew the fat but I can't. You just get a good night's sleep and I'll see you in the morning."

Mary stood in the doorway and waved as Louise pulled out of the drive, spraying gravel. She filled her lungs, to taste the air: it was tart and clear. She could see the stars in their figurations, and the vague streams of light that ran among the stars.

She still felt uneasy about reading Louise's work as her own. It would be her first complete act of plagiarism. It would change her. It would make her less—how much less, she did not know. But what else could she do? She certainly couldn't "wing it." Words might fail her, and then what? Mary had a dread of silence. When she thought of silence she thought of drowning, as if it were a kind of water she could not swim in.

"I want this job," she said, and settled deep into her coat. It was cashmere and Mary had not worn it since moving to Oregon, because people there thought you were pretentious if you had on anything but a Pendleton shirt or, of course, raingear. She rubbed her cheek against the upturned collar and thought of a silver moon shining through bare black branches, a white house with green shutters, red leaves falling in a hard blue sky.

Louise woke her a few hours later. She was sitting on the edge of the bed, pushing at Mary's shoulder and snuffling loudly. When Mary asked her what was wrong she said, "I want your opinion on something. It's very important. Do you think I'm womanly?"

Mary sat up. "Louise, can this wait?"

"No."

"Womanly?"

Louise nodded.

"You are very beautiful," Mary said, "and you know how to present yourself."

Louise stood and paced the room. "That son of a bitch," she said. She came back and stood over Mary. "Let's suppose someone said I have no sense of humor. Would you agree or disagree?"

"In some things you do. I mean, yes, you have a good sense of humor."

"What do you mean, 'in some things'? What kind of things?"

"Well, if you heard that someone had been killed in an unusual way, like by an exploding cigar, you would think that was funny."

Louise laughed.

"That's what I mean," Mary said.

Louise went on laughing. "Oh, Lordy," she said. "Now it's my turn to say something about you." She sat down beside Mary.

"Please," Mary said.

"Just one thing," Louise said.

Mary waited.

"You're trembling," Louise said. "I was just going to say—oh, forget it. Listen, do you mind if I sleep on the couch? I'm all in."

"Go ahead."

"Sure it's okay? You've got a big day tomorrow." She fell back on the sofa and kicked off her shoes. "I was just going to say, you should use some liner on those eyebrows of yours. They sort of disappear and the effect is disconcerting."

Neither of them slept. Louise chain-smoked cigarettes and Mary watched the coals burn down. When it was light enough that they could see each other Louise got up. "I'll send a student for you," she said. "Good luck."

The college looked the way colleges are supposed to look. Roger, the student assigned to show Mary around, explained that it was an exact copy of a college in England, right down to the gargoyles and stained-glass windows. It looked so much like a college that moviemakers sometimes used it as a set. *Andy Hardy Goes to College* had been filmed there, and every fall they had an Andy Hardy Goes to College Day, with raccoon coats and goldfish-swallowing contests.

Above the door of the Founder's Building was a Latin motto which, roughly translated, meant "God helps those who help themselves." As Roger recited the names of illustrious graduates Mary was struck by the extent to which they had taken this precept to heart. They had helped themselves to railroads, mines, armies, states; to empires of finance with outposts all over the world.

Roger took Mary to the chapel and showed her a plaque bearing the names of alumni who had been killed in various wars, all the way back to the Civil War. There were not many names. Here too, apparently, the graduates had helped themselves. "Oh yes," Roger said as they were leaving, "I forgot to tell you. The communion rail comes from some church in Europe where Charlemagne used to go."

They went to the gymnasium, and the three hockey rinks, and the library, where Mary inspected the card catalogue, as though she would turn down the job if they didn't have the right books. "We have a little more time," Roger said as they went outside. "Would you like to see the power plant?"

Mary wanted to keep busy until the last minute, so she agreed.

Roger led her into the depths of the service building, explaining things about the machine, which was the most advanced in the country. "People think the college is really old-fashioned," he said, "but it isn't. They let girls come here now, and some of the teachers are women. In fact, there's a statute that says they have to interview at least one woman for each opening. There it is."

They were standing on an iron catwalk above the biggest machine Mary had ever beheld. Roger, who was majoring in Earth Sciences, said that it had been built from a design pioneered by a professor in his department. Where before he had been gabby Roger now became reverent. It was clear that for him this machine was the soul of the college, that the purpose of the college was to provide outlets for the machine. Together they leaned against the railing and watched it hum.

Mary arrived at the committee room exactly on time for her interview, but the room was empty. Her two books were on the table, along with a water pitcher and some glasses. She sat down and picked up one of the books. The binding cracked as she opened it.

The pages were smooth, clean, unread. Mary turned to the first chapter, which began, "It is generally believed that . . ." How dull, she thought.

Nearly twenty minutes later Louise came in with several men. "Sorry we're late," she said. "We don't have much time so we'd better get started." She introduced Mary to the men, but with one exception the names and faces did not stay together. The exception was Dr. Howells, the department chairman, who had a porous blue nose and terrible teeth.

A shiny-faced man to Dr. Howells's right spoke first. "So," he said, "I understand you once taught at Brandon College."

"It was a shame that Brandon had to close," said a young man with a pipe in his mouth. "There is a place for schools like Brandon." As he talked the pipe wagged up and down.

"Now you're in Oregon," Dr. Howells said. "I've never been there. How do you like it?"

"Not very much," Mary said.

"Is that right?" Dr. Howells leaned toward her. "I thought everyone liked Oregon. I hear it's very green."

"That's true," Mary said.

"I suppose it rains a lot," he said.

"Nearly every day."

"I wouldn't like that," he said, shaking his head. "I like it dry. Of course it snows here, and you have your rain now and then, but it's a *dry* rain. Have you ever been to Utah? There's a state for you. Bryce Canyon. The Mormon Tabernacle Choir."

"Dr. Howells was brought up in Utah," said the young man with the pipe.

"It was a different place altogether in those days," Dr. Howells said. "Mrs. Howells and I have always talked about going back when I retire, but now I'm not so sure."

"We're a little short on time," Louise said.

"And here I've been going on and on," Dr. Howells said. "Before we wind things up, is there anything you want to tell us?"

"Yes. I think you should give me the job." Mary laughed when she said this, but no one laughed back, or even looked at her. They all looked away. Mary understood then that they were not really considering her for the position. She had been brought here to satisfy a rule. She had no hope.

The men gathered their papers and shook hands with Mary and told her how much they were looking forward to her class. "I can't get enough of the Marshall Plan," Dr. Howells said.

"Sorry about that," Louise said when they were alone. "I didn't think it would be so bad. That was a real bitcheroo."

"Tell me something," Mary said. "You already know who you're going to hire, don't you?"

Louise nodded.

"Then why did you bring me here?"

Louise began to explain about the statute and Mary interrupted. "I know all that. But why me? Why did you pick *me*?"

Louise walked to the window. She spoke with her back to Mary. "Things haven't been going very well for old Louise," she said. "I've been unhappy and I thought you might cheer me up. You used to be so funny, and I was sure you would enjoy the trip—it didn't cost you anything, and it's pretty this time of year with the leaves and everything. Mary, you don't know the things my parents did to me. And Ted is no barrel of laughs either. Or Jonathan, the son of a bitch. I deserve some love and friendship but I don't get any." She turned and looked at her watch. "It's almost time for your class. We'd better go."

"I would rather not give it. After all, there's not much point, is there?"

"But you *have* to give it. That's part of the interview." Louise handed Mary a folder. "All you have to do is read this. It isn't much, considering all the money we've laid out to get you here."

Mary followed Louise down the hall to the lecture room. The professors were sitting in the front row with their legs crossed. They smiled and nodded at Mary. Behind them the room was full of students, some of whom had spilled over into the aisles. One of the professors adjusted the microphone to Mary's height, crouching down as he went to the podium and back as though he would prefer not to be seen.

Louise called the room to order. She introduced Mary and gave the subject of the lecture. But Mary had decided to wing it after all.

Mary came to the podium unsure of what she would say; sure only that she would rather die than read Louise's article. The sun poured through the stained glass onto the people around her, painting their faces. Thick streams of smoke from the young professor's pipe drifted through a circle of red light at Mary's feet, turning crimson and twisting like flames.

"I wonder how many of you know," she began, "that we are in the Long House, the ancient domain of the Five Nations of the Iroquois."

Two professors looked at each other.

"The Iroquois were without pity," Mary said. "They hunted people down with clubs and arrows and spears and nets, and blow-guns made from elder stalks. They tortured their captives, sparing no one, not even the little children. They took scalps and practiced cannibalism and slavery. Because they had no pity they became powerful, so powerful that no other tribe dared to oppose them. They made the other tribes pay tribute, and when they had nothing more to pay the Iroquois attacked them."

Several of the professors began to whisper. Dr. Howells was say-ing something to Louise, and Louise was shaking her head.

"In one of their raids," Mary said, "they captured two Jesuit priests, Jean de Brébeuf and Gabriel Lalement. They covered Lalement with pitch and set him on fire in front of Brébeuf. When Brébeuf rebuked them they cut off his lips and put a burning iron down his throat. They hung a collar of red-hot hatchets around his neck, and poured boiling water over his head. When he continued to preach to them they cut strips of flesh from his body and ate them before his eyes. While he was still alive they scalped him and cut open his breast and drank his blood. Later, their chief tore out Brébeuf's heart and ate it, but just before he did this Brébeuf spoke to them one last time. He said—"

"That's enough!" yelled Dr. Howells, jumping to his feet.

Louise stopped shaking her head. Her eyes were perfectly round.

Mary had come to the end of her facts. She did not know what Brébeuf had said. Silence rose up around her; just when she thought she would go under and be lost in it she heard someone whistling in the hallway outside, trilling the notes like a bird, like many birds.

"Mend your lives," she said. "You have deceived yourselves in the pride of your hearts, and the strength of your arms. Though you soar aloft like the eagle, though your nest is set among the stars, thence I will bring you down, says the Lord. Turn from power to love. Be kind. Do justice. Walk humbly."

Louise was waving her arms. "Mary!" she shouted.

But Mary had more to say, much more; she waved back at Louise, then turned off her hearing aid so that she would not be distracted again.

Genuine Jerks and Genuine Jerk Organizations

by Carol Bly

We don't want there to be such a thing as a genuine jerk.

Decades ago a music critic hoped to shame a popular pianist by expressing contempt for his candlelit bowdlerizing of music. Liberace's famous response was: "I know. I cry about it all the way to the bank." Liberace's profit was taken from tastelessness, whereas a jerk's profit is taken from cruelty, but we have something in common with the music critic. Namely, we are galled.

We don't want to feel our natural indignation about any jerk's behavior only to find the jerk grinning, especially joking on the way to the bank. We find it less painful to *deny* that the jerk enjoys his or her cruelty. "He seems to be laughing at the harm he does; he seems to be grinning as he invests his profits," we tell ourselves. "But in fact he is in tremendous personal pain. He is acting out."[1]

Studies indicate that some bullies indeed are or have been in pain. Those who were but are not now in pain developed maladaptive behavior (bullying) at the time they experienced the psychological pain and then the behavior became habit.

But recent, other studies indicate that many bullies are not in pain and have not felt pain. Pushing other people around works for them. Until they are forced to stop they will keep jerking others around.

I used to glide along with the conventional wisdom that denial is mostly practiced by victims of bullying—battered wives, molested children—and most classically by numbers of German Jews during the 1930s who would not or could not make themselves believe the Nazis' intentions. Denial that there are genuine jerks, however, is practiced *not only* by victims but by those we least associate with unconscious behaviors like denial: social workers and psychotherapists. They cling to the idea that bullying is "a learned behavior."

The main idea of this chapter is that bullying is indeed a learned behavior, but the reason it is learned so skillfully by human beings starting as early as the age of one is that enjoyment of taking power over others is a potential in our brains. We are programmed for it.

That is the bad news. The good news is that we are also pro-grammed to develop conscious egos, and those conscious egos, when they develop and branch out to the fine points, put together a composite dislike of bullying—first in others, I expect, since we judge them first, and eventually in ourselves. What I called "putting together" is a very rough metaphor. Jean Piaget used the metaphor "adding a structure" for a person's refinement of an old paradigm. It will be a relief when neurophysiologists have got fur-ther with their present investigations into how brain circuitry steers attitude in us, and how attitude steers our brain circuitry. For a few years still, we rely on bright intuition about how the brain's own work improves the brain itself. As Richard Wilbur says, "Mind in its purest play is like some bat / That beats about in caverns all alone, . . . / The mind is like a bat. Precisely. Save / That in the very happiest intellection / A graceful error may correct the cave."[2] A small part of Wilbur's "happiest intellection" is Piaget's "adding a structure" or Jane Loevinger's "ego development."

If it is true that social workers for the most part, but also psy-chotherapists, journalists, and those thousands of us who read about social psychology, are practicing denial when we insist that bullies are people in pain, I would like to make some guesses at why we are practicing that denial. People in psychological pain are people for whom social workers and therapists have some helpful regimens. Perhaps these professionals want so much to change bullies that wishful thinking makes them want to put genuine jerks into the hopper of cases for which social work and psychotherapy are helpful.

A second possible explanation is that if helping professionals, as well as the growing number of eager amateurs in psychology, can only believe that far inside the bully is a badly frightened lit-tle boy or girl, then how much less galling the bully is! How re-lieved we are if we can tell ourselves, despite the jerk's apparent pleasure from behaving like a jerk, that his or her cruelty is only "acting out"!

So far, therapeutic practice with bullies falls into two parts. First, the professional makes it clear to the bully that jerk behavior is not acceptable and must be stopped immediately. The jerk, for example, may not continue to beat his wife or children. Second, the helping professional uses whatever communication skills and intuition he or she possesses to (1) determine the kind of pain the jerk is or has been experiencing, (2) raise the jerk's consciousness about that pain, and (3) help the jerk consider, choose, and plan better behavior patterns for the future.

How marvelous of helping professionals to be so detached and so fair-minded—how marvelous of them to be willing to work with such jerks! I admire them. I confess that my own response to hearing about some new savagery perpetrated upon people, animals, plants, water, or air is to long for prompt punishment and restitution. I feel exasperated, because in most cases of individual bullying the jerk seems to be getting away with it, and in *every* case of bullying by organizations that I know of the organization got away with it—at least for long enough to profit from the bullying behavior in question.

I have decided that there is such a thing as a genuine jerk, and also, it follows, jerk organizations, which are made up mostly of nice people following guidelines devised by genuine jerks.

A genuine jerk organization is typically a corporation depleting or poisoning the planet for the benefit of its senior management and shareholders. Such a corporation performs a cunning style of full-cost pricing: its experts project the value of what they can get from the planet—for example, old-growth trees, ores, water, fuels—against likely legal expenses for the same given period of time. In the ongoing, normal range, legal expenses include navigating the company's best route through existing regulations as well as manipulating government regulations to widen the road for the company. In the extraordinary range, legal expenses include projected costs the company might pay if caught and fined by the government. Projections for a decade or longer might show comparative fines for violating regulations balanced against profits realized as a result of the violations. A jerk organization considers, so to speak, the "shelf life" of its profitable activity.

A genuine individual jerk enjoys as many facets of jerk behavior as he or she possibly can. A genuine jerk corporation enjoys every possible facet of making money—the gutsiness of circumventing the law if need be, the pizzazz of outwitting or outmuscling smaller commercial groups, the pleasure of making the leadership of less avaricious organizations feel impotent. I have even seen the wives of executives from genuine jerk organizations subtly work in social situations to humiliate the wives of less powerful groups in the same field. It reminds one of the social caste system of naval officers and their wives, back when naval personnel and their dependents held the respectful interest of the public.

We have discussed the brutality of nature, staying in it, or leaving it. If bullying behavior comes naturally to us, our instinct for it must involve some fun. Our shirttail cousin is the cat who plays with her punctured mouse. After a quarter hour, the cat is still tossing the mouse into the air, trying to make it look more alive than it now is, so that when she bites it again she can echo her first pleasure in wounding it. If bullying is fun for people as well as for cats, what specific kind of fun is it? Sooner or later we shall want to design some better fun than hurting people so we can steer bullies to it.

If we pretend that we ourselves are the genuine bullies, we can imagine a number of pleasures in bullying. First, bullying is management, not factory-floor work. You get to design what you are going to do. Bullying is proactive, albeit in the wrong ways, and the brain likes being proactive.

As soon as one is proactive, one becomes a strategist. That is, one wants to achieve such and such, so one lays out strategies for doing so. The brain loves problem solving. A comparatively slumberous brain bestirs itself if there is a problem to solve.

We plan to bomb something or rape someone without anything backfiring on us. There is danger of discovery. Danger—our heart quickens. The brain goes nimbly, gratefully, around some of its circuitry: Stimulus! Let us surmise that the last time we felt *this* stimulated was when we were in a fight, preparing for a fight, being trained to fight, or when we stole or killed something.

And there will be collegiality, because we may need to band together. Human beings are tremendously eager to gather in groups, in any case.

Our project will feel akin to a spiritual endeavor, too, because it is not practical. If a person has very little experience in thinking about holiness, if one has never felt the holiness of certain places, or deliberately joined groups with altruistic goals, then holiness is inchoate: feelings of holiness easily attach to anything that isn't palpably practical. Feelings of holiness go back in our species. We are wired for such feelings. Like other feelings, feelings of holiness can slide around from object to object. If we don't find respectable activities to attach those feelings to we are at risk of attaching them to any project that comes along. We love to feel a quickened heartbeat, from perceived or real danger. We love collegiality, especially with a mix of both new and old friends who are engaged on some mission. We love that collegiality so much we are at risk of pooh-poohing our first misgivings about what the mission *is*.

It doesn't take an intellect as remarkable as Machiavelli's to see how these human proclivities would enable one to work up large or small bullying projects. Bullying in groups is all the more fun the more elaborate it is. The classic school recess bullying may engage boys and girls of age eight or nine, but human adults need finer-cast cruelty, and adults, being more experienced, usually write into the plan the escape procedure in case there is trouble. If one has a mixture of guts and common sense one figures out ahead of time how later to protest that it was all in fun. If one has a mixture of cowardice and common sense one figures out ahead how to be passive enough during the bullying so that later one can say one *(a)* wasn't involved, *(b)* felt pressured to participate and did so very unwillingly, or *(c)* protested vehemently all through the bullying but the others would pay no attention.

An intriguing instance: In 1981 the director of the Minnesota Humanities Commission, a woman, signed up for a mini-M.B.A. course offered at Stanford University. Officially known as the Stanford Executive Program, its students and faculty affectionately

called it Stanford's "sheep dip" course in philosophies of management. The eight-week course was brilliant, substantive, fast-
moving, and sophisticated.

One day it was this woman's turn to be leader of a small group
in the class. At that time the local newspaper had reported the
stabbing of a woman. Her all-male group had attached to the
blackboard the clipping. They had substituted for the victim's
name "Small Group Leader." The group refused to talk during the
session. The leader complained, but the person in charge of the
class paid no attention. At last, one man—only one—confessed to
the group leader privately that they had decided to make her cry.[3]

The usual explanation for such phenomena, especially among
people of satisfactory educational backgrounds getting M.B.A.s, is
that any male pack must either establish its alpha wolf of the day
or reaffirm the command hierarchy of the day previous. I believe
this is only part of it. The rest is that the heart rejoices in hurting
a creature that is *other*—in this case, not male, not a corporation
person, but the director of a humanities commission—*very* other.

My fear is that unless we keep our minds open to the idea that
some people may be genuine jerks, and pay attention to their behaviors as if there were such an entity as a genuine jerk, we may
fail to look at or misread psychological dynamics being enacted
right before us. Social psychologists who have spent their adult
lives using "good process" to change bad behavior lose heart at
the high rate of recidivism among rapists and other serious felons.
So far they can only make intelligent guesses as to how much of
the poor outcome is due to built-in criminality and how much of
it indicates that for all their efforts they have not yet found a good
technology for changing a person's evildoing purpose to a pro-
social purpose.

When we laypeople think about how people get a little kick
out of being cruel to one another, any cure seems doubtful. One
approach is to leave both the social sciences and literature alone
for the moment, and pretend that we ourselves are serious bullies.

When I first became interested in the idea of jerks, I put myself
through a scenario. I pretended that I was someone who had practiced trickery. I routinely and deftly clipped people who trusted

me. I figured out and implemented one or two outright and satisfying robberies. I pretended I had struck down some people who enraged me. (I kept a check on my own psychological material, too. I bore in mind the questions: What does it mean that someone wants to think about jerks? What does it mean if someone plans to fantasize being a jerk?)

Next, I imagined the perks. There was money in robbing, tricking, and clipping. What would ever make me give up the quick money, the quick emotional satisfaction?

By staying with the fantasy I began identifying some perks I hadn't thought of at first—glamour, for instance. Every field has its occupational blind spots: for ethicists I am sure a major blind spot is glamour. Those of us who take up the posture of mentoring on subjects of moral interest forget how wonderful glamour feels to all animals. How wonderful it is to swagger around and be known as a big shot! Why would I—now that I, imagining myself as a full-fledged bully, know what Tom McGrath calls in "Ode for the American Dead in Asia" "the rules" (of the world's game)—ever settle for the wormy, twining negotiations that people get into with therapy groups and business groups and family household groups? Bullies see therapy groups as an insipid jelly.

Building merciful human communication styles is cold oatmeal compared to the high one gets from cheating and dominating others—making them cry if you can quash them into crying. How could anyone get a high from those streaky, stippled conversations that counselors must advocate: "Eugene, it is your turn to *listen* now, while Marilyn explains her feelings." Even low-level business management conversations sound phony and chicken to someone whose savvy is in prying locks. The bland civilities, the modulated voices, those maddening, respectful, gluey eye contacts, the low-key glances across the table—what drivel all that looks and how much it sounds like mice squeaking!—at least, to someone who likes to move on impulse, and who is man or woman enough to live on the *edge*.

We can make some guesses as to how decent behavior looks to criminally inclined people by studying the attitudes of recess bullies toward kids who do not bully. The "good" kids look like sissies and pawns of the teachers. Tricky people look down on honest people, in the same way. Womanizers look down on faithful husbands. To a genuine bully, failure to bully is cowardice. Anyone with any backbone knows how to get what he or she wants.

These assumptions were made on the basis of an hour's pretending to be a bully. Then I learned something by chance. I had decided to carry the experiment further. At that time in my life I was working with a psychotherapist. She was teaching me how ethically useful the imagination can be. I was practicing the first level of imagination—pretending to be others, hypothesizing their motivations and responses.

By luck, I had been reading Sissela Bok's spacious study, *On Lying*. At the time, I had been lied to in both my personal and my professional life. I had an accurate feel for the force of being lied to. I was also sick of liberals around me constantly exclaiming, "I just can't understand how so-and-so could *do* such a horrible thing!" Not being able "to understand" a crime is mere rhetoric, not thinking. I wanted to find out, like a mathematician trying formulas, how so-and-so could indeed do such a horrible thing, for example, lying out of hand.

I decided deliberately to lie in order to see what that does for the liar. I found lying immensely satisfying. When you tell someone that something happened that did *not* happen you have power over history. So Orwell was right! *1984* is a horrifying book on any level—appearing the more horrifying to me once I had got a taste of the liars' motivation.

Lying made me feel, ironically, that I had control over my life—the great goal of millions. I noticed other returns. Lying was a practical deception, of course. It distanced me from whomever I lied to—of course—since it changed the diplomatic relations between us. Instead of being friends we were now merely indifferent, separate countries, connected only by foreign policies. I treated the other person like someone toward whom I directed a certain policy designed to benefit me. My intuition suggested that the person was digging trenches. Lying had reduced our social intercourse to Stage II in the general development scheme: we treated one another like instruments to be used or not used in this or that circumstance.

I remembered reading I had done about foreign policies. They by definition allow any behavior on one's part that redounds to the advantage of one's sovereign unit, provided that if it is foul behavior it can be kept disguised enough to evade indignation in fellow predators of equal or greater might. As in individual bullying, one need not grieve over the moral indignation of small nations or victims. So far so good. I was interested but not surprised. The next psychological result did surprise me, however. I found that my lying to others distanced me not just from my victim but from *everyone*.

Perhaps, then, a habituated liar is someone habitually distanced from everyone, not just from his or her designated mark. Perhaps this finding is old hat to social scientists, but it shook me.

Since there is still no sure, researched scientific word on how much jerk behavior comes of early bad psychological habitat and how much from genetic inheritance, I think the most useful and timesaving way to regard seriously bad behavior is to see it as either a practical move, a source of covert pleasure, or a mixture of both.

We laypeople want some cures for evildoing. We can make our project more nearly bite-sized, I believe, if we make two assumptions. We can abandon the assumptions if they should prove mistaken, but not to make any assumptions leaves us tottering and unable to make a plan.

Let us assume, first, that some regular evildoers might change if the right (psychological or medical or other) technology turned up and, second, that other evildoers may well not change in their lifetime because they enjoy hurting people, they have some level of skills at hurting people, and for the ninety-five years of their lives, being a jerk may well strike them as a brave mixture of risk taking and realism.

This category of people I call Genuine Jerks. I think force is the only reasonable response to their activities. The force can be law or it can be public shame assiduously kept up until such time as legislation is in place, in turn followed by adjudication and punishment.

If we are agreed that genuine jerks respond only to force, one form of which is public shame, then literature still has its ancient part to play. Literature traditionally shows us evil and begs readers to join in shaming or legislating. The intellectual work is to recognize jerk behavior when we see it. If we can, we must make jerks thoroughly miserable, in order to weaken their motivation to continue their brand of cruelty. That is the old crux of criminology: if one fails to motivate a person to be decent, at least one can work at spoiling the person's motivation to be indecent. In her poem "Dismantling the Castle," Linda McCarriston's first remark is her hope that the man who rapes his children will find them growing up to humiliate him publicly:

> May all of your children be writers,
> or makers of movies, or sculptors
> who will caste you in bronze forever
> and stand you in the village square

There are individual jerks in a number of the stories and poems of this anthology—either at center stage as with Donald in "The Woman Lit by Fireflies" and the father in "Brothers and Sisters," or offstage, so far as we can tell from Harrison's evidence, Donald's cynical son, Donald Jr. I congratulate Tobias Wolff on his creation of Louise, in "In the Garden of the North American Martyrs," one of the most impressive female jerks of contemporary literature.

This book includes a horror chest of jerk organizations behind the scenes whose activities affect those on stage in the poems and stories: the Atomic Energy Commission in "White Canyon"; the Nazis in "A Story about Chicken Soup"; the Iroquois in "In the Garden of the North American Martyrs," who appear as symbols for Louise and for all people who enjoy the elaborate torture of guileless people; the Department of Defense and the United States presidents during the Vietnam War in "Ode for the American Dead in Asia."

Before leaving the discussion of jerks I would like to suggest that the ever-democratic stage developmentalist wants to see them as people who have thus far failed at one of the tasks of childhood—character formation. But that definition gives us only a generality to guide by. Before writing off people we know as intrepid, unchangeable, genuine jerks, we might try a modern empathic role-playing game to see if it yields any hopeful ideas. We make some notes on that person's or those people's lives. Then we pretend to be any one or several of them. Next, we will write up a mini-stage-development format for the people, but this time the stage-development scheme should be based on *behavior* rather than on the kind of thinking. We can ask: I am pretending I am that person. If that person, which is to say myself, is a jerk, what were my various behavioral stages between my birth and my present customary activities?[4]

Stage I (self-oriented): I do everything for myself. If I get caught doing something that brings punishment, I am heartily sorry for myself, like Macbeth, for having been caught. By inference, the father in "Dismantling the Castle" is a Stage I person.

Stage II (tribe-oriented): I am still just a practical operator in the world. I now see others out there. If they are both big and near me, I make deals with them. If they are small and near me, I shove or eat them. Everyone is a useful tool to me—or they are no good as a tool. When I have reached this stage I give others their space. If they are far enough away I am truly nonjudgmental about them. If they are robbing a gas station far enough away so that it happens not to be a gas station I myself intend to rob, I leave them to it. It's a free world. If they use motorboats to rough up loons' nesting places, I do not call the Department of Natural Resources. Hey, I'm like, who's perfect? To accomplish my own practical goals I do, as President Bush succinctly put it, whatever it takes. Franzen, in "The Schreuderspitze," is a perfect Stage II person.

Stage III (wanting peer approval): I do what it takes to be well thought of. If pretending to be a radical is in, I pretend it. If being anti-Semitic is in, I am anti-Semitic. If mindless Gemütlichkeit is in, I turn hail-fellow-well-met, like Donald in "The Woman Lit by Fireflies." This stage is clearly illustrated in societies run by common denominator, such as small towns. Everyone who has spent any time in a small town knows about the rotten philanderer who gives talks on the 4-H to the Kiwanis.

Stage IV (loyal to sovereign group): I obey laws partly lest I get caught and partly because the old saw about patriotism being the last refuge of a scoundrel is true. Until now I have stretched away from self-love only as far as loving my own family or the tribal group—but now, in Stage IV, my imagination has brought me to love my country. It is a queer love. I cheat on my country's income taxes where I can make it stick, but I am willing to do whatever violence my country lays out for me to do. A Franzen can be a Stage IV person. Donald Jr., in "The Woman Lit by Fireflies," can be a Stage IV person.

A genuine jerk can be an outstanding soldier. People considered jerks in other situations have removed phosphorus shells from their aircraft bare-handed. The reason that suggests itself is that a jerk might well take to working in a large organization whose goal is to inflict as much death as possible upon foreign young people. Such an organization might feel like a good feisty extension of himself or herself.

There are no bad-behavior stages past Stage IV in the stage-development scheme of jerks. Loyalty to myself (1), laissez-faire (2), hiding in an attractive persona (3), and loyalty to country (4) is as far upward in ethics as a jerk is likely to reach and remain a jerk. Any stage above Stage IV would involve *principled* behavior—which is to say that it would require some short- or long-term sacrifice of some gratification.

On the stage scheme of *moral reasoning*, a jerk is always in the first four levels: (1) self-oriented, (2) feeling loyalty only to his or her own tribe, (3) taking as *good* whatever brings strokes from the community, and (4) taking as *good* whatever word comes down from authority, especially when that authority is one's church or one's sovereign nation. In those four levels of morality, the thinker considers *good* only as what will work or as what can be got without bringing down punishment. Punishment might be either psychological, such as losing popularity in the community, or actual, such as going to prison for refusing to serve in a war.

I love Mary McCarthy's unerring evaluation of Macbeth as a genuine jerk:

> Macbeth is not clever; he is taken in by surfaces, by appearance. He cannot think beyond the usual course of things. . . . In short, he has no faith, which requires imagination. He is literal-minded. . . . Macbeth has absolutely no feeling for others, except envy, a common middle-class trait. He *envies* the murdered Duncan his rest, which is a strange way of looking at your victim. What he suffers on his own account after the crimes is simple panic. He is never contrite or remorseful. . . .
>
> The idea of Macbeth as a conscience-tormented man is a platitude as false as Macbeth himself. Macbeth has no conscience.
>
> . . . Like so many unfeeling men, he has a facile emotionalism, which he turns on and off. Not that his fear is insincere but his loss of control provides him with an excuse for histrionics.[5]

McCarthy's description of Macbeth would fit Donald, who "could throw a successful fund raiser for a crack dealer." McCarthy wrote without reference to the work of Piaget or Kohlberg, and Kitwood and Loevinger came along too late for her. She would have known of at least the central philosophy of Piaget because she was an inquiring generalist. She was conversant with Freudian psychology, as were other radical intellectuals who graduated from very good liberal arts colleges in the 1930s. I think we should take from her remarks two points especially: her acuity in seeing Macbeth as just another pragmatist of the kind who make it through Sandhurst or West Point by the hundreds, and, second, of greater moral interest, her insistence that Macbeth *had no imagination.*

Imagination or the lack of it complicates the distinction between someone you could call seriously ethically stunted and someone you would call a genuine jerk.

Social scientists are seldom as comfortable writing off someone as an unchangeable jerk as we literary people are. We writers and readers recognize a sorry human being when we spot one. Literature traditionally shows up or straightforwardly denounces what is "bad," anyhow. No one asks literary people, "How would you work with Edmund in *King Lear* to free him from his sibling stress?" No one asks Shakespeare enthusiasts to design an "intentional group" that could help Iago redefine himself. In fact, the leaders in literary letters conventionally do not want explications or analyses of literary texts to serve something outside literature. Here is Donald Hall, advising students in the writing of literary criticism:

> Third, while writing and revising a paper, continually question whether your writing serves the work that you write about. Do not digress into subjects that lead away from the work into the outside world; avoid personal anecdotes or responses that explore your inside world.[6]

Hall's bidding rightly urges scholarly focus. In another sense, however, it cautions students not to make the connections to the outside; it implies that moral life and feeling are a digression from responsible focus. That is the message of any technology: stay on *how* a product was made or could be made. Keep off its impact on invisible people. I say "invisible people," because when one studies anything with single-minded focus, literature, for example, everyone beyond one's armchair is invisible.

Social workers, on the other hand, are supposed to exert themselves; they are supposed to keep asking themselves tirelessly, despite whatever the likelihood of failure, "How might we design a habitat that would discourage the subsequent adult behaviorial style of people like Donald?" They are supposed to think about America's loosely slung mixture of capitalism and governmental social administration. They need to worry about young men growing up to sacrifice everything to the profit-taking side of life, just as psychologists, especially criminologists, worry about young men growing up to treat people as objects:

> Young men, at the earliest feasible age, must be taught to interact with women in ways that are not exploitative. They must learn that sharing is a process more profound than a simple division of goods, services, money, or labor.[7]

Traditional literature is about heroes and genuine jerks. Much less has been written by the best writers about *genuine jerk organizations*. However many ways the 1960s peace movement may not have succeeded in America, one of its great successes has been the focus by artists on evildoing by groups. In the 1970s and 1980s, stories, essays, and poetry began to talk about how nice Americans engage in bad work in groups. Some of this attention came by extension from the beautiful groundbreaking work of Hannah Arendt, Viktor Frankl, Bruno Bettelheim, and others about how "decent Germans" managed to carry out evil in groups.

Group psychology came into its own. The group and systems approaches to family therapies, the fine-tuning of intentional *group psychology*, and popular group dynamics began giving people ways to be wary of what life in their workplaces might bring.

A good business makes as much money as it can without cheating others or wrecking the environment. A genuine jerk organization, on the other hand, has for its mission profiting any way it can. Generally speaking, this means profiting by hurting others (poisoning the earth, stealing workers' compensation, etc.) if that is what it takes, and limiting their harmful behaviors only when bad publicity or government chastisement might follow. Their top management typically pay themselves many times as much as the average salary of the firm (this average always figures in their salaries). They typically make a spread of good products or good services, along with some bad products—for example, the best in electronics, along with castration mines designed to jump upward three feet on contact so that whoever steps on one loses at least his or her genitalia.

When an individual performs a mixture of useful and deleterious tasks we are more conscious of it. For instance, we are aware of both the goodness and the wickedness in Giacomo's father in "The Soft Core." Although corporations not only make some good products and have some good policies, but also make other, very bad products or conduct very bad policy, we have not done much consciousness-raising about it. We would never admire a doctor who had cured 232 patients but deliberately murdered 14 patients, yet many people will defend a corporation by saying, "But they've done some great stuff!"

Genuine jerk organizations typically have a great many nice employees. These nice people either ignore the company's deplorable policies or don't know about them; some of them take some steps to alter bad policy (whistle-blowing being the extreme case). The environmental specialist who worked as Bristol-Myers Squibb's ecology officer "quit in frustration because her recommendations for complying with the Clean Water Act were not heeded."[8] Eventually Bristol-Myers Squibb, located on Onondaga Lake, pleaded guilty to spilling chemicals into the lake and was fined $3.5 million. The company, as was mentioned earlier in this book, had intended to do exactly what it did. It pleaded guilty when caught and only when caught.

The United States has done nothing that I know of to make children and young people aware that in the twentieth and twenty-first centuries, the moral crux of their lives will not be individual virtue, the kind of thing Sunday schools teach about, but whether or not they take employment from a corporation (or government agency) that brutalizes people or other creatures; how high up in that organization they will allow themselves to rise before they take "ownership" for the bad products of the organization; how much they will or will not exert themselves *(a)* to change the bad policies of that organization or *(b)* to report it to the public.

Even our ethics courses have mostly to do with individual integrity. The courses taught on business workplaces are only beginning to deal with the problem of the company's *exterior* behavior: hundreds of these ethics courses have let themselves swarm around what could be called microethics—sensitivity about this or that personnel issue.

High school job counselors hardly ever ask seniors to consider a company's procedures. If a company tortures rabbits, for instance, do you want to work for it? What is your attitude about working in one division of a scientific company that does its torturing of animals *in another division*? The Roman Catholic Church has a modern candidate for sainthood in Franz Jägerstätter, an ordinary devout Catholic from St. Radegund, Oberösterreich, Austria. Jägerstätter refused to return to the army after his preliminary training because the activities of the Nazis offended his faith. Everyone in authority—his local priest, his military superiors, the

Nazis in charge of his case—advised him to comply, to take medical service, for example. He held his line. In the end he was beheaded. When the Germans returned his ashes to his wife, she erected a little monument over them. It quoted Saint Matthew's declaration that you haven't really gained a life until you lose it over a moral issue. Jägerstätter's name was added to St. Radegund's list of World War II casualties—out of alphabetical order since it was added later.[9] The sociologist and peace worker Gordon Zahn, who first studied Jägerstätter's conscientious objection, discerned that the young Austrian recognized and took seriously a jerk organization when he saw one. Such discernment is as difficult for young people today as it was then.

We could easily educate eighteen-year-olds about working for bad organizations. Such education would bring them fresh pain because they must get jobs somewhere and few companies are pure. They would be forced into the humility one feels upon deciding to take a salary from an organization that does evil up to such and such a level. As soon as one wakes up ethically, nothing again is clean cut. What's more, what used simply to be a question of whether the work was interesting or not, whether it paid decently or not, now is complicated by whether it is all bad, middling-bad, or only peripherally bad.

I will use myself as an example of a case in which naming of a wrong or a right connected with my work would have sped me from mere fluttering of feelings into actual *thinking*.

When I was twenty-one, I worked a half year in the office of the Department of Nursing at the University of Minnesota. Once a week we smelled flesh burning. At any rate, we were told it was flesh burning, the flesh of dogs killed after surgical experimentation. A flurry went through me—a sensuous disturbance, not a thought. I was about as ethically conscious as someone who says, "Oh dear!" or "That's hard to believe!" My mind didn't suppose it should take the next step, connecting the stimulating thrill of dismay to some decision making. Was it or was it not ethical for the University of Minnesota Medical School to use dogs to give student-surgeons experience? Whatever moral flame I had was as flippy as a birthday candle before a child's breath.

One reading of a passage by Brenda Ueland would have set me
to work on the surgeons' use of dogs. I would have *decided* to
think it through, decide where my sympathies lay—with the dogs
or with future human patients of the surgeons—and then the
issue would have lodged for the rest of my life in my *imagination*.
Here is Brenda Ueland:

> Five vivisectors of the University [of Minnesota] Medical
> School and the University Hospital report that their experi-
> ments indicate that "cortisone administration to dogs DOES
> enhance peptic ulcer formations." They juggled the intestines
> of the animals by transplants and 3 or 4 days later injected
> them with 200 milligrams of cortisone daily for at least two
> months during which period the painful ulceration developed.
> The dogs, then—most of them—died. The U.S. Public Health
> Serv-ice and Donald J. Cowling and Jay and Rose Phillips Fund
> for Surgical Research financed these activities. Jay and Rose
> and Donald should go over and watch it all, the splendid
> progress made.[10]

As it was, I visited the upper-floor laboratory where some of the
animals were kept, but I did not insist on seeing all of them.

My college might have prepared and given a booklet to each
graduating senior explaining, so that we could imagine our own
future mind-sets ahead of time, how difficult it would be to make
ourselves take in bad information that we had much rather not
know about, how difficult it would be to decide to stay and work
in that bad place anyway. It would help to have words actually in
print to warn us where we would likely feel cowardly, where it
would be difficult. I would have been glad of a sentence in a pamphlet that would have run: "You will find making your first objection to vivisection easy: they will offer to show you the handsome
kennels, etc. What will be hard is the second step: insisting that
you see the business end of those kennels." I would have been
ready for the spurt of cowardice I felt after looking at the outer
kennels.

High schools could perfectly well offer pamphlets explaining
which oaths of loyalty enlisted personnel and officers must make.
The Uniform Code of Military Justice does not insist that an offi-

cer obey an order that is morally repugnant to him, but how many young people know that? Or, that before Lt. William Calley agreed to implement the My Lai massacre, a sergeant had turned down the proposal. The sergeant's decision brings the matter of moral choice into the issue. Young people might be told about those National Guard soldiers who refused to fire on industrial strikers in 1877. Such stories might wake people to a principal adult worker's issue: if I do wander by happenstance into lifelong employment with a jerk organization, when shall I refuse to do the dirty work?

Peace groups or environmental groups could undertake to publish all the stockholders' proposals to major corporations for a given year. Stockholders' proposals are a lively mixture of some sane and some quite mad righteousness. They make up a jetsam kind of moral activity peculiar to people who live partly on un-earned income—that is, who own profitable shares in American businesses.

More startling, especially in light of moral reasoning, is the in-variable directors' recommendation that shareholders vote against certain proposals. The directors seem to be saying: (1) we have to pay our top people this preposterous amount of money or they won't give us their talent;[11] and (2) all the other companies are doing it (this latter explanation being a grown-ups' version of grade-schoolers' excuses).

Melissa Everett's *Breaking Ranks*, mentioned earlier, describes the lives of ten people who profited by their positions in bad or-ganizations for years before quitting. If such people had been taken beforehand through a facsimile ethical thought process of quitting or not quitting, they might have quit after a few *months* instead of after several years. Perhaps the narrator in "White Canyon" would not have had a brain tumor and the Navajos, who are, only late in the 1990s, receiving any compensation for their illnesses and deaths by cancer from radioactivity, would not have sickened and died. Terry Tempest Williams's "clan of one-breasted women" would not have required mastectomies.[12]

Perhaps the father in "White Canyon" would have known to expect and ask about hazards in uranium mining and prospecting:

"But what about the hazards in this job?" [the uncle] asked.
"Hazards?" said my father.
"Radiation exposure. You're dealing with uranium, aren't you?"
"Small amounts," said my father, shrugging.
The A.E.C. [Atomic Energy Commission] had given his team a fleet of Jeeps and plenty of money, and he enjoyed the field work.
He himself asked none of the questions his brother put to him.

This issue was reported on again recently, with new particulars, in the *New York Times* of May 3, 1993, and in a recent book, *If You Poison Us: Uranium and Native Americans.*[13]

During the 1960s, liberal arts-educated protesters complained of strontium 90 and cobalt 60, but back then, liberal arts people read and philosophized totally differently from the way most scientists and engineers read and philosophized. People at MIT still sneered at the required humanities course.

Here is a rough psychological schedule of how people at different levels of ethical growth respond to evil done by genuine jerks, especially by genuine jerk organizations. Those in Stage IV of the moral reasoning chart—the stage in which one takes satisfaction in respecting and obeying established authority, such as the United States—have a terribly hard time protesting against *organizations*. Most people find it excruciating to stand up against a powerful organization that has attractive promotional materials, glamorous equipment sales, folksy barbeques, and so on.

Conventional wisdom suggests that different *types* of people respond to the need for ethical change in different ways: reformers grab hold of the situation and reform; passive people simply bear the injustice, whatever it is; psychologically unconscious people deny there is any injustice; and so forth. These are not really types of people, however; these are behavioral stages on a continuum: human beings are born as nonpolitical lovers of breast milk. Gradually, gradually, they wake up to what life is about and what life could, in the ideal case, be; they wake up enough to distinguish between such sorrows as are necessary (one's own eventual death, for instance) and the sorrows caused by selfish connivers (the illnesses and deaths of the Navajos and others who worked in the Southwest uranium mines). If they are brave enough they wake up enough to despise injustice wherever it shows. As an individual human being stays at one level in this continuum, he or she can be taken for a certain *kind* or *type* of person, but in fact the person is on the way (unless blocked) and will not always be in that stage.

In a chapter of *Soil and Survival* called "Psychological Pressures to Farm Badly," a list of kinds of responders to questions about farm ethics illustrates several moral-reasoning stages, and a description of genuine jerks with respect to farm issues:[14]

1. Those who propose an ethic about the evil in question (reformers).
2. Those who still see life as simply technical. They are apathetic about good or bad. Their language is about what works and what probably won't work.
3. Those who consciously break their own ethical code for now, but just for now. They agree to practice a little evil by joining a foul-purposed organization, but mean to stop it very soon. As soon as they are out of their current financial squeeze, they mean to return to ethicality—even generosity. Sam, in "Cider 5¢ a Glass," was of this ilk.
4. Those who regard themselves as unaffected by the evil in question. The issue is not in their backyard. They do not do the intellectual work of forming an opinion of it. (This is wise of them; for once one forms a conscious opinion, in so many words, of anything, that anything that once seemed to be on the opposite side of the earth suddenly looms very close and seems nearly connected to oneself.) Non-backyarders feel sanguine about most ethical questions. They count on being home free on most issues. Anyway, they are likely to add, life isn't some bloody Sunday school, after all.
5. Finally, those vicious few (genuine jerks) who mean to carry on unethically because it is profitable. They will bring adver-

sarial (legal process) measures to bear, if need be, to protect their interests.

Perhaps something so simple as writing lists takes us past moral-thinking Stages III and IV. Once past those stages, one is much less likely to be impressed by groups and organizations just because they *are* groups and organizations. List making gives us a few minutes away from our peers (a good thing), because constant peer presence seems to normalize general compliance. The world seems to be about sociability: the friendly faces of others are around us. We may find it hard to imagine distant victims of an organization when we are in a warm room of colleagues. Who would wish to decide that our group, our lovely group with its jokes, its understandings, our group that "goes a long way back with" us, with its uniforms perhaps, is a jerk group?

Even paranoids tend to agree that there are few all-around vicious members of our species—perhaps at any moment only a few tens of thousands. Yet there is a great deal of cruelty in the world. This suggests, unfortunately, that other people, people from one or more of the other four categories, are consciously or unconsciously doing the evil work of the vicious few *for* them.

We need to ask, again and again, perhaps phrasing the question several different ways in each of our generations, what is the mind-set of people willing to hire on to do projects that cause harm?

We might assume that if good people are doing bad work at the behest of comparatively few bad people, these good people are somehow being recruited from the second, third, or fourth group; that is to say, they are either *(a)* technically alert but morally still inchoate like children, *(b)* in a tight spot and therefore willing to do a little short-term wrong for financial or psychological reasons, or *(c)* not seeing the evil in question as evil because of the particular *kind* of evil or the *place* of it or the *size* of it. For example, residents of East 65th Street in New York might not worry about poisoned farm wells and landslides of mining slag; South Dakotans might not worry about political disappearances in Argentina; and all over the world people not given to making mental scenarios of possible outcomes might well not worry about a new virus making its way about.

I set myself to imagining that I am someone running a jerk organization. Unlike the Marines I don't need a few good men: I need thousands of good men and women from the preceding five categories of people. I will advertise for the easy ones first: I will say, "High starting pay. We need a few people with the backbone to stand by their colleagues ["colleagues" for college graduates, "fellow workers" for others]. Wimps need not apply."

Standing by fellow workers is only a Stage II ideal (tribal loyalty—the kind of loyalty that makes me feel that my squad is my comfortable group, and that personal rapport is real; universal principles are just talk). Just after World War II, an expression got going among diplomats and publicity people of the federal government: it was *team player.* When you criticized anyone for some *action* or *policy,* the defending response was, "He's a good team guy." The word *guy,* too, became fashionable. A hearty shoulder-to-shoulder coziness was in fashion, the very opposite sort of heroism to standing up for a principle alone. If enough shoulder-to-shoulder heartiness gets going in a group, its members can design and carry out some surprisingly wicked projects without feeling uneasy.

Women married to men working at Los Alamos reported over and over their sense of the fellowship, the pleasure in all being in the situation together. The women's emphasis on fellowship suggests that they were willing to live in contented ignorance about what the men were really doing. That was the perfect combination for using ethically neutral people in aid of a questionable project of magnitude. If I were a jerk organization recruiter, I would realize that if you do not ask casually educated people, "Were you anxious as you worked on the bomb?" or "Will you feel ethical anxiety if you work for us?" such questions will not come to their minds. If ethical anxiety is, as it appears to be, an acculturated emotion, one need only make a point of hiring people who have not yet been acculturated to it.

All I would need to do to hire people willing to do bad work on a temporary basis is corrupt them with the offer of a high starting salary. If they quaked at the prospect of some of the work, I would distract them from their scruples by putting before them the age-old question: What are you, a man or a mouse? "Can't you stand by your colleagues?" reinforces the ideals of Stage II, not Stage V or VI. "What are you, a man or a mouse?" reinforces Stage III (wanting to be well thought of), not Stage IV, V, or VI.

Financially squeezed people are the most easily recruited. Next easiest are habitually ethics-neutral people—young, technically educated, practical-minded people. The problem of those willing to do something frightful if it is presented as *(a)* science or *(b)* just a matter of practicality has been studied so much and so publicly we need only mention one famous study here. Stanley Milgram's experiment with both educated and comparatively uneducated subjects, whom he asked to press buttons that they believed were sending painful jolts of electricity to learners in order to teach those learners sets of data.[15]

Melissa Everett explains in *Breaking Ranks* that intelligence services, when they need people to learn the arts of torturing, don't hunt up sadists of record. They don't need to. The Nazis, for instance, went to farmboys from Saxony whose minds had been habituated to take all challenges as *practical* challenges.

In *The Genocidal Mentality* Robert Jay Lifton and Eric Markusen report on their inch-by-inch research into the ways Nazis recruited people from the third group—those who have felt at a distance from the evil in question. The job for which the SS needed workers was genocide and inhumane experimentation. Germany's Nazi culture had done the preliminary psychological manipulation: it had taught the we/they philosophy one needs for *any* wrongdoing. *We* are all right, but there is a *they* who are not all right, so it doesn't matter what *we* do to *them*. That much had already been inculcated by National Socialism. But how to make a decent doctor and a decent executive-type actually do the hands-on genocide?

I recommend *The Genocidal Mentality* for its description of how one offers mentorship to a newly recruited person and encourages what Lifton and Markusen call "doubling." One has only to make it clear to the recruit that there are some things a man has to do that he may not like. That's being a man. There likely isn't a state department in the world that hasn't explained to its people that now and again, as an agent of one's government, one must do something that one may not like doing. The men and women are being divided from the boys and girls: this is reality! This is *it*. This is being a professional. And in any case, it is only one's *daytime* work. After hours you are free to indulge your aesthetics or the moral philosophy you have always had. You can lead a double life.

Auschwitz duties were extreme, far at the horrible end of the continuum, but the same psychology the SS used to build and maintain its cadre of managers serves elsewhere, in businesses, in other, contemporary intelligence services—even, near the opposite end, in the tiny, crooked projects of rural county commissioners. I have heard elected officials jolly up someone to keep his mouth shut at a small-town city council meeting in the same way that Lifton and Markusen's "mentoring colleagues" handled new SS people. The commissioners convince their man that this is the real world, and he is now in with the group that is behind things, half hidden—the group that makes things happen.

This scenario illustrates "doubling" in a normal home setting, as practiced by heavy-drinking mothers raising small children: "Yes, I know we are not supposed to fib, but this will be our little secret from Daddy." That one sentence does this psychological work: it says that honor is not to be universally applied; it says that I am an adult mentor offering you cozy in-group feelings— there's nothing cozier than being told "our little secret": the club password, the personal identification number, the motto. Knowing a bottle is hidden behind the sofa is like knowing to say, "Open Sesame." Finally it says that this is *we* who are real, here, now, this minute, whereas Daddy is *they*, off at some assembly line or office, wherever he is, off, and other. Daddy slips from *we* to *they*. That corrupt mother, acting as one of the "vicious few," at the level appropriate to her mission—which is to get a child to do what she wants—uses the same sequence of psychological manipulations that the SS used to get their new people to go against their morals.

We have talked at length about how a bullying or jerk organization can fulfill its mission very well with a complement made up largely of ordinary, nice people. Apparently evil takes places in herds that none of these decent individuals would accommodate on his or her own.

Helping a jerk organization to accomplish its mission while still thinking of oneself as a nice person leads to a closely related psychological dynamic—*evil in the comfortable herd.*

Notes

1. *Acting out* is a social-psychological term for either unconscious signals of pain or inappropriate attempts to control others because one has not been able to control some part of one's own life.

2. Richard Wilbur, "Mind," in *Things of This World* (San Diego: Harcourt Brace Jovanovich, 1984).

3. Cheryl Dickson reporting in a talk to Horizon 100, St. Paul, Minnesota, November 2, 1994.

4. The stage-development scheme that follows is immensely influenced by the thinking of Lawrence Kohlberg, Jane Loevinger, and Tom Kitwood. Whenever we laypeople make enthusiastic use of professionals' findings, we amend the ideas according to our own common sense. Even if we *greatly* alter the original concepts, I think it is a good idea to give some credit to the original writers. If we had not read their work we might have spent thirty or forty years coming to their conclusions—or we might never have come to them. I shall always be especially grateful to the professional thinkers Kohlberg and Loevinger.

5. Mary McCarthy, "General Macbeth," in *The Writing on the Wall and Other Literary Essays* (New York: Harcourt, Brace and World, 1970), 3–14.

6. Donald Hall, *To Read Literature* (Fort Worth, Tex.: Harcourt Brace Jovanovich College Publishers, 1992), 1269.

7. W. J. Musa Moore-Foster, "Up from Brutality: Freeing Black Communities from Sexual Violence," in *Transforming a Rape Culture,* ed. Emilie Buchwald, Pamela Fletcher, and Martha Roth (Minneapolis: Milkweed Editions, 1993).

8. Constance L. Hays, "Bristol-Myers Pleads Guilty to Pollution," *New York Times,* April 25, 1992, 25.

9. Jägerstätter was first studied and reported on by Gordon Zahn, *In Solitary Witness* (New York: Holt, Rinehart and Winston, 1964).

10. Brenda Ueland, *Strength to Your Sword Arm* (Duluth, Minn.: Holy Cow! Press, 1993).

11. Virginia Gruber offered a stockholder proposal concerning executive compensation in *Notice of Annual Meeting of Stockholders,* April 27, 1993, in which she asked that shareholders vote that Merck & Company limit upper-level personnel to twenty-five times the income of the average employee. The board of directors of Merck recommended a vote against her proposal because

it "believes that a cap on executive compensation could prevent the Company from attracting, retaining and motivating the extraordinarily talented people essential to manage the Company for maximum stockholder value."

12. Terry Tempest Williams, "The Clan of One-Breasted Women," *Witness* 3, no. 4 (winter 1989): 99.

13. Keith Schneider, "A Valley of Death for the Navajo Uranium Miners," *New York Times*, May 3, 1993, Al. Peter Eichstaedt, *If You Poison Us: Uranium and Native Americans* (Santa Fe, N.Mex.: Red Crane Books, 1994).

14. Joe Paddock, Nancy Paddock, and Carol Bly, *Soil and Survival: Land Stewardship and the Future of American Agriculture* (San Francisco: Sierra Club Books, 1986), 58–59.

15. Stanley Milgram, *Obedience to Authority: An Experimental View* (New York: Harper and Row, 1983), 14.

CHAPTER 7

Evil in the Comfortable Herd

THE ILLUSTRATION

The Vote Is Now
Helen E. Hokinson

THE COMMENTARY
Carol Bly

The Vote Is Now

by Helen E. Hokinson

"The vote is now fifteen to one that we deplore Mussolini's attitude. I think it would be nice if we could go on record as <u>unanimously</u> deploring Mussolini's attitude."

from The New Yorker *(September 28, 1935)*

Evil in the Comfortable Herd

by Carol Bly

When we talk about evil in the comfortable herd, the ethical core of the whole issue is: can we be brave enough to be unpopular? This chapter gives a little psychological background to our passivity in groups and into insights from social thinkers on the subject. Our passivity in groups can be broken down into two kinds: the bystander effect, and a plain fear of being disliked if we stand apart from group flow.

The Bystander Effect

No wonder we take so naturally to waiting around for the word. Our childhoods were spent in groups, groups of siblings, or just the group of us and one or more parents or mentors. There we stood, smaller than the others, to see what was coming. We have to be bystanders while our parents figure out how to load the car. Sometimes the leaders of the group were involved in evil, not elsewhere but against *us*, but the family leaders were what carried the day. Whatever simple orders of papal bulls, whatever beatings or blessings, come down from our parents are seen by us children not as just or unjust but as reality, the way it is, the way it's done, the way it always will be.

What's more, people who have been passive generally haven't got a good sense of time. They don't distinguish between what is happening to them now, at this very minute, what has always been happening to them, and probably will happen again in the future. Since they are out of the loop of planning their own lives, their minds don't categorize time segments in the way minds must if they want to feel and be active. "I will do this now, that later": that is the conversation of an active personality, not someone who doesn't expect to take control. As children, most of us spend years hovering, happily or not, at the circumference of people in authority over us. No wonder we fall back easily into what has been termed "the bystander effect."

he bystander effect is watching some evil take place, but since we are watching with others who are watching, and no one seems to be doing anything about the evil, we go on watching and doing nothing about it. Instead of consulting our own feelings about what to do, we take our cue from the other bystanders. They are not doing anything. Therefore, we also do nothing. If something needed to be done, somebody would have done it.

Political thinkers and social psychologists who published brilliant insights into the bystander effect and moral drift and fear of singularity have not received the national acclaim they deserve. Their findings have not been generally welcomed. Few schools have decided to teach herd psychology to high school seniors. The several citizens' groups popping up around the United States for the training of public officials do not habitually teach useful, grassroots versions of psychologists' insight into groupthink and moral drift and the bystander effect.

Still, the last-mentioned aspect of herding, the bystander effect, became famous after thirty-five people watched from their apartment windows as an assailant pursued and repeatedly stabbed Kitty Genovese over a twenty-minute period in Kew Gardens, Queens. Kitty Genovese put up a good struggle, too. She screamed a lot. She ran from one place to another in the apartment courtyard. The thirty-five people watched, though, as the murderer stabbed her so many times she couldn't run anymore. Then he stabbed her to death. Not one of the witnesses called the police or intervened in any other way.

Pulling oneself into wakefulness when others look dazed does not come naturally. For one thing, passivity is in the short term a thousand times more practical than stepping forward to take action. One attracts attention from the enemy if one moves: if one freezes, the enemies in your line of sight continue killing whatever or whomever they have begun to kill and do not suddenly swing their attention to you. There is an African frog whose principal enemy is a comparatively large, long green snake. That snake is hunting precisely that frog, but it can pass (as shown in one of David Attenborough's dazzling videos) within a few inches of literal piles of the green frogs without seeing them providing none of them moves. A lesson of the most ancient part of our brain is to stay still and nothing will get you.

One needs learning from another part of the brain to overcome natural passivity. One needs a motivation more passionate than self-interested practicality. When a woman is being knifed to death the practical thing for those watching is to do nothing. The Kew Gardens onlookers acted quite naturally. One of the most difficult lessons children learn is how to make their minds shout at the passive psychological muscles inside them.

A gorgeous aspect of Charles Baxter's short story "Gryphon" (see chapter 9) is that the author presents a little boy who is actually an activist, despite his psychological habitat of ordinary classmates cheerfully adrift in the world the way children usually are—getting along, arriving at their haphazard insights, either brownnosing teachers or not, making jokes, automatically taunting strangers who behave in novel ways—and despite his depressed mother.

The *natural* thing is to go with fate, stand by unless shaken, figure the angles, and if the group commands it, kill someone.

Here is a creative-writing situation to demonstrate what hard work it is for an ordinary human being to *stop* being just a bystander. I pretend that I am a new writer. I pretend I am at that stage of a writer's development that George Orwell in his essay "Why I Write" called his "second stage": that is, I am past the first stage of wanting to write just anything that will get me published; I want to write something beautiful. Let us say I am between thirty and forty, which since the 1980s has been a typical decade for emerging creative writers. I know the conventional assumptions about what is beautiful and what is not: for example, one's childhood is more beautiful than one's adulthood, so I will write about that. After all, that is when Christmas was really Christmas. (Curiously, most beginning writers, if told to describe a sensitive situation, will choose a scene recalled from childhood, as if they supposed the sensibilities of childhood were superior to the sensibilities of adult life.)

This will be a story in which I start off thinking only of beauty and nostalgia, not of right or wrong.

"My brother and I were looking forward to an especially nice day. The weather was fine. It did not rain for the family picnic," I write. I stop there, however, not adding that the real reason the family did not get into the Volvo and drive to Ipswich was that Mom and Dad were both drunk and had fought physically. Both got bloodied. They went into their bedroom at 11 A.M., only an hour before the promised picnic time. We children did not try to wake them at noon. I put on the page, "It did not rain for the picnic." The creative-writing teacher had suggested, "If you feel you are getting stuck, just keep writing anyway." So I wrote again, "It did not rain for the picnic."

I go on. "We did not go on the picnic, though." Then I desist because it feels disloyal. Loyalty to parents comes naturally: the most microscopic observation that implies a fault in the parents is unnatural. Noticing and not denying faults in one's parents are often a child's first spark in the already set but not lit bonfire of ethical development. "All is not right after all!" is often the soul's first wakening to moral questions.

Why so much fuss about judging one's parents? I feel disloyal because already by the age of ten I have these two moral values: staying sober and keeping promises. My parents have failed in carrying out these two virtues. But I myself am really living at Stage II—loyalty to my particular tribal group, to my parents. So I leave off any further mention of the picnic. I will delay committing myself to judgment. I will hang around some more and see how things develop. I stop planning what to put on my writing pad. I had thought I would write something beautiful, but something else got in the way of it—so I stop.

That is how children have to live. If they don't develop out of the bystanding habit, they become adult bystanders.

A particular and fascinating kind of bystander effect has been identified and named *moral drift*. Let us say that eight people are discussing slavery. One person is strongly against it. Four are strongly in favor. Three suppose it is OK, or maybe not: they are backyardists; they have no feel for the subject because it hasn't come up in their own lives, and they have poor imaginations, being self-centered like Macbeth. The three who suppose that slavery is OK make no mental image of enslaving someone, or of being enslaved themselves.

That's the ambience of the room. The one antislavery person makes a strong objection to slavery. People defend slavery. Others shrug. The antislavery person speaks again. The others keep giving one another more and more eye contact, and less and less eye contact to this irritating speaker.

Nothing makes a strongly opinionated speaker yield so well as being denied eye contact. After ten minutes or an hour or a week or two weeks, the sometime strong dissenter says, "Well, I suppose there are *some* instances where slavery might be all right, of course."

Moral drift has taken place when a strong person of universal morals floats over to a position of cultural relativism or to a less pronounced objection to the evil in question. Incidentally, much of the "mellowing out" that forty- and fifty-year-olds smilingly observe in one another is simply moral drift. The conscientious dissenter has gotten tired and left the hustings.

Moral drift is a dynamic of people talking to other people on issues requiring conviction. For years I thought of groups as being venues in which one got all fired up about some project. In fact, groups tend toward more gentleness than firing. They damp things down to a mossy agreeableness. That is why very great poems, like very great short stories, are not written in groups.

Let us imagine that Louis Simpson is speaking to a group, instead of writing the poem called "A Story about Chicken Soup." He tells the group, "Actually, those relatives of mine who were killed in the concentration camps have some demand on me— they want me to be more serious than I want to be." Someone would say, "I can relate to that, but on the other hand, I think you are being too hard on yourself. You have a right *not* to stick in their mudhole where no one is elegant." Someone else would say, "I think the relatives have to come to terms with the fact that that was then and this is now. If they had to be poor and sleep in a room with many others, that was their situation. You have a right to stay centered on your situation." Someone else would pick up on the kindness of that remark and the apparent anguish of the poet. Kindness—so close to courtesy—is a powerful force in groups, especially kindness toward *those present in the group*. This group member would now say, "Louis, my feeling—I mean, in terms of what you're talking about, the tragic world and all—is that life is given to each of us. I think Wayne here is right in saying you have a right to your life. If your life is walking in the painted sunshine, then you have a right to walk in the painted sunshine, and I don't think you should be made to feel guilty about it."

Unfortunately, the very familiarity and popularity of the 1970s idea that no one should have to feel guilty for past events encourage anecdotal comments from other group members. These members hadn't felt clear about why Simpson was acting so bothered, or their grasp of German history between 1943 and 1945 may have been fuzzy. In any case, they now spot a chance to enter the discussion. "I don't let people do guilt trips on me anymore," one of them says.

By the end of an hour all poetic exactitude would have been mulched in with the other conversations. All particularity would have submitted to the general composting. Certainly the efforts of a poet to stop being a moral bystander would be forgotten.

What does this raveling process mean? It means that groups, because they are groups, are not happy with an intense ethical determination *to change something*. In their evaluations, group members may report, "We were fired up," or "We were excited," but groups often prefer a mild *aroma* of feeling rather than sharp feeling itself. I think that accounts for group members' so often reporting that in some recent discussion they talked about a particular issue. "Did you?" one asks. "What do people say should be *done* about it?" The group members reply, "It wasn't so much about what should be done. We all agreed, we feel changed."

Our very agreement sounds perverse. Why would we prefer things general, reminiscent, and without plan or plans for good change? One reason is frightening: unless there has been enough character development to stay with unpleasant data long enough to "process it," as they say, people find it hard to concentrate ten minutes on a subject outside their own lives. If we all knew how to practice empathy, we would ask questions of people who have just told us about their alien concerns. For example, let us say that Louis Simpson is visiting our group. He has just explained that he feels he hasn't the right to be a shallow-living aesthete because ours is a species that commits genocide. Anyone who has sat in any committee knows that such a remark is not the common run of remarks in committees.[1] You would expect that at least one of us might ask Simpson some small peripheral questions as to his definition of genocide, or the meaning of the painted sunshine and the tragic world. But most of us have never been taught how to ask questions. We haven't even been told that we should *expect* to ask questions.

So we begin to drift back to ourselves. We daydream. If we are having a bad day (and who does not?) we may even remark to ourselves or sotto voce to our neighbor that if that poet had not brought up that stuff he insisted on bringing up we'd have been out of here by now.

I have drawn that scene fully because something like it takes place in mortally important settings, such as in jury rooms. I would like to emphasize the devastating, yet comparatively unidentified, effect of moral drift in decision-making groups. In television programs about criminal justice, for example, juries are shown as people desperately weighing reasonable doubts against unreasonable doubts. None of them shows that five or ten or all twelve of the jurors may well be having difficulty keeping up moral intensity about the evidence given. Jurors might be so afflicted with absentminded self-centeredness that *(a)* they don't take in half the information given them and thus *(b)* haven't much feeling about the issues, so that *(c)* they might therefore militate against any colleague who *has maintained* strong feelings about the issues.

At such a level, moral drift is not just bovine behavior at a public meeting but a threat to justice.

As with any human proclivity, some people are more vulnerable to herding in groups than others. A marvelous and readable expert in this field is Dr. Alice Miller, who has given us scholarly and poignant portraits of Adolf Hitler and his father—of how psychological abuse of children gives them a poor self-image that they attempt to repair or replace with love of a charismatic leader.[2] Another wise counselor about herd mentality, especially as it operates in our commercial world today, is Tom Kitwood. He states that because modern people spend such a significant share of their lives working in large organizations, they scarcely can recover from the psychological effects in the time left them after retirement. His is a grim view. Accepting a low-level moral code during the day is bound to infiltrate one's off-time judgment as well. If one has to divide oneself into different selves (with different values), one is the more likely to become further fragmented:

> We need to consider, finally, the long-term effect of organizational membership on personality or, in moral terms, on character. From a purely cognitive-developmental point of view, those who have had to equilibrate over a long period to a low-level justice structure for the greater part of the day are likely to carry its effects in their whole moral outlook; one who has to be authoritarian at work will probably be authoritarian at home and at play. Depth psychology takes this matter much further. The typical organizational role, with its defensiveness, its selective inattention, its avoidance of responsibility, is the activation of a part-self; it is likely that a person who occupies such a role for a long period will enhance the division and fragmentation of his or her psyche. Perhaps this will especially be the case for one also identifies strongly with the role. The formal organizations of contemporary industrial society, then, create an enormous psychological problem for their members. The years of retirement, restricted in other ways as they are for very many people, do not always make for recovery.
>
> All this implies a vast moral project; it stares us in the face, and yet it is generally ignored.[3]

Of Kitwood's several gloomy insights, the gloomiest is the fact that although the ways in which we spoil our personalities by herding stare us in the face, we ignore them. Kitwood's observations are corroborated by the social work theory that some undesirable behavior, such as acting authoritarian around one's workplace and one's home, comes not of *present* bad feelings but of year-in, year-out habit. Such behavior will not respond, therefore, to ordinary psychotherapies: one needs to exert "character" —that is, willpower—to drop the bullying habit. Such character or willpower, however, is a quality typically undeveloped or atrophied by life in the "low-level justice structure" of the herd.

How, precisely, does the herd make moral mistakes? How can we spot the group dynamic as it starts up? For if we can spot a bad dynamic, we can stop it by showing it to the others.

I gratefully turn to Irving Janis's amazing collection of insights in his book *Groupthink*.⁴ Janis studied a number of groups who made poor decisions, such as the group responsible for the feasibility or nonfeasibility of the invasion later called the Bay of Pigs Project. Janis studied groups with first-rate outcomes, such as the long-range planning group chaired by George Kennan whose work was to implement the Marshall Plan. Janis focuses on how certain intricate dynamics lead to relaxation when what is needed is vigilance, to sloth when what is needed is exertion, to conviviality when instead, the members should have been listening to the small, dissenting voice. Human beings in herds have a terrible tendency to be comfortable together: they would plan World War XXX if it promised to make people feel shoulder-to-shoulder forever. The outcome of nearly all of what Janis calls "groupthink" is the human equivalent to lemmings' behavior. Groupthink is the outcome of doing what comes *naturally*, instead of each person making a point of stepping back, looking at what is being proposed, and being (here is the hard part) *willing to be unpopular with the group*.

A helpful project would be to give every child in every elementary school in the United States, Canada, and Britain a copy of Alan Arkin's *The Lemming Condition*.⁵ Class discussion of this book might stave off later unconsciousness about groups. Arkin's characters illustrate every principle of *groupthink* and a couple of the cures for it.

In *Groupthink*, Janis offers a list of eight specific kinds of thinking and feeling, divided into three general types, which characterize dangerous behaviors in human herds. Janis presents his symptoms so succinctly, and in such a neat form, that I offer them here for interest.

I have added, after each of Janis's symptoms, a short example to illustrate the case. The italicized heads and numbered concepts are Janis's.

Type I: Overestimation of the group — its power and morality

1. *An illusion of invulnerability, shared by most or all the members, which creates excessive optimism and encourages taking extreme risks*

A perfect instance of this illusion of invulnerability is the decision of Russian military commanders preceding World War I not to educate their officer corps in machine-gun technology. Holy Mother Russia had always been glorious with its charge of lancers and it would be glorious again. Younger officers who suggested they find out just what was involved in opposing machine-gun fire with cavalry charges were thrown out of the military academy. A similar illusion of invulnerability was exemplified by the French, who insisted that their military machine would conquer because it had superior esprit de corps or élan. Both cases are engagingly described in some detail by Barbara Tuchman in *The Guns of August.*

2. *An unquestioned belief in the group's inherent morality, inclining the members to ignore the ethical or moral consequences of their decisions*

Cold War enthusiasts, conducting classes at the War College and whose cool, rational lectures included language such as "we can figure on so many megadeaths," were certain they were right: they were to the best of their beliefs protecting the interests of the United States. Another example: When peace protesters marched outside the Pentagon, Secretary of Defense McNamara refused to speak to them from the window where he stood watching. He was sure they had nothing to teach him.

Type II: Closed-mindedness

3. *Collective efforts to rationalize in order to discount warnings or other information that might lead the members to reconsider their assumptions before they recommit themselves to their past policy decisions*

In church groups, no one wants to say unpleasant things such as, "What we did last year will no longer work because the situation is different," or worse, "What we felt proud of last year turns out, in retrospect, to have been a poor action. We need to talk to people who *know more than we know* to get a better perspective on our purpose here." Churches and other idealistic groups are especially vulnerable to this kind of groupthink because they try to keep their meetings so affectionate and high-spirited; they tend to be sure that there must be a group "high" or it won't be religiously correct. Hence such elevated language as "we were really excited" and "we felt such a oneness." When the goal of feeling good from minute to minute in a meeting is greater than the goal of being discerning about bad judgment, then a group is vulnerable to this aspect of groupthink. Another psychological dynamic that makes a group vulnerable is a membership made up of people at very differing levels of psychoethical development: those willing to be sober and think things over look antispiritual to those who want to feel high in the group; those who want unity and shouted allegiance look immature and prone to herd action to the sober thinkers and weighers.

4. *Stereotyped views of enemy leaders as too evil to warrant genuine attempts to negotiate, or as too weak and stupid to counter whatever risky attempts are made to defeat their purposes*

Type III: Pressures toward uniformity

5. *Self-censorship of deviations from the apparent group consensus, reflecting each member's inclination to minimize to himself the importance of his doubts and counterarguments*

Dislike of deviation from the apparent consensus is well illustrated by many committees formed to pass on honors candidates

at colleges and universities. I once sat on an undergraduate's committee for an honors project. I was the external member, the person chosen from outside the academic community in question.
The candidate's thesis had only two ideas, both of which were at
sophomore- or junior-, not senior-level, thinking. The bound thesis had forty-two substantial mistakes in grammar and usage, and
a computer had mispaginated every second page. The candidate
had not corrected that error. During our oral session, the candidate ducked several questions put by her professors, answered
others at too simple a level, and in one case answered at some
length a question that had not been asked. Aware of some intellectual shambling, the chairperson, who was the candidate's adviser, kindly asked a flurry of questions that the candidate could
easily answer, perhaps to stave off any further questioning by the
others. The candidate was asked to leave the room. I expressed
grave disappointment in the thesis itself and in the candidate's
presentation and answers to questions. The chairperson of the
committee turned to the others and said, "Well, I think we are all
agreed that S. passes our review—that is, if Carol can make herself
sign on." It was a classic case of a group leader's controlling dissenting opinion by implying it was fractious. I remarked equably
that since I was only the external member and had no ownership
in the academic reputation of the institution I would certainly
not stand in the candidate's way.

If we made a column of the mother cow's comments as to how
the herd received the information from The One Who Came
Back, in "A Mother's Tale," we would find a nearly perfect case of
someone's lying, first, to stay in good with the group in the story
of long ago and, second, to stay in good with the group of baby
steers standing around her now. There is no end to the mother
cow's fluctuations.

6. *A shared illusion of unanimity concerning judgments conforming*
   to the majority view (partly resulting from self-censorship of
   deviations, augmented by the false assumption that silence
   means consent)

Groups fond of consensus instead of voted majority opinion are
especially vulnerable to the illusion of unanimity. Sometimes, in

the generally excellent American Friends Service Committee, one sits through a long-range goals discussion in a workcamp setting and is aware that there are divergent opinions in the room that the group leaders and the others hope will vanish. There is a good deal of mention of "the spirit moving." Well, for the person with the divergent opinion, it must be an uneasy business to keep pointing out this or that particular point of the long-range plan only to be met with phrases like "perhaps in the spirit of the meeting . . ." and so forth.

A psychotherapist's solution might be to state the situation openly: "Look, friends, I feel a terrific desire around the room for us all to agree. Would it be all right if we *didn't* all agree? Could you look at the dissenting opinion here and see if by any chance it has something going for it—and don't lean on the dissenter at all, for, say, fifteen minutes? For these fifteen minutes let's not worry about finding common ground at all! Let's just learn all the truth we can! In fact, let's be worried together. Let's agree to be unsure of what we're doing, for fifteen minutes."

7. *Direct pressure on any member who expresses strong arguments against any of the group's stereotypes, illusions, or commitments, making clear that this type of dissent is contrary to what is expected of all loyal members*

There is familiar phrasing used by people who regard dissenting argument as a sign of ad hominem disloyalty to the group. "Wow, I don't know—the way you're talking—are you keeping in mind the interests of our project? We need a lot of real team spirit here!" Sometimes juries press a dissenting juror to the point where he or she is characterized as the only one who is keeping all twelve from their top priority—getting home early. Thousands of groups, if infected with groupthink of this kind, will forget the mission of the group altogether: it can become a group passion to accuse the dissenting minority of treason. The group forgets that it is not a nation, and one need not die (or lie) for it.

> 8. *The emergence of self-appointed mind guards—members who*
>   *protect the group from adverse information that might shatter*
>   *their shared complacency about the effectiveness and morality of*
>   *their decisions*

This is one of the shrewdest of Janis's insights. These mind guards will actually keep certain needed information away from the group, in the interests of "protecting morale." I was so impressed with the problem of the self-appointed mind guard that I invented a position that I now use with every creative-writing class I teach: it is a "truth keeper"—someone brave enough to protect the class from its teacher, to protect the small, weak voice from the majority opinion, and to carry dissent and complaints from individual people to the leader and the group. The mere presence of someone called the truth keeper causes a queer little relief in people: they laugh, but when the truth keeper is a good one, they are grateful for this preventer of corruption in the powerful leader or the class-herd.

Janis then observes that if a policy-making group:

> displays most of the symptoms of groupthink, we can expect to find that the group also displays symptoms of defective decision-making. Seven such symptoms were listed earlier [at the end of chapter 1 of Janis's book] on the basis of prior research on decision-making in government, industry, and other large organizations:
> 1. Incomplete survey of alternatives
> 2. Incomplete survey of objectives
> 3. Failure to examine risks of preferred choice
> 4. Failure to reappraise initially rejected alternatives
> 5. Poor information search
> 6. Selective bias in processing information at hand
> 7. Failure to work out contingency plans[6]

A suggestion to readers of this ethics anthology is that the cordial, proactive wisdom of Kitwood and the acuity of Janis's observations are too good *not* to apply to the works of literature included here. As mentioned, the Mother Cow embodied several group-think dynamics: her horrible cover-ups of the harsh truth; her desire to be admired by the calves; her dreadfully low-quality "information search"; her singing of the tribal song as if it were nothing but a chance to feel vaguely holy, and not an exhortation to revolution.

Although there are not specific examples in this book for each of the groupthink characteristics that Janis elaborated for us, we would find, if we jotted down an informal list of the groups *behind the scenes* in each literary selection, that *those* groups would constitute some perfect instances of groupthink—groupthink that vitally affects the people in the stories and poems. To offer just a few:

- Members of Sam's legal department in "Cider 5¢ a Glass." (That is, we cannot believe that every one of those men and women were delighted at the idea of swindling the hurt worker.)
- The various churches whose young people went off to the Vietnam War ("Ode for the American Dead in Asia"). Surely one or another of those clergypersons must have known of and wanted to suggest to young men that they seek "draft counseling," the most humane, nationwide, idealist-invented social structure of the 1960s.
- The eastern college faculty members who gave a hearing to Mary in "In the Garden of the North American Martyrs."

Other works illustrate Kitwood's "selective inattention" and other ideas. Some cause for our having any American dead in Asia at all is groupthink-driven decision making on the part of leaders. The aspect of groupthink having to do with members' wanting to please the leader rather than make a mental image of the victims of their decision making was discussed with respect to Secretary of Defense McNamara in chapter 9.

A word about the three professional fields that this book concerns itself with—literature, social work or psychotherapeutic communication skills, and stage-development philosophy: Each of these suffers some vulnerability to groupthink. Each is likely to accept research done in its own discipline as desirable and acceptable. Social workers, with their professional commitment to trying to change the system in which they work, might help client groups to consciousness of groupthink. Members of English departments across the country confess to feeling stymied by the heavy presence of affect-free and ethics-free textual criticism. Perhaps these professors might say to themselves, "If Irving Janis has any explanation for why people choose to look at literature as if it were simply grist for technical analysis, I will have a look at his ideas about groupthink. If any aspect of herd mentality is responsible for trivializing literature, then I want to break up that herd mentality. I want what English departments have properly always wanted—to teach good authors' best hopes, worst fears, and serious love of life to the young."

Notes

1. How great ideas and sacrifice in one individual leader (Charles Stewart Parnell) can get deintensified by a decade or two of committee banality is the subject of James Joyce's great short story "Ivy Day in the Committee Room," from *Dubliners* (1914; reprint, New York: Modern Library, n.d.), 148.

2. Alice Miller, *For Your Own Good: Hidden Cruelty in Child-Rearing and the Roots of Violence*, trans. Hildegarde and Hunter Hannum (New York: Farrar, Straus and Giroux, 1983).

3. Tom Kitwood, *Concern for Others: A New Psychololgy of Conscience and Morality* (London: Routledge, 1990), 180.

4. Irving Janis, *Groupthink: Psychological Studies of Policy Decisions and Fiascoes* (Boston: Houghton Mifflin, 1983).

5. Alan Arkin, *The Lemming Condition,* illus. Joan Sandin (New York: Harper and Row, 1976).

6. Janis, *Groupthink.*

CHAPTER 8

Evil by Pain Avoidance and Psychological Sloth

A Story about Chicken Soup

by Louis Simpson

In my grandmother's house there was always chicken soup
And talk of the old country—mud and boards,
Poverty,
The snow falling down the necks of lovers.

Now and then, out of her savings
She sent them a dowry. Imagine
The rice-powdered faces!
And the smell of the bride, like chicken soup.

But the Germans killed them.
I know it's in bad taste to say it,
But it's true. The Germans killed them all.

■   ■   ■

In the ruins of Berchtesgaden
A child with yellow hair
Ran out of a doorway.

A German girl-child—
Cuckoo, all skin and bones—
Not even enough to make chicken soup.
She sat by the stream and smiled.

Then as we splashed in the sun
She laughed at us.
We had killed her mechanical brothers,
So we forgave her.

■   ■   ■

The sun is shining.
The shadows of the lovers have disappeared.
They are all eyes; they have some demand on me—
They want me to be more serious than I want to be.

They want me to stick in their mudhole
Where no one is elegant.
They want me to wear old clothes,
They want me to be poor, to sleep in a room with many others—

Not to walk in the painted sunshine
To a summer house,
But to live in the tragic world forever.

Brothers and Sisters

by Alice Walker

We lived on a farm in the South in the fifties, and my brothers, the four of them I knew (the fifth had left home when I was three years old), were allowed to watch animals being mated. This was not unusual; nor was it considered unusual that my older sister and I were frowned upon if we even asked, innocently, what was going on. One of my brothers explained the mating one day, using words my father had given him: "The bull is getting a little something on his stick," he said. And he laughed. "What stick?" I wanted to know. "Where did he get it? How did he pick it up? Where did he put it?" All my brothers laughed.

I believe my mother's theory about raising a large family of five boys and three girls was that the father should teach the boys and the mother teach the girls the facts, as one says, of life. So my father went around talking about bulls getting something on their sticks and she went around saying girls did not need to know about such things. They were "womanish" (a very bad way to be in those days) if they asked.

The thing was, watching the matings filled my brothers with an aimless sort of lust, as dangerous as it was unintentional. They knew enough to know that cows, months after mating, produced calves, but they were not bright enough to make the same connection between women and their offspring.

Sometimes, when I think of my childhood, it seems to me a particularly hard one. But in reality, everything awful that happened to me didn't seem to happen to *me* at all, but to my older sister. Through some incredible power to negate my presence around people I did not like, which produced invisibility (as well as an ability to appear mentally vacant when I was nothing of the kind), I was spared the humiliation she was subjected to, though at the same time, I felt every bit of it. It was as if she suffered for my benefit, and I vowed early in my life that none of the things that made existence so miserable for her would happen to me.

394

The fact that she was not allowed at official matings did not mean she never saw any. While my brothers followed my father to the mating pens on the other side of the road near the barn, she stationed herself near the pigpen, or followed our many dogs until they were in a mating mood, or, failing to witness something there, she watched the chickens. On a farm it is impossible *not* to be conscious of sex, to wonder about it, to dream . . . but to whom was she to speak of her feelings? Not to my father, who thought all young women perverse. Not to my mother, who pretended all her children grew out of stumps she magically found in the forest. Not to me, who never found anything wrong with this lie.

When my sister menstruated she wore a thick packet of clean rags between her legs. It stuck out in front like a penis. The boys laughed at her as she served them at the table. Not knowing any better, and because our parents did not dream of actually *discussing* what was going on, she would giggle nervously at herself. I hated her for giggling, and it was at those times I would think of her as dim-witted. She never complained, but she began to have strange fainting fits whenever she had her period. Her head felt as if it were splitting, she said, and everything she ate came up again. And her cramps were so severe she could not stand. She was forced to spend several days of each month in bed.

My father expected all of his sons to have sex with women. "Like bulls," he said, "a man *needs* to get a little something on his stick." And so, on Saturday nights, into town they went, chasing the girls. My sister was rarely allowed into town alone, and if the dress she wore fit too snugly at the waist, or if her cleavage dipped too far below her collarbone, she was made to stay home.

"But why can't I go too," she would cry, her face screwed up with the effort not to wail.

"They're boys, your brothers, *that's* why they can go."

Naturally, when she got the chance, she responded eagerly to boys. But when this was discovered she was whipped and locked up in her room.

I would go in to visit her.

"Straight Pine,"* she would say, "you don't know what it *feels* like to want to be loved by a man."

* A pseudonym.

"And if this is what you get for feeling like it I never will," I said, with—I hoped—the right combination of sympathy and disgust.

"Men smell so good," she would whisper ecstatically. "And when they look into your eyes, you just melt."

Since they were so hard to catch, naturally she thought almost any of them terrific.

"Oh, that Alfred!" she would moon over some mediocre, square-headed boy, "he's so *sweet!*" And she would take his ugly picture out of her bosom and kiss it.

My father was always warning her not to come home if she ever found herself pregnant. My mother constantly reminded her that abortion was a sin. Later, although she never became pregnant, her period would not come for months at a time. The painful symptoms, however, never varied or ceased. She fell for the first man who loved her enough to beat her for looking at someone else, and when I was still in high school, she married him.

My fifth brother, the one I never knew, was said to be different from the rest. He had not liked matings. He would not watch them. He thought the cows should be given a choice. My father had disliked him because he was soft. My mother took up for him. "Jason is just tender-hearted," she would say in a way that made me know he was her favorite; "he takes after me." It was true that my mother cried about almost anything.

Who was this oldest brother? I wondered.

"Well," said my mother, "he was someone who always loved you. Of course he was a great big boy when you were born and out working on his own. He worked on a road gang building roads. Every morning before he left he would come in the room where you were and pick you up and give you the biggest kisses. He used to look at you and just smile. It's a pity you don't remember him."

I agreed.

At my father's funeral I finally "met" my oldest brother. He is tall and black with thick gray hair above a young-looking face. I watched my sister cry over my father until she blacked out from grief. I saw my brothers sobbing, reminding each other of what a great father he had been. My oldest brother and I did not shed a tear between us. When I left my father's grave he came up and introduced himself. "You don't ever have to walk alone," he said, and put his arms around me.

One out of five ain't *too* bad, I thought, snuggling up.

But I didn't discover until recently his true uniqueness: He is the only one of my brothers who assumes responsibility for all his children. The other four all fathered children during those Saturday-night chases of twenty years ago. Children—my nieces and nephews whom I will probably never know—they neither acknowledge as their own, provide for, or even see.

It was not until I became a student of women's liberation ideology that I could understand and forgive my father. I needed an ideology that would define his behavior in context. The black movement had given me an ideology that helped explain his colorism (he *did* fall in love with my mother partly because she was so light; he never denied it). Feminism helped explain his sexism. I was relieved to know his sexist behavior was not something uniquely his own, but, rather, an imitation of the behavior of the society around us.

All partisan movements add to the fullness of our understanding of society as a whole. They never detract; or, in any case, one must not allow them to do so. Experience adds to experience. "The more things the better," as O'Connor and Welty both have said, speaking, one of marriage, the other of Catholicism.

I desperately needed my father and brothers to give me male models I could respect, because white men (for example; being particularly handy in this sort of comparison)—whether in films or in person—offered man as dominator, as killer, and always as hypocrite.

My father failed because he copied the hypocrisy. And my brothers—except for one—never understood they must represent half the world to me, as I must represent the other half to them.*

---

* Since this essay was written [1975], my brothers have offered their name, acknowledgment, and some support to all their children.

Evil by Pain Avoidance and Psychological Sloth

by Carol Bly

Knowing your own mind morally is hard enough work.

Knowing one's own mind morally is different from what's commonly meant by knowing one's own mind—that is, feeling decisive on each issue as it comes up. A person who enters a dilemma of some sort and then makes a pronouncement with dispatch or decides on a course of action with dispatch is called someone who knows his or her own mind. Knowing one's own mind *morally*, however, involves being able to see the ethical meaning of a situation as well as its various concrete symptoms. One part of the human mind takes in the landscape quite thoroughly, but doesn't see the meaning of the components of the landscape. Later, perhaps, that person may ascribe some moral meaning to one or another item in the landscape. Police detectives need the habit of absorbing data that may appear to have no meaning at all, because later one or two bits of the data might be of dire importance to the case. Such absorption of apparently incidental data we associate with extroverts. "Oh, look at that," they say, pointing at something outside themselves. Although an extroverted person can of course know his or her own moral mind, that particular practice of noticing external minutiae or novelties of some minor interest is not the practice one wants in a moral dilemma. Knowing oneself morally means one notices the external data, just as the extrovert did, but one constantly runs the film of information back inward and asks, "Hey—all of you, my selves in there—what does this feel like? Is this tied to anything else I need to think about? Have I any choices here? I know I feel wretched about this, but I can't pinpoint the wretched feeling. Will you please turn up some memory that may put this in perspective for me? Will you please give your opinion, too: Am I being jerked around here? Is someone else being jerked around? Am I acting unrealistically? Help, you guys—help me."

Of course such a consultation with one's own mind is not done in so many words: movement from the ocular or aural nerves, which took in the data for which the speaker wanted help, toward the various neurons firing in the head is millions of times faster than one can form words. This hypothetical conversation is only an approximation on the page for lightning-speed chemo-electric messenger work.

On the surface, one might think, "Why would one ever *want* to do such deliberate agonizing? Why not just take in the land-scape, like it or dislike it, whatever, and lighten up?"

The answer is that unless we identify bad news in the land-scapes around us, as well as in the landscapes in our memories, we are hiding from pain. What is wrong with hiding from pain is that the hiding muscle, if one avoids pain a good deal of the time, gets so powerful, it inappropriately hides other feelings besides pain. It hides, for example, feelings of happiness.

Pain avoiders feel less spontaneous happiness, along with less spontaneous anguish, than they would if they could make them-selves be willing to feel anguish in the interests of truth. Learning to stop one's practice of psychological pain avoidance, and to do some pointing at and blaming of evil or perpetrators of evil, brings about a surprising and gorgeous return: one takes more joy in the world despite its failings. Such taking of joy is a sophisticated feeling. That kind of ebullient joy, half-philosophical and half-madcap, comes only from psychological consciousness.

Pain avoidance is still one of the most prevalent and ignored forces in people's lives. Psychotherapists rate it as a major force of blocking people from fully realized lives and fully engaged per-sonalities. From a moralist's point of view, pain avoidance, as much as any other kind of psychological unconsciousness in the normal range, causes evil.

In this chapter we will look at a few aspects of pain avoidance. We will also pay some attention to psychological sloth—a quies-cence in people toward serious living. Sloth is the lightweight's central characteristic. Sloth in labor means you don't work much. Sloth in psychology means you don't make the effort to contem-plate. Earlier here the speaker said, "Why would one ever *want* to do such deliberate agonizing? It sounds like *looking* for trouble! Why not just look at the landscape, enjoy it or dislike it, whatever, and lighten up." Two favorite phrases of psychological sloths inform that speech. The first—"whatever"—says that everything is much the same and that fussing about which idea or object differs in some way from some other idea or object sounds like work—work in aid of what, anyhow? This question brings us to the second favorite phrase of psychological sloths: "Lighten up." If there are no causes worth one moment's seriousness, one may as well lighten up.

I don't think anyone without formal training in psychology can reliably discern the several causes of pain avoidances or distinguish between pain avoidance and psychological sloth. Sometimes sloth seems so much a part of pain avoidance that only intellectual game playing would give them separate categories. At other times, however, psychological sloth seems so steady and self-confident, so morally indifferent, that it may be related to pain avoidance only in that long ago in the sloth's life, he or she repressed painful experiences, made a habit of the repressing, and then let that habit be a lifestyle from then on. By the time we meet such a person, we may very well not see any evidence in him or her of suppression of feelings or even neurosis: we are seeing repetitive behavior of such long standing it is now only a meaningless habit.

Alice Walker tells us, in essense, "I was brought up with constant insults to womanhood right in my face, although I was a girl." The psychological sloth would reply, "Whatever."

David Ignatow tells us, "I once really wanted to die 'but now that I am at [death's] door' I have decided the world's really terrific . . . in fact, 'In the next world,' if I remember this one, 'I will praise it / above everything.'" The psychological sloth replies, "All that about death and all—lighten up."

Those examples may be extreme, but so many millions of human beings conduct conversations like them at every stratum of society that we had better look into psychological sloth.

Churches, oddly enough, have always taken both pain avoidance and sloth seriously. The fact that church people don't always exercise even a rudimentary interviewing skill or two when they encounter pain avoidance or sloth doesn't mean that members of the clergy don't take those mind-sets seriously. With skimpy funding, churches try to educate their people in "counseling"; little of such training is comparable to even one course in master-level interactionary skills. Still, most clerics recognize and dislike sins of omission.

In traditional religious groups one often hears the expressions "sins of commission" and "sins of omission." Sins of omission, not doing something when something should have been done, are often products of the psychological dynamic called pain avoidance.

Therapists not only have been investigating pain avoidance for decades, they have been very successful in showing people how to stop doing it. Both their simple formats, of which I will offer an example of the one called "owning your own feelings," and their complex inquiries, conducted respectfully with their clients (too complex and too particular for us to discuss here), have helped people change their lives from jerky, repressive, stoical getting through each day to comparatively flexible, open-eyed, appropriately judgmental, engaging lives full of infuriated and sad and joyful moments.

The simplest format for attacking pain avoidance is "owning one's own feelings." Here is a still widely practiced format for *not* owning one's own feelings: one starts every sentence with the word "you."

A: How was it for you, B, when C insulted your mother?
B: You don't want that kind of thing. You can take just so much of that.

B's evasion of telling A anything personal in the example may or may not only emanate from the habit of starting all of his sentences with "you" instead of committing himself to what he, B, feels or thinks. In the following example, on the other hand, we hear B using "you" instead of "I" in order to make his feelings sound more altruistic and principled than they are. A will listen to the altruistic cover-up, and then the therapist will take over. The therapist will ask B about any other thoughts he may have. He may ask B to prioritize the various thoughts. If B gives a higher priority to one of the later thoughts stated than he gives to the first (altruistic) one, B will have owned up to a motivation that didn't sound as attractive to him as the first one. He will have heard himself as an unconscious liar. With luck, he will start always hearing himself when he uses sentences beginning with the word you.

In the story A is having the family reunion at his house:

A: Listen, B, everyone's coming a day earlier than planned, so come on the night of the tenth instead of morning of the eleventh. We're going to hang out.

B: You don't need one more hungry person around the place. That's the last thing in the world you need.

A: No—I'm asking you. I want you to come.

B: You don't get invited for three days and then show up a day early, too. That's the last thing a hostess needs.

A: Please come, B! Half the family's coming earlier than we thought, so come on.

B: (with a rueful, kindly laugh): What you need, it sounds to me, is someone to volunteer *not* to show up early!

And so forth. A plays the role, sincerely as far as we know, of enthusiastic hostess. B plays the role of a more considerate family member than the others, the one who doesn't want to impose.

Enter the therapist. Therapist asks B what the pros and cons are of showing up the night before with the others.

B: You don't just get offered an inch and take a mile, you know! A is being a good sport to have us all.

Therapist: Good for A. What would be some other reasons against your joining the others the night before the date originally set?

B: You can't just move things around at the last minute, you know.

Therapist (with interest): You said just "you" can't move things around at the last minute. What can't get moved?

B: You don't just change plans that were made a long time ago.

Therapist: Is that a rule? Is that a rule for all of us? I feel you have
    a principle about this.
B: Sure!
Therapist: And A's repeated welcoming remarks—they are not
    enough to overcome the principle of never changing plans
    at the last moment? A didn't seem concerned about the
    principle.
B: Well . . .

The therapist waits. He hopes that B is doing inward work,
now, perhaps for the first time. The therapist is silently cheering
him along. The therapist leaves time—silence—for it. B is deciding whether or not to tell the therapist that in this particular case
of the family reunion date, B had planned to go sailing the night
before with friends. B would infinitely rather go sailing on Lake
Huron than go to the family reunion for an extra evening and
night.

To summarize: B explains that to the therapist, who asks B to
revisit the conversation with A, but this time, B is to answer every
question about himself using the word *I* instead of the word *you,*
and simply to name his feeling. He must not make up and recite
little social strictures, as if the whole issue were a moral situation
in which one must act nobly. The therapist pretends to be A; he
asks, "Hey, B, come the day before! A lot of us are going to be here,
so come on! We want you here early!"

B says very slowly: "Thanks, A. I don't want to come a day early.
    I have plans. A bunch of us are going to sail, et cetera. But I
    am coming with bells on the next morning, as planned."
Therapist (pretending to be A): "I can't talk you out of the
    sailing?"
B: "No, but thanks. I am dying to go sailing but I am also very
    much looking forward to being with you on the eleventh."

Since so many people with awfully nice manners and a lifelong practice of pain avoidance pull off conversations like B's
with A, year after year, they begin thinking that one can't be honest about preferring sailing to family. When for years and years

one answers questions about oneself with made-up social formulas (as B did at first), one begins to suppose that some subjects are taboo between civilized human beings.

The assumption that some truths cannot be said or even reported in a journal is a psychological tool that bad persons use on their victims. They let the victim think, "I cannot say such rough things. I cannot be disloyal. I must act on principle. When there are only my rough feelings and no principles, I will say there is a principle anyway!"

The following is an example of avoiding pain by not reporting painful truth, a practice that, if the narrator and her brother Sandy grew up without ever confronting it, would work marvelously well for the perpetrators of suffering in their family.

We return to the creative nonfiction writer who stopped describing the day when their drunken parents broke their promise to take her and Sandy on a picnic.

First, we need to make a tentative assumption, namely, that someone learning to write a truthful and principled journal is doing psychological work that is similar to the psychological work of becoming more conscious of fairness and unfairness in life. The very reason that creative-writing teachers are so keen on everybody's writing journals is that it speeds up what ought to be a universal process for our species—that is, *noticing;* noticing and learning to have opinions—distinguishing one's honest feelings about one occasion from one's honest feelings about another occasion. Journal writing helps people say, "That person deserves praise. But so-and-so does not." And, "My parents were adventurous and sometimes they shared their madcap projects with Sandy and me. I will always remember that gratefully. On the other hand, their drunken fights and beatings were awful and should have been stopped. Also, it is possible that Dad wrecked my life, too."

The original journal entry we read about not going on the picnic although the weather was all right is several steps less painful than the writing I shall have to do if I want to say, "The United States Atomic Energy Commission should have warned uranium miners that they worked in extraordinary danger to themselves and their families." In turn, the statement about the Atomic Energy Commission is several steps more primitive, psychologically speaking, than Denise Levertov's saying that she loves Chekhov because he was so generous-spirited. The journal entry is at square one, psychologically, compared to David Ignatow's allowing that the world is beautiful and "should go on." That is, so far, the journal writer has not committed herself to revealing any feelings on a very major subject. David Ignatow has not only admitted to suicidal or nearly suicidal feelings but has told us that those feelings now are transformed into love of the world. To feel consciously suicidal is probably the most painful feeling there is. Anyone who says, "I feel suicidal," is not in that moment avoiding painful consciousness.

Naming any painful feelings is hard enough work at the beginning. The whole idea of psychotherapy is that if someone, like our would-be picnic goer, were to start truthfully naming feelings, that person might end up by taking joy in the world despite its failings. Taking joy is a gift of psychological sophistication.

We need to get our journal writer started toward such feelings, step by step. Making a judgment on drunkenness, violence, promise breaking, or irradiation of the innocent will lie many steps ahead; the step she needs to start off with right now is to move from "The weather was fine. It did not rain for the family picnic" to the following:

> It was a beautiful day today, no rain. Sandy and I did not get to go on the picnic because Mother and Daddy started a fight about who didn't get the Volvo's oil changed. They broke stuff in the dining room. Mother slapped Dad in the face with a yardstick and he slugged her back. Then they fought around and broke some stuff in the living room and knocked the answering machine onto the floor so hard a cassette popped out of it. Then they went to their bedroom, and we didn't dare knock to wake them. We stood outside the bedroom door a long time. We were old hands at this. We always knew the moment they were done slugging. We knew the moment when they were through lovemaking. Now we tried to read their breathing sounds. Were they asleep? If they slept well enough would they be nice when they woke up and maybe take us to

Crane's Beach after all? At this point, Sandy's thinking and my thinking diverged. He thought they would be hung over and then wouldn't take us. I agreed they would be hung over, but I supposed that Dad would offer me the usual deal. Sandy gets Mom to take him to get a Dilly bar and Dad takes me into the guestroom and then when they get back with the Dilly bars Dad tells Mom we may as well go to Crane's Beach. I didn't tell Sandy my thinking. There was no use to get up his hopes in case it didn't work out.

That is reportage. Reportage still makes no judgments. The narrator still tells no personal responses of her own, but she has proved that she can make herself take in, not deny, sad facts, and report them. If she hadn't been able to experience such painful truth as having to deliberate with one's sibling whether or not the parents will be kindly disposed enough to keep their promise, she would have stopped the journal at "The day was fine, but it turned out that we did not go on the picnic after all."

Arturo Vivante's story "The Soft Core" illuminates a fascinating mixture of dynamics in a family, most of them emanating from the totalitarian father. I don't know of a story that better illustrates pain avoidance. Giacomo, throughout the story's events and conversations, constantly evades looking into the face of evil and therefore is impotent to correct any of it.

"The Soft Core" is an unerring description of how a family of considerable advantage—cultivated background and financial substance—all contrived, unconsciously, to enable the father to be cruel to each of them in turn. He discounted his wife's art. He bullied one son out of the lifework he wanted. He somehow endowed the other son, Giacomo, with such psychological lassitude, or at least, ethical inattention, that he focused on how sweet his father was when sick, how his father had a "secret, gentle, tender core." This son did not feel constrained to intervene with his father on behalf of his mother or of his brother or even for himself. He seethed under his father's various everyday insults and rudenesses, but never got further than salving his feelings with the idea that underneath the brutality his father had a soft core.

Social workers could teach this story to everybody, not just to the *New Yorker* readers who saw it first and might read it only as a literary masterpiece. A social worker or therapist who happened upon Vivante would beg literary people to see the story as a perfect case of John Kenneth Galbraith's *accommodation* of evil.[1] One has "accommodated evil" if one has tried to comfort oneself about some tiny aspect of a bully instead of standing up to him.

Literature has this about it: one can love it as one does "The Soft Core," for its numinous tone, beauty of insight, and the will toward love that fills it. Literature is not hurt by a proactive approach. One can point out the following passage from Vivante's story and ask people to read it in connection with the abused children who, Alice Miller tells us, want so much to think well of their parents:

> When his father was well, he couldn't [talk to him], but now he was reaching the secret, soft core—the secret, gentle, tender core that is in each of us. And he thought, *This* is what my father is really like; the way he is now, this is his real, his naked self. For a moment it has been uncovered; he is young again. This was the young man his mother had met and fallen in love with; this was the man on whose knees he had played, who had carried him on his shoulders up the hills, who had read to him the poems he liked so much. His other manner was brought on by age, by a hundred preoccupations, by the years, by the hardening that comes with the turning of the years.
>
> Already, with coffee, with their talk, his father was recovering his memory. Soon he would be up and about, and soon Giacomo wouldn't be able to talk to him as he did now. But though he wouldn't, he would think of his father in the way he had been given back to him, the way he had been and somewhere—deep and secret and only to be uncovered sometimes—still was.

Vivante is one of the great literary artists of our time. His writing has so much character complication. He has a quality that only the most scrupulous artists have in common with only the most scrupulous therapists—a respect for *all* the sides of a person. This father of Giacomo's, for example: He is an appalling egoist, of course, but he has a quality we could wish Anne Frank's father had had—for the sake of the Frank family. Giacomo's father saw public, large-scale evil ahead—Italy's bow to fascism and then Nazism. He faced that bad news and took his family out. The psychiatrist Bruno Bettelheim was offended by the worldwide attention given Anne Frank's diary because it kept people from noticing that Anne Frank's father was such an avoider of pain that for the sake of his own psychological comfort he did what was, Bettelheim tells us, the very thing that enabled the Germans to find and kill the family: he couldn't bear the pain of dispersing the family, so he kept them together.

Further, Bettelheim wrote, with his acid ethics, Frank chose passive hiding with his family instead of sending them out of the country and himself joining the Underground to help oppose the occupation. How complex it is that a "good man," as Anne Frank's father is uniformly thought to be, should have made a decision, motivated by pain avoidance, that killed most of his family, whereas a harsh, unyielding character like Giacomo's father got his family out safely.

How complicated questions of ego strength are: one would need a strong ego to decide to get the family out, carry it off, make everybody cooperate, and so forth. Yet Giacomo's father was also what is called "needy": he needed constant, instantaneous praise of his projects, bolstering here and there, praise not just of his intellectual work but of his handiwork in the orchard.

We may be seeing two *kinds* of ego strength worth keeping distinguished from one another: first, the strength to oppose outside evils and not fall into the pain-avoiding quietism of "business as usual" (Bettelheim's term), and second, ego strength enough so one could eschew casual bullying of one's own dependents.

We can test these two kinds on the stories: the narrator's father, in "White Canyon," failed to protect his family from outside danger; in fact, no sooner did he hear about the dangers to his family than he pacified himself (ducked the painful thought) by concluding that the radioactivity level was minuscule.

Here is the dilemma of Louis Simpson's poem "A Story about Chicken Soup": do I admit the news is bad and that it does have an effect on me—I cannot or must not pretend it hasn't—and shall I (like John Donne) confess that one person's bad news is bad news for us all?

People whose egos have developed well enough do, sometimes by first-rate willpower, overcome the habit of denying bad news— avoiding painful considerations. If they are poets most of whose cousins and aunts and uncles were murdered by Nazis, they face the fact that their dead relations beg them not to write only prettily, "in the painted sunshine," but to suffer vicariously on their behalf. They ask the Louis Simpsons of the world and the rest of us not to spend too long in the aesthetic, dreaming stage of our lives, but to get sad if need be, by telling terrible truths when there are terrible truths to be told. Simpson's ironic "I know it's in bad taste to say it, / but it's true. / The Germans killed them all" is one of the best consciousness-raising passages in poetry. There is the voice of the social climber who knows the living-room rules, but whose moral development is such that he will break decorum for the sake of truth telling. Simpson's touch is subtle, too: we hear a little nostalgia for the psychological property he calls "good taste." *Taste*, in this sense, is not an individual but a class property; that is, it takes a classful of people to stretch a membrane of manners all over the graves of genocide.

A last word on pain avoidance and Giacomo. Let us look at Clare in "The Woman Lit by Fireflies" at the same time.

> As a child up near Petoskey on summer vacation her parents had allowed her to go to Daily Vacation Bible School with the maid's daughter. The maid was a mixed-blood Chippewa but her religion was Evangelical. Clare's parents had once discovered their daughter out in the garage praying over a three-legged cat that lived in the neighborhood. This was viewed as highly amusing and became part of a repertoire of "Clare stories" her parents shared with their friends during the rites of the martini hour. Now, to her surprise, this made Clare angry. What was the point of being angry at her parents for something that happened forty years ago, but then what was so funny about a child praying for a three-legged cat?

Here is Clare, late in life learning a major lesson that therapists teach: you may forgive if you can, but make sure you never forget. Do not erase history.

Clare had been especially prone to avoiding pain: she went to college just to read world literature, with the idea that anything else would be irritating. Going back over her own feelings about the parents' making fun of her is a serious change. Kitwood explains how very serious it is:

> Therapy, on its part, is designed to bring about integration in a fragmented psyche, self-deceived and torn apart by rival motivations: that is, there should, ideally, be a single centre of desire and value, a mind and body that are in harmony together, a unity and truthfulness in dealing with the many conflicting demands of a difficult world. As we have seen, it is an exacting and even terrifying process, against which a person may find enormously strong inner resistances. . . .
>
> . . . Further, integration requires a kind of general openness to experience, an awareness and acceptance of others, that must necessarily be accompanied by a greater vulnerability. . . . How, then, can a person continue to live according to the therapeutic idea in a world that is often superficial and corrupt, which is constantly pressing the psyche back towards disintegration and defence? In the long term, it would only appear to be possible if everyone with whom there is serious engagement were also moving towards a life that had integrity.[2]

Clearly we all want to be able to consider sad data and recognize cruelty when it is present. We don't want to let cruelty thrive, yet most of us in the ordinary range of life don't know many "models" for cutting through pain avoidance. Most of us don't read therapy models or go to the kinds of conferences where professionals do role playing to show pain avoidance versus confrontation. We don't know exactly how to go about quitting whatever defenses we indulge ourselves with each day.

People affected by substance abuse, in themselves or in their families, sometimes have this advantage: they have needed and therefore introduced themselves to expert psychological interventions. They often have been made conscious of the little repertoires of lies people tell themselves in order to avoid pain. They learn how to cut through them. But most of us don't want to think about that kind of thing, and the idea that there are some curatives for pain avoidance may leave us cold. Psychological jargon like the very phrase "pain avoidance" irritates us.

We can get past the annoyance and muddle by asking this question: What if Giacomo had *not* been a pain avoider? Might he have much earlier forced his father to respect his mother and brother? What would change someone like Giacomo, who is rather like the hummingbird in Mary Oliver's "Lilies"—who "whenever there is a fuss, / just rises and floats away"?

A quick list of cures for the habit of pain avoidance:

1. *Learning to confront.* This is the established practice of cutting through lying about evil. Confrontation is the classic start-up tool for consciousness of alcoholism in the alcoholic himself or herself. It brings about the "luxurious unlearning / of lies and fears" that Denise Levertov talks about in the last stanza of "Modulations"(quoted in chapter 1).
2. *Undergoing a startling psychological trauma in adult life.* This could be sudden despair or a startling view of someone else's psychological pain.
3. *Having friends who don't lie.* One must have friends who don't simply make supportive comments to everything one says to them. Dr. Roth, Clare's friend, wasn't a crusader, but he was a truth sayer (such as when he warned her not to use writing checks to charity as a way of assuaging guilt feelings for being rich). Some of his and Clare's conversations sound like the boasting drivel in *My Dinner with André;* most, however, are genuinely intellectual and poignant.
4. *Making sure we don't mistake lovely lifestyle for ethical awakening.* In our verbal U.S. culture, major words like *good* and *wrong* and, especially in the 1990s, *struggle* flood out to us on radio and television in shallow applications. Their meaning veers this way and that way. A football team is said to "struggle" if it hasn't got enough first-rate players. The team may

be said to "struggle" although no one is playing particularly hard, whereas in other circumstances, a team playing extraordinarily hard is not described as "struggling" because the word *struggle* has come to mean "low on needed resources of some kind." Twenty years ago the Chase Manhattan Bank took for its advertisement theme the Shaker hymn "It's a gift to be simple, it's a gift to be free." Then Vivaldi's *Four Seasons* became the theme of choice for many corporations and not-for-profit groups needing background music for slide shows and so forth. Auto parts are advertised to two refrains from the choral movement of Beethoven's Ninth Symphony. Mozart's "Eine kleine Nachtmusik" has helped sell bathroom cleaning chemicals. Words from psychology and ethics have been wafted about, separate from their serious meanings, in the same way great music has.

No wonder we experience some moral confusion. The word *good* gets used about everything from backpacking in some remote place to standing up against unkind federal policies. Clare does some nice heart-searching, as she sits in her cornfield, especially when having the phantom role-play with her straight-forward daughter, Laurel. But in the end, when she makes her break and goes off to Paris on her income of capital increment, all that she seems set to do is live out an old bohemian dream. She even wears the beret. Wearing a beret, going to museums, and having a nice time doesn't look like much of a way to stand up to Donaldism in our world. It has the look of pain avoidance. Harrison is a subtle writer, and this part of his story about Clare takes as careful reading as any other.

Perhaps Paris is to the rich what running off to the Foreign Legion was to poor and middle-class young people in the nineteenth century. Today, people sometimes talk about hiking in Montana as if they were leading a crusade. They are not aggrandizing the occasion, though they sound like privileged people pretending that their holiday is some sort of spiritual work. In fact, just departing from our ordinary places, especially going to unpeopled places, can be a holy step in life. Out there, feeling apart from others, we regroup the selves inside ourselves. We shed our old lifeskins—perhaps we have to, before we can gather our will. Asceticism has nothing to do with it. The Montana campers have laced hiking boots and handsome tents of expensive design and wonderful underwear that wicks away moisture. This is not the equipage of the poor, anymore than Clare's renting a place in the 6th arrondissement is the equipage of the poor.

All inner regrouping, no matter who is doing it, should be respected and given its time. Brave psychological regrouping is vital, wherever it takes place. It is scary work in character formation, whether one does it chewing trail mix or the provincial specialties of a good restaurant.

People whose psyches are stuck in pain avoidance sometimes seem merely indifferent. Sometimes a pain avoider looks merely slothful, the way depressed people sometimes look merely lazy. Rich people in genuine pain sometimes look perfectly comfortable and self-serving to others. Yet despite the customary luxuries, they may be doing hard work inside themselves, paying attention in places where they have been heretofore neglectful or flip.

Clare, who had never taken care of her well-being, will take care of it now. First she prayed for disabled animals. Now, very late, is her time to pray for herself.

Some evil comes less from immediate pain avoidance than from such a long practice of pain avoidance that even confrontation will do no good. At least, a pain avoider, like B in the conversation about the family reunion, responds to confrontation by a skilled therapist because the nervous feelings that B wants to deny are operative, and fairly close to consciousness. Confrontation, however, means little to psychologically slothful people. We can't ask them firmly, "You just said 'whatever!' in response to A's asking you to help at B's funeral. Will you say some more so I can get some idea of what you were feeling when you said that?" Such an inquiry comes to nothing because C, a psychological sloth of decades' standing, wasn't feeling anything much. C, therefore, immediately sees us, the therapist, as a personnel problem. We are coming off as a not very nice person. C thinks to himself, as he frequently does, "This is getting heavy." "This is getting heavy" and "Lighten up" are C's standby responses, second favorites to "Whatever." Several of the characters in Alice Walker's "Brothers and Sisters" are best described as indifferent to justice. One brother escapes this indifference, although not in time to help much. The other brothers cannot be called genuine jerks, pain avoiders, or psychological sloths: they are simply cultural products.

Tobias Wolff's "In the Garden of the North American Martyrs" gives us an extraordinary story in which the main character has our uneasy, not very respectful, sympathy. Mary lives in moral torpor, tricking out her life with jokes and prevarication and fragments of thoughts and changing the subject inside herself right at the moment of realizing she is being used. Only the most excruciating treachery rouses her, because her habitual kidding and ducking have been an acceptable workplace style.

Mary was not one bit physically lazy. She exerted energy and ongoing action to make up office jokes; she "founded the Brandon College chapter of a society dedicated to restoring the good name of Richard III." She was willing to work at *outer* things. When Louise woke her up in the middle of the night needing to talk, Mary was good enough to stay awake and listen to her. A *physically* lazy person will under no conditions be kind when wakened from the dearest activity of all, sleep.

But when we talk about someone being "psychologically" lazy or habituated to moral indifference a problem arises. The word *psychological* suggests something for which there may be a social-scientific cure, whereas the word *laziness* or *sloth* suggests a failure of character formation rather than or in addition to a failure in becoming conscious.

Why does Mary—in fact, why do thousands of Marys in the world—make a joke of her work? They are being careless of their own serious nature, yet the carelessness doesn't seem to come from mistakes of insight. Nor does apparent indifference to one's own serious nature always come of ill treatment by others in the past.

Such a person wakens in us readers little cognitive interest. I loved Wolff's story out of morbid curiosity about the series of appalling moral shambles the author could think up for the hero and the villain alike. A story is a tour de force of some sort when its author holds our interest all the way through but we would never want any discourse with its characters. We do not long to hear anything more that Mary might say. Background characters in Will Weaver's "The Undeclared Major" (Chapter 9), the uncles, the Main Street people, probably live lives of equally low intensity. Why fuss at such people? Why not let them be as they are, members of our species with the governor set on low, neither liking nor disliking virtue or evil, people who, if spoken to by Nathan Hale, might respond, "Whatever"? Their philosophies are the gelatin bricks of which public opinion is built.

Such people don't pursue evil. If they are just hanging in there, so to speak, why did psychological sloth make it onto the Roman Catholic Church's list of "seven deadly sins"? If we tolerantly decide to respect that list for a moment, we have to ask, "Now why did the church feel so warmly about mere sloth?" Should we, in fact, have another look at Mary in "In the Garden" and the minor characters in "Brothers and Sisters" and the minor characters in "The Undeclared Major" to see if what we wrote off as natural, harmless mediocrity causes more unkindness or injustice than we had noticed—in which case we want to devise a way to change it if we possibly can?

Psychological sloth never *causes* cruelty; it doesn't take up arms against it, either. Let us think about the older sister in "Brothers and Sisters." Although she got jeered at by her brothers and beaten up by her men, she cheerfully noted that cute boys made you feel like melting. Her inner life isn't unethical; it is just torpid. As Turgenev pointed out a century ago, most run-of-the-mill people stick to the surface of the world, not through grateful love, but casually, through force of gravity.

A crucial point about people who are morally indifferent is that they are present at most evildoings. They are there as watchers, as at Kew Gardens. They are the other faculty members at Mary's spurious interview. They are the ho-hum relations of little girls like Alice Walker. They are the people who do *not* grow up to draw people's attention to acts of cruelty that they witnessed as children.

The nineteenth century passed the morally indifferent off as an eternal verity. They were natural followers. For every alpha-wolf family there are six or seven other wolf families: this is how nature operates, the idea went. A species has a few leaders who give us the punctuated evolution that Stephen Jay Gould discusses. Then there are the millions of followers.

The twentieth century, on the other hand, has given us this new idea: some mediocrity of spirit may be changed. Indifferent people can be invited into the life of painful awareness in the interests of finding strong stimuli inside oneself.

I open the question for any readers or groups of readers of this book who may already be working on this problem: is there a way to increase the ratio of psychologically *eager* human beings to psychologically *lazy* human beings?

Here are two tentative sample questions, based on Walker's "Brothers and Sisters":

1. What kind of discussion could be invented for the oldest brother, the one capable of love and of being responsible for his children, that might have enabled him to stand up for the little girl Alice?
2. What kind of empathic questioning could be devised for first, reassuring, and second, challenging, the Marys in universities, the lightweights in "The Undeclared Major," and the older sister in "Brothers and Sisters"?

Here is the end of our century, another century in which the only recourse a good dissenter in a house full of bullies seems to have is to grow up and get away. If someone or some profession has already worked up a stunning psychosocial model by which a good person can reenter and transform a suffocating family or community in order to hearten its younger victims, we all want to know that model.

Of course, and always, our suffering comes first from genuine jerks and next from psychologically *blocked* people, the pain avoiders. But certainly a good deal of cruelty continues simply for the reason that some psychologically *lazy* person at the meeting was wondering if the coffee pot had anything left in it or was thinking up a cute skit just when the proposal came up that the military test out some of our innovative weaponry on our own people.

What's more, genuine jerks at the white-collar level deliberately keep their tone of voice casual and cordial when making evil proposals: intuitive jerks know that the psychologically lazy, morally random people in the room pick up on *tone*. They may not know one idea from another, but they are influenced by *tone*. Jerks know that people as ungathered as that have a wistful longing for bland and friendly tone. To them, when things look pointless, witty but friendly, life feels pleasing. One can attend to the tiny rustles and specks of consciousness. One can plan to pick up fresh asparagus for dinner. Incidental meanderings of the mind seem superb to a psychologically lazy person. A fragment of an old sermon comes to mind. Try to recognize the mountain peaks in your life, the old fellow had said. Remember them when you are in a valley. Not bad, the dreaming committee member thinks. Not bad. It puts one in a grateful frame of mind. One feels like helping. Someone has called the question, "All in favor?" One raises one's hand good-naturedly.

A true psychological sloth typically makes or seconds several motions at a meeting because that speeds the business smoothly. The secretary checks the tape. A skillful genuine jerk chairperson sends the psychological sloth a grateful look.

If *this* is any part of how the world's evil is accomplished, we want to take seriously not only pain avoidance but psychological sloth. When people interested in ethics decide to take something or someone *seriously,* they are saying in effect that we should cast a glance around to see who the invisible victims of that something or someone are. Checking for invisible victims is the essential work of social scientists, the central work of ethicists, and the passionate, if occasional, work of authors.

I love it that Tobias Wolff made such a devastating and funny story out of one hundred percent mediocre people. Every single person in his story is either a little dreadful or very dreadful. "In the Garden of the North American Martyrs" gives us a trial case for looking for *invisible victims*. If we think of Mary and of Louise and the steam-plant-admiring student and the awful faculty members at the eastern college, we feel easy scorn. Since none of those people is a murderer or rapist or child molester and none of them advocates the overthrow of the United States or the wreckage of our planet, who cares what they do?

Their invisible victims are their English literature students. Students whose teachers participate in Mary's kind of cordial, even earnest dishonor are culturally deprived. They get cynical. They revolt and leave, or they themselves slide into cordial, earnest dishonor. They don't remember how they voted at the meeting.

Wolff's Louises get by them. Boys like those in Walker's essay keep getting something on their stick.

Notes

1. John Kenneth Galbraith, *The Nature of Mass Poverty* (Cambridge, Mass.: Harvard University Press, 1979), 92–93.
2. Tom Kitwood, *Concern for Others: A New Psychology of Conscience and Mortality* (London: Routledge, 1990), 211.

CHAPTER 19

Culture and Enthusiasm:
A Secret Kept from Most People

THE READINGS

THE COMMENTARY

Gryphon

by Charles Baxter

On Wednesday afternoon, between the geography lesson on ancient Egypt's hand-operated irrigation system and an art project that involved drawing a model city next to a mountain, our fourth-grade teacher, Mr. Hibler, developed a cough. This cough began with a series of muffled throat-clearings and progressed to pro-pulsive noises contained within Mr. Hibler's closed mouth. "Listen to him," Carol Peterson whispered to me. "He's gonna blow up." Mr. Hibler's laughter—dazed and infrequent—sounded a bit like his cough, but as we worked on our model cities we would look up, thinking he was enjoying a joke, and see Mr. Hibler's face turning red, his cheeks puffed out. This was not laughter. Twice he bent over, and his loose tie, like a plumb line, hung down straight from his neck as he exploded himself into a Kleenex. He would excuse himself, then go on coughing. "I'll bet you a dime," Carol Peterson whispered, "we get a substitute tomorrow."

Carol sat at the desk in front of mine and was a bad person—when she thought no one was looking she would blow her nose on notebook paper, then crumple it up and throw it into the waste-basket—but at times of crisis she spoke the truth. I knew I'd lose the dime.

"No deal," I said.

When Mr. Hibler stood us in formation at the door just prior to the final bell, he was almost incapable of speech. "I'm sorry, boys and girls," he said. "I seem to be coming down with something."

"I hope you feel better tomorrow, Mr. Hibler," Bobby Kryzanowicz, the faultless brown-noser, said, and I heard Carol Peterson's evil giggle. Then Mr. Hibler opened the door and we walked out to the buses, a clique of us starting noisily to hawk and raugh as soon as we thought we were a few feet beyond Mr. Hibler's earshot.

Since Five Oaks was a rural community, and in Michigan, the supply of substitute teachers was limited to the town's unemployed community college graduates, a pool of about four mothers. These ladies fluttered, provided easeful class days, and nervously covered material we had mastered weeks earlier. Therefore it was a surprise when a woman we had never seen came into the class the next day, carrying a purple purse, a checkerboard lunchbox, and a few books. She put the books on one side of Mr. Hibler's desk and the lunchbox on the other, next to the Voice of Music phonograph. Three of us in the back of the room were playing with Heever, the chameleon that lived in a terrarium and on one of the plastic drapes, when she walked in.

She clapped her hands at us. "Little boys," she said, "why are you bent over together like that?" She didn't wait for us to answer. "Are you tormenting an animal? Put it back. Please sit down at your desks. I want no cabals this time of the day." We just stared at her. "Boys," she repeated, "I asked you to sit down."

I put the chameleon in his terrarium and felt my way to my desk, never taking my eyes off the woman. With white and green chalk, she had started to draw a tree on the left side of the blackboard. She didn't look usual. Furthermore, her tree was outsized, disproportionate, for some reason.

"This room needs a tree," she said, with one line drawing the suggestion of a leaf. "A large, leafy, shady, deciduous . . . oak."

Her fine, light hair had been done up in what I would learn years later was called a chignon, and she wore gold-rimmed glasses whose lenses seemed to have the faintest blue tint. Harold Knardahl, who sat across from me, whispered, "Mars," and I nodded slowly, savoring the imminent weirdness of the day. The substitute drew another branch with an extravagant arm gesture, then turned around and said, "Good morning. I don't believe I said good morning to all of you yet."

Facing us, she was no special age—an adult is an adult—but her face had two prominent lines, descending vertically from the sides of her mouth to her chin. I knew where I had seen those lines before: *Pinocchio.* They were marionette lines. "You may stare at me," she said to us, as a few more kids from the last bus came into the room, their eyes fixed on her, "for a few more seconds, until the bell rings. Then I will permit no more staring. Looking I will permit. Staring, no.

It is impolite to stare, and a sign of bad breeding. You cannot make a social effort while staring."

Harold Knardahl did not glance at me, or nudge, but I heard him whisper "Mars" again, trying to get more mileage out of his single joke with the kids who had just come in.

When everyone was seated, the substitute teacher finished her tree, put down her chalk fastidiously on the phonograph, brushed her hands, and faced us. "Good morning," she said. "I am Miss Ferenczi, your teacher for the day. I am fairly new to your community, and I don't believe any of you know me. I will therefore start by telling you a story about myself."

While we settled back, she launched into her tale. She said her grandfather had been a Hungarian prince; her mother had been born in some place called Flanders, had been a pianist, and had played concerts for people Miss Ferenczi referred to as "crowned heads." She gave us a knowing look. "Grieg," she said, "the Norwegian master, wrote a concerto for piano that was . . ."—she paused— "my mother's triumph at her debut concert in London." Her eyes searched the ceiling. Our eyes followed. Nothing up there but ceiling tile. "For reasons that I shall not go into, my family's fortunes took us to Detroit, then north to dreadful Saginaw, and now here I am in Five Oaks, as your substitute teacher, for today, Thursday, October the eleventh. I believe it will be a good day: all the forecasts coincide. We shall start with your reading lesson. Take out your reading book. I believe it is called *Broad Horizons,* or something along those lines."

Jeannie Vermeesch raised her hand. Miss Ferenczi nodded at her. "Mr. Hibler always starts the day with the Pledge of Allegiance," Jeannie whined.

"Oh, does he? In that case," Miss Ferenczi said, "you must know it *very* well by now, and we certainly need not spend our time on it. No, no allegiance pledging on the premises today, by my reckoning. Not with so much sunlight coming into the room. A pledge does not suit my mood." She glanced at her watch. "Time *is* flying. Take out *Broad Horizons.*"

She disappointed us by giving us an ordinary lesson, complete with vocabulary and drills, comprehension questions, and recitation. She didn't seem to care for the material, however. She sighed every few minutes and rubbed her glasses with a frilly handkerchief that she withdrew, magician-style, from her left sleeve.

After reading we moved on to arithmetic. It was my favorite time of the morning, when the lazy autumn sunlight dazzled its way through ribbons of clouds past the windows on the east side of the classroom and crept across the linoleum floor. On the playground the first group of children, the kindergartners, were running on the quack grass just beyond the monkey bars. We were doing multiplication tables. Miss Ferenczi had made John Wazny stand up at his desk in the front row. He was supposed to go through the tables of six. From where I was sitting, I could smell the Vitalis soaked into John's plastered hair. He was doing fine until he came to six times eleven and six times twelve. "Six times eleven," he said, "is sixty-eight. Six times twelve is . . ." He put his fingers to his head, quickly and secretly sniffed his fingertips, and said ". . . seventy-two." Then he sat down.

"Fine," Miss Ferenczi said. "Well now. That was very good."

"Miss Ferenczi!" One of the Eddy twins was waving her hand desperately in the air. "Miss Ferenczi! Miss Ferenczi!"

"Yes?"

"John said that six times eleven is sixty-eight and you said he was right!"

"*Did* I?" She gazed at the class with a jolly look breaking across her marionette's face. "Did I say that? Well, what *is* six times eleven?"

"It's sixty-six!"

She nodded. "Yes. So it is. But, and I know some people will not entirely agree with me, at some times it is sixty-eight."

"When? When is it sixty-eight?"

We were all waiting.

"In higher mathematics, which you children do not yet understand, six times eleven can be considered to be sixty-eight." She laughed through her nose. "In higher mathematics numbers are . . . more fluid. The only thing a number does is contain a certain amount of something. Think of water. A cup is not the only way to measure a certain amount of water, is it?" We were staring, shaking our heads. "You could use saucepans or thimbles. In either case, the water *would be the same.* Perhaps," she started again, "it would be better for you to think that six times eleven is sixty-eight only when I am in the room."

"Why is it sixty-eight," Mark Poole asked, "when you're in the room?"

"Because it's more interesting that way," she said, smiling very rapidly behind her blue-tinted glasses. "Besides, I'm your substitute teacher, am I not?" We all nodded. "Well, then, think of six times eleven equals sixty-eight as a substitute fact. "

"A substitute fact?"

"Yes." Then she looked at us carefully. "Do you think," she asked, "that anyone is going to be hurt by a substitute fact?"

We looked back at her.

"Will the plants on the windowsill be hurt?" We glanced at them. There were sensitive plants thriving in a green plastic tray, and several wilted ferns in small clay pots. "Your dogs and cats, or your moms and dads?" She waited. "So," she concluded, "what's the problem?"

"But it's wrong," Janice Weber said, "isn't it?"

"What's your name, young lady?"

"Janice Weber."

"And you think it's wrong, Janice?"

"I was just asking."

"Well, all right. You were just asking. I think we've spent enough time on this matter by now, don't you, class? You are free to think what you like. When your teacher, Mr. Hibler, returns, six times eleven will be sixty-six again, you can rest assured. And it will be that for the rest of your lives in Five Oaks. Too bad, eh?" She raised her eyebrows and glinted herself at us. "But for now, it wasn't. So much for that. Let us go on to your assigned problems for today, as painstakingly outlined, I see, in Mr. Hibler's lesson plan. Take out a sheet of paper and write your names on the upper left-hand corner."

For the next half hour we did the rest of our arithmetic problems. We handed them in and then went on to spelling, my worst subject. Spelling always came before lunch. We were taking spelling dictation and looking at the clock. "Thorough," Miss Ferenczi said. "Boundary." She walked in the aisles between the desks, holding the spelling book open and looking down at our papers. "Balcony." I clutched my pencil. Somehow, the way she said those words, they seemed foreign, mis-voweled and mis-consonanted. I stared down at what I had spelled. *Balconie.* I turned the pencil upside down and erased my mistake. *Balconey.* That looked better, but still incorrect. I cursed the world of spelling and tried erasing it again and saw the paper beginning to wear away. *Balkony.* Suddenly I felt a hand on my shoulder.

"I don't like that word either," Miss Ferenczi whispered, bent over, her mouth near my ear. "It's ugly. My feeling is, if you don't like a word, you don't have to use it." She straightened up, leaving behind a slight odor of Clorets.

At lunchtime we went out to get our trays of sloppy joes, peaches in heavy syrup, coconut cookies, and milk, and brought them back to the classroom, where Miss Ferenczi was sitting at the desk, eating a brown sticky thing she had unwrapped from tightly rubber-banded waxed paper. "Miss Ferenczi," I said, raising my hand. "You don't have to eat with us. You can eat with the other teachers. There's a teacher's lounge," I ended up, "next to the principal's office."

"No, thank you," she said. "I prefer it here."

"We've got a room monitor," I said. "Mrs. Eddy." I pointed to where Mrs. Eddy, Joyce and Judy's mother, sat silently at the back of the room, doing her knitting.

"That's fine," Miss Ferenczi said. "But I shall continue to eat here, with you children. I prefer it," she repeated.

"How come?" Wayne Razmer asked without raising his hand.

"I talked to the other teachers before class this morning," Miss Ferenczi said, biting into her brown food. "There was a great rattling of the words for the fewness of the ideas. I didn't care for their brand of hilarity. I don't like ditto-machine jokes."

"Oh," Wayne said.

"What's that you're eating?" Maxine Sylvester asked, twitching her nose. "Is it food?"

"It most certainly *is* food. It's a stuffed fig. I had to drive almost down to Detroit to get it. I also brought some smoked sturgeon. And this," she said, lifting some green leaves out of her lunchbox, "is raw spinach, cleaned this morning."

"Why're you eating raw spinach?" Maxine asked.

"It's good for you," Miss Ferenczi said. "More stimulating than soda pop or smelling salts." I bit into my sloppy joe and stared blankly out the window. An almost invisible moon was faintly silvered in the daytime autumn sky. "As far as food is concerned," Miss Ferenczi was saying, "you have to shuffle the pack. Mix it up. Too many people eat . . . well, never mind."

"Miss Ferenczi," Carol Peterson said, "what are we going to do this afternoon?"

"Well," she said, looking down at Mr. Hibler's lesson plan, "I see that your teacher, Mr. Hibler, has you scheduled for a unit on the Egyptians." Carol groaned. "Yessss," Miss Ferenczi continued, "that is what we will do: the Egyptians. A remarkable people. Almost as re-markable as the Americans. But not quite." She lowered her head, did her quick smile, and went back to eating her spinach.

After noon recess we came back into the classroom and saw that Miss Ferenczi had drawn a pyramid on the blackboard close to her oak tree. Some of us who had been playing baseball were messing around in the back of the room, dropping the bats and gloves into the playground box, and Ray Schontzeler had just slugged me when I heard Miss Ferenczi's high-pitched voice, quavering with emotions. "Boys," she said, "come to order right this minute and take your seats. I do not wish to waste a minute of class time. Take out your geography books." We trudged to our desks and, still sweating, pulled out *Distant Lands and Their People*. "Turn to page forty-two." She waited for thirty seconds, then looked over at Kelly Munger. "Young man," she said, "why are you still fossicking in your desk?"

Kelly looked as if his foot had been stepped on. "Why am I what?"

"Why are you . . . burrowing in your desk like that?"

"I'm lookin' for the book, Miss Ferenczi."

Bobby Kryzanowicz, the faultless brown-noser who sat in the first row by choice, softly said, "His name is Kelly Munger. He can't ever find his stuff. He always does that."

"I don't care what his name is, especially after lunch," Miss Ferenczi said. *"Where is your book?"*

"I just found it." Kelly was peering into his desk and with both hands pulled at the book, shoveling along in front of it several pencils and crayons, which fell into his lap and then to the floor.

"I hate a mess," Miss Ferenczi said. "I hate a mess in a desk or a mind. It's . . . unsanitary. You wouldn't want your house at home to look like your desk at school, now, would you?" She didn't wait for an answer. "I should think not. A house at home should be as neat as human hands can make it. What were we talking about? Egypt. Page forty-two. I note from Mr. Hibler's lesson plan that you have been discussing the modes of Egyptian irrigation. Interesting, in my view, but not so interesting as what we are about to cover. The pyramids, and Egyptian slave labor. A plus on one side, a minus on the other." We had our books open to page forty-two, where there was a picture of a pyramid, but Miss Ferenczi wasn't looking at the book. Instead, she was staring at some object just outside the window.

"Pyramids," Miss Ferenczi said, still looking past the window. "I want you to think about pyramids. And what was inside. The bodies of the pharaohs, of course, and their attendant treasures. Scrolls. Perhaps," Miss Ferenczi said, her face gleeful but unsmiling, "these scrolls were novels for the pharaohs, helping them to pass the time in their long voyage through the centuries. But then, I am joking." I was looking at the lines on Miss Ferenczi's skin. "Pyramids," Miss Ferenczi went on, "were the repositories of special cosmic powers. The nature of a pyramid is to guide cosmic energy forces into a concentrated point. The Egyptians knew that; we have generally forgotten it. Did you know," she asked, walking to the side of the room so that she was standing by the coat closet, "that George Washington had Egyptian blood, from his grandmother? Certain features of the Constitution of the United States are notable for their Egyptian ideas."

Without glancing down at the book, she began to talk about the movement of souls in Egyptian religion. She said that when people die, their souls return to Earth in the form of carpenter ants or walnut trees, depending on how they behaved—"well or ill"—in life. She said that the Egyptians believed that people act the way they do because of magnetism produced by tidal forces in the solar system, forces produced by the sun and by its "planetary ally," Jupiter. Jupiter, she said, was a planet, as we had been told, but had "certain properties of stars." She was speaking very fast. She said that the Egyptians were great explorers and conquerors. She said that the greatest of all the conquerors, Genghis Khan, had had forty horses and forty young women killed on the site of his grave. We listened. No one tried to stop her. "I myself have been in Egypt," she said, "and have witnessed much dust and many brutalities." She said that an old man in Egypt who worked for a circus had personally shown her an animal in a cage, a monster, half bird and half lion. She said that this monster was called a gryphon and that she had heard about them but never seen them until she traveled to the outskirts of Cairo. She wrote the word out on the blackboard in large capital letters: GRYPHON. She said that Egyptian astronomers had discovered the planet Saturn but had not seen its rings. She said that the Egyptians were the first to discover that dogs, when they are ill, will not drink from rivers, but wait for rain, and hold their jaws open to catch it.

"She lies."

We were on the school bus home. I was sitting next to Carl Whiteside, who had bad breath and a huge collection of marbles. We were arguing. Carl thought she was lying. I said she wasn't, probably.

"I didn't believe that stuff about the bird," Carl said, "and what she told us about the pyramids? I didn't believe that, either. She didn't know what she was talking about."

"Oh yeah?" I had liked her. She was strange. I thought I could nail him. "If she was lying," I said, "what'd she say that was a lie?"

"Six times eleven isn't sixty-eight. It isn't ever. It's sixty-six, I know for a fact."

"She said so. She admitted it. What else did she lie about?"

"I don't know," he said. "Stuff."

"What stuff?"

"Well." He swung his legs back and forth. "You ever see an animal that was half lion and half bird?" He crossed his arms. "It sounded real fakey to me."

"It could happen," I said. I had to improvise, to outrage him.

"I read in this newspaper my mom bought in the IGA about this scientist, this mad scientist in the Swiss Alps, and he's been putting genes and chromosomes and stuff together in test tubes, and he combined a human being and a hamster." I waited, for effect. "It's called a humster."

"You never." Carl was staring at me, his mouth open, his terrible bad breath making its way toward me. "What newspaper was it?"

"*The National Enquirer*," I said, "that they sell next to the cash registers." When I saw his look of recognition, I knew I had him. "And this mad scientist," I said, "his name was, um, Dr. Frankenbush." I realized belatedly that this name was a mistake and waited for Carl to notice its resemblance to the name of the other famous mad master of permutations, but he only sat there.

"A man and a hamster?" He was staring at me, squinting, his mouth opening in distaste. "Jeez. What'd it look like?"

When the bus reached my stop, I took off down our dirt road and ran up through the backyard, kicking the tire swing for good luck. I dropped my books on the back steps so I could hug and kiss our dog, Mr. Selby. Then I hurried inside. I could smell brussels sprouts cooking, my unfavorite vegetable. My mother was washing other vegetables in the kitchen sink, and my baby brother was hollering in his yellow playpen on the kitchen floor.

"Hi, Mom," I said, hopping around the playpen to kiss her. "Guess what?"

"I have no idea."

"We had this substitute today, Miss Ferenczi, and I'd never seen her before, and she had all these stories and ideas and stuff."

"Well. That's good." My mother looked out the window in front of the sink, her eyes on the pine woods west of our house. That time of the afternoon her skin always looked so white to me. Strangers always said my mother looked like Betty Crocker, framed by the giant spoon on the side of the Bisquick box. "Listen, Tommy," she said. "Would you please go upstairs and pick your clothes off the floor in the bathroom, and then go outside to the shed and put the shovel and ax away that your father left outside this morning?"

"She said that six times eleven was sometimes sixty-eight!" I said. "And she said she once saw a monster that was half lion and half bird." I waited. "In Egypt."

"Did you hear me?" my mother asked, raising her arm to wipe her forehead with the back of her hand. "You have chores to do."

"I know," I said. "I was just telling you about the substitute."

"It's very interesting," my mother said, quickly glancing down at me, "and we can talk about it later when your father gets home. But right now you have some work to do."

"Okay, Mom." I took a cookie out of the jar on the counter and was about to go outside when I had a thought. I ran into the living room, pulled out a dictionary next to the TV stand, and opened it to the Gs. After five minutes I found it. *Gryphon*: variant of griffin. *Griffin*: "a fabulous beast with the head and wings of an eagle and the body of a lion." Fabulous was right. I shouted with triumph and ran outside to put my father's tools in their proper places.

Miss Ferenczi was back the next day, slightly altered. She had pulled her hair down and twisted it into pigtails, with red rubber bands holding them tight one inch from the ends. She was wearing a green blouse and pink scarf, making her difficult to look at for a full class day. This time there was no pretense of doing a reading lesson or moving on to arithmetic. As soon as the bell rang, she simply began to talk.

She talked for forty minutes straight. There seemed to be less connection between her ideas, but the ideas themselves were, as the dictionary would say, fabulous. She said she had heard of a huge jewel, in what she called the antipodes, that was so brilliant that when light shone into it at a certain angle it would blind whoever was looking at its center. She said the biggest diamond in the world was cursed and had killed everyone who owned it, and that by a trick of fate it was called the Hope Diamond. Diamonds are magic, she said, and this is why women wear them on their fingers, as a sign of the magic of womanhood. Men have strength, Miss Ferenczi said, but no true magic. That is why men fall in love with women but women do not fall in love with men: they just love being loved. George Washington had died because of a mistake he made about a diamond. Washington was not the first *true* President, but she didn't say who was. In some places in the world, she said, men and women still live in the trees and eat monkeys for breakfast. Their doctors are magicians. At the bottom of the sea are creatures thin as pancakes who have never been studied by scientists because when you take them up to air, the fish explode.

There was not a sound in the classroom, except for Miss Ferenczi's voice, and Donna DeShano's coughing. No one even went to the bathroom.

Beethoven, she said, had not been deaf; it was a trick to make himself famous, and it worked. As she talked, Miss Ferenczi's pigtails swung back and forth. There are trees in the world, she said, that eat meat: their leaves are sticky and close up on bugs like hands. She lifted her hands and brought them together, palm to palm. Venus, which most people think is the next closest plant to the sun, is not always closer, and, besides, it is the planet of greatest mystery because of its thick cloud cover. "I know what lies underneath those clouds," Miss Ferenczi said, and waited. After the silence, she said, "Angels. Angels live under those clouds." She said that angels were not invisible to everyone and were in fact smarter than most people. They did not dress in robes as was often claimed but instead wore formal evening clothes, as if they were about to attend a concert. Often angels *do* attend concerts and sit in the aisles, where, she said, most people pay no attention to them. She said the most terrible angel had the shape of the Sphinx. "There is no running away from that one," she said. She said that unquenchable fires burn just under the surface of the earth in Ohio, and that the baby Mozart fainted dead away in his cradle when he first heard the sound of a trumpet. She said that someone named Narzim al Harrardim was the greatest writer who ever lived. She said that planets control behavior, and anyone conceived during a solar eclipse would be born with webbed feet.

"I know you children like to hear these things," she said, "these secrets, and that is why I am telling you all this." We nodded. It was better than doing comprehension questions for the readings in *Broad Horizons.*

"I will tell you one more story," she said, "and then we will have to do arithmetic." She leaned over, and her voice grew soft. "There is no death," she said. "You must never be afraid. Never. That which is, cannot die. It will change into different earthly and unearthly elements, but I know this as sure as I stand here in front of you, and I swear it: you must not be afraid. I have seen this truth with these eyes. I know it because in a dream God kissed me. Here." And she pointed with her right index finger to the side of her head, below the mouth where the vertical lines were carved into her skin.

Absentmindedly we all did our arithmetic problems. At recess the class was out on the playground, but no one was playing. We were all standing in small groups, talking about Miss Ferenczi. We didn't know if she was crazy, or what. I looked out beyond the playground, at the rusted cars piled in a small heap behind a clump of sumac, and I wanted to see shapes there, approaching me.

On the way home, Carl sat next to me again. He didn't say much, and I didn't either. At last he turned to me. "You know what she said about the leaves that close up on bugs?"

"Huh?"

"The leaves," Carl insisted. "The meat-eating plants. I know it's true. I saw it on television. The leaves have this icky glue that the plants have got smeared all over them and the insects can't get off 'cause they're stuck. I saw it." He seemed demoralized. "She's tellin' the truth."

"Yeah."

"You think she's seen all those angels?"

I shrugged.

"I don't think she has," Carl informed me. "I think she made that part up."

"There's a tree," I suddenly said. I was looking out the window at the farms along County Road H. I knew every barn, every broken windmill, every fence, every anhydrous ammonia tank, by heart. "There's a tree that's . . . that I've seen . . ."

"Don't you try to do it " Carl said. "You'll just sound like a jerk."

I kissed my mother. She was standing in front of the stove. "How was your day?" she asked.

"Fine."

"Did you have Miss Ferenczi again?"

"Yeah."

"Well?"

"She was fine. Mom," I asked, "can I go to my room?"

"No," she said, "not until you've gone out to the vegetable garden and picked me a few tomatoes." She glanced at the sky. "I think it's going to rain. Skedaddle and do it now. Then you come back inside and watch your brother for a few minutes while I go upstairs. I need to clean up before dinner." She looked down at me. "You're looking a little pale Tommy." She touched the back of her hand to my forehead and I felt her diamond ring against my skin. "Do you feel all right?"

"I'm fine, " I said, and went out to pick the tomatoes.

Coughing mutedly, Mr. Hibler was back the next day, slipping lozenges into his mouth when his back was turned at forty-five-minute intervals and asking us how much of his prepared lesson plan Miss Ferenczi had followed. Edith Atwater took the responsibility for the class of explaining to Mr. Hibler that the substitute hadn't always done exactly what he, Mr Hibler, would have done, but we had worked hard even though she talked a lot. About what? he asked. All kinds of things, Edith said. I sort of forgot. To our relief, Mr. Hibler seemed not at all interested in what Miss Ferenczi had said to fill the day. He probably thought it was woman's talk: unserious and not suited for school. It was enough that he had a pile of arithmetic problems from us to correct.

For the next month the sumac turned a distracting red in the field, and the sun traveled toward the southern sky, so that its rays reached Mr. Hibler's Halloween display on the bulletin board in the back of the room, fading the pumpkin head scarecrow from orange to tan. Every three days I measured how much farther the sun had moved toward the southern horizon by making small marks with my black Crayola on the north wall, ant-sized marks only I knew were there.

And then in early December, four days after the first permanent snowfall, she appeared again in our classroom. The minute she came in the door, I felt my heart begin to pound. Once again, she was different: this time, her hair hung straight down and seemed hardly to have been combed. She hadn't brought her lunchbox with her, but she was carrying what seemed to be a small box. She greeted all of us and talked about the weather. Donna DeShano had to remind her to take her overcoat off.

When the bell to start the day finally rang, Miss Ferenczi looked out at all of us and said, "Children, I have enjoyed your company in the past, and today I am going to reward you." She held up the small box. "Do you know what this is?" She waited. "Of course you don't. It is a Tarot pack."

Edith Atwater raised her hand. "What's a Tarot pack, Miss Ferenczi?"

"It is used to tell fortunes," she said. "And that is what I shall do this morning. I shall tell your fortunes, as I have been taught to do."

"What's fortune?" Bobby Kryzanowicz asked.

"The future, young man. I shall tell you what your future will be. I can't do your whole future, of course. I shall have to limit myself to the five-card system, the wands, cups, swords, pentacles, and the higher arcanes. Now who wants to be first?"

There was a long silence. Then Carol Peterson raised her hand.

"All right," Miss Ferenczi said. She divided the pack into five smaller packs and walked back to Carol's desk, in front of mine. "Pick one card from each one of these packs," she said. I saw that Carol had a four of cups and a six of swords, but I couldn't see the other cards. Miss Ferenczi studied the cards on Carol's desk for a minute. "Not bad," she said. "I do not see much higher education. Probably an early marriage. Many children. There's something bleak and dreary here, but I can't tell what. Perhaps just the tasks of a housewife life. I think you'll do very well, for the most part." She smiled at Carol, a smile with a certain lack of interest. "Who wants to be next?"

Carl Whiteside raised his hand slowly.

"Yes," Miss Ferenczi said, "let's do a boy." She walked over to where Carl sat. After he picked his five cards, she gazed at them for a long time. "Travel," she said. "Much distant travel. You might go into the army. Not too much romantic interest here. A late marriage, if at all. But the Sun in your major arcana, that's a very good card." She giggled. "You'll have a happy life."

Next I raised my hand. She told me my future. She did the same with Bobby Kryzanowicz, Kelly Munger, Edith Atwater, and Kim Foor. Then she came to Wayne Razmer. He picked his five cards, and I could see that the Death card was one of them.

"What's your name?" Miss Ferenczi asked.

"Wayne."

"Well, Wayne," she said, "you will undergo a great metamorphosis, a change, before you become an adult. Your earthly element will no doubt leap higher, because you seem to be a sweet boy. This card, this nine of swords, tells me of suffering and desolation. And this ten of wands, well, that's a heavy load."

"What about this one?" Wayne pointed at the Death card.

"It means, my sweet, that you will die soon." She gathered up the cards. We were all looking at Wayne. "But do not fear," she said. "It is not really death. Just change. Out of your earthly shape." She put the cards on Mr. Hibler's desk. "And now, let's do some arithmetic."

At lunchtime Wayne went to Mr. Faegre, the principal, and informed him of what Miss Ferenczi had done. During the noon recess, we saw Miss Ferenczi drive out of the parking lot in her rusting green Rambler American. I stood under the slide, listening to the other kids coasting down and landing in the little depressive bowls at the bottom. I was kicking stones and tugging at my hair right up to the moment when I saw Wayne come out to the playground. He smiled, the dead fool, and with the fingers of his right hand he was showing everyone how he had told on Miss Ferenczi.

I made my way toward Wayne, pushing myself past two girls from another class. He was watching me with his little pinhead eyes.

"You told," I shouted at him. "She was just kidding."

"She shouldn't have," he shouted back. "We were supposed to be doing arithmetic."

"She just scared you," I said. "You're a chicken. You're a chicken, Wayne. You are. Scared of a little card," I singsonged.

Wayne fell at me, his two fists hammering down on my nose. I gave him a good one in the stomach and then I tried for his head. Aiming my fist, I saw that he was crying. I slugged him.

"She was right," I yelled. "She was always right! She told the truth!" Other kids were whooping. "You were just scared, that's all!"

And then large hands pulled at us, and it was my turn to speak to Mr. Faegre.

In the afternoon Miss Ferenczi was gone, and my nose was stuffed with cotton clotted with blood, and my lip had swelled, and our class had been combined with Mrs. Mantei's sixth-grade class for a crowded afternoon science unit on insect life in ditches and swamps. I knew where Mrs. Mantei lived: she had a new house trailer just down the road from us, at the Clearwater Park. She was no mystery. Somehow she and Mr. Bodine, the other fourth-grade teacher, had managed to fit forty-five desks into the room. Kelly Munger asked if Miss Ferenczi had been arrested, and Mrs. Mantei said no, of course not. All that afternoon, until the buses came to pick us up, we learned about field crickets and two-striped grasshoppers, water bugs, cicadas, mosquitoes, flies, and moths. We learned about insects' hard outer shell, the exoskeleton, and the usual parts of the mouth, including the labrum, mandible, maxilla, and glossa. We learned about compound eyes, and the four-stage metamorphosis from egg to larva to pupa to adult. We learned something, but not much, about mating. Mrs. Mantei drew, very skillfully, the internal anatomy of the grasshopper on the blackboard. We learned about the dance of the honeybee, directing other bees in the hive to pollen. We found out about which insects were pests to man, and which were not. On lined white pieces of paper we made lists of insects we might actually see, then a list of insects too small to be clearly visible, such as fleas; Mrs. Mantei said that our assignment would be to memorize these lists for the next day, when Mr. Hibler would certainly return and test us on our knowledge.

Above Everything

by David Ignatow

I wished for death often
but now that I am at its door
I have changed my mind about the world.
It should go on; it is beautiful,
even as a dream, filled with water and seed,
plants and animals, others like myself,
ships and buildings and messages
filling the air—a beauty,
if ever I have seen one.
In the next world, should I remember
this one, I will praise it
above everything.

Like Loving Chekhov

by Denise Levertov

Loving this man who is far away
is like loving Anton Chekhov.
It is true, I do love Anton Chekhov,
I have loved him longer than I have known this man.
I love all the faces of Chekhov in my collection
of photos that show him in different years of his life,
alone, or with brothers and sisters, with actors,
         with Gorki,
with Tolstoi, with his wife, with his undistinguished
endearing pet dogs; from beardless student to pince-nez'd
famous and ailing man.
      I have no photo
of the man I love.

I love Chekhov for travelling alone
to the prison island without being asked.
For writing of the boiling, freezing, terrible seas
around the island and around the lives of its people
that they 'resembled the scared dreams
of a small boy who's been reading
        Lost in the Ocean Wastes
before going to sleep, and whose blanket has fallen off,
so he huddles shivering
and can't wake up.'
For treasuring the ugly inkstand a penniless seamstress
gave him in thanks for his doctoring.
If there's an afterlife,
I hope to meet Anton Chekhov there.

    Loving the man I love
is like that, because he is far away,
and because he is scrupulous, and because surely
nothing he says or does can bore me.
But it's different too. Chekhov had died

long before I was born. This man is alive.
He is alive and not here.
This man has shared my bed, our bodies
have warmed each other and given each other
delight, our bodies
are getting angry with us for giving them to each other

                and then

allowing something they don't understand to

                pry them apart,

                  a metallic

cruel wedge that they hear us call
necessity.
      Often it seems unreal to love
a man who is far away, or only real to the mind,
the mind teasing the body. But it's real,
he's alive, and it's not in the afterlife
I'm looking to see him,
but in this here and now, before I'm a month older,
before one more gray hair has grown on my head.
If he makes me think about Chekhov it's not because
he resembles him in the least but because the ache
of distance between me and a living man I know and

              don't know

grips me with pain and fear, a pain and fear
familiar in the love of the unreachable dead.

The Schreuderspitze

by Mark Helprin

In Munich are many men who look like weasels. Whether by genetic
accident, meticulous crossbreeding, an early and puzzling migra-
tion, coincidence, or a reason that we do not know, they exist in
great numbers. Remarkably, they accentuate this unfortunate
tendency by wearing mustaches, Alpine hats, and tweed. A man
who resembles a rodent should never wear tweed.

One of these men, a commercial photographer named Franzen,
had cause to be exceedingly happy. "Herr Wallich has disappeared,"
he said to Huebner, his supplier of paper and chemicals. "You
needn't bother to send him bills. Just send them to the police. The
police, you realize, were here on two separate occasions!"

"If the two occasions on which the police have been here had
not been separate, Herr Franzen, they would have been here only
once."

"What do you mean? Don't toy with me. I have no time for
semantics. In view of the fact that I knew Wallich at school, and professionally, they sought my opinion on his disappearance. They
wrote down everything I said, but I do not think that they will find
him. He left his studio on the Neuhausstrasse just as it was when he
was working, and the landlord has put a lien on the equipment. Let
me tell you that he had some fine equipment—very fine. But he was
not such a great photographer. He didn't have that killer's instinct.
He was clearly not a hunter. His canine teeth were poorly developed;
not like these," said Franzen, baring his canine teeth in a smile
which made him look like an idiot with a mouth of miniature castle
towers.

"But I am curious about Wallich."

"So is everyone. So is everyone. This is my theory. Wallich was
never any good at school. At best, he did only middling well. And it
was not because he had hidden passions, or a special genius for
some field outside the curriculum. He tried hard but found it difficult
to grasp several subjects; for him, mathematics and physics were
pure torture.

"As you know, he was not wealthy, and although he was a nice-looking fellow, he was terribly short. That inflicted upon him great scars—his confidence, I mean, because he had none. He could do things only gently. If he had to fight, he would fail. He was weak.

"For example, I will use the time when he and I were competing for the Heller account. This job meant a lot of money, and I was not about to lose. I went to the library and read all I could about turbine engines. What a bore! I took photographs of turbine blades and such things, and seeded them throughout my portfolio to make Herr Heller think that I had always been interested in turbines. Of course, I had not even known what they were. I thought that they were an Oriental hat. And now that I know them, I detest them.

"Naturally, I won. But do you know how Wallich approached the competition? He had some foolish ideas about mother-of-pearl nau-tiluses and other seashells. He wanted to show how shapes of things mechanical were echoes of shapes in nature. All very fine, but Herr Heller pointed out that if the public were to see photographs of mother-of-pearl shells contrasted with photographs of his engines, his engines would come out the worse. Wallich's photographs were very beautiful—the tones of white and silver were exceptional—but they were his undoing. In the end, he said, 'Perhaps, Herr Heller, you are right,' and lost the contract just like that.

"The thing that saved him was the prize for that picture he took in the Black Forest. You couldn't pick up a magazine in Germany and not see it. He obtained so many accounts that he began to do very well. But he was just not commercially-minded. He told me himself that he took only those assignments which pleased him. Mind you, his business volume was only about two-thirds of mine.

"My theory is that he could not take the competition, and the demands of his various clients. After his wife and son were killed in the motorcar crash, he dropped assignments one after another. I suppose he thought that as a bachelor he could live like a bohemian, on very little money, and therefore did not have to work more than half the time. I'm not saying that this was wrong. (Those accounts came to me.) But it was another instance of his weakness and lassitude.

"My theory is that he has probably gone to South America, or thrown himself off a bridge—because he saw that there was no future for him if he were always to take pictures of shells and things. And he was weak. The weak can never face themselves, and so cannot see the practical side of the world, how things are laid out, and what sacrifices are required to survive and prosper. It is only in fairy tales that they rise to triumph."

Wallich could not afford to get to South America. He certainly would not have thrown himself off a bridge. He was excessively neat and orderly, and the prospect of some poor fireman handling a swollen, bloated body resounding with flies deterred him forever from such nonsense.

Perhaps if he had been a Gypsy he would have taken to the road. But he was no Gypsy, and had not the talent, skill, or taste for life outside Bavaria. Only once had he been away, to Paris. It was their honeymoon, when he and his wife did not need Paris or any city. They went by train and stayed for a week at a hotel by the Quai Voltaire. They walked in the gardens all day long, and in the May evenings they went to concerts where they heard the perfect music of their own country. Though they were away for just a week, and read the German papers, and went to a corner of the Luxembourg Gardens where there were pines and wildflowers like those in the greenbelt around Munich, this music made them sick for home. They returned two days early and never left again except for July and August, which each year they spent in the Black Forest, at a cabin inherited from her parents.

He dared not go back to that cabin. It was set like a trap. Were he to enter he would be enfiladed by the sight of their son's pictures and toys, his little boots and miniature fishing rod, and by her comb lying at the exact angle she had left it when she had last brushed her hair, and by the sweet smell of her clothing. No, someday he would have to burn the cabin. He dared not sell, for strangers then would handle roughly all those things which meant so much to him that he could not even gaze upon them. He left the little cabin to stand empty, perhaps the object of an occasional hiker's curiosity, or recipient of cheerful postcards from friends traveling or at the beach for the summer—friends who had not heard.

He sought instead a town far enough from Munich so that he would not encounter anything familiar, a place where he would be unrecognized and yet a place not entirely strange, where he would have to undergo no savage adjustments, where he could buy a Munich paper.

A search of the map brought his flying eye always southward to the borderlands, to Alpine country remarkable for the steepness of the brown contours, the depth of the valleys, and the paucity of settled places. Those few depicted towns appeared to be clean and well placed on high overlooks. Unlike the cities to the north—circles which clustered together on the flatlands or along rivers, like colonies of bacteria—the cities of the Alps stood alone, *in extremis,* near the border. Though he dared not cross the border, he thought perhaps to venture near its edge, to see what he would see. These isolated towns in the Alps promised shining clear air and deep-green trees. Perhaps they were above the tree line. In a number of cases it looked that way—and the circles were far from resembling clusters of bacteria. They seemed like untethered balloons.

He chose a town for its ridiculous name, reasoning that few of his friends would desire to travel to such a place. The world bypasses badly named towns as easily as it abandons ungainly children. It was called Garmisch-Partenkirchen. At the station in Munich, they did not even inscribe the full name on his ticket, writing merely "Garmisch-P."

"Do you live there?" the railroad agent had asked.

"No," answered Wallich.

"Are you visiting relatives, or going on business, or going to ski?"

"No."

"Then perhaps you are making a mistake. To go in October is not wise, if you do not ski. As unbelievable as it may seem, they have had much snow. Why go now?"

"I am a mountain climber," answered Wallich.

"In winter?" The railway agent was used to flushing out lies, and when little fat Austrian boys just old enough for adult tickets would bend their knees at his window as if at confession and say in squeaky voices, "Half fare to Salzburg!," he pounced upon them as if he were a leopard and they juicy ptarmigan or baby roebuck.

"Yes, in the winter," Wallich said. "Good mountain climbers thrive in difficult conditions. The more ice, the more storm, the greater the accomplishment. I am accumulating various winter records. In January, I go to America, where I will ascend their highest mountain, Mt. Independence, four thousand meters." He blushed so hard that the railway agent followed suit. Then Wallich backed away, insensibly mortified.

A mountain climber! He would close his eyes in fear when looking through Swiss calendars. He had not the stamina to rush up the stairs to his studio. He had failed miserably at sports. He was not a mountain climber, and had never even dreamed of being one.

Yet when his train pulled out of the vault of lacy ironwork and late-afternoon shadow, its steam exhalations were like those of a man puffing up a high meadow, speeding to reach the rock and ice, and Wallich felt as if he were embarking upon an ordeal of the type men experience on the precipitous rock walls of great cloud-swirled peaks. Why was he going to Garmisch-Partenkirchen anyway, if not for an ordeal through which to right himself? He was pulled so far over on one side by the death of his family, he was so bent and crippled by the pain of it, that he was going to Garmisch-Partenkirchen to suffer a parallel ordeal through which he would balance what had befallen him.

How wrong his parents and friends had been when they had offered help as his business faltered. A sensible, graceful man will have symmetry. He remembered the time at youth camp when a stream had changed course away from a once gushing sluice and the younger boys had had to carry buckets of water up a small hill, to fill a cistern. The skinny little boys had struggled up the hill. Their counselor, sitting comfortably in the shade, would not let them go two to a bucket. At first they had tried to carry the pails in front of them, but this was nearly impossible. Then they surreptitiously spilled half the water on the way up, until the counselor took up position at the cistern and inspected each cargo. It had been torture to carry the heavy bucket in one aching hand. Wallich finally decided to take two buckets. Though it was agony, it was a better agony than the one he had had, because he had retrieved his balance, could look ahead, and, by carrying a double burden, had strengthened himself and made the job that much shorter. Soon, all the boys carried two buckets. The cistern was filled in no time, and they had a victory over their surprised counselor.

So, he thought as the train shuttled through chill half-harvested fields, I will be a hermit in Garmisch-Partenkirchen. I will know no one. I will be alone. I may even begin to climb mountains. Perhaps I will lose fingers and toes, and on the way gather a set of wounds which will allow me some peace.

He sensed the change of landscape before he actually came upon it. Then they began to climb, and the engine sweated steam from steel to carry the lumbering cars up terrifying grades on either side of which blue pines stood angled against the mountainside. They reached a level stretch which made the train curve like a dragon and led it through deep tunnels, and they sped along as if on a summer excursion, with views of valleys so distant that in them whole forests sat upon their meadows like birthmarks, and streams were little more than the grain in leather.

Wallich opened his window and leaned out, watching ahead for tunnels. The air was thick and cold. It was full of sunshine and greenery, and it flowed past as if it were a mountain river. When he pulled back, his cheeks were red and his face pounded from the frigid air. He was alone in the compartment. By the time the lights came on he had decided upon the course of an ideal. He was to become a mountain climber, after all—and in a singularly difficult, dangerous, and satisfying way.

A porter said in passing the compartment, "The dining car is open, sir." Service to the Alps was famed. Even though his journey was no more than two hours, he had arranged to eat on the train, and had paid for and ordered a meal to which he looked forward in pleasant anticipation, especially because he had selected French strawberries in cream for dessert. But then he saw his body in the gently lit half mirror. He was soft from a lifetime of near-happiness. The sight of his face in the blond light of the mirror made him decide to begin preparing for the mountains that very evening. The porter ate the strawberries.

Of the many ways to attempt an ordeal perhaps the most graceful
and attractive is the Alpine. It is far more satisfying than Oriental
starvation and abnegation precisely because the European ideal is to
commit difficult acts amid richness and overflowing beauty. For that
reason, the Alpine is as well the most demanding. It is hard to deny
oneself, to pare oneself down, at the heart and base of a civilization
so full.

Wallich rode to Garmisch-Partenkirchen in a thunder of proud
Alps. The trees were tall and lively, the air crystalline, and radiating
beams spoke through the train window from one glowing range to
another. A world of high ice laughed. And yet ranks of competing
images assaulted him. He had gasped at the sight of Bremen, a port
stuffed with iron ships gushing wheat steam from their whistles
as they prepared to sail. In the mountain dryness, he remembered
humid ports from which these massive ships crossed a colorful
world, bringing back on laden decks a catalogue of stuffs and
curiosities.

Golden images of the north plains struck from the left. The salt-
white plains nearly floated above the sea. All this was in Germany,
though Germany was just a small part of the world, removed almost
entirely from the deep source of things—from the high lakes where
explorers touched the silvers which caught the world's images, from
the Sahara where they found the fine glass which bent the light.

Arriving at Garmisch-Partenkirchen in the dark, he could hear
bells chiming and water rushing. Cool currents of air flowed from
the direction of this white tumbling sound. It was winter. He hailed
a horse-drawn sledge and piled his baggage in the back. "Hotel
Aufburg," he said authoritatively.

"Hotel Aufburg?" asked the driver.

"Yes, Hotel Aufburg. There is such a place, isn't there? It hasn't
closed, has it?"

"No, sir, it hasn't closed." The driver touched his horse with the
whip. The horse walked twenty feet and was reined to a stop. "Here
we are," the driver said. "I trust you've had a pleasant journey. Time
passes quickly up here in the mountains."

The sign for the hotel was so large and well lit that the street in
front of it shone as in daylight. The driver was guffawing to himself;

the little guffaws rumbled about in him like subterranean thunder. He could not wait to tell the other drivers.

Wallich did nothing properly in Garmisch-Partenkirchen. But it was a piece of luck that he felt too awkward and ill at ease to sit alone in restaurants while, nearby, families and lovers had self-centered raucous meals, sometimes even bursting into song. Winter took over the town and covered it in stiff white ice. The unresilient cold, the troikas jingling through the streets, the frequent snowfalls encouraged winter fat. But because Wallich ate cold food in his room or stopped occasionally at a counter for a steaming bowl of soup, he became a shadow.

The starvation was pleasant. It made him sleepy and its constant physical presence gave him companionship. He sat for hours watching the snow, feeling as if he were part of it, as if the diminution of his body were great progress, as if such lightening would lessen his sorrow and bring him to the high rim of things he had not seen before, things which would help him and show him what to do and make him proud just for coming upon them.

He began to exercise. Several times a day the hotel manager knocked like a woodpecker at Wallich's door. The angrier the manager, the faster the knocks. If he were really angry, he spoke so rapidly that he sounded like a speeded-up record: "Herr Wallich, I must ask you on behalf of the other guests to stop immediately all the thumping and vibration! This is a quiet hotel, in a quiet town, in a quiet tourist region. Please!" Then the manager would bow and quickly withdraw.

Eventually they threw Wallich out, but not before he had spent October and November in concentrated maniacal pursuit of physical strength. He had started with five each, every waking hour, of push-ups, pull-ups, sit-ups, toe-touches, and leg-raises. The pull-ups were deadly—he did one every twelve minutes. The thumping and bumping came from five minutes of running in place. At the end of the first day, the pain in his chest was so intense that he was certain he was not long for the world. The second day was worse. And so it went, until after ten days there was no pain at all. The weight he abandoned helped a great deal to expand his physical prowess. He was, after all, in his middle twenties, and had never eaten to excess.

Nor did he smoke or drink, except for champagne at weddings and municipal celebrations. In fact, he had always had rather ascetic tendencies, and had thought it fitting to have spent his life in Munich— "Home of Monks."

By his fifteenth day in Garmisch-Partenkirchen he had increased his schedule to fifteen apiece of the exercises each hour, which meant, for example, that he did a pull-up every four minutes whenever he was awake. Late at night he ran aimlessly about the deserted streets for an hour or more, even though it sometimes snowed. Two policemen who huddled over a brazier in their tiny booth simply looked at one another and pointed to their heads, twirling their fingers and rolling their eyes every time he passed by. On the last day of November, he moved up the valley to a little village called Altenburg-St. Peter.

There it was worse in some ways and better in others. Altenburg-St. Peter was so tiny that no stranger could enter unobserved, and so still that no one could do anything without the knowledge of the entire community. Children stared at Wallich on the street. This made him walk on the little lanes and approach his few destinations from the rear, which led housewives to speculate that he was a burglar. There were few merchants, and, because they were cousins, they could with little effort determine exactly what Wallich ate. When one week they were positive that he had consumed only four bowls of soup, a pound of cheese, a pound of smoked meat, a quart of yogurt, and two loaves of bread, they were incredulous. They themselves ate this much in a day. They wondered how Wallich survived on so little. Finally they came up with an answer. He received packages from Munich several times a week and in these packages was food, they thought—and probably very great delicacies. Then as the winter got harder and the snows covered everything they stopped wondering about him. They did not see him as he ran out of his lodgings at midnight, and the snow muffled his tread. He ran up the road toward the Schreuderspitze, first for a kilometer, then two, then five, then ten, then twenty—when finally he had to stop because he had begun slipping in just before the farmers arose and would have seen him.

By the end of February the packages had ceased arriving, and he was a changed man. No one would have mistaken him for what he had been. In five months he had become lean and strong. He did two hundred and fifty sequential push-ups at least four times a day. For the sheer pleasure of it, he would do a hundred and fifty push-ups on his fingertips. Every day he did a hundred pull-ups in a row. His midnight run, sometimes in snow which had accumulated up to his knees, was four hours long.

The packages had contained only books on climbing, and equipment. At first the books had been terribly discouraging. Every elementary text had bold warnings in red or green ink: "It is extremely dangerous to attempt genuine ascents without proper training. This volume should be used in conjunction with a certified course on climbing, or with the advice of a registered guide. A book itself will not do!"

One manual had in bright-red ink, on the very last page: "Go back, you fool! Certain death awaits you!" Wallich imagined that, as the books said, there were many things he could not learn except by human example, and many mistakes he might make in interpreting the manuals, which would go uncorrected save for the critique of living practitioners. But it didn't matter. He was determined to learn for himself and accomplish his task alone. Besides, since the accident he had become a recluse, and could hardly speak. The thought of enrolling in a climbing school full of young people from all parts of the country paralyzed him. How could he reconcile his task with their enthusiasm? For them it was recreation, perhaps something aesthetic or spiritual, a way to meet new friends. For him it was one tight channel through which he would either burst on to a new life, or in which he would die.

Studying carefully, he soon worked his way to advanced treatises for those who had spent years in the Alps. He understood these well enough, having quickly learned the terminologies and the humor and the faults of those who write about the mountains. He was even convinced that he knew the spirit in which the treatises had been written, for though he had never climbed, he had only to look out his window to see high white mountains about which blue sky swirled like a banner. He felt that in seeing them he was one of them, and was greatly encouraged when he read in a French mountaineer's memoirs: "After years in the mountains, I learned to look upon a given range and feel as if I were the last peak in the line. Thus I felt the music of the empty spaces enwrapping me, and I became not an intruder on the cliffs, dangling only to drop away, but an equal in transit. I seldom looked at my own body but only at the mountains, and my eyes felt like the eyes of the mountains."

He lavished nearly all his dwindling money on fine equipment. He calculated that after his purchases he would have enough to live on through September. Then he would have nothing. He had expended large sums on the best tools, and he spent the intervals between his hours of reading and exercise holding and studying the shiny carabiners, pitons, slings, chocks, hammers, ice pitons, axes, étriers, crampons, ropes, and specialized hardware that he had either ordered or constructed himself from plans in the advanced books.

It was insane, he knew, to funnel all his preparation into a few months of agony and then without any experience whatever throw himself alone onto a Class VI ascent—the seldom climbed *Westgebirgsausläufer* of the Schreuderspitze. Not having driven one piton, he was going to attempt a five-day climb up the nearly sheer western counterfort. Even in late June, he would spend a third of his time on ice. But the sight of the ice in March, shining like a faraway sword over the cold and absolute distance, drove him on. He had long passed censure. Had anyone known what he was doing and tried to dissuade him, he would have told him to go to hell, and resumed preparations with the confidence of someone taken up by a new religion.

For he had always believed in great deeds, in fairy tales, in echoing trumpet lands, in wonders and wondrous accomplishments. But even as a boy he had never considered that such things would fall to him. As a good city child he had known that these adventures were not necessary. But suddenly he was alone and the things which occurred to him were great warlike deeds. His energy and discipline were boundless, as full and overflowing as a lake in the mountains. Like the heroes of his youth, he would try to approach the high cord of ruby light and bend it to his will, until he could feel rolling thunder. The small things, the gentle things, the good things he loved, and the flow of love itself were dead for him and would always be, unless he could liberate them in a crucible of high drama.

It took him many months to think these things, and though they might not seem consistent, they were so for him, and he often spent hours alone on a sunny snow-covered meadow, his elbows on his knees, imagining great deeds in the mountains, as he stared at the massive needle of the Schreuderspitze, at the hint of rich lands beyond, and at the tiny village where he had taken up position opposite the mountain.

Toward the end of May he had been walking through Altenburg-St. Peter and seen his reflection in a store window—a storm had arisen suddenly and made the glass as silver-black as the clouds. He had not liked what he had seen. His face had become too hard and too lean. There was not enough gentleness. He feared immediately for the success of his venture if only because he knew well that unmitigated extremes are a great cause of failure. And he was tired of his painful regimen.

He bought a large Telefunken radio, in one fell swoop wiping out his funds for August and September. He felt as if he were paying for the privilege of music with portions of his life and body. But it was well worth it. When the storekeeper offered to deliver the heavy console, Wallich declined politely, picked up the cabinet himself, hoisted it on his back, and walked out of the store bent under it as in classic illustrations for physics textbooks throughout the industrialized world. He did not put it down once. The storekeeper summoned his associates and they bet and counterbet on whether Wallich "would" or "would not," as he moved slowly up the steep hill, up the steps, around the white switchbacks, onto a grassy slope, and then finally up the precipitous stairs to the balcony outside his room. "How can he have done that?" they asked. "He is a small man, and the radio must weigh at least thirty kilos." The storekeeper trotted out with a catalogue. "It weighs fifty-five kilograms!" he said. "Fifty-five kilograms!" And they wondered what had made Wallich so strong.

Once, Wallich had taken his little son (a tiny, skeptical, silent child who had a riotous giggle which could last for an hour) to see the inflation of a great gas dirigible. It had been a disappointment, for a dirigible is rigid and maintains always the same shape. He had expected to see the silver of its sides expand into ribbed cliffs which would float over them on the green field and amaze his son. Now that silver rising, the sail-like expansion, the great crescendo of a glimmering weightless mass, finally reached him alone in his room, too late but well received, when a Berlin station played the Beethoven Violin Concerto, its first five timpanic D's like grace before a feast. After those notes, the music lifted him, and he riveted his gaze on the dark shapes of the mountains, where a lightning storm raged. The radio crackled after each near or distant flash, but it was as if the music had been designed for it. Wallich looked at the yellow light within a softly glowing numbered panel. It flickered gently, and he could hear cracks and flashes in the music as he saw them delineated across darkness. They looked and sounded like the bent riverine limbs of dead trees hanging majestically over rocky outcrops, destined to fall, but enjoying their grand suspension nonetheless. The music traveled effortlessly on anarchic beams, passed high over the plains, passed high the forests, seeding them plentifully, and came upon the Alps like waves which finally strike the shore after thousands of miles in open sea. It charged upward, mating with the electric storm, separating, and delivering.

To Wallich—alone in the mountains, surviving amid the dark massifs and clear air—came the closeted, nasal, cosmopolitan voice of the radio commentator. It was good to know that there was something other than the purity and magnificence of his mountains, that far to the north the balance reverted to less than moral catastrophe and death, and much stock was set in things of extraordinary inconsequence. Wallich could not help laughing when he thought of the formally dressed audience at the symphony, how they squirmed in their seats and heated the bottoms of their trousers and capes, how relieved and delighted they would be to step out into the cool evening and go to a restaurant. In the morning they would arise and take pleasure from the sweep of the drapes as sun danced by, from the gold rim around a white china cup. For them it was always too hot or too cold. But they certainly had their delights, about which sometimes he would think. How often he still dreamed, asleep or awake, of the smooth color plates opulating under his hands in tanks of developer and of the fresh film which smelled like bread and then was entombed in black cylinders to develop. How he longed sometimes for the precise machinery of his cameras. The very word *"Kamera"* was as dark and hollow as this night in the mountains when, reviewing the pleasures of faraway Berlin, he sat in perfect health and equanimity upon a wicker-weave seat in a bare white room. The only light was from the yellow dial, the sudden lightning flashes, and the faint blue of the sky beyond the hills. And all was quiet but for the music and the thunder and the static curling about the music like weak and lost memories which arise to harry even indomitable perfections.

A month before the ascent, he awaited arrival of a good climbing rope. He needed from a rope not strength to hold a fall but lightness and length for abseiling. His strategy was to climb with a short self-belay. No one would follow to retrieve his hardware and because it would not always be practical for him to do so himself, in what one of his books called "rhythmic recapitulation," he planned to carry a great deal of metal. If the metal and he reached the summit relatively intact, he could make short work of the descent, abandoning pitons as he abseiled downward.

He would descend in half a day that which had taken five days to climb. He pictured the abseiling, literally a flight down the mountain on the doubled cord of his long rope, and he thought that those hours speeding down the cliffs would be the finest of his life. If the weather were good he would come away from the Schreuderspitze having flown like an eagle.

On the day the rope was due, he went to the railroad station to meet the mail. It was a clear, perfect day. The light was so fine and rich that in its bath everyone felt wise, strong, and content. Wallich sat on the wooden boards of the wide platform, scanning the green meadows and fields for smoke and a coal engine, but the countryside was silent and the valley unmarred by the black woolly chain he sought. In the distance, toward France and Switzerland, a few cream-and-rose-colored clouds rode the horizon, immobile and high. On far mountainsides innumerable flowers showed in this long view as a slash, or as a patch of color not unlike one flower alone.

He had arrived early, for he had no watch. After some minutes a car drove up and from it emerged a young family. They rushed as if the train were waiting to depart, when down the long troughlike valley it was not even visible. There were two little girls, as beautiful as he had ever seen. The mother, too, was extraordinarily fine. The father was in his early thirties, and he wore gold-rimmed glasses. They seemed like a university family—people who knew how to live sensibly, taking pleasure from proper and beautiful things.

The littler girl was no more than three. Sunburnt and rosy, she wore a dress that was shaped like a bell. She dashed about the platform so lightly and tentatively that it was as if Wallich were watching a tiny fish gravityless in a lighted aquarium. Her older sister stood quietly by the mother, who was illumined with consideration and pride for her children. It was apparent that she was overjoyed with the grace of her family. She seemed detached and preoccupied, but in just the right way. The littler girl said in a voice like a child's party horn, "Mummy, I want some peanuts!"

It was so ridiculous that this child should share the appetite of elephants that the mother smiled. "Peanuts will make you thirsty, Gretl. Wait until we get to Garmisch-Partenkirchen. Then we'll have lunch in the buffet."

"When will we get to Garmisch-Partenkirchen?"

"At two."

"Two?"

"Yes, at two."

"At two?"

"Gretl!"

The father looked alternately at the mountains and at his wife and children. He seemed confident and steadfast. In the distance black smoke appeared in thick billows. The father pointed at it. "There's our train," he said.

"Where?" asked Gretl, looking in the wrong direction. The father picked her up and turned her head with his hand, aiming her gaze down the shimmering valley. When she saw the train she started, and her eyes opened wide in pleasure.

"Ah . . . there it is," said the father. As the train pulled into the station the young girls were filled with excitement. Amid the noise they entered a compartment and were swallowed up in the steam. The train pulled out.

Wallich stood on the empty platform, unwrapping his rope. It was a rope, quite a nice rope, but it did not make him as happy as he had expected it would.

Little can match the silhouette of mountains by night. The great mass becomes far more mysterious when its face is darkened, when its sweeping lines roll steeply into valleys and peaks and long impossible ridges, when behind the void a concoction of rare silver leaps up to trace the hills—the pressure of collected starlight. That night, in conjunction with the long draughts of music he had become used to taking, he began to dream his dreams. They did not frighten him—he was beyond fear, too strong for fear, too played out. They did not even puzzle him, for they unfolded like the chapters in a brilliant nineteenth-century history. The rich explanations filled him for days afterward. He was amazed, and did not understand why these perfect dreams suddenly came to him. Surely they did not arise from within. He had never had the world so beautifully portrayed, had never seen as clearly and in such sure, gentle steps, had never risen so high and so smoothly in unfolding enlightenment, and he had seldom felt so well looked after. And yet, there was no visible presence. But it was as if the mountains and valleys were filled with loving families of which he was part.

Upon his return from the railroad platform, a storm had come suddenly from beyond the southern ridge. Though it had been warm and clear that day, he had seen from the sunny meadow before his house that a white storm billowed in higher and higher curves, pushing itself over the summits, finally to fall like an air avalanche on the valley. It snowed on the heights. The sun continued to strike the opaque frost and high clouds. It did not snow in the valley. The shock troops of the storm remained at the highest elevations, and only worn gray veterans came below—misty clouds and rain on cold wet air. Ragged clouds moved across the mountainsides and meadows, watering the trees and sometimes catching in low places. Even so, the air in the meadow was still horn-clear.

In his room that night Wallich rocked back and forth on the wicker chair (it was not a rocker and he knew that using it as such was to number its days). That night's crackling infusion from Berlin, rising warmly from the faintly lit dial, was Beethoven's Eighth. The familiar commentator, nicknamed by Wallich Mälzels Metronom because of his even monotone, discoursed upon the background of the work.

"For many years," he said, "no one except Beethoven liked this symphony. Beethoven's opinions, however—even regarding his own creations—are equal at least to the collective pronouncements of all the musicologists and critics alive in the West during any hundred-year period. Conscious of the merits of the F-Major Symphony, he resolutely determined to redeem and . . . ah . . . the conductor has arrived. He steps to the podium. We begin."

Wallich retired that night in perfect tranquillity but awoke at five in the morning soaked in his own sweat, his fists clenched, a terrible pain in his chest, and breathing heavily as if he had been running. In the dim unattended light of the early-morning storm, he lay with eyes wide open. His pulse subsided, but he was like an animal in a cave, like a creature who has just escaped an organized hunt. It was as if the whole village had come armed and in search of him, had by some miracle decided that he was not in, and had left to comb the wet woods. He had been dreaming, and he saw his dream in its exact form. It was, first, an emerald. Cut into an octagon with two long sides, it was shaped rather like the plaque at the bottom of a painting. Events within this emerald were circular and never-ending.

They were in Munich. Air and sun were refined as on the station platform in the mountains. He was standing at a streetcar stop with his wife and his two daughters, though he knew perfectly well in the dream that these two daughters were meant to be his son. A streetcar arrived in complete silence. Clouds of people began to embark. They were dressed and muffled in heavy clothing of dull blue and gray. To his surprise, his wife moved toward the door of the streetcar and started to board, the daughters trailing after her. He could not see her feet, and she moved in a glide. Though at first paralyzed, as in the instant before a crash, he did manage to bound after her. As she stepped onto the first step and was about to grasp a chrome pole within the doorway, he made for her arm and caught it.

He pulled her back and spun her around, all very gently. Her presence before him was so intense that it was as if he were trapped under the weight of a fallen beam. She, too, wore a winter coat, but it was slim and perfectly tailored. He remembered the perfect geometry of the lapels. Not on earth had such angles ever been seen. The coat was a most intense liquid emerald color, a living light-infused green. She had always looked best in green, for her hair was like shining gold. He stood before her. He felt her delicacy. Her expression was neutral. "Where are you going?" he asked incredulously.

"I must go," she said.

He put his arms around her. She returned his embrace, and he said, "How can you leave me?"

"I have to," she answered.

And then she stepped onto the first step of the streetcar, and onto the second step, and she was enfolded into darkness.

He awoke, feeling like an invalid. His strength served for naught. He just stared at the clouds lifting higher and higher as the storm cleared. By nightfall the sky was black and gentle, though very cold. He kept thinking back to the emerald. It meant everything to him, for it was the first time he realized that they were really dead. Silence followed. Time passed thickly. He could not have imagined the sequence of dreams to follow, and what they would do to him.

He began to fear sleep, thinking that he would again be subjected to the lucidity of the emerald. But he had run that course and would never do so again except by perfect conscious recollection. The night after he had the dream of the emerald he fell asleep like someone letting go of a cliff edge after many minutes alone without help or hope. He slid into sleep, heart beating wildly. To his surprise, he found himself far indeed from the trolley tracks in Munich.

Instead, he was alone in the center of a sunlit snowfield,

walking on the glacier in late June, bound for the summit of the Schreuderspitze. The mass of his equipment sat lightly upon him. He was well drilled in its use and positioning, in the subtleties of placement and rigging. The things he carried seemed part of him, as if he had quickly evolved into a new kind of animal suited for breathtaking travel in the steep heights.

His stride was light and long, like that of a man on the moon. He nearly floated, ever so slightly airborne, over the dazzling glacier. He leaped crevasses, sailing in slow motion against intense white and blue. He passed apple-fresh streams and opalescent melt pools of blue-green water as he progressed toward the Schreuderspitze. Its rocky horn was covered by nearly blue ice from which the wind blew a white corona in sines and cusps twirling about the sky.

Passing the bergschrund, he arrived at the first mass of rock. He turned to look back. There he saw the snowfield and the sun turning above it like a pinwheel, casting out a fog of golden light. He stood alone. The world had been reduced to the beauty of physics and the mystery of light. It had been rendered into a frozen state, a liquid state, a solid state, a gaseous state, mixtures, temperatures, and more varieties of light than fell on the speckled floor of a great cathedral. It was simple, and yet infinitely complex. The sun was warm. There was silence.

For several hours he climbed over great boulders and up a range of rocky escarpments. It grew more and more difficult, and he often had to lay in protection, driving a piton into a crack of the firm granite. His first piton was a surprise. It slowed halfway, and the ringing sound as he hammered grew higher in pitch. Finally, it would go in no farther. He had spent so much time in driving it that he thought it would be as steady as the Bank of England. But when he gave a gentle tug to test its hold, it came right out. This he thought extremely funny. He then remembered that he had either to drive it in all the way, to the eye, or to attach a sling along its shaft as near as possible to the rock. It was a question of avoiding leverage.

He bent carefully to his equipment sling, replaced the used piton, and took up a shorter one. The shorter piton went to its eye in five hammer strokes and he could do nothing to dislodge it. He clipped in and ascended a steep pitch, at the top of which he drove in two pitons, tied in to them, abseiled down to retrieve the first, and ascended quite easily to where he had left off. He made rapid progress over frightening pitches, places no one would dare go without assurance of a bolt in the rock and a line to the bolt— even if the bolt was just a small piece of metal driven in by dint of precariously balanced strength, arm, and Alpine hammer.

Within the sphere of utter concentration easily achieved during difficult ascents, his simple climbing evolved naturally into graceful technique, by which he went up completely vertical rock faces, suspended only by pitons and étriers. The different placements of which he had read and thought repeatedly were employed skillfully and with a proper sense of variety, though it was tempting to stay with one familiar pattern. Pounding metal into rock and hanging from his taut and colorful wires, he breathed hard, he concentrated, and he went up sheer walls.

At one point he came to the end of a subtle hairline crack in an otherwise smooth wall. The rock above was completely solid for a hundred feet. If he went down to the base of the crack he would be nowhere. The only thing to do was to make a swing traverse to a wall more amenable to climbing.

Anchoring two pitons into the rock as solidly as he could, he clipped an oval carabiner on the bottom piton, put a safety line on the top one, and lowered himself about sixty feet down the two ropes. Hanging perpendicular to the wall, he began to walk back and forth across the rock. He moved to and fro, faster and faster, until he was running. Finally he touched only in places and was swinging wildly like a pendulum. He feared that the piton to which he was anchored would not take the strain, and would pull out. But he kept swinging faster, until he gave one final push and, with a pathetic cry, went sailing over a drop which would have made a mountain goat swallow its heart. He caught an outcropping of rock on the other side, and pulled himself to it desperately. He hammered in, retrieved the ropes, glanced at the impassable wall, and began again to ascend.

As he approached great barricades of ice, he looked back. It gave him great pride and satisfaction to see the thousands of feet over which he had struggled. Much of the west counterfort was purely vertical. He could see now just how the glacier was riverine. He could see deep within the Tyrol and over the border to the Swiss lakes. Garmisch-Partenkirchen looked from here like a town on the board of a toy railroad or (if considered only two-dimensionally) like the cross-section of a kidney. Altenburg-St. Peter looked like a lady-bug. The sun sent streamers of tan light through the valley, already three-quarters conquered by shadow, and the ice above took fire. Where the ice began, he came to a wide ledge and he stared upward at a sparkling ridge which looked like a great crystal spine. Inside, it was blue and cold.

He awoke, convinced that he had in fact climbed the counterfort. It was a strong feeling, as strong as the reality of the emerald. Sometimes dreams could be so real that they competed with the world, riding at even balance and calling for a decision. Sometimes, he imagined, when they are so real and so important, they easily tip the scale and the world buckles and dreams become real. Crossing the fragile barricades, one enters his dreams, thinking of his life as imagined.

He rejoiced at his bravery in climbing. It had been as real as any-thing he had ever experienced. He felt the pain, the exhaustion, and the reward, as well as the danger. But he could not wait to return to the mountain and the ice. He longed for evening and the enveloping darkness, believing that he belonged resting under great folds of ice on the wall of the Schreuderspitze. He had no patience with his wicker chair, the bent wood of the windowsill, the clear glass in the window, the green-sided hills he saw curving through it, or his brightly colored equipment hanging from pegs on the white wall.

Two weeks before, on one of the eastward roads from Altenburg-St. Peter—no more than a dirt track—he had seen a child turn and take a well-worn path toward a wood, a meadow, and a stream by which stood a house and a barn. The child walked slowly upward into the forest, disappearing into the dark close, as if he had been taken up by vapor. Wallich had been too far away to hear footsteps, and the last thing he saw was the back of the boy's bright blue-and-white sweater. Returning at dusk, Wallich had expected to see warmly lit windows, and smoke issuing efficiently from the straight chimney. But there were no lights, and there was no smoke. He made his way through the trees and past the meadow only to come upon a small farmhouse with boarded windows and no-trespassing signs tacked on the doors.

It was unsettling when he saw the same child making his way across the upper meadow, a flash of blue and white in the near darkness. Wallich screamed out to him, but he did not hear, and kept walking as if he were deaf or in another world, and he went over the crest of the hill. Wallich ran up the hill. When he reached the top he saw only a wide empty field and not a trace of the boy.

Then in the darkness and purity of the meadows he began to feel that the world had many secrets, that they were shattering even to glimpse or sense, and that they were not necessarily unpleasant. In certain states of light he could see, he could begin to sense, things most miraculous indeed. Although it seemed self-serving, he concluded nonetheless, after a lifetime of adhering to the diffuse principles of a science he did not know, that there was life after death, that the dead rose into a mischievous world of pure light, that something most mysterious lay beyond the enfolding darkness, something wonderful.

This idea had taken hold, and he refined it. For example, listening to the Beethoven symphonies broadcast from Berlin, he began to think that they were like a ladder of mountains, that they surpassed themselves and rose higher and higher until at certain points they seemed to break the warp itself and cross into a heaven of light and the dead. There were signs everywhere of temporal diffusion and mystery. It was as if continents existed, new worlds lying just off the coast, invisible and redolent, waiting for the grasp of one man suddenly to substantiate and light them, changing everything. Perhaps great mountains hundreds of times higher than the Alps would arise in the sea or on the flatlands. They might be purple or gold and shining in many states of refraction and reflection, transparent in places as vast as countries. Someday someone would come back from this place, or someone would by accident discover and illumine its remarkable physics.

He believed that the boy he had seen nearly glowing in the half-darkness of the high meadow had been his son, and that the child had been teasing his father in a way only he could know, that the child had been asking him to follow. Possibly he had come upon great secrets on the other side, and knew that his father would join him soon enough and that then they would laugh about the world.

When he next fell asleep in the silence of a clear windless night in the valley, Wallich was like a man disappearing into the warp of darkness. He wanted to go there, to be taken as far as he could be taken. He was not unlike a sailor who sets sail in the teeth of a great storm, delighted by his own abandon.

Throwing off the last wraps of impure light, he found himself again in the ice world. The word was all-encompassing—*Eiswelt.* There above him the blue spire rocketed upward as far as the eye could see. He touched it with his hand. It was indeed as cold as ice. It was dense and hard, like glass ten feet thick. He had doubted its strength, but its solidity told that it would not flake away and allow him to drop endlessly, far from it.

On ice he found firm holds both with his feet and with his hands, and hardly needed the ice pitons and étriers. For he had crampons tied firmly to his boots, and could spike his toe points into the ice and stand comfortably on a vertical. He proceeded with a surety of footing he had never had on the streets of Munich. Each step bolted him down to the surface. And in each hand he carried an ice hammer with which he made swinging, cutting arcs that engaged the shining stainless-steel pick with the mirrorlike wall.

All the snow had blown away or had melted. There were no traps, no pitfalls, no ambiguities. He progressed toward the summit rapidly, climbing steep ice walls as if he had been going up a ladder. The air became purer and the light more direct. Looking out to right or left, or glancing sometimes over his shoulders, he saw that he was now truly in the world of mountains.

Above the few clouds he could see only equal peaks of ice, and the Schreuderspitze dropping away from him. It was not the world of rock. No longer could he make out individual features in the valley. Green had become a hazy dark blue appropriate to an ocean floor. Whole countries came into view. The landscape was a mass of winding glaciers and great mountains. At that height, all was separated and refined. Soft things vanished, and there remained only the white and the silver.

He did not reach the summit until dark. He did not see the stars because icy clouds covered the Schreuderspitze in a crystalline fog which flowed past, crackling and hissing. He was heartbroken to have come all the way to the summit and then be blinded by masses of clouds. Since he could not descend until light, he decided to stay firmly stationed until he could see clearly. Meanwhile, he lost patience and began to address a presence in the air—casually, not thinking it strange to do so, not thinking twice about talking to the void.

■　■　■

He awoke in his room in early morning, saying, "All these blinding clouds. Why all these blinding clouds?"

Though the air of the valley was as fresh as a flower, he detested it. He pulled the covers over his head and strove for unconsciousness, but he grew too hot and finally gave up, staring at the remnants of dawn light soaking about his room. The day brightened in the way that stage lights come up, suddenly brilliant upon a beam-washed platform. It was early June. He had lost track of the exact date, but he knew that sometime before he had crossed into June. He had lost them early in June. Two years had passed.

He packed his things. Though he had lived like a monk, much had accumulated, and this he put into suitcases, boxes, and bags. He packed his pens, paper, books, a chess set on which he sometimes played against an imaginary opponent named Herr Claub, the beautiful Swiss calendars upon which he had at one time been almost afraid to gaze, cooking equipment no more complex than a soldier's mess kit, his clothing, even the beautifully wrought climbing equipment, for, after all, he had another set, up there in the *Eiswelt*. Only his bedding remained unpacked. It was on the floor in the center of the room, where he slept. He put some banknotes in an envelope—the June rent—and tacked it to the doorpost. The room was empty, white, and it would have echoed had it been slightly larger. He would say something and then listen intently, his eyes flaring like those of a lunatic. He had not eaten in days, and was not disappointed that even the waking world began to seem like a dream.

He went to the pump. He had accustomed himself to bathing in streams so cold that they were too frightened to freeze. Clean and cleanly shaven, he returned to his room. He smelled the sweet pine scent he had brought back on his clothing after hundreds of trips through the woods and forests girdling the greater mountains. Even the bedding was snowy white. He opened the closet and caught a glimpse of himself in the mirror. He was dark from sun and wind; his hair shone; his face had thinned; his eyebrows were now gold and white. For several days he had had only cold pure water. Like soldiers who come from training toughened and healthy, he had about him the air of a small child. He noticed a certain wildness in the eye, and he lay on the hard floor, as was his habit, in perfect comfort. He thought nothing. He felt nothing. He wished nothing.

Time passed as if he could compress and cancel it. Early-evening darkness began to make the white walls blue. He heard a crackling fire in the kitchen of the rooms next door, and imagined the shadows dancing there. Then he slept, departing.

On the mountain it was dreadfully cold. He huddled into himself against the wet silver clouds, and yet he smiled, happy to be once again on the summit. He thought of making an igloo, but remembered that he hadn't an ice saw. The wind began to build. If the storm continued, he would die. It would whittle him into a brittle wire, and then he would snap. The best he could do was to dig a trench with his ice hammers. He lay in the trench and closed his sleeves and hooded parka, drawing the shrouds tight. The wind came at him more and more fiercely. One gust was so powerful that it nearly lifted him out of the trench. He put in an ice piton, and attached his harness. Still the wind rose. It was difficult to breathe and nearly impossible to see. Any irregular surface whistled. The eye of the ice piton became a great siren. The zippers on his parka, the harness, the slings and equipment, all gave off musical tones, so that it was as if he were in a place with hundreds of tormented spirits.

The gray air fled past with breathtaking speed. Looking away from the wind, he had the impression of being propelled upward at unimaginable speed. Walls of gray sped by so fast that they glowed. He knew that if he were to look at the wind he would have the sense of hurtling forward in gravityless space.

And so he stared at the wind and its slowly pulsing gray glow. He did not know for how many hours he held that position. The rape of vision caused a host of delusions. He felt great momentum. He traveled until, eardrums throbbing with the sharpness of cold and wind, he was nearly dead, white as a candle, hardly able to breathe.

Then the acceleration ceased and the wind slowed. When, released from the great pressure, he fell back off the edge of the trench, he realized for the first time that he had been stretched tight on his line. He had never been so cold. But the wind was dying and the clouds were no longer a corridor through which he was propelled. They were, rather, a gentle mist which did not know quite what to do with itself. How would it dissipate? Would it rise to the stars, or would it fall in compression down into the valley below?

It fell; it fell all around him, downward like a lowering curtain. It fell in lines and stripes, always downward as if on signal, by command, in league with a directive force.

At first he saw just a star or two straight on high. But as the mist departed a flood of stars burst through. Roads of them led into infinity. Starry wheels sat in fiery white coronas. Near the horizon were the few separate gentle stars, shining out and turning clearly, as wide and round as planets. The air grew mild and warm. He bathed in it. He trembled. As the air became all clear and the mist drained away completely, he saw something which stunned him.

The Schreuderspitze was far higher than he had thought. It was hundreds of times higher than the mountains represented on the map he had seen in Munich. The Alps were to it not even foothills, not even rills. Below him was the purple earth, and all the great cities lit by sparkling lamps in their millions. It was a clear summer dawn and the weather was excellent, certainly June.

He did not know enough about other cities to make them out from the shapes they cast in light, but his eye seized quite easily upon Munich. He arose from his trench and unbuckled the harness, stepping a few paces higher on the rounded summit. There was

Munich, shining and pulsing like a living thing, strung with lines of amber light—light which reverberated as if in crystals, light which played in many dimensions and moved about the course of the city, which was defined by darkness at its edge. He had come above time, above the world. The city of Munich existed before him with all its time compressed. As he watched, its history played out in repeating cycles. Nothing, not one movement, was lost from the crystal. The light of things danced and multiplied, again and again, and yet again. It was all there for him to claim. It was alive, and ever would be.

He knelt on one knee as in paintings he had seen of explorers claiming a coast of the New World. He dared close his eyes in the face of that miracle. He began to concentrate, to fashion according to will with the force of stilled time a vision of those he had loved. In all their bright colors, they began to appear before him.

He awoke as if shot out of a cannon. He went from lying on his back to a completely upright position in an instant, a flash, during which he slammed the floorboards energetically with a clenched fist and cursed the fact that he had returned from such a world. But by the time he stood straight, he was delighted to be doing so. He quickly dressed, packed his bedding, and began to shuttle down to the station and back. In three trips, his luggage was stacked on the platform.

He bought a ticket for Munich, where he had not been in many, many long months. He hungered for it, for the city, for the boats on the river, the goods in the shops, newspapers, the pigeons in the square, trees, traffic, even arguments, even Herr Franzen. So much rushed into his mind that he hardly saw his train pull in.

He helped the conductor load his luggage into the baggage car, and he asked, "Will we change at Garmisch-Partenkirchen?"

"No. We go right through, direct to Munich," said the conductor.

"Do me a great favor. Let me ride in the baggage car."

"I can't. It's a violation."

"Please. I've been months in the mountains. I would like to ride alone, for the last time."

The conductor relented, and Wallich sat atop a pile of boxes, looking at the landscape through a Dutch door, the top of which was open. Trees and meadows, sunny and lush in June, sped by. As they descended, the vegetation thickened until he saw along the cinder bed slow-running black rivers, skeins and skeins of thorns darted with the red of early raspberries, and flowers which had sprung up on the paths. The air was warm and caressing—thick and full, like a swaying green sea at the end of August.

They closed on Munich, and the Alps appeared in a sweeping line of white cloud-touched peaks. As they pulled into the great station, as sooty as it had ever been, he remembered that he had climbed the Schreuderspitze, by its most difficult route. He had found freedom from grief in the great and heart-swelling sight he had seen from the summit. He felt its workings and he realized that soon enough he would come once more into the world of light. Soon enough he would be with his wife and son. But until then (and he knew that time would spark ahead), he would open himself to life in the city, return to his former profession, and struggle at his craft.

Love Calls Us to the Things of This World

by Richard Wilbur

The eyes open to a cry of pulleys,
And spirited from sleep, the astounded soul
Hangs for a moment bodiless and simple
As false dawn.
              Outside the open window
The morning air is all awash with angels.

   Some are in bed-sheets, some are in blouses,
Some are in smocks: but truly there they are.
Now they are rising together in calm swells
Of halcyon feeling, filling whatever they wear
With the deep joy of their impersonal breathing;

   Now they are flying in place, conveying
The terrible speed of their omnipresence, moving
And staying like white water; and now of a sudden
They swoon down into so rapt a quiet
That nobody seems to be there.
                    The soul shrinks

   From all that it is about to remember,
From the punctual rape of every blessèd day,
And cries,
             "Oh, let there be nothing on earth but laundry,
Nothing but rosy hands in the rising steam
And clear dances done in the sight of heaven."

   Yet, as the sun acknowledges
With a warm look the world's hunks and colors,
The soul descends once more in bitter love
To accept the waking body, saying now
In a changed voice as the man yawns and rises,

"Bring them down from their ruddy gallows;
Let there be clean linen for the backs of thieves;
Let lovers go fresh and sweet to be undone,
And the heaviest nuns walk in a pure floating
Of dark habits,
　　　　　　keeping their difficult balance."

Poem in Three Parts

by Robert Bly

I

Oh, on an early morning I think I shall live forever!
I am wrapped in my joyful flesh,
As the grass is wrapped in its clouds of green.

II

Rising from a bed, where I dreamt
Of long rides past castles and hot coals,
The sun lies happily on my knees;
I have suffered and survived the night
Bathed in dark water, like any blade of grass.

III

The strong leaves of the box-elder tree,
Plunging in the wind, call us to disappear
Into the wilds of the universe,
Where we shall sit at the foot of a plant,
And live forever, like the dust.

Daddy Longlegs

by Ted Kooser

Here, on fine long legs springy as steel,
a life rides, sealed in a small brown pill
that skims along over the basement floor
wrapped up in a simple obsession.
Eight legs reach out like the master ribs
of a web in which some thought is caught
dead center in its own small world,
a thought so far from the touch of things
that we can only guess at it. If mine,
it would be the secret dream
of walking alone across the floor of my life
with an easy grace, and with love enough
to live on at the center of myself.

The Undeclared Major

by Will Weaver

In his gloomy periods Walter Hansen saw himself as one large
contradiction. He was still twenty, yet his reddish hair was in full retreat from the white plain of his forehead. He had small and quick-
moving blue eyes, eyes that tended skyward, eyes that noted every
airplane that passed overhead; his hands and feet were great, heavy
shovels. As Walter shambled between his classes at the University of
Minnesota in Minneapolis, he sometimes caught unexpected sight
of himself in a tall glass doorway or window. He always stopped to
stare: there he was, the big farm kid with a small handful of books.
Walter Hansen, the only twenty-year-old Undeclared Major on the
whole campus.

But even that wasn't true. Walter Hansen had declared a major
some time ago; he just hadn't felt up to telling anyone what it was.

At present Walter sat in the last, backward-facing seat of the
Greyhound bus, reading *The Collected Stories of John Cheever*. Occasionally he looked up to stare at the blue-tinted fields, which in their
passing pulled him, mile by mile, toward home. Toward his twenty-
first birthday this very weekend.

By the third hour of the trip Walter had a headache from reading.
He put away Cheever and began to watch the passing farms. It was
a sunny, wet April in central Minnesota. Farmers were trying to
spread manure. Their tractors left black ruts in the yellow corn stub-
ble, and once Walter saw two tractors chained together straining,
the big rear wheels spinning, throwing clods in the air, as they tried
to pull free a third spreader sunk to its hubs beneath an overenthusi-
astic load of dung.

At the end of the fourth hour Walter's hometown came onto the
horizon. It was low and scattered, and soon began to flash by in the
windows of the slowing bus like a family slide show that was putting
to sleep even the projector operator. A junkyard with a line of shining hubcaps nailed on the fence. A combination deer farm and
aquarium with its stuffed black bear wearing a yellow hula skirt, and
wheels that stood by the front door. Then the tall and narrow white

wooden houses. The square red brick buildings of Main Street, where the bus sighed to a stop at the Shell station. Ducking his head, Walter clambered down the bus steps and stood squinting in the sunlight.

Main Street was three blocks long. Its two-story buildings were fronted with painted tin awnings or cedar shake shingles to disguise the brick and make the buildings look lower and more modern. At the end of Main Street was the taller, dull gray tower of the feed mill. A yellow drift of cornmeal lay on its roof. A blue wheel of pigeons turned overhead. At the stoplight a '57 Chevy chirped its tires, accelerated rapidly for half a block, then braked sharply to turn down Main Street.

Which Walter planned to avoid. On Main Street he would have to speak to people. They would ask him things.

"Walt—so how's the rat race?"

"Walt—where does a person park down there?"

"So Walt, what was it you're going into again? Business? Engineering? Vetinary?"

Carrying his small suitcase, and looking neither left nor right, Walter slipped undetected across Main Street. He walked two blocks to the railroad crossing where he set out east.

The iron rails shone blue. Between the rails, tiny agates glinted red from their bed of gravel, and the flat, sun-warmed railroad ties exhaled a faint breath of creosote. On Walter's right, a robin dug for worms on the sunny south embankment; on the north side, the dirty remnant of a snowbank leaked water downhill. Walter stopped to poke at the snowbank with a stick. Beneath a black crust and mud and leaves, the snow was freshly white and sparkling—but destined, of course, to join the muddy pond water below. Walter thought about that. About destiny. He stood with the chill on his face from the old snowbank and the sun warm on his neck and back. There was a poem buried somewhere in that snowbank. Walter waited, but the first line would not visit him. He walked on.

Walter was soon out of town and into woods and fields. Arms outstretched, suitcase balanced atop his head, he walked one rail for twenty-two ties, certainly a record of some sort. Crows called. A red-headed woodpecker flopped from east to west across the rails. The bird was ridiculously heavy for the length of its wings, a fact which made Walter think of Natural Science. Biology. Veterinary Medicine and other majors with names as solid and normal as fork handles.

Animal Husbandry.

Technical Illustration.

Mechanical Engineering.

Ahead on Walter's left was a twenty-acre field of new oat seeding, brown in the low spots, dusty chartreuse on the higher crowns of the field.

Plant Science.

He could tell people he was developing new wheat strains for Third World countries, like Norman Borlaug.

He walked on, slower now, for around a slight bend he could see, a half mile ahead, the gray dome of his father's silo and the red shine of the dairy barn. He neared the corner post of the west field, where his father's land began. Half the field was gray, the other half was freshly black. He slowed further. A meadowlark called from a fence post. Walter stopped to pitch a rock at the bird.

Then he heard a tractor. From behind a broad swell in the field rose his father's blue cap, tan face, brown shirt, then the red snout of the Massey-Ferguson. The Massey pulled their green four-row corn planter. His father stood upright on the platform of the tractor. He stood that way to sight down the tractor's nose, to keep its front tires on the line scuffed in the dirt by the corn planter's marker on the previous round. Intermittently Walter's father swiveled his neck for a glance back at the planter. He looked, Walter knew, for the flap of a white rag tied around the main shaft; if the white flag waved, the main shaft turned, the planter plates revolved, pink kernels fell— Walter knew all that stuff.

He stopped walking. There were bushes along the fencerow, and he stooped to lower his profile, certain that his father hadn't seen him. First Walter wanted to go home, talk to his mother, have a cup of coffee. Two cups, maybe. A cinnamon roll. A bowl of bing cherries in sauce, with cream. Maybe one more splash of coffee. Then. Then he'd come back to the field to speak with his father.

Nearing the field's end, his father trailed back his right arm, found the cord, which he pulled at the same moment as he turned hard to left. Brakes croaked. Tripped, the marker arms rose, the Massey came hard around with its front wheels reaching for their new track, the planter straightened behind, the right arm with its shining disk fell, and his father, back to Walter, headed downfield.

Except that brakes croaked again and the tractor came to a stop. His father turned to Walter and held up a hand.

Walter waved once. He looked briefly behind him to the rails that led back toward town, then crossed the ditch and swung his suitcase over the barbed wire.

His father shut off the tractor. "Hey, Walt—" his father called.

Walter waved again.

His father waited by the corn planter. He smiled, his teeth white against the tan skin, the dust. Walter came up to him.

"Walt," his father said.

They stood there grinning at each other. They didn't shake hands. Growing up, Walter believed people shook hands only in the movies or on used-car lots. None of his relatives ever shook hands. Their greeting was to stand and grin at each other and raise their eyebrows up and down. At the university Walter and his circle of friends shook hands coming and going, European style.

"How's it going?" Walter said, touching his boot to the corn planter.

"She's rolling," his father said. "Got one disk that keeps dragging, but other than that."

People in Walter's family often did not complete their sentences.

"A disk dragging," Walter said.

"Yep," his father said. He squinted at Walter, looked down at his clean clothes. "What would you do for a stuck disk?" he asked.

"I'd take out the grease zerk and run a piece of wire in there. That failing, I'd take off the whole disk and soak it in a pan of diesel fuel overnight," Walter said.

Father and son grinned at each other.

His father took off his hat. His forehead was white, his hair coppery.

"So how's the rat race, son?"

"Not so bad," Walter said.

His father paused a moment. "Any . . . decisions yet?" his father said.

Walter swallowed. He looked off toward town. "About . . . a major, you mean?" Walter said.

His father waited.

"Well," Walter said. His mouth went dry. He swallowed twice. "Well," he said, "I think I'm going to major in English."

His father pursed his lips. He pulled off his work gloves one finger at a time. "English," he said.

"English," Walter nodded.

His father squinted. "Son, we already know English."

Walter stared. "Well, yessir, that's true. I mean, I'm going to study literature. Books. See how they're written. Maybe write one of my own some day."

His father rubbed his brown neck and stared downfield.

Two white sea gulls floated low over the fresh planting.

"So what do you think?" Walter said.

His father's forehead wrinkled and he turned back to Walter. "What could a person be, I mean with that kind of major? An English major," his father said, testing the phrase on his tongue and his lips.

"Be," Walter said. He fell silent. "Well, I don't know, I could be a . . . writer. A teacher maybe, though I don't think I want to teach. At least not for a while. I could be . . ." Then Walter's mind went blank. As blank and empty as the fields around him.

His father was silent. The meadowlark called again.

"I would just be myself, I guess," Walter said.

His father stared a moment at Walter. "Yourself, only smarter," he added.

"Yessir," Walter said quickly, "that's it."

His father squinted downfield at the gulls, then back at Walter. "Nobody talked you into this?"

Walter shook his head no.

"You like it when you're doing it?" his father asked. He glanced across his own field, at what he had planted.

Walter nodded.

His father looked back to Walter and thought another moment. "You think you can make a living at it?"

"Somehow," Walter said.

His father shrugged. "Then I can't see any trouble with it myself," he said. He glanced away, across the fields to the next closest set of barns and silos. "Your uncles, your grampa, they're another story, I suppose."

"They wouldn't have to know," Walter said quickly.

His father looked back to Walter and narrowed his eyes. "They ask me, I'll tell them," he said.

Walter smiled at his father. He started to take a step closer, but at that moment his father looked up at the sun. "We better keep rolling here," he said. He tossed his gloves to Walter. "Take her around once or twice while I eat my sandwich."

Walter climbed onto the tractor and brought up the RPMs. In another minute he was headed downfield. He stood upright on the platform and held tightly to the wheel. The leather gloves were still warm and damp from his father's hands. He sighted the Massey's radiator cap on the thin line in the dirt ahead, and held it there. Halfway downfield he remembered to check the planter flag; in one backward glance he saw his father in straight brown silhouette against the chartreuse band of the fencerow bushes, saw the stripe of fresh dirt unrolling behind, the green seed canisters, and below, the white flag waving. He let out a breath.

After two rounds, Walter began to relax. He began to feel the warm thermals from the engine, the cool breath of the earth below. Gulls hovered close over the tractor, their heads cocked earthward as they waited for the disks to turn up yellow cutworms. A red agate passed underneath and was covered by dirt. The corn planter rolled behind, and through the trip rope, a cotton cord gone smoothly black from grease and dusty gloves, Walter felt the shafts turning, the disks wheeling, the kernels dropping, the press wheel tamping the seed into four perfect rows.

Well, not entirely perfect rows.

Walter, by round four, had begun to think of other things. That whiteness beneath the old snowbank. The blue shine of the iron rails. The damp warmth of father's gloves. The heavy, chocolate-layer birthday cake that he knew, as certain as he knew the sun would set tonight and rise tomorrow, his mother had hidden in the pantry. Of being twenty-one and the limitless destiny, the endless prospects before him, Walter Hansen, English Major.

As he thought about these and other things, the tractor and its planter drifted a foot to the right, then a foot to the left, centered itself, then drifted again. At field's end his father stood up. He began to wave at Walter first with one hand, then both. But Walter drove on, downfield, smiling slightly to himself, puzzling over why it was he so seldom came home.

Culture and Enthusiasm:
A Secret Kept from Most People

by Carol Bly

Enthusiasm versus Indifferent Feelings

To modern psychologists, joy is a sophisticated emotion. That is because joy comes of someone's having consciously or half-consciously decided to enjoy individual moments as if they were all time. One old story and one old saying contain that idea. In the story, after a fisherman has saved its life, a flounder repeatedly comes out of the sea to offer status and wealth to the fisherman's wife. She wants a better cottage, then by degrees, a mansion, a castle, and retinues of servants. She wants to be king. When finally, in her mounting, frenetic discontent, she insists the flounder make her lord god of the universe, all the acquisitions disappear and she is back to being a poor fisherman's wife. Her downfall was of course greed, as most teachers tell listeners to the story, but more to our purpose here, her failure came of her being unable to shut off mental images of the future during any instant of the present. That is, as soon as she sat upon the throne in her royal castle, her mind made another image: herself ruling over the universe. She could not make a specific image stick and take whatever pleasure it had to offer.

The saying that carries the same warning about control of one's own imagination is: "Be ye even as a little child."

That particular advice has been a spiritual curiosity to sages and a conundrum to fools, not to mention a puzzle to the millions of us in between. We wobble through our perceptions. We make guesses, try them, reject interpretations that don't work. What has a little child got that I haven't got? is where I begin. The answer is that a child's experience is small and its level of cognition still simple. If that is true of kids, how should such small experience and limited cognition be good for getting into the kingdom of heaven or anything like it?

If one cannot make mental images of future likelihoods one's concentration in any given moment is undiluted. One feels thoroughgoing happiness at any gift just received (unlike the fisherman's wife). One's mind is too inexperienced to drop cynicism or fear into that happiness. "Here's a doll whose face breaks my heart," I think, not adding, "But doll or no doll, the Serbs are killing Bosnians and they are perfecting even more complicated biological warfare at Fort Detrick." I also add, "Yes, the doll gets all my love, but what if it gets left in the alley and someone drives over it?"

A child's joy in the moment is protected by ignorance and not yet having developed the acculturated mental process called tying one experience to others by dint of imagination. Making a mental image of something not here, or not yet here, or of something that may or may not become reality, is making connections, the great characteristic work of human brains. We need and want to learn to construct mental images, but when we hold one thing in our hands (this doll or this moment) and imagine another, far away or in the future, the brain is not acting "even as a little child." The major purpose of ego development is to be able to identify the meaning of what is here and what is now but at the same time to imagine what ought to be here and what we might try to bring about.

Yet full-hearted enthusiasm at any one moment involves deliberately cutting off those mental pictures of other realities or other ideal realities. A secret kept from most people is that, once one is educated, one has to use one's conscious willpower in order to feel intense joy.

Making a deliberate act of will to feel unmitigated enjoyment of the moment is not much taught by parents or schools in the United States. I am not sure it is taught by any nationality of parents and schools, but other cultures still give their children poetry and poetry contains sharp feelings of the moment. Poets get hold of the tiniest thing and decide it is wonderful. They not only give an unusual focus of attention to a tiny thing, but being adults with grown-up cognitive habits, they often race into their own cloakroom of emotions, grab something, and bring it back out to set alongside the tiny object they have just paid attention to. Ted

Kooser's "Daddy Longlegs" is a case in point. Some parents show their children spiders and much else, and invite children to enjoy them, but most probably do not. Levelheadedness is our mood in the late 1990s. Unfortunately, by levelheadedness what most of us mean is levelheartedness. Solitude and deliberate acts of will, like thinking about a spider, are what we need, but life in groups and ignorance of stories is our modern style.

Most of us are in groups all day. We work in groups. There are people around us in our apartment buildings and in our houses. Hour after hour we are ringed with acquaintances at the gym, colleagues at work, family members, other directors on the board. Being in the presence of others is so common now, as opposed to a century ago, that lots of people choose to play radios or televisions constantly so that even when they *are* alone they hear the sounds of other people.

Intense feeling about life, not genial fellowship, is what all good literature and the nonmanipulative kinds of psychology are about. Yet because we spend hours and hours of each day in the low-level feelings that suit communal life, we may snort at the idea of intense feelings being a good thing. Literature and psychology get snorted at, generally, by people who aren't familiar with either. The gift of enthusiasm is a secret, in the way that the satellite navigation signals hold life-giving information but are a secret to people who don't know how to pick them up.

How do literature and psychotherapy go about bringing us enthusiasm for life? Both rely a good deal on this expectation: when we get unsnarled from the rigid lies told us by the culture, told us often by parents, then carried into our own minds and told us by ourselves to ourselves, over and over, then sharp, fresh feelings can take their place inside us. Psychologists seem to see the rigid lies or fears as a mangrove tangle: one chops one's way clear of this binding root, then that binding root, either fast through therapy or taking a lifetime by just getting older. Once one is out of the tangle, one's own will is freed to dash around through the beautiful joys and thoroughgoing sorrows for which our species has some taste.

Once the will is free, we become expressive, feeling people.

Literary people regard expressiveness as a natural trait inside each of us until someone or some circumstance represses it. People write stories and poems, and read stories and poems, with the idea of checking into that old burrow of intense feeling. A reader is something like a mole coming across the old wonderful scent of home. Psychologists talk about freeing a person from outdated or inappropriate strictures. Their image is nearer the mangrove image.

The idea of both psychology and good literature is that such a home is the rightful inheritance of everyone. A wide range of feeling is good, not bad. In serious literature, the good guys are those with strong takes on the world, like the curious, spontaneous Tommy in "Gryphon," not the depressed mother or Mr. Hibler or Wayne Razmer. The reason is that Tommy is moving toward the gorgeous high expectations of our species.

The point of poor literature is to do the opposite: it is to distract us from much intensity. Human beings write and publish more sluggish literature than high-spirited literature, a cultural factor that makes it sound a little crazy to say, "Let's have wider mood swings! Let's move from enjoyable distraction to passionate intensity!"

We are an ill-behaved species, generally speaking. Still, we have invented and carved into the stones of nearly every religion three ideas that no other animal has recorded so far. No animal would stop licking the red off its paws for an abstract idea, never mind a moral abstraction.

The first idea is that you shouldn't hurt the innocent of your own species, even if they happen not to be known to you personally. The second is that mercy is a positive good, not just a default activity of the weak. The third idea is that it is good to stand apart from the group when the group is unjust, even if the group responds with muscle and scorn. Motivation for standing apart from the group has to come from integrity, never from wanting profit. No practical extrovert would go to the grief of such loneliness.

I have been visualizing what it is like for someone to entertain

his or her first powerful ethical conviction. Let u
again the sister and brother who had been prom
Crane Beach. Let us say that the first powerful ethic
little girl's life is that her father's savaging of her bod
bedroom is not "just the way it goes" but a bad thing

This inner idea comes to the girl in a sluggish wa   very
idea of applying the notion of *wrongness* to a member of her own
family feels unpromising. Still standing outside her parents' bedroom door with her little brother, she feels apologetic. A minute
passes, and her mind has made the jump. She is now thinking
right and wrong about something in her own life. She is cognitively not the same person she was a minute before.

"That's right," she says, wonderingly but with growing confidence. "Brutalization in my family is not all right. It is bad." (She
might not say "brutalization," but she would mean precisely that.)

Here is an image for the little girl's brain. We can imagine the
dendritic trees of the brain, neurons with branches that thicken
and complicate just as a tree's branching out thickens and grows
complex if the tree gets enough nutrients and fair sky to fulfill its
fate as a tree. If we now change our image slightly, we get close to
an actual brain process: let us imagine that the tree is not a tree of
wood or of human flesh, but of electric fire, like the trees of lightning one sometimes sees in a hot sky. The neuron pattern is like
that. When the little girl realizes that what is merely familiar,
merely a thing of practical nature such as her mother and father,
is also a group of ethical or unethical potentials, new electrical firing goes branching about in her brain's circuit. Next time she considers some personal reality and asks herself, "What is the ethics
of this?" the brain will do it faster, because it has been over the
new electric routing and knows the shape of that new tree. She
learns to snub all decision making for a moment in order to practice discernment. The very process of such deliberation, such paying attention, excites the mind. Another new surge of fiery idea
whips along some branching route that it, in turn, will try again
and again. For example, say that she asked, "Is Dad's having raped
me either fair or unfair and not just a values-free event?" Such a

question in itself is enhancement to the brain. The brain puts an increased value on given sets of paths just from having used them. As it does more and more complex referencing it develops a taste for ever more complex referencing.

But now the little girl asks, "Is the fact that it was a sunny day for the picnic (as it was) a question of right or wrong?" She decides, "No, it is not. Weather is appropriate to nature and I need not double-think it, ethically." Now she has practiced a civilized process we might call "quietly, not frantically, taking counsel with herself"—or, to use the conventional theological word, *discernment.* The moment she discerns, her brain is further enhanced.

Discernment between what is ethical and therefore our passionate business and what is nature and therefore only our practical business distinguishes a cultural life, no matter how problematic, from mere primitive nervousness. I count it as primitive nervousness if one sees lightning and says, "That is punishment because I or we have done such and such." We have these sorts of illogical, self-centered suppositions lying around near the base of our brains like sunken and sea-furred shipwrecks. If we get so scared that we become demoralized we sometimes stumble backward into those ancient emotions. It is not by chance that we use the word *demoralization* to describe our condition when we are not thinking at the most realistic level we can.

This book has paid a lot of attention to what I call the American psychological class system. Here is the final mention of the subject: culturally lucky people have a safe refuge that they don't publicize much—just as financially lucky people who have chosen to isolate themselves in walled estates with their own power systems do not publicize their arrangements. The children of educated people get the liberal arts educations that reinforce and develop *intense feeling and freedom of feeling.* The children of less educated or of uneducated people, even at the end of the twentieth century, are usually led to believe that education is a means for getting high starting salaries. They are usually told to focus upon technical, extroverted subjects. They are led to believe that the thinking that counts for anything is *how-to* thinking.

Over and over, the message of school systems, both explicitly and implicitly, has been that education is the road to technology, and technology is the road to profit. Those who peddle that message are not consciously committing a cultural wrong. At one level of understanding, they are right: America steps on people who haven't "taken up" something at the college level. Teachers know that and don't want their kids stepped on. All those Main Street characters in Will Weaver's story believe that the sensible question to ask young people is, "What was it you're going into again? Business? Engineering? Vetinary?" Certainly not, "Hey, Walt! Are you taking up literature or social psychology in order to fulfill your potential, or what?"

The good news about our class system is that more and more teachers in elementary schools feel called to enable young people to write their own stories and to appropriate literature for their own uses. The increasing presence of therapy and ethics programming in American public life is slowly—slowly—undoing the old idea that only girls and upper-class boys care for inner feelings. They are undoing the old dynamic that boys and engineers and soldiers and scientists are to regard feeling as either pansy fluff or disagreeable *affect*. When we get rid of that idea completely we will have removed most of the psychological kind of bullying that goes on in the education system. At that point, young people, such as the victims in Tom McGrath's "Ode for the American Dead in Asia," will no longer be empty-headed tennis players who have no access to noble feelings except through the tinsel patriotism offered them.

In a fair, democratic educational system, every kid and every adult would sense validation or self-recognition in Ted Kooser's "Daddy Longlegs." They would recognize not just the spider: they would feel how one's own personality wants to live "springy" above bottom-level cant, not flat in it. I think of the ground here as the omnipresent tepid life, with its tepid communal doctrines breeding their tepid emotions.

I will make a rough guess at a few of the inner, acculturated ideas that help us live springily above boredom:

Wanting to live at some level of virtue
Wanting to live in love with everything
Hating any injustice that we catch sight of

What first showed me that joy and horror and everything in between is for everyone, not for only certain "types," was my use of "continuum lines" during the early 1980s.

The 1970s had been the decade of the facilitator. Facilitators were then a new cultural artifact. They invented more ingenious "tools" for group dynamics in one decade than you could use in a thousand retreats or seminars. There were even whole facilitated games that took groups of fifteen or twenty people several hours to play. Facilitated games and group dynamics were always what social workers call "intentional"; that is, they were designed to raise people's awareness of ethical issues they hadn't noticed.

A common dynamic was the "continuum line," and its goal was threefold: getting half strangers in an ongoing group acquainted with one another, making them conscious of their own opinions on the particulars of an ethical issue, and showing them that it is not disastrous to talk about thoughts and feelings.

We were a group of Farmers Union members studying the humanities. Our ethics issue had to do with family farming: was family farming culturally valuable to America, or was it merely nostalgic but out-of-date, like shocking wheat?

Those who felt one way about it were designated Opinion A people; those who felt the opposite were Opinion B. Everyone had to stand up and arrange themselves in a line across the room, taking places according to the intensity of their convictions.

A few people leaped out of their conference chairs. They raced for the far ends, A and B: these were the strong thinkers, people who were used to expressing themselves. They were comparatively fearless and jostled one another, down there at either end, each trying to get the actual end position, like crew members who all want to row stroke. After they took their positions, they began enjoying themselves; they baited the crowd in the middle.

In the middle were the unpracticed people. They could hardly tell where to place themselves on the line. Some didn't even talk: they guessed, because, as they later explained during the debriefing, they felt it was intrusive to ask others the questions they would need to ask in order to place themselves either A-ward or B-ward of others. The middle people kept twining around, changing places, looking anxious. They peered into one another's faces, listening, explaining, assessing, but there was a piteous quality to it.

I stopped the process in order to announce that only half the purpose of the continuum line was educational: it was supposed to be a chance to communicate, too. Now some of the middle people looked more anxious than before. They interviewed each other now, with shy, brittle, courageous smiles.

What struck me, in the end, was not that the extreme-opinion people found their places so easily. Of course they would. It was that the low-key-opinion people could not get the hang of any playfulness about it. If they are naturally low-key, I had thought, they will enjoy the middle position all right. They will find one another in the middle and be glad of like-feathered birds. They weren't. I learned something that has stuck with me ever since: intense feeling is for all of us. If it were not, the middle people that day would have been as happy as the End-A and End-B people. They were not happy because deep in their unconscious minds were End-A and End-B convictions (if conviction is thought and feeling wrapped around each other). But somewhere between birth and joining the National Farmers Union, our culture had told them to respect only low-key feelings, so they had dutifully done that. Therewith much cognitive playfulness had seeped away from their imaginations.

Great art had better be dealt to everyone—not murder mysteries and romances for the many and Weaver and Levertov and Helprin and Kooser and Baxter and Robert Bly and Wilbur and Ignatow for the few. The authors in this chapter should by rights be taught to everybody. If there has been cultural abuse—if we are serious about cultural abuse—then there must be therapeutic restitution. Somehow we must release the victims of low-key opinion and low-key emotion from the lies they have drunk up

and the fears that someone has slapped into them, just as Denise
Levertov said.

Here is her democratic stanza again:

> . . . All humankind
> women and men,
> hungry,
> hungry beyond the hunger
> for food, for justice,
> pick themselves up and stumble on
> for this: to transcend barriers, longing
> for absolutions each of each by each,
> luxurious unlearning
> of lies and fears,
> for joy, that *throws down the reins*
> on the neck of
>   *the divine animal*
> *who carries us through the world.*[1]

And here is Paula Gutlove of the Center for Psychology and Social
Change on the same subject: "disrupting old patterns" is an undoing of lies.

> Family systems theory emphasizes relationships, interactive
> patterns, and context. Nations, like families, must be able to
> recognize when their belief systems are based on obsolete and
> constricted habits of thought that lead to undesirable actions
> and outcomes. Family systems therapy strives to disrupt and
> transform old patterns of belief and behavior, while fostering
> an openness to new information and the creation of fresh so-
> lutions. Family therapists have a repertoire of techniques to ef-
> fect such changes.[2]

I am going to make a short paraphrase of a group dynamics
scheme designed by one of the greatest thinkers about group therapy, Irvin D. Yalom. Dr. Yalom developed ways for a number of
human beings to sit around together in a regularly convened
group with the express purpose of teaching people with aimless or
mixed-up feelings to find their *own* deep truths. (Dr. Yalom's description of this process is presented in the Appendix to this book.)

Dr. Yalom developed a list of principles that one after another, in order, gradually show a person who relates poorly, to others and to himself or herself, how to shake free of false, useless assumptions—and how to lay aside ancient fears. Although a major purpose of Dr. Yalom's particular groups was to develop workable communication styles with other people, its process makes a person able to discern his or her own ideas more clearly. The reason for this surprising improvement was that the "patient" (Dr. Yalom's groups were formed of hospital residents) heard for the first time which of his or her characteristics drove other people away, and therefore saw (also for the first time) that the whole of the self was not worthless or bad. If you have been thinking that you were all around a bad person, it is cheering to find that it is only your poor friendship skills that are tripping you up. These patients brighten up and feel supported enough, therefore, so they can begin to observe their own behavior with a little detachment. Next, they can see that they are the people to make the changes: they are responsible for their own behavior. They are the makers of their own worlds. Such a feeling—that one makes one's own world—is stronger stuff than most of us carry in our psyches.

Dr. Yalom's group members were every day up for more ego risk-taking. They were shown how to look at their own behavior and decide which of it was all right and which wasn't. Soon they saw that other things, if they looked at them straight, could do with some change, too. "Social anxiety decreases; self-esteem rises."

Here is how the rest of us get into the act. If one can break apart one's own behavior, putting different judgments on different parts of it, then one can in like manner break apart one's heretofore rigid, all-of-a-piece doctrines. Let us say that someone desperately clings to family loyalty. If that person can mount enough confidence so that he or she can honor *some* of the family ways, and abandon others, then the fear is gone. The family will be all right! But no one may intrude on anyone else. The good parts won't be lost—only the bad.

It is no accident that Denise Levertov saw how closely lie two experiences—better interpersonal relationships (an expression I am grateful does not show up in her work) and better spiritual insight:

> [Human beings] transcend barriers, longing
> for absolutions each of each by each,
> luxurious unlearning
> of lies and fears . . .

What is an all-purpose way to use Yalom's group dynamics? I propose that we pretend our whole *self* is the group: it is the outlying organization that has members (things inside ourselves) somehow relating to each other, badly or well, tidily or untidily in our personality. Then we pretend that each opinion, each idea, each feeling, about nearly anything—even tiny feelings like the pleasure of watching a daddy longlegs cross the floor—are members of the group, and that they all have been badly cared for. But now they are going to be well cared for. We will pay attention to intricate insights and feelings, the way artists do in themselves, the way therapists do in others—and we will promise our whole self and each individual feeling we have that this is a safe place. Such a decision means we have to *make* ourselves a safe place for our insights and emotions.

No matter what society we live in, the waste of strong feelings is the mode a good deal of the time. Just living along, kidding, in what Tom McGrath called "summer follies," teasing anyone who is sensitive, the way Clare's parents teased her, or asking one another, "Walt—so how's the rat race?"—hundreds of hours of normal, even culturally privileged life goes into that cheery, tinny life.

Even people who are much loved may not have a safe place for their own serious nature. They resort to diaries. Anne Frank reported herself as a lucky person (she probably enjoyed a thousand times the self-confidence of the average mental hospital patient), yet she had only a diary as a safe place for her serious nature.

I especially liked an expression of hers that was translated to a handy British phrase, "the common round." It reminds us of what befuddles people in the middle of a continuum line:

> Let me put it more clearly, since no one will believe that a
> girl of thirteen feels herself quite alone in the world nor is it so.
> I have darling parents and a sister of sixteen. I know about
> thirty people whom one might call friends—I have strings of

boyfriends, anxious to catch a glimpse of me through mirrors in class. I have relations, aunts and uncles, who are darlings, too, a good home, no—I don't seem to lack anything. But it's the same with all my friends, just fun and joking, nothing more. I can never bring myself to talk of anything outside the common round.[3]

It must be this "common round" that actually discourages our private seriousness. I note how Dr. Yalom says of our own worlds (which we make ourselves) that "the depth and meaningfulness of this awareness is directly proportional to the amount of affect associated with the sequence." That is terrible social science language for this marvelous point: the stronger our feelings about our own outlook and our own world, and the more passionately we realize that we ourselves must make any moral changes we want, the more exhilarating and meaningful is our life.

Culture as a Task of Adulthood

Will Weaver's story is about deliberately educating oneself for the 201,480 hours of life in which an adult between the ages of twenty-one and ninety is not asleep or at work, as opposed to educating oneself for the 88,000 hours an employed adult between the ages of twenty-one and sixty-five, omitting two-week holidays, spends in the workplace.

Anyone would readily agree that it would be better to educate for 201,000 hours than for 88,000 hours, but that is a liberal arts idea, and the liberal arts idea is not yet the guiding principle of rural communities. In theory, the liberal arts—majoring in English, for example—lead you to principled thinking and therefore intense feelings. From Weaver's "The Undeclared Major," for example, we learn that something dirty and ordinary-looking on the outside can in fact be quite brilliant inside (like a snowdrift, like deciding to read and write literature). In *theory* we know that, but in fact it is a secret to do with ecstasy and art that is kept from nearly everybody.

Nothing illustrates this secret better than Weaver's story in which he shows us the unswerving track of the straight, Western

European/American class system—the boy scared to tell towns-folk that he means to major in English, not in "business, engineering, or vetinary." He is afraid to tell his father, too. Still, it is the weekend of his twenty-first birthday, the event symbolic of becoming an adult, so he has gathered his spunk to tell.

This story is eagerly read in Minnesota as a piece of humorous site-specific sociology. Reading "The Undeclared Major" as local color is like painting TAXI on the door of a stretch DC-9 and then driving it back and forth on the taxiways.

Weaver tells his story with such an accurate ear for midwestern rural life that it lends itself to sociological interpretation. The author's theme, however, is not sociology. "The Undeclared Major" is about what happens when one member of a community and a family decides to escape the practical conventions of his class and to study human nature instead.

From then on, life is *culture*, with what culture involves—some separation from the pack, renewed love of natural beauty, a wider range of strong feelings than one allowed oneself or even was aware of before. The story of the herd back there on Main Street may be sociology; Walt's own story is about how the individual personality uses culture to wake itself up. He uses culture the way the Prodigal Son used travel into the world. The Prodigal Son deepened his feelings, including affection for his own father. Into the bargain he risked, and lost, his economic stake. Walt's venture into reading and writing literature intensifies his feelings, and, even in the time of the story, keeps his affection for the father. Both the Prodigal Son and Walt challenge their families' systems. Whenever one person escapes from the behavioral expectations of a family, the other members divide into those who will empathically hear out the new notions, thus keeping their love for the errant member intact, and those who are overchallenged—threatened—and offended. We haven't much to go on regarding Walt's grouping: Weaver never suggests that the mother expresses any ideas other than love-through-baking.

A surprising sociological tangent to this story is that farm boys are the last enclave of people whose childhood and teenage work is done in solitude. They are therefore well out of the loop of most of the ethics conversations that wash back and forth in our mass culture. The deliberations at Nuremburg and Kent State and on the decks of Greenpeace ships are not farm boys' ethics. Farm boys who go to college and study the liberal arts come across and usually love Wendell Berry and grow from reading his thoughts, but by then they are in their twenties: in those twenty years they have not discussed whether or not, like Thoreau, to part from the values of their own nation.

They are ethically at risk, not because they have been taught bad morals but because they have a kind of moral vacuum. In *Breaking Ranks*, as pointed out in chapter 6, Melissa Everett reports that farm boys, being comparatively empty of ethical convictions other than the goodness of hard work, have classically been fodder for intelligence recruiters.

If hours of solitude and freedom from American popular culture leave one in a kind of ethical vacuum, those hours of solitude can also work to set a person free of our sluggish culture. In "The Undecided Major" we see a farm boy who has had hours empty of American sound—free of the rock beat, free of the kidding around in groups—so he is at risk for exploring his own potential. His brain, hour for hour, has been less "happy in [his] summer follies" than the brains of the boys in McGrath's poem. No one put a tennis racquet into his hand. Eighty-eight percent of Americans farmed in President Lincoln's time; now between one and three percent of Americans farm. In the 1990s, by far the majority of young people are in each other's company most of the time. They normalize one another. They suffer from the bystander effect with regard to their own individuality; that is, their own individuality stands outside the group. If the group notices another's individuality at all, they might only gape, the way groups gape at some passing source of stimulus—a knifing or something on television or an unusual dog in the back of a passing pickup. They don't make much of whatever the passing stimulus may be. Nor does that part of a young person who is a member of the group make much of whatever some passing sense of his inner self may be.

I bring this up because of an unlikely sociological truth about who reads serious literature, expecting something from it, and who doesn't. English majors tend to stop reading the *best* literature within two or three years of their leaving college. Most former English majors over thirty years old have never heard of Will Weaver or Susan Lowell or Ted Kooser. They have heard of Wendell Berry because he is so famous, but they don't know his work. They have not read Mark Helprin or Louis Simpson or David Ignatow. They may have derided Robert Bly for male separatism, but they don't know his exquisite poems. Too few literary people of thirty and forty know Charles Baxter's work, although his short stories are wonderful and often about sensitive people in their thirties and forties.

The cultural expectation used to be that you find a field that suits you, "study what you most affect," as Shakespeare put it, in order to nourish some deep part of your own personality. That would suggest that English majors would look to the best in literature, but perhaps the new no-man's land of American culture tells us of a new pattern: ethics seminars in corporate workplaces are using serious literature. The MOTHEREAD programs for teenage mothers, started in North Carolina and picked up by the Minnesota Humanities Commission and other cultural groups, are using serious literature, written and oral. Psychology professors use literature. Graduate schools of social work use literature.

Perhaps learning from profound *story*, one's own or others', is passing into surprising hands. The whole question of who uses literature *how* is fascinating. Jim Harrison's Clare and Donald Hall's narrator have read more literature than any other characters in the literary selections of this book. They are literature major *types*, but neither of them used literature as a means of confrontation in their own lives. Perhaps their cultural training, with its supposedly thoughtful reading of literature, simply immunized them to the uses literature can provide in moral development.

Will Weaver's Walter Hansen, unlike Clare or Hall's narrator, is vulnerable to whatever his reading can give him:

> As Walter shambled between his classes at the University of Minnesota in Minneapolis, he sometimes caught unexpected

sight of himself in a tall glass doorway or window. He always stopped to stare: there he was, the big farm kid with a small handful of books.

And here is Weaver's symbolic remark about taking literature seriously, taking any given moment seriously:

> Walter stopped to poke at the snowbank with a stick. Beneath a black crust and mud and leaves, the snow was freshly white and sparkling—but destined, of course, to join the muddy pond water below. Walter thought about that.

The surface of things may be covered with snirt (dirt and snow mixed, crusted over a field or a ditch, because the beastly practice of fall plowing lets the wind blow the topsoil together during the winter). The surface may be dark, but once you look inside something, the way you have to poke your unconscious inner life with a stick, there is the pure beauty still.

At the moment when Walter has finally told his father he will major in English, two white gulls float low over the fresh planting. Everyone who knows midwestern farming knows that seagulls do in fact follow tractors plowing or disking and planting, because the bottoms and disks and chains go hooking through the soil turning up a million Christmas dinners of worms. So a cynic might say Weaver's having the two white birds pass is just a nice piece of mild realism like any other piece of accurate realism. Not two white birds at just that moment. The birds tell us: this Walt has got up his nerve and said it and now he is going to have some spiritual good luck. And he has the good luck of having an empathic father: the man has just asked him what he hopes to become (with this English major):

> "I would just be myself, I guess," Walter said.
> His father stared a moment at Walter. "Yourself, only smarter," he added.
> "Yessir," Walter said quickly, "that's it."

In that cupful of conversation lies some hint of why Walter, rather than Clare, will get clear of a merely practical life. He has a

wonderful father. His father engages in three psychotherapeuti-
cally sophisticated practices:

1. He brings out into the open the central problem between
   them (Walter's major).
2. He makes up his mind to hear out whatever explanation
   Walter gives. He tries to get the feel of the son's idea: "'An
   English major,' his father said, testing the phrase on his
   tongue and his lips."
3. Then the rarest piece of communication between American
   parents and children: the father repeats back to the son what
   the son has said, adding the interpretation he makes of it:
   "'Yourself, only smarter.'"

The first two of these three steps are called very good manners
by traditional people. All three together are called good communication or the first three levels of "basic empathy" by social
workers. Step 3, the *reflecting back* of Walter's own philosophy in
the father's voice, plus the father's own take on the son's idea
("'Yourself, only smarter'"), is one of the greatest stimuli to cognitive and ethical growth in the son or whoever the speaker is
whose ideas are being respectfully "reflected back." Such reflection leads a child to delight in human conversation, and in fact
gives such high expectation of human conversation that a child
might well never settle for bullying someone just to break up the
boredom. I wish we had trustworthy statistics on exactly which
children set themselves to humiliating or beating up others in
third-grade playgrounds: perhaps we would find that the recess
bullies had seldom or never had their remarks about life "reflected
back" to them by adults in authority.

Then two charming points about this particular son of the
father: Walt is afraid to leave the herd, even though he has already left it. He is afraid of the opinions of his uncles and
grampa. I always feel cheered by someone else's cowardice.
"'They wouldn't have to know,' Walter said quickly."

But the father wasn't a coward to be trifled with. He "narrowed
his eyes. 'They ask me, I'll tell them.'" That line reminds me of

Chekhov's telling his brother Nicolai that cultivated people despise lies. They hate lying worse than anything else. The father reminds us of Professor Jane Loevinger's remark that character formation is the work of children. Walt has work left to do: he must quit being a coward.

After Walter confesses he will major in English he gets onto his dad's planter for a few passes up and down the field. The tractor veers left, the tractor veers right. Walt doesn't stay in the row— well, thinking people rejoice in their contemplations and they tend to get out of row. Habitués of convention, not thinkers, feel secure and validated when they cannot hear the stamp of their own feet because they are in perfect cadence with the group.

But Walter also feels the warmth that lingers in his father's gloves. This detail gives the balance and complication that both beginning writers and beginning psychologists work hard to keep in mind. Someone may be driving a Massey-Ferguson out of row, but he also is blessed by the warmth of his father's hands. That gloves detail in this story is the gift of a pro.

Weaver's story is entirely unromantic. It is about culture—that mixture of love of life and looking forward to as much as one can make of it, getting pulled looking backward to old simple answers, and finally, getting up your nerve to become a change agent. If you want to find any pure white under a dirty crust of snow you have to poke at it with a sharp stick. We can ask ourselves, too, about Weaver's striking observation that Walter couldn't get a poem out of it. We remember Joyce Carol Oates trying willfully to write a poem, "something short, tight, mean," and ending up instead with a not particularly lovely insight into her own character. Spiritually speaking, can one or can one not turn a swift moment's gift—like poking a stick through the snirt to the white snow—to one's own uses, such as writing a work of art? I would guess that a Zen master would slap our heads just then.

In theory, we know that if one *fails* to contemplate life, life will be brutal. People were whining about it a long time before Thoreau did. When we are children we know intuitively that contemplation is wonderful. The dullest young human being knows that anticipating anything like Christmas or the coming of spring doubles and triples the pleasure of it. Putting a name on feelings intensifies the feelings. Why should naming things make any difference to our level of feelings? It is odd that abusive parents are more likely to call their children "honey," "hon," and "sweetie" than to use their names. Emotionally repressed people call one another by name less than people in touch with their own expressiveness. And when we ask ourselves why *naming* is so refreshing to us, we can also ask how *not* naming something—such as love, honor, and gratitude—affects us. We had better ask this question, since not naming things is an intensifying phenomenon of our culture.

Using words for experience redoubles our passions. We know that much, on a humorous level, when we read Irish curses. If I were so angry at some fellow Irish American as to call her a "whey-faced slut"—a term from a famous Irish curse—I would feel all the more strongly what a slut she was after hearing my voice say so. On a serious level, however, the same dynamic seems to operate. When we love, it is not enough merely to cling, trembling, to each other; we want to *say* that we love each other, as well. That's why lovers are always getting caught with incriminating packets of letters. You would think people who should theoretically not be thinking of each other's bodies could shut up about their feelings, but no, the enormous pleasure of putting words to invisible feelings seduces them into writing letters. Anything once said acquires some holiness, whether or not it really is holy. Many of us ask one another with exasperation, "Goodness! Do you believe everything you read?" The cunning answer to that is, "No, I do not believe everything I read, but I *like* ideas for which I have words a little more than feelings without words."

We do a number of tasks in the name of culture, only one of which is to commit ourselves, as Walt did, to *invisible values*. Another is to gather and organize information not of immediate practical value. A third task of culture is *enthusiasm for the large scene*. The very definition of a "cultivated person" is someone who keeps scanning around outside of his or her own immediate surroundings, and even better, likes to see parallels between any private life and the great public lives of history.

A person of culture has enough willpower to drop his or her own goals and expertise from time to time—in order to pay attention to an untoward or sudden happening. Even though one happens to be engaged in listening to birdsong, a person of culture pays attention to the chuffing of a bear.

One of the happy works of Garrison Keillor has a scene in which, as a small boy, he stood near grown men at a wake. He heard the deep sounds of their quiet voices. How dignified their quiet sharing and mourning, he thought. He crept closer and found they were comparing chassis of two different makes of car. The little boy was disappointed: even at a wake, shallow everyday life called to them the way people holding their breath under water long to return to the surface. A job of culture is to teach us how to stay longer in the depths.

Not just Keillor but children in general love their parents' serious talk; they love odd conversations about queer subjects to tumble about at suppertime. Children have the greatest taste for everyone's weighing any preposterous information someone else brings to the group. Since children have so little information in their docket so far, all news seems somewhat preposterous to them. They joyfully tolerate very wild stuff.

One can hardly exaggerate the joy and freedom of mind it gives a child to have parents who are interested in all sorts of things. Apropos, note the dreadful limitation of culture in the mother, in "Gryphon." Her son comes home with fascinating conversational offerings, but she has no curiosity. Culturally speaking, she is a deadbeat—someone who destroys enthusiasm.

The core of Mortimer J. Adler's mourning what he calls "the disappearance of culture" is that we are mostly specialists. Universities do not teach students to be generally "cultured people," as Ortega y Gasset pointed out as long ago as 1930. Specialization has grown geometrically since then, and Adler is indignant over the fact that people do not study the "basic ideas that are everybody's business."[4]

In his famous "Letter to Nicolai," Chekhov upbraids a worth-less brother for being a selfish slob: "You have only one fault. Your false position, your unhappiness, your intestinal catarrh are all due to it. It is your utter lack of culture."

Then Chekhov goes on to define cultured people in one of the most lucid letters anyone has ever written. Chekhov's cultured person is a dignified, unself-centered, and honest person. Cul-tured people, Chekhov says, "are candid, and dread lying as they dread fire. They do not lie even about trifles."[5] In Chekhov's thinking, cultured people are as anxious not to be too easy on themselves as 1990s pundits are happy to tell each other not to be so hard on themselves.

Enthusiasm for flights of fancy is an idiosyncratic task of cul-ture. The most curious children and the most speculative adults are those who are open to extreme ideas and to wild hypotheses. Stephen Jay Gould has suggested that a few members of a species presumably do the testing around the edges of the whole group's knowledge. They nudge things along the road. They stick their noses and paws and hands into water. "Gryphon" gives us Tommy as someone at a child's level paying attention to a new stimulus even though it sounds crazy.

"Gryphon" is funny only as Kafka is funny. The circumstances are wretched and, alas, so like life in most schools and homes, a reader can't read it for the gags. Tommy kisses those who don't re-spond. He gives ideas to those who not only don't think but don't respect thinking. He stands up, as Walt Whitman tells us to do, for the crazy.

He is starving for culture in Mr. Hibler's crummy class. He longs for any word about heroic virtue. That longing is one of the gifts of culture. Tommy has a tolerant nature, as one must if one goes to grade school and lives in a dull household. He is marking the sun's progress on the north wall of the classroom as if it were the pyramids the substitute teacher told them of.

Before speaking more of Tommy, I would like to point out how carefully this story is made: the half-crazy substitute teacher's speeches to the children start with her adjuring them to mercy.

She asks the boys if they are tormenting an animal. Her last advisory to the children is her telling them that death is a transformation. She appears to be someone moving into a manic episode of a bipolar disorder, so much of what she says is grandiose and her judgment is appalling. Obviously, Miss Ferenczi would not pass the simplest reality checkpoint. Yet she is talking about mercy and truth and perspective.

We can borrow from the social scientists a way to read this story. We make a list of everything she says, with an analytic remark or two of our own at the right of each item. The list might resemble one we could make of our own thoughts for a whole day. We expect to remove any grandiosity from our own thoughts. We can remove grandiosity and purely insane observations from Miss Ferenczi's offerings. It helps to bear in mind that if Miss Ferenczi is manic, Tommy's mother is depressive, and people in both those states inhabit our children's worlds. My idea is to try some of the ways in which Irvin Yalom's "group" members handle one another's ideas: they call one another on the crazy stuff, yet stay respectful enough of the other ideas. The charm of Charles Baxter's Tommy is that he is trying to practice discernment. He also wants to get into the act: Tommy's main passion is to escape the vapid center of life with the deadbeats, the Wayne Razmers of the world, the Mr. Hiblers, with their lists of hard-shelled things that are hollow. He does not want to be something with a hard outer shell and a hollow inside.

The cultural, moral life is not easily come by, it would seem. What a mind killer the conversation below is—although it is such a normal middle-class conversation one hardly notices the mother's unremitting mean-spiritedness:

> "Hi, Mom," I said, hopping around the playpen to kiss her. "Guess what?"
>
> "I have no idea." [This response alone is sardonic, signaling more coolness to come.]
>
> "We had this substitute today, Miss Ferenczi, and I'd never seen her before, and she had all these stories and ideas and stuff."
>
> "Well. That's good." My mother looked out the window. . . .

In the 1990s parents are instructed *not* to look out the window when the "stories and ideas and stuff" come into the conversation. The good news is that so many parents now deliberately tell stories to children and deliberately listen to stories that their children save up to tell them.

As an aside, note that the names of characters and objects in Baxter's story are wonderful: Ferenczi, like the classical psychoanalyst; *Broad Horizons*, the textbook; Hibler, a mix of *crippler* and *hobble* and *Hitler*.

"Gryphon" seems to say that intellectual boredom and poor communication between people are a chilling enough combination so that a smart kid will tolerate lots of craziness and cruelty just to escape the boredom. The little boy in this story is interested not only in new, wider philosophies but also in how intellectual life hangs in balance with character: One of his classmates "was a bad person . . . but at times of crisis she spoke the truth."

Innovative ideas are nothing if you don't protect them from cynics and power brokers. In the end, Tommy punches out the kid who tells on Miss Ferenczi. Of the literary selections in this book, Baxter's story is the only one in which a champion appears to save the princess of truth. In the other poem-stories and short stories, the heroes bravely arrive at hard truths, but there is no one outside themselves to shout hurrah. All of the embattled seekers in these narratives could have used a champion—Clare might have had one in Zilpha, but Zilpha died. Her daughter served as well as she could from a distance. Wallich had an enemy to his spirit, Franzen, so he used Beethoven and the champion inside himself, the dreamer. This sounds coarse, but I can't help thinking that if someone like Tommy had told off Franzen, in front of Wallich, the way Tommy told off Wayne Razmer, Wallich would have slung himself past the Schreuderspitze and into his proper life faster. This is not an observation that noncombatants will like.

As in Weaver's story, Baxter's has no accidents. There is ebullience in literature whenever the author feels his or her ideas surely enough to turn everyday circumstance into symbol. For example, at the end of "Gryphon," Tommy strides out from under the children's slide with its depression where all the children have landed.

Culture as Lifesaving: "The Schreuderspitze"

The more cultured people are, the more invisible their equipment for life. A humanities education, for instance, is invisible. Its uses are utterly invisible if one is looking for a set of building tools.

"The Schreuderspitze" is as intricate and complex as any short story in English. It is about how an inward, ethical, aesthetically developed, even talented, photographer is so wracked when his wife and child are killed that he loses his self and falls outside his life. His conscious struggles lead him away from the very thing that will let him return to his own "true occasion."

I will not interpret this story, other than to make this observation: Wallich's grief is brought about by several kinds of grief that he himself was not responsible for: first, the death of his family in an accident; second, his having a vicious professional colleague in Franzen; and third, his own slight, rather soft physiology.

From the beginning of the story his inner equipment is honesty and civility. The man is neither cheat nor manipulator, and he has a classic desire to develop his character further. Here and there in Helprin's work one sees this classical, unmodern passion—someone standing apart, trying to decide, by will, what kind of a person to become, and then exerting fierce effort to realize that willed personhood. Wallich's story never wanders into repetition, dreaminess, or irresolution.

Mark Helprin peoples Wallich's workplace with the kind of moral lightweights whom Socrates constantly tried to teach—people whose first question is, "But what would be in it for me?" Franzen, whom we can take for the villain of "The Schreuderspitze," reminds me gratefully of the ego-developmentalist Jane Loevinger: she made such a point of saying that building our character is one of our jobs on earth.

Wallich wanders off his "center" because of grief. He makes a psychological mistake typical of psychologically unconscious people: he tries to solve a spiritual problem with determination and physical muscle and asceticism. His is a mind-set that psychotherapists see much of. Tremendous pain has come into the client's life. The client knows he or she can hardly bear it, perhaps actually cannot bear it. The client's instinct is to toughen up so that he or she *can* bear this new pain. The client's instinct is not to look at the pain, because that would count as self-pity, but rather to distract the self from it by energetic projects. In general, as the author of this story knows, anyone trying to toughen up through expending energy will choose crazy or violent projects. A psychotherapist asks the client to translate all that brave energy into the brave contemplation of his or her own pain. This is the lifesaving practice for which the twentieth century has given us so many dull names: consciousness-raising, getting centered, giving oneself permission to be, finding out "who you are." Too bad about the language.

Three circumstances, in order, serve to save Helprin's hero: First, he sees a perfect family at the railway station when he goes to pick up rope for descending the Schreuderspitze. Second, he listens to Beethoven's Violin Concerto. And third, he learns to dream.

Here are Wallich's saving experiences arranged for general use:

1. Facing our own grief at last, through seeing an outside parallel
2. Then letting our culture help us heal ourselves (for Wallich, a German, this meant Beethoven)
3. And finally, being open to instruction from a profound if mercurial teacher whom we all have—our dreams

Humor and Gaiety as Gifts of Moral Feeling

Denise Levertov is one of the great nonliars of our culture. "Like Loving Chekhov" is a plain poem, compared with much of this poet's work. Some of its many lines bring sound too scattered to be resonant. When Levertov wants to be resonant she is resonant; when she is not it is because her mission for the particular poem in question is to have a contemplative, cordial conversation with the reader. "Like Loving Chekhov" is the best conversational poem I have ever read.

Its plot is simple: the poet misses a lover who has to go out of town on business, and at the same time she is reminded of her feeling for Anton Chekhov. This poem talks with a full heart about two kinds of enthusiasm—physical love and moral admiration. Levertov's humor is serious because she never forgets the griefs and annoyances of life, and in her consciousness she does not forget to keep company with her own hatred of chill hearts and cruelty. She is a writer who rejoices in the physical pleasure of love but doesn't try to make it do work it doesn't do, such as heal or cover up other problems. In this poem she reverses that wisdom: she rejoices in the *character* of Chekhov, but she does not try to make that admiration pinch-hit for the pleasure of physical lovemaking. This tendency—trying to spread one joy to do more than it can do—is where thousands of poets slip into wishful thinking. Levertov doesn't engage in wishful thinking:

> . . . our bodies
> have warmed each other and given each other
>   delight, our bodies
> are getting angry with us for giving them to each
>   other and then
> allowing something they don't understand to pry
>   them apart,
> a metallic cruel wedge that they hear us call
>   *necessity.*

The moxie of the poem comes from its no-nonsense distinctions. Why call it "moxie"? The reason is that if one's self-confidence is low, one finds it extraordinarily difficult to admit that one is feeling two such different feelings at the same time (physical longing and admiration for a dead physician). When we are wobbly and unsure, we feel that we ought at least to be consistent. When the mind pops up with a second feeling that has no apparent connection to the feeling we had thought we were having, if we are unconfident, we will deny or reject that second feeling. Those who think they are longing to have their lover back in bed would give scant focus to this new feeling floating toward them (how terrific Chekhov was, my goodness, Chekhov certainly was terrific). We would not dream of putting that fragmentary feeling about Chekhov into our poem about bed. That is why much poetry is dull.

An artist takes a risk whenever he or she puts two human emotions into the same work. If we admire Denise Levertov for being both funny and interested in ethical behavior, why not set out to read or write humorous verse? What does it mean that some people want to have fun? Why can't we teach kids to enjoy light literature? This is a problem for idealists: what is the relationship between our right to have fun and our potential for making human behavior better than it now is?

The distinctions between Levertov's humor and ordinary joking are matters of taste and content, but experientially one must forget certain current injustices and cruelties in order to laugh at jokes and giggle at light verse, whereas to enjoy Levertov's poetry we needn't forget any bad thing that human beings have ever done to one another. We don't have to endure pain avoidance, denial, or temporary escape from reality in order to feel her gaiety.

We want *not* to forget psychological history because all history is psychological history. The saw about our being doomed to repeat history if we don't read it applies to things psychological. Dan Olweus's research into Scandinavian schoolyard bullying discussed in chapter 4 suggests that some bullying is done for the fun of it. We want to remember incidents of bullying done for the fun of it because that is the history we don't want repeated. We want to keep remembering that in August of 1993 Senator Jesse Helms entered an elevator where Senator Carol Moseley-Braun stood. She said, "He saw me standing there, and he started to sing, 'I wish I was in the land of cotton . . .' And he looked at Senator Hatch and said, 'I'm going to make her cry. I'm going to sing 'Dixie' until she cries.'"[6] What we want is *not* to forget or deny that the Atomic Energy Commission sickened and killed people with its war games. And we want *not* to forget that the president chose to bomb Baghdad in June of 1993. We *want* to see ourselves darkly mirrored behind the names of our Vietnam dead on the monument, and we want to get up our nerve, having read

McGrath, and say to ourselves, "They *did* die in vain," and many fewer would have died if the Secretary of Defense had spoken up then instead of decades later.

To hold out for the luxury that Levertov talks about in "Modulations," "unlearning lies," we have first to remember what the lies were. Light verse, like kidding around, does not help with the psychological and ethical work of remembering evil. A strange, almost blessed result of having made up one's mind to remember evil is gaiety—a form of which is "[throwing] *down the reins* on the neck of *the divine animal"* that Levertov refers to in "Modulations."

A characteristic of any country run by advertising is a general conviction that people should "lighten up" and "not get heavy" and "not lay some sad trip on others." Products cannot be sold to people who are in a resonating, contemplative mood. You couldn't sell Socrates a Town Car for five dollars. Products cannot be sold to people who are about to speak up in dissent to some policy or other. Products cannot be sold to people who have just decided to risk their livelihood or right not to be incarcerated for a cause. Therefore, advertisers quite sensibly keep serious thought, dissent, and the whole issue of sacrificing anything for any reason out of television as much as they can. The ideal television watcher and products buyer would be Tobias Wolff's Mary, in "In the Garden of the North American Martyrs," before she hit bottom and found her principles. Mary was everything an advertiser could wish for in a potential customer—a human being who has decided not to form her character and not to stick by her feelings:

> When she was young, Mary saw a brilliant and original man lose his job because he had expressed ideas that were offensive to the trustees of the college where they both taught. She shared his views, but did not sign the protest petition. She was, after all, on trial herself—as a teacher, as a woman, as an interpreter of history.
>
> Mary watched herself. Before giving a lecture she wrote it out in full, using the arguments and often the words of other, approved writers, so that she would not by chance say something scandalous. Her own thoughts she kept to herself, and

the words for them grew faint as time went on; without quite disappearing they shrank to remote, nervous points, like birds flying away.

I remind us of Mary, because of her relationship to Levertov's happiness—and to Wilbur's, Bly's, Kooser's, and Ignatow's inner happiness. If we imagine ourselves as a large task force with many kinds of vessels, Mary is the ship that somehow wandered out of the convoy, early in the sailing. We are trying to get clear of the "ancient lies," but here is Mary lying out of fear, self-censoring out of fear, thus making herself seriously vulnerable to joking (as in her promoting a group that seeks to restore the good name of Richard III)—an actual creator of the "common round" of kidding that Anne Frank, even at fourteen, knew to be trivial and dismal.

As a gift to the readers of this book, I have decided to limit my comments on the poetry in this chapter to the one point just made: that true gaiety comes of remembering as much history as we can, never denying evil, and not forgetting to praise kindness and courage. I have chosen Denise Levertov's work to look at in detail because one might miss some of its originality. As for the other poems in chapter 9, I want to point out that each of the poets practices what literary critics since the 1940s often call "irony": that is, every image carries both good news and bad news.

A livelier phrase for that practice of tying the good news of a thing to its bad news is *psychological health*. The poems in this chapter come from happiness. They give off a happiness, too, and yet there is nothing of escapism in them. These poets—Robert Bly, David Ignatow, Ted Kooser, Denise Levertov, and Richard Wilbur—tell us in one breath about trouble in the world, and in the next breath about how much they love the queerest bunch of things—spiders, clothes, second-rate trees, the buildings of New York City.

None of these poems suggests that we can get free of nature's teeth. That is, we will not get free of illness, mistaken choices, failed religious faith, and death. We will end up like dust.

The poems charge us to talk about everything we know of that goes wrong and everything that we know of that goes right.

I think a helpful way to introduce ourselves to what serious literature and serious social work and serious psychology are about is to pretend for a moment that the world is an outsize music room, where everyone has shown up to practice what instruments they can. The bright people, the jerks, the lucky, the scared children, our well-intentioned relations, our ill-intentioned relations, the busybodies and moralists, the ghosts of those whom we have loved—everyone has shown up. The authors and therapists and social workers are passing out the same scores for rehearsal. As soon as we get our sheets, we glance around at the others—we feel we are connected by *work*.

What will the work be that this unimaginable crowd could do together? Well, the work of beauty, music—that is why we thought we had got together. The scores we peer at are musical instructions, not some other kind. But as we look around at the faces we realize that beauty is not all we want. Music, or beauty, is not even what we want to attend to first. Here's what we want to look at first.

We want everyone to stop knocking everyone else around. We want them simply to stop it. We aren't sure exactly how to stop it. No one has passed out score sheets for this kind of work. There is no conductor, either. If we want saving angels, as Wilbur has told us, we shall have to make them up.

We will imagine the selves we need. The rehearsal room, frankly, is full of a very motley looking bunch. People will have to talk enough to each other so everyone can clearly make out everyone else. Then we will imagine all those selves, the others' selves and the various surprising selves inside us.

We should do that first.

Notes

1. From Denise Levertov, "Modulations," in *Life in the Forest* (New York: New Directions, 1978).

2. Paula Gutlove, "Transforming the Confrontation Mentality," *Center Review* 5, no. 2 (fall 1991). (Project on Promoting Effective Dialogue, Center for Psychology and Social Change, 1493 Cambridge St., Cambridge, MA 02139.)

3. Anne Frank, *The Diary of a Young Girl* (New York: Modern Library, 1994).

4. Mortimer J. Adler, "The Disappearance of Culture," *Newsweek*, August 21, 1978, 15.

5. Avrahm Yarmolinsky, ed., *The Portable Chekhov* (Harmondsworth: Penguin, 1947), 598.

6. Deborah Mesce, "Dixie Hits a Sour Note," *St. Paul Pioneer Press*, August 6, 1993, 1.

APPENDIX

A Small Reading List

Andrews, Lewis M. *To Thine Own Self Be True: The Relationship between Spiritual Values and Emotional Health.* New York: Doubleday, 1989.

Berry, Wendell. *What Are People For?* San Francisco: North Point Press, 1990.

Bettelheim, Bruno. *The Informed Heart.* New York: Free Press, 1960.

Block, Gay, and Malka Drucker. *Rescuers: Portraits of Moral Courage in the Holocaust.* Prologue by Cynthia Ozick. New York: Holmes and Meier, 1992.

Bly, Carol. "Kidding in the Family Room: Literature and America's Psychological Class System." *Iowa Review,* 22, no. 3 (Fall 1992): 18–42.

Bowen, Murray. *Family Therapy in Clinical Practice.* Northvale, N.J.: Jason Aronson, 1987.

Frankl, Viktor. *Man's Search for Meaning: An Introduction to Logotherapy.* Part I translated by Ilse Lasch. Preface by Gordon W. Allport. Boston: Beacon Press, 1962.

Griffin, Susan. *Chorus of Stones.* New York: Doubleday, 1992.

Janis, Irving. *Groupthink.* Boston: Houghton Mifflin, 1983.

Kohlberg, Lawrence. *The Philosophy of Moral Development: Moral Stages and the Idea of Justice.* San Francisco: Harper and Row, 1981.

Levi, Primo. *The Drowned and the Saved.* Trans. Raymond Rosenthal. New York: Vintage Books (Random House), 1989.

Lewis, C. S. *The Abolition of Man.* London: Macmillan, 1947.

Lickona, Thomas, ed. *Moral Development and Behavior: Theory, Research, and Social Issues.* New York: Holt, Rinehart and Winston, 1976.

Lifton, Robert Jay, and Eric Markusen. *The Genocidal Mentality: Nazi Holocaust and Nuclear Threat.* New York: Basic Books, 1990.

Loevinger, Jane. E*go Development: Conceptions and Theories.* San Francisco: Jossey-Bass, 1976.

Miller, Alice. *For Your Own Good: Hidden Cruelty in Child-Rearing and the Roots of Violence.* Translated by Hildegarde and Hunter Hannum. New York: Farrar, Straus and Giroux, 1983.

Oliner, Samuel P., and Pearl M. Oliner. *The Altruistic Personality.* New York: Free Press, 1988.

Orwell, George. "Why I Write." In *Eight Modern Essayists,* 5th ed. Ed. William Smart. New York: St. Martin's Press, 1990.

Sichrovsky, Peter (compiler). *Born Guilty: Children of Nazi Families.* Trans. Jean Steinberg. Introduction and postscript by Peter Sichrovsky. New York: Basic Books, 1988.

Staub, Ervin. *The Roots of Evil: The Origins of Genocide and Other Group Violence.* Cambridge (England): Cambridge University Press, 1989.

True, Michael. *An Energy Field More Intense than War: The Non-Violent Tradition and American Literature.* Syracuse, N. Y.: Syracuse University Press, 1995.

Tuchman, Barbara W. *The Guns of August.* New York: Macmillan, 1962.

Vaillant, George E. *Adaptation to Life.* Boston: Little, Brown, 1977.

Vidich, Arthur J., and Joseph Bensman. *Small Town in Mass Society: Class, Power, and Religion in a Rural Community.* New York: Anchor, 1960.

Wolf, Christa. *Accident: A Day's News.* Trans. Heike Schwarzbauer and Rick Takvorian. New York: Farrar, Straus and Giroux, 1989.

Yalom, Irvin D. *Existential Psychotherapy.* New York: Basic Books, 1980.

———. *The Theory and Practice of Group Psychotherapy.* 8th printing. New York: Basic Books, 1970.

Some Milestones of Ego Development
by Jane Loevinger

Stage	Code	Impulse Control, Character Development	Interpersonal Style	Conscious Preoccupations	Cognitive Style
Presocial			Autistic		
Symbiotic	I–1		Symbiotic	Self vs. non-self	
Impulsive	I–2	Impulsive, fear of retaliation	Receiving, dependent, exploitative	Bodily feelings, especially sexual and aggressive	Stereotyping, conceptual confusion
Self-Protective	Δ	Fear of being caught, externalizing blame, opportunistic	Wary, manipulative, exploitative	Self-protection, trouble, wishes, things, advantage, control	
Conformist	I–3	Conformity to external rules, shame, guilt for breaking rules	Belonging, superficial niceness	Appearance, social acceptability, banal feelings, behavior	Conceptual simplicity, stereotypes, clichés
Conscientious-Conformist	I-3/4	Differentiation of norms, goals	Aware of self in relation to group, helping	Adjustment, problems, reasons, opportunities (vague)	Multiplicity
Conscientious	I–4	Self-evaluated standards, self-criticism, guilt for consequences, long-term goals and ideals	Intensive, responsible, mutual, concern for communication	Differentiated feelings, motives for behavior, self-respect, achievements, traits, expression	Conceptual complexity, idea of patterning
Individualistic	I-4/5	*Add:* Respect for individuality	*Add:* Dependence as an emotional problem	*Add:* Development, social problems, differentiation of inner life from outer	*Add:* Distinction of process and outcome

Note: *"Add"* means in addition to the description applying to the previous level.

(Source: Jane Loevinger, Ego Development: Conceptions and Theories *[San Francisco: Jossey-Bass, 1976], 24–25.)*

Stage	Code	Impulse Control, Character Development	Interpersonal Style	Conscious Preoccupations	Cognitive Style
Autonomous	I-5	Add: Coping with conflicting inner needs, toleration	Add: Respect for autonomy, interdependence	Vividly conveyed feelings, integration of physiological and psychological, psychological causation of behavior, role conception, self-fulfillment, self in social context	Increased conceptual complexity, complex patterns, toleration for ambiguity, broad scope, objectivity
Integrated	I-6	Add: Reconciling inner conflicts, renunciation of unattainable	Add: Cherishing of individuality	Add: Identity	

Comparison of Rogers's Process of Psychotherapy with Ego Development

by Jane Loevinger

Ego Development	Process of Psychotherapy	
Stage *Description*	*Description*	**Stage**
I–2 S tends to dichotomize the world; stereotyping is the most conspicuous sign.	Personal constructs are rigid.	1
Affects are seen as bodily states or impulses rather than as differentiated inner feelings.	Feelings and personal meanings are not recognized or owned. Communication is about externals only.	
There is a limited emotional range.		
Trouble is located in a place rather than a situation.	No problems are recognized or perceived; there is no desire to change.	
Δ S does not see himself as responsible for trouble or failure; you are lucky or unlucky, or other people are to blame; or blame is external and impersonal.	Problems are perceived as external to self; S has no sense of personal responsibility for problems.	2
Δ/3 Obedience and conformity to norms are simple, absolute rules.	Personal constructs are rigid and thought of as facts, not recognized as constructs.	
Emotions are seen as quasi-physiological.		
I–3 Inner life is mentioned in generalities; feelings are denied or mentioned in a vague, evasive, or noncommittal way.	Differentiation of personal meanings and feelings is limited and global.	
Inner conflict may be manifest, but it is not acknowledged.	Contradictions may be expressed but without recognition as contradictions.	
I–3/4 Self-consciousness and rudimentary self-awareness and self-criticism are characteristic.	There is freer flow of expression about self, self-related experiences, and self as reflected in others.	3
There is stronger awareness of feelings than before. S is more aware of individual differences in attitudes, interests, and abilities, but still in global and banal terms.	Differentiation of feelings and meanings is slightly sharper and less global than before.	
S sees multiple possibilities and alternatives in situations; there are contingencies, exceptions, and comparisons, though global and banal ones.	There is recognition of contradictions in experience.	
I–4 S has a richly differentiated inner life; experiences are savored and appreciated.	Past feelings are described as intense; present feelings are still distrusted and feared.	4
S is aware of the problem of impulse and control.		
I–4 Interpersonal interaction is intensive.		
S sees patterns in behavior and has a vivid sense of individual differences in the long-term dispositions that underlie behavior.	There is an increased differentiation of feelings, constructs, and personal meanings, seeking exactness of symbolization.	

(Source: Jane Loevinger, Ego Development: Conceptions and Theories, [San Francisco: Jossey-Bass, 1976], 154–55.)

Ego Development		**Process of Psychotherapy**	
Stage	*Description*	*Description*	*Stage*

	Descriptions of people are more realistic because S perceives more complexities.		
	S is aware of self, reflects on self, and describes self and others in terms of reflexive traits. S sees intentions and motives as well as consequences of behavior.	S is concerned about contradictions and incongruities between experience and self.	
	S distinguishes appearances from underlying feelings.		
	S has a strong sense of responsibility.	There are feelings of self-responsibility in problems, though such feelings vacillate.	
	S sees life as presenting choices; he holds the origin of his own destiny.		
I–4/5	Where the I–4 S sees polar, incompatible opposites, the I–4/5 S is more likely to see a paradox, a quasi-contradiction in nature rather than a forced choice.	There is increasingly clear facing of contradictions and incongruities in experience.	5
	S becomes aware of conflicting or contrasting emotions.	Feelings are close to being fully experienced.	
	There is greater complexity in conception of interpersonal interaction. The idea of communication and expression of feelings is deepened and made more complex. Psychological causality replaces vague statements of "reasons" and "problems" at lower levels. S gives vivid and personal versions of ideas presented as clichés at lower levels.	There are fresh discoveries of personal constructs and a critical examination of them. There is a strong tendency towards exactness in differentiation of feelings and meanings. There is increased acceptance of self-responsibility for problems and freer internal communication.	
	S distinguishes inner life from outer, appearances from reality. Maintaining one's own individuality is perceived as a problem.	There is increasing ownership of self-feelings and a desire to be the "real me."	
I–5	S feels the full force of inner conflict and tries to cope with it or transcend it.	New feelings are experienced with immediacy and richness of detail.	6
	S is concerned with communicating feelings.	Differentiation of experiencing is sharp and basic.	
	Emotions are differentiated and vividly conveyed. Sensual experiences come through vividly. S displays spontaneity, genuineness, intensity.	There is acceptant ownership of changing feelings, a basic trust in his own process.	7
	S has a high tolerance for ambiguity; conflicting alternatives are construed as aspects of many-faceted life situations.	Personal constructs are tentatively formulated and loosely held.	

Note: Descriptions of stages of ego development are excerpted from Jane Loevinger and Ruth Wessler, *Measuring Ego Development* (San Francisco: Jossey-Bass, 1970), chapter four, 54–109. Descriptions of stages of psychotherapy are excerpted from Carl R. Rogers, *On Becoming a Person: A Therapist's View of Psychotherapy* (Boston: Houghton Mifflin, 1961), chapter seven, 125–59.

Stage Development of Motives and Values

by Lawrence Kohlberg

Motive Given for Rule Obedience or Moral Action	The Value of Human Life
1 Obey rules to avoid punishment.	Value of life confused with value of physical objects and is based on social status or physical attributes of the possessor.
2 Conform to obtain rewards, have favors returned, and so on.	Value of human life seen as instrumental to the satisfaction of the needs of its possessor or of other people.
3 Conform to avoid disapproval and dislike by others.	The value of human life is based on the empathy and affection of family members and others toward its possessor.
4 Conform to avoid censure by legitimate authorities and resultant guilt.	Life is conceived as sacred in terms of its place in a categorical moral or religious order of rights and duties.
5 Conform to maintain the respect of the impartial spectator judging in terms of community welfare.	Life is valued both in terms of its relation to community welfare and in terms of life being a universal human right.
6 Conform to avoid self-condemnation.	Human life is sacred—a universal human value of respect for the individual.

(Source: Lawrence Kohlberg, The Philosophy of Moral Development: Moral Stages and the Idea of Justice, vol. 1, Essays on Moral Development [San Francisco: Harper and Row, 1981], 19–20.)

The Six Moral Stages
by Lawrence Kohlberg

Content of Stage

Level and Stage	What Is Right	Reasons for Doing Right	Social Perspective of Stage
Level I: **Preconventional** *Stage 1: Heteronomous Morality*	To avoid breaking rules backed by punishment, obedience for its own sake, and avoiding physical damage to persons and property.	Avoidance of punishment, and the superior power of authorities.	*Egocentric point of view.* Doesn't consider the interests of others or recognize that they differ from the actor's; doesn't relate two points of view. Actions are considered physically rather than in terms of psychological interests of others. Confusion of authority's perspective with one's own.
Stage 2: Individualism, Instrumental Purpose, and Exchange	Following rules only when it is to someone's immediate interest; acting to meet one's own interests and needs and letting others do the same. Right is also what's fair, what's an equal exchange, a deal, an agreement.	To serve one's own needs or interests in a world where you have to recognize that other people have their interests, too.	*Concrete individualistic perspective.* Aware that everybody has his own interest to pursue and these conflict, so that right is relative (in the concrete individualistic sense).
Level II: **Conventional** *Stage 3: Mutual Interpersonal Expectations, Relationships, and Interpersonal Conformity*	Living up to what is expected by people close to you or what people generally expect of people in your role as son, brother, friend, etc. "Being good" is important and means having good motives, showing concern about others. It also means keeping mutual relationships, such as trust, loyalty, respect and gratitude.	The need to be a good person in your own eyes and those of others. Your caring for others. Belief in the Golden Rule. Desire to maintain rules and authority which support stereotypical good behavior.	*Perspective of the individual in relationships with other individuals.* Aware of shared feelings, agreements, and expectations which take primacy over individual interests. Relates points of view through the concrete Golden Rule, putting yourself in the other guy's shoes. Does not yet consider generalized system perspective.

(Source: Thomas Lickona (ed.), Moral Development and Behavior: Theory, Research, and Social Issues [New York: Holt, Rinehart and Winston, 1976], 35–36. Based on work by Lawrence Kohlberg.)

Content of Stage

Level and Stage	What Is Right	Reasons for Doing Right	Social Perspective of Stage
Stage 4: Social System and Conscience	Fulfilling the actual duties to which you have agreed. Laws are to be upheld except in extreme cases where they conflict with other fixed social duties. Right is also contributing to society, the group, or institution.	To keep the institution going as a whole, to avoid the breakdown in the system "if everyone did it," or the imperative of conscience to meet one's defined obligations. (Easily confused with Stage 3 belief in rules and authority; see text.)	*Differentiates societal point of view from interpersonal agreement or motives.* Takes the point of view of the system that defines roles and rules. Considers individual relations in terms of place in the system.
Level III: Post-Conventional, or Principled *Stage 5: Social Contract or Utility and Individual Rights*	Being aware that people hold a variety of values and opinions, that most values and rules are relative to your group. These relative rules should usually be upheld, however, in the interest of impartiality and because they are the social contract. Some nonrelative values and rights like *life* and *liberty*, however, must be upheld in any society and regardless of majority opinion.	A sense of obligation to law because of one's social contract to make and abide by laws for the welfare of all and for the protection of all people's rights. A feeling of contractual commitment, freely entered upon, to family, friendship, trust, and work obligations. Concern that laws and duties be based on rational calculation of overall utility, "the greatest good for the greatest number."	*Prior-to-society perspective.* Perspective of a rational individual aware of values and rights prior to social attachments and contracts. Integrates perspectives by formal mechanisms of agreement, contract, objective impartiality, and due process. Considers moral and legal points of view; recognizes that they sometimes conflict and finds it difficult to integrate them.
Stage 6: Universal Ethical Principles	Following self-chosen ethical principles. Particular laws or social agreements are usually valid because they rest on such principles. When laws violate these principles, one acts in accordance with the principle. Principles are universal principles of justice: the equality of human rights and respect for the dignity of human beings as individual persons.	The belief as a rational person in the validity of universal moral principles, and a sense of personal commitment to them.	*Perspective of a moral point of view* from which social arrangements derive. Perspective is that of any rational individual recognizing the nature of morality or the fact that persons are ends in themselves and must be treated as such.

A Sequence in Growth in Interpersonal Style as a Result of Group Theory
by Irvin D. Yalom

If these principles are organized into a logical sequence, the mechanism of interpersonal learning as a curative factor becomes more evident.

1. Psychiatry, the study of human behavior, is the study of interpersonal relationships. Psychiatric symptomatology has both its origins and its contemporary expression in disturbed interpersonal relationships.
2. The psychotherapy group, provided its development is unhampered by severe structural restrictions, evolves into a social microcosm, a miniaturized representation of each patient's social universe.
3. The group members, through consensual validation and self-observation, become aware of significant aspects of their interpersonal behavior: their strengths, their limitations, their parataxic distortions, and their maladaptive behavior which elicits unwanted responses from others. Often the patient in the past has had a series of disastrous group experiences in which he has been rejected and consequently has gradually internalized a derogatory self-image. He has failed to learn from these experiences because the members, sensing his general insecurity, have not communicated to him the reasons for his rejection. He has never learned to discriminate between objectionable aspects of his behavior and a picture of himself as totally objectionable. The therapy group with its encouragement of accurate feedback makes such a discrimination possible.
4. The depth and meaningfulness of this awareness is directly proportional to the amount of affect associated with the transaction. The more real and the more emotionally laden the experience, the more potent is the impact; the more objectified and intellectualized the experience, the less effective the learning.

5. As a result of this awareness, the patient may gradually change or may more abruptly risk new types of behavior and expression. The likelihood that change will occur is a function of:
   a. the patient's motivation for change; the amount of personal discomfort and dissatisfaction with current modes of behavior;
   b. the patient's involvement in the group, his need for acceptance by the group, his respect and appreciation of the other members;
   c. the rigidity of the patient's character structure and interpersonal style.
6. The change in behavior may generate a new cycle of interpersonal learning via self-observation and feedback from other members. Furthermore, the patient appreciates that some feared calamity which had hitherto prevented such behavior was irrational; his new behavior did not result in such calamities as death, destruction, abandonment, derision, or engulfment.
7. The social microcosm concept is a bi-directional one; not only does outside behavior become manifest in the group, but behavior learned in the group is eventually carried over into the patient's social environment and alterations appear in his interpersonal behavior outside the group.
8. Gradually an *adaptive spiral* is set into motion, at first inside and then outside the group. As the patient's interpersonal distortions diminish, his ability to form rewarding relationships is enhanced. Social anxiety decreases, self-esteem rises, there is less need to conceal himself; others find his behavior likable and show more approval and acceptance to the patient, which further increases self-esteem and enhances further change. Eventually the adaptive spiral achieves such autonomy and efficacy that professional therapy is no longer necessary.

(Source: Irvin D. Yalom, The Theory and Practice of Group Psychotherapy, *8th printing [New York: Basic Books, 1970], 44–45.)*

Two Math Problems Set to High School Students in Nazi Germany

An example of dehumanization dressed as neutral arithmetic [C. B.]:

Problem 94

In one region of the German Reich there are 4,400 mentally ill in state institutions, 4,500 receiving state support, 1,600 in local hospitals, 200 in homes for the epileptic, and 1,500 in welfare homes. The state pays a minimum of 10 million RM/year (RM = Reichsmarks) for these institutions.

    I. What is the average cost to the state per inhabitant per year?

    II. Using the result calculated from I, how much does it cost the state if:
        A. 868 patients stay longer than 10 years?
        B. 260 patients stay longer than 20 years?
        C. 112 patients stay longer than 25 years?

Problem 95
The construction of an insane asylum requires 6 million RM. How many housing units @ 15,000 RM could be built for the amount spent on insane asylums?

(Source: Quoted by Robert Proctor, Racial Hygiene: Medicine under the Nazis *[Cambridge, Mass.: Harvard University Press, 1988], 184, note 26. Based on Adolf Dorner,* Mathematik im Dienste der nationalpolitischen Erziehung *[Frankfurt, 1935].)*

Women of Los Alamos during World War II:
Some of Their Views
by Kathleen E. B. Manley

Professor Manley was interested in how the combination of being young, very busy, of feeling aware that they were associated with a project bigger than any private project of one's ordinary life, and delight with the camaraderie of like-minded people (other wives of scientists, in this case) apparently relieved the women of the Los Alamos project of any moral doubts. Nor did they express, in hindsight, feelings of guilt. Their reminiscences indicate that several of them were pathetically glad to have rubbed shoulders with famous people. [C. B.]

The calibre of the people who were members of the community of Los Alamos during World War II appears to have been one of the most significant factors in the women's attitude. Of twenty-nine women interviewed, seventeen, either gratuitously or when asked about the best part of the wartime years on the Hill, mentioned the people they knew or the camaraderie they experienced. Many of the scientists' wives and the laboratory workers already knew members of the community when they arrived, and they were delighted to see them again; the people in the community were extremely interesting to be around. Peggy Hemmendinger, for example, mentioned the brilliance of the people involved; Sara Dowson Prestwood thought she was privileged to have known such special people; Jean Parks Nereson commented on people's knowledge and how intensively they studied everything—the Indians, for instance; Josephine Elliott Powers appreciated the chance to work with many famous people on a worthwhile project. Elsie McMillan, looking back in 1975, said, ". . . I don't think I shall ever live in a community that had such deep roots of cooperation and friendship."

(Source: Kathleen E. B. Manley, "Women of Los Alamos during World War II: Some of Their Views," New Mexico Historical Review 65, no. 2 [April 1990]: 251–66.)

Finding a Good Therapist and Creating Moral Communities among Therapists

by William J. Doherty

I have argued that many well-trained therapists hold a worldview that blinds them to issues of moral responsibility in their clients' lives and deemphasizes the character of the therapist and the needs of the larger community. I have also argued that therapists who are open to these issues are well situated to provide moral consultation along with traditional psychotherapy. So how do you choose a morally sensitive therapist? This is a question for therapists and nontherapists alike, since therapists themselves refer many people to other therapists and frequently seek out therapy for themselves. Therapists may advertise their credentials and clinical specialty areas, but they don't advertise their virtues and moral sensitivity. And I wouldn't trust anyone who did.

Following are some positive qualities to look for in a morally sensitive therapist, along with warning signs to watch out for. I am assuming, of course, that the therapist you are considering (or already seeing) has appropriate professional credentials and training. Moral sensitivity is no substitute for lack of clinical competence.

What to Look for in a Good Therapist

1. *Caring*—the therapist seems genuinely compassionate and values you as a person. This sense of being cared for should start from your first contact with the therapist, whether on the phone or in the office, and should never be in serious doubt as you move through the difficult parts of therapy. I suggest trusting your intuition in the first contacts you have with the therapist. If you don't feel warmth and respect, look elsewhere.

2. *Courage*—the therapist is willing to challenge you when you are off base, even if you get angry or defensive in response. Therapy should not be just a feel-good exercise, and a therapist who does not annoy you at times is probably not doing a good job. The therapist should show you, over time if not at the outset of

therapy, a willingness to persevere in facing issues that you would prefer to avoid.

3. *Prudence*—the therapist's feedback and suggestions about your life decisions seem realistic and reasonable, neither too timid nor too risky. Most good therapists are cautious about giving direct advice about a client's decisions, but when they do, the advice makes good sense, such as the classic suggestions to "sleep on it" before sending an angry letter or to not make major decisions when seriously depressed. Prudence should be visible in the first contacts with the therapist and should not flag through the course of treatment.

4. *Willingness to use moral language*—the therapist is willing to engage in moral discussion about what is fair, right, honest, or responsible. The therapist appears comfortable talking with you about your values and your religious beliefs and about your sense of right and wrong. This quality should be visible from the first time you raise these kinds of issues.

5. *Respect for your interpersonal commitments and responsibilities*— the therapist honors your inclinations to act responsibly toward people you are committed to in your life, even when he or she is sometimes pointing out the destructive elements in these relationships. Good therapists respect their clients' pace for making difficult decisions on morally loaded decisions such as whether to divorce a spouse or whether to institutionalize an ill or disabled family member.

6. *Respect for your community commitments and responsibilities*—the therapist honors your efforts to contribute to your community, even though he or she may challenge you at times to achieve a better balance in your life. The therapist focuses not only on what your community involvement does for you but also on what it contributes to others. The therapist encourages you to talk about this part of your life and about your values and does not immediately turn the discussion back to your inner life.

What to Be Wary of in a Therapist

1. *The therapist discourages all use of moral language.* A good therapist will distinguish between "shoulds" that are moral in nature,
   such as "I should not put my ex-wife down in front of the children," and those that are based on nonmoral, sometimes op-
   pressive standards, such as "I should finish any job I start," or,
   "I should look like the fashion models I see in the magazines."
   In the latter examples, a good therapist is likely to challenge the
   meaningfulness of the "should" and explore where this injunc-
   tion came from in your life. In the former case, a good therapist
   will take the moral dimension of postdivorce parenting very
   seriously.

2. *The therapist is quick to urge or support cutoffs from other family
   members.* As I mentioned in chapter 2, a friend of mine was told
   by her therapist that she was showing an inability to "grieve"
   and "move on with her life" when she was not ready to give up
   on a long-term marriage after her husband's out-of-the-blue announcement, just three weeks prior, that he was having an affair
   and wanted a separation. Fortunately, my friend fired the therapist. Some therapists are also quick to suggest cutoffs from parents when clients come to understand the abuse they suffered
   as a child. The therapist may move too soon to recommend
   that the client write a letter stating, "You abused me, so goodbye," without a full exploration of this decision and its consequences for all concerned, including the client. Often such
   cutoffs include siblings who were completely innocent but are
   swept away in a premature, therapist-inspired "family-ectomy."
   These therapists are like gynecologists who perform unnecessary hysterectomies. I suggest asking a prospective therapist on
   the phone for his or her philosophy about cutting off contact
   with family members in cases of abuse.

3. *The therapist sees only negatives in your family or spouse.* A good
   therapist will demonstrate a realistic but caring attitude toward
   people close to you. A bad therapist will paint your family members or partner in negative colors only and will interpret your
   defense of them as denial. This therapist sees others in your life

primarily in terms of their poor treatment of you, not as people whom you may care for deeply despite their actions.

4. *The therapist always portrays you as the victim of others, not as someone who also can harm others.* Some therapists work so hard to help abuse victims not blame themselves for the abuse that they lose sight of the here-and-now ways in which the client is hurting or taking advantage of others. A physically abused wife is not responsible for her beatings, but she is responsible for continually telling her son that his father is scum. If your therapist does not challenge behavior you sense is harmful to others, you are not getting good therapy.

5. *The therapist disparages your sense of duty toward others.* When you talk about how hard it is to visit your failing mother in the nursing home, does the therapist ask you to do a cost-benefit analysis—what do you get out of going, and what does it cost you?—without honoring the moral obligation involved? Or when you are struggling to maintain your disabled child in your home, does the therapist continually make the case for your own needs without at the same time supporting your sense of duty to keep your child at home as long as you can? Ditto for community commitments: does the therapist suggest that you are trying to "save the world" to avoid dealing with your personal problems, without acknowledging and supporting the moral imperative you feel to give something back to your community? If so, you are seeing the wrong therapist.

Unfortunately, you may not be able to see many of either the positive qualities or the red flags before getting into therapy. But they can guide your initial inquiries about what the therapist is like and your first talks with the therapist on the phone. When you are already in therapy and your therapist shows behaviors or attitudes that I have classified as warning signs, I encourage you to raise your concerns directly. A caring, brave, and wise therapist will listen carefully to your concerns and work with you to achieve a better balance in the therapy. When I have been pushing too hard for parents to look at the negative side of keeping a child with serious disabilities at home, sometimes they will say, in effect, "Read our lips. We want to find a way to keep our child at home for now." I almost always realign my energies to support their commitment. Good therapists are willing to discuss, and be challenged about, their stance toward moral responsibilities.

My greatest concern about promoting the moral consultation role for therapists is that most of us have not been trained to do it, nor do we have a forum in which to talk about moral and community issues. But there is no going back. We already do provide moral consultation disguised as psychological consultation. I am suggesting that we begin to do it more consciously and explicitly—and hopefully better. Nevertheless, I am still concerned about setting therapists loose without moorings in the moral arena. There are already some therapists out there who feel free to impose their moral judgments on clients— telling couples to stay married, for example. I don't want to expand the number of therapists who see morality in psychotherapy as the straightforward prescription of unambiguous moral standards, instead of a delicate blend of clarifying, exploring, thinking together, and occasionally challenging. And we do not need therapists promoting ill-conceived moral positions that they have never aired and discussed with colleagues. Idiosyncratic moral philosophies that are not subject to dialogue and challenge can be as dangerous in therapy as they are in politics and other settings.

As I mentioned in chapter 1, most practicing therapists are members of a case consultation group in which they discuss difficult clinical cases and get feedback and suggestions. These meetings are often pressed for time, since there are usually more than enough cases to discuss. The result is that most case consultations do not lend themselves to careful evaluation of the therapist's mode of dealing with issues of interpersonal moral responsibility, professional ethics in the changing health care system, and better communities. Strictly clinical concerns swamp other concerns. Graduate school and clinical training settings are better suited to this kind of exploration, but instructors have to make a place for moral and community issues in the curriculum and in supervised internships, not just in the mandatory ethics courses, which often focus mainly on the ethical appropriateness of the therapist's behavior in areas such as confidentiality and informed consent. And training programs rarely pay explicit attention to the development of the character of the trainee.

Therapists need to create groups to educate one another about moral consultation in psychotherapy and about the role of therapists in promoting community well-being. Inspired by the salon movement created by *Utne Reader* magazine, my colleague Patrick Dougherty and I approached an influential magazine for therapists, *Family Therapy Networker,* about the idea of creating a national network of forums or discussion groups for therapists to explore the reenvisioning of psychotherapy as a moral and community-sensitive enterprise. The editor, Richard Simon, immediately liked the idea and offered to sponsor it, first in the Twin Cities and then nationally.

Following is the description we used to invite therapists of all clinical persuasions (not just family therapists) to join the movement. The Minnesota forums began in September 1994, and the National Network forums are being launched in the spring and summer of 1995. Therapists are welcome to use these ideas and materials to develop groups with their own colleagues. Or they can contact *Family Therapy Networker* for assistance at 7705 13th Street N.W., Washington, DC 20012.

Network Forums for Therapists on Moral, Ethical, and Community Issues

What Are Network Forums?

Network forums are discussion groups of therapists who meet to explore moral, ethical, and community concerns that generally are not addressed in other professional settings.

What Kinds of Issues Are Discussed?

Although each forum is autonomous and free to pursue its members' interests, the following questions about moral, ethical, and community concerns can be used to open discussion:

1. Can psychotherapy be value-free, or should it even try to be? What is the role of morality in psychotherapy? Where do issues such as justice, honesty, and responsibility to others fit in? How

do we deal with moral issues in the lives of our clients without preaching to them, invading their autonomy, or pretending that moral concerns are merely psychological issues in disguise?

2. What virtues must therapists have to practice good therapy? What is the role of character traits such as integrity, truthfulness, caring, and courage? How can therapists exhibit these qualities in the current health care marketplace?

3. What is the role of psychotherapy in promoting the survival and well-being of community? Are we helping clients create psychological cocoons for themselves at the expense of their communities?

4. What should therapists be contributing to our communities beyond our work with specific clients? What values do we "profess" to the larger world, and how can we enact those values?

5. How can the profession and practice of psychotherapy change in a way that is consistent with our values and also responds to the legitimate demands of managed care companies and the government for accountability in the use of fiscal and human resources?

6. In promoting widely available mental health care, how can therapists separate out self-interest from the needs of citizens and consumers? How can therapists maintain their professional integrity as healers in a health care system that is demanding more and more adjustment in therapists' standards of care?

What Is the Spirit of the Forums?

We hope the forums will be supportive and challenging both professionally and personally, that they will be open to a range of ideas and persuasions, and that most discussions will touch on clinical practice, the person of the therapist, and the needs of the larger community. Rather than just critiquing the status quo, we hope forum participants will take the next difficult steps by asking, "How are we part of this problem?" and, "How can we contribute to its solution?"

Traps to Avoid in Conducting Forums

- Duplicating case consultations
- Getting into debates about therapy models
- Losing the focus on moral and ethical issues by reducing every-thing to pragmatic considerations or legalities
- Losing the focus on community issues (many therapists are more comfortable at the personal and clinical levels)
- Letting professional guild issues predominate
- Blaming other systems and forces in society without also exam-ining our part

How Will the Forums Work?

Based on the experience of the Minnesota forums, we suggest the following logistics to begin the groups. Once formed, the forums will be autonomous.

- Holding monthly two-hour meetings
- Inviting about fifteen members to join
- Designating someone to host the meetings
- Designating someone to facilitate the discussions
- Designating someone to serve as liaison with the *Family Therapy Networker* forum movement
- Deciding at the first meeting on topics, format, future places to meet, and other logistical issues

Psychotherapy is at a crossroads in the United States at the end of the twentieth century. One road leads to increased medicalization—reducing psychotherapy to a technique for treating narrowly con-ceived mental disorders when medication is not sufficient—and increased commodification—reducing psychotherapy to a cost item in the health care budget that must be carefully rationed and con-trolled. If the field takes that road, the argument of this book will be essentially irrelevant and the practice of moral lobotomy in clinical and public discourse will go unchallenged by the community of therapists.

The other road leads to an expansion of psychotherapy beyond its pretenses to being a value-free form of treatment and beyond its love affair with expressive individualism, its preference for technique over character, and its lack of social conscience. There are no maps that clearly show how to take this road. In fact, we will have to build it as we go, in partnership with our clients and our communities. If we build it well, someday it may become the road more traveled.

(Source: William J. Doherty, Soul Searching: Why Psychotherapy Must Promote Moral Responsibility *[New York: Basic Books, 1995], 181–90.)*

Empathy in Literature: A Sequence of Five Steps in Empathy
by Mary Peterson and Carol Bly

What are the actual steps in practicing empathy? Practicing empathy is deliberately hearing the point of view of the other: the conversation is not random. It is *intentional*.

1. The first step is the one most often missed: it is making the decision that you *are going to hear.*

It is work. For example, to ask a child or student or anyone another question about what that child or student or person has just said reassures him or her that someone is taking a serious interest. "This adult actually seems to respect what I just said or they wouldn't be asking a *second* question!" (How many Americans have *ever* been asked another question about something they just spoke of? It is so rare. It is such a civil experience and it is so rare! It is amazing any of us have any self-image at all.)

2. Emptying yourself (for the moment, since you can always come back to it) of your own point of view.

3. Asking open-ended, not yes–or–no, and not "leading" questions. "How was it when . . . ?" "What was it like when . . . ?"

4. Stating back to the person in your own words what you understand him or her to have said—and then asking if you have it right.

5. Asking this: given all the comments made, the feelings or meanings reported, where do we go from here? What do you see as the direction, or the future aspects?

There are slight variations, but in both their philosophy and sequence, the five steps above are classical empathy. When we use empathy in *literature*, it means we can ask the questions above of each separate character in a story, or of the author, and inevitably, when we are used to hearing and telling and reading stories, we ask these questions of ourselves.

(Source: Empathy-in-Literature Theory [To Hear*], Collaborative of Teachers and School Social Workers, St. Paul, Minnesota.)

*We can grow and deepen *only* when we have been heard out. . . .

Shakespeare and the Psychological Work of Listing Particulars:
An Excerpt from Henry VI, *part 3, act 2, scene 5*

This monologue illustrates one kind of list making that both therapists and writing teachers suggest to their clients. Henry starts off with a generalization, "For what is in this world but grief and woe?" That generalization is in the genre of clients' opening remarks in a therapy session. ("Everything's been so unbelievably awful . . .") General remarks are endemic to first drafts of essays, too. General remarks, in fact, are how we start out most discourse, even in journals. ("Today was a wonderful day. Everything went wonderfully. The wedding ceremony went off just the way we'd hoped.")

In psychological work, the mentor then asks the speaker to partialize. "What is one of the ways in which 'everything has been so awful'?"

In the case of the journal writer, the creative-writing teacher asks for particulars. "What was one good thing about that wedding, for example? What else went well?"

Shakespeare was ingenious at discourse that starts with a generalization. To give a few examples: the world is just "grief and woe"; everyday life keeps proceeding at this petty pace; if you want to keep the dread-of-death factor low, don't let yourself perseverate or fantasize about it — to mention a few familiar cases. Then he invariably lists particulars.

Henry's listing of particulars accomplishes the classic side effect of all listings of particulars: as the thinker jots down the concrete details, his or her enthusiasm for life, memories of this or that gorgeous aspect of nature ("a fresh tree's shade"), small, sturdy pleasures (such as "cold thin drink out of his leather bottle") come to the top of the mind and tell us what a rich mixture life is, whatever its evils. List making does not lead one to denial of the grief originally complained of. Lists give balance, the balance that makes therapists say, "Some of the affect of the presenting complaint gets diluted." Lists lead writing teachers to say, "The particulars have given their gift of irony: now the author recognizes the several feelings felt about a subject at the same time."

Authors and therapists urge us to make lists because lists invite us to remember, cordially, aspects of life that we had forgotten we love. [C. B.]

For what is in this world but grief and woe?
O God! methinks it were a happy life,
To be no better than a homely swain;
To sit upon a hill, as I do now,
To carve out dials quaintly, point by point,
Thereby to see the minutes how they run,
How many makes the hour full complete,
How many hours brings about the day,
How many days will finish up the year,
How many years a mortal man may live.
When this is known, then to divide the times:
So many hours must I tend my flock,
So many hours must I take my rest,
So many hours must I contemplate,
So many hours must I sport myself;
So many days my ewes have been with young,
So many weeks ere the poor fools will ean,
So many years ere I shall shear the fleece.
So minutes, hours, days, months, and years,
Pass'd over to the end they were created,
Would bring white hairs unto a quiet grave.
Ah, what a life were this! how sweet! how lovely!
Gives not the hawthorn-bush a sweeter shade
To shepherds looking on their silly sheep,
Than doth a rich embroider'd canopy
To kings that fear their subjects' treachery?
O, yes, it doth; a thousand-fold it doth.
And to conclude, the shepherd's homely curds,
His cold thin drink out of his leather bottle,
His wonted sleep under a fresh tree's shade,
All which secure and sweetly he enjoys,
Is far beyond a prince's delicates, —
His viands sparkling in a golden cup,
His body couched in a curious bed,
When Care, Mistrust, and Treason waits on him.

More familiar examples of Shakespeare's list making are the "petty pace" speech in Macbeth, *act 5, scene 5, and Hamlet's list of "whips and scorns" in* Hamlet, *act 3, scene 1.*

List of Readings

Agee, James. "A Mother's Tale." In *The Collected Short Prose of James Agee*. Edited and with a memoir by Robert Fitzgerald. Boston: Houghton Mifflin, 1968, pp. 221–43. Copyright © 1968 by The James Agee Trust.

Baxter, Charles. "Gryphon." In *Through the Safety Net*. New York: Viking, 1985, pp. 165–84. Copyright © 1985 by Charles Baxter. Used by permission of Viking Penguin, a division of Penguin Books USA Inc.

Berry, Wendell. "Solving for Pattern." In *The Gift of Good Land*. San Francisco: North Point Press, 1981, pp. 134–45. Copyright © 1981 by Wendell Berry. Reprinted by permission of North Point Press, a division of Farrar, Straus & Giroux, Inc.

Bly, Robert. "Poem in Three Parts." In *Silence in the Snowy Fields*. Middletown, Conn.: Wesleyan University Press, 1962, p. 21. Copyright © 1962 by Robert Bly. Reprinted by permission of Robert Bly.

Hall, Donald. "Cider 5¢ a Glass." In *Old and New Poems*. New York: Ticknor and Fields, 1990, pp. 197–202. Copyright © 1990 by Donald Hall. Reprinted by permission of Ticknor and Fields / Houghton Mifflin Company. All rights reserved.

Harrison, Jim. "The Woman Lit by Fireflies." In *The Woman Lit by Fireflies*. Boston: Houghton Mifflin / Seymour Lawrence, 1990, pp. 177–247. Copyright © 1990 by Jim Harrison. Reprinted by permission of Houghton Mifflin Company / Seymour Lawrence. All rights reserved.

Helprin, Mark. "The Schreuderspitze." In *Ellis Island and Other Stories*. New York: Delacorte Press / Seymour Lawrence, 1981, pp. 1–32. Copyright © 1976, 1977, 1979, 1980, 1981 by Mark Helprin. Used by permission of Delacorte Press / Seymour Lawrence, a division of Bantam Doubleday Dell Publishing Group, Inc.

Hokinson, Helen E. "The Vote Is Now." Illustration in *The New Yorker*, September 28, 1935. Copyright © 1935, 1963, The New Yorker Magazine, Inc. Reprinted by permission.

Ignatow, David. "Above Everything." In *New and Collected Poems, 1970–1985*. Middletown, Conn.: Wesleyan University Press, 1986. Copyright © 1986 by David Ignatow. Reprinted by permission of University Press of New England.

Kooser, Ted. "Daddy Longlegs." In *One World at a Time*. Pittsburgh: University of Pittsburgh Press, 1985, p. 19. Copyright © 1985 by

Ted Kooser. Reprinted by permission of the University of
Pittsburgh Press.

Levertov, Denise. "Like Loving Chekhov." In *Life in the Forest.* New
York: New Directions, 1978, pp. 77–78. Copyright © 1978 by
Denise Levertov. Reprinted by permission of New Directions
Publishing Corp.

Lowell, Susan. "White Canyon." In *Ganando Red.* Minneapolis,
Minn.: Milkweed Editions, 1988, pp. 13–26. Copyright © 1988
by Susan Lowell.

McCarriston, Linda. "Dismantling the Castle." From *Eva-Mary,* by
Linda McCarriston. Evanston, Ill.: TriQuarterly Books / Northwest-
ern University Press, 1991, pp. 49–50. Copyright © 1991 by Linda
McCarriston. All rights reserved. Reprinted by permission of
Northwestern University Press.

McGrath, Thomas. "Ode for the American Dead in Asia." In
Minnesota Writes: Poetry. Edited by Jim Moore and Cary Waterman.
Minneapolis, Minn.: Milkweed Editions, 1987, pp. 37–38.

Oates, Joyce Carol. "Against Nature." In *Antaeus* 57 (Autumn 1986):
236–43. Copyright © 1986 *The Ontario Review.* Reprinted by
permission of the author.

Oliver, Mary. "Lilies." In *House of Light.* Boston: Beacon Press, 1990,
pp. 12–13. Copyright © 1990 by Mary Oliver. Reprinted by permission of Beacon Press.

Pollitt, Katha. "Marooned on Gilligan's Island: Are Women Morally
Superior to Men?" In *The Nation,* 28 December 1992, pp. 799–808.
Copyright © The Nation Company, Inc. Reprinted with permis-
sion from *The Nation.*

Sanders, Scott Russell. "Death Games." In *The Paradise of Bombs.*
Athens: University of Georgia Press, 1987, pp. 118–33. First
appeared in *The North American Review* as "Bang, Bang, You're
Dead." Copyright © 1987 by Scott Russell Sanders. Reprinted by
permission of the author and Virginia Kidd, Literary Agent.

Simpson, Louis. "A Story about Chicken Soup." In *At the End of the
Open Road.* Middletown, Conn.: Wesleyan University Press, 1963,
pp. 25–26. Copyright © 1963 by Louis Simpson. Reprinted by
permission of University Press of New England.

Vivante, Arturo. "The Soft Core." In *The Tales of Arturo Vivante.*
Selected and with an introduction by Mary Kinzie. Riverdale-on-
Hudson, N. Y.: Sheep Meadow Press, 1990, pp. 70–79. Copyright ©
1990 by Arturo Vivante. Reprinted by permission from the
author.

Walker, Alice. "Brothers and Sisters." In *In Search of Our Mothers' Gardens: Womanist Prose.* New York: Harcourt Brace Jovanovich, 1983, pp. 326–31. Copyright © 1975 by Alice Walker. Reprinted by permission of Harcourt Brace and Company.

Weaver, Will. "The Undeclared Major." In *A Gravestone Made of Wheat.* New York: Simon and Schuster, 1989, pp. 169–75. Copyright © 1989 by Will Weaver. Reprinted by permission of Simon and Schuster.

Wilbur, Richard. "Love Calls Us to the Things of This World." In *Things of This World.* New York: Harcourt Brace Jovanovich, 1956, pp. 5–6. Copyright © 1956 and renewed 1984 by Richard Wilbur. Reprinted by permission of Harcourt Brace and Company.

Wolff, Tobias. "In the Garden of the North American Martyrs." In *In the Garden of North American Martyrs.* New York: Ecco Press, 1981, pp. 123–35. Copyright © 1976, 1978, 1980, 1981 by Tobias Wolff. Reprinted by permission from The Ecco Press.

Cited Works

Material from the following publications is quoted in this book:

Adler, Mortimer J. "The Disappearance of Culture." *Newsweek* 21 (August 1978): 15.

Agee, James. *The Collected Short Prose of James Agee*. Edited and with a memoir by Robert Fitzgerald. Boston: Houghton Mifflin, 1968. Copyright © 1968 by The James Agee Trust.

Anscombe, *G. E. M. The Collected Philosophical Papers of G. E. M. Anscombe*. Vol. 3. of *Ethics, Religion, and Politics*. Minneapolis: University of Minnesota Press, 1981.

Arkin, Alan. *The Lemming Condition*. Illustration by Joan Sandin. New York: Harper and Row, 1976.

Arlen, Michael J. *Passage to Ararat*. New York: Farrar, Straus and Giroux, 1975.

Baxter, Charles. *Through the Safety Net*. New York: Viking, 1985. Copyright © 1985 by Charles Baxter. Used by permission of Viking Penguin, a division of Penguin Books USA Inc.

Belenky, Mary Field, Blythe McVicker Clinchy, Nancy Rule Goldberger, and Jill Mattuck Tarule. *Women's Ways of Knowing*. New York: Basic Books, 1986.

Berry, Wendell. *The Gift of Good Land*. San Francisco: North Point Press, 1981. Copyright © 1981 by Wendell Berry. Reprinted by permission of North Point Press, a division of Farrar, Straus and Giroux, Inc.

Binder, David. "Black Bears, Up Close and Personal." *New York Times*, 4 April 1995, sec. C1.

Bly, Carol and Mary Peterson. *Empathy-in-Literature Theory [To Hear*]*. Collaborative of Teachers and School Social Workers. St. Paul, Minn.

Bly, Robert. *Silence in the Snowy Fields*. Middletown, Conn.: Wesleyan University Press, 1962. Copyright © 1962 by Robert Bly. Reprinted by permission of Robert Bly.

Chira, Susan. "An Ohio College Says Women Learn Differently, So It Teaches That Way." *New York Times*, 13 May 1992, sec. A1. Copyright © 1992 by The New York Times Company. Reprinted by permission.

Chomsky, Noam. "1984: Orwell's and Ours." Introduction by John M. Dolan. *Thoreau Quarterly 16*, (winter-spring 1984): 13.

Chomsky, Noam. *Chronicles of Dissent: Interviews with David Barsamian.* With an introduction by Alexander Cockburn. Monroe, Maine: Common Courage Press, 1992.

Chomsky, Noam and Edward Herman. *Manufacturing Consent: The Political Economy of the Mass Media.* New York: Pantheon, 1988.

Dember, W. N. "The New Look in Motivation." *American Scientist* 53, (1965): 409-27.

Dickson, Cheryl. Reported in a talk to Horizon 100, St. Paul, Minn., 2 November 1994.

Doherty, William J. *Soul Searching: Why Psychotherapy Must Promote Moral Responsibility.* New York: Basic Books, 1995.

Earth Works Group. *Fifty Simple Things You Can Do to Save the Earth.* Berkeley, Calif.: Earthworks, 1989.

Eichstaedt, Peter. *If You Poison Us: Uranium and Native Americans.* Santa Fe, N.Mex.: Red Crane Books, 1994.

Everett, Melissa. *Breaking Ranks.* Philadelphia: New Society Publishers, 1989.

Ferreira, Antonio. "Emotional Factors in Pre-Natal Environment." *Journal of Nervous and Mental Disease* 141 (1965): 108-17.

Frank, Anne. *The Diary of a Young Girl.* New York: Modern Library, 1994.

Frankl, Viktor E. *Man's Search for Meaning: An Introduction to Logotherapy.* Part 1 translated by Ilse Lasch. Preface by Gordon W. Allport. Boston: Beacon Press, 1962.

Galbraith, John Kenneth. *The Nature of Mass Poverty.* Cambridge, Mass.: Harvard University Press, 1979.

Ginsberg, Allen. *Howl.* San Francisco: City Lights Books, 1956.

Goleman, Daniel. "The Brain Manages Happiness and Sadness in Different Centers." *New York Times,* 28 March 1995, sec. C1.

Groves, Betsy McAlister, Barry Zuckerman, Steven Marans, and Donald J. Cohen. "Silent Victims: Children Who Witness Violence." Division of Developmental and Behavioral Pediatrics, Boston City Hospital, Talbot 214, 818 Harrison Avenue Boston, MA 02118.

Gutlove, Paula F. "Transforming the Confrontation Mentality." *Center Review* 5, no. 2 (1991). Reprinted by permission of author.

Hall, Donald. *Old and New Poems.* New York: Ticknor and Fields, 1990. Copyright © 1990 by Donald Hall. Reprinted by permission of Ticknor and Fields / Houghton Mifflin Company. All rights reserved.

Hall, Donald. *To Read Literature*. Fort Worth, Tex.: Harcourt Brace Jovanovich College Publishers, 1992.

Harrison, Jim. *The Woman Lit by Fireflies*. Boston: Houghton Mifflin / Seymour Lawrence, 1990. Copyright © 1990 by Jim Harrison. Reprinted by permission of Houghton Mifflin Company / Seymour Lawrence. All rights reserved.

Harvard Mental Health Letter 9, no. 11. (May 1993): 2-3.

Hays, Constance L. "Bristol-Myers Pleads Guilty to Pollution." *New York Times,* 25 April 1992, 25. Copyright © by The New York Times Company. Reprinted by permission.

Healy, Jane M. *Endangered Minds: Why Our Children Don't Think*. New York: Simon and Schuster, 1990.

Heinz, John P., and Edward O. Laumann. *Chicago Lawyers: The Social Structure of the Bar*. 1983. Reprint, Evanston, Ill.: Northwestern University Press, 1994.

Helprin, Mark. *Ellis Island and Other Stories*. New York: Delacorte Press / Seymour Lawrence, 1981. Copyright © 1976, 1977, 1979, 1980, 1981 by Mark Helprin. Used by permission of Delacorte Press / Seymour Lawrence, a division of Bantam Doubleday Dell Publishing Group, Inc.

Hokinson, Helen E. "The Vote Is Now." Illustration in *The New Yorker,* 28 September 1935. Copyright © 1935, 1963, The New Yorker Magazine, Inc. Reprinted by permission.

Ignatow, David. *New and Collected Poems, 1970–1985*. Middletown, Conn.: Wesleyan University Press, 1986. Copyright © 1986 by David Ignatow. Reprinted by permission of University Press of New England.

Janis, Irving L. *Groupthink*: *Psychological Studies of Policy Decisions and Fiascoes*. 2nd edition. Boston: Houghton Mifflin, 1983. Copyright © 1982 by Houghton Mifflin Company. Used with permission.

Kitwood, Tom. *Concern for Others: A New Psychology of Conscience and Morality*. London: Routledge, 1990. Reprinted by permission of Routledge.

Kohlberg, Lawrence. *The Philosophy of Moral Development: Moral Stages and the Idea of Justice*. Vol. 1, *Essays on Moral Development*. San Francisco: Harper and Row, 1981.

Kooser, Ted. *One World at a Time*. Pittsburgh: University of Pittsburgh Press, 1985. Copyright © 1985 by Ted Kooser. Reprinted by permission of the University of Pittsburgh Press.

Levertov, Denise. *Life in the Forest*. New York: New Directions, 1978. Copyright © 1978 by Denise Levertov. Reprinted by permission of New Directions Publishing Corp.

Levin, Michael. "Ethics Courses: Useless." *New York Times,* 25 November 1989, p. 23. Copyright © 1989 by The New York Times Company. Reprinted with permission.

Lickona, Thomas, ed. *Moral Development and Behavior: Theory, Research, and Social Issues.* New York: Holt, Reinhart and Winston, 1976.

Lifton, Robert Jay, and Eric Markusen. *The Genocidal Mentality: Nazi Holocaust and Nuclear Threat.* New York: Basic Books, 1990.

Loevinger, Jane. *Ego Development: Conceptions and Theories.* San Francisco: Jossey-Bass, 1976. Copyright © 1976 by Jossey-Bass Inc., Publishers. Reprinted by permission.

Loevinger, Jane, and Ruth Wessler. *Measuring Ego Development.* San Francisco: Jossey-Bass, 1970.

Lowell, Susan. *Ganado Red.* Minneapolis, Minn.: Milkweed Editions, 1988. Copyright © 1988 by Susan Lowell.

Manley, Kathleen E. B. "Women of Los Alamos during World War II: Some of Their Views." *New Mexico Historical Review* 65, no. 2 (April 1990): 251–66. Reprinted by permission from *New Mexico Historical Review.*

McCall, Nathan. *Makes Me Wanna Holler: A Young Black Man in America.* New York: Random House, 1994.

McCarriston, Linda. *Eva-Mary.* Evanston, Ill.: TriQuarterly Books / Northwestern University Press, 1991. Copyright © 1991 by Linda McCarriston. All rights reserved. Reprinted by permission of Northwestern University Press.

McCarthy, Mary. *The Writing on the Wall and Other Literary Essays.* New York: Harcourt, Brace and World, 1970. First published in *Harper's Magazine.* Copyright © 1962 by Mary McCarthy. Reprinted by permission of the The Mary McCarthy Literary Trust.

McGrath, Thomas. "Ode for the American Dead in Asia." In *Minnesota Writes: Poetry.* Edited by Jim Moore and Cary Waterman. Minneapolis, Minn.: Milkweed Editions, 1987.

Mesce, Deborah. "'Dixie' Hits a Sour Note." *St. Paul Pioneer Press,* 6 August 1993, p. 1.

Milgram, Stanley. *Obedience to Authority: An Experimental View.* New York: Harper and Row, 1983.

Miller, Alice. *For Your Own Good: Hidden Cruelty in Child-Rearing and the Roots of Violence.* Translated by Hildegarde and Hunter Hannum. New York: Farrar, Straus and Giroux, 1983.

Moore-Foster, W. J Musa. "Up from Brutality: Freeing Black Communities from Sexual Violence." In *Transforming a Rape Culture.* Edited by Emilie Buchwald, Pamela Fletcher, and Martha Roth. Minneapolis, Minn.: Milkweed Editions, 1993.

Oates, Joyce Carol. *Antaeus* 57 (Autumn 1986): 236–43. Copyright © 1986 *The Ontario Review*. Reprinted by permission of the author.

Oliver, Mary. *House of Light*. Boston: Beacon Press, 1990. Copyright © 1990 by Mary Oliver. Reprinted by permission of Beacon Press.

Olweus, Dan. "Bullying Among School Children: Intervention and Prevention." In *Aggressions and Violence throughout the Lifespan*. Edited by R. D. Peters, R. J. McMahon, and V. L. Quincy. Newbury Park, Calif.: Sage Publications, 1992.

Orwell, George. *Down and Out in Paris and London*. 1933. Reprint, New York: Harcourt Brace Jovanovich, 1961.

Paddock, Joe, Nancy Paddock, and Carol Bly. *Soil and Survival: Land Stewardship and the Future of American Agriculture*. San Francisco: Sierra Club Books, 1986.

Pipher, Mary. *Reviving Ophelia: Saving the Selves of Adolescent Girls*. New York: Ballantine Books, 1994.

Pollitt, Katha. "Marooned on Gilligan's Island: Are Women Morally Superior to Men?" In *The Nation*, 28 December 1992, pp. 799–808. Copyright © The Nation Company, Inc. Reprinted with permission from *The Nation*.

Proctor, Robert. *Racial Hygiene: Medicine under the Nazis*. Cambridge, Mass.: Harvard University Press, 1988.

Rawls, John. "Two Concepts of Rules." *Philosophical Review* 64, no. 1 (January 1955): 3-32.

Rogers, Carl R. *On Becoming a Person: A Therapist's View of Psychotherapy*. Boston: Houghton Mifflin, 1961.

Sanders, Scott Russell. *The Paradise of Bombs*. Athens: University of Georgia Press, 1987. First appeared in *The North American Review* as "Bang, Bang, You're Dead." Copyright © 1987 by Scott Russell Sanders. Reprinted by permission of the author and Virginia Kidd, Literary Agent.

Schaeffer, Heinz. *U-Boat 977*. New York: W. W. Norton, 1952. Reprint, New York: Bantam Books, 1981. Reprinted by permission of Curtis Brown, Ltd.

Schneider, Keith. "A Valley of Death for the Navajo Uranium Miners." *New York Times*, 3 May 1993, sec. A1.

Shakespeare, William. *Henry VI*.

Simpson, Louis. *At the End of the Open Road*. Middletown, Conn.: Wesleyan University Press, 1963. Copyright © 1963 by Louis Simpson. Reprinted by permission of University Press of New England.

Sontag, L. W. "Parental Determinants of Post Natal Behavior." In *Fetal Growth and Development*. Edited by Harry W. Waisman and George R. Kerr. New York: McGraw-Hill, 1970.

Spelt, D. K. "The Conditioning of the Human Fetus in Utero." *Journal of Experimental Psychology 38* (1948): 338-346.

Ueland, Brenda. *Strength to Your Sword Arm: Selected Writings*. Duluth, Minn.: Holy Cow! Press, 1993.

Vaillant, George E. *Adaptation to Life*. Boston: Little, Brown, 1977.

Verny, Thomas, and John Kelly. *The Secret Life of the Unborn Child*. New York: Dell, 1981.

Vivante, Arturo. *The Tales of Arturo Vivante*. Selected and with an introduction by Mary Kinzie. Riverdale-on-Hudson, N. Y.: Sheep Meadow Press, 1990. Copyright © 1990 by Arturo Vivante. Reprinted by permission from the author.

Walker, Alice. *In Search of Our Mothers' Gardens: Womanist Prose*. New York: Harcourt Brace Jovanovich, 1983. Copyright © 1975 by Alice Walker. Reprinted by permission of Harcourt Brace and Company.

Weaver, Will. *A Gravestone Made of Wheat*. New York: Simon and Schuster, 1989. Copyright © 1989 by Will Weaver. Reprinted by permission of Simon and Schuster.

Wilbur, Richard. "Mind." In *Things of This World*. San Diego: Harcourt Brace Jovanovich, 1984. Copyright © 1956 and renewed 1984 by Richard Wilbur. Reprinted by permission of Harcourt Brace and Company.

Wilbur, Richard. *Things of This World*. New York: Harcourt Brace Jovanovich, 1956. Copyright © 1956 and renewed 1984 by Richard Wilbur. Reprinted by permission of Harcourt Brace and Company.

Williams, Terry Tempest. "The Clan of One-Breasted Women." *Witness* 3, no. 4 (1989).

Wolff, Tobias. *In the Garden of North American Martyrs*. New York: Ecco Press, 1981. Copyright © 1976, 1978, 1980, 1981 by Tobias Wolff. Reprinted by permission from The Ecco Press.

Yalom, Irvin D. *Existential Psychotherapy*. New York: Basic Books, 1980.

Yalom, Irvin D. *The Theory and Practice of Group Psychotherapy*. 8th printing. New York: Basic Books, 1970.

Yarmolinsky, Avrahm, ed. *The Portable Chekhov*. Harmondsworth: Penguin, 1947.

Zahn, Gordon. *In Solitary Witness: The Life and Death of Franz Jägerstätter*. New York: Holt, Rinehart and Winston, 1964.

Carol Bly's second collection of stories, *The Tomcat's Wife and Other Stories* (HarperCollins, 1991), won the Friends of American Writers Award. Five of her essays are included in *Eight Modern Essayists*, edited by William Smart (St. Martin's Press, 1990). She is the author of *Backbone*, her first book of short stories (Milkweed Editions, 1985), the essay *Bad Government and Silly Literature* (Milkweed Editions, 1987), and the acclaimed book of essays, *Letters from the Country* (Harper and Row, 1981). Recent work anthologized includes the forthcoming "My Dear Republican Mother," to appear in Constance Warloe's 1997 anthology *I've Always Meant to Tell You: Letters to Our Mothers.*

Bly is the coauthor of *Soil and Survival: Land Stewardship and the Future of American Agriculture* (with Joe Paddock and Nancy Paddock, Sierra Club Books, 1986). She was the Benedict Distinguished Visiting Professor of English at Carleton College (spring 1990). Bly has taught Ethics-in-Literature in the University of Minnesota's Master of Liberal Studies program. She regularly teaches creative-writing workshops in the University of Minnesota's Split Rock Summer Arts Program, at the Vermont Studio Center, and in Northland College's Lifelong Learning Program. She has received the Distinguished Christian Service Award from Seabury-Western Seminary and an honorary doctoral degree from Northland College.

Carol Bly lives in St. Paul, Minnesota.

Interior design by Will Powers.
Typeset in Stone Sans and Stone Serif
by Stanton Publication Services, Inc.
Printed on acid-free Glatfelter paper
by Edwards Brothers, Inc.

More essays from Milkweed Editions:

The Passionate, Accurate Story:
Making Your Heart's Truth into Literature
Carol Bly

Transforming a Rape Culture
Edited by Emilie Buchwald,
Pamela Fletcher, and Martha Roth

Rooms in the House of Stone
Michael Dorris

Grass Roots: The Universe of Home
Paul Gruchow

The Mythic Family
Judith Guest

The Art of Writing:
Lu Chi's Wen Fu
Translated from the Chinese by Sam Hamill

Coming Home Crazy:
An Alphabet of China Essays
Bill Holm

The Heart Can Be Filled Anywhere on Earth:
Minneota, Minnesota
Bill Holm

I Won't Learn from You!
The Role of Assent in Learning
Herbert Kohl

Basic Needs:
A Year with Street Kids in a City School
Julie Landsman

Tips for Creating a Manageable Classroom:
Understanding Your Students' Basic Needs
Julie Landsman

Planning to Stay: Learning to See
the Physical Features of Your Neighborhood
William R. Morrish and Catherine R. Brown

The Old Bridge:
The Third Balkan War and the Age of the Refugee
Christopher Merrill

A Male Grief:
Notes on Pornography and Addiction
David Mura

Homestead
Annick Smith

What Makes Pornography "Sexy"?
John Stoltenberg